W9-DEJ-753

Developmentally Appropriate Curriculum
Best Practices in Early Childhood Education
Third Edition

Marjorie J. Kostelnik
University of Nebraska, Lincoln

Anne K. Soderman
Michigan State University

Alice Phipps Whiren
Michigan State University

PEARSON

Merrill
Prentice Hall

Upper Saddle River, New Jersey
Columbus, Ohio

Library of Congress Cataloging-in-Publication Data

Kostelnik, Marjorie J.
   Developmentally appropriate curriculum : best practices in early childhood education / Marjorie J. Kostelnik,
Anne K. Soderman, Alice Phipps Whiren.—3rd ed.
      p. cm.
Includes bibliographical references (p.   ) and index.
   ISBN 0-13-049658-8
   1. Early childhood education—United States.   2. Early childhood education—Curricula—United States.
3. Child development—United States.   I. Soderman, Anne Keil.   II. Whiren, Alice Phipps.   III. Title.
   LB1139.25 .K67 2004
   372.21—dc21

                                                                                          2003009821

Vice President and Executive Publisher:
   Jeffery W. Johnston
Assistant Vice President and Publisher:
   Kevin M. Davis
Editorial Assistant: Autumn Crisp
Production Editor: Sheryl Glicker Langner
Production Coordination: *The GTS Companies/*
   York, PA Campus.

Design Coordinator: Diane C. Lorenzo
Photo Coordinator: Kathy Kirtland
Cover Designer: Brian Huber
Cover photo: Corbis
Production Manager: Laura Messerly
Director of Marketing: Ann Castel Davis
Marketing Manager: Amy June
Marketing Coordinator: Tyra Poole

This book was set in Century Schoolbook by *The GTS Companies*/York, PA Campus. It was printed and bound
by Banta Book Group. The cover was printed by Phoenix Color Corp.

Photo Credits: CEM/Merrill, p. 341; Scott Cunningham/Merrill, pp. 13, 35, 91, 134, 261, 278, 313; Karen
Mancinelli/Pearson Learning, p. 39; Kevin Fitzsimons, p. 171; Jean Greenwald/Merrill, p. 157; Richard
Hutchings/Silver Burdett Ginn, p. 382; Anthony Magnacca/Merrill, pp. 377, 401; Barbara Schwartz/Merrill,
pp. 102, 181, 287; Anne Vega/Merrill, pp. 53, 65, 119, 205, 210, 241; Todd Yarrington/Merrill, pp. 431, 436;
all other photos by David Kostelnik

Pearson Prentice Hall™ is a trademark of Pearson Education, Inc.
Pearson® is a registered trademark of Pearson plc
Prentice Hall® is a registered trademark of Pearson Education, Inc.
Merill® is a registered trademark of Pearson Education, Inc.

Pearson Education Ltd.
Pearson Education Singapore Pte. Ltd.
Pearson Education Canada, Ltd.
Pearson Education—Japan

Pearson Education Australia Pty. Limited
Pearson Education North Asia Ltd.
Pearson Educación de Mexico, S.A. de C.V.
Pearson Education Malaysia Pte. Ltd.

10 9 8 7 6 5 4 3
ISBN: 0-13-049658-8

Preface

Every adult needs a child to teach. It's the way adults learn. —Anonymous

❑ What are developmentally appropriate practices, and how effective are they?

❑ How can we create the best programs for young children?

❑ As early childhood educators, what is our role in shaping children's educational experiences? What is the child's role? What is the role of the family and community?

❑ How can we tell if children are actually learning?

Questions such as these are typically asked by early childhood professionals–in–training as well as by seasoned practitioners in the field. Our work with students and increasing numbers of educators probing for answers indicated the need for a comprehensive guide to support the exploration, planning, and implementation of developmentally appropriate programs. Thus, our goal in writing *Developmentally Appropriate Curriculum: Best Practices in Early Childhood Education* was to bring together the best information currently available for developing an integrated approach to curriculum and instruction in the early years. We also hoped to bridge the worlds of child care and early education, as well as those of preprimary and primary programs. The resulting volume addresses *early childhood professionals–in–training and professionals working in formal group settings with young children from 3 to 8 years old*. We realize that early childhood education spans birth to age 8 years; however, we see infancy and toddlerhood as unique ages within this period, requiring specialized knowledge beyond the scope of this text. For this reason, we did not focus on infants or toddlers in our discussions.

We believe the information in this book will be *valuable to both novices and master practitioners*. The ideas in this text have been extensively field-tested and found to be effective. All are designed to give you a cohesive view of the *"what," "why," and "how" of developmentally appropriate practices.*

Finally, we have had many years of experience working directly with young children and their families and with educators in preprimary and primary settings. We have been in urban, suburban, and rural programs; large–medium and small classes; public, private, not-for-profit, and profit-seeking organizations; half- and full-day programs; preschool classes; and the elementary grades. Currently, all of us are actively engaged in educating young children and/or the professionals who work with them.

DISTINCTIVE FEATURES OF THIS TEXT

Developmentally Appropriate Curriculum: Best Practices in Early Childhood Education offers instructors and readers several unique features that increase reader understanding and skill development:

❑ The text addresses the classroom as an ecosystem. This ecosystem includes contributions by children and adults, the physical and social environments, and contextual factors leading to learning.

❑ The concept of developmentally appropriate practices is pervasive throughout the volume. Each chapter addresses principles of age appropriateness, individual appropriateness, and socio cultural appropriateness.

❑ This book spans the early childhood years from 3 to 8. It provides a comprehensive, cohesive approach that results in greater continuity for children and practitioners.

❑ Each chapter progresses clearly from theory and research to practice.

❑ We use developmental domains to address the early childhood curriculum. Doing so helps practitioners better understand the link between child development and program implementation.

❑ Every curriculum chapter includes sample activities.

❑ The text addresses individual curricular domains as well as curriculum integration.

❑ Detailed directions facilitate the application of developmentally appropriate practices.

❑ We demonstrate the interaction of developmental goals, developmentally appropriate practices, and relevant curriculum content.

❑ Readers learn a comprehensive approach to conceptualizing, planning, implementing, and evaluating curriculum.

❑ Chapter-end activities provide readers the opportunity to extend their understanding of chapter content to their professional lives. *Discussion questions* focus on essential information in each chapter and give readers an opportunity to explore ideas with classmates and colleagues. *Journal recommendations* enhance readers' reflective thinking. Sample *observations* help readers recognize developmentally appropriate practices in operation. *Classroom activities* enable readers to apply chapter content and processes in interactions with children, families, or professionals in the field. Finally, if readers complete the *portfolio entries* in each chapter, they will create a comprehensive portfolio including artifacts (things generated in class and then used in a portfolio), reproductions (things reproduced by camera, video, or audio for use in the portfolio), productions (things specifically produced for placement in the portfolio), and testimonials (others attesting to their abilities), all centered around developmentally appropriate practices.

FORMAT AND CHAPTER SEQUENCE

Developmentally Appropriate Curriculum: Best Practices in Early Childhood Education is divided into four parts. Part 1, Foundations of Early Childhood Education, consists of the Introduction as well as chapters 1 and 2 and addresses the philosophy of developmentally appropriate practice. Characteristics of the field, principles associated with developmentally appropriate practice, and critical issues in early childhood education are all outlined in part 1. "Setting the Stage for Learning" is the focus of part 2, chapters 3 through 8. In these chapters, we describe the overall understandings and skills necessary to create effective programs for young children. We begin with planning, implementing, and organizing small-group, then whole-group, activities. Organizing

the physical space and materials used in the classroom; creating a schedule for the day; and determining how to group children to achieve certain aims are discussed next. Child guidance, authentic assessment, and family involvement are treated as fundamental building blocks of effective teaching, with individual chapters devoted to each of these topics. In part 3, chapters 9 through 14, the curriculum is explained within the context of six developmental domains: aesthetic, affective, cognitive, language, physical, and social. Each of the domain chapters has a discussion of theory, research, and educational issues related to children's development and learning in that particular arena, a suggested outline of ultimate goals and intermediate objectives, teaching strategies that characterize the domain, and examples of classroom activities. The curriculum domains are presented in alphabetical order to underscore the idea that no one domain is more important than any of the others. However, you may find knowing that each domain refers to five kinds of knowledge useful. These kinds of knowledge are physical, logical-mathematical, representational, social-conventional, and metacognitive. If you are familiar with these terms, reading chapters 9 through 14 in order will make sense. However, if you are unfamiliar with them, first reading chapter 11, in which the terms are explained, will be useful. The last section of the book is part 4, Integrating Curriculum. This part includes chapters 15 and 16, both focused on creating a cohesive whole. First, we consider the integrative nature of pretend play and construction; second, we consider the integrative aspects of using projects and theme teaching.

STRUCTURAL FEATURES

Each chapter begins with a series of questions that pique readers' interest in the material and provide a framework for reflecting on the chapter's content following an initial reading. In addition, a series of culminating activities enables readers to review and apply the material in their professional lives. Thus, every chapter ends with discussion questions, potential observations to make in early childhood settings, application activities, guidelines for journal entries, and suggested items to add to a portfolio. These learning aids will hone readers' understanding and skill and serve as resource materials for the future.

WHAT REMAINS THE SAME

Among the popular elements we transferred from the second edition are our focus on developmental domains, a strong research basis for the information provided, and an emphasis on practical applications. Because readers liked the clear link between theory and practice provided by the "Implications" sections in the early chapters, those remain. The curriculum chapters still include rationales and sample teaching strategies specific to each domain, objectives, issues practitioners face, and illustrative activities. Examples featuring children, families, and professionals from a variety of backgrounds continue to be a feature of the chapters that compose the book.

SIGNIFICANT CHANGES

Content Changes This edition has been extensively updated. On the basis of feedback from our readers, we have pruned some material from each chapter so that the book remains comprehensive but more reader friendly. In chapter 1, we added the Montessori model to demonstrate the variety of developmentally appropriate practices. Chapter 2 has been expanded to include the newest of Gardner's intelligences—the naturalist. The section on direct instruction in chapter 3 has been completely revised. In chapter 4, the emphasis is on two forms of whole-group activity—group time and field trips. The organization of space, materials, and time, discussed in chapter 5, has been streamlined, but the material on how to structure the environment and diagrams and examples of various ways to do teaching schedules and arrange classrooms have been retained. Material on the uninvolved discipline style as well as a new diagram of the authoritative teaching continuum has been added to chapter 6. We embellished the section on creating whole-school discipline plans, but dropped the elaborate model we used in the past. The chapter on authentic assessment has been moved to become chapter 7. This was done to make the link among assessing, planning, and implementing clearer. "Strengthening Developmentally Appropriate Programs Through Family Involvement" is now chapter 8. Additional material on fathers has been added to this chapter as well as suggestions for how to involve fathers more fully in early childhood programs.

The domain chapters retain many of the features readers found useful in the last edition. However, new material has been added to each, including at least one example per chapter focused on adapting activities to support children with special needs. Chapter 9, the Aesthetic Domain, places greater emphasis on exploration in the arts, focusing on the aesthetic process more fully. Practices include providing time for meaningful aesthetic learning while avoiding wasting children's time with adult-designed product art. Readers will find new sections on children's development of emotional awareness and emotional intelligence in chapter 10, covering the affective domain. Chapter 11, on the cognitive domain, includes the latest neuroscience findings related to young children and the implications of such findings for classroom practices. In addition, the objectives in this chapter reflect the latest work by the National Council of Teachers of Mathematics, *Principles and Standards for School Mathematics, Prekindergarten through Second Grade*. The language domain, covered in chapter 12, provides expanded material on literacy, written language, and phonological awareness. The Physical Domain, chapter 13, includes new material on fitness, health, safety, and perceptual awareness. Chapter 14, which addresses the social domain, has been amplified with additional examples, particularly in relation to the anti bias curriculum.

Pretend play and construction continue to be combined in chapter 15. Our aim is to highlight the integrative nature of play and its importance at all levels of early childhood education. We have striven to make the connection between the curriculum and play stronger and more evident. The chapter on themes, chapter 16, has been enlarged to include more information on the Project Approach. A guest segment by Sylvia Chard describes projects more fully and offers a case study focused on a project in action.

All these revisions address current issues in early childhood curriculum development and implementation. Their inclusion should better prepare readers to face the realities of teaching young children on a day-to-day basis.

SUPPLEMENTARY MATERIALS

Instructor's Manual With this edition we are introducing a comprehensive instructor's manual to supplement the textbook. In it, we describe how to organize a course by using the textbook; how to find, select, and maintain appropriate field placements for students; how to model skills for students to imitate; and how to provide feedback to students assigned to field placements on campus or in the community. In addition, we have included a series of role-playing activities meant to be carried out in class. They are designed to familiarize students with how to use particular skills prior to implementing them with children and to clarify basic concepts as they emerge during class discussions. A third section of the instructor's manual provides a test bank of multiple-choice, true–false, short-answer, and essay questions for each chapter. Finally, the instructor's manual contains a criterion-referenced observation tool, the CSI (Curriculum Skills Inventory). This is a unique feature of *Developmentally Appropriate Curriculum: Best Practices in Early Childhood Education*. It can be used by instructors and practitioners to evaluate the degree to which students demonstrate the skills taught.

Web Site In addition to the instructor's manual, teachers may make use of an early childhood Web site created by Prentice Hall that includes a syllabus manager, a message board, and other educational resources.

ACKNOWLEDGMENTS

We would like to recognize the major contributions to this text by seven of our colleagues in early childhood education: Barbara M. Rohde, Director of Children's Programs at Child Abuse Prevention Services in Lansing, Michigan, contributed chapter 9; in addition, she supplied artwork for the classroom floor plans and the pictograph that appear in chapter 5. Laura C. Stein, Early Childhood Consultant, Stein Associates, East Lansing, Michigan, produced chapter 14. Carolyn Pope Edwards, Professor of Family and Consumer Sciences and Psychology, University of Nebraska, Lincoln, contributed the section "The Reggio Emilia Approach to Early Childhood Education"; Mary Hohmann, Senior Consultant, Program Division, High/Scope Educational Research Foundation, wrote the portion entitled "The High/Scope Approach to Early Childhood Education"; and, Joy Turner, editor of *Montessori Life,* the official publication of the American Montessori Society, authored the information entitled "The Montessori Approach to Early Childhood Education." These three segments appear in chapter 1. Sylvia Chard, Professor of Elementary Education, University of Alberta, wrote the material describing the Project Approach, featured in chapter 16. These individuals' work has broadened the scope of the text and has enabled us to present multiple voices describing developmentally appropriate curriculum.

We appreciate the generous assistance of David Kostelnik, photographer, who provided excellent images taken at a number of preschool and elementary sites. We are also indebted to the teachers in the Child Development Laboratories at Michigan State University for their early work on curriculum, for providing continuous and easy access to their classrooms for observation, and for inspiring many of the ideas represented in this book. We are grateful to Deborah Sharpe, Haslett Public Schools, and Grace Spalding, Department of Family and Child Ecology, for the group times described in chapter 4; and to Donna Howe, of the Creation Station, for materials related to learning centers (chapter 5) and theme-related material (chapter 16). Dr. John Haubenstricker, Department of Physical Education and Exercise Science, Michigan State University, graciously shared his research and the figures that illustrate gross-motor skills (chapter 13).

We thank the following reviewers for their comments and suggestions: Pamela Chibucos, Owens Community College; Marcia P. Rysztak, Lansing Community College; Vernelle Tyler, University of South Carolina, Aiken; and Jean Maakestad Wolf, Western Illinois University.

Christina Tawney, our editor at Merrill/Prentice Hall, was a tremendous support, as were all members of the production team. During the preparation of this manuscript, we discussed our ideas with and received feedback from a number of University of Nebraska and Michigan State University students as well as Head Start, Chapter 1, child care, nursery school, and elementary school teachers and administrators. We heard the concerns of many parents of young children and listened to the children themselves as they responded to diverse program practices in their classrooms. We are especially grateful for all these contributions in shaping our vision of appropriate practices and in motivating us to share this vision with others.

Marjorie Kostelnik
Anne Soderman
Alice Whiren

Discover the Companion Website Accompanying This Book

THE PRENTICE HALL COMPANION WEBSITE: A VIRTUAL LEARNING ENVIRONMENT

Technology is a constantly growing and changing aspect of our field that is creating a need for content and resources. To address this emerging need, Prentice Hall has developed an online learning environment for students and professors alike—Companion Websites—to support our textbooks.

In creating a Companion Website, our goal is to build on and enhance what the textbook already offers. For this reason, the content for each user-friendly website is organized by topic and provides the professor and student with a variety of meaningful resources. Common features of a Companion Website include:

For the Professor—

Every Companion Website integrates **Syllabus Manager™**, an online syllabus creation and management utility.

- **Syllabus Manager™** provides you, the instructor, with an easy, step-by-step process to create and revise syllabi, with direct links into Companion Website and other online content without having to learn HTML.
- Students may log on to your syllabus during any study session. All they need to know is the web address for the Companion Website and the password you've assigned to your syllabus.
- After you have created a syllabus using **Syllabus Manager™**, students may enter the syllabus for their course section from any point in the Companion Website.
- Clicking on a date, the student is shown the list of activities for the assignment. The activities for each assignment are linked directly to actual content, saving time for students.
- Adding assignments consists of clicking on the desired due date, then filling in the details of the assignment—name of the assignment, instructions, and whether or not it is a one-time or repeating assignment.

- In addition, links to other activities can be created easily. If the activity is online, a URL can be entered in the space provided, and it will be linked automatically in the final syllabus.

- Your completed syllabus is hosted on our servers, allowing convenient updates from any computer on the Internet. Changes you make to your syllabus are immediately available to your students at their next logon.

For the Student—

- **Introduction**—General information about the topic and how it will be covered in the website.
- **Web Links**—A variety of websites relted to topic areas.
- **Timely Articles**—Links to online articles that enable you to become more aware of important issues in early childhood.
- **Learn by Doing**—put concepts into action, participate in activities, examine strategies, and more.
- **Visit a School**—Visit a school's website to see concepts, theories, and strategies in action.
- **For Teachers/Practitioners**—Access information you will need to know as an educator, including information on materials, activities, and lessons.
- **Current Policies and Standards**—Find out the least early childhood policies from the government nd various organizations, and view state, federal, and curriculam standards.
- **Resources and Organizations**—Discover tools to help you plan your classroom or center and organizations to provide current information and standards for each topic.
- **Electronic Bluebook**—Paperless method of completing homework or essays assigned by a professor. Finished work can be sent to the professor via email.
- **Message Board**—Virtual bulletin board to post and respond to questions and comments from a national audience.

To take advantage of these and other resources, please visit the The Child in the Family and the Community, Third Edition, Companion Website at

www.prenhall.com/kostelnik

About the Authors

Marjorie J. Kostelnik, Ph.D., is Dean of the College of Human Resources and Family Sciences at the University of Nebraska, Lincoln. A former child care, Head Start, and nursery school teacher, as well as elementary school specialist, Dr. Kostelnik has been actively involved in helping educators in early childhood programs explore the implications of developmentally appropriate practices. Her work has taken her to many settings throughout the United States and abroad. Dr. Kostelnik completed a 4-year term as Vice President of the National Association for the Education of Young Children in 1998 and is currently on the advisory board of Project TEACH for the State of Nebraska.

Anne K. Soderman has had 14 years of classroom experience working with children in both public and nonpublic educational settings prior to joining Michigan State University, where she is currently Professor of Family and Child Ecology. In addition to carrying out teaching assignments in a number of international settings, she consults with public school systems in early childhood curriculum, instruction, and evaluation, with a particular focus on early literacy for children who are at risk. She has also recently coauthored *Creating Phonological and Print Awareness in the Early Years: Developmentally Appropriate Practices* with Kara M. Gregory and Louise T. O'Neill.

Alice Phipps Whiren is a professor in the Department of Family and Child Ecology, College of Human Ecology, Michigan State University. She teaches curriculum in early childhood and child development to undergraduate and graduate students. Early in her career, she taught young children in an inner-city public school in Michigan. She also served as a Head Start assistant director and has provided a variety of training sessions for preprimary teachers nationally and internationally. Most recently, she has been a consultant to public school systems as their staffs implement more developmentally appropriate programs for children.

CONTRIBUTORS

Barbara Rohde is the Director of Children's Programs at Child Abuse Prevention Services in Lansing, Michigan, where she works with teachers in child care, school readiness preschool, Even Start, and Early Head Start classrooms. She taught for 17 years in public and private school settings, including the laboratory schools at Michigan State and Florida State Universities, and as elementary art teacher in Rochester, New York. She spent 6 years as an early childhood consultant to preprimary and elementary teachers in the Owasso Public Schools.

Laura C. Stein, a former Head Teacher of the Child Development Laboratories at Michigan State University, is an early childhood consultant living in East Lansing, Michigan. For the past 25 years, she has worked with college students as well as 4- and 5-year-old children. She is a coauthor of a textbook on children's social development, has contributed numerous chapters and articles to books and journals, and speaks extensively to professional audiences.

Brief Contents

Contents

Contents _____ **xix**

Note: Every effort has been made to provide accurate and current Internet information in this book. However, the Internet and information posted on it are constantly changing, it is inevitable that some of the Internet addresses listed in this textbook will change.

Educator Learning Center:
An Invaluable Online Resource

Merrill Education and the Association for Supervision and Curriculum Development (ASCD) invite you to take advantage of a new online resource, one that provides access to the top research and proven strategies associated with ASCD and Merrill—the Educator Learning Center. At **www. Educator Learning Center.com** you will find resources that will enhance your students' understanding of course topics and of current educational issues, in addition to being invaluable for further research.

How the Educator Learning Center will help your students become better teachers

With the combined resources of Merrill Education and ASCD, you and your students will find a wealth of tools and materials to better prepare them for the classroom.

Research

- More than 600 articles from the ASCD journal *Educational Leadership* discuss everyday issues faced by practicing teachers.

- A direct link on the site to Research Navigator™ gives students access to many of the leading education journals, as well as extensive content detailing the research process.

- Excerpts from Merrill Education texts give your students insights on important topics of instructional methods, diverse populations, assessment, classroom management, technology, and refining classroom practice.

Classroom Practice

- Hundreds of lesson plans and teaching strategies are categorized by content area and age range.

- Case studies and classroom video footage provide virtual field experience for student reflection.

- Computer simulations and other electronic tools keep your students abreast of today's classrooms and current technologies.

Look into the value of Educator Learning Center yourself

Preview the value of this educational environment by visiting www.EducatorLearningCenter.com and clicking on "Demo." For a free 4-month subscription to the Educator Learning Center in conjunction with this text, simply contact your Merrill/Prentice Hall sales representative.

Introduction

If you are a practicing teacher, you probably know the joy of getting a love note from a child. If you are an aspiring early childhood educator, you might receive a letter like this someday, a hug, a smile, or some other sign that you have become an integral part of a young child's life. Knowing that you make a difference to children and families is one of the best aspects of being an early childhood professional. Another is knowing that you are helping children at the start of life, a time of amazing potential and tremendous opportunity.

A GOOD BEGINNING IS ESSENTIAL

> *You know that the beginning is the most important part of any work, especially in the case of a young and tender thing.*
>
> —Plato

During the early years, children develop the dispositions and attitudes toward education and themselves as learners that will stay with them all their lives. As children move from the early childhood period to middle childhood, many have also reached one of the following conclusions:

School is exciting/challenging/fun, and I am a good learner.

or

School is boring/difficult/painful, and I can't learn.

Youngsters whose conclusions are positive have a strong foundation for subsequent life success. However, the future for children whose school evaluations and self-evaluations are negative is bleak. These children are the most likely to require extensive remedial assistance, encounter mental health problems, endure academic failure, and drop out of school (R. P. Doyle, 1989; Goleman, 1995). The particular opinions children form are greatly influenced by their educational experiences in the first few years of life.

As an early childhood professional, you play a major role in shaping these experiences. The more you know about the field you are entering, the better prepared you will be to create effective early childhood programs. This Introduction provides an overview of early childhood education today. We define the profession and discuss its significance now and in the future. In addition, we describe the children, families, and professionals who learn together in early childhood settings. Let us begin.

WHAT IS EARLY CHILDHOOD EDUCATION?

Which of the following programs would you classify as early childhood education programs?

Nursery school classroom
Second-grade classroom
Family child care home

If you answered "All of the above," you were correct. Early childhood education involves any group program serving children from birth to 8 years that is designed to promote children's intellectual, social, emotional, language, and physical development and learning (Bredekamp & Copple, 1997). Such education translates into a wide array of programs attended by children of many ages. Early childhood education includes programs for infants and toddlers, as well as preschool, kindergarten, and primary programs. These programs may be half day or full day; public or private; enrichment or remedial in focus; targeted at low-, middle-, or high-income families; and administered by a variety of community institutions.

At one time, our view of early childhood education and its focus group was limited. In the not-too-distant past, the term *early childhood* was used only in reference to children 5 years old and younger. Parents and educators alike recognized that such youngsters differed significantly from older children. Under this traditional interpretation, entry into primary school (usually first grade) divided early childhood from later childhood. Thus, preschoolers and kindergartners were categorized as one group, and school-age children as another (Smart & Smart, 1972). Following this line of reasoning, you might assume that first and second graders would be more like fifth graders than like kindergartners. However, research and practical experience refute this. Evidence related to children's intellectual, social, and physical powers suggests that significant shifts in young children's development occur more likely around age 7 or 8 years than at age 5 years. Consequently, psychologists and educators have conceptualized early childhood as extending through the eighth year of life. This period crosses traditional programmatic boundaries, including preschool children, kindergartners, and students in the early primary grades. Currently, more children than ever are involved in early childhood programs.

CHILDREN AND FAMILIES DIFFER IN EARLY CHILDHOOD EDUCATION

Mary Hughes was making name tags for the children in her class: Juan, Un-Hai, Rachel, Steven, LaTanya, Clarissa, Heidi, Mohammed, Molly, Sally, Keiko, Mark, LeRoy, Indira, Jennifer, and Sasha. As she finished each name tag, she thought about how different each child was. The youngsters represented many racial, ethnic, and cultural backgrounds. The children varied greatly in terms of their parents' educational level and their

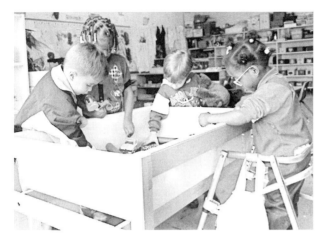

Early childhood education programs are inclusive, which enhances the development and learning of all the children enrolled.

families' socioeconomic status. Some children spoke English, and several spoke languages other than English at home. Some had prior preschool experience, and some had none. Some children lived at home with two parents, some were living in single-parent households, and one youngster was a foster child, newly arrived in her foster home. The children also functioned at varying developmental levels. Mary marveled at the group's diversity.

Early Childhood Programs Serve a Diverse Population of Children and Families

Like Mary, you will likely work with a diverse array of children and families throughout your career in early childhood education. You will do so because the United States is becoming more diverse each year. For instance, racial and ethnic diversity has increased substantially

in the United States since 1980. According to the U.S. Census Bureau (2001), the population of White children in the United States is declining, while the proportion of children who are non-White is growing. See Figure 1. In addition, within the next 5 years, perhaps as many as one third of the children between the ages of 3 and 8 years will speak home languages other than English (Washington & Andrews, 1998). Such linguistic diversity means the mix of languages in early childhood classrooms will be greater than it is now.

Family structures are also shifting. As mentioned previously, today children may live in a variety of family arrangements—two-parent families, single-parent families, blended families, interracial families, families with different-sex parents and families with same-sex parents, adoptive families, and foster families. Family income is another differentiating variable. You might work with children whose families have limited financial resources as well as with children whose families have large financial reserves. Some programs serve families whose income levels are within the same range; other programs serve families whose socioeconomic circumstances vary widely. Another factor that has influenced diversity in early childhood classrooms is inclusion. Since the passage of Federal Law 94–142 in 1975, children with disabilities have been provided access to free public education in the least restrictive setting. In 1986, Public Law 99–457 extended such services to children 3 to 5 years old. The Individuals With Disabilities Education Act (IDEA) of 1997 provided additional protections to people with disabilities, including freedom from discrimination and equal access to public programs. All these laws underscore a U.S. commitment to educate all children, to the maximum extent appropriate, in regular classrooms on a full-time basis. Support services are brought to children as needed; the children are not removed from the early

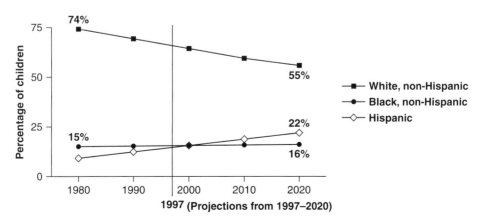

FIGURE 1 Shifting Population
Source: U.S. Census Bureau (2001).

childhood setting to receive the services. Thus, children with disabilities are not clustered into groups of persons with similar disabilities. They are no longer served only in separate classrooms labeled "learning disabled" or "emotionally impaired" (Kostelnik, Onaga, Rohde, & Whiren, 2002). As a result of this mainstreaming, more children with disabling conditions are being served in regular early childhood classrooms.

These trends mean that early childhood educators must create responsive early childhood programs that treat all people with respect. Rather than viewing one set of life experiences or demographics as "appropriate" and others as "inappropriate," we must integrate children's beliefs, history, and experiences into our programs in ways that make sense to children and enable them to flourish as learners (E. Garcia, 1993).

Families Are Children's First Teachers

During early childhood, the immediate context of the family has the greatest influence on the child. The family is responsible for meeting children's physical needs and for socializing the younger generation. Family members provide children with their first social relationships, their models for behaviors and roles, a framework of values and beliefs, and intellectual stimulation (Bobbitt & Paolucci, 1986; Gable & Cole, 2000). All these functions take place through direct and indirect teaching, in constructive and sometimes destructive ways, more or less successfully. In addition, most environmental influences are channeled to some extent through the family. For instance, through their families, children gain access to economic resources and learn the customs of their cultural group. The first attitudes toward education, work, and society that children encounter are in the family. Parents arrange for out-of-home care and make the initial entrée into a school for their children. They also promote or inhibit opportunities for peer and community contact. If parents are stressed by the hardships of poverty, the uncertainty of losing a job, or the prospects of marital dissolution, their ability to meet the needs of their young children is jeopardized. If such parents receive help or support from relatives, friends, or social institutions, the home environment they create for their children may be enhanced.

EARLY CHILDHOOD PROGRAMS VARY IN STRUCTURE AND SCOPE

During your years as an early childhood professional, you will most likely work in a variety of settings and programs. Education programs for young children come in all forms. Programs for young children operate under different funding sources (public or private) and vary in

location and size (private home, church or temple, small-group center, or large school). Such programs encompass a wide range of educational philosophies and curricula. Early childhood education programs also vary in their target audience, their scope (full day to half day; full year to partial year; every day to some days), and the training background of key personnel. An overview of the vast array of services currently available is offered in Table 1.

These variations in programs serving young children evolved from distinct needs and traditions. For instance, modern child care programs were devised in response to societal demands for protected child care environments during parents' working hours. Historically, child care programs have emphasized the health and safety of the children enrolled, and, although currently some involve government subsidies, many rely on corporate or private sponsorship and parent fees. Supplementing the learning experiences children have at home has long been the function of the nursery school movement. Usually financed through parent fees, the nursery school has nurturance, enrichment, and school readiness as its primary aims. More recent early intervention programs, such as Head Start and Chapter 1, are the result of federally mandated and supported efforts to remediate unfavorable developmental or environmental circumstances. These compensatory education programs focus on a particular segment of the population—children who are disadvantaged. Such programs are designed to change these children's life opportunities by altering the course of the children's development for the better. Conversely, primary education reflects a history that emphasizes the commitment of public funds to mass education. The goals of primary education have focused on transmitting society's accumulated knowledge, values, beliefs, and customs to youngsters of all backgrounds and educational needs. Compulsory in some states, not required in others, but available in all, kindergarten straddles the two "worlds" of early childhood. Long considered a transition into formal schooling, kindergarten programs have been the center of much current controversy. Should they be structured more like nursery school or more like the elementary grades? Traditionally more similar to the former than to the latter, today's kindergarten programs vary greatly depending on the philosophy of the school or district. Awareness that many children have previously attended early education programs and concern about children's subsequent school success have resulted in increasingly adult-centered, academic kindergarten programs (Krogh & Slentz, 2001b). This trend not only has ignited renewed debate, not yet resolved, about the true function of kindergarten and its role in children's lives, but also has spawned new early

TABLE 1   Early Childhood Education Programs for Children Aged 3–8 Years

Program	Children Served	Ages	Purposes	Funding
Nursery schools	Mostly middle class	2–5 years	Enrichment experiences aimed at whole-child development	Parent tuition
Parent cooperative preschools	Children of participating parents	2–5 years	Enrichment experiences aimed at whole-child development and parent education	Parent tuition and support services
Religious preschools	Children of church, temple, or mosque members and the religious community	2–5 years	Enrichment experiences aimed at whole-child development and spiritual training	Church subsidies and parent tuition
Group child care programs	All	6 weeks–12 years	Comprehensive care of children covering all aspects of development	Varies. Sources include employer subsidies; parent tuition; state agencies; the federal government by means of Title XX funds, the USDA Child Care Food Program, and child care tax credits; and private and charitable organizations.
Family child care homes	All	6 weeks–12 years	Comprehensive care of children covering all aspects of development	Varies. Sources include employer subsidies; parent tuition; state agencies; and the federal government by means of Title XX funds, the USDA Child Care Food Program, and child care tax credits; and private and charitable organizations.
Head Start	Children from low-income families, children with disabilities	3–5 years	Comprehensive development program addressing children's educational, nutritional, and medical needs, as well as parent education	Federal funds
Even Start	Children and parents from low-income families	1–7 years	Integration of early childhood education and adult education of parents	Federal funds
Follow Through	Children from low-income families	5–8 years	Continuation of educational support for former Head Start participants	Federal funds

(continued on the next page)

TABLE 1 *(continued)*

Program	Children Served	Ages	Purposes	Funding
Chapter 1	Children who are educationally deprived (migrants, disabled, neglected, or delinquent)	4–12 years	Supplemental education for children and parents	Federal funds
State-sponsored 4-year-old programs	Children identified as at risk for economic, developmental, or environmental reasons	4–18 years	Development of readiness skills for future schooling	State taxes and special allocations
Developmental kindergarten	Children identified by school or parents as not ready for regular kindergarten	5 years	Development of readiness skills	State and local taxes or, in the case of private schools, parent tuition
Kindergarten	All	5–6 years	Introduction to formal schooling	State and local taxes or, in the case of private schools, parent tuition
Transition rooms (pre- or junior first grade)	Children identified by school as not ready for first grade following a year or more of kindergarten	6–7 years	Development of readiness skills (most likely related to reading)	State and local taxes or, in the case of private schools, parent tuition
First, second, and third grade	All	6–8 years	Transmission of society's accumulated knowledge, values, beliefs, and customs to the young	State and local taxes or, in the case of private schools, parent tuition

childhood programs such as developmental kindergartens and transition rooms.

The program variations just described are implemented by a wide array of practitioners trained to work with young children. Let us briefly consider how people become early childhood professionals and what distinguishes a professional from an amateur.

EARLY CHILDHOOD PROFESSIONALS COME TO THE FIELD IN MANY WAYS

When Scott arrived at Lakeland College, he majored in business administration. After taking some classes, he realized business was not his forte, but he had no clear idea of what he wanted to do. One afternoon he went with some friends to help supervise a Halloween party for kindergartners at the local YMCA. He had a great time with the children. They were fun and so smart. After several more experiences with children at the Y,

Scott decided to talk to his adviser about the school's major in early childhood education.

Jackie is the mother of three children. When she began working in a Head Start classroom as a parent volunteer, she became intrigued with preschoolers' development and learning in the classroom. She vowed that someday she would earn her associate's degree in child development. Today she is close to fulfilling that dream—just one class to go!

Lourdes knew she wanted to have a classroom of her own from the time she was a little girl. She played teacher with her friends and took a child development course in high school. Every chance she had, Lourdes found ways to work with children. She tutored at the local elementary school and participated in the Big Sister program in her town. During her freshman year, Lourdes signed up for courses in early childhood education, determined to make her lifelong dream come true.

What Makes Someone an Early Childhood Professional?

As evidenced by Scott, Jackie, and Lourdes, early childhood educators come to the field in a variety of ways. Some begin their training on the job; others start in a 2- or 4-year institution. Some are hoping to fulfill a long-held goal; others "discover" the field as a result of different life experiences. Whatever their motivation and entry point, individuals eventually decide to move from layperson status to the professional world of early childhood education. This shift is the result of education and training, not simply desire. Thus, certain characteristics differentiate the professional early childhood educator from a layperson (Kostelnik, Whiren, Soderman, Stein, & Gregory, 2002; Morrison, 2001).

Access to Knowledge Professionals have access to specialized knowledge and skills that are unavailable to amateurs and that are acquired as a result of prolonged education and specialized training. The Association of Childhood Education International (ACEI) and the National Association for the Education of Young Children (NAEYC) have made recommendations for the training of professionals at all levels of early childhood education. Recommended course content and skills include general studies (humanities, mathematics, technology, social sciences, biological and physical sciences, the arts, physical health and fitness), child development and learning, curriculum development and implementation, family and community relationships, assessment and evaluation, professionalism, and field experiences with young children under appropriate supervision.

Although valuable, life experience alone is insufficient to provide the full range of technical know-how and professional skills necessary for maximum effectiveness on the job.

Demonstrated Competence Professionals also differ from amateurs in having to demonstrate competence in their field before they can enter the profession. The most formalized evidence of mastery requires earning a license or certification, which is usually governed by state or national standards. Slightly less formal monitoring involves having to take tests, pass courses, and demonstrate proficiency either in a practicum setting or on the job. All these experiences occur under the supervision of qualified members of the profession.

Standards of Practice Professionals perform their duties in keeping with standards of excellence generally accepted for the field. Such standards arise from research and professional reflection. Some standards are enforced through self-monitoring within the profession, whereas others are maintained through governmental regulation. Whatever the case, professional standards provide a gauge by which early childhood practitioners assess their performance and the overall quality of the services they offer children and families.

Lifelong Learning To keep up with the standards in their field, early childhood professionals constantly upgrade their knowledge and skills both informally and formally. Such efforts include attending workshops, consulting with colleagues, participating in professional organizations, reading professional journals, and pursuing additional schooling. Regardless of the means, professionals treat learning as a lifelong process.

Code of Ethics Although useful, the personal moral code most people bring to their work is inadequate to govern professional behavior. What is common sense to an individual may or may not be congruent with agreed-on standards within the profession. Thus, professionalism requires adoption of an ethical code of conduct that has been formally approved within the field. Such codes provide guidelines for determining acceptable and unacceptable behavior on the job. Specific ethical codes govern professionals whose work involves children. Although the particulars may vary, all ethics codes focus on ensuring confidentiality, providing safe and beneficial experiences, and treating people with respect regardless of sex, race, culture, religion, and ability.

HOW DOES PROGRAM QUALITY AFFECT EARLY CHILDHOOD EDUCATION?

How will you know if the program in which you are participating benefits young children? According to materials prepared for prospective clients, all early childhood programs claim to be outstanding. Is this true? Let us look at some examples.

Brochure describing the early childhood program at the Westover Child Development Center:

Here at the Westover CDC, we offer a high-quality early childhood program for children from three to five years of age. Our teachers all have degrees in child development or early education. We focus on all aspects of children's learning using a play-based curriculum.

Advertisement posted on the community bulletin board of a local grocery store:

High-quality child care in my home. Loving environment. Lots to do. Fun, safe, reliable. References available.

Headline of an editorial in a local newspaper:

Blue Ribbon Panel Outlines Criteria for High-Quality Elementary Schools

Although each example focuses on a different early childhood program, they all mention quality. People who talk about "high quality" are referring to excellence. When something is described as having high quality, we understand that it represents more than the minimum standards and has value exceeding the ordinary. Conversely, "poor quality" suggests an image of substandard conditions and negative outcomes. These variations in quality are particularly important in relation to early childhood education.

Quality Makes a Difference

Quality is a term early childhood professionals often use in describing their programs. Parents, too, are concerned about the quality of their children's education and care. This is true for all families, regardless of background or income level. In a recent national poll, 97 percent of the parents surveyed cited quality as their top priority in determining which early childhood programs they wanted their child to attend (T. M. Smith, Young, Bae, Choy, & Alsalam, 1997). Yet there is a difference in the quality of education and care that children receive. Some children are in high-quality early childhood programs, but many others have poor-quality experiences. High-quality programs benefit children and their families; poor-quality programs are detrimental to them.

Poor-Quality Programs Every day, thousands of children are subjected to program practices that threaten their immediate health and safety as well as their long-term development and learning (Cost, Quality and Child Outcomes Study Team, 1995; Whitebook, Sakai, & Howes, 1997). For instance, poor-quality experiences lead to increased behavioral problems and poorer academic progress in children. Such children are also more likely to have poor social skills (Jambunathan, Burts, & Pierce, 1999; Vandell & Corasanti, 1990). These negative effects appear to be long lasting: Evidence of poor quality is apparent as long as 5 years later. To make matters worse, families may not be able to compensate for the negative impact of poor-quality programs, at least for children who spend 20 or more hours a week in such circumstances (Doherty-Derkowski, 1998). Because high-quality care and education may be more expensive, children in low-income families are the most likely to be enrolled in poor-quality programs at both the preprimary and primary levels. In this way, poor-quality programs compound the challenges such children face.

High-Quality Programs Children whose education and care are described as high quality enjoy a variety of benefits. Such children demonstrate higher levels of language development, greater social competence, a better ability to regulate their behavior, and better academic performance than do their peers in poor-quality programs (National Research Council, 2001). Additional evidence indicates that children who have high-quality early childhood program experiences outperform peers who have no such experiences prior to entering school. These results hold true in the short term and across time. Therefore, our aim as early childhood professionals is to create high-quality early childhood programs for children and families. To do this, we must have a better picture of what such programs involve.

What Do High-Quality Programs Look Like?

With so much at stake, we must ask, "What do high-quality programs look like?" Fortunately, there is a growing research base we can draw on for the answer. The essential components of high-quality early childhood programs are given in the following list (Biddle & Berliner, 2002; Kontos & Wilcox-Herzog, 2001; Stronge, 2002; Whitebook et al., 1997):

Practitioners are well prepared and well compensated.

❏ Adults have specific training in child development, early childhood education, and subject matter content such as literacy, math, and science.

❏ Adults have specific training in content and subject matter relevant to what they are teaching.

❏ Adults vary their teaching strategies and expectations on the basis of what they believe is age appropriate, individually appropriate, and socially and culturally appropriate for each child.

❏ Adults in higher quality programs are paid reasonable wages and receive satisfactory benefits.

Staffing is stable.

❏ Teachers remain with the program and the same group of children long enough for children to develop a trusting relationship with an adult outside the home.

Group sizes are small, and a small number of children are assigned to each practitioner.

❏ The group size and adult–child ratios are small enough that children can engage in firsthand interactions with adults, receiving individualized instruction and personal feedback about their learning experiences.

Warm, attentive relationships are established between adults and children.

❏ Adults are warm, respectful, understanding, affectionate, and friendly toward children.

❏ Adults listen to children and comfort, support, and guide them in ways that make sense to children and help them become more successful in their social interactions.

Environments are safe and healthy.

❏ Health and safety provisions are in place to support children's well-being.

Environments are stimulating.

❏ Adequate, appropriate materials are available to support children's explorations and development of more-advanced knowledge and skills.

❏ The curriculum is designed to support and enrich children's aesthetic, affective, cognitive, language, physical, and social development and learning.

Family involvement is evident.

❏ The program is designed to support and complement families in their child-rearing role.

❏ Family members are welcome to observe, discuss, and recommend policies and to participate in the program's activities.

Links to comprehensive community services are made.

❏ Families are referred and have access to a wide array of services necessary to support their child-rearing responsibilities.

All these quality indicators set the stage for the best possible interactions between children and the early childhood professionals who will help prepare them for the 21st century.

LOOKING TOWARD THE FUTURE

The children with whom you are now working will be adults in a world we have yet to know. Although specific details are difficult to predict, researchers generally agree that to function successfully in the mid-21st century, people will have to demonstrate the following core abilities (Bredekamp & Copple, 1997; Resnick, 1996):

Possess a solid education and be able to apply what they know and can do in relevant situations: Demonstrate knowledge and skills in the areas of literacy, numeracy, science, social studies, music and the visual arts, physical education, and health.

Work well with others: Communicate well, respect others, engage with colleagues to resolve differences of opinion, and function well as members of a team.

Act as problem solvers: Analyze situations, make reasoned judgments, and solve new problems.

Successful citizens of the 21st century need to know how to work together and be flexible thinkers.

Utilize skills broadly and engage in flexible thinking: Apply knowledge and skills across multiple areas, generalize knowledge and skills from one situation to another, and regroup and try alternative approaches when standard solutions fail.

Function as information seekers: Gain access to information through various modes, including spoken and written languages, and intelligently use complex new tools and technologies.

Envision themselves as lifelong learners: Continue to learn new approaches, skills, and knowledge as conditions and needs change.

As early childhood educators, we are becoming increasingly aware that in addition to *what* children learn, we must consider *how* children learn so that we can best promote the development of these core abilities (Slentz & Krogh, 2001a). In trying to describe how to achieve programs that enhance this kind of learning, educators have created the concept of **developmentally appropriate practice.** The remainder of this book is devoted to exploring this concept as a means for achieving high quality.

In chapter 1 we define developmentally appropriate programs and describe the rationale that drives decision making in such programs. In chapter 2 we examine principles of development and learning and the implications these principles have for developmentally appropriate practices. Setting the stage for learning in developmentally appropriate ways is the focus of chapters 3 through 8. In chapter 3 we discuss how to plan small-group activities for children and the typical teaching strategies you will use daily. Planning whole-group activities is the subject of chapter 4, including planning both circle times and field trips. In chapter 5 you learn how to organize indoor and outdoor space, classroom materials, and groups of children to promote optimal learning. Appropriate child guidance is fundamental to all other forms of instruction and provides the foundation for a developmentally appropriate classroom. This critical topic is addressed in chapter 6. In chapter 7 we discuss how authentic assessment can be used to guide children's learning and to plan the early childhood curriculum. The focus of chapter 8 is on integrating home and school perspectives through family involvement. The curriculum is highlighted in chapters 9 through 14. Each of these six chapters centers on one developmental domain: aesthetic, affective, cognitive, language, physical, or social. All six provide an overview of content and developmental processes related to the domain, relevant issues, sample goals for children, developmentally appropriate teaching strategies, and activities you might use to reach the goals of the domain. Although the curricular domains are presented separately, in practice they are integrated throughout the day and across the entire early childhood program. Therefore, integrating the curriculum is the topic of chapters 15 and 16. In chapter 15 we describe how you might use pretend play and construction activities to help children synthesize what they learn in a holistic way. Themes and projects are an additional strategy you might use to integrate the curriculum, and they are described in chapter 16.

We designed this book to help you develop the knowledge base you will need to function as a professional in the field. While you are reading, we encourage you to reflect on the content in terms of your experiences with children and early childhood programs. We hope you will select some topics to explore further and that you will ask questions and challenge concepts you have doubts about. Most important, we urge you to use the material provided in this book to develop personal ideas about how to create and implement high-quality programs for children. You are the emerging generation of early childhood educators. We are looking to you to add to our store of knowledge about best practices in early childhood education.

Part 1

Foundations of Early Childhood Education

Developmentally Appropriate Practice

An Evolving Framework for Teaching Young Children

You may wonder:

Exactly what do people mean when they say a program uses *developmentally appropriate practices*?

How well do developmentally appropriate practices work?

Should all programs for young children use developmentally appropriate practices?

What do developmentally appropriate practices look like in action?

How do your experiences with young children support or challenge the idea of developmentally appropriate practice?

In this chapter on developmentally appropriate practice in early childhood education, we present information to help you answer the preceding questions.

A visitor asked, "How will I know good teaching practices when I see them?"

The principal replied, "Basically, look for action in the learning environment."

Good practice is children in action: children busy constructing, creating with multimedia, enjoying books, exploring, experimenting, inventing, finding out, creating, and composing throughout the day.

Good practice is teachers in action: teachers busy holding conversations, guiding activities, questioning children, challenging children's thinking, observing, drawing conclusions, and planning and monitoring activities throughout the day (Paciorek & Munro, 1995).

Good practices like these are sometimes described as *developmentally appropriate practice*, or *DAP*. DAP has had a powerful influence on people's ideas about early childhood education. In little more than a decade, DAP has moved to center stage in the discussion of what constitutes a good program for young children. In this chapter we explore DAP and what it means for you as an early childhood educator. First, you will read about the origins of DAP, the philosophy, and the general practices associated with it. Empirical support for DAP is also described, as well as critics' opinions of its universal application. Second, you will read about three model programs—the High/Scope approach, the Reggio Emilia approach, and the Montessori approach—all of which illustrate DAP in their operations. These models are just three examples of how the general practices associated with DAP can be combined to create effective programs for children and families. In the third portion of the chapter we review some of the misperceptions about and half-truths associated with DAP. More-accurate interpretations are provided for each. The chapter ends with an outline of the professional practice implications of DAP. This outline was prompted by the material that preceded it. Our hope is to highlight the link between theory and practice. Taken altogether, this information will increase your understanding of an idea that has strongly influenced the field you will be entering. Now, let us look at how and why DAP was created.

WHY IS THERE A NEED FOR DAP?

The Edgewood School Board voted last night to eliminate morning recess for kindergarten and grades 1, 2, and 3.

Board member Roger McPherson says, "This will give us more time for classroom instruction. That's really necessary if the Edgewood Schools are going to improve their math and reading scores on the state assessment."
—*The Edgewood Schools Weekly Register*

Kindergarten teachers are reminded there will be a meeting after school to review the new math workbook series we will be using next year. Refreshments will be served.
—*Morning announcement, Spring Arbor Elementary*

The children look like they're having fun. But when do you get down to the real learning?
—*Prospective parent observing the program for 3- and 4-year-olds at the Spartan Nursery School*

These real-life events illustrate a continuing trend in the United States—the "pushing down" of curriculum from the primary grades into kindergarten and preschool. Practices that only a decade ago were not encountered until first grade or later—such as whole-class instruction, teacher-centered instruction, formal reading instruction, written instruction out of workbooks, and frequent grading—have become commonplace in kindergarten and some preschools (Stipek, Feiler, Daniels, & Milburn, 1995). First and second graders, too, are expected to perform tasks previously reserved for the upper grades, such as taking standardized achievement tests and dealing with possible retention. Parental demands for more academics and a "back to the basics" philosophy have supported such practices.

These trends arose as a result of society's increased recognition that the early years are significant and that early intervention can have beneficial outcomes. Such trends also resulted from our desire to remain competitive with other nations and to help our children "get ahead." The unfortunate result of this competitive urge has been reinforcement of the belief that "earlier is better." Consequently, more and more young children find themselves sitting at desks, filling out workbook sheets, and taking tests to get into kindergarten and first grade. Teachers feel pressured to engage in classroom practices they believe are not in the best interests of young children. Child advocates are alarmed at what they view as an erosion of childhood and the "miseducation" of the youngest members of society. Physicians report a dramatic increase in the numbers of young children who visit them for stress-related illnesses and conditions. Nationwide, people who understand child development warn that children are being hurried into functioning in ways that do not match their natural modes of learning (Elkind, 1989).

The Early Childhood Profession Responds

In response to these circumstances, the National Association for the Education of Young Children (NAEYC) developed a position paper in 1986 defining the concept of DAP. This paper was quickly followed by an NAEYC statement describing examples of appropriate and inappropriate practices for programs serving children aged birth to 8 years (Bredekamp, 1987). "The goal of DAP was to 'open up' the curriculum . . . and move away from the narrow emphasis on isolated academic skills and the drill and practice approach to instruction" that was dominating many programs for young children (Bredekamp & Rosegrant, 1992, p. 4). Several important education associations such as the National Council for the Social Studies, the National Council of Teachers of Mathematics, the Association for Childhood Education International, and the Association for Supervision and Curriculum Development endorsed the NAEYC papers. Within a few years, other organizations such as the National Association of State Boards of Education (1988), the National Association of Elementary School Principals (1990), and the National Education Association (Gullo, 1994) published papers and reports corroborating the basic principles associated with DAP. Today,

> the DAP guidelines have been widely embraced by many early childhood practitioners who view them as formalization of practices they have long advocated. Increasing numbers of school districts in the United States have instituted policies which recognize DAP guidelines as the source of instructional principles for kindergarten and the primary grades. In addition, child care and preschool settings in a wide range of contexts (e.g., employee-sponsored child care, nonprofit, and Head Start) have begun to revise curricula to meet these expectations. *(E. L. Klein, Murphy, & Witz, 1996, p. 144)*

This trend has led thousands of practitioners to use DAP as a basis for examining their practices and those of the programs for which they are responsible.

WHAT IT MEANS TO BE DEVELOPMENTALLY APPROPRIATE

Practitioners who use DAP make decisions about the well-being and education of young children on the basis of three important sources of knowledge (Bredekamp & Copple, 1997):

1. What they know about how children develop and learn

2. What they know about the strengths, needs, and interests of individual children

3. What they know about the social and cultural contexts in which children live

Using this knowledge to guide their thinking, early childhood educators ask themselves, "Is this activity, interaction, or experience age appropriate? Is it individually appropriate? Is it socially and culturally appropriate?"

DAP Is Age Appropriate

Although age is not an absolute measure of a child's capabilities and understandings, it does help establish reasonable expectations of what might be interesting, safe, achievable, and challenging for children to do (Bredekamp & Copple, 1997). To address age appropriateness, we first think about what children are like within a general age range. Next, we develop activities, routines, and expectations that accommodate and complement these characteristics. Mrs. Omura, the teacher in the 4-year-old class, was thinking about age appropriateness when she selected wooden puzzles that contain 8 to 25 pieces for the fine-motor area of her classroom. She made her selections on the basis of her observations of the number of pieces 4-year-olds typically find doable but challenging to complete. Mr. Allison, the second-grade teacher, also made an age-related choice when he chose jigsaw puzzles consisting of 50 to 100 pieces for the youngsters in his group. He was aware that 7- and 8-year-old children find the more complex puzzles stimulating and fun to try. In both cases, the teachers made decisions about age appropriateness on the basis of their understanding of child development, which was gleaned through study and observation.

DAP Is Individually Appropriate

All children within a given age group are not exactly alike. Each child is a unique person with an individual pattern and timing of growth, as well as an individual personality and learning style (Berk, 2003). Certain children are more verbal than others; some enjoy solitude; others crave company; some children are skillful readers at 5 years of age; others may achieve reading proficiency 2 years later. All these variations must be considered in the design, application, and evaluation of activities, interactions, and expectations. For instance, both Mrs. Omura and Mr. Allison chose puzzles that ranged in complexity, knowing that some children would need simpler puzzles to match their current levels of functioning and that other children would benefit from more challenging versions.

In addition, individual children bring certain levels of previous knowledge and skill to each new experience they encounter. Children with little or no exposure to a particular situation should not be expected to perform at the same level of competence as children whose backlog of experience is greater. Thus, Josh, a 6-year-old newly arrived in North Dakota from Florida, might take longer than his same-aged peers the first time he puts on all his winter gear because doing so is entirely new to him. On the basis of the notion of individual appropriateness, his teacher recognizes his need for more time. To ignore his lack of experience and expect Josh to "keep up" with his classmates the first day would be inappropriate according to this principle.

DAP Is Socially and Culturally Appropriate

We must also look at children and families within the context of their community and culture before we can create meaningful, supportive early childhood programs. Let us consider the following examples:

❑ Kyoko eats rice for breakfast at home. During a nutrition activity at school, some children insist that rice is only a dinner food. The teacher points out that people eat rice sometimes at breakfast, sometimes at lunch, and sometimes at dinner. Later she reads a story called *Everybody Cooks Rice,* which describes people eating rice prepared in various ways and at different meals.

❑ In Nathan's family, children are taught to cast their eyes downward to show respect for their elders. Knowing this, the teacher does not demand that Nathan look her in the eye when she talks to him about why he and another child were arguing.

❑ Powwows are very important in First Nations Cree culture, and most of the children in the Grade 2–3 combined class on a First Nations Reserve in Alberta, Canada, have experienced powwows. However, the teacher realizes that few of them know much about the traditions behind these important community events. This realization prompts her to introduce the topic "powwows" for the children to investigate.

In each preceding situation, the early childhood practitioner demonstrated respect for the child and his or her family by taking into account the social and cultural contexts in which they live. Understanding social and cultural contexts requires early childhood professionals to recognize differences among children as well as characteristics children have in common with others in a cultural group (C. B. Phillips, 1991). Culture is defined by values, traditions, and beliefs that are shared and passed down from one generation to the next. Groups of people develop common bonds based on their ethnic or linguistic heritage, geography, customs, social class, income, lifestyle, or particular life events (Berns, 2001). Thus, people may share certain values, traditions, and beliefs because they have one or more of the following characteristics:

Are Mexican American

Can trace their roots to Lebanon

Live in western Nebraska

Speak Mandarin

Consider themselves middle class

See themselves as part of the baby-boomer generation

Are family members of a child with a disability

Grew up in a single-parent home

> Growing up as members of a family and community, children learn the rules of their culture—explicitly through direct teaching and implicitly through the behavior of those around them. Among the rules they learn are how to show respect, how to interact with people they know well as compared to those they just met, how to organize time and personal space, how to dress, what and when to eat, how to respond to major life transitions and celebrations, how to worship, and countless other behaviors that humans perform with little apparent thought everyday. Individual children may be members of more than one cultural group and may be embedded in their cultures to different degrees. *(Bredekamp & Copple, 1997, p. 42)*

Because of the amount of variation among people, no single "correct" set of cultural beliefs exists. Instead, adults who work with children must recognize the legitimacy of multiple perspectives, including those very different from their own. For example, "It is important to know the family's view of child rearing and their expectations, both personally and culturally. . . . To set up programming that promotes independent functioning and adaptive skills with a family that values dependency is almost sure to fail" (Deiner, 1993, p. 333). Similarly, home visits may be welcome by some families but perceived as intrusive by others. On the basis of the community context in which they live, young children in an urban neighborhood might find a class project on public transportation useful, whereas children in a rural community (where no such transportation is available) might find the same content less relevant. The more that strategies and content build on what is familiar to children and families, the more comfortable they feel. The more congruent that expectations are between home and the early childhood environment, the more productively children learn.

When we ignore these contexts, we lose access to the rich backgrounds children bring to the classroom from home. Likewise, we cannot take advantage of the full range of children's interests and abilities to help them achieve the learning goals of the program (Bredekamp & Copple, 1997). Even worse, we communicate to chil-

dren that they are unacceptable or deficient in the eyes of the program (Chipman, 1997; Hale, 1994). This lack of sensitivity and respect for social and cultural contexts leads to negative results for children and programs alike. Thus, understanding what may be interpreted as meaningful to and respectful of children and their families is a key element in determining developmental appropriateness.

The Essence of Developmental Appropriateness

Weaving the strands of age appropriateness, individual appropriateness, and sociocultural appropriateness into a cohesive philosophy requires deliberate effort and continuous reflection by early childhood practitioners. First, we as educators must recognize the unique ways in which children are children, not miniature adults. Experiences and expectations planned for children should reflect that early childhood is a time of life qualitatively different from that of the later school years and adulthood. This means we must take into account everything we know about how children develop and learn and match it to the content and strategies planned for them in early childhood programs. Second, we must think of children as individuals, not as a cohort group. This means recognizing that even children who

These children are learning by doing.

share many similar characteristics are still singular human beings. Finally, we must treat children with respect. This requires us to learn about and value the families, communities, and cultures that shape children's lives. These beliefs and intentions form the essence of DAP. As you read the next section of this chapter, consider how these strands are apparent in the practices described.

GENERAL PRACTICES TYPICALLY ASSOCIATED WITH DAP

DAP provides a resource for thinking about, planning, and implementing high-quality programs for young children. It informs our decision making and gives us a basis for continually scrutinizing our professional practices. Within the NAEYC document, examples of appropriate and inappropriate practices are outlined for infants and toddlers, children aged 3 to 5 years, and children aged 6 through 8 years. (Refer to Table 1.1 for an example.)

As you can see from Table 1.1, *inappropriate* practice sometimes reflects errors of omission (ignoring parental concerns) as well as errors of commission (communicating with parents only about problems and conflicts). *Appropriate* practices are often defined between these extremes (working in partnership with parents and listening to and talking with parents not only about concerns, but also about children's strengths). Although the NAEYC document contains many examples of appropriate and inappropriate practices, 10 fundamental practices characterize the DAP philosophy (Gullo, 1994; Hart, Burts, & Charlesworth, 1997; D. F. Miller, 2004):

1. *Addressing the "whole child."* Early childhood professionals address child development and learning from a holistic perspective, creating curricula to meet children's emotional, social, cognitive, and physical needs.
2. *Individualizing the program to suit particular children.* Program planning and implementation are adapted to meet the different needs, levels of functioning, and interests of children in the group.
3. *Recognizing the importance of child-initiated activity.* Children are active decision makers in the learning process. Teachers accept a wide range of constructive child responses.
4. *Recognizing the significance of play as a vehicle for learning.* Play is valued and facilitated both indoors and outdoors.
5. *Creating flexible, stimulating classroom environments.* Teachers actively promote children's learning, using direct and indirect instruction as appropriate.
6. *Using an integrated curriculum.* Program content and curriculum areas (e.g., science, math, literacy, and social studies) are combined in the context of daily activities.
7. *Learning by doing.* Children engage in concrete experiences with real materials. The activities in which they participate are relevant and meaningful to them.
8. *Giving children choices about what and how they learn.* Teachers provide a wide range of activities and materials from which children may choose and within which children pursue educational goals in many ways.
9. *Continually assessing individual children and the program as a whole.* Practitioners use a variety of assessment strategies, including formal and informal techniques. Standardized assessment is deemphasized in favor of performance-based documentation.
10. *Forming partnerships with family.* Parents and other significant family members are valued as partners and decision makers in the education process. Their involvement in their children's education is viewed as desirable and essential.

Practices that negate those just described are often characterized as developmentally inappropriate. These include the following:

❏ Focusing on limited aspects of child development and learning (e.g., cognitive or social) to the exclusion of all others
❏ Expecting all children to learn the same things at the same time in the same way
❏ Creating programs dominated by teacher-centered activities in which the children's role is passive and only one response is judged acceptable
❏ Treating play as superfluous or unacceptable
❏ Creating rigid, uninteresting classroom environments
❏ Fragmenting and compartmentalizing curricula into isolated lessons that have no relation to one another
❏ Expecting children to learn mostly through listening and engaging in abstract activities that have little meaning or relevance to them
❏ Denying children opportunities to make choices or to function as active decision makers in the learning process
❏ Assessing children's learning sporadically and in ways that are unrelated to their classroom experiences
❏ Treating parents and family members as adversaries or as inconsequential

TABLE 1.1 Examples of Appropriate Practices and Inappropriate Practices Related to Establishing Reciprocal Relationships with Families

Age Group	Appropriate Practices	Inappropriate Practices
Infants and toddlers	Caregivers work in partnership with parents, communicating daily to build mutual understanding and trust and to ensure the infant's welfare and optimal development. Caregivers listen carefully to what parents say about their children, seek to understand parents' goals and preferences, and are respectful of family and cultural differences.	Caregivers communicate with parents only about problems or conflicts, ignore parents' concerns, or avoid difficult issues rather than resolving them with parents.
3- to 5-year-olds	Parents are always welcome in the program, and home visits by teachers are encouraged. Opportunities for parent participation are arranged to accommodate parents' schedules. Parents have opportunities to be involved in ways that are comfortable for them, such as observing, reading to children, or sharing a skill or hobby.	Teachers view parents' visits to the program as intrusive and discourage parents from visiting. Parent participation is so limited that visits rarely disrupt the classroom. Parent meetings or other participation opportunities occur only during the day, when many employed parents are unavailable.
6- to 8-year-olds	Educators and parents share decisions about children's education. Teachers listen to parents and seek to understand their goals for their children. Teachers work with parents to resolve problems or differences of opinion and are respectful of cultural and family differences.	School personnel do not involve parents in decisions about how best to handle children's problems or support their learning. They see parents in a negative light, complaining that the parents have not raised their children well or blaming the children's poor school performance on the home environment. Teachers make only formal contacts with parents through report cards and one yearly conference.

IT REQUIRES JUDGMENT TO DETERMINE DEVELOPMENTAL APPROPRIATENESS

Referring to the practices just outlined, can you determine which of the following situations are developmentally appropriate and which are not?

Twenty 4-year-olds have been in circle time for 40 minutes.—DAP or not DAP?

Suzanne wants the easel all to herself. Bianca wants a turn. The first-grade teacher helps the girls develop a timetable for sharing during the next several minutes.—DAP or not DAP?

Jamie, a kindergartner, laboriously copies a series of words onto lined paper.—DAP or not DAP?

Your first impression may be that a 40-minute circle time is too long for most 4-year-olds and that copy work is not the best way to teach children to write. If so, you

probably decided that these scenarios were examples of developmentally inappropriate practices. You may also have assumed that helping two children learn to share clearly illustrates DAP. However, closer scrutiny may prompt you to reassess your original judgments. For instance, you might revise your opinion about the circle time after learning that the children are enthralled by a storyteller who actively involves them in the storytelling process and that the group time has been prolonged in response to the children's request, "Tell us another one." Likewise, helping children to share is usually a worthwhile aim. However, in this case, Suzanne's aunt, uncle, and cousins recently lost most of their belongings in a household fire. They are staying with Suzanne's family, and Suzanne is having to share many things for the first time—attention at home, her room, and most of her things. Knowing this, we might determine that making her share the easel on this occasion is unnecessarily stressful. Helping Bianca find an alternative activity that will satisfy her desire to paint could be a better course of action for now. A second look at Jamie reveals that he is working hard to copy the words "I love you" for a present he is making for his mom. He is using a model created by another child and is writing on paper he selected himself. Within this context, Jamie's being engaged in copy work no longer seems questionable (Kostelnik, 1993).

Scenarios such as these illustrate that determining what does or does not constitute DAP requires more than simply memorizing a set of do's and don't's or looking at children's activities in isolation. It involves considering every practice within the context in which it is occurring and making a judgment about what is happening to a particular child in a particular place at a particular time (Kostelnik, 1998). The best judgments are those you make consciously.

Faced with having to determine the extent to which their actions are developmentally appropriate, many early childhood educators find asking the following three questions useful:

1. Is this practice in keeping with what I know about child development and learning?
2. Does this practice take into account children's individual strengths and needs?
3. Does this practice demonstrate respect for children's social and cultural lives?

These queries can address immediate concerns or serve as the basis for long-term deliberations. They can stimulate individual thinking or consideration of program practices by an entire staff. In every circumstance, the answer to all three questions should be "yes." A "no" answer to any of them is a strong sign that the practice should be reconsidered, revamped, or discarded. If uncertainty exists about a question in relation to a certain practice, that practice is worth examining further. Your response will depend on your interpretation of what is age appropriate, individually appropriate, and socioculturally appropriate in terms of specific children. Your knowledge of child development and learning, your understanding of curriculum development and implementation, your awareness of family and community relationships, your knowledge of assessment and evaluation, and your interpretation of your professional role will also influence what you do (NAEYC, 1996b). All these factors, combined with an understanding of DAP, should guide early childhood decision making.

DAP HAS HISTORIC ROOTS

The practices associated with developmental appropriateness did not emerge all at once, nor were they the

Children in developmentally appropriate classrooms are excited about school and eager to learn.

product of any one person's thinking. Although strongly influenced by the theories of Jean Piaget, Lev Vygotsky, and Eric Erickson, certain ideas such as whole-child teaching and hands-on learning evolved during hundreds of years. Table 1.2 provides a brief description of some early philosophers and child advocates whose contributions laid a foundation for general practices that characterize DAP classrooms. This list is not complete, but it will give you a sense of some of the people who helped shape practices in early childhood education today.

Now that we considered the basic components of DAP, let us explore the effectiveness of this approach. For any framework to stand the test of time, it must be supported by demonstrable results.

THERE IS EMPIRICAL SUPPORT FOR DEVELOPMENTALLY APPROPRIATE PROGRAMS

Facts, Watson. We must have facts.
—The Adventures of Sherlock Holmes (1939)

What began as a "feeling" for many people is becoming a documented reality. The evidence is mounting that flexible curriculum models, which incorporate DAP principles into their programs, lead to positive educational outcomes. In contrast to programs that ignore such principles, DAP-based programs are more likely to produce long-term gains in children's intellectual development,

TABLE 1.2 People Whose Work Contributed to Current Practices

Person	Contribution
John Amos Comenius (1592–1670) Moravian philosopher "All material of learning must be divided according to age levels."	Wrote that multisensory learning was more relevant than verbal learning alone Maintained that learning progresses from general to specific and from easier to more difficult Urged parents to become involved in their children's education
John Locke (1632–1704) English philosopher "None of the things children are to learn should be made a burden to them."	Discussed individual differences among children Believed that education should begin early and be enjoyable to children Suggested that teaching was best accomplished through modeling, using praise, providing opportunities for children to practice what they learned, and adapting to each child's current capacity
Jean Jacques Rousseau (1712–1778) French philosopher "A child should neither be treated as an irrational animal, nor as a man, but simply as a child."	Recognized individual patterns of development within children Promoted the idea that children's natural curiosity was a strong source of learning Believed that the school should fit the child, not that the child must fit the school
Johann Heinrich Pestalozzi (1746–1827) Swiss philosopher and teacher "Success depends upon how well what is taught to children commends itself to them as true, through being closely connected with their own personal observation and experience."	Emphasized child-initiated activities and sensory learning Advocated specialized teacher training that was focused on children, not just subject matter
Robert Owen (1771–1858) Welsh industrialist and social reformer "Physical punishment in a rationally conducted infant school will never be required and should be avoided as much as giving children poison in their food."	Created an employer-sponsored infant school that was a forerunner of the North American preschool Favored multiage groupings among children 2, 3, 4, and 5 years old Focused on hands-on learning and field trips as a way to observe how real things existed in the world Emphasized the importance of positive discipline Advocated relevant assessment based on children's individual progress
Friedrich Wilhelm Froebel (1782–1852) German philosopher "The prime purpose throughout is not to impart knowledge to the child but to lead the child to observe and think."	Became known as the father of the kindergarten Stressed the significance of play and the value of childhood as a time of importance for its own sake, not simply as preparation for adulthood Created the first curriculum—including a planned program for children to follow, routines (songs, finger plays, and circle time), and specialized objects for learning (called *gifts*—objects for children to handle) Encouraged women to receive special training to become teachers
Margaret McMillan (1860–1931) British reformer and teacher "Every slum child is a power-house of energy, once given a chance to grow."	First used the term *nursery school* Focused on whole-child learning through play, sensory experience, and open-air classrooms Advocated performing daily health checks and teaching children self-care as ways to combat health problems brought on by poverty Emphasized working with parents, and suggested doing home visits

(continued)

TABLE 1.2 *(continued)*

Person	Contribution
John Dewey (1859–1952) American educator "Education therefore is a process of living and not a preparation for future living."	Advocated children's learning by doing through hands-on activities, projects, units of study, and a child-centered, integrated curriculum
	Highlighted the value of play
	Promoted respect for children's individuality
	Founded the first "laboratory" school for the study of child development and teaching methods through systematic research and practice
Patty Hill Smith (1868–1946) American educator "Observe the children and follow their lead."	Emphasized the importance of the kindergarten experience in children's lives
	Promoted hands-on learning, experimentation, and self-discovery
	Wrote the song "Happy Birthday"
	Wrote a kindergarten manual that attempted to systematically define best practices for young children
	Founded the National Committee on Nursery Schools (1926), which eventually became the National Association for the Education of Young Children (NAEYC)

social and emotional skills, and life-coping capabilities (Dunn & Kontos, 1997; Hart et al., 1997; Marcon, 1999). Although much remains to be learned, following are the facts about the effectiveness of DAP as we currently know them.

Cognitive Outcomes

Children's creative-thinking and problem-solving skills are enhanced when children participate in developmentally appropriate preschool or primary classrooms (Hirsh-Pasek, Hyson, & Rescorla, 1990; Hyson, Hirsh-Pasek, & Rescorla, 1990). Equally important, children recognize their cognitive competence, accurately perceiving themselves as having the know-how to work through intellectual challenges (Mantzicopoulos, Neuharth-Pritchett, & Morelock, 1994).

Children in developmentally appropriate classrooms have been found to be more involved in the process of understanding mathematics than have children who are taught mathematics with more didactic methods. The former group displays a better grasp of mathematical concepts and is more adept at generalizing numeracy skills across situations (Nicholls, Cobb, Wood, Yackel, & Patashnick, 1991). In other research, second graders who had been in DAP programs since kindergarten scored significantly higher on mathematics achievement tests than did youngsters who were not (Sherman & Mueller, 1996).

Likewise, children participating in developmentally appropriate reading programs demonstrate better letter–word identification, better comprehension of literature read to them, and better understanding of what they have read than do youngsters who participate in classrooms in which DAP is not evident (Huffman & Speer, 2000; Palincsar & Brown, 1989). Children whose teachers embrace DAP also demonstrate better listening skills and are more verbally adept (Dunn, Beach, & Kontos, 1994; Marcon, 1992). Reading achievement tests have yielded mixed results about which strategies are most generally effective. Some studies indicate that didactic teaching leads to higher scores in letter recognition at the preschool and kindergarten levels (Stipek et al., 1995). Other research shows that children who were in DAP classrooms for at least 3 years outscored other children in reading achievement by the second grade (Sherman & Mueller, 1996). Such results may indicate that didactic methods have short-term effects but do not sustain these benefits with time. These results may also demonstrate that certain teaching methods are better suited for certain skills and that a mix of strategies will ultimately be necessary to obtain the best results. More research is needed before any conclusions can be made. However, DAP-oriented strategies now appear to have many long-lasting benefits for children who are learning to read (Figure 1.1).

FIGURE 1.1   Developmentally Appropriate Practice: Mathematics and Language Arts

Sara, a budding writer, brings over her math journal [to the observer]. It is January. The entry illustrates Sara's capabilities for inventing her own math problems, as well as her composing, spelling and grammar capabilities.

there Were 4
Boys playing
Baskitball. And they
Lost it. And a girl
Finded it. How Many
is there now?
                5

Later, the students divide into several small groups. Their teacher has read them the story One Gorilla, *by Atsuko Morozumi. Each illustration contains the wandering gorilla and increasing numbers of different animals. The children are to use crayons, pencil, paper and Unifix Cubes to calculate the number of animals. They are to draw their solutions and write at least two sentences describing their method. A buzz of activity begins as each group organizes itself and goes to work. When everyone is finished, each group presents its solution to the class. A variety of approaches have been used. For example, one group has counted out Unifix Cubes, and then, using one-to-one-correspondence, written tally marks; another group has one long row of cubes stuck together. The accompanying written explanations were:*

We did unafick cubes and then we did tally Marcks and there were 56

We counted them up and there was 56. It was fun!

Source: Charlesworth, R. (1998). Developmentally appropriate practice is for everyone. *Childhood Education, 74*(5), 278.

Social Outcomes

Children enrolled in developmentally appropriate classrooms exhibit fewer negative social behaviors, better social problem-solving skills, and more cooperation than do children in more traditional classrooms (Jambunathan, Burts, & Pierce, 1999; Mantzicopoulos et al., 1994; Marcon, 1992). Children whose teachers act in developmentally appropriate ways exhibit significantly fewer stress-related behaviors than those exhibited by children whose teachers rely on strategies described as developmentally inappropriate (Burts, Hart, Charlesworth, & Kirk, 1990, 1992; Hart, Burts, Durland, Charlesworth, DeWolf, & Fleege, 1998; Love, Ryer, & Faddis, 1992). Although children in DAP groups are not completely stress free, both the number of incidents and the total amount of stress they display are far less than those exhibited by children whose time in school is dominated by whole-group instruction, paper-and-pencil tasks, and oral drills.

Children's self-esteem is positively influenced when teachers treat them in ways congruent with DAP (N. E. Curry & Johnson, 1990). Student attitudes toward school and teachers are apt to be more favorable as well (Hyson et al., 1990; Wiltz & Klein, 2001).

Let Us Consider Diversity

One important question is how well DAP contributes to the positive development, learning, and academic success of diverse children. Many people speculate that DAP is well suited for some youngsters but not appropriate for others. In response to these concerns, current evidence indicates that DAP has the potential to "provide strong foundational experiences for males and females from different racial and socioeconomic backgrounds" (Hart et al., 1997, p. 8). For instance, the positive program results associated with DAP that were described previously are evident for boys and for girls, for children from higher income families and lower income families, and for European American, Native American, and African American youngsters. These results seem to support the idea that children benefit from DAP even when their backgrounds are diverse. Conversely, substantial inequities exist for children in classrooms categorized as developmentally inappropriate. In such programs, females, children of higher socioeconomic status, and White children all perform better and report less stressful experiences than do males, children of lower socioeconomic status, Native American children, and African American children (Charlesworth, Hart, Burts, Thomasson, Mosely, & Fleege, 1993; Dunn & Kontos, 1997; Hart et al., 1998; Little-Soldier, 1992).

Initial results indicate that DAP is a promising approach for working with diverse populations of children. However, additional studies specifically structured to answer questions of diversity are necessary before we can comfortably say as a fact that DAP meets the needs of all the children and families that early childhood educators serve.

DAP Has Its Critics

To imply that DAP has met with universal approval and acceptance within the field would be a misrepresentation of the facts. Since its inception, thoughtful critics have suggested that DAP fails to meet the needs of diverse children and families in defining what constitutes "appropriate practice." Many of these criticisms question the theories that underpin DAP as well as gaps in the knowledge base on which DAP is founded. The most common concerns are summarized as follows:

❏ Early childhood professionals have been cautioned that DAP's focus on child-centered teaching supports middle-class values, while negating the more didactic programs frequently preferred by lower income families (D. Powell, 1994).

❏ Many critics believe the DAP philosophy is too narrow to support the optimal development and learning of ethnic, racial, and linguistic minority children and families (Delpit, 1995; Lubeck, 1994).

❏ Special educators warn that although many points of congruence can be found between DAP and special education practices, DAP alone is insufficient to address the wide-ranging problems faced by children with disabilities (Carta, Schwartz, Atwater, & McConnell, 1993; Wolery, Strain, & Bailey, 1992).

❏ Concern has been expressed that DAP's emphasis on child development as a foundation for practice is flawed. This criticism hinges on two points. First, critics point out that much of the current knowledge base related to child development relies on data dominated by European American biases. Evidence from cross-cultural investigations of child development conducted since 1980 challenges current beliefs regarding normative child development and processes as well as optimal child development settings (New, 1994). Second, early childhood professionals are reminded that child development theory and research is part but not all that is necessary to design comprehensive education programs (L. Katz, 1996; Spodek & Brown, 1993). Factors such as learning theory, research on teaching, subject-matter content, and cultural, political, and economic factors are also essential to consider.

❏ Theoretically, DAP has been criticized as emphasizing the role of maturation in children's learning more than it has emphasized the social environment (T. Cross, 1995; Fleer, 1995; Lubeck, 1998). Critics protest that teachers assume they have no direct input into children's learning. Educators and researchers who express this concern believe that children do not experience enough intellectual challenge in DAP-oriented programs.

❏ As DAP has become more widely implemented, educators say that it is often used in too prescriptive a fashion. When this happens, DAP becomes a rigid set of criteria rather than a tool for guiding teachers' judgments and decision making (Kessler, 1991; Kostelnik, 1993).

❏ Scholars outside the United States have voiced concern about transplanting the child-centered focus of DAP to other cultures such as South Korea, Australia, or China (Fleer, 1995; Hsue & Aldridge, 1995; Jackson, 1997).

Criticisms such as these have fostered vigorous debate and much reflection regarding early childhood education. The exchange of views that has resulted has vitalized the field and broadened the conversation. It has also led to new research and deeper understandings, which in turn have stimulated greater refinements in DAP and the theories and practices that support it. In response to input from many sources, the NAEYC published *Developmentally Appropriate Practice in Early Childhood Programs* (Bredekamp & Copple, 1997). The revised document maintains the fundamental principles of the original version but includes new emphases that address many of the concerns just listed. These new focus points are as follows:

❏ Whereas the original document spoke primarily to age appropriateness and individual appropriateness, the revised edition of DAP more clearly stresses the role of culture in children's development and learning. The idea of social and cultural appropriateness is equal in importance to the first two criteria in defining developmentally appropriate practices.

❏ The significance of families in early childhood education is discussed in more detail.

❏ Emphasis on the social environment and its relation to childhood learning has increased. Also, the importance of teachers as active participants in children's development and learning is more fully described.

❏ The need for multiple sources of information (beyond child development theory) to inform practice is underscored in the revised edition of DAP.

❏ Examples of appropriate and inappropriate practices are presented along a continuum, not as polar opposites. The hope is that the document will less likely be used "cookbook" fashion. Instead, the new edition of DAP emphasizes decision making based on principles that take into account the varying needs of children, families, and communities.

It is still too early to tell how well the revised edition of developmentally appropriate practices will satisfy concerns elicited by the original concept. Theoretical arguments aside, the "proof of the pudding" will be in whether the diverse population of children and families is better served. It is also not possible to clearly identify new issues that may arise as people use the revised DAP guidelines in their daily work with children and families. What we do know is that the concept of DAP will continue to evolve with time. People will still debate and discuss professional practice. These discussions will play a significant part in the forward progress of the field.

WHAT DOES THE DAP DEBATE MEAN FOR EARLY CHILDHOOD PRACTITIONERS?

The debate about DAP is not simply a philosophical argument being carried out by a few academicians in the field. Every day, people at all levels of the profession are engaged in discussions about DAP—what it is, how to enact it effectively, and how to revise it to better support their work with children and families. This ongoing discussion is important for three reasons. First, it tells us that we are part of a "thinking" profession. As early childhood educators, we face many challenges. Some are economic (how to obtain better wages); some are political (how to move children up on the political agenda); and others are physical (how to get through the day without being totally exhausted). However, our work poses intellectual demands as well, requiring clear, creative thinking. Thus, we must continually ask ourselves, "Is our current understanding of DAP comprehensive and inclusive? Does it provide a useful framework? How can DAP be adapted to accommodate the differences among us while maintaining the integrity of its guiding principles?" These critical issues remain open to question and will require our best efforts to answer.

Second, the DAP debate reminds us that the knowledge base undergirding the field is continually changing. We can never sit back and assume that what we know now is all we will ever need to know. Instead, we must approach our profession as lifelong learners—examining, revising, and expanding our thinking with time.

Finally, the debate has made clear that a one-size-fits-all approach to teaching is neither functional nor desirable. No single set of strategies is automatically best for every situation. A strategy appropriate for one child may be less appropriate for another child in another circumstance. Instead, we must adapt our methods to fit the strengths and needs of the children and families we serve. Keeping these ideas in mind, let us examine how programs that exemplify DAP are similar and how they sometimes differ from one another.

DAP PROGRAMS VARY IN STRUCTURE AND CONTENT

LaJoya Gatewood and her husband are looking for an early childhood program in which to enroll their 3-year-old son and 7-year-old daughter. During their search, they visit three facilities, all of which are self-described as using DAP.

The literature for the Burcham Hills Child Development Center states, "We offer a developmentally appropriate array of activities for children designed to foster the development and well-being of the whole child. With the support of caring teachers, children play and experiment, making their own discoveries about the physical and social worlds in which they live. Children learn indoors and outside, in the classroom, at home, and in the neighborhood. Fieldtrips are an integral part of the program as are visits to the classroom by parents and other family members. Parents receive suggested home activities related to what is happening in the classroom on a weekly basis. Every September the staff conduct home visits. During these times, teachers and parents talk about and then develop relevant goals for each child. The staff keep careful records of children's progress and share these with parents throughout the year."

During a visit to the Christian Children's Center they are told, "The philosophy that guides the program at CCC is based on Christian values and developmentally appropriate practice. One of the obvious distinctions of our center is the Christian atmosphere we strive to maintain. Strong efforts are made to incorporate the loving presence of Jesus Christ throughout our program. This includes saying a short prayer before meals, having Bible stories in our book corner and at story times, and teaching children simple Bible verses. We also stress, as Jesus did, the importance of loving and caring for one another. In addition, we appreciate that children develop at varying rates and create programs that allow children to progress at a comfortable pace in learning the skills and concepts necessary for later success in school."

The brochure for the Rosa Parks Community School says, "At the Rosa Parks Community School, children experience a dynamic infusion of African American culture into the early childhood curriculum. Framed within the context of developmentally appropriate practice, children come away with a love of learning and positive self-esteem gained through meaningful activity. Hands-on learning is central to the program. Children learn about Africa and their rich cultural heritage; they learn about African American and African heroes and heroines, music, arts and crafts, and folktales. Teachers come from Africa as well as the United States, and all have first-hand knowledge of African culture."

All these programs have features the Gatewoods like, but each is distinct from the others. The family wonders, "How can programs that differ so greatly in focus all be described as developmentally appropriate?" The answer to their question lies in the fact that DAP is a philosophy, a framework, and an approach to working with children. It is not a single curriculum (Bredekamp & Rosegrant, 1992). Consequently, early childhood programs that incorporate developmentally appropriate practices into their overall design vary in structure and content. At the same time, they share a common commitment to the principles that are a hallmark of the philosophy.

We asked early childhood educators highly involved in the design of three program models to summarize the key elements of their work. The three models they describe are the High/Scope approach, the Reggio Emilia approach, and the Montessori approach. As you read these descriptions, consider how each program demonstrates DAP principles in its operations.

The High/Scope Approach to Early Childhood Education

Mary Hohmann

High/Scope Educational Research Foundation

Origins

The High/Scope educational approach, currently used in settings serving the full range of preschool-aged and early elementary–aged children, was originally developed to serve "at-risk" children in Ypsilanti, Michigan. In 1962, David P. Weikart, former president of the High/Scope Educational Research Foundation, initiated the Perry Preschool Project to see if early education could counteract the persistent school failure of high school students from Ypsilanti's poorest neighborhoods. During this project, teachers worked with 3- and 4-year-old children in a classroom setting for 3 hours a day, conducted daily staff meetings, and made weekly home visits. The basic framework of the High/Scope approach emerged with active learning, a plan–do–review process, and small-group activities as its core. A longitudinal study of the students in the Perry Preschool Project found that at age 27 the preschool students, compared to a group of children from the same neighborhood with no preschool experience, were less likely to have been arrested or receive social services, and more likely to be high school graduates, to earn at least $2,000/month, and to own a home.

Central Principles

Five basic principles—active learning, supportive adult–child interactions, a materials-rich learning environment, a consistent daily routine, and ongoing child assessment—form the framework of the High/Scope approach. Through *active learning*—having direct and immediate experiences and deriving meaning from them through reflection—young children construct knowledge that helps them make sense of their world. The power of active learning comes from personal initiative. Young children act on their innate desire to explore; they ask and search for answers to questions about people, materials, events, and ideas that arouse their curiosity; they solve problems that stand in the way of their goals; and they generate new strategies to try. As

FIGURE 1.2 High/Scope Key Experiences

The areas of key experiences for preschool children are as follows:

Creative representation   Classification
Language and literacy   Seriation
Initiative and social relations   Number
Movement   Space
Music   Time

The areas of key experiences for elementary children related to language and literacy, mathematics, and science are as follows:

Language and Literacy
  Speaking and listening
  Reading
  Writing

Mathematics
  Collections of objects   Measurement of continuous quantity
  Number and numerical operations   Movement, time, and speed
  Geometry and space   Language, symbols, and graphing

Science
  Observing   Designing, building, fabricating, and modifying
  Classifying and ordering materials   structures or materials
  Measuring, testing, and analyzing   Reporting and interpreting data and results
  Observing, predicting, and
  controlling change

Source: Mary Hohmann, High/Scope Educational Research Foundation.

they follow their intentions, children engage in key experiences—creative, ongoing interactions with people and materials that support children's mental, emotional, social, and physical growth. A brief summary of the High/Scope key experiences is available in Figure 1.2.

Active learning depends on *supportive adult–child interactions.* Mindful of the importance of providing a psychologically safe climate for young learners, adults using the High/Scope approach strive to be supportive as they converse and interact with children. Throughout the day, guided by an understanding of how young children think and reason, adults practice supportive interaction strategies—sharing control with children, focusing on children's strengths, forming authentic relationships with children, supporting children's ideas, and adopting a problem-solving approach to social conflict. For example, when a child talks, an adult listens attentively, makes related comments and observations, and asks open-ended questions directly related to what the child is doing, thinking, and saying. This interaction style enables the child to confidently express thoughts and feelings, construct an understanding of concepts, and experience partnership in dialogue. Adults rely on encouragement and use a problem-solving approach to deal with everyday classroom situations rather than a child-management system based on praise, punishment, and reward.

Because the *physical setting* has a strong impact on the behavior of children and adults, the High/Scope approach places a strong emphasis on planning the layout of the classroom or center, selecting appropriate materials, and making them accessible to children. An active-learning environment provides children with ongoing opportunities to make choices and decisions. Thus, adults organize the learning space into specific interest areas well stocked with natural, found, commercial, and homemade materials that provide many opportunities each day for children to engage in the key experience in creative purposeful ways.

In addition to arranging the setting, adults also plan a *consistent daily routine* that supports active learning. The routine enables young children to anticipate what happens next and gives them a great deal of control over what they do during each part of their day. The High/Scope daily routine includes the plan–do–review process, which enables children to express their intentions, carry them out, and reflect on what they have done. Small-group times (for younger children) and workshops (for older children) encourage children to explore and experiment with materials and concepts adults have selected based on their daily observations of children's interests, abilities, and the key experiences.

In the High/Scope approach, *assessment* includes a range of tasks teachers undertake to ensure that observing children, interacting with children, and planning for children receive full adult energy and attention. Each day, teachers gather accurate information about children by observing and interacting with children and taking anecdotal notes based on what they see and hear. Periodically, they use the child observations they have noted to complete a key experience–based child assessment for each child—the High/Scope Child Observation Record (COR).

Where Readers Can Find Out More

The High/Scope approach is described in *Educating Young Children* (1995), by Mary Hohmann and David P. Weikart, and *Foundations in Elementary Education: Overview,* by Charles Hohmann and Warren Buckleitner, available from High/Scope Press, 600 North River, Ypsilanti, MI 48198-2898; telephone: 1-800-407-7377. For up-to-date information about High/Scope training, research, publications, and videos, visit the High/Scope home page: http://www.highscope.org

The Reggio Emilia Approach to Early Childhood Education

Carolyn Pope Edwards

University of Nebraska—Lincoln

Origins

Reggio Emilia is a city in northern Italy where a volunteer group of educators, parents, and children came together after World War II with a shared vision for a new kind of school for young children. After the suffering and destruction of the war, they wanted to offer hope to society and improve life for children and families. Under the leadership of the founding director, Loris Malaguzzi (1920–1994), the system then evolved from a parent cooperative movement into a city-run system of first preschools and then also infant–toddler centers. The system exercises a leadership role in educational innovation in Italy and Europe, and now increasingly the world. Through their experience in the Reggio Emilia preschools, children learn to engage in dialogues and debates with others in a nonviolent and constructive manner and develop problem-solving skills. Children (and families) are also encouraged to express and discuss ideas in open-democratic meetings and to form close, long-term relationships with others in the school. The schools are publicly funded and inclusive, giving first priority to children with disabilities or social service needs.

Goals

The Reggio Emilia approach is not an educational model in the formal sense, with defined methods, teacher certification standards, and accreditation processes. Instead, educators speak of their "experience" and how it can be a source of reflection to others. Loris Malaguzzi was a social constructivist, influenced by progressive educators and psychologists such as Dewey, Piaget, and Vygotsky. He drew a powerful image of the child, who comes into the world social from birth, intelligent, curious, and competent. Malaguzzi's vision, "education based on relationships," focuses on children in relation to people, things, and ideas. The goal is to activate and support children's network of connected ideas and their participation in a world of peers, community members, and the physical environment. Children, teachers, and parents all have their respective rights to be part of the system, contribute to it, and learn within it. In fact, children are expected to be active and resourceful and to generate changes in the systems in which they are involved. Teachers seek to hold before them this powerful image of the child as they support children in exploring and investigating. Children grow in competence to symbolically represent their ideas and feelings through any of their "hundreds of languages" (expressive, communicative, and cognitive), including words, gestures, drawing, painting, building, sculpture, shadow play, collage, wirework, dramatic play, music, dance, puppets, and computers, to name a few that they systemically explore and combine. Adults follow the children's interests and do not provide focused instruction in reading and writing; however, they foster emergent literacy as children record and manipulate their ideas and communicate with others. They try to understand as fully as possible the children's viewpoints and abilities, seeing each child as full of strengths rather than full of needs.

Content/Focus

Teaching and learning are negotiated, emergent processes between adults and children, involving generous time and in-depth revisiting and reviewing. Close, long-term relationships are formed because children and teachers usually stay together in the same group for 3 years, so that a strong link is formed for the child between home and school. Furthermore, long-term, open-ended projects are important vehicles for collaborative work, and these become longer and more elaborate as children grow older and more experienced in this way of learning. Classroom environments are carefully prepared to offer complexity, beauty, organization, and a sense of well-being and ease. The physical space receives much attention so that it supports exchange and relationships through physical qualities of transparency, reflectiveness, openness, harmony, softness, and light. The space conveys to children, parents, and teachers that their presence is valued and respected. A classroom atmosphere of playfulness and joy should prevail in this kind of environment. Time, too, is treated with special care. Children's own sense of time and their personal rhythm are considered in planning and carrying out activities and projects. Children have time to explore their ideas and hypotheses fully and in-depth. Projects and themes follow the children's ideas and development of concepts. Projects, activities, and experiences such as field trips and celebrations build upon one another over time. Children review and revise their original work and ideas, refining them as they have further experiences, consider further questions, notice more details, make more connections, and acquire improved skills. Learning and development advance at their own pace, in widening and deepening cycles of understanding, not stepwise sequences.

Methods

The methods used in the Reggio approach are flexible and allow for input and decision making on the part of all participants. The methods must be adapted to each context and situation, with its own particular history, set of problems, and resources. The most important principle is that teaching should be based on careful observation of children. Teachers begin by actively soliciting children's ideas and thoughts, considering what knowledge, questions, and preferences the children have before formulating plans and projects. Teachers usually work two to a classroom, and collaboration/mentoring is strongly promoted. A *pedagogista* (pedagogical specialist or education coordinator) works with several schools to guarantee high-quality services. In addition, each school usually has a specialist (*atelierista*, specialist trained in the visual arts) to work with teachers and children to encourage expression through different media and symbol systems. Collaboration is encouraged among children through the use of small groups working together in common pursuit of an investigation or a project. These can last for a couple of days, weeks, or months depending on the age and interest level of the children.

Role of the Teacher

Teachers seek to be partners and guides to the children as they learn. They carefully prepare the environment to ensure that it provides strong messages about respect for the children and for their learning. In working with children, teachers play a role of *artful balancing* between engagement and attention. They ask questions to draw out the children's ideas, hypotheses, and theories. Then teachers discuss together what they have recorded and make flexible plans and preparations. They are an endless source of possibilities and provocations to the children. They also act as recorders for the children, helping them trace and revisit their words and actions. Teachers offer new ways of looking at things to children, and provide related experiences and materials. They provide instruction in tool and material use when needed, help children to find materials and resources, and scaffold children's learning—sometimes coming in close and interacting actively, sometimes remaining attentively nearby. They also nurture the children's emotional needs, and support and develop relationships with each family. They act as advocates for high-quality services to the public and the government.

Role of the Children

Children are active participants in their learning. They make many choices throughout the day, including where to go in their classroom and building and what to work on. In addition to ongoing projects, children engage in many other forms of activity and play, including pretend play, singing, group games, storytelling, reading, cooking, outdoor play, rest, and sociable meals together. They become part of a close-knit group, with their own unique rituals and ways of expressing friendship and affection for one another.

Assessment

Children's progress is tracked in nontraditional ways. Documentation is a cooperative practice that helps teachers listen to and see their children, thus guiding curriculum decisions and fostering professional development through collaborative study and reflection. Teachers keep extensive notes on the children and portfolios of children's individual and group work. Then they construct panels, slide shows, booklets, or videos to record memorable projects and to explore and interpret the learning process. The portfolios are shared with families at the end of the year, and teachers also meet frequently with parents to discuss developmental issues. Teachers may also prepare "diaries," or memory books, to trace the experience of each child in the school and become a precious good-bye gift to the family. The memory books help children reflect on themselves as individuals and group members, and help them incorporate their memories into their self-identity and autobiographical narrative of their life. Finally, teachers help older children to create elaborate constructions, artworks, and performances to summarize project learning. Documentation helps teachers to follow and study the ways the group of children develops ideas, theories, and understandings.

There are no checklists of skills, tests, or diagnostic evaluations in a Reggio Emilia program. It is felt that standard assessment tools limit children by focusing on their shortcomings or lack of skills, not their strengths and potential. The research community distinguishes between types of research based on the purposes for which it is conducted. The documentation favored by educators in Reggio Emilia promotes reflective practice and program improvement through formative methods that help educators to better understand their problems, assess the needs of children, and analyze "what works and what does not" on an ongoing basis. It is intended to assist educators to refine and improve their work in process, not to allow outside audiences to understand outcomes and measure impacts over time.

Where Readers Can Find Out More

The Reggio Emilia approach is described in *The Hundred Languages of Children: The Reggio Emilia Approach: Advanced Reflections* (2nd ed.), edited by C. P. Edwards, L. Gandini, and G. Forman (1998), published by Ablex Publishing Corporation and available from Redleaf Press (1-800-423-8309). The Web site of the ERIC Clearinghouse for Elementary and Early Childhood Education has an extensive Reggio link (http://ericeece.org/reggio.html) that presents information about Reggio Children/USA and a list of self-nominated schools in North America with programs based on or inspired by the approach used in Reggio Emilia.

The Montessori Approach to Early Childhood Education

Joy Starry Turner

Montessori Greenhouse Schools, American Montessori Society

Origin

Maria Montessori (1870–1952), Italy's first female physician, was instrumental in founding that country's first state-supported institution for children with disabilities and served as the first director (1900–1901). A unique synthesis that developed from the work of her medical/pedagogical predecessors, Montessori's system was a spectacular success in assisting the children to maximize their potentials. Later opportunities to design settings for "normal" children in Rome's slum clearance projects proved just as effective, and schools bearing Montessori's name blossomed in more than 80 countries around the world. Although the approach began with children between ages 2 and 7, many of the estimated 5,000 schools in the United States now encompass a wider age range, from infant–toddler into even the secondary level. About 5% of programs are located in public school districts.

As developer of the world's first day care centers, Montessori contributed a legacy of "first concepts" now widely accepted by early childhood educators: the significance of early stimulation for later learning; the importance of the learning environment; child-scaled furnishings; active, self-directed learning through play and developmentally appropriate educational materials; the multiage class; the teacher as guide; freedom within limits; the school as community; and parent partnership.

Goals, Content, and Focus

The Montessori system aims to foster the whole child's realization of fullest potential toward becoming an independent, competent, adaptable, responsive, and responsible citizen. Montessori's first concern was the quality of a child's life, though her goals went far beyond the immediate, to nothing less than world reconstruction resulting in a peaceful, sustainable universe. Montessorians frequently describe the system as a dynamic interaction among three basic elements (Figure 1.3): child, adult, and environment.

When Montessori observed the spontaneous behaviors of young children free to act in a supportive environment,

FIGURE 1.3 The Montessori Triangle

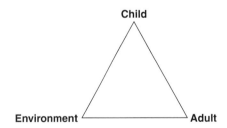

Source: The Montessori Approach, Joy Starry Turner, Montessori Greenhouse Schools, American Montessori Society.

she found that they exhibited four surprising characteristics not usually associated with 3- to 6-year-olds:

1. The ability to concentrate
2. The need for and enjoyment of meaningful activity or work that led to competence and independence
3. The ability to evidence self-discipline or self-regulation
4. Sociability or the desire to be a responsible and contributing member of a community (Loeffler, 2002)

Reflecting Montessori's medical-anthropological background and insightful observations, her writings indicate that human growth is hierarchical and unfolds in stages or "planes" of development, each with its own developmental imperative and inherent complex of attributes (Figure 1.4).

The goal Montessori sought is the nourishing and retention of the four essential characteristics through each plane of development into a new level of thought and actions (Loeffler, 2002).

FIGURE 1.4 Montessori's Planes of Development

> ***Birth–6: Formation of character and intelligence.*** Children respond most positively to environments with concrete, sequential materials that help them interact with and learn about the limits and realities of their world.
> ***Age 6–12: Acquisition of the culture:*** Children are highly social, interested in the world around them and in finding their own "place in the universe." A more complex cognitive style enables the use of reason in development of imagination, leading to a lifelong love of learning.
> ***Age 12–18: Independence through physical and psychic transformations.*** Key materials are replaced by key experiences that enable the young adult to explore the world of human affairs, community, and culture; interdependence supports development of personality and exploration of ways to make contributions to the world.
> ***Age 18–24: Maturity through practical work and experience.***

Source: The Montessori Approach, Joy Starry Turner, Montessori Greenhouse Schools, American Montessori Society.

Methods

The Montessori system is an *individualized* approach facilitated by the teacher's careful observation, knowledge of development, and organization of the environments (physical and psychological). It allows children to learn from one another, make choices, progress at their own pace, and work at their own levels. The liberty of the child is limited by the collective interest. An aesthetically attractive, well-organized, and open-ended *environment* supports independence and spontaneity in learning, provides many forms of both concrete and abstract representation to assist the learner in conceptual understanding, and offers the use of many types of mediators (color, shape, maps, charts, activity units, spatial arrangements, etc.) to assist and guide the child in self-directed learning. Outside environments (museums, nature walks, camping trips, civic work, etc.) provide enrichment beyond the walls of the classroom. *Multiage grouping,* usually in a 3-year span, facilitates a sense of community, peer teaching, flexible group work, and collaborative learning. *Curriculum and materials* are concrete, multidimensional, and multidisciplinary. Large time blocks allow ample opportunity for both exploration and repetition relevant to emergent abilities.

Roles of Child and Teacher

The child's role is to create the adult he or she will become. The adult's role is to provide the necessary nourishment. The early environment encourages a "natural learning cycle" observable in almost any family with young children. First the child observes as a trusted model performs a task the child is interested in mastering; then the child begins to interact and participate in the model's performance of the task, which becomes a collaborative effort suitable to the child's level of competence. A period of role-playing practice follows: self-regulated repetition in which the child assumes responsibility for the action, learns from trial and error, and moves toward refinement. Soon comes a "Eureka moment": The child achieves a sense of accomplishment, an "I know how to do this" feeling. And finally the child reaches the performance level, reveling in mastery and using the newly acquired skill in a context of social purpose (Turner, 1992). As shown in Figure 1.5, the adult's process is complementary to the child's. At older levels, small-group and collaborative project work plays a larger part, as children grow in their ability to locate resources and organize their own work.

Assessment

As the adult observes, records, analyzes, and interprets the child's behavior, assessment is an ongoing part of the cycle. Many schools include more-formal testing as part of assessment above the preschool level, but it is only one of many ways teachers document child strengths and progress. Montessorians are committed to formats (portfolios, presentations, multimedia projects, etc.) that more authentically gauge the ability to interrelate ideas, think critically, and use information meaningfully. Several times each year, information is shared in parent conferences that often involve students as a way of supporting their reflection on their own learning and goals.

FIGURE 1.5 The Teaching–Learning Cycle

THE ADULT'S PROCESS

Preparation:
Organization of Program (goals, criteria)
Organization of environments

Assessment & Planning — Performance Mastery — Demonstration (Instruction/Modeling)

THE CHILD'S PROCESS
(Natural Learning)

Eureka Moment — Observation of Demonstration

Analysis/Interpretation — Practice — Participation — Invitation/Involvement

Feedback
(Observation/Recording)

Source: The Montessori Approach, Joy Starry Turner, Montessori Greenhouse Schools, American Montessori Society.

Where Readers Can Find Out More

Montessori's own books (about 15), three biographies, and a number of contemporary books about Montessori education are widely available from libraries and publishers. Several Montessori organizations publish a journal or magazine. Organizational Internet sites include the American Montessori Society: http://www.amshq.org, the Association Montessori Internationale: http://www.montessori-ami.org, The Montessori Foundation: http://www.montessori.org, the National Center for Montessori Education: http://www.montessori-ncme.org, the North American Montessori Teachers' Association: http://www.montessori-namta.org, and the *Public School Montessorian:* http://www.jolapub.com

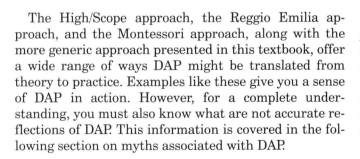

The High/Scope approach, the Reggio Emilia approach, and the Montessori approach, along with the more generic approach presented in this textbook, offer a wide range of ways DAP might be translated from theory to practice. Examples like these give you a sense of DAP in action. However, for a complete understanding, you must also know what are not accurate reflections of DAP. This information is covered in the following section on myths associated with DAP.

MYTHS ASSOCIATED WITH DAP

As DAP has become more widely known, it has also been subject to misinterpretation. This is especially true as people try to translate the DAP philosophy into classroom practices. As a result, some early childhood educators implement practices they consider to be developmentally appropriate that are not. Other educators reject DAP because what they believe to be true about the philosophy is false. Following are some typical examples.

Dennis Avery read an article about DAP and asked his principal to allow him to purchase a variety of hands-on learning materials. He decided to give the youngsters in his class a 2-hour period for self-directed learning while he prepared lessons for the next day. However, this approach was not working out as he had hoped. Children wandered aimlessly around the room, arguments about materials and who could play with whom were frequent, and the noise level grew worse each day. After the teacher in the next room complained for the third time about the chaos in Dennis's class, he decided to give up on the idea and go back to his traditional way of teaching.

The third-grade teachers were angry. During the summer, an early childhood committee, consisting of kindergarten, first-grade, and second-grade teachers, had put together a document entitled "Developmentally Appropriate Practice in Early Childhood." The third-grade teachers had heard about DAP—they were fairly sure there would be no phonics instruction, and children would not be required to spell correctly. They complained that their workload would certainly increase because they would have to make up for everything the early elementary teachers neglected to teach in the new "watered down" curriculum.

After observing a preschool classroom in a program espousing DAP, a parent was overheard to say, "It was all very nice. But I'm not sure the children were learning much. All they did was play all day. I never saw anyone teach them anything."

These real-life happenings illustrate some of the erroneous ideas people have about DAP. For instance, Dennis Avery was under the mistaken impression that DAP does not require teachers to do anything more than put out a variety of "manipulatives" for children to use each day. The third-grade teachers erroneously believed that academic subjects are ignored in DAP classrooms. The parent observer misunderstood what she saw and assumed the teachers were not teaching. Such misinterpretations have led to tremendous confusion about what developmentally appropriate practices actually are. In the absence of true understanding, myths have sprung up representing popular opinions based on false assumptions or faulty reasoning. Some of these myths have evolved from people's attempts to oversimplify a complex idea to the point of inaccuracy. Others have resulted from people's intuitive interpretations of child behavior or from superficial understanding of child development and learning-related theories and research (Kostelnik, 1992). Still more myths have been created as people try to make finite and absolute a concept that is open ended and responsive to many variations. Unfortunately, these myths are rampant, which has caused widespread misapplications, resistance, and anxiety among practitioners and the public. What follows is a selection of the five most common misunderstandings that we encounter and that you might encounter too. We answer each myth with an alternative explanation. On the basis of what you have learned about young children and your experiences in early childhood settings, think about how your answers compare with ours.

Myth There is One "Right" Way to Implement DAP in the Classroom. As you have seen from the High/Scope model, the Reggio Emilia approach, and the Montessori model, developmentally appropriate practices can be combined in varying ways to create different programs to enhance children's learning and development. This openness to variation is also true for individual practices within the classroom. However, when we talk

about DAP with any group of educators, we often hear statements such as these:

> "You always use learning centers."
> "You never use whole-group instruction."
> "You always let children determine the content of the lesson."
> "You never teach children directly."
> "You always let children figure out their own spellings for words."
> "You never use lined paper."

Likewise, teachers and administrators may ask,

> "Is it ever OK to show children how to hold a pencil?"
> "Is it wrong to spell words for children when they ask?"
> "Exactly when should we introduce cursive writing?"

These kinds of statements and questions represent efforts to establish a single, correct approach to instruction. They are based on the belief that one method of teaching suits all children and all situations. Unfortunately, the reality is that *teaching is complex;* no single solution fits every circumstance. Actually, individual teaching episodes can and should be qualified by "It depends" (J. M. Newman & Church, 1990). It depends on variables such as the child's current level of comprehension, experiences, and previous knowledge and skills. Contextual elements including time, human resources, the physical environment, material resources, parental expectations, and the values and expectations of the school and community must also be considered. The goals, strategies, and standards early childhood personnel finally choose are all affected by these constraints as well as by the DAP requirements.

This means practitioners must continually assess their actions in relation to their knowledge about how children develop and learn. To translate this knowledge into teaching strategies, they must be willing to explore a variety of practices in the classroom and allow themselves to make mistakes. Moreover, teachers must continually examine their assumptions and learn from the children as they evaluate the effectiveness of their teaching. What meets the needs of several children in a group may not be appropriate for others. What was optimal for last year's class may not be so this year. Educators' search, then, is not simply for "right" answers but for the best answers to meet the needs of children representing a wide range of abilities, learning styles, interests, and social and cultural backgrounds. Finally, practitioners also differ from one another and require a flexible approach to teaching that is compatible with their beliefs and comfortable for them as well as for their students. These variations in both children's and teacher's needs necessitate different strategies. As mentioned previously in this chapter, every educational decision requires judgment, made on the spot or with time, but always with certain children in mind. Perpetuation of the "one way" myth ignores the important role such judgments play in determining what is appropriate and what is not.

Myth All You Need to Create Developmentally Appropriate Programs Are the Right Materials. Some people mistakenly believe that DAP simply involves trading one set of materials (workbooks, basal readers, and lined paper) for other materials (manipulatives, picture books, and unlined paper). They assume that nothing more is necessary. If this myth were true, the guidelines for DAP would consist solely of an equipment list supplemented by the names of several early childhood materials catalogs. Although equipment does enrich the educational environment, research shows that the teacher is the essential ingredient in determining the quality of education received by children. In turn, program quality is directly linked to the teacher's knowledge of and ability to apply developmentally appropriate principles in his or her classroom (Bredekamp & Copple, 1997; Kontos & Wilcox-Herzog, 2001). Thus, the proper equipment must be accompanied by trained staff who know how to use this equipment to enhance child development and learning.

Myth Developmentally Appropriate Classrooms are Unstructured and Chaotic. The myth that DAP yields chaos is perpetuated by people who mistake the active learning of DAP classrooms for chaos and disorganization. They sometimes describe what they see as "unstructured," assuming that structure requires silence and lack of movement. This assumption is a misinterpretation of the term (Kostelnik, 1998). *Structure* refers to the extent to which teachers develop an instructional plan and then organize the physical setting and social environment to support the achievement of educational goals (Spodek, Saracho, & Davis, 1991).

By this definition, developmentally appropriate classrooms are highly structured. Both teachers and children contribute to their organization. Teachers generate educational goals for students on the basis of programmatic expectations tempered by their understanding of individual children's needs, abilities, and interests. All of the day's activities and routines are planned to promote these goals. Keeping their instructional plan in mind, teachers determine the arrangement of the furniture, which specific materials to offer children, the nature and flow of activity, the approximate time to allocate to various instructional segments, and the grouping of chil-

dren throughout the session. As teachers interact with children, teachers observe, listen, instruct, guide, support, and encourage the children. Consequently, while teachers carefully consider long-range objectives, their moment-to-moment decision making remains fluid so that they can capitalize on the children's input (J. M. Newman & Church, 1990). Children ask questions, suggest alternatives, express interests, and develop plans that may lead the instruction in new directions. In this way, overall instructional goals are merged with more immediate goals, which thereby creates a flexible, stimulating classroom structure.

Developmentally appropriate classrooms are active classrooms in which both teachers and students learn from one another. Such learning requires a constant interchange of thoughts and ideas. As a result, sometimes during the day many people are talking or moving about the room all at once. To the untrained eye these conditions may appear chaotic, but a closer look should reveal children on task constructively involved in their learning.

Myth In Developmentally Appropriate Classrooms, Teachers are Not Teaching. The myth that teachers do not actually teach in developmentally appropriate classrooms stems from the stereotypical idea that teachers are people who stand in front of a group of students, telling them what they need to know, and that the teacher's most important duties consist of assigning work to children and checking for correct and incorrect answers. According to this scenario, teachers are always at center stage. People who envision teachers this way may not recognize all the teaching that is going on in developmentally appropriate classrooms. For example, teachers create physical environments and daily schedules that enable children to engage in purposeful activity. Curricular

Teachers in developmentally appropriate classrooms are often down on the floor with the children.

goals are frequently addressed through pervasive classroom routines such as dressing to go outside, preparing for snack, and cleaning up. Although whole-group instruction does occur, teachers spend much of their classroom time moving throughout the room and working with children individually and in small, informal groups. During these times, teachers influence children's learning indirectly by providing certain activities that are focused on children's self-discovery and exploration. Teachers also teach children directly, using a variety of instructional strategies. Teachers initiate learning activities and respond to children's initiatives. They pose questions, offer procedural suggestions, suggest explorations, and provide information. As opportunities arise, teachers present children with challenges that help them move beyond their current understandings and strategies (Bodrova & Leong, 1996). In addition, teachers constantly reflect on what is happening in the classroom. They make judgments about children's progress and introduce variations or changes in focus as children's needs warrant. All these activities are essential teaching behaviors.

Myth Academics Have No Place in Developmentally Appropriate Programs. Academics represent the traditional content of the schools. In most people's minds this means reading, writing, and arithmetic. People who *wish* that the myth that academics have no place in developmentally appropriate programs were true believe young children are not ready for academics. They proudly announce that students in their programs are not expected to read, use numbers, or write. People who *fear* that this myth is true express concern that children who participate in developmentally appropriate programs are not learning the essentials. They worry that such children will lack critical skills necessary for achievement. Both claims are based on an overly narrow interpretation of academic learning. They equate academics with technical subskills (e.g., reciting the alphabet or writing numerical equations) or with rote instruction (e.g., emphasizing worksheets and drills). Each of these definitions is too narrow in scope. Both confuse concepts with methods and ignore how reading, writing, and number-related behaviors and understandings emerge in young children's lives.

Children do not wait for elementary school to demonstrate an interest in words and numbers. They manifest literacy-related interests as infants when they mouth a book or pat the bunny and again as toddlers when they beg, "Read it again." Likewise, young children count one cookie, two shoes, and three birthday candles. They compare: "Which has more?" "Who still needs some?" Children calculate: "Will it fit?" "Now I have two; I need one more." These kinds of activities form the beginnings of literacy and mathematical thinking—the true essence of academics.

Children continue in this manner as they mature, seeking new knowledge and skills as their capacities to know and do increase. Thus, there is no specific time when such learning is either appropriate or inappropriate. These evaluative labels are better applied to the parameters within which academics are defined and the strategies teachers use to address academic learning. Programs that focus on isolated skill development and rely on long periods of whole-group instruction or abstract paper-and-pencil activities do not meet young children's needs. Programs that emphasize concepts and processes and utilize small-group instruction; active manipulation of relevant, concrete materials; and interactive learning provide a solid foundation for academics within a context of meaningful activity.

Using children's interests and ways of learning as guides, early childhood teachers do four things to promote academic learning. First, they understand the broad nature of literacy and mathematics and are familiar with the concepts, processes, and content that compose them. They recognize that reading is more than reciting the alphabet or making letter–sound associations out of context, that writing is not the same as penmanship, that mathematics goes beyond rote memorization of number facts. Second, they recognize manifestations of academic interest and exploratory behavior in the children they teach (e.g., "Teacher, what does this say?" "How many do we need?" "Look what I made!"). At the same time, they recognize the importance of phonics or number facts as part of the learning process and incorporate these elements into their teaching in ways that make sense to children. Third, teachers provide concrete materials and relevant experiences to enhance children's academic learning. They read to children often and invite them to respond to and interpret the story. They sing songs, read poems, and play rhyming games in which sound associations are addressed. They give children materials to sort, sequence, count, combine, or divide and make estimations about. They offer children many ways to express themselves both orally and in writing. Fourth, teachers introduce new information, materials, and problems that stimulate children to make observations and comparisons, question, experiment, derive meaning, make predictions, and draw their own conclusions. In this way academics become an integral part of classroom life.

IMPLICATIONS OF DAP FOR PROFESSIONAL PRACTICE

Now that you are familiar with DAP as well as some people's reactions to DAP, take a moment to consider the implications this educational philosophy could have for your work with children and families. Also, ask yourself, "How will the issues that surround DAP affect my development as a professional in the field?" Then read the implications we thought of and see how they match your ideas.

Implications

As early childhood professionals in training or as practitioners in the field, we should do the following:

❏ Have a thorough knowledge of what DAP is and what it is not

❏ Continually examine our practices, reflecting on our work with children and families and revising our actions in accordance with new knowledge and understandings

❏ Combine our understanding of DAP with knowledge of child development and learning, curriculum goals and content, instructional practices, family and community relationships, assessment, and professionalism to create high-quality programs for children and families

❏ Become adept at articulating the rationale behind our practices and connecting what we do in the classroom to the fundamental principles of DAP

❏ Share information about DAP with parents and colleagues

❏ Listen thoughtfully to questions raised and concerns expressed about DAP and strive to clarify points of agreement and disagreement

❏ Challenge people who make blanket statements or inaccurate overgeneralizations about DAP

❏ Respond to misinformation about DAP with accurate facts and relevant information

❏ Recognize that early childhood education is a vital profession in which new ideas are constantly being explored

SUMMARY

This chapter chronicles an evolving concept in early childhood education: developmentally appropriate practice. Developmentally appropriate programs match how children develop and learn with how they are taught. Such programs are founded on faith in children's capacity to learn as well as on respect for children as individuals and people who are shaped by the social and cultural contexts in which they live. Educators working with youngsters aged 3 to 8 years recognize that young children's learning differs significantly from that of older children and adults and approach their work with this understanding in mind. Thus, the application of DAP makes the nature and well-being of children the central focus of professional practice. Research supports the idea that developmentally appropriate programs represent positive educational experiences for young children. Not only do children perform well academically, but their attitudes toward school remain enthusiastic and optimistic. This is not the case for many children enrolled in classes that ignore children's unique educational needs.

DAP has not been without its critics. Concern has been expressed that the approach may not meet the needs of all children and that the basic premises underlying the approach are flawed. These concerns led to a revised version of DAP, which was published in 1997. Only time will tell how well the ideas presented in the second edition of the NAEYC document will satisfy the concerns expressed. In addition to these concerns, the misinterpretations that sometimes arise from people's efforts to understand DAP are covered, as are the realities associated with each. Therefore, the entire focus of this chapter is to establish the foundation on which developmentally appropriate programs are based. As you explore the ramifications of this concept in the chapters that follow, you will repeatedly encounter the ideas expressed in this chapter. There is no element of early childhood education they do not touch. Activities and routines, materials, the physical environment, classroom management, methods of family involvement, and assessment procedures are all influenced by these principles.

✋ Applying What You Read in This Chapter

1. Discuss

a. On the basis of your reading and your experiences with young children, discuss each of the questions that open this chapter.

b. Reread the sections on the High/Scope approach and the Reggio Emilia approach to early childhood education. Find examples of how these approaches utilize strategies associated with DAP.

2. Observe

a. Observe a teacher who has adopted a DAP philosophy. Identify concrete examples of this philosophy in the classroom.

b. Observe a preschool classroom and a classroom for children older than 5 years. Describe ways the adults use the principle of age appropriateness in terms of materials, activities, and routines in each classroom. Find the similarities and the differences between the two rooms with regard to the notion of age appropriateness.

3. Carry out an activity

a. Talk to an early childhood practitioner about how he or she tries to make the children's program age appropriate, individually appropriate, and socioculturally appropriate. Write a summary of what he or she tells you.

b. Read a journal article about DAP. Is the author in favor of the concept or opposed to it? Describe how convinced you are by his or her position.

c. Select one of the program models described in this chapter. Gather additional information about the approach. Summarize what you discover.

d. Review written information describing an early childhood program in your community. On the basis of the program's written philosophy and program description, discuss to what extent the program reflects DAP principles.

4. Create something for your portfolio

a. Provide three examples of your work with children: one in which you address the idea of age appropriateness, one in which you demonstrate individual appropriateness, and one that illustrates your efforts related to sociocultural appropriateness.

5. Add to your journal

a. What is the most significant concept about DAP that you learned from your readings and your experience with children?

b. In what ways have you used DAP in your work with children? What goals do you have for yourself in this regard?

Principles of Development and Learning

Implications for Effective Teaching

You may wonder:

Why do so many early childhood teacher preparation programs include child development as a significant part of the curriculum?

What difference do child development and learning make in the design of effective early childhood programs?

How might programs for children aged 3 to 8 years look similar to or different from programs designed for adolescents or adults?

Is having knowledge about child development and learning sufficient to ensure high-quality programs for young children?

In this chapter on principles of child development and learning, we present information to help you answer the preceding questions.

Imagine you are interviewing for an early childhood teaching position. The interviewer asks you the following questions:

What kinds of activities will you design for the children in your classroom?

How will you meet the needs of children who vary in age and ability?

When should children stop playing and concentrate on learning?

What role will families play in your classroom?

What will you do if an activity is too simple or too difficult for a particular child?

How will you answer? Although there is no single response to any of these queries, the answers you give will reflect your ideas about how young children develop and learn. Such knowledge is the hallmark of the early childhood professional and a major factor in the delivery of high-quality programs for children.

EDUCATORS NEED TO KNOW ABOUT CHILD DEVELOPMENT AND LEARNING

Zeal without knowledge is like fire without light.
—Thomas Fuller (1608–1661)

Many adults enjoy working with young children. However, those who have specialized knowledge about child development and learning are the most likely to engage in developmentally appropriate practices (National Association for the Education of Young Children, 1996b; Stronge, 2002). Instead of treating their interactions with children as wholly intuitive, they bring factual information to bear on how they think about children and interact with them in the classroom. Thus, early childhood education, like all education, demands well-prepared personnel who appreciate the unique characteristics of the children they serve. Knowledge of child development and learning contributes to this preparation and appreciation.

Child development principles help us to recognize commonalities among children and characteristics typical within age ranges. Although no two children are alike, we know that 4-year-olds are more like other 4-year-olds than they are like 10-year-olds. Likewise, we recognize that certain behaviors emerge at fairly predictable times. For instance, most children begin to talk between 12 months and 2 years. Four- and five-year-olds typically engage in various forms of verbal humor. Around 6 years of age, children develop the auditory abilities necessary to discriminate consonant blends such as *sp* (*space*) or *tr* (*train*). Losing their front teeth is a common experience for most 6-, 7-, and 8-year-olds. Such developmental milestones are a natural part of growing up. When teachers know about child development, they gain insights into how and why children behave as they do. These insights make understanding typical variations among children easier. They also make recognizing potential problems that may require specialized intervention more possible. Familiarity with child development also offers clues about the order in which activities might be presented to children and the degree of developmental readiness children must demonstrate to achieve program goals. Therefore, knowledge of child development helps adults predict strategies, materials, interactions, and experiences that will be safe, healthy, interesting, achievable, and challenging to children (Bredekamp & Copple, 1997).

Theory and research related to childhood learning yields additional information. Although researchers are far from unanimously agreeing on every aspect of learning, increasing evidence indicates that young children think and acquire knowledge in ways that differ significantly from those used by older children and adults (Berk & Winsler, 1995; R. Shore, 1997). Awareness of these differences helps us to create programs that support rather than undermine children's natural ways of acquiring new knowledge and abilities. The physical environments we design, the methods we use, and the routines, activities, and assessments we create can all be made better by taking into account principles of childhood learning.

However, simply knowing about child development and learning is not sufficient to ensure that early childhood programs will be high quality (Dunn & Kontos, 1997). *Practitioners must link what they know with what they do.* This connection between theory and practice is essential if children are to experience positive outcomes. Keeping this in mind, let us review some basic development and learning principles and then explore their implications for action.

PRINCIPLES OF CHILD DEVELOPMENT

Children Develop Holistically

Aesthetic, affective, cognitive, language, physical, and social development are all interrelated. No single facet of development exists independently from the others, nor is any one facet the most valuable. For example, adults observing children engaged in a vigorous game of

dodgeball might categorize their activity as purely physical. Yet the children's ability to play the game is influenced by many developmental processes:

Aesthetic—Appreciating the grace of another player's movements, enjoying the rhythm of the game

Affective—Coping with the disappointment of being "out," accepting compliments and criticism from other players, expressing anger over a disputed call

Cognitive—Determining the sequence in which the game is played, discerning how many children can fit in the space available, remembering who has had a chance to be "it" and who has not, analyzing the best angle for hitting a fleeing player

Language—Determining what "scripts" to use to get into or out of the game, using words to describe the rules, responding to the teacher's directions

Physical—Catching, dodging, and throwing the ball; developing stamina

Social—Negotiating the rules of the game, signaling others about a desire to have a turn, making way for a new player, working out disagreements over boundaries and teams

Likewise, reading and computing are both intellectual functions that also have social, affective, aesthetic, language, and physical elements. The same is true for any task that children encounter. Social processes shape cognitive processes, cognitive processes promote or restrict social capabilities, physical processes influence language and cognition, and so on. Consequently, when we are thinking about children, we must remember that they are whole human beings whose development is enhanced when educators concern themselves with *all* aspects of their development. This orientation is referred to as focusing on the whole child (Hendrick, 2001; Hymes, 1998).

In support of the whole-child philosophy, researchers have found that serious problems arise when one facet of development is emphasized to the exclusion of all others. For instance, children who participate in classrooms in which academic achievement is the only priority suffer from lack of attention to social and emotional development. For children whose poor social skills lead to rejection by peers, the results can be devastating. Such youngsters are likely to engage in delinquent acts or succumb to mental health problems (Goleman, 1995).

Equally negative effects occur when physical development is neglected. Children exhibit increasingly poor fitness and health-related behaviors across time (V. G. Payne & Rink, 1997). This negative effect is a problem both in the short term (children fail to develop optimal

TABLE 2.1 Developmental Facets of Whole-Child Learning

Aesthetic	Affective	Cognitive
Developing sensory awareness	Developing a positive, realistic self-concept	Developing thinking processes (observing, recalling, comparing, patterning, classifying, generalizing, integrating, and evaluating)
Imagining and visualizing		
Exploring	Accepting and expressing emotions in socially appropriate ways	
Creating		Constructing knowledge
Responding	Coping with change	Developing memory skills
Interpreting	Developing decision-making skills	Acquiring facts
Developing critical awareness	Accepting challenge	
Expressing and representing through a variety of forms	Developing independence	
	Feeling pride in accomplishments	
	Increasing instrumental know-how	
	Enjoying living and learning	

Adapted from *Kindergarten Curriculum Guide and Resource Book,* 1985, Victoria, British Columbia: Ministry of Education; and *Teaching Young Children Using Themes,* M. Kostelnik (Ed.), 1991, Glenview, IL: Good Year Books.

cardiovascular functioning, physical strength, endurance, and physical skills) and in the long run (children grow up to be sedentary adults at risk for heart disease and other physical ailments). The notion of whole-child teaching is so important that in early childhood education the curriculum and the whole child are seen as indivisible. This fact has four important implications for early childhood programs.

Implications

1. Activities and routines are designed so that all aspects of child development are addressed each day. A sample of developmental processes associated with whole-child learning is offered in Table 2.1.

2. Educators think of subject matter (e.g., spelling or reading) in terms of how it relates to child development. For example, reading is viewed within the context of overall language development. This means that reading is considered in relation to listening, speaking, and writing, not in isolation. Likewise, handwriting is treated as a product of fine-motor development and visual perception. Writing instruction and expectations for children's writing are created with these developmental processes in mind.

3. Daily time allocation is an important consideration. Because all facets of child development are important, huge amounts of time are not devoted to some areas (e.g., spelling or art and crafts) to the preclusion of others (e.g., science or social studies, problem-solving activities or games).

4. Classroom activities and routines are designed so that children have opportunities to participate in

integrated, rather than isolated, experiences. This design includes integration across developmental domains, subject matter, and traditional lines of responsibility. For example, children participate in activities that incorporate language, physical, and social processes simultaneously. They have experiences that combine reading, science, and math. The adults with whom they come in contact often work in teams. The responsibility for creating an effective learning environment is shared among students, teachers, specialists, administrators, and parents.

Child Development Occurs in an Orderly Sequence

Try putting these developmental milestones in the order in which they tend to appear during childhood.

> *Fear of ghosts.*
>
> *Fear of animals.*
>
> *Fear of being embarrassed in front of others.*
>
> *Stranger anxiety.*

What did you decide? Sample progressions like these illustrate the notion of developmental sequence.

Development is sequential, and changes across time occur fairly predictably. Scientists worldwide have identified typical sequences of behavior or understanding related to language; social, emotional, and personality development; graphic and symbolic representation; problem solving; logical-mathematical understanding; moral development; and physical development (Berk, 2003). For

Language	Physical	Social
Responding and communicating through listening, speaking, writing, and reading	Developing competence in using large and small muscles	Developing internal behavior controls
Experimenting with language	Taking care of and respecting your body	Helping
Representing through language	Being aware of and practicing good nutrition habits	Cooperating
	Developing physical fitness	Respecting and accepting others
	Appreciating and enjoying human movement	Learning from others
		Seeking and giving companionship
		Developing friendships
		Becoming a responsible citizen
		Appreciating and respecting the cultural identity and heritage of others
		Respecting the environment

instance, before children walk, they first learn to lift their heads, then sit up, then stand with assistance, then crawl, and then stand on their own. Eventually they toddle, then run. Similarly, children's earliest attempts to write messages are the creation of scribbles. In cultures in which the alphabet is used, scribbles gradually give way to letter-like forms, then to single consonants representing entire words, then to combinations of letters in phonetic attempts at spelling, until eventually more and more standard spelling is used. Childhood fears tend to emerge in the following order: stranger anxiety, fear of animals, fear of ghosts, and fear of potential embarrassment.

Such changes are often uneven rather than smooth. Individual children spend more or less time on each step; they may move forward a bit, back a little, then forward again. Some children may even skip some phases that are less relevant to them. However, the sequences tend to remain predictable, with the increments for each emerging in the same order. Applying this principle implies the use of four early childhood practices.

Implications

1. Educators read about development and observe young children carefully to become familiar with relevant developmental sequences in every domain.
2. Practitioners use their knowledge of developmental sequences to determine reasonable expectations for individual children.
3. Teachers use their understanding of child development to determine the new understandings or behaviors that might logically expand children's current

levels of functioning. Doing so enables them to challenge youngsters appropriately in the classroom.
4. Teachers avoid unduly pressuring children to accelerate their progress through certain developmental sequences such as those associated with spelling, number recognition, or handwriting.

Child Development Proceeds at Varying Rates Within and Among Children

Emahl is 5; so is Lawrence. Emahl was walking at age 1 year and talking in complete sentences by age 2 years. He still has difficulty sharing people and toys. Lawrence did not walk until he was 14 months old and began talking fluidly only at 3 years old. He knows several strategies for sharing, which he uses well. Emahl and Lawrence are alike yet different—both are developing normally.

As illustrated by Emahl and Lawrence, every child develops according to his or her "biological clock." No two children are exactly alike. Differences in development manifest in two ways: intrapersonally and interpersonally.

Within every individual, various facets of development are dominant at different times throughout childhood. For instance, infancy is a time of rapid physical growth; although language development is also progressing, it is doing so more slowly. The same trends reverse as children enter the preschool and elementary years; physical growth slows while children simultaneously make spectacular strides in using language. These are examples of *intrapersonal variations* in development. Such internal variations explain why the same child may be easily moved to tears, have difficulty with

These second graders share the same birthday but vary in their rates of physical, language, cognitive, and socioemotional development.

oral expression, climb nimbly to the highest part of the jungle gym, recite the alphabet backward, and have moderate success cutting with scissors. Such unevenness in development is to be expected.

Interpersonal variations in rates also occur. Although the typical sequences still apply, the pace at which youngsters move through them differs. Hence, children of the same age may exhibit behaviors and understandings unlike those of one another. If you were to chart the normal development of an entire classroom of children, the time at which each child reached certain milestones would vary considerably. For instance, you could expect some first graders to come to school in September reading words and phrases. Other children might just be starting to make the association between various letters and sounds. At the same time, certain children in the class may group objects by function only, others may group objects by more than one property at a time, and still others may be exploring how to regroup objects in different ways. All these variations are normal, and similar differences could be found across all domains.

If you are familiar with age-level expectations or norms, you may be wondering how they correspond to the variation-in-rates principle. Profiles of typical age expectations for certain skills such as walking, speaking, counting, and participating in games are commonly available for the early childhood years. However, the ages identified do not represent exact points in time. Such figures are based on averages. So, even though skipping may be listed at age 6 years, sometimes this capacity emerges later, say, at age 8 years, whereas

occasionally it can be seen as early as age 5 years. Norms guide us in understanding the *order* in which certain behaviors appear and approximately when they may occur. They are not meant to be used as absolute standards or rigid timetables for growth and development. There is always a range of variation in human development. Also, *when* a milestone is achieved does not necessarily predict proficiency with time. By age 10 years, little difference may be evident between children who began skipping at age 5 years and those who mastered this skill later. Likewise, children who began talking early in their second year do not necessarily talk more or less or with greater or lesser skill than youngsters for whom age 30 months marked the beginning of fluent oral communication. Understanding the wide-ranging variations among children is a key consideration in the creation of developmentally appropriate educational programs.

Implications

1. Teachers expect children in early education classrooms to exhibit a wide range of abilities.

2. Early childhood professionals avoid focusing on a single index (e.g., IQ, reading test score, child's ability to draw a person, etc.) as a measure of children's overall potential or achievement.

3. Teachers carefully observe children to discover behavioral patterns for each child within various developmental domains. Teachers use this knowledge to individualize their instruction rather than expecting all children to learn the same thing in the same way at the same time.

4. Educators create daily schedules in which children have opportunities to pursue activities at their own pace. Children are seldom required to rotate from activity to activity on a predetermined schedule. Practitioners adjust or change their plans to meet the current needs of individuals in the group.

5. Developmental norms are not used as rigid standards against which children are labeled "ahead" or "behind" others in the group.

6. Classroom activities are designed to encompass multiple learning objectives, not just one. Such activities allow children more than one opportunity to be challenged and to experience success.

7. Teachers repeat activities more than once during the year so that children can gain different benefits from the activity according to their changing needs and capabilities.

8. Practitioners document children's individual patterns of progress. They keep continuous records based on observations of children's movement from one phase of a developmental sequence to another.

New Development Is Based on Previous Development

If you plant an acorn, it will grow up into an oak-tree. But it doesn't follow that if you plant a honeycomb, it will grow up into a beehive.
—Piglet to Pooh (Milne, 1995)

Development is based on a foundation; past, present, and future are related and build on each other in succession. New capabilities and understandings arise out of and elaborate on what is already there. The idea that children develop a sense of independence only after establishing an adequate sense of trust illustrates this principle. Similarly, children's writing evolves from scribbling, expressive language is founded on earlier babbling, and children's understanding of numbers is based on their first achieving such milestones as object permanence and one-to-one correspondence. In all these instances, certain developmental threads are carried forward across time, which provides continuity from one phase of development to the next. The six implications of this principle for practitioners are obvious but essential.

Implications

1. Practitioners interact with children and observe them to discover what children know and can do.

2. Educators plan instruction on the basis of each child's level of performance and understanding.

3. Ample opportunities are made available for children to explore and practice what they have learned prior to educators' expecting them to learn something new.

4. Teachers help children make connections between new experiences and past experiences and support children's progress toward more elaborate concepts or skills as they exhibit interest, mastery, and understanding.

5. Concepts and skills are not addressed in isolation or out of context relative to children's experiences.

6. Educators do not expect children to exhibit behaviors and understandings that are far beyond the current developmental foundations on which they are building.

Development Has Both Cumulative and Delayed Effects

What we live through is who we become.
—Oprah Winfrey (1996)

Beginning at birth, children accumulate a history of repeated, frequent experiences that may have positive or negative effects on their development depending on the circumstances. How this happens is illustrated by

infants who usually have their needs met and so develop a sense of trust in themselves and the world. Youngsters whose needs are often ignored develop mistrust. These outcomes result from not one or two incidents but a long-term pattern of interactions that children come to view as typical (Seligman, 1995). Likewise, children who occasionally see a violent television program may not experience long-term damaging effects. However, children who spend hours, weeks, and years watching violence depicted on television eventually demonstrate increased levels of aggression in their daily interactions (Friedrich & Stein, 1973; Shaffer, 2002). Along similar lines, L. G. Katz (1987) and Katz and Chard (1989) made an eloquent case for considering the long-term negative effects of such typical school practices as flash-card drills and daily worksheet sessions. They pointed out that the sporadic use of such techniques is probably harmless. However, the cumulative result for children who receive a steady diet of such experiences seems to be lack of intellectual confidence and an erosion of inquiry and problem-solving strategies. These researchers' concerns are echoed by other educators who fear that practices such as these undermine children's conceptual development, participatory skills, grasp of essential meanings, breadth of knowledge, and interest in school (Jensen, 1998; Marcon, 1995). Cumulative effects like these are difficult to reverse.

In addition to accumulated impacts, developmental outcomes may be delayed. That is, early experiences may influence children's functioning in ways that become obvious only later in life (Kohn, 1993; Wieder & Greenspan, 1993). For instance, some children of abusive parents may appear remarkably well adjusted while growing up but experience serious mental health problems in adolescence and adulthood as a result of their tumultuous past. On the positive side, the benefits of reasoning with children as a way of teaching them how to behave are not always immediately apparent. However, when adults consistently provide reasons for rules and prohibitions, children eventually become better able to reason on their own. This increases their ability to exercise self-discipline (Kostelnik, Onaga, Rohde, & Whiren, 2002).

Implications

1. Professionals consider the long-range implications of their practices as well as short-term outcomes. When current strategies undermine long-term goals, they are revised in favor of the long term. In this way, teachers ensure that their methods support their goals.

2. Researchers conduct longitudinal studies of children's learning. Program evaluators assess children's progress and program effectiveness across time.

3. Developmentally appropriate practices are explained to parents, colleagues, and decision makers in terms of how such practices support children's learning during the life span.

PRINCIPLES OF CHILDHOOD LEARNING

Children are learning all the time. They learn to say things such as "Excuse me" when they bump into someone; they learn to count, catch a ball, play bingo, recognize letters and numerals, find ways to solve problems, and derive pleasure from sharing with a friend. True learning in each of these instances occurs only when children make a relatively permanent change in their thinking or behavior as a result of the interaction between maturation and experience. Children who clean up messes, even when no one else is around, have learned. Children who remember a telephone number for 5 minutes and then forget it have not. Certain universal principles describe children's learning throughout the early childhood years.

Children Are Active Learners

Sung Won is talking to herself as she works on a three-dimensional puzzle. "Gee!" "How can I do it?" "That's really funny." "How come . . . ?" "Wait! Wait!" "Oh, I know!"

Surprise, puzzlement, struggle, excitement, anticipation, and dawning certainty—those are the [elements] of intelligent thought. As virtues, they stand by themselves—even if they do not on some specific occasion lead to the right answer. In the long run, they are what count.
—Duckworth (1987)

When we say children are "active," we must recognize the multidimensional nature of their activity. First, young children are motoric beings. They are genetically programmed to reach out, pull up, stand upright, move forward, and move about (Sanders, 2002). As children move, they seek stimulation, which increases their opportunities for learning.

Second, children use their whole bodies as instruments of learning, taking in data through all their senses. Young children are compelled to taste, touch, listen to, look at, and smell objects and spaces to find out about them—what their properties are, how they function, and how they fit in with the rest of the world. In this way children connect thought with action.

Third, children are active participants in their experiences. They are not empty vessels passively waiting to be "filled up" with information and experiences determined by others. On the contrary, they energetically

seek ways to achieve their maximum potential in both structure and function. Children do this by observing, acting on objects, and interacting with people (Bredekamp & Copple, 1997).

Finally, if the usual avenues are unavailable, children search for substitute sources of satisfaction (Smart & Smart, 1982). Consequently, youngsters find alternative ways of satisfying their needs when ordinary paths are blocked. A child who is deprived of approval from adults may seek it from peers instead; a student who finds seatwork boring may rush through it, heedless of accuracy, to gain satisfaction from moving on to another kind of task.

Implications

1. Practitioners provide children with many multisensory opportunities to explore and handle objects directly every day. This kind of hands-on learning dominates the teaching strategies implemented.
2. Substantial segments of time are planned during which children can move about the classroom freely.
3. Teachers create schedules for the day in which quiet times are followed by active times and in which times when children are to be passive are minimized.
4. Opportunities for gross-motor activities are made available to children each day, both indoors and outdoors.
5. Educators observe children carefully to see whether some of children's "unacceptable" behavior may be the result of blocked goals. If this is the case, teachers and administrators work with the child to determine better alternatives for meeting his or her needs. These strategies sometimes involve restructuring some aspect of the classroom that is developmentally inappropriate or assisting the child in adopting new behaviors.

Children's Learning Is Influenced by Maturation

Suppose you have a friend with a 6-month-old son who is just learning to sit up. She wants to impress her mother-in-law, who will be visiting in a few weeks. She decides the way to do this is to teach her baby to walk and asks your advice about the best exercises to use.

Chances are you will tell your friend that no matter how much exercise she provides, her 6-month-old will not be walking in the next few weeks because he is too immature to accomplish the task. His legs cannot support his body, and he lacks the balance and strength necessary to hold himself upright. Practice as they might, her son is simply not ready to walk. Just as expecting a 6-month-old to walk independently is inappropriate, other demands can be equally unrealistic if suitable maturation has not occurred. For instance, most young children lack the eye control to accurately shift from a near focus (e.g., the paper on their desk) to a far focus (e.g., words or numerals on a blackboard). Such coordination tends to mature sometime after the 7th year. This lack of coordination makes the task of copying work from a blackboard generally inappropriate for most kindergartners and many first graders (Soderman, 1997).

In contrast, through maturation new possibilities for learning are created that could not have been realized earlier. This fact is illustrated by children's increasing ability to understand other people's emotions with time. Between 2 and 5 years of age, children identify someone else's emotional state on the basis of how that person looks—crying equals sadness, and laughter equals joy. They have little idea that the context of the situation also contributes to people's feelings. However, as their cognitive skills expand, 6- and 7-year-olds take into account situational circumstances, too. Children this age recognize that Sonia could be sad because her dog is lost. They also know that Sonia might feel happy again if the dog returns. By age 9 or 10 years, many youngsters are aware that memories may produce feelings even though the original event is long past. When 10-year-old Raymond says, "Yoko is sad. She's lonesome for her dog she used to have," he is demonstrating an increasingly mature concept of how and why emotions occur (Kostelnik et al., 2002).

In all the preceding examples, the maturation process established a general timetable for the emergence of new capabilities and understandings. These timetables could be retarded by environmental insults such as malnutrition or could be accelerated through environmental stimulation. However, maturation is not completely elastic, and stimulation can accelerate development only within the parameters dictated by each child's biological blueprint. This fact was illustrated by the scenario that introduced this principle. As you can see, maturation plays an important role in deciding the appropriateness of certain tasks for young children.

Implications

1. Early childhood professionals learn about how children mature and what might reasonably be expected of children across time. They communicate this understanding to other significant adults in children's lives.

2. Teachers simplify, maintain, or extend activities in response to children's demonstrated levels of functioning and comprehension.

3. The school curriculum is designed so that some flexibility exists in the grade placement of learning objectives. For example, no single grade level encompasses both the introduction and the mastery of particular knowledge or skills. Instead, these are spread out across more than one grade. Also, the accomplishment of certain milestones such as counting to 100 or being able to carry out a forward roll fit into the expectations for multiple grades. Restructuring school schedules and grade configurations to allow children to progress at a more self-determined rate rather than a calendar year–determined rate also supports flexibility.

Children's Learning Is Influenced by the Environment

Although they cannot profit from certain experiences without the appropriate neurological and physical structures, *children do not gain knowledge and skills from maturation alone.* Environment plays a critical role in the learning process. The environment runs the gamut from the biological environment of nutrition, medical care, physical exercise, and drugs, to the physical environment of clothing, shelter, materials available, and climate, to the social environment of family, peers, schools, community, media, and culture (Santrock, 2000). Such environmental variables either enhance or detract from children's ability to learn.

For instance, we know that children who are well rested, physically comfortable, and generally healthy get more out of early childhood programs than do children for whom these basic needs are not fully met (CDF, 1997.). Also, children are better able to acquire new understandings when they are free of strong biological urges such as hunger or having to go to the bathroom (Maslow, 1954).

Children learn best when they feel psychologically safe and secure (Bredekamp & Copple, 1997). This translates into knowing that they are in a place where routines and rules or expectations are predictable and suited to their capacities. Being in the company of adults who respect and like them, tolerate mistakes, teach them constructive ways to satisfy their aims, and support their efforts to explore and experiment helps children feel secure. Thus, children who have positive, consistent relationships with adults at home and in the early childhood program feel more at ease and confident than do children who are denied such relationships.

In a like manner, the design of indoor and outdoor spaces and the choices of materials and equipment encourage or restrict children's experiences, affecting children's behavior and emotions. For instance, positive peer interactions are facilitated when children have ample (but not too much) space in which to move around and when play spaces are arranged so that small numbers of peers can work together rather than in isolation (Weinstein & Mignano, 2003). As another example, children display better problem-solving skills when classrooms have a large variety of age-appropriate materials from which to choose. Poor variety prevents children from combining materials and exploring new problems to solve (Hayes, Palmer, & Zaslow, 1990).

Optimal learning also requires a stimulating social environment. Because young children develop new understandings from observing and participating with other children and adults, they need numerous opportunities to interact with others in stimulating, satisfying ways.

Implications

1. Teachers and administrators highlight the importance of the environment on learning by ensuring that the program facility is safe and secure and complies with the legal requirements of the appropriate licensing or accrediting agency.

2. Early childhood programs are structured to ensure that children's biological and physical needs are addressed. For instance, children may use the toilet whenever they need to, they may rest when they are tired, and they receive snacks and meals as appropriate. Classrooms and outdoor areas offer ample space for safe, unencumbered movement. Adequate ventilation is provided, and room temperatures are maintained at a comfortable level. Children's wet or soiled clothing is changed promptly.

3. A daily schedule is established that is relatively stable and predictable to children. Changes in routine are explained in advance so that children can anticipate what will happen next.

4. Educators design activities, transitions, and routines in keeping with children's attention span, physical development, and needs for activity, social interaction, and attention from caring adults.

5. Consistent adult supervision is provided so that children can readily identify a specific adult from whom to seek help, comfort, attention, and guidance.

6. Children are treated with warmth, respect, and caring (regardless of socioeconomic, cultural, ethnic, or family background; appearance; behavior; or any disabling condition).

7. Early childhood professionals use positive discipline techniques aimed at enhancing children's self-esteem and self-control.

8. Practitioners create classroom environments that support and challenge children's abilities.

Children's Learning Is Influenced by Early Dispositions and Perceptions

The entire time children are acquiring knowledge and skills, they are also developing dispositions toward learning. Dispositions are the typical reaction patterns people develop toward various life events. Tendencies and attitudes are other words that describe such reactions. For example, when confronted with a new idea, a child might have the disposition to be curious or apathetic, open minded or rejecting. The reaction that the child habitually displays indicates that he or she has developed a disposition in that direction.

Dispositions have their foundations in early childhood and last a lifetime. As children see certain dispositions modeled by the people around them and as children are reinforced for displaying like behaviors, they adopt these dispositions (L. G. Katz & Chard, 1989). Dispositions are not taught directly, nor do they come about as the result of a single incident. Instead, they emerge through accumulated experiences. Consequently, dispositions can be strengthened or weakened by the educational practices children encounter each day.

To illustrate this concept, let us consider a classroom in which children's questions are treated as interruptions, the pursuit of one correct answer is emphasized, and a strict timetable governs children's activities. These kinds of strategies detract from children's disposition toward curiosity. Conversely, to strengthen this disposition, the teacher could provide children with intriguing materials to examine, encourage questioning and other investigative behaviors, allow children to pursue self-determined projects, modify the classroom schedule in line with children's interests, and promote students' search for multiple solutions to problems. Likewise, the disposition to be cooperative is weakened when competition is used to spur children's performance but promoted when teachers encourage group problem solving and implement group rewards.

In addition to dispositions, children form perceptions about themselves and about school. These perceptions are subjective, personal evaluations children make regarding their sense of competence, worth, and security. Interactions with others at school and the overall school climate are major contributors to the conclusions children draw. Depending on whether such experiences are predominantly positive or negative, children may perceive themselves as secure or insecure, capable or incapable, or belonging or not belonging. In addition, they may come to perceive school as worthwhile or useless, rewarding or punitive, enjoyable or tedious.

Like dispositions, perceptions evolve gradually. Initially, they are difficult to discern from children's outward behaviors. For instance, youngsters required to master isolated skills prematurely may willingly perform as desired while simultaneously formulating a negative perception of school and themselves as learners. Only after such perceptions are well grounded do they become evident. By that time, they have become relatively enduring. Consequently, we can surmise that the early childhood years are an optimal period for the development of dispositions and perceptions. Therefore, early childhood educators must exercise particular care to create program environments in which children's favorable dispositions and perceptions are enhanced.

Implications

1. Teachers and administrators strengthen positive dispositions and perceptions among children when they carefully consider the dispositions and perceptions they hope children will develop in their programs (e.g., enthusiasm for learning, curiosity, absorption in tasks, derivation of pleasure from effort and mastery, friendliness, generosity, honesty, cooperation, self-confidence).

2. Early childhood educators model the dispositions they want to strengthen in children.

3. The early childhood program climate promotes children's feelings of competence, worth, and security.

4. Adults consider to what extent program procedures and structures may undermine the dispositions and perceptions they hope children will develop. Such analyses take into account not only direct and indirect strategies, but also intended and unintended outcomes. When incongruities are discovered, practices and routines are restructured to promote more favorable results.

Children Learn Through a Combination of Physical Experience, Social Interaction, and Reflection

Maria: "Teacher, am I first on the story list?"
Teacher: "So far you are the only one on the list."
Molly: "I'm first."
Maria: "You can't be first if I'm first, Mollie. You have to be called next."
Pause
Molly: "Okay then, Maria. I'm next-first."
—Paley (1988)

Physical Experience Children have a powerful need to make sense of everything they encounter. From birth, their efforts focus on organizing their knowledge more coherently and adapting to environmental demands by directly manipulating, listening to, smelling,

Physical experiences and social interaction enhance children's learning.

tasting, and otherwise acting on objects to see what happens (Kamii, 1985; Shaffer, 2002). From such investigations children generate a logic or knowledge of the properties of things, how they work, and how they relate to one another. This knowledge accrues not simply from the passive act of observing, but also from the more complex mental activity of interpreting and drawing conclusions about what happens. Such conclusions either add to children's existing ideas or cause children to reformulate their thinking.

Social Interaction Children's experiences with physical objects are further influenced by their interactions with people (Bodrova & Leong, 1996; Vygotsky, 1978). As youngsters play, talk, and work with peers and adults, they exchange and compare interpretations and ideas. They generate hypotheses, ask questions, and formulate answers (Bredekamp & Copple, 1997). In doing so, they often face contradictions in the way people or objects respond, and these discrepancies force children to extract new understandings from what has occurred. Through such experiences *children construct knowledge internally,* continually shaping, expanding, and reorganizing their mental structures. Dominating the preschool and elementary years, constructed learning like this encompasses all the operations and conceptual knowledge children require to function in the everyday world (Berk, 2003).

Social experiences also provide children with factual information they cannot construct solely on their own. Through their interactions with others, children are instructed in culturally determined knowledge and skills necessary for successful functioning in society. Examples include the following:

Names of things (door, window, or porte, fenêtre)

Historical facts (Martin Luther King's birthday is January 20; you were born in St. Louis)

Customs (when some children are 7 years old, they take their first holy communion; some children who lose a tooth hide it under their pillow)

Rules (wash your hands before eating; walk with scissors)

Skills (how to form the letter *A*; how to throw a football correctly)

Children learn this body of knowledge through observation, imitation, memorization, and reinforcement.

Whether their knowledge is constructed or instructed, "research shows that children need to be able to successfully negotiate learning tasks most of the time if they are to maintain their motivation to learn. Confronted by repeated failure, most children will simply stop trying" (Bredekamp & Copple, 1997, p. 14). At the same time, increasing evidence indicates that children are highly motivated to adopt concepts and skills that are slightly beyond their current level of independent mastery (Bodrova & Leong, 1996). That is, children are eager to learn what they nearly, but do not quite, comprehend—what they can almost do but not quite carry out on their own. Thus, children learn best when teachers provide experiences just beyond what children can do on their own but within what they can do with assistance from someone whose skills are greater. This situation is sometimes called teaching within the child's *zone of proximal development* (Berk & Winsler, 1995; Vygotsky, 1978). For instance, Irma is speaking in two-word phrases (e.g., "Big cookie"). In conversations with Irma, her child care provider expands the child's sentences, adding more language and grammar than Irma can currently produce ("You have a big cookie" or "You like that big cookie"). If the provider's "lesson" is too complex or beyond Irma's understanding, she will not take it in. However, if Irma can simply "stretch" her thinking to encompass the new language, higher order learning is possible. Under these conditions she will gradually expand her language skills to a higher level of mastery than she would have been able to manage independently. More about the zone of proximal development is covered in chapter 11. For now, what is important to recognize is that simply giving children access to a variety of experiences is not sufficient to foster optimal learning. Adults must monitor such situations to ensure that they are manageable for children. Adults

must also provide the assistance necessary to prompt higher order learning. A youngster who is overwhelmed may be unable to understand or apply knowledge gained, regardless of how potentially useful it may be. In contrast, children who experience no challenge beyond their current level of functioning will fail to progress in their understandings and abilities. Thus, learning is most likely to flourish when children feel both successful and stimulated.

Reflection

"How did you decide this bridge was longer than that one?"

"What do you want to know about insects? How will you find that out?"

"You thought that container had more. What do you think now?"

Questions such as these are aimed at helping children reflect on what they have done or how they know what they know. Such strategies support increased self-awareness and recognition of potential learning strategies. Children who make a plan of how they want to proceed with an activity, then later recall and analyze how closely their actions matched the original plan, deepen their knowledge and understanding (Hohmann & Weikart, 1995). Children who generate ideas about how to remember a list of items (e.g., chunking, making associations, and using imagery) and then use one or more of these strategies to aid their memory at another time also deepen their knowledge. Although this kind of learning emerges most prominently during the later elementary years, evidence shows that all children benefit from reflective opportunities to think about their own thinking (Perkins, 1995).

Educators demonstrate an understanding of the importance of physical experience, social interaction, and reflection in relation to children's learning when they do the following.

Implications

1. Support learning by encouraging children to explore and act on the environment and by providing experiences that stimulate children to discover and construct knowledge for themselves

2. Interact with children, posing questions and introducing new elements to challenge children's current thinking

3. Provide daily opportunities for children to interact with their peers

4. Offer information, ask questions, demonstrate, point out, and explain in an effort to help children

acquire knowledge or skills they cannot discover on their own

5. Provide experiences that enable children to link new information with what they already know and understand

6. Give children opportunities to reflect on their experiences and help children develop strategies for doing so

Children's Learning Styles Differ

Sarah likes to work on her own.

Consuelo prefers working with a friend.

Wilma has been interested in numbers since toddlerhood.

Carlos has a way with words.

Jerome seems to have a special feel for the outdoors.

Steve enjoys the thrill of competition.

Different children—different ways of approaching the world.

If you and your classmates were trying to get directions to a place where you had never been, some of you might prefer using a map, others would like to hear the directions several times aloud, and still others would physically need to go through the motions of orienting their bodies to the left or right as they went over the directions in their mind. These differences in how each person might best process the directions occur because every person has a preferred modality that works best for him or her (Kovalik, 1997). Modalities are the sensory channels (visual, auditory, kinesthetic, and tactile) through which people perceive the world. For example, people who are primarily *visual learners* respond best to what they see. Often they envision things in their mind as a way to recall them. Youngsters who rely on hearing and speaking as their primary means of learning are referred to as *auditory learners*. For them, sound is the message. These youngsters sometimes move their lips or talk themselves through tasks. Kinesthetic and tactile learners are children who must move and constantly touch things as a way to grasp concepts. Often, they also have to touch themselves in some way to remember or process information. All people use all four modalities to learn; however, all people also function more effectively in the context of their preferred modalities.

Howard Gardner of Harvard University took the idea of preferred modalities further than the four just described by expanding the construct beyond simple perceptual processing. He believes that everyone possesses at least eight intelligences, or "frames of mind," and that

a person's blend of competencies in each area produces a unique cognitive profile (Gardner, 1993a). The eight intelligences are linguistic, logical-mathematical, musical, spatial, bodily-kinesthetic, intrapersonal, interpersonal, and naturalistic. Gardner suggested that "each of these (intelligence/competency) areas may develop independently (in the brain), although ultimately they all work together" (Hatch & Gardner, 1988, p. 38). He emphasized that people possess varying degrees of know-how in all eight categories and that individuals may be "at promise" in some areas, while being average or below average in others. Most people have the potential to develop further in each of the intelligences. The eight intelligences and how they influence children's learning are summarized in Table 2.2.

Differences in learning style may also exist as a result of temperament or cultural factors. For instance, some children think quickly, spontaneously, and impulsively; others are deliberate and reflective. Some children focus on the "big idea"; some think more about the details. Some children constantly look for connections among ideas; others take a single thought and follow it in many directions. Some children organize their thoughts in sequence; others think in a more circular fashion. Some children are socially oriented, working best cooperatively and in groups. Other children value individual achievement and enjoy competition (Guild, 2001).

All these variations in learning style suggest that there is no single "correct" way to learn and that there are many ways to be "smart." This concept has not always been understood. For many years, educational settings that emphasized seatwork and listening to lectures from the teacher favored verbal, or linguistic, and logical-mathematical learners. In these settings, active children (bodily-kinesthetic learners), social children (interpersonal learners), and spontaneous thinkers were treated as though their natural learning styles were inappropriate. Children with learning styles dominated by visuospatial, musical, or naturalistic intelligences found few opportunities to use these intelligences in daily classroom life. Today, we are much more aware of the many ways in which children learn. Early childhood educators demonstrate respect for this diversity when they engage in the following six practices.

Implications

1. Observe children carefully to discover which learning opportunities might best match each child's learning style

2. Provide activities for children that represent a variety of modalities or intelligences

TABLE 2.2 Children's Frames of Mind: Corresponding Learning and Teaching Practices

Type of Intelligence	Child Enjoys	Child Excels in	Child Learns Best by	The Classroom Should Provide Opportunities for
Verbal, or linguistic, learner "The Word Player"	Reading, writing, telling stories	Memorizing names, places, dates, and trivia	Seeing, saying, and learning language	Many language-based materials, which should be print rich
Logical-mathematical learner "The Questioner"	Doing experiments, figuring things out, working with numbers, asking questions, exploring patterns and relationships	Math, reasoning, logic	Looking for patterns and relationships	Handling objects, exploring new ideas, and following the scientific process naturally
Spatial learner "The Visualizer"	Drawing, building, designing, creating things	Imagining things, sensing changes, doing mazes and puzzles	Visualizing, dreaming, using the mind's eye	Children to work with art and construction materials and to create "projects"
Musical learner "The Music Lover"	Singing, humming, whistling, listening to instruments, responding to music	Picking up sounds; remembering melodies, pitches, and rhythms; keeping time	Using rhythm and melody	Information to be presented through rhythm and melody
Bodily-kinesthetic learner "The Mover"	Moving around, touching and talking, using body language	Physical activities (sports/dance/acting), crafts	Touching, moving, interacting with space, processing knowledge through bodily sensations	Role-playing, drama, creative movement, gross-motor, and other whole-body activities
Interpersonal learner "The Socializer"	Having lots of friends, talking to people, joining groups	Understanding people, leading others, organizing, communicating, manipulating, mediating conflicts	Sharing, comparing, relating, cooperating, interviewing	Cooperative, collaborative activities and projects; children to express selves to others
Intrapersonal learner "The Individual"	Working alone, pursuing own interest, engaging in self-imagery	Understanding people; focusing inward, on feelings or dreams; following instincts; pursuing interests or goals; being original	Working alone, doing individualized projects, following self-paced instruction, having own space	Self-paced activities, individualized projects, private space, and time for children to work on own
Naturalistic learner "The Nature Lover"	Experiencing the outdoors, animals, and plants.	Recognizing plants and animals, sorting, categorizing, matching, classifying, comparing, sequencing, making associations and patterns with natural objects, recording relationships	Observing nature, interacting with plants and animals, making relationships among natural things	Spending time outdoors, caring for the earth (recycling, composting), caring for plants, caring for animals, and having hands-on experiences with natural objects

Adapted from *Frames of Mind: Theory of Multiple Intelligence*, H. Gardner, 1993a. New York: Basic Books; *Seven Styles of Learning*, September 1990, *Instructor Magazine*, p. 52; Using the Multiple Intelligences Theory to Assess Early Childhood Curricula, A. Carlisle, *Young Children*, 56(6), 2001, 77–83; and Are There Additional Intelligences? The Case for Naturalist, Spiritual, and Existential Intelligences, H. Gardner, 1998, in J. Kane (Ed.), *Education, Information, and Transformation: Essays on Learning and Thinking* (pp. 111–131). Upper Saddle River, NJ: Prentice Hall.

3. Address the same concept or skill through multiple modalities and multiple intelligences

4. Review programs for balance, ensuring activities take into account multiple modalities and multiple intelligences, and revise the curriculum as necessary to achieve better balance

5. Provide an array of activities each day, from which children may choose, so that children can self-select those that best suit their learning needs

6. Give children a variety of ways to show what they have learned, taking into account multiple modalities and intelligences

Children Learn Through Play

Play is fun, imaginative, meaningful, active, voluntary, intrinsically motivated, and rule governed.	It is pleasurable. It is not constrained by reality. It connects and relates experiences to one another. Children are doing things. No one must force children to play. Curiosity, the desire for mastery, and the desire for affiliation are some reasons children play. Rules may be implicit or explicit and are created by the children.

Children play at home, at school, and everywhere between. They play with people, things, and ideas (Whiren, 1995). When more fundamental needs are met—when children are not sleeping, eating, or seeking emotional support from others—children choose to play and can remain occupied that way for hours. Play is the province of children from the time they are born throughout the elementary school years.

All areas of development are enhanced through children's play activities. Play is the fundamental means by

Play is the primary medium through which children learn.

which children gather and process information, learn new skills, and practice old skills (Fromberg, 2002). Within the context of their play, children come to understand, create, and manipulate symbols as they take on roles and transform objects into something else. Children explore social relationships, too—experimenting with various social roles, discovering points of view in contrast to their own, working out compromises, and negotiating differences. Play enables children to extend their physical skills, language and literacy capabilities, and creative imaginations. The safe haven that play provides for the release of tensions, the expression of emotions, and the exploration of anxiety-producing situations has also been well documented (Santrock, 2000). In fact, the amount of research touting the value of play in children's lives is substantial, and most scientists agree that play is central to children's learning. Why, then, does so much resistance to letting children play exist in some early childhood programs, especially in elementary school?

Some educators suggest that the problem has arisen because adults in our society have traditionally considered play the opposite of valuable work and therefore the opposite of learning (Fields & Spangler, 2000). Other educators believe that adults are unaware of the benefits of play and thus categorize this essential activity as "just playing," equating it with frivolous or extraneous endeavors (Eiferman, 1971). Still other researchers claim that adults confuse educational play (supported by the teacher with educational aims in mind) with random activity (which results when teachers fail to support play properly; Spodek, 1985). The first two misconceptions are best addressed through better communication about how play helps children develop and learn. Therefore, early childhood professionals who already believe that play is essential for children must become more knowledgeable and eloquent in defending play to colleagues, parents, administrators, and other program decision makers. The third misperception will be rectified only when teachers and administrators understand the ways in which play can vary in the classroom and the ways in which they can support educational play.

Bergen (1988b) developed a schema of play and learning consisting of four categories depicted along a continuum. These categories progress from play to nonplay, child centered to adult centered, and discovery learning to rote learning. Briefly, the four categories are as follows:

1. *Free play* Free play is the most child-centered, discovery-oriented category of play. Children choose whether to play, how to play, what to play, and when to play. Such play requires the teacher to provide a safe environment, supported by a variety of props, and minimal

restrictions regarding how the play will proceed. Children's creating a grocery store out of a refrigerator box or turning the outdoor climber into a spaceship could illustrate this type of play. Making up their own card game and playing with language sounds are other possibilities.

2. *Guided play* Guided play has many of the elements of the preceding category, but the teacher carefully structures the experiences so that certain discoveries are more likely to occur. Thus, guided play has more rules, fewer alternatives, and closer adult supervision than free play does. Examples might include play at the workbench or computer or in a pretend grocery store in which the teacher asks questions or models behaviors aimed at helping children focus more closely on the roles of customer and employee.

3. *Directed play* When the adult designates that children may choose one of three board games or asks all the children to play Duck, Duck, Goose, he or she is directing the play. The children's participation is required, and the means by which the children play is often adult determined. The primary kind of learning that occurs within this mode of play is receptive, with the emphasis on oral instructions and explanations.

4. *Work disguised as play* Work disguised as play involves task-oriented activities that the teacher attempts to transform into directed- or guided-play episodes. Playing a spelling game and conducting an addition facts race are typical examples. Most work disguised as play involves rote learning. Although such activity may be a more enjoyable way to engage in practice and drill, it is no longer play because it contains none of the elements of play described at the onset of this section.

Bergen (1988b) pointed out that the school day for preschoolers and children in the lower elementary grades should include many opportunities for free play and guided play. There are limited benefits to devoting much time to directed play and even fewer for the fourth category. Teachers who transpose these desired emphases by focusing on the last two categories to the exclusion of free play and guided play are not promoting the kind of play from which children benefit the most. The same is true for teachers who take an entirely hands-off view of play (Whiren, 1995), which happens when they allow play but do nothing to enhance or facilitate it. Practitioners who fail to provide a rich background of experiences as a foundation for play—who neglect to rotate props, ask questions, or provide information periodically to enlarge children's perceptions—are depriving children of valuable opportunities to develop and extend their play. Neither overcontrolling the play nor failing to support it is consistent with developmentally appropriate practice.

Implications

1. Early childhood professionals support children's play when they talk to parents and colleagues about the value of play and its relationship to children's development and learning.

2. One or more long blocks of time during the school day are devoted to playful activities.

3. Classroom space and materials are organized to enable children to engage in both solitary play and collaborative play.

4. Play is integrated into all curricular domains.

5. A variety of props and other materials are available with which to play.

6. Adults are joyful and playful as they work with children and stimulate children's play by modeling, taking roles, offering information, asking questions, playing with language, and avoiding interrupting the play when they are not needed.

7. The sound and activity levels within the classroom reflect the quality of children's play—high-quality play is often noisy and active.

WHAT ARE THE CONTEXTS OF CHILDHOOD DEVELOPMENT AND LEARNING?

Rules of development are the same for all children, but social contexts shape children's development into different configurations.
—Bowman (1994)

Children are born and carry out their lives within many contexts, including the *biological* makeup bestowed on them by their parents and the *environment* in which they develop. This environment comprises the immediate family and the extended family; extrafamilial settings such as the neighborhood, a child care center, or school; and the culture and society. These contexts often overlap and are embedded within one another (Bronfenbrenner, 1989). They can be depicted as a series of concentric rings, as shown in Figure 2.1, with each system influencing and being influenced by the others.

The Biological Context

The child is at the core of everything. Each youngster is born possessing a unique biological heritage. Genetic givens include gender, temperament, and a timetable for the emergence of intellectual, emotional, and physical capacities. In addition, children are born with a predisposition to act on the environment, learn, and seek social stimulation as well as form bonds with other people (DeHart, Sroufe, & Cooper, 2000). In combination, these

FIGURE 2.1 The Ecological Context of Child Development and Learning

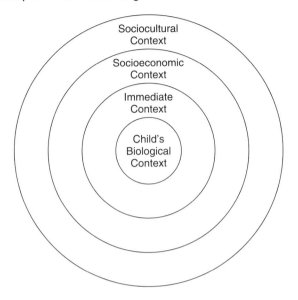

traits provide the biological boundaries within which development and learning occur.

The Immediate Context

Development and learning are further influenced by the immediate environment—all the people, objects, settings, and resources with which the child has direct contact. At birth, this context is dominated by the family. Eventually, additional settings (e.g., a child care home, a child care center, school, the playground, the neighborhood, or a 4-H group) become increasingly influential.

The Socioeconomic Context

All the immediate settings in which children find themselves are further embedded in a broader socioeconomic context. The impact of social and economic factors on children's development is frequently indirect but profound. For instance, the materials provided in a classroom and the curricula children encounter at school are shaped by educators, parents, and school boards using resources within a particular community. General economic factors and community-based beliefs also contribute to the educational program offered students. Indirectly, all these factors have an impact on each child even though the parties may have no direct contact with one another or the children.

The Sociocultural Context

Individuals, families, schools, and communities exist within a society and a culture and are greatly influenced by these, the broadest of all environments. The

sociocultural context, the outermost ring in Figure 2.1, is defined by the belief patterns shared by groups of people. These beliefs shape the structure of various societal institutions (e.g., legal, economic, religious, and political systems) and other social structures such as social class. In addition, within and across societies cultural groups exist that share more narrowly defined beliefs, norms, and values and that differ from one another in their basic approaches to living. Essential cultural variations exist regarding the way human beings relate to one another, the significance of time, the personality types most valued, how humans relate to nature, and the fundamental notions of whether human beings are innately good or bad (Berns, 2001). As a result of how different groups approach these issues, some children learn that cooperation is more highly valued than competition, and others learn the reverse. One cultural group might interpret a child's assertive behavior as a positive sign of independence, whereas another would be dismayed at the child's lack of deference. In some groups children are encouraged to revere nature; in some they are taught to control it. The belief system that prevails for children is a function of the cultural context in which they find themselves.

Contextual Relationships and Impacts

None of the contexts just described exists in isolation or exerts its influence apart from the rest. They are all interdependent, both influencing and being influenced by the others. For instance, children are not passive recipients of environmental impacts. They actively contribute to their own development and to the creation of the contexts in which they live and learn. For example, knowing this, we may observe that a "resistant" child frequently elicits rule-related confrontations from adults and that such behavior, in turn, prompts the child to become increasingly resistant. Similarly, the family environment may be strengthened or weakened by changes that occur in the socioeconomic context surrounding it. However, because influence is bidirectional, families also affect socioeconomic forces, demanding alterations in services and community organizations to support their changing needs. This interdependence among contexts means that intervention with the child will have an impact on the other contexts within which he or she functions, such as the family. Also, what occurs in the family or neighborhood will influence the child's behavior in the early childhood program.

Finally, the significance that biological variables, other immediate environments, socioeconomic factors, and sociocultural factors have for young children is always mediated by decisions and interactions within their families (DeHart et al., 2000). As discussed in the

Introduction, families are children's first teachers. The interrelationships among contexts and the dynamic nature of their influence on child development and learning suggest four important implications for early childhood educators.

Implications

1. Professionals must take into account many dimensions when considering children's early education and determining appropriate intervention methods.
2. The collective influence of all the contexts referred to in Figure 2.1 is unique for each child. Although some effects may be shared among a group of children, the total milieu for one youngster is unlike that of any other. This means each child is distinct from all others and requires individual consideration at all times.
3. Early childhood programs not only influence children and families, but also are influenced by the contexts within which they operate. It is neither possible nor desirable to try to work with children in isolation.
4. Because children function within a variety of social settings, communication among practitioners in these settings is essential. This means that continuity among the programs children attend simultaneously (e.g., child care center and elementary school) must be natural and well planned. The same is true as children move from one setting one year (e.g., Head Start) to another the next year (e.g., kindergarten).

THE OVERARCHING PRINCIPLE OF DEVELOPMENTAL DIRECTION

Both development and learning proceed in predictable directions. In other words, development and learning progress from a beginning point. The principle of developmental direction defines this forward progress. For instance, in the body, maturation proceeds from top to bottom (head to tail) and midline to outer extremities, which is why infants are born with large heads and proportionately smaller lower bodies. The head region, containing the brain, on which all life depends, is more developed than the posterior region, which is not immediately necessary for survival. For the same reason, babies gain control of their head and neck muscles (lifting, turning, and holding up the head) prior to mastering control of their legs and feet. Likewise, the heart and other internal organs are fully coordinated in the newborn, whereas hand coordination occurs much later. These outward manifestations of developmental direction are obvious to even the casual observer, but other,

FIGURE 2.2 Developmental Directions in Children's Learning

Simple	Complex
Known	Unknown
Self	Other
Whole	Part
Concrete	Abstract
Enactive	Symbolic
Exploratory	Goal directed
Inaccurate	More accurate
Impulsive	Self-controlled

more subtle, examples of internal change are equally important for educators to know about. Such changes influence child development and learning throughout the preschool and elementary years.

Development and learning proceed from simple to complex, known to unknown, self to other, whole to part, concrete to abstract, enactive to symbolic, exploratory to goal directed, inaccurate to more accurate, and impulsive to self-controlled (Figure 2.2).

Simple to Complex

There are hundreds of examples of how developmental progression from simple to complex influences children's lives. To conserve space, let us consider just one—how children develop categories. At first, toddlers may categorize all fuzzy living creatures into one simple category: "doggies." Gradually, as children gain experience and their cognitive powers expand, they differentiate among fuzzy creatures, thereby creating multiple categories: "doggies" and "kitties." With time, these categorizations become increasingly complex as children differentiate breeds of cats and dogs, friendly versus unfriendly characteristics of each, and real and pretend examples.

Complexity increases as the numbers of variables multiply and as the discriminations among these variables become less acute. Also, combining elements is more complex than dealing with them separately. Thus, putting together a puzzle containing eight large pieces is more complicated for a child than putting together one containing four, and putting together puzzles in which the color and shape of the pieces are extremely different is easier than putting together puzzles in which pieces are varied in color but shaped alike. Teachers have this principle in mind when they gradually introduce challenge to children by increasing numbers of elements, offering finer discriminations for children to consider, and asking children to group and regroup objects and events differently.

Known to Unknown

Children base what they learn and do on what is familiar. They build skills on previously learned behaviors. More-sophisticated concepts grow out of those that already exist for them. When children can make connections between their prior knowledge and new experiences, these experiences become meaningful. When children cannot, the experiences are irrelevant. Thus, this fact means teachers must discover what children know and can do prior to introducing new material. This fact also provides the rationale for addressing concepts within a context that makes sense to the children. Therefore, a teacher would introduce mammalian characteristics by using examples of animals common in the children's environment, not animals they had seen only in pictures.

Self to Other

The young child's world revolves around him- or herself. All new experiences are considered within this sphere. It is not surprising then that among children's first words are *me* and *mine*. This preoccupation with the self is the child's way of learning about what is closest to him or her and of relating new experiences to familiar experiences. At first, children's egocentric interpretations result from an erroneous assumption that all views of the world are identical and thus must resemble theirs. As experiences occur in which this perspective is challenged and as children develop greater cognitive sophistication, their interpretations expand. They eventually recognize that multiple perspectives are possible and that these perspectives might differ. As this understanding takes hold, children become more adept at recognizing, valuing, and accommodating others' needs, reactions, and experiences. This principle further underscores the importance of relating knowledge and skills to children in ways that have personal meaning. Explanations and experiences that make sense to adults but not to children do not enhance children's development and learning. This principle should also serve as a reminder that children's egocentric world view is a function of their development, not an aberration.

Whole to Part

Children perceive and experience the world in integrated, unified ways, moving from wholes to parts and general to specific understandings. Something like this happens to adults when they go to a movie for the first time. They usually come away with a basic understanding of the plot and sensory impressions of color, sound, and feelings. On seeing the same movie again, people often perceive things they missed initially because they are moving from the holistic sensation of the first experience to paying more attention to detail. A third or fourth trip could reveal even more specifics, contributing to better comprehension of subtle plot nuances as well as the mechanics of filmmaking.

Children take in experiences holistically in much the same way. Only after they have grasped the essentials of an experience do the details become meaningful to them. Hence, children might hear a song several times before differentiating some of the words. Likewise, the value of paying attention to letter–sound associations develops only after children have formulated a concept of print and how it relates to their daily lives. Introducing the specifics prematurely or out of context renders them meaningless. Much the same result would occur if people were shown a brief clip of movie dialogue and then asked to analyze it. This mechanical exercise would not lead to substantive gains in their understanding of the story or increase its personal relevance. In fact, if it happened often enough, it might promote the perception that films are boring or purposeless, which would thereby decrease their appeal.

Teachers who think about the whole-to-part principle offer children a broad array of rich, multisensory experiences. They repeat activities often, giving children plenty of time to explore and formulate their impressions and conceptualizations. As children express interest and understanding, teachers draw children's attention to relevant details that enlarge youngster's perceptions and challenge them to try alternatives or reconsider old ideas. Conversely, teachers are careful not to teach children skills or facts in isolation. They work from the general to the specific rather than the other way around.

Concrete to Abstract

The most concrete experiences are tangible experiences that involve physical contact with real objects. They are those in which children taste, touch, and smell as well as see and hear. The further removed an experience is from this tangible state and the fewer senses children are required to use, the more abstract it becomes. Providing children with real leaves to look at, handle, take apart, smell, and taste is a concrete way to enhance children's interest in and knowledge about leaves. Giving children pictures to explore or having them cut leaves from magazines is a step removed from the real thing and thus is more abstract. Even further removed is having children watch the teacher point to leaves in a book or on the bulletin board. The most distant and therefore most abstract activity involves having children think about leaves as the teacher talks about them.

Children throughout the preschool and elementary years benefit from concrete experiences in all developmental domains and across all subject areas. The more unfamiliar the object or phenomenon, the more this is true. Even adults who are learning something for the first time do better when given opportunities for real-life experiences rather than just seeing something modeled or having it explained. The danger in ignoring this principle is that children may parrot what the adult wants to hear but not truly understand essential concepts. For this reason teachers provide children with many firsthand experiences and tangible objects on which to base their learning.

Enactive to Symbolic

Enactive Representation Children first represent the world enactively. They use their bodies to reconstruct or act out events and roles by using objects, gestures, sounds, and words. This way to think through an experience is very tangible and concrete and is the most basic form of representation (Lawton, 1987). Teachers observe enactive representation when, after taking a field trip to feed the ducks, the children return to the classroom imitating duck sounds, waddling, and making "quacking" gestures with their hands. Such representations duplicate and preserve many of the distinctive qualities associated with the actual phenomenon—ducks.

Iconic Representation A more abstract mode of representation involves children's making pictures or constructing three-dimensional images of what they see and think about. These pictures are iconic representations. Youngsters who reproduce or create personal interpretations of objects and events by using art or construction materials such as blocks are demonstrating iconic representation. Thus, following the duck field trip, some youngsters might paint what they saw, and others might sculpt ducklike shapes in clay. Although these pictorial representations share many of the same characteristics as those of real ducks (e.g., color and shape), other concrete cues such as sound and motion are less obvious.

Symbolic Representation The ultimate and most abstract means of representation is symbolic. In this mode, children manipulate words and symbols, such as letters and numerals, to interpret and represent particular objects and events. Youngsters returning from a field trip could represent what occurred by dictating or writing descriptions of the trip. However, the symbols they use no longer bear any resemblance to real ducks, which makes this level of representation the most removed from the children's actual experience.

Enactive representation occurs in its most rudimentary form within the first year of life. Infants think in terms of actions and about objects by acting on them. Gradually, these enactive episodes become more elaborate, blossoming into pretend play in toddlerhood. Iconic representation first appears at about age 18 months, with symbolic representation following soon after. As one form of representation emerges, children do not discard earlier forms. Rather, they build on and combine the different modes to enhance their conceptualizations and understandings.

The importance of these different modes of representation provides a rationale for including materials and experiences related to all three in early childhood classrooms. Children do not outgrow their need for pretend play, art, or construction materials when moving into the elementary grades. Nor is toddlerhood too early to encourage children to experiment with drawing or writing surfaces and related tools and implements. This continuum also suggests that the developmentally appropriate early childhood curriculum gives children ample opportunity to explore concepts through enactive representation prior to being introduced to the more abstract iconic and symbolic representations related to these concepts.

Exploratory to Goal Directed

Exploration Educators have many notions of how children move along the continuum from randomly experimenting with objects and relationships to purposefully applying the knowledge and skills they gain. However, even theories that represent otherwise incompatible interpretations begin at the exploration phase. That is, children experiment and "play around" with objects and materials prior to using them in prescribed ways. Exploration is a time of self-discovery that occurs through the spontaneous manipulation of objects and through informal social interactions with peers and adults. Knowledge grows as these interactions are mentally organized, which is why children who have never seen a lotto game would have difficulty beginning to play it immediately. They would need time to handle the pieces, look at the different pictures on the cards and boards, and experiment with making some matches. Prior to seeing this particular game, youngsters would need many previous chances to explore the whole notion of game playing, working with others in a group, and so forth. If they were to plunge into the game without this exploratory experience, chances are they would explore anyway and thereby miss some of the directions or not pay attention to the course of the action. The adult, trying to keep the children on task, would be fighting children's natural tendencies to explore. Neither adult nor children would benefit from the experience. For the adult, playing lotto might turn into a discipline-focused confrontation; for the children, the cognitive aspects of the game would not necessarily register.

The early childhood years mark a time when much of children's attention and energy is focused on exploring the world around them. As Hymes (1980) said, children are the aliens to the planet; they are the new beings for whom experiences are fresh and unfamiliar. We "old-timers" sometimes forget how novel it all is for children and how much there is to discover. Also, all the discovering is not over by ages 4 or 5 or 7 or 8 years. The exploration phase is the threshold from which children gradually acquire knowledge and skills, practice their newfound understandings and behaviors, and eventually generalize what they have discovered across a variety of situations. It is the foundation of all understanding.

Acquisition Once children have thoroughly explored a phenomenon, they display signs of being ready to move to the acquisition phase of learning. Children signal this when they ask, "How do you play this game?" "What comes next?" or "Why is the grass green?" Using a variety of indirect and direct instructional strategies, teachers respond to children's cues. In doing so, they help children refine their understanding, guide their attention, and make connections (Bredekamp, 1991; Deiner, 1993). This form of inquiry is usually more goal oriented for both teachers and children than is characteristic of pure exploration. However, it is neither rigid nor unidirectional. Children still have a lot of latitude in how they proceed and in the paths they take.

Practice Acquisition of new knowledge and skills is followed by a time during which children concentrate on practicing what they have learned. They use the new behavior or knowledge repeatedly and in a variety of circumstances. This is exemplified by the child who, having learned to play lotto, wants to play again and again, enjoying rather than tiring of the repetitions. Children who have just learned to wash the dishes beg to do them, at least for a while, and youngsters who have learned to dribble a basketball try it out in the hall, on the playground, in the gym, and on the sidewalk. In every case, the child's practice is self-motivated and self-initiated. It represents the tangible way in which children gain mastery. Teachers facilitate children's practice when they allow children time to play out the same scenarios repeatedly and when they follow children's lead in repeating activities more than once as well as varying the practice conditions.

Generalization Eventually, children have enough grounding to apply their newfound knowledge or skills to novel situations. When this happens, they enter the generalization phase of learning, which is the most advanced and goal-directed phase along the learning continuum. Within this phase children apply what they have learned in many ways and adjust their thinking to fit new circumstances or demands. They also formulate novel hypotheses, which may prompt them to initiate new explorations and thereby begin the cycle again (Bredekamp, 1991). It is worth noting that the goal orientation so prominent in the generalization phase remains internally inspired. Therefore, the teacher's role becomes that of creating vehicles for children to make applications to real-world situations and providing meaningful situations children can use for learning.

Children proceed from exploratory to goal-directed activity within all realms of learning: aesthetic, affective, cognitive, language, physical, and social. Where they are in the process depends on their backlog of experiences and understandings as well as the learning opportunities available to them. Therefore, each child's progress along the continuum will differ for various threads within each realm as well as from realm to realm. In other words, children are not in any one phase of learning for everything simultaneously. Instead, youngsters may just be starting to explore some concepts or skills while acquiring, practicing, or generalizing others.

To accommodate such differences within and among children, teachers have to provide them with broad-based, open-ended activities. From these, children extrapolate experiences that correspond to the phase of learning most relevant to them. Thus, several children working with puzzles may use them for different purposes—exploration, practice, and so forth. Repeating activities is also a good idea because children need many opportunities to progress along the learning continuum. Furthermore, teachers must support children in whatever phase of learning they are in for a given activity by using different instructional strategies as necessary (e.g., providing many varied materials for exploration; offering feedback, providing information, or asking questions as appropriate; giving children chances to practice what they have learned under different conditions; and encouraging children to apply what they have learned to new situations). Such adaptations are more easily made within individualized and small-group instructional formats than in whole-group formats.

Inaccurate to More Accurate

Children develop hypotheses about the world in which they live according to the internal processes of acquiring, structuring, and restructuring knowledge. Subsequently, young children's natural thinking and reasoning processes are filled with trial and error and incorrect conclusions. All these result from children's continuous efforts to order the world into understandable patterns. These so-called mistakes are central to children's mental development. They serve as the means by which children refine their thinking and enlarge it. As children experience the mental conflict that arises through events that challenge their deductions, they resolve the dilemma through further mental activity and thus gradually develop more accurate thinking.

Because of this principle, educators must be cautious about focusing on children's producing "right" answers. A child who answers "correctly" may be responding from rote memorization or inaccurate conclusions rather than accurate reasoning processes. For this reason, emphasis should be on how children derive answers. Activities that involve children's developing predictions, evaluating their experiences, solving problems, and determining what they know as well as how they know should be featured throughout the day.

Impulsive to Self-Controlled

Young children are active, noisy beings who come about these characteristics naturally. Controlling their impulses to touch, make sounds, move, or go after what they want is difficult for them. Waiting and holding back are acquired skills that develop in tandem with children's cognitive, physical, emotional, and social concepts and behaviors. The acquisition of these skills is supported when teachers and administrators create classroom environments in which children have opportunities to move about freely, express themselves openly, learn alternative strategies for achieving their goals, and practice ways of delaying gratification that are in keeping with their comprehension and abilities.

Forcing children into a passive, inactive state is unnatural and interferes with all other aspects of their development and learning.

Implications of Developmental Direction

1. Practitioners use the principle of developmental direction as a guide for designing activities to support children's progress from less mature or complex levels of knowledge and skill to more sophisticated levels.
2. Early childhood educators assume that within each activity, individual children will be in different places along the continuums associated with developmental direction. Their plans reflect this understanding.
3. Practitioners use the principle of developmental direction as a guide for simplifying and extending activities and routines in accordance with children's needs and interests.

SUMMARY

In this chapter, we outline fundamental principles of childhood development and learning as well as the overarching principle of developmental direction. Corresponding implications for program design and classroom practice are identified for each. As readers explore the ramifications of these concepts in the chapters that follow, the ideas expressed in this chapter will be revisited. There is no element of early childhood education they do not touch. Activities and routines, materials, the physical environment, classroom management, methods of parental involvement, and assessment procedures are all influenced by these principles. With this understanding, let us turn our attention to setting the stage for children's learning.

Applying What You Read in This Chapter

1. **Discuss**
   a. On the basis of your reading and your experiences with young children, discuss each of the questions that open this chapter.
   b. Select two principles of development and learning that you believe are most important for people untrained in early childhood education to know about. Explain your choices and what you would emphasize about each.
2. **Observe**
   a. Observe two children of approximately the same age who are involved in the same activity. Note similarities in their behavior as well as differences.
   b. Observe a teacher carrying out an activity with one or more children. Identify which of the following continuums related to developmental direction were evident throughout the time you observed:
      Simple to complex
      Known to unknown
      Self to other
      Whole to part
      Concrete to abstract
      Enactive to symbolic
      Exploratory to goal directed
      Inaccurate to more accurate
      Impulsive to self-controlled

Provide examples to illustrate your observations.
3. **Carry out an activity**
   a. First, choose one of the following early childhood activities:

      Child learning to button her coat

      Child learning to tell a familiar story from beginning to end

      Child stacking nesting cups in order

      Child learning to wait her turn at the snack table

      Child learning to wash his hands properly

      Next, select one of the principles of developmental direction outlined in this chapter. Then explain how you would use this principle to support children's forward progress in the activity you chose.

   b. Select a trade book, aimed at parents, describing some aspect of child development. Describe to what extent the book you chose supports or fails to support the principles of development and learning that you read about in this chapter.

   c. Create a bumper sticker that captures the essence of one of the principles of development or learning described in this chapter.

   d. Review written information describing an early childhood program in your community. On the basis of the program's written philosophy and program description, discuss to what extent the program is congruent or incongruent with the principles described in this chapter.

4. **Create something for your portfolio**
   a. Select a fundamental belief you have about child development and learning. Think both about children in general and specifically about the ages of the children in a program where you are working, volunteering, or doing a practicum. Describe how this belief would affect the following program dimensions: the children's program, staff, materials, physical space, budget, and family involvement. Identify practices that would be incompatible with the principle you chose.

5. **Add to your journal**
   a. What is the most significant concept about child development and learning that you learned from your readings and your experience with children?

   b. Reflect on the extent to which the content of this chapter corresponds to what you have observed in the field. What is your reaction to any discrepancies you perceive?

   c. In what ways have you used child development and learning principles in your work with children? What goals do you have for yourself in this regard?

Part 2

Setting the Stage for Learning

Planning and Implementing
Effective Small-Group Activities

You may wonder:

Why do teachers write lesson plans? Why are plans necessary?

Is formal planning as important for children in child care settings or nursery schools as it is for children enrolled in elementary programs?

As a teacher with my own class, will I have to write the same kind of plans as I am writing now?

As an early childhood professional, what kinds of teaching strategies should I use?

How can I implement a single plan that accommodates developmental differences among children?

---

n this introduction to planning and implementing effective small-group activities, we present information to help you answer the preceding questions.

Estaban Ramirez is student teaching in the kindergarten of an employer-sponsored child care center. His roommates are amazed at the time and care he puts into writing lesson plans. After all, the children are only 5 and 6 years old. His friends cannot understand how planning for children that age could be so involved.

Sometimes people are surprised at how much planning is necessary to ensure a smoothly running early childhood classroom. They may erroneously assume that in an early childhood classroom little more is required than simply putting out materials for children to use. However, the difference between providing children with truly educational experiences and merely keeping them busy or entertained is *planning* (Krogh & Slentz, 2001a). In fact, planning is a key element of high-quality early childhood programs, and the ability to plan developmentally appropriate activities distinguishes effective practices from ineffective practices (Doherty-Derkowski, 1998).

WHY PLAN?

Thorough planning provides the foundation for effective teaching. Early childhood professionals plan ahead to create positive environments for teaching and learning (Freiberg & Driscoll, 2000). Although the design of teachers' plans varies from program to program, the aims of planning are universal. Planning helps teachers to do the following:

❑ Organize their thoughts and actions
❑ Think creatively about what they want to do
❑ Gather needed equipment and materials in advance
❑ Map ways to address immediate instructional objectives and long-term educational aims
❑ Address the needs of the "whole child"
❑ Tailor programs to accommodate the needs of specific children
❑ Address differences among learners
❑ Communicate to others what they are doing
❑ Identify a standard by which learning and teaching can be accurately and appropriately evaluated

Appropriate planning leads to purposeful, comprehensive instruction, which conveys a sense of direction and order that children perceive and appreciate. Implementing carefully sequenced plans gives teachers valuable information about children, materials, teaching methods, and outcomes. As a result, teachers are better able to chart the progress of individual students and the group as a whole, noting where advances are being made and where change might be necessary (Dodge, 1995). In these ways, early childhood professionals use their plans as a basis not only for their teaching, but also for assessing children's development and learning.

In contrast, lack of planning results in chaos. Children may wander aimlessly or engage in inappropriate behavior for lack of something better to do. Other negative consequences of inadequate planning include meeting the needs of some youngsters but not all and creating superficial, irrelevant activities that fail to stimulate children's learning. In each instance, poor planning yields poor-quality programs for children. To prevent these negative results, early childhood practitioners must acquire effective planning skills.

CHARACTERISTICS OF EFFECTIVE PLANNING

Effective early childhood planning involves taking into account individuals and groups of children. It also involves addressing immediate objectives and long-term goals as well as what is currently going on in the classroom and what might be needed in the future. Such planning reflects the teacher's knowledge and understanding not only of how young children develop and learn, but also of the context in which children's learning occurs. A strong grasp of relevant subject matter is also necessary (Bredekamp & Copple, 1997; Stronge, 2002). In addition, whether the planning is for a single activity or for the program as a whole, good planning is flexible enough to allow teachers to accommodate children's changing needs and to take advantage of teachable moments as they happen.

TEACHERS AS PLANNERS

The act of planning involves purpose, organization, foresight, preparation, and deliberate decision making. Most important, early childhood educators must keep in mind the children for whom their plans are being developed: the children's needs, interests, and strengths (Slentz & Krogh, 2001b). Effective planners also take into account the materials at their disposal, the physical space in which the plan will be carried out, and the context of classroom, family, and community. Thus, teachers engaged in developmentally appropriate prac-

tices recognize the ecological nature of planning. They understand that although a plan may be technically correct, if it is created without consideration for specific children and for context, it could be inappropriate. Janet Fowler learned this lesson her first day on the job.

Janet arrived at the Willow Street Cooperative Preschool to begin work as the new head teacher. Among the activities she planned for the day was marble painting at the art table during free-choice time. She wanted to provide an open-ended art activity the children would enjoy. She also thought allowing them to create decorations for the room would be nice. Janet reasoned that doing so would be a good way for the children to make the classroom their own as well as have fun.

Getting to the classroom early, Janet set up the materials: four metal pie pans, marbles, circles of paper cut to fit the bottom of the pans, baby food jars half filled with thick poster paint, plastic spoons for retrieving the marbles from the jars, and smocks. She posted a sign, on which four figures were drawn, illustrating that four children at a time could participate in the activity. She covered the table with newspaper to protect it and positioned a drying rack nearby on which children could hang their finished paintings. Looking over the area, she felt satisfied that everything was ready and went to the door to greet the children and the parent volunteer as they came into the classroom.

The materials at the art table intrigued the children. However, before Janet could ask everyone to put on a smock, Carl poured some of the paint onto the newspaper, treating it like finger paint. As he tried to push his sleeves out of the way, paint ran down his elbows and onto his shirt. LaTanya tried to roll her marble in a pan with no paper but a lot of paint. As she moved the marble in the pan, paint sloshed over the sides. Soon six or seven children were crowded around the table trying to get to the materials. Voices rose as children became upset about not getting a turn or stepping in spilled paint. While Janet struggled to help the children, she wondered how she had lost control of the activity so quickly. This problem had not occurred when she had tried the same activity last spring with the 4-year-olds in the Head Start center where she had worked.

What Janet did not realize was that the children at the Willow Street Cooperative Preschool had never tried marble painting before. Moreover, none of the children had access to similar paints at home. Because poster paints had only rarely been used at the school in the past, even returning children had little background with the medium. In addition, the youngsters had no prior experience with the use of signs to indicate how many children could participate in one area. Although such symbols are generally a good structuring tool, children do not automatically know what they mean. Finally, Janet forgot that children who are in a classroom from fall to spring know much more about classroom routines and expectations than do youngsters coming together for the first time. Her plan for marble painting, which worked well with one group of children, was ineffective with this group at this time. Although Janet had a good plan, which included a goal and careful preparation, she forgot to consider the contextual nature of planning. To avoid such mistakes, effective planners assume each of the following roles as they plan: diagnostician, designer, organizer, evaluator, and writer. (Brewer, 2001; Saracho, 1993).

Teachers as Diagnosticians The first phase of planning involves thinking about the children in relation to what is being taught. This phase enables the teacher to make an appropriate match between instruction and the knowledge, skills, and understandings children bring to the activity. In their diagnostic role, teachers ask themselves questions such as the following:

What experiences have the children had?

What are the children interested in knowing or finding out?

What abilities and skills do the children possess?

What do families hope their children will learn?

What goal does the program or school district have for the children?

What are my short-term goals for the children?

What are my long-term goals for individual children and the entire group?

What is the correct level of challenge for this child (these children) in relation to this activity?

Practitioners find the answers to these questions by observing children carefully, talking with children, and keeping records of children's interactions with materials, peers, and adults. Asking families to supply relevant information is another strategy that can be used in the diagnostic phase of planning. Informal assessments throughout the day's activities are the primary source for such information at both the preprimary level and the primary level. More-formal strategies such as designing specific activities to garner information about children's ideas and skills and asking for periodic work samples are also useful.

Teachers as Designers After making an initial diagnosis of children's needs and capabilities, teachers consider how to frame their instruction within the guidelines of developmentally appropriate practice. Doing so requires

thinking about ways to apply the principles of child development and learning described in chapter 2. The overarching principle of developmental direction is a further consideration. Sample questions related to the designer role include the following:

How does what I know about child development and learning relate to this plan?

How does what I know about developmental direction relate to this plan? For instance, how might children proceed from simple to complex within this plan? Or, how might children proceed from concrete to abstract within this plan?

How can I start with the children's knowledge of this and relate it to what I want to teach?

Teachers as Organizers Using the information from the previous planning phases, teachers next plan to organize the instruction. Organizing involves analyzing resources, considering long-term goals, determining short-range objectives, identifying potential materials, and matching goals and objectives with strategies. Teachers as organizers ask these typical questions:

What is the purpose of this plan?

What abilities, skills, and understandings must children possess to successfully participate?

What is the sequence in which learning might logically occur?

Which materials are necessary to carry out the plan?

When and where will the plan be implemented?

How will I know that the children are learning?

How will I measure children's learning and document their progress?

Teachers as Evaluators A significant role for every teacher is that of evaluator. This role requires teachers to think about the match between what they plan and what occurs. Teachers plan evaluation questions to answer when the activity is over. Answers to these questions help teachers analyze the current state of affairs and plan for the future. Typical questions considered within the evaluator role include these:

Did the plan meet the children's instructional needs?

Who benefited and who did not benefit from participating in the plan and why?

What are ways to extend this plan in the future?

How should the plan be changed and why?

What unanticipated events occurred that should be considered in future planning?

Teachers as Writers Working your way through the dimensions of planning just described is best done in writing (Driscoll & Nagel, 2002). Written plans provide a tangible record of your thinking and give you a foundation for creating new plans in the future. They also offer a means for communicating with others. Most significant, writing plans can help you think your ideas through from start to finish. In fact, some people claim that the main value of writing plans is not the final product achieved but the thinking process that produces them (Shoemaker, 1995, p. 55).

The amount of detail that goes into written plans varies with the writer's experience. In general, inexperienced planners profit from writing their ideas out in great detail. Doing so makes checking for accuracy and completeness easier. As teachers gain practice writing and thinking about planning, the need for extensive written detail gradually decreases. With time, teachers become better able to think comprehensively while writing only what is necessary for someone else (e.g., a parent volunteer, assistants in the program, or the substitute teacher) to follow their plan successfully. In this way, learning to plan proceeds from the concrete act of representing all your thinking to the more abstract form of conveying only its essence. Planning also shifts from focusing mostly on enhancing your comprehension to helping other people understand what you intend.

In this text we first present detailed activity plans to help you think through all the necessary steps involved in effective planning. Later, we present an abbreviated form that many experienced teachers use in their day-to-day work with children. Regardless of whether you are a new planner or an experienced planner, you must think about certain factors so that you can create developmentally appropriate plans for children. These considerations are basic to all planning.

PLANNING BASICS

Teachers plan activities for solitary children, for small groups of children, and for the entire class to participate in together. All these activity types can be thought about in similar ways, with minor variations. In this chapter we focus on activity plans in which five or six children participate together. Such experiences are often featured during small-group times or free-choice periods in early childhood classrooms. These kinds of activities form the building blocks for teachers' daily, weekly, and yearly planning. In chapter 4, we discuss how to plan and implement activities in which the entire class participates together. All the elements that should be incorporated into a typical activity plan are outlined in Figure 3.1. A sample plan follows in Figure 3.2.

CREATING DEVELOPMENTALLY APPROPRIATE PLANS

All the components of the activity plan, described in Figure 3.1, are critical to the planning process. Considered individually, each makes an important contribution to your understanding of how to translate goals for children into developmentally appropriate learning experiences.

FIGURE 3.1 Activity Plan Format

Domain   One of the six curricular domains identified in this text: aesthetic, affective, cognitive, language, physical, and social.

Activity Name   The title of the activity.

Intermediate Objective   Intermediate objectives are listed in each of the chapters describing the curriculum. These objectives identify desirable behaviors relevant to children's development and learning within the domain.

Immediate Objectives   A list of specific instructional objectives leading to the intermediate objective and tailored to meet the needs of the children involved.

Content   The content that will be addressed in the activity. This content identifies the terms (vocabulary), facts, and principles relevant to the lesson.

Materials   A list of all necessary props or equipment.

Procedures   A step-by-step description of how to implement the activity. Procedures may include multiple teaching strategies.

Simplifications   Ideas for reducing the complexity or abstractness of the activity. Ways to adapt the activity for children with less experience or special needs.

Extensions   Ideas for making the activity more challenging as children demonstrate the desire and ability to expand their knowledge and skills.

Evaluation   Ways to assess children's learning and the teaching methods used.

FIGURE 3.2   Sample Activity Plan

Domain Language   **Activity Name** Turnip Story Sequence

Intermediate Objective   Children will listen to a story and then discuss the story sequence (chapter 12, The Language Domain, Intermediate Objective 8).

Immediate Objectives
The child will be able to do the following:

1. Listen to the story one time through
2. Name the characters in the story as the teacher points to them following his or her enactment of the story
3. Assist the teacher in retelling the story in the correct sequence

Content
1. *Sequence* refers to the order in which events occur.
2. A *story* describes a series of events that progresses from beginning to end.
3. Changing the sequence of events in a story may change the story's meaning.

Materials   Flannel figures corresponding to the characters in the story "The Big, Big Turnip"; a flannel board

Procedures
  Objective 1:   The child will *listen* to the story one time through.

  Invite children to listen to the story "The Big, Big Turnip." Tell the story with enthusiasm and expression, placing the flannel board pieces on the board at appropriate points. Emphasize the characters' names and the sequence in which they appear by repeating them each time a new character is introduced. Leave the characters on the board when the story is over.

  Objective 2:   The child will *name* the characters in the story as the teacher points to them following his or her enactment of the story.

  Encourage the children to name the characters in order. Point to each one in line, beginning with the farmer. Ask the children to say the character's name when you point to it.

  Objective 3:   The child will *assist the teacher* in retelling the story in the correct sequence.

  Hide the characters behind the flannel board. Ask the children to help tell the story by telling you which character to put on the board next.

  Repeat this part of the activity more than once. Vary the procedure by giving each child a character that he or she is to put on the board when it is time for that character to appear in the story.

Simplification   Put the flannel board pieces at the bottom of the board, facing the children. Raise them to the top of the board in sequence as you tell the story.

Extension   Tell the story and make mistakes in the sequence. Ask the children to help by correcting mistakes they hear. Ask children to talk about how the meaning of the story changed when the sequence varied. Another option is to encourage children to tell the story on their own.

Evaluation   Using a performance checklist, identify which of the three objectives outlined in this activity plan individual children met. On the basis of your observations of children's participation, describe how this information will influence your future instruction related to story sequence.

Taken altogether, they address the diagnostic, design, organization, and evaluation roles of the effective planner. Let us recap what must be considered for each element.

Domain

The Children's Comprehensive Curriculum, described in part 3, is divided into six domains representing the various aspects of whole-child learning that are discussed in chapter 2. Although curriculum integration is our ultimate aim, we have discovered that planners are most effective when they concentrate on one domain at a time until they are thoroughly familiar with the curriculum and are skilled in writing plans (Kostelnik, 1997). With this in mind, choose a domain within which to write your plan: aesthetic, affective, cognitive, language, physical, or social. Then, start writing.

Activity Name

The name you select for your activity should be brief and descriptive. Cute titles that are difficult to decipher are not as useful as functional names that clarify the main focus of your plan.

Intermediate Objective

Select an intermediate objective on which to concentrate within the domain you selected. Intermediate objectives are listed in the curriculum chapters of part 3. The intermediate objective answers the question "What is the purpose of this plan?"

Immediate Objectives

Immediate objectives represent the step-by-step progression a child could go through to pursue a certain intermediate objective. This segment of the plan outlines the order in which children's learning might logically occur. Consequently, the intermediate objective and the immediate objectives are closely related. To create such a sequence, you will find the principle of developmental direction particularly useful. This principle gives you a tool for thinking about how to break down the broadly stated intermediate objective into a graduated series of more specifically defined aims. For instance, the intermediate objective of having children organize objects and events by classification can be broken into several substeps. Possibilities include the following: exploring the objects, grouping them by at least one similar property, describing how they are alike, and regrouping them in a new way. These substeps progress from simple to more complex, from concrete to more abstract, and from exploratory to more goal directed and can be applied to any set of objects—leaves, seashells, rocks, toy vehicles, keys, or buttons.

When formulating immediate objectives, think in terms of behavior (Charlesworth & Lind, 1995; Schmoker, 1996). That is, identify specific child actions that will signify that an objective has been achieved. With this in mind, characterize immediate objectives by action words that you can observe as they occur, such as *name, point, show, tell, describe, make, find, circle, select, compare, sort, measure, count, observe, predict, estimate,* and *evaluate.* The immediate objectives for a leaf-sorting activity might be as follows. The child will (a) explore the various properties of the leaves (size, color, shape, edge, flexibility, and so on); (b) group the leaves according to one common property of his or her choosing; (c) tell what property he or she used to group the leaves; and (d) regroup the objects, changing from one property to another of his or her choosing. When objectives are stated in behavioral terms, you can determine the extent to which children successfully engage in the activity. If all the objectives are achieved, the children are ready for more-challenging experiences. However, if the children do not achieve some objectives, repeat the activity, create an alternative plan, or try a different presentation mode. Breaking the objectives into even smaller steps may also be appropriate.

What objectives do you think the teacher has for the children participating in this activity?

Because children develop and learn at varying rates, groups of children commonly perform at differing levels of the immediate objectives sequence. Some youngsters may spend a great deal of time exploring the leaves; others may be interested in grouping the leaves almost immediately; still others may be ready to move beyond single-property classification to grouping the leaves according to multiple criteria. Your job is to follow the children's lead and challenge them with the next step of the sequence as appropriate. Not every child will, in a single day, go through the entire sequence that you plan. Some children might take all year or even longer to achieve the most advanced objectives, so you should repeat activities several times during the year, and your developmentally appropriate activity plans should include at least three immediate objectives.

Content

The content segment of the plan identifies the information you plan to address. It should be based on your diagnosis of what the children already know and what would be useful and worthwhile for them to learn. Content addresses terms, facts, and principles relevant to the domain and the intermediate objective you chose. *Terms* are the vocabulary that describe activity-related objects and events (e.g., a *lamb* is a baby sheep, or *piglet* is the name given to a baby pig). Something known to exist or to have happened is a *fact* (e.g., sheep give birth to lambs; pigs give birth to piglets). *Principles* refer to combinations of facts and the relationships among them (e.g., animals give birth only to their own kind).

Accuracy is critical. Research your terms, facts, and principles and be able to explain what the lesson is about. Write down these ideas so that you or anyone else who is carrying out the plan will have a clear understanding of its content.

Materials

Part of organizing your plan involves creating a complete list of the materials required for you to carry it out. Effective planners consider everything necessary for the setup, implementation, and cleanup phases of the activity. Enough detail should be provided so that someone else would know what was needed in your absence. Also, if you are doing something you have never tried before, you should experiment with the materials prior to using them with the children. For instance, Mr. Buthelezi discovered that to make a "tornado in a bottle," he needed stronger tape than he had initially planned to use. During a test run, he found that the connection between the two inverted soft-drink bottles leaked after the liquid in the bottles was swirled several times. Duct tape held better than the masking tape he had originally selected. Trying the materials in advance prevented a classroom mess and allowed children to concentrate on the experiment rather than on leaky bottles.

Procedures

Planning the procedures requires both design and organizational skills. The primary focus of your planning is to select the processes you will use to facilitate children's achievement of the immediate objectives. To determine these procedures, you will have to apply knowledge of child development and learning as well as an understanding of effective instructional techniques. More information about how to do this is given in the Common Teaching Strategies section of this chapter. For now, what is most important is to understand that procedures are designed to support the intermediate and immediate objectives associated with your activity plan. For every objective, corresponding processes must be selected. This congruence between objectives and procedures is illustrated in Figure 3.2. The easiest way to accomplish congruence is to plan procedures in a stepwise fashion that matches the immediate objectives. For instance, if the activity involves children's sorting leaves, the writer must plan to make a variety of leaves available for children to explore, provide opportunities for children to examine the leaves, include a process by which children will be encouraged to group the leaves, and make sure a process is planned to facilitate children's talking about their groupings. You cannot assume that such procedures happen automatically. Instead, planners must decide which strategies will enable children to move in the desired direction but must remain open to child-initiated interests and learning. To achieve this, most planners use an array of strategies rather than relying on just one.

Simplifications

Simplifications are ways to modify the activity for children who are not achieving the objectives you identified. Sometimes the simplifications address inaccurate assumptions you made. For instance, in the previous example of marble painting, Janet Fowler assumed that children at the Willow Street Cooperative Preschool were familiar with marble painting. On discovering that her assumption was incorrect, she should have revised the activity to make it less complex. Because the children had not had access to poster paint in the past, she could have provided paint and brushes at the easel so that children could become familiar with the paint without the added complication of manipulating several objectives at once. After the children became more experienced painters, she could have introduced the marbles and pie tins, knowing that the children would be more successful.

At other times, simplifications serve as a further breakdown of a particular task. To *simplify* a task means to make it simpler, more known, more focused on self, more focused on the whole rather than the parts, more concrete, more enactive, or more exploratory. Thus, a girl who is trying to button her coat with minimal success may do better if you start the button for her and then have her pull it through the hole. Similarly, a youngster who is having difficulty solving a mathematical word problem (symbolic representation) might benefit from drawing it on paper (iconic representation) or even representing it by using objects (enactive representation). Such simplifications are especially useful when you are working with children who have special needs.

Extensions

Children who achieve all the objectives you identified benefit from trying more-advanced steps. The extension ideas you create provide such challenges. To extend an activity means to make it more complex, more unknown, more focused on others than on self, more focused on its components, more abstract, more symbolic, more goal directed, more accurate, and more independent. For instance, children who can group objects according to single properties could be invited to classify them according to multiple properties such as size and shape at the same time. Children who can think of one way to share an item could be challenged to think of alternative ways as well. Youngsters who can write certain words with adult assistance could be helped to develop strategies for remembering how to write these words on their own or for using these known words to create a story. All these strategies move children beyond their current level of functioning to more-advanced performance levels in accordance with their needs and abilities.

Evaluation

The evaluation portion of each activity plan is both an ending and a beginning relative to planning. Evaluation information can assist you in assessing the accuracy of your assumptions, the lesson content, the effectiveness of your teaching methods, and child outcomes. These data help you to gauge your learning as well as the children's. However, appropriate evaluation does not simply describe the past. It also provides ideas for the future. What did you discover that will be useful to consider next time? How will you use what you learned? How might you change the direction of your planning? Answers to these questions will inform your plans for days and weeks to come.

To guide your thinking, pose specific evaluation questions and answer them in writing. Typical evaluation questions are listed in Figure 3.3. Some of them are answered by the planners, some by other members of the teaching team, and some by the children. In this way, evaluation becomes a dynamic, communal part of early childhood education. Most planners select three or four self-evaluation or activity-evaluation questions to answer for each plan. Varying the questions from day to day and from one plan to the next allows you to gain a lot of information in a short time. Such information might be gathered through observations, anecdotal records, performance checklists, rating scales, samples of children's work, participation charts, and children's assessments of their work or progress. More about the specific strategies for gathering evaluative data is described in chapter 7.

DEVELOPMENTALLY APPROPRIATE TEACHING STRATEGIES

Children learn in many ways, so the strategies that best support their learning vary too. These variations are important to consider when you are planning activities. Following are three examples of different approaches to enhancing children's learning.

A teacher plans for 3-year-olds to match plastic jars to their lids. To support the children's learning, the teacher will provide them with a collection of containers and lids that vary in size, color, and shape. Because the children are familiar with the materials, the teacher plans for them to carry out the activity with minimal adult direction. However, she also plans to stop by the area periodically to describe the size, shape, and color of the lids as she talks to the children about their experiences.

FIGURE 3.3 Typical Evaluation Questions Regarding Children's Learning and Teaching Effectiveness

---

Children's Participation
1. Who participated in this activity?
2. To what extent was the activity of interest to the children? How do you know?
3. How did you get the children involved in the activity?
4. How accurate were your assumptions?

What Children Learned
1. Which children achieved which objectives?
2. Did children appear to understand the content of the lesson? How do you know?
3. What did children say or do in the activity to demonstrate that they were learning?
4. What indicated that the activity was developmentally appropriate for children in the group?

Teaching Effectiveness
1. How did advance preparation (or lack of it) contribute to the success (or lack of success) of the activity?
2. How did the materials meet the needs of the children who participated?
3. Was the activity carried out as planned? What changes were made and why? Did the changes enhance or detract from the activity?
4. If you were to use this activity again, what would you repeat and what would you change? Why?
5. What activities might be implemented to strengthen children's comprehension?
6. What did you learn from this activity?

The kindergartners at Fairview School have been placing planks to form inclined planes in the block area for several days. They have enjoyed racing their toy cars down the ramps to see how far the cars will go. Capitalizing on their interests, the teacher plans an activity in which children will observe, predict, and discover ways to make the cars go farther by varying the ramp angles. The teacher also plans for the children to analyze and interpret their experimental results. To help the children engage in these scientific processes, the teacher plans what she will do and say to gain the children's attention, help them recall their past observations of the cars going down the ramps, make predictions about what they think will happen when the ramp angle is changed, and then evaluate their predictions. The procedure she plans combines questioning, informing, listening, paraphrasing, and recording the children's ideas.

Today, Mr. Rosenshine wants to teach the children in his second-grade class new motions to a familiar song. He plans to demonstrate the song first, then have the children imitate his movements several times, then have them catch him making mistakes, and finally have the children do the song independently without watching him model the actions. He assumes that several repetitions will be necessary before the children will be able to sing the words and do the motions simultaneously on their own.

In each of the preceding activities, the teacher carefully considered the teaching strategies he or she would use to facilitate children's learning. The planned procedures ranged from providing opportunities for exploration to verbally underscoring children's discoveries to developing step-by-step methods aimed at guiding children through set processes. Although these strategies varied in type, degree of formality, complexity, and directiveness, they shared the characteristic of having been selected in concert with teachers' goals for children. As such, they were designed to support the learning objectives associated with each plan.

WHICH TEACHING STRATEGIES ARE BEST?

At one time, early childhood educators wondered if direct instructional methods such as explaining and demonstrating were best for teaching children or if indirect teaching techniques such as inviting and paraphrasing were more effective (Evans, 1975). More recently, we have begun to realize that both direct and indirect instruction can be more or less appropriate depending on the goals for the activity and individual children's needs. For instance, indirect strategies that enhance children's exploratory behavior are well suited to children's discovering the properties of modeling dough, different ways they can move their bodies, or the operation of levers. However, such approaches are less well suited to children's learning the names of the stars, the specific procedures involved in a tornado drill, or the precise rules for a particular game. Likewise, demonstrations (a form of direct instruction) may help children learn the motions to a song but inhibit children from creating their own motions to the words. The strategies you choose will depend on what you want children to learn. Thus, you must ask yourself, "Which strategies are most suitable for meeting the goals and objectives of this lesson?" (Pica, 2000). When a good match exists among goals, objectives, and teaching strategies, children benefit. Creating such a match requires you to become familiar with not only an array of potential teaching strategies, but also methods for incorporating these strategies into your activity plans.

COMMON TEACHING STRATEGIES

So many teaching strategies are available that outlining them all in this chapter would be impossible. However, what follows is representative of common instructional methods that early childhood professionals use. The first three strategies—sensory engagement, preparation of environmental cues, and task analysis—are preparatory methods that shape your plans before they are carried out. The other dozen strategies that follow are those you think about in advance but implement only after children are on the scene. All are used alone or in combination to enhance children's learning in a variety of activities.

Sensory Engagement

Ensuring that ways are available for children to be actively engaged in the instruction by using as many senses as possible is paramount. All learning begins with perception: seeing, hearing, touching, tasting, and smelling. Children learn best by using all their senses (Bredekamp & Copple, 1997; Hendrick, 2003). Because most researchers agree about the importance of hands-on learning, you might assume that every activity for young children would naturally include a high level of sensory engagement by children. However, anyone who has ever seen children sit through a 15-minute talk on the color *green,* watched children listen to a compact disk for the sound of an instrument they have never seen or heard in person, or listened to children read a story about pomegranates (a fruit with which many have had no experience) knows that appropriate sensory engagement is not guaranteed without careful planning.

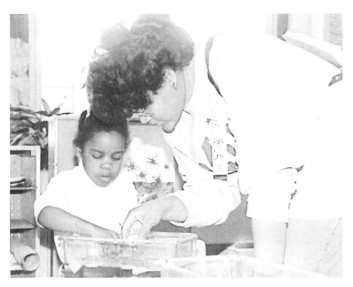

Firsthand experiences are best!

The most effective means of sensory engagement is firsthand experience. This means you must consider ways to give children direct contact with real objects, people, places, and events (Vance, 1973). If you are teaching children about the color *green,* provide objects of many shades of green for children to see and handle. If you are teaching children to listen for the sound of an oboe, first show them an oboe and let them touch the instrument. Have someone play the instrument while children watch. If you are teaching about pomegranates, show children real pomegranates and give them opportunities to examine them through taste, touch, and smell. If no firsthand experience is possible, seriously reconsider whether the activity is age appropriate. The younger the children, the less valid is relying on secondhand experience rather than firsthand involvement. As children mature and express curiosity about people, objects, and events somewhat removed from their immediate experience, continue to plan activities that provide the maximum sensory involvement, keeping the following guidelines in mind:

❏ Firsthand experiences are best.
❏ Firsthand experiences should precede representational or more-abstract experiences (e.g., show real fruit prior to pictures of fruit).
❏ Models are more concrete than pictures; pictures are more concrete than words.
❏ Plan activities so that sensory engagement occurs earlier in the procedure rather than later.

Environmental Cues

Children can learn much from observing environmental cues (Hendrick, 2003; Hildebrand, 1997). Environmental cues signal the children about expectations for tasks or learning areas that may not be specified verbally. Four chairs around the snack table provide evidence that four children may participate at one time. A sign on the cracker basket with a hand showing three fingers or the numeral *3* indicates that each child may take three crackers. Children can learn to turn on and shut down the computer by referring to a pictograph outlining the appropriate steps. If six children are participating in an art activity in which only two pairs of scissors are available, an unspoken message is that children must share the scissors if everyone is to have the chance to use them. These nonverbal signals support objectives related to independence, cooperation, and self-regulation.

Task Analysis

Task analysis involves breaking whole tasks into smaller parts so that they are easier for children to master. Such analysis is an essential early childhood planning strategy (Essa, 2003; Krogh & Slentz, 2001a). For instance, expecting 4-year-old children to learn how to set an entire table is unrealistic. Instead, teachers analyze the knowledge, skills, and procedures necessary to achieve the goal of setting the table. Next, they create a logical sequence of small steps, planning to introduce new steps as children master previous steps. This process is depicted in Figure 3.4. What should be

FIGURE 3.4   Sample Steps in Setting a Table

1. What is the goal? Set the table.
2. What will the finished arrangement look like?

3. What are the skills or steps involved?
   a. Get out plates.
   b. Put a plate at each person's place.
   c. Fold napkin.
   d. Place napkin to left of each plate.
4. What do children need to know?
   a. Where to find plates
   b. How to fold napkin
   c. Where utensils are positioned
5. What part will I teach first?

covered early and what comes later becomes clear in the analysis. The result of performing a task analysis is purposeful instruction through which children expand their repertoire of skills, experiencing success all along the way. The combination of intermediate objective, immediate objectives, simplifications, and extensions required in the activity plans you are learning to write is a form of task analysis. The principle of developmental direction, described in chapter 2, provides a useful set of criteria for devising logical sequences around which to create your plans. Other sequences are presented in the curriculum portions of this text in part 3.

Scaffolding

Scaffolding is the process of providing and then gradually removing external support for children's learning. During the scaffolding process, the original task is not changed, but how the child participates in the task is made easier with assistance. As children take more responsibility for pursuing an objective, assistance is gradually withdrawn (Bodrova & Leong, 1996). For example, Mr. Kaye has planned a counting activity. Children select a bag of "treasures" and count the number of objects inside. As Mr. Kaye works with the children, he notices that Cathleen knows the names of the numbers but counts some objects more than once and others not at all. He recognizes this as a situation in which scaffolding could be used to enhance Cathleen's ability to count accurately. In this case, the teacher might take Cathleen's hand, pointing with her to each object and counting them one at a time, orally. With repetition, Mr. Kaye will stop counting aloud but continue to help Cathleen point to the objects. Eventually, Cathleen will be able to count each object, one at a time, without Mr. Kaye's physical or verbal assistance. The scaffolding process begins with the teacher's providing maximum assistance and taking primary responsibility for pursuing the objective (counting). However, gradually this responsibility shifts to Cathleen until she is able to achieve the objective unassisted. The same principles are at work when teachers plan activities to teach children how to decide who goes first during a board game (Berk & Winsler, 1995; Fox, 1993). At first, the adult may serve as a group member, providing direct support as the children work through this social dilemma. However, with time, the teacher will take a more passive role, providing fewer cues, which enables children to lead one another to mutual resolution. Eventually, children will be able to carry out this cooperative task with minimal adult presence.

Naturally, children's capacity to achieve higher levels of functioning will be influenced by their development and past experiences. Previously in this text we discussed the idea that children learn best when they have opportunities to engage in activities that are slightly beyond their current mastery level. Scaffolding provides a means for helping individual children move from a level of assisted performance to independent functioning. In other words, children benefit when they have chances to stretch their cognitive, language, social, and physical skills in joint activity with "experts" who can help them perform at levels higher than they could achieve on their own (Davidson, 1996). Such experts may be adults or peers. The scaffolding techniques may be verbal or physical and may or may not include props.

Effective planners think about their activity plans in terms of potential scaffolding opportunities. They consider who could serve as the experts and ways in which the activity could promote joint interactions. In addition, they think of types of supports (physical or verbal) that could be put in place as well as how to gradually withdraw these supports in accordance with children's needs.

Guided Practice

Four-year-old Tony heads for the puzzle area every day. At the beginning of the year, he mostly enjoyed knob puzzles that had a few distinct pieces. Then he moved on to interlocking puzzles that varied in color and shape. Most recently, he has become intrigued with the new floor puzzle of a bus. He has tried this puzzle each day, sometimes on his own, sometimes with other children, and sometimes with the teacher's help. Tony's teacher supports his learning by providing time, space, and materials for him to practice his puzzle-making skills. When she plans for the puzzle area, she considers ways to maintain the children's interest and provide them with appropriate challenges. Each week, she holds over a few favorites from the week before and then adds new puzzles for novelty. She also includes different types of puzzles and puzzles of varying degrees of difficulty. Tony's teacher is using the strategy of *guided practice*.

One basic premise of early childhood education is that children learn through repetition. Real learning does not occur in a single episode. Children need many opportunities to engage concepts, explore ideas, and try out skills to gain mastery. In other words, children need a chance to practice what they are learning and to generalize what they have learned to new situations (Slentz & Krogh, 2001b). Such practice is most beneficial when the conditions under which it occurs vary slightly from one time to the next. Such practice episodes may occur within a day or during several weeks' time. Thus, Tony increases his puzzle-making skills by working on some of the same puzzles, as well as a few new puzzles, as time passes. An-Sook learns to hop by hopping on one foot and then the other; hopping sideways and backward; hopping inside and outside; hopping on even surfaces and uneven surfaces; and hopping alone and with friends. The first graders in Mrs. Hamouz's room become more proficient at forming their letters by writing in the pretend grocery, making signs to post around the room, writing in their journals, making lists, and writing notes to themselves to help them remember "important stuff." Deliberately setting the stage for these kinds of practice opportunities is essential to effective planning.

Invitations

Verbal invitations encourage children to participate in activities by creating openings for them to explore materials or to interact with you or other children. Samples include the following: "Come and see what we're doing here," "Here's a place for you right next to LaKesha," and "Check out the new materials in the reading center. I saw a book I'm sure you'll enjoy." Planning a few invitations is a good idea so that you have a better idea of how to motivate children to try various activities.

Behavior Reflections

Sometimes called *information talk* or *descriptive feedback, behavior reflections* are verbal descriptions of children's actions (Kostelnik, Onaga, Rohde, & Whiren, 2002; Sharp, 1987). They are nonjudgmental statements made to children regarding some aspect of their actions.

Situation: Outdoors, a child is sorting leaves into small piles.
Adult: You found some red and brown leaves. (Or either of the following: You have several different leaves in your piles; You're putting together the leaves that are alike.)
Situation: Two children are matching lids to jars.
Adult: You two are working together. (Or: Each of you has found a lid to match a jar; Mareesa, your lid is square. Kyoko, your lid is round. You both found different-shaped lids.)

Behavior reflections help draw children's attention to certain aspects of an experience that they may only faintly perceive and expose them to vocabulary that describes their experience. Such reflections also summarize children's actions in a way that is informative without being intrusive. For instance, children acting on materials might hear their teacher say, "Your fingers are moving gently over the water, making small ripples" or "When you turned the puzzle piece around, it fit." Summarizations like these do not interrupt children's actions. Youngsters do not have to stop what they are doing to attend to the lesson. However, they do prompt children to focus specifically on their actions, which in turn helps them to solidify and internalize these actions. Behavior reflections may also induce children

to explore additional ways of moving their fingers over the water or turning other pieces in the puzzle to make them fit (Trepanier-Street, 1991, p. 195). Thus, behavior reflections increase children's self-awareness and understanding.

Paraphrase Reflections

Similar in form to behavior reflections, *paraphrase reflections* are restatements, in your words, of something the child has said. These nonevaluative comments are sometimes referred to as *verbal expansions* or *active listening* (Kostelnik, Onaga, et al., 2002; Sharp, 1987). Using words slightly different from those spoken by the child, paraphrase reflections broaden children's vocabulary and grammatical structures. At times such reflections also prompt children to expand on what they are saying. Verbal expansion helps them to refine and clarify key concepts and messages. When children respond to your reflections, you also gain valuable insights into their thinking. Such insights will influence how you proceed with the activity as well as help shape the direction of future planning. Finally, because paraphrase reflections allow children to take the lead in adult–child conversations, children interpret their use as a signal of adult interest and caring. Such feelings enhance the learning climate in early childhood classrooms.

Situation: Outdoors, a child is sorting leaves into two piles. He says, "These leaves are pointy. These leaves are round."
Adult: You found two kinds of leaves. (Or: You noticed that the edges of the leaves made them look different from each other. You're sorting the leaves according to their shape.)
Child: These (pointing to three leaves on the side) have holes.
Adult: You made a special pile just for leaves with holes. You have three piles altogether.

Modeling

Children learn many things by imitating others (Bandura, 1989; Pica, 2000). Watching a friend play a game, seeing the teacher use a sculpting tool in a certain way, listening to a peer "think aloud" about how to solve a math problem, and observing how one person greets another are all lessons from which children may profit. Even though much of what children imitate is unplanned, teachers can enhance the effectiveness of classroom activities when they deliberately use modeling to help children learn new or appropriate behaviors. For example, when Ms. Pritchard holds a snake gently, she is modeling a positive attitude toward snakes that she hopes the children will emulate. Likewise, when Mrs. Levine visits the pretend restaurant, she models being a customer by sitting down and saying things to the children such as, "Hmm, now what will I have? Do you have a menu? Oh, that sounds good. I'd like a salad and a milkshake. How much will that cost?" Her modeling provides children with examples of how a customer might behave. When Mr. Petricic models looking up information he does not know, he is conveying to children ways of using reference materials to answer questions. Models such as these have the greatest impact when their behavior is obvious to the children. Thus, children are best able to imitate a model with whom they can interact or whose behavior is pointed out to them (Kostelnik, Onaga, et al., 2002). Self-descriptions such as "I'm not sure how many stomachs a cow has. I'll have to look that up" are useful signals of the modeling that is about to occur. Similarly, peer models are highlighted when teachers say, for example, "Look, John has discovered a new way to use the paint" or "Natalie found another way to add three columns of numbers."

The teacher uses effective praise when she says, "You found a way to surprise the reader at the end!"

Effective Praise

Planners often assume that praise automatically promotes children's positive behaviors and encourages children to persist at tasks. Unfortunately, some praise has the potential to lower children's self-confidence and inhibit their achievement (Kamii, 1985; D. F. Miller, 2004). Thus, there is a difference between ineffective praise and effective praise. *Ineffective praise* is general, repetitive, and not genuine. It evaluates children, compares them with one another in unfavorable ways, links their success to luck, and tends to interrupt their work and concentration. Conversely, *effective praise* is specific, acknowledges children's actions, and compares their progress with their past performance. It links their success to effort and ability, is individualized to fit the child and the situation, and is nonintrusive. The differences between ineffective praise and effective praise are illustrated in Table 3.1.

Telling, Explaining, and Informing

During their field trip to the animal barns, Jonathan points to a llama and asks the man who is leading the tour, "What's that?" The man answers, "That's called a llama." Jonathan repeats the new word, "llama." The children are full of questions: "Where do llamas come from?" "Why do they have such heavy coats?" "Do big llamas have baby llamas?" "How big is the biggest llama in the world?" The tour guide answers each question simply and directly. Simultaneously, he draws the children's attention to the sights, sounds, and smells associated with the llamas. Anyone who wants may touch the animal's coat, look into the llama's feed trough, and handle some of the feed pellets. When Jonathan sees his mom at the end of the day, the first thing he says is, "Guess what we saw today? A llama! And they get real big and people use their hair to make

TABLE 3.1 Comparison of Ineffective Praise and Effective Praise

Ineffective Praise	Effective Praise
Good job. Nicely done.	You spent a lot of time on this story. You looked up some important information that made the setting more exciting.
You are a great writer.	You found a way to surprise the reader at the end.
Look at Rodney. Everyone should try to write as neatly as he does.	In this story, you used two words that you never wrote before.
You were lucky to come up with such a good idea.	The time you spent editing paid off. You were able to come up with just the right words to finish your story.
Mary, good job.	Mary, you used a lot of animal sounds in your story.
Carl, good job.	Carl, you added a joke to your story to make it funny.

hats." Obviously, Jonathan is pleased with his newly acquired knowledge.

On their field trip to the barn, children discovered that the llama's coat was thick by looking at and touching it. However, they could not discover the name of the animal in the same way—they had to be told it was a llama. Information such as the names for things, historical facts, and customary behaviors are learned through social transmission. That is, people tell you either directly through verbal communication or indirectly through books, television, or computer technology. In any case, important information can be conveyed to children through telling and explaining.

Effective explanations build on children's firsthand experiences and take place within a context that is meaningful to them. Such is the case when the teacher plans to teach a new game by referring to situations and skills already familiar to the children. One example of this was given by Lay-Dopyera and Dopyera (1993):

> Remember how you always take turns outside riding the bikes? You can play this game (pick-up sticks) by taking turns, too. First, Peter, let John pick up all the sticks he can without moving any of the others. And then, John, you let Peter do it next. (p. 242)

By explaining new concepts in relation to familiar skills and situations, you can incorporate relevant information into the ongoing conversations you have with children each day.

In early childhood programs, most information is introduced on a just-in-time basis. That is, as children demonstrate a need to know something, the appropriate information is offered. For instance, children in the pretend grocery store get into a squabble over the cash register. Five children want to "work" in the store, but there is only one register. The teacher observes to see whether the children can resolve the difficulty themselves; however, they seem stumped. The only job they know about is the cashier's job. The teacher decides that the time is ripe to offer some useful information. She enters the store saying, "Hello, I'm the district manager. Have you done an inventory yet? One of the jobs for people who work at the grocery store is to count all the items on the shelves. Another job is to make sure each item has a price tag. Who will make the price tags for our store?" Armed with this new information, the children's play resumes, and the children have a broader idea of the possible roles they might play.

At other times, adults predetermine that they want to teach children certain information. Such decisions may be based on interests previously expressed by children, or they may be dictated by social expectations such as how to wash your hands properly or behave during a fire drill. In any case, teachers plan activities to teach children specific vocabulary, facts, or routines. Teachers convey such information through telling, explaining coupled with modeling, and including some form of hands-on involvement by the children.

In all these examples, telling, explaining, and informing in early childhood education involves more than merely reciting facts. Such information is tied to children's experiences and requires involvement by them that goes beyond simply listening. Effective planners look at each activity plan in terms of the explanations or information that may be necessary to support children's learning. Such planners also make sure they have sufficient background to answer children's questions and provide accurate explanations as necessary.

Do-It Signals

Simple directions to children such as "Look here," "Tell me what you see," "Show me how you like to dance," "Put together the leaves that are alike," "Find a key that doesn't fit," and "Guess how many are in the jar" are called *do-it signals*. Beginning with a verb, do-it signals are short statements that prompt children to engage in an action. In other words, they tell children to do something. When children follow the do-it direction, their actions demonstrate to the teacher what children do and do not understand. For instance, if, as part of a lesson aimed at examining the parts of fruits, the teacher gives a do-it signal to a boy in her class to show her the rind and he hands her a seed, the child's action tells the teacher the child may not know the difference. The teacher would respond with additional experiences and information as appropriate.

Do-it signals should not be phrased as questions, such as "Can you count to five for me?" or "Who can count to five for me?" Queries like these fail to lead children into action. The appropriate do-it signal would be to say, "Count to five for me." These kinds of positive statements give children a clearer idea of what to do.

Challenges

"Show me how tall you can be." "Find a way to make a tower by using five different block shapes." "Figure out two ways to make this wooden board sink." Challenges are open-ended variations of do-it signals. Challenges motivate children to create their own solutions to teacher-suggested tasks (Pica, 2000). In this way, challenges provide shared opportunities for children and adults to control activity outcomes. Adults shape the initial direction of the activity, and children determine its application.

A variation on the basic challenge occurs when adults challenge children to think about something in a new or different way. For example, Elliot has divided a set of keys into three groups. One group includes all the round gold keys, a second group has all the angular gold keys, and a third group includes all the silver keys. Having observed Elliot at work, the teacher approaches with a round copper-colored key and says, "I just found this key. Show me where it belongs with the keys that you've sorted." Elliot is now faced with the challenge of reconsidering his groupings to accommodate a new element that does not exactly fit. The children are faced with a similar challenge when they declare that only men can be firefighters. A few days later, the teacher invites a female firefighter to visit the class and talk about her work. Again the children are challenged to reconsider their thinking in light of new evidence that does not match their previous conceptions.

Effective teachers carefully observe and listen to children as they participate in activities. On the basis of the information gleaned directly from the children, teachers plan challenges to stretch children's thinking beyond their current perceptions. As part of the challenge, teachers talk with children, encouraging them to put their thinking into words. Throughout this process, teachers are careful not to expect children to accomplish every challenge during a single activity or to change their thinking simply because they are faced with conflicting information.

Questions

Questions are basic instructional tools common to every early childhood classroom. However, the kinds of questions adults ask dictate the quality of the answers they receive. Effective questions are purposeful (tied directly to the objectives you are trying to teach), thought provoking (going beyond the obvious to stimulate higher levels of thinking), clear (understandable), and brief (to the point). Questions that meet these standards are the most likely to gain children's attention and help them learn. When questions are used simply to pass the time or when they are too many in number or become intrusive, children stop paying attention, and the quality of their responses decreases (Kostelnik, Onaga, et al., 2002). Also, questions should never be used to demonstrate children's lack of knowledge and understanding when no previous experience or instruction has been provided. Such use is a negative form of pretesting, such as when Ms. Johnson shows a picture of an aardvark to a group of 4-year-olds and asks, "What is the name of this animal?" When adults ask questions that they have no reason to believe children can answer, children respond with silence or mistakes. In both cases, youngsters get the message that they should know the answer and that their failure to respond correctly is a

fault. Using poor-quality questions like these is something to avoid.

Many taxonomies describe possible questions to ask children. Although they differ in terminology, questions that go beyond simple yes–no and one-word answers are generally the most desirable. In addition, using a variety of questions is preferable to relying on only one kind (Charlesworth & Lind, 1995). On the basis of the criteria just outlined, in Table 3.2 we offer several categories of questions for teachers to incorporate into their plans. Besides considering the range of questions you plan to pose to children, you should think about a few other factors as well (Kilmer & Hofman, 1995; B. J. Taylor, 2003b):

Limit amount.	❑ Ask only one question at a time. Plan your questions carefully.
Provide time.	❑ Give children enough time to respond to your questions. Wait several seconds for children to answer. Do not appear impatient or undermine their thinking by answering your own questions.
Use do-it signals.	❑ Phrase some of your questions as do-it signals to add variety: "Tell me what happened when we put the snowball in the hot water."
Ask all.	❑ Phrase questions to the entire group of children, not only to individuals: "Let's all think of the ways these two piles of leaves are alike. Jake, you begin."
Listen and reflect.	❑ Listen carefully to children's responses. Acknowledge their remarks by using behavior reflections and paraphrase reflections. Focus on the process of their thinking, not merely the correctness of their response.
Redirect.	❑ If a child's answer seems wrong or off track, follow up by saying something such as "What made you think . . . ?" or "Tell us more about . . ." Children sometimes make connections that are less obvious to grown-ups.
Address misconceptions.	❑ If the child's answer to a question indicates a true misconception, handle the situation matter-of-factly. Paraphrase the child's idea and then offer more-accurate information: "You thought this was an apple because it is red. This is a tomato. Tomatoes are sometimes red, too."

TABLE 3.2 Types of Questions and Examples

You Plan to Enhance Children's Ability to	Sample Questions
Observe	What do you see/hear/smell/taste/feel?
Reconstruct previous experiences	What do you remember about the people at the pizza parlor? What happened the last time we put the rock in the sunshine?
Relate cause and effect	What can you do to make it happen? What happens when/if you do ____? When does it happen?
Predict	What do you think will happen next?
Evaluate	What happened? You thought ____ would happen? How did that compare with what actually happened? Which poem is your favorite? Why? How will you know the art area is clean enough? What will help you decide?
Generalize	Now that you saw what we found when we cut open the lemon, what do you think we will find when we cut open this orange?
Compare	How are they alike/different? Which things go together?
Reason	How did you decide those went together?
Discriminate among objects and events	Which one does not belong? Which one is not an oak tree?
Solve problems	What can we do to find out how many marbles are in the jar?
Quantify	How many? How long? How far?
Imagine something	What would it be like if people had long tails?
Propose alternatives	In what other way could you group these objects?
Utilize factual knowledge	Where do you suppose we could find a worm at this time of year?
Infer	What else can you think of that works like this? Why do you think it happened? How do your observations compare with other children's?
Become aware of their thinking processes	How did you know . . . ? What made you decide . . . ?
Apply	How can you use what you learned?
Make decisions	What do you think we should do now that we know _____?
Communicate	How can you show/remember/share with others what you did/learned?

Silence

Six children are in the block area. They have used almost every block for an elaborate building that stretches from one side of the rug to the other. They are laughing and talking to one another, sharing materials, and taking on the roles of construction workers. Mr. Moon observes silently from nearby, noting that Teisha has become part of the group. Today is the first time she has moved into a learning center involving more than one or two children. He writes a quick anecdotal record to remind himself of this milestone. Mr. Moon also notices that the children are sustaining the activity well. He does not interrupt but remains nearby to provide support if needed.

The children and their teacher are investigating a large horseshoe crab shell one of the children brought back

from a week at the beach. The teacher has just said, "Tell me what you notice about this big shell." She remains silent for several seconds to give the children a chance to answer.

Coral and Aiysha are engaged in a story-mapping activity in which they are determining the distinguishing characteristics of each character. They are deeply absorbed in their discussion. Their teacher listens attentively for a few moments and then moves to another group of children. The girls continue their analysis.

In each of these situations, the teacher used silence to support children's learning. Remaining quiet can be an effective teaching strategy, especially when it is coupled with attentive observation of children and the context in which they are functioning (Kostelnik, Onaga, et al., 2002). Too much adult talk, inappropriate adult talk, or adult talk at the wrong time detracts from a positive learning environment. For instance, researchers have documented that many teachers are too quick to respond to their own questions or too swift to move from one child to the next when a child fails to respond immediately to a question or a do-it signal (Freiberg & Driscoll, 2000). Children need at least 3 to 5 seconds to process what has been said and to formulate a response. Getting into the habit of giving children a few seconds of "wait time" is an effective use of silence. Likewise, children perceive the learning environment as more supportive when teachers refrain from inserting themselves into the center of every interaction and when they avoid interrupting children who are deeply engaged in communicating with one another. In these cases, children interpret the adult's silence as a sign of warmth and respect.

COMBINING STRATEGIES TO PROMOTE LEARNING IN DIFFERENT WAYS

Although children's sensory involvement is integral to every lesson, the other teaching strategies just described can be combined in different ways to create activities that vary in function and form. The most significant variation among activities is the extent to which either children or adults determine processes and outcomes. For some activities, how and what is learned is mostly determined by the children; in other activities, children and teachers share responsibility for how the activity transpires and what ends are achieved; still other activities place primary control for what happens with the adult. Because of what we know about how young children learn best, child-directed experiences and shared activities are much more prevalent in high-quality early childhood programs than are adult-controlled activities. However, all three variations can be used appropriately at one time or another to support children's learning.

With these ideas in mind, we describe six generic activity types that form the basis for planning and teaching in early childhood education today: (a) exploratory play, (b) guided discovery, (c) problem solving, (d) discussions, (e) demonstrations, and (f) direct instruction. We selected these activity types because they represent common approaches to teaching in the early years. They are appropriate for use with the entire range of children aged 3 through 8 years because they span child-centered and shared and adult-controlled methods and because they are adaptable to each curricular domain. These six activity types do not cover all the possibilities, but they represent the foundations on which most other activity variations build. More specific techniques commonly associated with particular domains, such as story mapping or conflict mediation, are addressed in the domain-related chapters to which they apply.

Exploratory Play

Much of what young children learn evolves through playful explorations of the environment. Through self-initiated examinations of people, places, objects, and events, children construct their own knowledge rather than having information imposed on them. Exploratory play enables children to carry out firsthand investigations, proceeding at their own pace and making most of the decisions about what is done and how and when it is done (Slentz & Krogh, 2001b). Because there are no prescribed answers, children discover things for themselves, taking the activity in whatever direction suits their interests.

Even though children assume primary responsibility for the direction of exploratory play, teachers do more than just make materials available for children to use. Teachers consider which broad experiences they want children to have and the best ways to support children's involvement in these experiences. For instance, Ms. Habibi encourages children's exploration of sand by putting damp sand in the sand table one day, and dry sand on another. She provides various props such as sifters, measuring cups, sieves, containers, shovels, slotted spoons, and nonslotted utensils and gives children plenty of time to engage in the activity. She also invites children to the area, occasionally commenting on what they are doing and saying as a way to acknowledge individuals and support children's involvement.

To enhance children's learning to the fullest, educators must plan exploratory play carefully. In exploratory play, teachers rely heavily on the strategies of sensory involvement and environmental cues to stimulate children's interest and enable them to participate freely and safely. Teachers use behavior reflections and paraphrase reflections to acknowledge children's actions and discoveries. However, because they have no predetermined agenda for what they want the children to learn, teachers avoid potentially leading strategies such as do-it signals or questions that guide children's thinking in particular directions.

Guided Discovery

Teachers plan guided-discovery experiences by focusing on the learning process, not on children's generating particular solutions. The educator's aim is for youngsters to make connections and build concepts through interactions with people and objects. The children's role in guided-discovery activities is to construct knowledge for themselves: making choices and decisions, experimenting and experiencing, raising questions, and finding their own answers (J. Klein, 1990). The adult's role is to serve as a resource: emphasizing how to find answers, providing information and tools as necessary, and supporting children's progress through domain-related processes (Bredekamp & Copple, 1997). Both children and adults influence the direction of guided-discovery activities. Adults provide the broad parameters in which learning occurs; children determine the essence of what is learned.

Guided-discovery activities build on exploration, incorporating the additional teaching strategies of modeling, using effective praise, telling and explaining, using do-it signals, posing challenges, and posing questions. Therefore, when the sand table is being used for guided discovery, the activity looks different from when the sand is being used for an exploratory activity. For instance, Ms. Jamison plans a guided-discovery activity in which she wants children to think about the idea that volume, shape, and color are distinct properties of objects. She sets out several 1-cup measures of different colors and shapes and dampens the sand. As children pack the sand and mold it by using the measuring cups, she comments on the size and shape of the cups and the sand structures the children are building. She also asks questions such as "Which measuring cup holds the most? How could you find out? What is the same about these measuring cups? What is different? How do you know? You discovered that the blue cup and the red one hold the same amount of sand. Look at this yellow cup. Will it hold more or less sand than those cups?" Such verbalizations are interspersed with periods of attentive adult silence to allow children opportunities to talk about their ideas and what interests them about the materials and one another. Using this combination of strategies, Ms. Jamison gently guides children's thinking along certain lines but allows children to come to their own conclusions based on the evidence of their experience. Sometimes the children's conclusions are not scientifically correct. When this happens, Ms. Jamison offers a challenge to stimulate children to think about the objects in new ways. However, because this project is a guided-discovery activity, she ultimately accepts the children's ideas no matter what they are. She does not tell children they are wrong or make them parrot "correct" answers. Instead, she uses what she finds out about children's thought processes to plan guided-practice experiences through which children gradually construct more-accurate concepts for themselves. The activity described in Figure 3.2 is a guided-discovery example. Another example can be found in the Appendix.

Problem Solving

Problem-solving activities are variations of guided-discovery experiences. Children plan, predict, make decisions, observe the results of their actions, and form conclusions while adults serve as facilitators (Hendrick, 2003). Young children are intrigued by movement problems (How many different ways can you move from Point A to Point B?), discussion problems (What would happen if . . . ?), strategy problems (What strategies do you need to play a board game?), and skill problems (How many different ways can a set of objects be grouped?). Sometimes these problems arise out of naturally occurring events, and sometimes adults plan them. The best problems for children to think about engage them in various ways, allow them to gather information concretely, and have more than one possible solution. The more immediate, observable, and obvious the problem, the more easily children can evaluate their actions and come to their own conclusions. All good problems prompt children to analyze, synthesize, and evaluate events, information, and ideas, which thereby encourages children to make new mental connections and construct fresh ideas (Freiberg & Driscoll, 2000).

The problem-solving process is similar for every curricular domain. A typical five-step sequence is associated with scientific problem solving:

1. Becoming aware of a problem (noticing, observing, and identifying)
2. Hypothesizing or proposing an explanation (thinking of possible reasons why things happen, gathering

These children are listening carefully to one another's ideas as they participate in a problem-solving activity.

information, making intelligent guesses based on experience, and predicting)

3. Experimenting (testing ideas)

4. Drawing conclusions (observing results, making generalizations, determining whether alternative hypotheses are needed, and reflecting on the results of their actions)

5. Communicating results (talking about what happened, recording what happened, and making plans for further experimentation with a new hypothesis)

Mrs. Radechek is using scientific problem solving when she supplies materials at the water table for children to use in a sink-and-float experiment. Having encouraged children to explore similar materials in the water table on many previous occasions, she prepares to guide them in discovering which properties of objects seem to have a bearing on whether they sink or float. Mrs. Radechek thinks carefully about the materials she will provide as well as what she will say and do to help children proceed through the steps of the scientific process. Her ultimate aim is for children to generate ideas about the following:

❏ What they see (John says, "The bottle cap floats. The plastic boat floats. The rock is on the bottom.")

❏ Why things happen (John says, "The blue stuff stays on top. The brown thing sank.")

❏ What will happen when another object is placed in the water (John predicts, "The 'brown' popsicle stick will sink.")

❏ The outcomes of their predictions (John says, "It floated.")

❏ Alternative hypotheses (John says, "Maybe being long is what makes things float.")

Although John generated a hypothesis that was incorrect (e.g., color is related to floating and sinking), his investigations eventually led him to reject color as a significant property and switch to something else. By observing, hypothesizing, experimenting, and drawing conclusions many times and with many variations, John will gradually construct more-accurate concepts. In this problem-solving activity, John acted on objects in purposeful ways, applied his notions of how the world works, and reflected on his experiences, with his teacher's help. Mrs. Radechek's role included supporting John's investigation ("Tell me what you see. You noticed the bottle cap is blue and the boat is blue. You've decided being blue is what makes things float") as well as asking questions and offering challenges as appropriate ("What do you think will happen when you put the popsicle stick in the water?"). The process of problem solving was the ultimate goal, not the physics

of water displacement (floating). By observing and listening carefully, the teacher gleaned valuable information to use for future planning. This sink-and-float activity was one in which adult and child shared control and from which both learned.

The six steps characteristic of social inquiry are similar to those associated with the scientific method:

1. Becoming aware of a problem (noticing, observing, and identifying)

2. Gathering information (thinking of possible reasons why things happen, gathering information, and making intelligent guesses based on experience)

3. Designing a plan or a solution

4. Trying out a plan or a solution

5. Drawing conclusions (observing results, making generalizations, and determining whether alternative plans are needed)

6. Communicating results

Children might engage in social inquiry as they generate ideas for rules in the block area, determine how to resolve a conflict between the boys and the girls on the playground, choose a name for the class iguana, or develop an equitable plan for using the computer.

The Appendix provides a sample problem-solving plan.

Discussions

There is much to talk about in early childhood classrooms:

❏ *What is happening in the program?* Who will water the plants? What are ways cooperative reading partners can help each other when someone is absent? Why are some people upset with what is going on in the block area? Where should we hang the graphs we made? When will be the best time to celebrate Flopsy Bunny's birthday? How does it feel when someone makes a mistake and other people laugh?

❏ *What is happening to children away from the program?* Jessica has a new baby at her house. Tanya's grandma is visiting. Rudy's dog died. Carlos went to the Panthers game over the weekend. Roger became scared when he heard people yelling and banging outside his window. Selma will be moving with her family soon.

❏ *What is happening in the community and world at large?* Children notice many things: There was a big storm last night. A new shopping center is being built. The Pirates won the game yesterday. People will be voting next week. Children wonder many things: Can women be firefighters or just men? Why do some trees lose their leaves and other trees do not? How high is the sky? What happened to all the dinosaurs? What does it mean to vote?

Discussion implies reciprocal interactions among teachers and children; adults talk to children, children talk to adults, and children talk to one another. Using invitations, reflections, questions, and statements, teachers guide the conversation but encourage children to express themselves and communicate their ideas aloud. Throughout the discussion, teachers talk, but children talk as much as, if not more than, the adults. Sometimes a record is made of the discussion, such as when a group makes a list of classroom rules, generates ideas for names for the guinea pig, or lists suggestions for a new ending to a familiar story. Sometimes no tangible record is made. In both cases, responsibility for discussion is a shared endeavor, in which children and adults influence processes and outcomes together.

A sample discussion plan can be found in the Appendix.

Demonstrations

Generally, demonstrations involve one person's showing others how something works or how a task is to be carried out. When people demonstrate something, the direction of the activity is completely up to them. Teachers use demonstrations to illustrate instructions, offer children a preview of something they will do later, or open a lesson in a dramatic way. Demonstrations combine do-it signals and modeling and generally consist of three steps: (a) gaining children's attention, (b) showing children something, and (c) prompting children to respond, in words or actions, to what they saw. For instance, teachers at the Tree Top Child Development Center open each day with a greeting time, during which they demonstrate one of the materials that will be available to children in the room throughout the free-choice portion of the day. Typical items are games (e.g., lotto, dominoes), experiments (e.g., dissolving substances in water), and novel materials. Today the children will have a chance to scrape vegetables to make "Stone Soup." Their teacher plans to demonstrate the safe way to scrape the potatoes and other items that will go into the soup. She hides some vegetables and a scraper in a paper bag and places it behind her chair. Following one or two opening songs, she pulls out the bag. Giving the children a few introductory hints, she encourages them to guess what they think might be inside (gaining the children's attention). After some guesses are made, she reveals the vegetables and the scraper and proceeds to show the children how to scrape away from their bodies and over a plastic bowl (showing the children something). Finally, she asks the children to make the appropriate scraping motion, as they pretend to scrape a favorite vegetable (children respond). The demonstration ends. The teacher assumes the children will need additional support as they attempt to scrape vegetables

for real. However, she is satisfied that she has introduced the safe way to handle the scrapers in a manner children understood and enjoyed.

Demonstrations may constitute an entire activity, as illustrated by the vegetable scraper demonstration. Alternatively, demonstrations are sometimes only a small part of a larger interaction. For instance, a teacher or a peer might demonstrate the proper amount of food to feed the guinea pig, how to reboot the computer, or how to capture air in a jar by putting the jar straight into the water upside down. Even in these brief situations, the same instructional process is followed: gain attention, model, and prompt children to respond in some way. The children's response may be verbal or involve an action of some type, such as shaking out the approximate amount of food, telling the first step in rebooting the computer, or trying to capture air in their jars. When demonstrations of any kind are planned for young children, they must be kept short, and sensory involvement should be ensured early in the procedure. A sample demonstration plan is presented in the Appendix.

Direct Instruction

If we were to create a continuum of teaching strategies, direct instruction would be at the opposite end from exploratory play. It is the most structured, teacher-centered strategy discussed in this chapter. Direct instruction is used to teach children information or routines created by others; it is not focused on children's constructing these things for themselves. For instance, a child who wants to ride a bike must master the appropriate hand signals before he or she may ride on the street. Such signals have been socially agreed on and handed down from one generation to the next. It is not safe for children to rely on a personally constructed signal system because such a system would not be meaningful to others on the road. In early childhood classrooms, direct instruction is used to teach children certain terms, facts, strategies, rules, and routines (Freiberg & Driscoll, 2000). The advantages of direct instruction are that it is efficient, produces immediate results, teaches children to follow directions, and lends itself to on-the-spot evaluation (Pica, 2000).

Sam Borazage is using direct-instruction techniques when he points to one of three kiwis from among the many fruits the children are examining and says, "This is a kiwi. You say it, *kiwi*." The children repeat the word *kiwi*, and Sam acknowledges their response. After two more repetitions of the word *kiwi*, Sam points to a red apple and says enthusiastically, "Is this a kiwi?" The children say in chorus, "No!" Sam smiles and says, "You knew this wasn't a kiwi. Let me see if I can fool you." Sam points to an orange and whispers, "Is this a kiwi?"

The youngsters laugh and say, "No!" Sam laughs, too. He points to a kiwi and says in a squeaky voice, "Is this a kiwi?" The youngsters loudly say, "Yes!" Sam says, "Good. You knew that was a kiwi." He points to a lime, which is green like the kiwi. "Is this a kiwi?" he queries. The children are not so sure. Sam says matter-of-factly, "This is not a kiwi." He points to the kiwi, "*This* is a kiwi." After two or three instances of discriminating kiwis from other fruits, Sam says, "Show me a kiwi." Most of the children are able to point to a kiwi from among the fruits on the table. The lesson has taken only a few minutes, and Sam is pleased to hear the children using the word *kiwi* in their conversations with one another. He then shifts the activity into a guided-discovery mode by cutting open some of the fruit and encouraging children to investigate them as they choose.

Direct instruction is more than simply telling or showing children something. It includes performing task analysis, modeling, using effective praise, informing and explaining, using do-it signals, and posing challenges. Teachers either ignore inappropriate responses or provide corrective feedback as necessary. This emphasis on working toward a correct response is a significant distinction between direct-instruction activities and exploration or guided-discovery activities. In direct instruction, the adult combines a variety of teaching strategies to allow children to be correct most of the time and to lead children through the required steps in such a way that youngsters learn correct responses relatively quickly. As Sam illustrated in the kiwi activity, teachers vary their voices, their facial expressions, and the pace of the activity as part of direct instruction. They also use gestures, intentional mistakes, surprises, pauses, and enthusiasm to stimulate children's interest and to draw their attention to essential lesson elements. Key elements of a typical direct-instruction sequence are outlined in Table 3.3.

During direct-instruction activities, adults make most of the decisions regarding what, how, and when students will implement certain tasks (Slentz & Krogh, 2001b). This level of control requires teachers to plan such lessons very carefully and to use the method sparingly. Short lessons are best. Also, something taught through direct instruction (e.g., learning a polite way to answer the telephone) is best supplemented by child-centered instruction in which there is shared responsibility for the activity (e.g., using the phone in the pretend-play area, incorporating answering the telephone in role-play or puppet-play activities). In this way, direct instruction can be combined with other activity types to provide children with a well-rounded set of experiences. In fact, strong evidence indicates that direct instruction makes a positive difference when it is used with child-centered and shared activities as part of whole-language teaching, mathematics education, social skills development, and physical education (Baroody, 1993; Delpit, 1991; Spear-Swerling & Sternberg, 1994). Conversely, classrooms in which direct instruction is ignored yield less-positive learning outcomes for children (McIntyre & Pressley, 1996).

Direct Instruction as Part of a Larger Learning Experience One way to ensure that direct instruction is used appropriately and effectively with young children is to consider its place in supporting the principle of

TABLE 3.3 Direct-Instruction Steps with Accompanying Oral Cues

Sequence of Steps	Sample Oral Cues
Step 1 *Attend* Draw children's attention to the task.	Look up here. I have something to tell you. Find a spot where you can see the pictures. Listen to this.
Step 2 *Show or tell* Show or tell children something.	Here is a _____. This is how to _____. This is what to do first.
Step 3 *Differentiate* Help children recognize examples and nonexamples.	Which is the _____? Show me something that is not _____.
Step 4 *Apply* Have children apply what they are learning.	Make a _____. Tell how to _____. Show how to _____. Give me an example of _____. What will happen if _____?

exploratory to goal-directed learning. As you may remember from chapter 2, children move along a continuum from randomly experimenting with objects and relationships to purposefully applying the knowledge and skills they gain. This developmental sequence consists of exploration, acquisition, practice, and generalization. Direct instruction is most supportive of the acquisition phase of learning. Keeping this in mind, remember that exploration always precedes any prescribed use of materials or actions. Children need lots of time to explore before moving on to acquisition. For instance, children who have had few chances to examine flowers in real life will have difficulty learning facts about them. Exploration can take place on previous occasions as well as immediately prior to encountering factual information. The decision to move into acquisition is often signaled by the children (e.g., "Teacher, what's this?" or "How does the water get in the leaves?"). When children start to ask questions about an experience or when they can describe or show some basic understanding of a phenomenon, they are ready to acquire new knowledge and skills. In the acquisition phase, teachers or peers provide instruction, and children do things to demonstrate understanding. After a small amount of instruction has been offered, children need to practice what they have learned prior to moving on to something else. For this reason, teachers use guided practice within the same activity or in other activities to reinforce the original experience. Eventually, children will generalize or apply what they have learned in one situation to a circumstance new to them. Often, children's generalization activities occur spontaneously (e.g., children generalize what

they have learned about flowers in the garden to blossoms they see growing on trees). At other times, teachers set up subsequent experiences that make such generalizations more likely to happen. The relationship among exploratory to goal-directed learning, teacher's strategies, and children's responses is outlined in Table 3.4.

Planning for Differences Among Children as Part of Direct Instruction In every activity, children differ as to which phase of the learning continuum is occupying their attention. For instance, when learning about ladybugs, one child might be involved in exploration because he has not previously encountered a ladybug. Another child, who has seen or had a ladybug land on her hand in the past, may be ready to learn some facts about these insects. This child is at the acquisition phase of learning. Yet another child, who knows many facts about ladybugs, may want to practice identifying and temporarily catching the insects outdoors. Other children may know so much about ladybugs that they focus on using what they know to help them better understand other flying insects. These youngsters are at the generalization phase of learning about ladybugs. To meet the needs of all the children, teacher's direct-instruction plans must address all four phases. However, effective planners recognize that individual children will not progress from exploration to generalization in one lesson. Instead, the teacher's written plan will be used again and again throughout the year. An example of a complete direct-instruction activity plan is presented in the Appendix.

TABLE 3.4 Relationship Among Exploratory to Goal-Directed Phases of Learning, Sample Teaching Strategies, and Children's Behavior

Learning Phase	Teaching Strategy (Procedures)	Child's Response (Objectives)
Explore	Invite, offer, provide, encourage, reflect, imitate, use silence	Observe, touch, smell, taste, hear, examine, talk about, ask questions
Acquire	Elaborate, reflect, model, demonstrate, ask questions, tell/explain/inform, use do-it signals, use effective praise, correct, ignore inaccurate responses	Carry out an action
Practice	Invite, offer, provide, encourage, reflect, vary, simplify, expand	Repeat previous action with variations
Generalize	Reflect, ask child to describe his or her thinking	Transfer knowledge from one situation to another

MAKING AND IMPLEMENTING PLANS

Now that you are familiar with all the parts of a plan, sample teaching strategies, and typical activity types, you are ready to create and carry out your own plans. As you do so, keep the following guidelines in mind:

❏ Choose a curricular domain within which to plan your activity. Practice writing plans in each of the six domains: aesthetic, affective, cognitive, language, physical, and social.

❏ Do *not* confine your planning to only the domains with which you are most comfortable.

❏ Select an intermediate objective that supports the domain you choose. Refer to the list of intermediate objectives presented in part 3 for each curricular domain. Choose one that fits the learning needs of the children for whom you are planning. Remember that the most basic intermediate objectives are listed first, followed by more-advanced objectives. Use the initial intermediate objectives when planning for preschoolers or inexperienced first and second graders. Choose intermediate objectives farther down the list as children gain experience and demonstrate mastery.

❏ Do *not* write any part of the activity before you choose the intermediate objective.

❏ Brainstorm activity ideas that could support the intermediate objective you selected. Choose one idea to develop into an activity plan. Make sure the activity is appropriate and of potential interest to children. Consider both developmental factors and contextual factors when making a final choice. As time passes, be sure to plan activities that encompass all six activity types described in this chapter.

❏ Do *not* select activities just because you have a particular prop or saw a great idea in an activity book. Remember to tailor your plans to meet the specific needs of the children with whom you are working.

❏ Write your plan. At first write down as much detail as possible. After you gain experience, use a shorter format but still think through your plans, referring to all the parts outlined in this chapter. Use the writing process to help you think comprehensively and creatively about the activities you plan.

❏ Do *not* assume that you will be able to remember everything without writing it down.

❏ Verify each element of your plan for accuracy. Make sure that the individual segments of your plan comply with the definitions presented in Figure 3.1. These definitions should help you develop appropriate activity names, assumptions, objectives, material lists, procedures, hints for success, simplifications, exten-

sions, and evaluation items. Also refer to the Appendix for sample plans.

❏ Do *not* suppose that effective planning happens quickly or easily. It will take time to perfect your planning skills.

❏ Complete your plan. Include all the elements listed in Figures 3.1 and 3.2.

❏ Do *not* skip or combine parts of the activity plan.

❏ Check that all the elements of your plan are congruent. The activity name, assumptions, content, objectives, procedures, simplifications, extensions, and evaluation should all relate to the intermediate objective. For instance, if the intermediate objective focuses on story sequence, as illustrated in Figure 3.2, the objectives should be about story sequence, not about choosing favorite illustrations or describing the difference between fiction and fact. In a congruent plan the procedures will be closely linked to the objectives. When the objective states, "Children will listen to the story one time through," the procedure must be planned to include reading the story aloud. Likewise, the content of the activity should revolve around story sequence, not information about how turnips grow in the ground. If growing turnips is what you really want children to know about, the intermediate objective would be "Children will learn facts about the natural world," and the rest of the plan would support this aim. If story sequence is the focus of the activity, the simplifications and extensions should build on this idea or break it down into smaller steps for children to manage. Extensions that have children drawing pictures of turnips or mashing them with a hand masher do not support children's development of the story sequence concept. Paying attention to congruence lends substance to your plans.

❏ Do *not* assume that congruence happens simply because materials remain constant. To create the necessary curricular match throughout the entire activity, keep the intermediate objective in mind at all times. Make all parts of the plan relate to it.

❏ Prepare to carry out your plan. Gather materials in advance. Think about who will implement the activity and about when, where, and how to do it. Experiment with unfamiliar activities and rehearse procedures you have not tried before. Anticipate how children might respond, and consider ways of supporting them under these circumstances.

❏ Do *not* wait until the last minute to collect what you need or to think about how you will prepare, supervise, and clean up after the activity.

❏ Implement your plan. Try to follow the plan as written, adapting as necessary. Make note of the children's participation, the achievement of objectives, and the effectiveness or lack of effectiveness of the teaching methods you chose.

❑ Do *not* abandon your plan in the excitement of carrying it out. Neither should you rigidly follow a plan merely because of what is written if children's behavior indicates some changes are necessary. Strike a balance between implementing plans as anticipated and remaining flexible enough to respond to children's cues.

❑ Reflect on the children's learning experiences as well as on yours. Keep written records of what was accomplished. Make notes about what to change next time and how to build on the children's interests and accomplishments. Use this information to create new activity plans and to make records of children's progress.

❑ Do *not* fail to follow through on what children learn as a result of the activity. For instance, if several children meet all the objectives of the story sequence plan, prepare to move into the extensions another time soon. Avoid thinking that you will remember what you observed. With so much happening every day, forgetting important details is easy. Write anecdotes, keep work samples, and answer the evaluation questions in writing to provide a resource for future planning.

SUMMARY

Planning is a key ingredient in creating developmentally appropriate programs for young children. Early childhood professionals use planning for organizational, educational, and accountability purposes. Effective planning requires consideration of many factors simultaneously. These factors include individual children and groups of children as well as past, present, and future needs and expectations. When planning, educators must first think about the children in relation to what is being taught. This initial diagnostic step enables teachers to make an appropriate match between instruction and the knowledge, skills, and understandings children bring to the classroom. Following this diagnosis, early childhood professionals design, organize, and evaluate their plans. All these functions are best expressed in writing. Novice planners write in much detail. More-experienced planners keep in mind the same elements of planning that they wrote as beginners but record only the essence of their thinking.

A typical written activity plan includes the following 10 components:

1. The curricular domain in which the activity is planned
2. A name for the activity
3. An intermediate objective from within the chosen domain
4. At least three immediate objectives focusing on child performance
5. Content covering relevant terms, facts, and principles
6. All necessary materials
7. Sample procedures
8. Ideas about how to simplify the activity
9. Ideas about ways to extend the activity
10. Three or four evaluation questions

Children learn in many ways. The teaching strategies that support their learning vary accordingly. Some strategies are more appropriate in certain situations than are others. Which strategies professionals use depends on what they want children to learn. Thus, establishing congruence between the goals and objectives of the activity and the selected strategies outlined in the procedure portion of the plan is essential. Four common teaching strategies are (a) ensuring children's sensory involvement, (b) performing task analysis, (c) using scaffolding, and (d) using guided practice. These strategies influence activity design and the ways in which tasks are presented to children. Issuing invitations; using behavior and paraphrase reflections; modeling; using effective praise; telling, explaining, and informing; using do-it signals; posing challenges; and posing questions are all verbal strategies that support children's learning more or less directively. Using silence can also be an effective teaching strategy when it is done to deliberately facilitate children's peer interactions and self-discoveries.

All the teaching strategies described in this chapter can be combined in different ways to create activities that vary in function and form. Another dimension along which activities contrast has to do with who controls processes and outcomes—children or adults. Some activities are primarily child controlled, others involve shared responsibility between children and adults, and some activities are directed primarily by adults. The first two kinds of activities are the most prevalent in high-quality early childhood programs. However, all three have an appropriate place in the overall delivery of effective early childhood education. With this understanding in mind, six generic activity types that form the basis for planning are presented in this chapter in a sequence that proceeds from an entirely child-centered orientation to more-adult-directed forms. The six types are exploratory play, guided discovery, problem solving, discussions, demonstrations, and direct instruction. Definitions and examples of each activity type are provided in this chapter. A step-by-step description of the do's and don't's involved in making plans is also provided. Sample plans are presented in the Appendix.

Applying What You Read in This Chapter

1. Discuss

a. On the basis of your reading and your experiences with young children, discuss each of the questions that open this chapter.

b. Imagine that you are planning to interact with children by using art materials. The supplies available include modeling dough and various utensils such as forks, spatulas, cookie cutters, and rolling pins. Discuss what you would do to promote children's learning in an exploratory activity. Discuss how your strategies might change if you switched to a problem-solving mode. What kinds of problems might children pursue with the dough?

c. You observe a classroom in which the children are to learn about the relative size of objects by circling the largest items in rows depicted on a ditto sheet. How does this activity correspond with your ideas about how children learn best? What other, if any, teaching strategies and types might you suggest to support children's learning?

2. Observe

a. Observe the exploratory play of a younger child (younger than 5 years old) and an older child (6, 7, or 8 years old) in an open-ended activity such as sand play, block play, or water play. Describe similarities and differences between the two children in terms of what they say and do in their explorations.

b. Watch a seasoned practitioner interact with children in an activity for at least 15 minutes. Refer to the teaching strategies outlined in this chapter and identify no fewer than three strategies used by the adult. Describe what the adult said and did that fit the definitions offered. Conclude this observation by identifying the generic activity type that you believe you saw. Explain your answer.

3. Carry out an activity

a. Refer to the turnip story sequence activity outlined in Figure 3.2. Review the procedures portion of the plan. Talk about which of the sample teaching strategies outlined in this chapter are represented in the procedures. On the basis of your understanding of the generic activity types described in this chapter, assign this plan to one of those categories. Explain your answer.

4. Create something for your portfolio

a. Develop a statement of no more than one page that describes your beliefs about planning and the ways in which you intend to engage in effective planning as you work with children.

b. Select a written plan that you have implemented with children. Evaluate the effectiveness of your teaching. Finally, write a synopsis of how you might teach the lesson again with the same group of children.

5. Add to your journal

a. What is the most significant concept that you learned about planning and teaching from your readings and your experience with children?

b. Reflect on the extent to which the content of this chapter corresponds with what you have observed in the field. What is your reaction to any discrepancies you perceive?

c. What goals do you have for yourself related to planning and teaching activities for young children? How do you intend to pursue these goals?

Planning and Implementing
Effective Whole-Group Activities

You may wonder:

With so much emphasis on individual learning, is teaching all the children the same thing at the same time ever appropriate?

What makes a good group time for preschoolers? for school-age children?

What are some pitfalls to avoid when I am carrying out whole-group activities with young children?

What do I need to know to manage a successful field trip for a whole group of children?

In this introduction to planning and implementing whole-group instruction for young children, we present information to help you answer the preceding questions.

Every day the 3-year-olds come together at about 10:00 in the morning for a 10-minute circle time. Today, the teacher starts by singing, "There was a farmer had a dog, and Bingo was his name-o." The children clap as they join in, singing the familiar song.

A firefighter has come to show the kindergarten children the special equipment firefighters use. Youngsters sit in a circle, trying on hats and boots as the firefighter explains their use. The children are especially intrigued by the oxygen tanks and masks she shows them.

The second graders in Mr. LaFontane's class gather on the rug for a short class meeting on measuring. The teacher invites them to watch as Louie shows how he solved the problem of measuring the size of the class guinea pig.

All the children and adults just described are engaged in whole-group instruction. Whole-group activities are events during the day when all or most of the children gather in one place to share the same learning experience simultaneously. Nearly every early childhood classroom includes periods of whole-group

activity, which are commonly referred to as *group times* and are implemented with children aged 3 to 8 years old. Half-day programs usually include one or two group times; full-day programs may have as many as three or four. The curricular focus of a particular group time might be aesthetic, affective, cognitive, linguistic, physical, or social. Consequently, group times incorporate a wide range of activities (Henninger, 2002). On any given day, the whole class may come together to do the following:

❏ Sing, dance, and experience music
❏ Act out stories or hear them read aloud
❏ Play games
❏ Participate in movement activities
❏ Receive instructions
❏ Interact with a resource person
❏ Learn about what is coming next
❏ Discuss a problem in the room
❏ Observe a demonstration
❏ Plan for the session
❏ Report on work or show others what they have accomplished
❏ Reflect on the day

Naturally, adults select only one or two of these activities per group time. Thus, although some group-time routines are the same from day to day, others are varied to maintain children's interest and address different aspects of the curriculum.

Carried out appropriately, group times benefit everyone involved. Most important, they foster cohesive group feelings. Group times are ideal for conveying important information everyone needs—a visitor is coming, the guinea pig died, these are the activities from which to choose today, or this is where we are going on the field trip. No one is left out, and everyone hears the same thing at the same time, which facilitates communication among group members. In addition, looking around the circle, children see the faces and hear the ideas of all the children in the class, not just a few as in the case of small-group activities. The joyous experience of singing together or dictating a story to which everyone contributes prompts satisfaction and pleasure in one another's company. Children who share their work, talk about their day, or otherwise engage in group discussions construct shared meanings and explore together the give-and-take of group membership. All these experiences foster a sense of community.

In contrast, when whole-group instruction is carried out *inappropriately,* it is an unpleasant experience dominated by children's lack of attention, distracting behaviors, adult reprimands, and frustration for all (D. McAfee, 1985). The difference between positive and negative whole-group experiences is careful planning and preparation.

PLANNING EFFECTIVE GROUP TIMES

All group times have four parts: (a) the *opening,* when children are gathering and starting to become engaged in the group; (b) the *body,* when the teacher and the children are focusing on the main purpose of the group time; (c) the *closing,* when the teacher summarizes the activity and guides children into the next portion of the day; and (d) the *transitions,* the times between each activity included in the group time. All these segments must be considered both separately and in relation to one another for the educator to provide a comprehensive whole-group experience.

The Opening

The primary purpose of the opening is to signal the beginning of group time and capture children's interest. This portion usually consists of two or three short activities (e.g., an action rhyme, followed by a "stretching" poem, followed by a quiet song aimed at bringing the children's energy level down and focusing their attention on the *body* of the group time). Experi-

enced group leaders plan to be at the large-group area to greet children as they arrive. Such leaders do not expect children to sit on the rug waiting while the adult engages in last-minute cleanup or searches for needed items. As soon as two or three children are ready, the leader begins, rather than waiting until the last child appears. Finger plays, songs, and humorous poetry attract children to the circle and make entering the circle at any point easy for the children to do. Turn-taking songs and discussions are left for the *body* of the group time because children find joining groups engaged in such activities more difficult. Youngsters who are still cleaning up or finishing an activity elsewhere soon recognize the opening activities as a signal that whole-group instruction is about to start. Effective planners think of ways to securely gain children's involvement before moving on to the body of the group time. For instance, these educators plan to sing a song a few times—not just once—with variations (e.g., singing the "Eency Weency Spider" using normal pitch; singing it again as a tiny spider with a high-pitched voice; and singing it one last time as a huge spider with a deep-pitched voice). Another strategy is for the educator to move fluidly from one song or finger play to another, being careful not to interrupt the flow of the opening by talking between the activities. Thus, the group leader might start by chanting, "Five little hot dogs frying in a pan" (Figure 4.1) and use this finger play as a way to shift into a song involving hand motions, such as "My Finger Is Starting to Wiggle" (Figure 4.2). Likewise, in a first- or second-grade group, the teacher might move from a familiar action rhyme such as "Three Short-Necked Buzzards" (Figure 4.3) to introducing a factual lesson on identifying birds by their beaks and claws. The sequence of activities and the transition from one to another are thought out in advance.

FIGURE 4.1 Five Little Hot Dogs

Five little hot dogs frying in a pan (Hold right hand up showing five fingers),
the grease got hot (Hold left hand palm side up, rub with right palm in circular motion),
and one (Hold up one finger) went bam!
(clap hard)
(Repeat words counting down four, three, two, and one)

No little hot dogs frying in a pan (Hold right hand up showing closed fist),

The grease got hot, and the pan went BAM! (End with BIG CLAP!)

FIGURE 4.2 My Finger Is Starting to Wiggle
(tune: "The Bear Went Over the Mountain")

> My finger is starting to wiggle, my finger is starting to
>   wiggle,
> my finger is starting to wiggle, wiggle all around.
>
> My foot is starting to wiggle, my foot is starting to wiggle,
>   my foot is starting to wiggle, wiggle all around.
> (Repeat with different body parts and corresponding
>   motions)

The Body

When most of the children are participating in the opening, the leader moves into the main purpose of the activity. Children participate most successfully when they understand what will happen each step of the way (Hendrick, 2001). The group leader introduces the body of the group time by telling the children about the activity and then inviting their participation through strategies such as asking an open-ended question or posing a problem. Props are used to stimulate children's curiosity and interest. For instance, in introducing a guided-discovery activity about animals hatched from eggs, the first-grade teacher shows the children a real egg and says, "Look at what I have. See this egg? Today you will hear a story all about eggs. While I'm reading the story, listen for the names of animals hatched from eggs. Afterward, we'll talk about them." The teacher gives clear, specific directions to the children and uses effective praise to acknowledge appropriate behavior. Teaching strategies such as inviting, reflecting, modeling, telling, explaining, using do-it signals, posing challenges, and asking questions can help support children's learning. Using an expressive face, voice, and gestures, and using props, demonstrations, pictures, humor, and mime are other ways to keep children involved and attentive.

FIGURE 4.3 Three Short-Necked Buzzards
(This rhyme is said while standing.)

> Three short-necked buzzards (Hold up three fingers,
>   raise shoulders, scrunch neck, resume natural
>   posture),
> three short-necked buzzards (Repeat motions described
>   in preceding line),
> three short-necked buzzards (Repeat motions just
>   described),
> sitting on a dead tree (Hold arms out in an uneven
>   position like the branches of a tree, stand on one foot).
> (Repeat words and motions for two, one, and no
>   short-necked buzzards)

During group time, children gain a sense of community in the classroom.

The Closing

The closing signals the end of the group experience and serves as a transition to the next part of the day. Group leaders use this time to summarize key ideas and direct individual children into other learning activities. These leaders never simply send children away from the group; instead, the leaders direct the children toward a different activity. In some cases, early childhood professionals explain which activities are available and ask the children to choose one. An alternative is for group leaders to lightly tap the children one at a time (or use some other signal) to release them from the group. In other classrooms, teachers say something such as "All the people wearing red may get up and put on their coats to go outside. Now the people wearing blue may start getting dressed." This approach staggers the children's exit from the area, which enables them to shift more easily from whole-group instruction to the next scheduled activity (Machado, 2002).

Group-Time Transitions

Group-time is a series of short activities connected by transitions, which are the glue that fuses the individual group-time elements into a cohesive whole. For example, a traditional group time might include the following events: introductory song, movement rhyme, short story told with props, stretching rhyme, another song, and exit from group. How well the group flows from beginning to end has much to do with how smooth and interesting the transitions are. It is at transition points that either children become intrigued by what is coming next or their attention begins to wander. Consider the difference between the following transitions from a finger play to the song "Old MacDonald":

Group Leader 1:   "Okay, everybody! Let's sing Old MacDonald. Ready? Come on, let's get ready. Okay? One, two, three, Old MacDonald had a farm, Ee-i-ee-i-oh. . . ."

Group Leader 2:   (said with great enthusiasm) "There was so much block building going on today! I noticed a lot of you were making pens for the animals. I said to myself, "It looks just like Old MacDonald's farm." *Adult begins singing,* "Old MacDonald had a farm, Ee-i-ee-i-oh. . . ."

The first example was not interesting and did nothing to engage the children's attention. The adult's words sounded like directions, not an invitation to become involved. Group Leader 2 capitalized on the children's earlier activity to stimulate their interest and lead them into singing the song. Linking the song to the children and using an expressive voice were two strategies the second adult used to make the transition to music. The leader's words served as a bridge from a finger play she had just finished to a new activity—the song "Old MacDonald."

Gene Casqueiro, kindergarten teacher, uses the element of surprise to capture children's attention during the opening to a group time focused on storytelling (Educational Productions, 1988).

As children come to the group-time area, Gene sits on a chair facing them, holding a small carton of milk and a 4-ounce paper cup in his hands. The children are intrigued.

Taking a dark gray tray lined with waxed paper from under his chair, he balances it on his knees. All the while, he talks softly to the children, describing his actions as he carries them out and explaining that he will be reading a story in just a minute. He goes on to say that his throat is dry, and he wants to take a little drink so that he can read more comfortably.

When children make comments such as "My throat is dry, too," the teacher uses paraphrase reflections to incorporate their remarks into the interaction. "You're thirsty. After group time you may get something to drink at the snack table."

Gene pours a little milk into the paper cup. Taking a sip, he places the cup on the tray and says, "That's better. Now, where is my book? Oh, there it is." He continues to talk, maintaining eye contact with the children the entire time.

Picking up a paperback copy of the book he will read, he says, "One thing you have to be careful of is that you

don't end up . . . oh no . . . it spilled. (He gently knocks over the cup on the tray.) Oh well, you know what they say, you can't cry (he pauses dramatically) . . . over spilt milk." Some children say the last words with him in chorus.

The teacher holds the tray where the children can see the milk make little pools of various shapes on the waxed paper. After a moment or two, Gene puts the tray on a nearby shelf. Showing the children the cover of the book, he says, "Today the story happens to be It Looked Like Spilt Milk. *And I just happened to spill my milk. What a coincidence." The children laugh.*

Gene continues, "Well, let's see what this story is all about." Opening the book, he begins to read. The children listen with rapt attention.

This teacher combined words, gestures, and props to capture the children's interest and lead up to the title of the book. This opening was much more fun and did more to help children become engaged than if he had simply said, "Here's today's book. It's called *It Looked Like Spilt Milk.*"

Transitions need not be elaborate. However, they should be thought out in advance. The aim is to have the opening, the body, and the closing flow smoothly, one after the other in a way that makes sense to children and helps them focus on what the leader is trying to convey. Thus, transitions require the same careful planning that goes into selecting the music, stories, demonstrations, and games that make up each portion of group time.

WRITING GROUP-TIME PLANS

Just as with all other forms of planning, whole-group experiences require a written plan. Written plans help ensure that group time has an educational focus each day and prompts teachers to use a variety of teaching strategies and activity types (D. McAfee, 1985). Many elements of the activity plan format outlined previously in this book also apply when you are writing plans for group times. However, in this chapter the format has been adjusted to take into account planning decisions unique to whole-group instruction, such as the sequence of each lesson (opening, body, and closing) and the transition from group time to the next event in the day. As with activity plans, when practitioners are first learning to plan group times, they benefit from writing out all the parts of the plan. Later, a more abbreviated form can be used. A sample plan appropriate for whole-group instruction of all types is presented in Figure 4.4.

FIGURE 4.4 Sample Group-Time Plan

Date: Monday, March 17, 2003   **Activity Name:** Whole-Group Storytelling

Age of Children: 5 to 7 years

Intermediate Objective(s): Children will take on roles and act out their interpretations of these roles to tell a familiar story.

Content
1. Stories are sometimes told by one person, sometimes by groups of people.
2. The people or animals portrayed in a story are called the story *characters.*
3. Storytellers combine words, sounds, facial expressions, gestures, and other body motions to communicate the story.

Materials: None

Opening
1. Sing the songs "Hello Everybody" (incorporate the children's names into the song) and "I Had a Cat and the Cat Pleased Me."
2. Transition to the body by talking about the animals in the song; lead into the animals in the story.

Body
3. Introduce whole-group storytelling: "Earlier this morning you heard me tell the story 'The Three Billy Goats Gruff.' Now, I will tell the story, and we will all act it out together."
4. Set the scene. Briefly review the characters and major events in the story. Explain that each child may be any character he or she wants or may decide to be several in turn (first the "littlest" billy goat, then the middle-size billy goat, and so on). Explain that you will be the storyteller and perhaps take on a role or two as well.
5. Begin the story ("Once upon a time . . ."), and continue the story, moving from event to event until the conclusion.
6. Announce "The End."
7. Transition into the closing by having the children clap for themselves.

Closing
8. Review with the children the ways in which they acted like the billy goats and the troll.
9. Acknowledge the children's participation by using effective praise: "That was fun. You pretended so well. Some children pretended to be the biggest billy goat, some children pretended to be all three billy goats, and some children pretended to be the troll. We will play this story again soon. You can even play it yourselves when we go outside."

Transition to Next Portion of the Day
10. Dismiss the children by shoe color or type to go outdoors.

Evaluation Questions
1. In what ways did children enact their roles?
2. How did the children differ in their interpretation of the three goats?
3. How adequate were the initial directions in helping children to interpret the story successfully? What changes might be necessary in explaining or supporting this activity another time?

GROUP-TIME PREPARATIONS AND STRATEGIES

Location

Effective early childhood professionals locate the whole-group instruction area away from attractive items such as dress-up clothes and open shelves, or they temporarily cover such items to minimize distractions. Arranging for comfortable seating where children can easily see the group leader and can sit close enough together to hear one another's voices is another consideration. Some teachers prefer having children sit in a circle, others have children sit in a clustered group, and still others prefer having children sit in a horseshoe-shaped configuration, with the adult facing the group at the open end. Sometimes the shape is marked with tape on the floor in a continuous line or as a series of *x*s. This approach gives each child a specific spot on which to sit. In every case, making sure everyone has enough room to see, hear, and move comfortably is critical. Children who are crammed together pay more attention to protecting personal space or touching their neighbors than focusing on the whole-group activity.

Focus

The foundation for planning a good group time is knowing what you want children to learn and then selecting activities to support this aim. Having no learning objectives leads to confusion, superficial treatment of content, and a haphazard approach to skill development. Conversely, trying to address too many objectives in one experience yields the same outcomes. Experienced group leaders choose one or two intermediate objectives around which to plan. As a way to enhance children's understanding and provide some depth of experience, teachers relate one activity to the next. They also vary the curricular focus featured in the body of the group time from day to day. Doing so keeps group times fresh and enables teachers to address different learning objectives across time. Thus, Monday's group time may be dominated by language-related activities, and Tuesday's group time may highlight social learning. On Wednesday, the main focus may shift to the physical domain.

Pace and Variety

Experienced professionals change the pace and variety of each whole-group activity. Quiet segments are followed by more-active times; listening is interspersed with doing; teacher-directed activities are counterbalanced by child-initiated and shared types of activities. Activities demanding much concentration or effort by children, such as learning a new song or watching a demonstration, are addressed early in the body of the circle time, when children are still fresh (Hendrick, 2001). As the group time winds down, children sing familiar songs and engage in relaxing activities, such as stretching or listening to soothing music, before starting something new.

Materials

Group times are kept interesting by using a variety of props (Stephens, 1996). Such props may include books, flannel boards, puppets, musical instruments, audiotapes or compact disks, sections of videotape, nature items, real objects, pictures, charts, posters, and storybooks large enough for children to see. Group leaders can better attend to the children when they have selected their materials in advance and are thoroughly familiar with the stories, songs, poems, or instructions they intend to convey. They do not simply pull a book from the shelf at the last minute, nor do they begin a demonstration they have not thought through. These educators carefully select materials, keeping in mind the objectives of the circle time as well as ongoing emphases such as appreciation of diversity. Ms. Richards illustrates this blend of foci when she carries out a demonstration of household utensils by using spatulas, tortilla turners, and chopsticks. This array of real materials is useful in addressing the intermediate objective of increasing children's awareness of tools and their function. Such materials also support Ms. Richards's desire for multicultural inclusion. She stores all the necessary items close at hand but out of the children's sight until she needs them. To remind herself of the exact sequence of the activities she planned for group time, Ms. Richards posts a large

agenda near the whole-group area, which she glances at from time to time to remind herself of what comes next. Other teachers post the words to new songs or poems at eye level near the group area, not only for their reference, but also for the children's.

Preparation

To increase their confidence and to prevent potential problems, group leaders practice new stories or songs before trying them with the children. Before the children arrive on the rug, the leaders determine the best place to position the puppet stage so that everyone can see. They arrange the flannel board pieces in the correct order to prevent fumbling with them during the story. They make sure in advance that they have enough jingle bells for each child to have one. They rehearse the words they will use for the transition from one group activity to another. Strategies such as these increase the likelihood that group time will proceed smoothly and enjoyably for everyone.

Active Involvement

Remembering to give children firsthand experiences is as critical for group time as it is for all other learning activities. Thus, high-interest activities and activities in which children can become actively engaged are desirable for children of all ages. In addition, whole-group instruction is appropriate only when all the children in the group are able to participate in the learning. If the activity is relevant for only certain class members, it is better offered during small-group or learning center–based activity times.

Group-Time Teaching Methods

All the teaching strategies described in chapter 3 are applicable to whole-group instruction (ensuring sensory involvement; preparing environmental cues; performing task analysis; using scaffolding; using guided practice; issuing invitations; using behavior and paraphrase reflections; employing effective praise; telling, explaining, and informing; using do-it signals; posing challenges; asking questions; and using silence). Likewise, all the activity types described in chapter 3, including exploration, guided discovery, problem solving, discussion, cooperative learning, and direct instruction, are applicable to whole-group instruction. Following are some additional strategies that effective group leaders use regularly (Dodge, 1995; Stephens, 1996; Torgeson, 1996).

❑ Make whole-group experiences a predictable part of the daily schedule (e.g., group time always follows cleanup or is usually the first activity in the morning or the last activity in the afternoon)

❏ Seat themselves where they can see *all* the children

❏ Continually scan the group to determine children's interest level and involvement

❏ Make sure all the children can see them (e.g., they do not have children sit in their laps or directly at their sides, where children cannot see the leader's face; some sit on a low chair just a little above the group or on the floor at the front of a horseshoe shape to enable children to focus on what the leader is doing)

❏ Create an atmosphere to support group-time activities (e.g., use audiotaped sounds of a meadow to introduce an insect activity, dim the lights to tell a nighttime story)

❏ Use facial expressions, gestures, and variations in voice to maintain children's attention

❏ Involve children in setting guidelines for appropriate group-time behavior

❏ Clarify the expectations for children's group-time behavior

❏ Pass out materials for children to handle when they need them, not before, and collect them before going on to the next activity

❏ Allow children to influence the group-time agenda by giving them choices (e.g., children decide which motions to make or choose between two stories to hear or two games to play)

❏ Change, shorten, or eliminate whole-group activities that are not working

❏ Extend or repeat activities that children enjoy

❏ Practice, practice, practice (experience brings effectiveness)

Preparation of Other Adults for Supporting Group-Time Learning

Some teachers have sole responsibility for an entire group of youngsters, whereas other educators work in a team with staff or volunteers. When multiple people are present during group time, children benefit most when everyone is familiar with the group-time procedures. Although there is no one correct way to do things, adults should have a mutual understanding of their roles and responsibilities during the activity. Typical expectations include the following: (a) Adults are expected to sit among the children, not next to each other or off to the side; (b) adults should sing along and do the motions; and (c) adults should help children focus on the leader or wait their turn to talk. Taking time to define everyone's level of participation, identifying strategies for helping children become engaged, and determining ways to support children who are easily distracted are important in the preparation phase of planning. Like-

wise, all adults should understand the extent to which children are expected to come to the circle-time activity and what to do if children refuse to participate. The best way to arrive at a mutual understanding is to discuss these issues beforehand and to communicate group-time expectations to both adults and children.

VARIATIONS ON STANDARD GROUP-TIMES

The standard group time carried out in most early childhood programs combines a variety of activities, such as singing songs, listening to stories, and engaging in movement, and typical routines, such as using a job chart or a weather wheel. In addition, early childhood professionals sometimes incorporate specialty groups into the daily schedule. Specialty-group times are periods of whole-group instruction whose purpose is more specific than that of the general group times described so far. They are called by names such as *greeting time, planning time, music time,* and *author's circle.* Early childhood professionals may regularly use one or more of these specialized group times once or twice during the week. Some common variations are described as follows.

Greeting Time

Hello everybody, yes indeed,
hello everybody, yes indeed,
hello everybody, yes indeed,
sing, children, sing!

Hello to Marsha, yes indeed,
hello to LaToya, yes indeed,
hello to Samson, yes indeed,
sing, children, sing.

Greeting time occurs at the beginning of the classroom session, welcoming children and helping them make the transition from home to the early childhood program (Graves, Gargiulo, & Sluder, 1996). Children have an opportunity to say hello to one another and share daily news before dispersing into more-individualized activities. Greeting time may also be used to introduce children to activities and materials available during the day. Sometimes this introduction involves simply telling children what their choices are, and sometimes it includes demonstrations of materials that children will have a chance to use later in learning centers, individually, or in small groups. Other typical greeting-time activities include daily routines such as reporting on the weather or asking children to volunteer to do certain classroom jobs such as watering the plants or carrying around the cleanup sign. Greeting time is generally brief and is often followed by free-choice or learning center time. A second, more traditional, group time usually follows later in the session.

Planning Time

Some children start their day by planning how they will spend some of their time in the classroom (Hohmann & Weikart, 1995). Although planning time may take place individually, often children plan or at least announce their plans during a short group time. The purpose of planning time is to encourage children to make decisions and set goals. Plans may be oral or written, using pictures or words. A sample picture plan is presented in Figure 4.5. After children become familiar with the activities that are available during the day, they choose two or three to do and (sometimes) the order in which to do them. At times, only the children make these decisions. In other circumstances, children collaborate with peers or adults in making their choices. Some plans include "have-to" activities (those that the teacher requires) as well as "choice" activities, from which children may freely select. As the day progresses, children periodically refer to their plans to determine how well they are following them. Some programs end with a whole-group closing time during which children describe the extent to which they followed plans made earlier in the day. In other programs, this reflection on the day is carried out one-to-one with an adult or in small-group time.

Storytelling Time

"Once upon a time . . ." Few children can resist the enjoyment promised by these words. Everyone likes a good story. Telling a story without a book; telling stories with flannel boards, puppets, or props; and enacting stories through dramatic movement are all activities well suited to whole-group instruction. Effective storytellers use various techniques to capture children's

FIGURE 4.5 Planning/Reporting

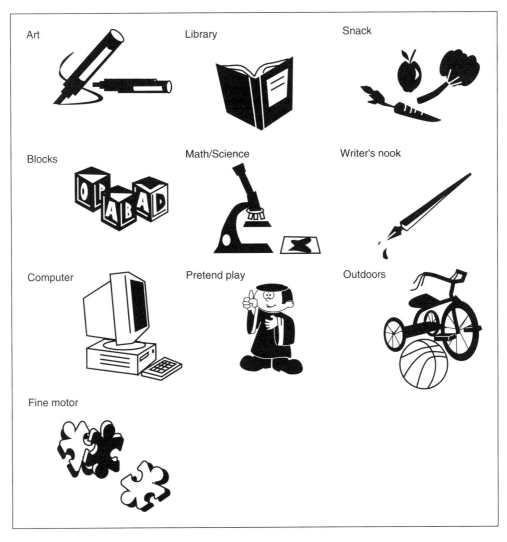

interest and hold it from the beginning of the story to the end (Machado, 2002). They do the following:

- ❏ Choose stories related to the children's interests
- ❏ Tell both familiar stories and new stories
- ❏ Know their story well (which often includes practicing the story beforehand)
- ❏ Begin the story in a dramatic voice to get children's attention
- ❏ Maintain eye contact with individual children by continually scanning the group
- ❏ Change the speed, pitch, volume, and rhythm of their voice to correspond to the meaning of the story
- ❏ Articulate each word clearly
- ❏ Use dramatic pauses to build suspense or facilitate transitions between events in the story
- ❏ Change their voice for each character in the story
- ❏ Provide an opportunity for children to participate in the story by making sounds or appropriate gestures or having them say repeated phrases in chorus (such as "I'll huff and I'll puff and I'll blow your house down")

Music Time

In many programs music time is an essential feature of the daily schedule. Singing, experimenting with rhythm and beat, and moving to music are typical activities during these specialty-group activities (Andress, 1998). See chapter 9 for guidelines related to several kinds of music activities. In each case, music time emphasizes mutual enjoyment and interactive learning.

Read-Aloud Time

During read-aloud time, adults read to children. The aim is to provide adult reading models and to share literature with youngsters in the group. Teachers may also address such literacy goals as oral language, print concepts, and story sense. Picture books with large, colorful illustrations; Big Books; and chapter books make suitable reading materials, depending on the children's age and their interests. During read-aloud time, children do not sit in a circle but rather cluster around the adult, who often sits in a chair so that children can see and hear more easily. When illustrations are shown, the adult turns the pages from the bottom so that children have a clear view of the pictures. Holding the book up high enough for everyone to see is another essential strategy. Books with complex illustrations or small pictures are better read to children individually than in a large group. In many programs, read-aloud time is a daily activity.

In addition to whole-group approaches to reading aloud, young children need opportunities for close per-

sonal interactions around books (Davidson, 1996). Such opportunities are often better afforded in groups of four or five than with the whole class looking at the same book. Dividing the circle of children into smaller groups, with each group having a copy of the book, is an alternative to trying to show 20 children the pictures in a single book. Another alternative is to read a familiar book, such as *If You Give a Mouse a Cookie,* with children reading along in their own paperback copies.

Class Meetings

Class meetings deal with life in the classroom and are a form of children's self-government (Gartrell, 2003; Musson, 1994). They are usually aimed at topics and issues that directly affect the group as a whole, such as how to manage the use of the new computers, what to do when children tease each other, or what the class iguana's name should be. These meetings are primarily discussion activities in which both adults and children become actively involved. During these times, children explore problems, suggest solutions, and develop plans. Just as with any group time, class meetings have a clear purpose and are guided by rules everyone knows (e.g., one person talks at a time, children listen respectfully, participants have a choice to speak or not). Children as young as age 3 years can successfully participate in short meetings involving the whole group. Such meetings create a sense of community among children, which leads to increased cooperation and ownership of classroom decision making (Castle & Rogers, 1994). As children gain maturity and experience, class meetings may be scheduled regularly to ensure smooth classroom functioning and to provide opportunities for children to practice skills associated with democratic living (Glasser, 1985). Reaching consensus, learning to compromise, and making decisions by voting are typical skills that children gain by participating in class meetings.

Brainstorming Groups

K = What do we *K*now?
W = What do we *W*ant to know?
H = *H*ow do we want to find out?
L = What did we *L*earn?
H = *H*ow did we learn?

The KWHLH formula describes the content of specialty-group times that early childhood professionals use to increase children's understanding and involvement in their learning. Such instruction times are usually tied to a theme or a project that the children are studying. At an initial whole-group gathering, children brainstorm a list of what they know about a particular topic (Kohn, 1993). The adult does not comment on the accuracy of what children think they know. As a result, the first list often combines faulty ideas and accurate information. Next, the children create a list of what they want to find out and a third list of the means they may use to obtain answers to their questions. The information on these three lists influences both the teacher's planning and the children's. Once the theme or project is under way, the children add to the lists or revise them as appropriate. To conclude the unit, the group comes together to discuss what they learned and the strategies that led to their increased knowledge. This meeting becomes an additional brainstorming session in which children have an opportunity to consider a wide-ranging array of possibilities. Comparing their original ideas with what was true or with the processes actually used to discover what was true is an additional way children analyze their learning strategies and the outcomes of their involvement with the topic. An example of a set of KWHLH lists related to spiders that was generated by children in a multiage class (kindergarten through second grade) is presented in Figure 4.6.

Minilessons

On some occasions early childhood professionals want to convey specific information to the whole group. Providing instructions about how to carry out a fire drill, demonstrating place value, and teaching children map-reading strategies are examples. The best minilessons are concise. They also incorporate all the characteristics of active learning associated with developmentally appropriate practice; they are not simply lectures. This kind of whole-group instruction usually precedes small-group or individualized learning experiences that build on what was presented to the entire class. For instance, Felicitas Moreno wants to teach the first graders in her class some of the same writing processes professional writers use—gathering ideas before writing, writing more than one draft, revising what they have written, and editing their work for capitalization, punctuation, and spelling with the help of older peers or adults (McGee & Richgels, 2000). With this in mind, she conducts a *writer's workshop* for a few minutes each morning. Each writer's workshop is a minilesson on a single topic such as how to brainstorm ideas for something to write about or how to put ideas in order from beginning to end. Sometimes

FIGURE 4.6 KWHLH Lists About Spiders

What do we *know* about spiders?
Spiders are insects.
Spiders make webs.
Spiders crawl on walls.
Spiders are black.
Spiders are sometimes found in basements.

What do we *want* to know about spiders?
What do spiders do all day?
Why do they make webs?
What are baby spiders called?
How long do spiders live?

***How* do we want to find out about spiders?**
We can look in books.
We can watch spiders outside.
We can look for other places that spiders might live.
We can talk to people who know a lot about spiders.
We can watch a show about spiders.

What did we *learn* about spiders?
~~Spiders are insects.~~ Spiders are arachnids.
Spiders make webs. Most spiders spin webs.
    Webs help spiders catch insects to eat. Webs help to keep the spider safe. Some spiders are "wandering" spiders. They do not make webs.
Spiders eat bugs.

Spiders lay eggs.
Spiders crawl on walls.
Spiders are black. They can also be brown, white, and purple.
Most spiders are not poisonous. Do not touch a spider unless you know it is not harmful.
Spiders have eight legs.
Spiders are sometimes found in basements.
Baby spiders are called *spiderlings*.
Spiders live about 1 year.
Spiders help people by eating insects that are harmful to plants.
People make up stories about pretend spiders like "Anansi."

***How* did we learn about spiders?**
We talked to Mr. Boyle (farmer) and Ms. Kumar (librarian).
We made a spiderweb from string.
We found spiderwebs outside and at school.
We looked in books. We visited the library.
We made our own book about spiders.
We played a spider game.
We made "toothpick" spiders.
We watched two spiders.

Ms. Moreno demonstrates how to do something; sometimes the children work as a group to help one another. These minilessons are followed by a 15-minute writing period during which children work individually or in pairs.

Author's Chair

The author's chair specialty-group time gives children an opportunity to read something they have written (such as journals or self-designed books) to the group as a whole (McGee & Richgels, 2000). Usually two or three children who have indicated they are ready to share their writing are given a chance to read each day. After the reading, listeners ask questions (e.g., "What is going to happen next?" "How did you decide on the name of the story?"). They also provide feedback (e.g., "You thought up a really good title. It told exactly what the story was going to be about"; "The joke you added on the last page was a fun way to end the story"; "Those facts about toads were cool"). Such comments may be offered by children or adults. Author's circles highlight children's efforts to communicate their thoughts through writing and give group members a chance to celebrate one another's accomplishments.

Reporting Time

Reporting time provides an organized opportunity for children to describe something they have done or to

This young writer proudly shares her work from the author's chair.

show their work to peers. For instance, the 4-year-olds in Mrs. Reed's class have returned from a field trip to a bakery. Each child has a chance to describe one thing he or she saw. All the items are compiled on a master list that is later posted in the room. In John Kamwi's first-grade class, the children meet three times a week in the late afternoon to report on something they have learned that is related to the theme. Usually four or five children have a chance to report each day. Their reports may be completely oral or may involve showing the others things they have made or classroom materials (such as books or artifacts) related to what they are talking about. Some children complete a reporting form such as that presented in Figure 4.5 as a way to record how they spent their time during the day. Reporting time provides closure to the day's activities and fosters a sense of group involvement in each person's efforts.

COMMON QUESTIONS PRACTITIONERS ASK ABOUT WHOLE-GROUP INSTRUCTION

Having successful group times requires careful consideration of the answers to the following six questions.

1. *Should all children be required to participate in group time?* Early childhood professionals are divided in their response to this query. Some teachers believe that the goals of group time are so critical that every child should participate to the best of his or her ability, which means each child must go to the group and remain there. Other practitioners assume that, if group time is interesting enough, most children will want to join the group anyway but believe that children should not be required to do so. Youngsters who do not want to participate may engage in quiet activities away from the group so long as they do not disturb others. Such expectations often vary according to the children's age and developmental abilities. Consequently, younger, less experienced children may have more flexibility about participation than may older, more experienced youngsters. Whichever approach is used, the educator's expectations must be clear and consistent so that children know what is appropriate and which behaviors demonstrate compliance.

2. *What are some strategies for facilitating conversations among a large group of children?* Many group-time activities involve engaging children in conversation. However, some adults are so worried that the discussion might get away from them that they hesitate to carry out this form of whole-group instruction. Instead, they rigidly enforce a "no talking" rule. Other group leaders attempt discussions only to have them end in chaos or with little accomplished. Both problems can be avoided by helping children learn skills associated

with the art of conversation (Freiberg & Driscoll, 2000). The place to begin is in small groups of two or three children with an adult. Even grown-ups find conversing in groups of 20 people difficult. Conversations can occur at various times of the day, formally or informally, and indoors or outdoors. Prompting discussions with open-ended questions, reminding children about oral turn taking, paraphrasing one child's words to another child, and helping children relate their response to the idea expressed by their peer are all ways to enhance children's conversational abilities.

Some tips for facilitating group conversations follow: Introduce whole-group discussions by incorporating children's spontaneous remarks into the normal flow of the group-time activities. Eventually move to purposeful group conversations. Use the strategies described in chapter 3 related to guided-participation, problem-solving, and discussion activities. If several children want to speak at once, create a conversation lineup: "First we'll listen to LaVelle, then Duane, then Grace." Periodically remind children of the central question they are answering, and recap what has been said so far. Avoid setting up situations in which children must answer in ways that are absolutely correct or incorrect. Conversations are not oral tests. If a child says something that is obviously incorrect, do not say, "Wrong!" but do not ignore the remark. Otherwise, you may perpetuate the acquisition of erroneous information. Instead, find something correct in the response, then add a strategy or information to make it more accurate. For example, the children were talking about fish. One child pronounced that little fish eat big fish. The teacher replied, "You know that fish sometimes eat each other. I'm not sure who eats whom. Let's spend some time this afternoon finding out if little fish eat big fish or if big fish eat the little ones. During our reporting group, we can tell people what we discovered." Another strategy is to ask for group responses as well as individual replies to questions you pose. Mr. Gogglin does this as part of an estimating activity when he says, "Earlier today some people thought there might be 100 marbles in this jar. Who here estimates that the number of marbles in this jar is 100?" On a large easel pad nearby, he records the names of children who say they agree or who make some physical sign of agreement. Next, he asks, "Who estimates that there are fewer marbles than that?" Children respond, and he records their names. Returning to a one-person-at-a-time procedure, Mr. Gogglin says, "Stephen, you said you thought there were fewer marbles. Tell us how you decided that."

Finally, keep initial group discussions short. Gradually increase their length and complexity as children become more comfortable and adept.

3. *What should the group leader do when children interrupt a story or a presentation?* The best way to avoid interruptions is to make sure children are comfortable and in a good position to see before you begin. Doing so prevents complaints of "Teacher, I can't see" or "Teacher, she's squishing me." Another strategy is to tell children before you begin that they will have a chance to talk when you are finished. However, children who make a connection between what you are doing and their own lives may find waiting too difficult. Two options are available when this happens: Incorporate their remarks into the ongoing presentation, or remind them to save their comments for the end. Sometimes the two can be combined. For example, a teacher is reading the book *Green Eggs and Ham,* by Dr. Seuss. Jeremy interrupts excitedly, "I had eggs for breakfast. Mine were scrambled." Immediately, the other children chime in with comments about eggs and breakfast. The teacher treats their remarks as signs of interest and says, "It sounds like you know a lot about eggs and breakfast. Let's hear what Sam did about those green eggs he had, and we'll talk about your eggs when the story is over." She continues reading. This kind of gentle redirection is more helpful and less disruptive than a long discourse on how impolite interrupting is. If the children continued, she might momentarily close the book and say something such as "You have lots to say. This story is most fun when you can hear the rhythm of the words. If you keep interrupting, the rhythm will be spoiled. Wait until the story is over; then we will have a good long talk." After the story is over, she waits a moment to savor the mood and then expresses her appreciation to the children for waiting. Turning her attention to Jeremy, she says, "Now, Jeremy, tell me about those eggs you had for breakfast."

4. *What can be done to support easily distractible children?* If the group as a whole is having difficulty paying attention, such inattention may be a sign that group time has gone on too long or that the content is not relevant or engaging. In these situations, revise your group-time plans on the spot and rethink them for the future. However, if only one or two children consistently have difficulty remaining focused, more-targeted techniques are advisable. These techniques, which are designed to help children be more successful and get the most out of whole-group experiences, are as follows.

❑ Tell children who have difficulty settling down in group what will be happening during group time before they enter it. For instance, during cleanup time each day, the teacher tells Carlita the topic or main activity that will be featured at circle time. This prompt helps Carlita make the mental transition from cleanup to group more comfortably.

❑ Have easily distractible children sit near an adult who can cue them as necessary (e.g., "Look up at the book" or "See the shell she is holding" or "Listen for what comes next"). If no other adult is available, the child could sit within arm's length of the leader (not on the leader's lap) to see and hear more clearly, without being the center of attention.

❑ With time, use a scaffolding strategy to help the child function more independently within the group. For instance, the child may begin the year by sitting on an adult's lap. Gradually supports would be withdrawn by having the child sit next to the adult, then sit one or two people away from the adult, and finally sit wherever in the circle he or she chooses.

❑ Give the child something for which to watch or listen (e.g., "This is a song about an animal. When I've sung it through, tell me what animal it was about"). This strategy could be implemented privately or with the whole group.

❑ Give the child something to do in the group—turn the pages or pass out the rhythm instruments.

❑ Ask the child to begin by participating in the group and then allow him or her to leave group time midway through and work quietly nearby. Gradually increase the amount of time the child stays with the group.

❑ Break the larger group into smaller groups so that easily distractible children have more opportunities for personal attention, less waiting, and fewer competing stimuli with which to cope.

5. *What should the group leader do when children become unhappy or angry during group time?* Clarissa is not pleased with the choice of rhythm instruments that are left when it is her turn to select one. Luellen cries when she does not get her favorite colored ribbon for creative movement. Jeremiah becomes angry when he does not get to sit next to a special friend in the circle. In each of these situations, the group leader is faced with having to tend to the needs of an individual child while trying to keep the activities going for the whole group. Group leaders can use several strategies in such circumstances.

❑ *Minimize potential problems over materials.* Ensure that enough materials are available so that even the last child has at least two or three items from which to select. Although the child may still not get his or her favorite, making a choice is a more palatable option to children than settling for the one that is left. Also, if children are using rhythm instruments or some other items, have them trade midway through the activity. Announce that this will happen before you pass out the

materials so that children will know that they will have more than one opportunity to select the object of their choice.

❑ *Acknowledge children's emotions with a simple nonevaluative statement.* "You really wanted the pink ribbon." "You were hoping to sit next to Carlos at group." When adults underscore children's emotions orally, they exhibit sensitivity and caring in a way children can understand. This acknowledgement makes children feel heard and accepted. Although such statements do not necessarily resolve the dilemma, they serve as a foundation for eventual problem solving. They also provide some comfort to children for whom no other satisfactory solution is possible at the time.

❑ *Problem solve whenever possible.* Give children information that may help them deal with their feelings (e.g., "In a few minutes we will be trading ribbons. You will have another chance to get a pink one"). When problems arise among children who have adequate conversational abilities, invite the child or others in the group to help devise a solution for now or the next time (e.g., "Jeremiah really wants to sit next to Carlos, but so do Ralph and Lauren. What can people do when more than one person wants to sit in the same place?"). This kind of problem solving could go on within the whole group or be carried out quietly between the concerned parties a little away from the group area. Depending on the flexibility of your agenda, such conversations could occur during group time or afterward.

❑ *If other adults are available, solicit their help rather than trying to deal with each problem yourself.* Signal the other adult nonverbally or use words: "Mrs. Johnson, please help Jeremiah find a spot to sit." "It looks like Luellen is sad. Please see what comfort you can give her."

❑ *When necessary, state clear, matter-of-fact limits.* Sometimes children may behave inappropriately. If this happens, acknowledge the child's concern, then give the child a positive direction about what to do next.

6. *What about show-and-tell?* Show-and-tell is a routine whole-group experience in many early childhood classrooms. However, the practice gets mixed reviews from teachers and parents (Hendrick, 2001; Spangler, 1997). Some people see show-and-tell as a means for children to develop both listening skills and speaking skills. Some like the idea that children have a chance to become the center of attention in an approved way. In contrast, some people express concern that children may become bored by sitting for long periods or

may feel coerced into speaking before the group. Still other individuals worry that children develop competitive feelings in the process or feel left out if they think they have nothing worthwhile to share. Each teacher must decide what to do about show-and-tell. If teachers choose to carry out this experience, they should have a clear curricular goal in mind and then select strategies to match the goal. For example, if the goal relates to listening and speaking, teachers must remember that children initially practice these skills best in small groups. Thus, having one day when groups of three or four children share items from home is a more appropriate strategy than having several children try to show and tell about their items in front of the entire class each day. To minimize the idea that show-and-tell is a time to show off, ask children to bring in items that fit particular criteria. For instance, "Bring in something blue or something that begins with the letter *k*, or something you found in your front yard." Also, make sure that children who have no items to share or who forget can find something to talk about by using materials available in the program. Before show-and-tell gets under way, establish some simple rules to govern how items will be supervised. Some early childhood educators require that items remain put away until the appointed time. Some teachers ask children to designate in advance whether the item is something they can only look at or can touch. Such precautions do much to prevent tears and conflicts. Finally, be prepared to ask children one or two open-ended questions about the items they brought. Telling children in advance what these questions will be often helps. Many young children have difficulty answering on the spot. They do better with some time to think about what they might say.

ADAPTATION OF WHOLE-GROUP INSTRUCTION FOR CHILDREN OF DIFFERENT AGES AND ABILITIES

Although the guidelines for whole-group instruction are the same for all children, some accommodations based on age and ability are necessary to enhance children's enjoyment and learning. Younger, less experienced children enjoy group times that share these characteristics:

Are short (10 to 15 minutes long)

Involve a lot of participation

Involve minimal talk

Include short songs and stories

Begin with a familiar activity each time (e.g., a song the children know well or a favorite finger play)

Older, more experienced children enjoy group times that are structured as follows:

Are longer (20 to 30 minutes long)

Involve a lot of participation

Include discussion

Include songs with several verses and more-complex stories

Involve both familiar and novel activities

Include an element of surprise

Focus on factual information as well as problem solving

Teachers working with children in mixed-age groups must consider all the children in the group rather than simply teaching "to the middle." Such consideration could involve starting with a whole group, implementing a short agenda, then dividing children into smaller groups to better accommodate their varying abilities and interests. Another strategy is to carry out an action-oriented body of the group time with everyone and then invite children who want to stay for a longer story or conversation to do so but dismiss the others to carry out quiet activities elsewhere in the room.

Sample group-time plans for younger preschoolers and a mixed-age group of children aged 6 through 8 years are presented in Figure 4.7. Review the sample group times presented in Figure 4.7. Decide how the two group times are similar and different. Look for evidence of how each group time was tailored to meet the needs of younger or older children.

PITFALLS TO AVOID DURING GROUP-TIME PLANNING

As described previously, whole-group instruction has many potential benefits for children. Unfortunately, these benefits are not always realized. Many of the problems associated with whole-group instruction could be averted by better planning. In the following subsections, we describe a few common mistakes educators make and ways to avoid them.

Failing to Prepare Adequately

Early childhood professionals are busy people. There are so many things to do in a day that planning whole-group instruction may seem impossible or unnecessary. Some practitioners assume that changing the songs and the book featured at group time each day is enough variety. Others may gather the children and do whatever comes to mind until the whole-group portion of the daily schedule is over. Still others have a general idea of

FIGURE 4.7 Sample Group Times for a 3-Year-Old Group and a Primary
School Mixed-Age Group

3-Year-Olds

Date: Monday, August 18, 2003   **Activity Name:** Rhythm Stick Fun

Age of Children: 3 years

Intermediate Objective(s): Children will explore the use of a musical instrument (rhythm sticks).

Content

1. Rhythm sticks are usually played by making a sound on the beat of the music.
2. *Beat* is the recurring pulse heard or sensed through the music.
3. There is more than one way to play rhythm sticks.
4. Playing rhythm sticks involves knowing when and when not to make sounds.

Materials: Rhythm sticks, enough for two per child and adult

Opening

1. Song, "Everybody, sit down, sit down, sit down, everybody, sit down, sit down here" (tune: "Everybody Do This"). Clap on the beat as you sing.
2. Transition to body—continue song, making motions in time with the beat. "Everybody, clap your hands, clap your hands, clap your hands, everybody, clap your hands, just like me. Everybody, tap your feet . . . everybody, shake your head . . ."

Body

3. Say: "We just sang a song using our hands and feet to make special sounds with the song. We'll sing that song again using musical instruments called *rhythm sticks*. Watch me as I show you how to use the rhythm sticks."
   Do: Take two of the rhythm sticks and demonstrate to the class how they work. Tap them together quietly, then louder; tap them quickly, then slowly; rub them together in a circular motion to make a gentle swishing sound. Tell the children what you are doing as you make the various sounds.
4. Say: "Before I pass out the sticks, I want to show you a signal that I will use when everyone's sticks must be quiet. When I hold the ends of my rhythm sticks on my shoulders like this, it means be quiet. When I play my sticks, that means it's time for you to play.

   "Now it's time to pass out the sticks. As you get your sticks, place them on your shoulder like this in the 'be quiet' position."
   Do: Ask the adults to pass out the rhythm sticks, and remind the children to hold the sticks against their shoulders. Model this behavior as the children receive their sticks.
5. Say: "Now that everyone has a rhythm stick, let's practice how to use them. Take your sticks and tap them together like this. Try tapping them fast like this. Now slowly. Tap them loud. Now softly. Rub your sticks together like this to make another kind of soft sound. You're doing a great job! Now let's sing a song while we play our instruments."

   Now sing, "Everybody, tap your sticks, tap your sticks, tap your sticks, everybody, tap your sticks, just like this." Keep singing the song, each time changing the method of tapping the sticks as practiced earlier. Match the way you sing the words with the way you play the sticks. For example, as you are tapping quietly, sing in a very quiet voice.

Closing

6. Say: "We have had a great time playing the rhythm sticks. That was fun. It's time now to pass your rhythm sticks to an adult."

Transition to Next Portion of the Day

7. Say: "Let's get in our jack-in-the-boxes."
   Do: Model huddling low to the floor on hands and knees, face in arms resting on the floor.
   Say: "Jack in the box, you sit so still. Won't you come out? Yes, I will."
   Do: On the last words, pop up on knees, hands outstretched above head. Repeat once more.
   Say: "This time stay in your jack-in-the-box until I tap you. Then you may get up and find a place to play."
   Do: Tap each child one at a time until all have been released from the group.

Evaluation Questions

1. To what extent were children able to use the rhythm sticks as modeled?
2. Did anyone have difficulty finding the beat? If so, what scaffolding strategy might you use to help him or her next time?
3. What future activities will you create based on the children's experience in this activity?

FIGURE 4.7 *(continued)*

Primary School Mixed-Age Group

Date: Monday, April 14, 2003   **Activity Name:** Global Fun

Age of Children: 6, 7, and 8 years

Intermediate Objective(s): Children will gain knowledge related to social studies (maps and globes).

Content

❑ A *globe* is a sphere on which a map of the earth is drawn.

❑ The brown and green shapes on the globe represent land.

❑ The blue shapes on the globe represent water.

❑ The earth's surface contains more water than land.

Materials: Books in book basket, calendar materials, poem chart with acetate cover, large flat map of the United States, "Waldo" character, state coloring chart, crayons, box with individual cards giving information about each of the 50 states, three plastic globes (about the size of a basketball), very small stickers (enough for each child to have one)

Transition into Opening

❑ **Books:** As children enter the room each day, they are greeted by the teacher and then choose books from a book basket on the group-time rug. Children read individually or with other children.

After 15 minutes the "book leader" collects the books and puts them in the basket while children sing the "bookworm" song.

Opening

❑ **Songs/chants:** One or two class favorites

❑ **Calendar:** Calendar helper locates yesterday, today, and tomorrow on calendar. Child adds a popsicle stick to the "ones" box to represent the number of days the children have been in school this year and writes the corresponding numeral.

❑ **Poem of the week:** (Poem about traveling) One child points to the words on the poetry chart as the group recites it together. The teacher calls on children to circle and read the words with *th, sh,* or *ch* digraphs.

Transition to Body

❑ **Movement activity:** Short stretching exercise that refers to geographic features (climb up the mountain, swim through the sea, etc.)

Body

❑ **State review:** Teacher says, "It's Cara's turn to choose a new state. She will move Waldo to a new state on the map of the United States." Cara chooses any state. Teacher asks her why she chose that state, asks the group if they know anything about the state or anyone who lives there, or if anyone has traveled there. Cara locates the state she chose on the coloring map and colors it in any color. Adult pulls the corresponding state card out of the state box and gives children some information about the state. Cara uses the pointer and points to each state previously chosen as children recite the names of the states.

❑ **Land or water game:** Adult divides children into three groups. Each group gets a globe.

Adult explains that this is a globe and that globes are a type of map. Adult uses guided-discovery strategies as children examine globes.

What do you notice about this object?

What do you think the colors mean?

(Adult provides information as necessary.)

What do you think you see more of—land or water?

Adult collects globes, puts two aside, and explains: "We're going to play a game to help us locate land and water on the globe. Raise the hand that you write with in the air. Now point to the ceiling with your pointer finger, and I am going to come around and put a sticker on your fingernail. Here are the rules to the game. When you have the globe, decide whom you will roll it to, then call out his or her name. Be sure to roll the globe." Adult demonstrates. "When you catch the globe, look at your sticker finger and decide if it has landed on land or water." Adult writes the words *water* and *land* on the board or on chart paper. "If your finger touches land, I will put a tally mark under that word. If your finger touches water, I will put a tally mark under that word. Which do you predict will have more tally marks, land or water? Why?"

(continued)

FIGURE 4.7 *(continued)*

> Group plays game until everyone has had a chance to catch the globe and identify land or water. At the game's end, adult and children count the tally marks and talk about the results.
>
> **Closing**
> ❏ Adult lets children know globes will be available if they would like to play the land and water game during free-choice time. Suggests the children could see if they get the same basic results each time.
>
> **Transition to Next Portion of the Day**
> ❏ Adult briefly describes choices available during free-choice time. Adult asks who would like to start on their journals (and so forth) and then dismisses children in small numbers as they indicate their choices.
>
> **Evaluation Questions**
> ❏ To what extent were children able to identify land and water?
> ❏ How accurate were children's observations?
> ❏ What unexpected outcomes may have occurred during this group time?
> ❏ What future activities will you create based on the children's experience in this activity?

Source: For 3-year-olds: Grace Spalding, Child Development Laboratories, Department of Family and Child Ecology, Michigan State University, East Lansing, Michigan. For primary school mixed-age group: Deborah Sharpe, Wilkshire Early Childhood Center, Haslett Public Schools, Haslett, Michigan.

what they want to accomplish but continually interrupt themselves or halt the group because they do not have everything they need immediately at hand. When this happens, children become restless and inattentive. Control problems proliferate under these circumstances, and children leave group time having gained little of educational value. The antidote for this problem is to plan ahead for whole-group instruction. Joanne Hendrick (2003), a long-time early childhood teacher/director and professor emerita at the University of Oklahoma, says,

> Providing educationally worthwhile group times takes self-discipline and energy combined with sincere convictions . . . self-discipline to sit down and plan such experiences in advance, energy to carry out plans once they have been made, and conviction that group time is valuable enough to make careful planning a consistent part of the program . . . not just once in a while, but daily. (p. 387)

At first, writing a whole-group plan for each group time will be necessary. Once the decision-making steps involved are internalized, written plans will become briefer, often encompassing only the educational objective and the highlighted feature activity for each whole-group segment of the day. An abbreviated group-time agenda for "The Three Billy Goats Gruff" group time featured previously in this chapter is presented in Figure 4.8.

Relying on Whole-Group Instruction to Meet Objectives Better Addressed in Smaller Groups

Sometimes practitioners plan activities using a whole-group format when children would benefit more from

working on the task with fewer peers. For instance, attending to others and waiting your turn to speak are important receptive-listening skills. Children learn these behaviors just as they learn everything else—gradually. Being expected to wait long enough for 10 or 20 other youngsters to say an idea, have a turn to touch the turtle, or come to the front of the group, one at a time, is inappropriate for most youngsters aged 3 to 8 years old. Although children need practice improving their

FIGURE 4.8 Abbreviated Group-Time Agenda

Activity Name: Whole-Group Storytelling

Intermediate Objective(s): Children will take on roles and act out their interpretations of these roles to tell a familiar story.

Opening: Sing the songs "Hello Everybody" and "I Had a Cat and the Cat Pleased Me."
Transition to the body—Talk about the animals in the song; lead into the animals in the story.

Body: Introduce whole-group storytelling.
Begin "The Three Billy Goats Gruff" story; continue by encouraging children to act out various roles.
Announce "The End."

Closing: Review with the children the ways in which they acted like the billy goats and the troll. Acknowledge the children's participation.

Transition to Next Portion of the Day: Dismiss by shoe color or type to go outdoors.

turn-taking skills, task analysis would suggest that the wait time must be reduced. One way to accomplish this time reduction is to divide the children into smaller groups for discussions and other turn-taking activities. For example, during scheduled group times, preschoolers could be divided into smaller groups according to the number of adults available. First- and second-grade children could be divided into self-directed groups of four or five children each. Children would complete a task and then reconvene as a whole. For example, the teacher has a variety of seashells for children to examine. Rather than passing the seashells around the entire circle one at a time, she has the children form four smaller groups within the large-group area. Each group is given four or five seashells to look at, which allows the youngsters to handle and examine the seashells without much waiting. After several minutes, all 20 children come together again to talk about what they observed.

Another strategy is to reserve activities that require much waiting for periods in the day other than group time. This does not mean that children should never have to wait as part of whole-group instruction. However, such periods should be brief.

Selecting Inappropriate Materials

Picture books with illustrations that are too small, too pale, or too busy for children to see clearly; songs that have too many verses; flannel board pieces that do not stick; incomplete items; and equipment that malfunctions are examples of inappropriate group-time materials. Whole-group activities that rely heavily on talk with few other sensory prompts are also poor choices. Likewise, items that support the theme but undermine other curricular goals should be avoided or revised to make them more appropriate. This was the case for Marlene Grubbs, who wanted to teach children about settings in which community workers functioned. Searching through the program's picture file, she found a set of community helper pictures that were large, colorful, and supportive of her main idea. Unfortunately, they depicted only male workers and did not represent the full range of possibilities for boys and girls that Marlene wanted to portray. Rather than being satisfied with the pictures as they were, Marlene sought additional images that included women. This kind of attention to detail helped Marlene ensure that her group-time materials were appropriate both in terms of her short-range objectives (supporting the theme) and her long-range goals (promoting respect for both genders).

Incorporating Too Many Routinized Activities

In some classrooms, daily activities such as using the calendar, completing a weather chart, assigning class-room jobs, having show-and-tell, and taking roll all take place during whole-group instruction. Furthermore, often many of these routines are combined in the same time period. This practice makes group times longer and shortens the time available for other whole-group activities. Consequently, children's enthusiasm for group time may be dulled, children wait long periods, and they are exposed to the core of group-time activities when they are no longer fresh and interested. Several ways to prevent these negative outcomes are available. One is to eliminate some routines. Some early childhood professionals strongly believe activities such as using the calendar and having show-and-tell are developmentally inappropriate because of their abstract nature and their use of procedures that may create competition or unfavorable comparisons among children (Brewer, 2001; L. Katz, 1996). However, many practitioners believe that certain classroom rituals add to the predictability of the day and that children benefit from making choices or participating in discussions relative to such matters. No matter which routines you decide are appropriate for the children in your class, always remember to consider each in terms of what children are learning and whether whole-group instruction is the best mode for approaching such learning. For instance, attendance could be completed as children arrive, and completing the weather chart could be a learning center activity instead of a mandatory whole-group endeavor each day. Similarly, show-and-tell could shift from being a whole-group activity to an activity carried out in small groups. In addition, because many programs have more than one group time a day, essential routines can be divided among them. Doing so frees time for children and teachers to engage in other, more varied whole-group activities.

Waiting Too Long to Engage Children in Active Learning

Diane (4 years old): It's [circle time] boring. We just have to be listening, listening, listening, and I don't like that.
—*Wiltz and Klein (2001, p. 225)*

A long-winded opening that consists of 15 minutes of telling and explaining before the educator gets to something more engaging in the body of the group time is too long for most children aged 3 to 8 years old. Likewise, asking 3- and 4-year-olds to sit through using the calendar, singing four songs, and listening to a story before dancing with scarves is pushing the limits of their abilities. Even youngsters in the first and second grade find sitting so long with no other form of engagement demanding. Group time is not a synonym for *sit time,* nor does whole-group instruction have to be passive.

The best group times include periods of active movement.

Planning appropriate group times means getting children actively involved early in the procedure and often. Such engagement can take many forms. For example, children who are singing a song can do the motions, clap or slap their thighs in time to the music, change positions (stand up, sway, crouch, put their hands over their head, and so forth), listen for certain words or phrases in the song, vary the volume and pitch of their voices, vary the speed of the words, and engage in call and response. Children listening to a story can become more active participants by responding with a motion to various instructions within the story, saying a repeated line in chorus, miming some of the characters' actions, or filling in a word or a line as relevant.

A guided-discovery activity could include items for children to handle as well as questions to answer as they go along rather than having all the talk at the end of the procedure. During a demonstration children might watch for certain things to happen or signal the leader in a special way when they note a process is beginning or ending. Youngsters may also talk the leader through a demonstrated procedure, catch the leader making "mistakes," or imitate actions by pantomiming or using objects.

Allowing Group-Times to Go on Too Long

Donnie (whining): I don't like doing circle.
Adult: Why?
Donnie: Because it always takes too long.
—Wiltz and Klein (2001, p. 220)

Early childhood professionals have different beliefs regarding the suitability of large-group time for preschoolers. Some individuals counsel against using whole-group instruction with children 3 and 4 years old (Brewer, 2001). Others caution that such times should last only a few minutes a day and lengthen gradually as children become more experienced (Hendrick, 2001). As children in kindergarten and first and second grade develop group-time skills, their overall ability to enjoy and benefit from whole-group activities as long as 20 to 30 minutes increases. However, this fact remains true only as long as the other criteria defining appropriate group times, such as active involvement and purposeful activity, are maintained. No matter what age the children are, group time is best ended before children lose interest. Thus, group time follows the theatrical adage, "Always leave them wanting more." Remember, too, that activities carried out in group time should be repeated or supplemented beyond the whole-group instruction period. For instance, a flannel board story featured during group time could be made available in the library corner for children to use to reenact the story, the materials to conduct an experiment demonstrated at group time could be offered to smaller groups of children later in the day, and the book written, published, and read by a first- or second-grade "author" can be displayed for children to reread on their own.

All the whole-group instruction activities described so far occur daily or at least weekly. Other whole-group activities that occur less frequently but are also important to children's learning are field trips into the community.

FIELD TRIPS

A walk around the block, a trip to the grocery store, and an excursion to the local arboretum all provide active, concrete opportunities for children to learn about people, places, and things outside the immediate realm of the classroom. Excursions into the community broaden children's understanding of the world in which they live and offer ways to diversify the curriculum through firsthand experience (B. J. Taylor, 2003a). Such trips may be as simple as visiting the mailbox on the corner or as elaborate as a day at the museum. They may take only 20 minutes to complete or occupy most of the session. Sometimes they may require transportation. No matter what the circumstances, all field trips require careful planning, implementation, and follow-up.

Field Trip Planning

Planning a successful field trip requires generating thoughtful answers to the following questions.

1. *What is the purpose of the trip?* Because the function of field trips is to help children make sense of the

world, they, like all other educational activities, must have a definite purpose clearly tied to the curriculum (Eliason & Jenkins, 2003). The best way to ensure that this happens is to plan around one or two objectives within any of the curricular domains described in this book. For example, a trip to a garden could focus on plant identification (cognitive domain), or it could emphasize children's using all their senses to experience the wonder and beauty of the garden (aesthetic domain). Although one focus does not entirely preclude the other, the activities you carry out at the garden will differ depending on the goal you choose. For instance, to foster plant identification skills, Eileen Verstoefel organized a plant scavenger hunt to stimulate children's interest in recognizing certain plants. Each small group of children had a plant book and notepad to use to record their observations. Adult comments at the garden centered around labeling the plants and promoting children's observations aimed at differentiating one plant from another.

The strategies associated with an aesthetic goal would not be the same. For instance, to encourage children to use their senses, the teacher might have them sit in a circle, close their eyes, listen quietly, and then describe the sounds they hear. Youngsters would be urged to smell the plants and touch them gently. Arranging with garden personnel to allow children to taste some edible plants would also contribute to children's aesthetic awareness. The names of the plants would not be emphasized nearly so much as the sensory impressions children were having. In each case, children would learn from their garden experience, but the primary result of such learning would have been shaped by the purpose of the trip.

2. *What is your destination?* Many wonderful places are available for children to visit in their communities. Refer to Table 4.1 for a partial listing of these. However, not every site is appropriate for every group of children. For instance, a place that is fascinating to 8-year-olds (such as the local television station they watch every day) could be incredibly boring and incomprehensible to 3-year-olds. Likewise, visiting a greenhouse could be interesting if the plants are low enough for children to see easily but frustrating and ineffective if the plants are on high shelves far above the children's eye level. Thus, after you choose a potential site on the basis of what you want the children to learn, visiting the site in advance to determine its suitability is important.

During this preliminary visit, do the following:

❏ *Consider to what extent the site allows children to act like children.* This consideration includes allowing children to (a) move about freely, (b) make some noise, and (c) participate in a hands-on activity rather than remaining passive observers (Hendrick, 2001). The more closely the site meets these conditions, the more successful the trip will be.

❏ *Determine how well the site will support your educational goals.* Preview what children will actually see, hear, and do. If on-site personnel are to be involved, talk with them in advance, discussing the developmental needs of the children involved, the amount of time available, and the group size. Remember that a field trip that worked well with a previous group of children may or may not be suitable for the current group with whom you are working. Also, people and places change. Make a preliminary visit even if you have been to a location before.

TABLE 4.1 Potential Field Trip Sites

Orchard	Dentist's or doctor's office	Bakery
Greenhouse	Veterinarian's office	Retail store
Garden	Artist's studio	Restaurant
Natural wooded area	Television or radio studio	Museum
Park	Newspaper office	Garage
Butterfly house	Construction site	Car wash
Fish hatchery	Fire station	Bus ride
Stream or pond	Post office	Library
Farm	Train, truck, or air terminal	Grocery store or market
Nature center	Boat dock or marina	Pet store
Planetarium	Home for the elderly	Water treatment plant
Aviary	Hairstyling shop	Recycling center
Aquarium	Weather station	Theater
Meadow or plain	Lumber yard	Laundromat
Bridge	Gymnasium	Stadium
City fountain	Ice rink or roller rink	Teacher's home

❑ *Determine how long the trip will take.* Inexperienced and younger children as well as children enrolled in half-day programs should spend no more than 20 minutes walking or riding (one way) to the site. Older, more experienced youngsters enrolled in full-day programs can tolerate as much as 1 hour of riding time in one direction without ill effect (Eliason & Jenkins, 2003; Michigan Family Independence Agency, 1996). No matter how attractive the final destination is, if children have been walking or riding too long to get there, they will neither enjoy nor benefit from the experience.

❑ *Consider how to meet children's biological needs during the trip.* Such needs include using the toilet, having access to food and water, and resting periodically. If meeting these needs is not possible, choose another place to visit.

❑ *Check the site for accessibility to persons with special needs.* Will everyone have easy access to all areas of the site where the group will be visiting? Excluding any member of your party because of inaccessibility is not acceptable. In addition, think through how children, family members, or staff members with special needs will benefit from traveling to this site. If the benefits are few, choose another site.

❑ *Check for potential safety hazards,* both at the site and getting there and back. Make every effort to ensure all participants' safety. Any place in which safety is questionable is inappropriate.

❑ *Determine logistical details specific to the site.* For instance, determine a potential meeting place outside or inside the facility, suggest a sequence through the facility, identify where to take shelter in case it rains or is too hot, and describe what to be sure to see or avoid.

Once the site has been selected and confirmed, early childhood professionals continue planning by answering the next seven questions.

3. *When will the trip occur?* The time and date of the trip will be influenced by site availability, access to transportation (if necessary), availability of adult support, and the time of day when children are most alert and comfortable. Another factor to consider is whether the trip will serve as an introduction on which future classroom experiences will build or function as a summary experience aimed at helping children synthesize what they have learned. For example, on the one hand, if the children are engaged in a project about public transportation, a trip to the bus station early in their investigation could enrich subsequent activities. On the other hand, visiting the bus station later in their study might prompt children to make connections that would not be obvious earlier. Either point in time has its advantages and its disadvantages, and these should be considered as part of your planning.

4. *How will children get to the site?* Whether you have planned a walking field trip or a field trip requiring transportation, you must think through the route you will take and anticipate any problems that might arise on the way.

For a walking field trip, walk the route yourself, remaining alert to potential dangers such as construction or fast-moving traffic. Plan how you want the children to walk: single file, as partners, holding hands, or paired with an adult. Prepare to take along a lightweight STOP sign for an adult to hold up in case you reach a difficult corner without crossing assistance. Be realistic about how far your class can walk in comfort. If necessary, plan to walk in only one direction. For example, children may walk to the post office several blocks away and then return by van to the center or school.

For field trips requiring transportation, the program may provide drivers as well as buses or vans. In many programs, transportation must be arranged several weeks in advance, and permission must be obtained from appropriate program supervisors. Other programs rely on parent volunteers to drive. When you are soliciting adult drivers from children's families, provide advance notice so that you can be sure enough vehicles and seat belts are available. In addition, make sure every driver has a legal driver's license and appropriate insurance. Soliciting backup drivers in case someone cannot go at the last minute is a good idea as well. If you are going by car, each vehicle should have these items:

a. A map showing the route between the program and the field trip site
b. A written record of the telephone numbers of the early childhood program and the site you will be visiting
c. A list of all persons riding in the vehicle
d. A seat belt for each person
e. A field trip first-aid kit (bandages, soap, moist towelettes, paper cups, a fresh container of potable water)
f. An emergency card for each child riding in the vehicle, listing a place to reach the parent and emergency medical information (these are required by law for all children enrolled in most state-licensed preschool programs and are a good idea for elementary children, too)
g. A list of sample songs to sing or information for adults to share with children on the way to the site or while returning to the program
h. A schedule for the day, including specified times for gathering, such as snack and lunch times; a designated time for leaving; and a list of procedures in case someone gets lost or becomes ill

Prepare all these items in advance and have them on hand the day of the trip.

5. *What kind of supervision will be necessary?* Adult supervision involves keeping children safe as well as drawing their attention to relevant features of the trip, extending concepts, and answering questions. Plan supervision on the basis of the number of children going as well as logistical considerations such as having to cross busy streets or going to a crowded location in which keeping track of more than two or three children at once may be difficult for any one adult. If possible, the group leader should not be responsible for a particular group of children. Such leeway will allow him or her to keep a global view of the group as a whole, to more easily address unexpected problems that may arise, and to interact with resource people at the site as necessary. For children aged 3 to 5 years, a ratio of one adult to every three or four children is desirable; for youngsters 6 to 8 years old, one adult should be assigned to every five or six children (Eliason & Jenkins, 2003; Michigan State University Child Development Laboratories, 1997). Regardless of how small the group might be, at least two adults should always go along. If you are going by car, van, or bus, plan to have two adults in each vehicle: one to drive and one to supervise the children. In addition, at least one adult must be available to stay at the center or the school if a child does not have permission to go on the trip or if a child refuses to participate. If not enough adults are available to carry out the trip safely and enjoyably, the trip should be postponed until adequate supervision is available.

6. *How will permission be obtained for children to participate?* In most states, parents or guardians must grant permission before children can take part in any excursion away from the center or school. In some programs, families are asked to sign a blanket form once a year to allow children to take part in program-sponsored field trips; in other programs, separate permission slips are required for each trip. A sample consent form is presented in Figure 4.9. Even when parents provide blanket permission, they must be notified before each field trip and told when and where the children will be going. *No child may go on a field trip without written permission from his or her parent or guardian.* Follow-up telephone calls or written reminders are sometimes necessary to acquire all appropriate permissions.

7. *In what ways might parents or other family members be involved in the field trip?* Field trips provide great opportunities to include parents and other family members in children's educational experiences. Inviting

FIGURE 4.9 Field Trip Announcement/Consent Form

Part 1: Introduction: Where (name and location of site), when (day and date), and why (purpose of trip) you are going.

Part 2: Permission for child to participate: (Child's name) has my permission to participate in the field trip described above. I understand that transportation will be provided by (private automobile/program vehicles) and that the group will be leaving (name of program) at approximately (insert time) and returning at approximately (insert time).

_____
(parent/guardian signature/date)

Part 3: Opportunity to decline participation: I prefer that my child not participate in the field trip described above and will make alternate arrangements for her/his care on that day.

(Or, depending on program policy)

I prefer that my child not participate in the field trip described above and expect that he or she will remain at the program site that day.

_____
(parent/guardian signature/date)

Part 4: Request for drivers: I would be willing to drive. My vehicle is in safe operating condition, it is insured, and I have a valid driver's license. My vehicle has _____ seat belts in addition to one for the driver.

This permission form was created by Donna Howe, specialist, Department of Family and Child Ecology, Michigan State University.

parents to come along on a trip to the farm, to the river to feed the ducks, or to the bicycle shop promotes home–school interaction and contributes to a sense of community among children and adults. Moreover, family members can provide supervision or transportation to make certain trips possible. Another option is to visit a parent's workplace and have him or her serve as tour guide. In any case, if you plan to have parents participate, they must be given ample notice of when and where the trip will take place, its purpose, and what their role will be. Written notification is a must. When this information is supplemented by personal invitations, parents know they are truly welcome.

8. *How will the lesson continue after the field trip?* For children to get the most out of a field trip, they must have opportunities to tell what they have learned and to build on their experience after they return to the center or school. Plan how this will happen. Do not leave such learning to chance.

9. *What is your backup plan?* Anticipate what might go wrong and have an alternative strategy in mind for these dilemmas. What will you do if a driver calls in sick, how will you handle someone's getting lost en route, what will you do if at the last minute a parent says his or her child cannot participate? The time to determine what to do in such circumstances is beforehand, not afterward. In addition, sometimes unexpected events happen that prompt cancellation of the trip—a site might unexpectedly close, or it may rain on field trip day. Thus, every field trip plan should include what you will do if the original activity falls through or does not take the full amount of time you allotted.

Only after you have answered all these questions satisfactorily are you ready to carry out the field trip you have planned.

Field Trip Day

Children learn best and support personnel are most helpful when they have an idea of what will happen before, during, and after a field trip. Thus, the first step in field trip implementation is preparing children and adults for what to expect.

Preparing the Children

At the Hilltop Nursery School, children have been involved for several days in a variety of activities focused on vehicles and vehicle repair. Today, Ms. Oblicki uses a whole-group information time to prepare children for a trip to a local garage. She explains that during this trip they will have a chance to see mechanics using a variety

of tools and machines to work on vehicles. The teacher describes how the children will be divided into small groups and that each group will be assigned to a particular adult. The children are cautioned to remain with their group at all times. Ms. Oblicki explains what will happen once they arrive at the garage and the rules everyone must follow with regard to the tools and the vehicles. Next, she invites the children to talk about what they think they will see. She makes a list of their ideas and encourages them to look for these items when they get to their destination. The teacher says they will refer to this list when the group returns from their outing.

The children at the Walnut Acres after-school program will walk several blocks to see different kinds of buildings along the route. The children have traveled this path many times before but with different purposes in mind. Prior to assembling the children, the teacher follows the route, taking pictures of distinctive buildings along the way. Back at the school, he puts the pictures on a bulletin board and invites the children to look at them throughout the week, explaining that these are sites they will see during their walk. The morning of the outing, the children select partners. They are reminded that they will be walking side by side, not running. Next, the teacher challenges the children to look along the way for the places they saw in the pictures. Each pair of children is given one building to find. He mentions that when they get back, they will have a chance to talk about "their buildings." They may even try to arrange the pictures in the order in which they appeared during the walk.

In each teacher's preparation of the children for the field trip, he or she included the following information: a reason for the trip, group assignments, what to expect, what to look for, safety precautions, and necessary limits. Such information helps children behave in constructive, safe ways and get the most out of their field trip experience. Final details include making sure the children have had a chance to use the toilet and minimizing the amount of wait time required for them to stand in line or sit bundled up in a vehicle before the trip begins. Providing the children with colorful tags to wear on which the program name and telephone number are prominently displayed is a safety precaution required by many programs. These tags provide valuable information in case a child becomes separated from the group, but they do not reveal the child's name to strangers.

Preparing the Adults Just as children benefit from advance knowledge, so do adults. Adults accompanying children on a field trip need to hear everything involved in the children's preparation as well as guidelines regarding their supervisory responsibilities. Adults feel more comfortable when they have been informed of the rules and any special considerations, such as how to interact with a child who moves only with the aid of a walker or strategies to help an easily frustrated child feel more relaxed during the trip. Volunteers and support staff will be better able to support the field trip focus if you clarify what it is and provide a few ideas of things they might do or say in keeping with the focus. Provide such guidelines in writing as well as orally. Ask volunteers to arrive a few minutes early so that there is enough time to orient them to the trip, and allow them to ask questions as necessary.

Supervising at the Field Trip Site Four phrases characterize what should happen while any field trip is in progress: count, teach, remain flexible, enjoy.

Count Know exactly how many youngsters are in the group. Count the children frequently throughout the time you are away. *Never* leave the field trip site itself or any stop along the way without making certain every child is present.

Teach Remember that field trips are firsthand experiences aimed at enhancing children's understanding of the world around them. Teaching strategies associated with guided-instruction and problem-solving activities are well suited to these experiences. Brief instances of direct instruction may also be appropriate. With these strategies in mind, follow through on the curricular focus you planned for the trip. Draw children's attention to relevant cues in the environment, and respond to children's remarks with this focus in mind. If you have prepared the adults adequately, they should support the educational aims of the trip. If you notice that some people seem to have forgotten these purposes, offer gentle reminders or model a few sample things to say or do.

Remain Flexible Take advantage of spontaneous events from which children might benefit. For instance, the children were visiting the Sun Rise Restaurant to see noodles being made by hand. The purpose of the field trip was for children to develop an awareness of and respect for the traditions and culture of others. While they were there, several children noticed the restaurant owner's many songbirds kept in large bamboo cages in the garden. They were intrigued. Did people eat the birds, they wondered? Why were there so many birds? Did the birds have names? Clearly, the birds had captured the children's interest. Rather than ignoring the children's queries, the field trip leader asked the owner if he would talk about the birds and if the children could see them. What followed was

a delightful exchange between owner and children in which children learned about a Hong Kong custom the owner was proud to share. Noodle making was no longer a central focus as youngsters admired the birds and interacted with them in the garden. Although the original activity was revised, the goal of the trip was fulfilled. The teacher's flexibility enabled the children to follow through on their interests while simultaneously engaging in an activity that supported the trip's purpose.

Enjoy If you have planned well, the implementation of the field trip should proceed relatively smoothly. You should not be so frazzled with last-minute adjustments and details that there is no time to appreciate the site you have visited or to interact with the children during the time there. Appropriate planning and preparation will make field trip day more relaxed and enjoyable.

After the Field Trip

Activities A field trip does not end when children return to the early childhood program. Youngsters need opportunities to reflect on what they saw, heard, and experienced. Field trip plans should include one or more follow-up activities in which children

Back in the classroom after a field trip to an animal hospital, these boys recreate what they saw.

- Participate in group discussions
- Look at pictures or make an album of pictures taken on the trip
- Draw pictures or make a collage related to the trip
- Dictate stories about what they experienced
- Write in their journals or create a group newsletter to send home to family members, outlining the key concepts they learned
- Reconstruct the field trip experience during pretend play or with blocks
- Role-play in relation to the trip
- Use items collected during the trip to create something back at the center or school (e.g., children make soup from vegetables purchased at the grocery, or they make a classroom reference book from the leaves they gathered on a nature walk)
- Visit the site again, with a new goal in mind (e.g., children make repeated visits to a pond during the year, attending to different details each time)

Thank-You Note Every field trip should end with the children's drawing pictures or writing letters thanking volunteers who provided supervision on the trip or people who guided their visit at the field trip site. These tokens of appreciation can be created individually or generated by the group. Not only do thank-you activities provide a sense of closure to the trip, but they also demonstrate the role of courtesy in community living.

Evaluation As soon after the field trip as possible, the experience should be evaluated (B. J. Taylor, 2003a). What did the children gain from the trip? How well was the educational purpose of the trip fulfilled? To what extent did the trip proceed as expected? What were some things you did not anticipate? What were the strengths of the trip? How could the trip have been improved? Would you recommend returning to the same place another time? Why or why not? What follow-up activities would best support the children's learning? What might family members like to know about the children's experience? Questions such as these could be answered by the children and the adults. The answers should be incorporated into future planning.

Field Trip Example

Early in the fall, teachers at the El Shabaz Child Development Center decided to capitalize on the children's enjoyment of citrus fruit by taking them to see oranges growing in a grove. Following preliminary visits to two sites, the teachers selected Bird's Orange Grove as a field trip destination. A summary of what they thought about when they were planning, carrying out, and following up on the field trip is presented in Figure 4.10.

Field Trip Alternatives

Field trips are wonderful learning opportunities for children and adults, but sometimes they are not the best option for a particular group of children at a particular time. For instance, early in the year, when children are not accustomed to program routines or are just beginning to develop trusting relationships with program adults, field trips may cause unnecessary disruptions in the daily routine. On other occasions, the field trip site may be too far away, too costly, or too difficult to reach to make the journey worthwhile. One option is to make on-site excursions in the building or on program grounds to acclimatize children to functioning in a whole group away from the classroom. A visit to the office, the boiler room, the kitchen, or the marshy area outside, or a hunt for insects on program property provides an excellent opportunity for expanding children's learning beyond classroom boundaries.

SUMMARY

Most early childhood classrooms include some whole-group instruction each day. The most common whole-group experiences are group times. Group times can be used to enhance learning across the curriculum and to develop a sense of community within the classroom. The extent to which such benefits are derived is directly influenced by the quality of the planning and preparation that go into them. The format for writing group-time plans maintains some of the same planning elements described for other kinds of activity plans. One difference is that the procedures section outlines the opening, the body, and the closing of the activity. Another difference is that a specific strategy is identified for helping children move from group time to the next portion of the day. Group times may be traditional in form or serve specialty functions in early childhood classrooms. Typically both types of group times are used sometime during the day. Pitfalls to avoid in planning or implementing group-time activities include the following: failing to prepare adequately, using whole-group instruction when an individual or small-group experience would better facilitate children's learning, selecting inappropriate materials, making too many routinized activities part of group time, waiting too long to engage children in active learning, and failing to end whole-group instruction soon enough. The bad news is that these mistakes can negate the positive benefits children could potentially derive from group-time learning

FIGURE 4.10 A Field Trip to the Orange Grove

I. Planning and Preparation
 A. Planning
  1. Purpose: For children to learn how oranges grow
  2. Destination: Bird's Orange Grove
  3. When: Friday, September 19, 9 A.M.
  4. Travel: Fifteen minutes by car one way; volunteer drivers needed. At least 23 seat belts necessary for children and staff; adult volunteers would add to this total.
  5. Supervision: One adult for every four children; at least two adults needed beyond current staff.
  6. Permission: All families notified beforehand of location, time, and goal of trip. Written permission obtained from all parents/guardians for children to participate.
  7. Family Involvement: Weekly newsletter used to invite adult family members to drive and to request family orange recipes.
 B. Preparing the Children
  1. One week before: Trip culminated the week's activities about oranges: Children tasted oranges, made orange juice, saw pictures of oranges growing, and pretended to sell oranges in a make-believe fruit stand; books were available about oranges and how they grow.
  2. Day before: Talked with children about what they thought they would see at the orange grove. Asked them to generate a list of questions they wanted answered on the visit. Talked about strategies such as asking and observing to get answers.
  3. Field trip day: Told children purpose of trip, reminded them of questions generated day before, divided them into groups of four children per adult (this was accomplished by using color-coded tags), reminded children of appropriate behavior in cars and on the trip.
 C. Preparing the Adults
  1. One week before: Arranged transportation including backup drivers, collected and prepared necessary materials (map, lists of children, field trip first-aid kits, snack items). Made sure there were one driver and one adult rider per vehicle.
  2. Day before: Confirmed drivers and volunteers one last time.
  3. Field trip day: Prepared adults with specific guidelines and relevant information. Described purpose, key vocabulary, and things to look for or point out to children at the orchard. Talked about what to do if a group became separated from the others, where the bathrooms were, and how to support James (a child with Down's syndrome). Emphasized that adults were to keep track of the four children assigned to them.
II. At the Orange Grove
 A. Used questions generated by the children as a basis for what to look for and ask about at the grove.
 B. Made sure each child had a chance to see the grove, the orange press, and the fruit market.
 C. Took photographs of the experience.
 D. Purchased some oranges to take back to the program.
 E. Counted frequently: made sure children stayed with the group.
III. After the Trip
 A. Thanked all adult participants for their help.
 B. Carried out follow-up discussions and activities with the children. (That day the children participated in a group time during which they talked about answers to the questions they had generated earlier. The following Monday they wrote a thank-you note to the grove owner and tasted oranges purchased at the grove. On Tuesday, the children looked at pictures taken during the trip and wrote an experience story about the grove. They also added items to pretend play on the basis of what they saw during their outing and created a classroom recipe book by using orange recipes provided by their families.)
 C. Evaluated trip in terms of goals and educational value for children.
 D. Evaluated adult support during trip.
IV. Backup Plan
 A. In case of heavy rain, the trip would have been canceled until the following Tuesday. Children would have participated in regularly scheduled activities in the classroom. Most of these were carryovers from the previous day; one or two were originally scheduled for the following Tuesday. Group time would include the song "There Was a Tree" and the flannel board story "The Life of an Orange Tree" made up by the teacher.

experiences. The good news is that such problems are avoidable through appropriate planning, preparation, practice, and experience.

Field trips are other potential whole-group activities. The success of such trips depends on how well thought out they are and how carefully children, adults, and resource people are prepared and supported throughout the experience. Follow-up activities and backup plans are additional factors group leaders must consider before a field trip is taken.

Applying What You Read in This Chapter

1. **Discuss**
   a. On the basis of your reading and your experiences with young children, discuss each of the questions that open this chapter.
   b. Discuss three ways in which you could create a group time around the story "The Little Red Hen."
   c. Imagine that a person from the Humane Society has brought a very friendly dog to your classroom to use while he or she is talking about animal care. One of the children is extremely frightened. How will you handle the situation?

2. **Observe**
   a. Watch a group time in an early childhood program. On the basis of your observations, identify the purpose of the group time and create an agenda that corresponds to what you saw. Critique the effectiveness of what you observed.
   b. Observe a group of children being prepared to go on a field trip. What strategies were used to help children anticipate what was going to happen? What instructions did they receive? Critique the effectiveness of what you observed.
   c. Observe a classroom visitor who is interacting with the children. What do you believe was the main purpose of the visit? Describe how well you believe this purpose was achieved.

3. **Carry out an activity**
   a. Plan a group time for a specific group of children. Create a detailed written plan for what you will do. If possible, carry out the group time and eval-uate the results in writing. Another option is to ask a friend to observe you and provide feedback.
   b. Plan a field trip for the children with whom you are working. Use the corresponding steps in this chapter to guide your planning. Carry out the activity and evaluate the results.

4. **Create something for your portfolio**
   a. Describe a group time that you planned and carried out with children. Identify the learning objectives for children and evaluate the results.
   b. Videotape a group time that you implemented with children. Make the tape no more than 10 to 15 minutes long. On an index card, identify relevant learning objectives for children.
   c. On one page, describe a field trip that you arranged for the children. Describe what you learned from this experience.

5. **Add to your journal**
   a. What is the most significant concept that you learned about whole-group planning and implementation from your readings and your experience with children?
   b. Reflect on the extent to which the information in this chapter corresponds to what you have observed in the field. What is your reaction to any discrepancies you perceive?
   c. What goals do you have for yourself related to whole-group instruction for young children? How do you intend to pursue these goals?

CHAPTER

5

Organizing Space, Materials, Time, and Children's Groups

You may wonder:

How do I arrange a classroom?

What materials will I need?

How do I decide the order of the activities in the day?

How can I provide for active learning?

Which combinations of children should be grouped for instruction?

In this chapter on organization, we present information to help you answer the preceding questions.

Surveying the rich array of materials available, a kindergarten child sighed contentedly and said, "I must be special. Look at the party they made for me," as she entered her sunny, comfortable classroom for the first time.

Entering the basement classroom of his child care program, a 4-year-old child pronounced the gloomy setting a "dooky place" (Greenman, 1988) even though his teacher had made efforts to make the setting more cheerful.

Even the youngest children are aware of and responsive to their physical environment. They pay attention to aesthetics, function, and the social and learning opportunities provided there. Preschoolers also have opinions about what would make their child care center more appealing, as became clear when some of them were asked to complete the following sentence:

"I wish my classroom had . . ."

❏ *a fountain that squirted orange soda.*
❏ *a pig. I can't have one at home.*
❏ *more boys. There's too many girls here.*
❏ *blue walls.*
❏ *lots more books.* (Kostelnik, 1997)

Primary-grade children also want classrooms that stimulate, provide a variety of choices, and offer both social and solitary opportunities. Professionals who organize the environment with children's needs and desires in mind provide these opportunities and support the children's learning at the same time.

ORGANIZING THE PHYSICAL ENVIRONMENT

The facilities, many of the major furnishings, and most equipment are usually in place before you enter an environment for the first time. However, you will be able to add to or delete from the environment or to adjust it in other ways to meet children's developmental needs. Organizing learning centers indoors and outdoors, preparing the daily schedule, and developing groups of children to work and learn together are all regular tasks of early childhood educators. Practitioners engaging in developmentally appropriate practices also strive to provide materials that suit the age and skill of children in their group, provide for youngsters' comfort and safety, and create a sense of community and beauty.

Safety

Early childhood educators are responsible for overseeing building, room, and playground safety and for training children to use materials and equipment safely. Three- to five-year-olds will need much more careful supervision for all safety practices than will children aged 6 to 8 years because the former group is less likely to have learned safe practices well. However, you can expect that all children during the early childhood period will need help in learning what is safe and what is dangerous. As a result, children should never be left unsupervised. In fact, one half to two thirds of all accidents involving 3- to 5-year-olds occur outdoors (S. I. Taylor & Morris, 1996). Supervision can be simplified by adjusting the physical environment to minimize potential hazards. Consider the following 22 guidelines:

Indoors

1. Cover electrical outlets except when they are in use.
2. Use extension cords, of adequate size, only when necessary. Never string them together for long distances or across pathways.
3. Supervise any electrical appliance in use while children are present.
4. Remove (and repair if possible) any materials or pieces of equipment that appear unsafe.
5. When you must attend to other things, place tools on high shelves or block off equipment that may be unsafe when an adult is not present. For example, to prevent 4-year-old children from touching a cooling iron after completing a project in which crayon shreds were melted between sheets of wax paper, put the iron in an inaccessible spot.
6. Place all chemicals (plant fertilizer, cleaning compounds, medicines, etc.) out of the reach of children.
7. Scan the environment regularly for safety hazards such as water or sand on pathways, clutter near exits, and improper equipment use.
8. Include teaching children the safe use of materials as a normal part of instruction.
9. Teach children to recognize common symbols indicating a dangerous situation or object, such as the symbols for poison or STOP.
10. Teach children to keep pathways free of objects so that they do not fall.
11. Maintain first-aid kits, including plastic gloves and hazardous-waste disposal bags, for treating minor injuries. Use universal precautions when you are exposed to blood, indoors and outdoors (American Public Health Association & American Academy of Pediatrics, 1992).

Outdoors

1. Take children to play on playgrounds designed for their age group. A playground for children aged 3 to 5 years is different from one designed for children aged 6 to 12 years.
2. Scan the playground for materials that do not belong there (e.g., glass or refuse) and remove it. Scan the playground periodically during the growing season for poisonous plants such as poison ivy and have them removed if any are found. Many decorative, common plants have poisonous parts, so all vegetation should be checked for safety.
3. Periodically check wooden equipment for splinters; sand and treat it annually.
4. Wet metal slides during the summer so that the surface is cool enough on which to slide, and check that metal is not dangerously cold during the winter.
5. Report maintenance needs and follow up on them to ensure completion of the work.
6. Check the force-absorbent material under climbers, slides, swings, and other equipment at the time of installation; these materials must be level to ameliorate falls.
7. Check for the possibility of these common hazards: entrapment of the head or other body parts, falls from heights, equipment that can pinch or crush fingers, protrusions, sharp areas, and slippery surfaces or objects in pathways, which lead to abrasions, bruises, and cuts (S. K. Allen & Johnson, 1995). Report maintenance needs to the appropriate administrators.
8. Maintain pathways so that they are not slippery. Sweep sand off sidewalks during the summer. Apply sand or salt to icy spots during the winter.
9. Store children's play materials after use, and keep pathways free from hazards.
10. Scan the area for objects that might trip children. Remove objects in pathways. Contain loose material parts in areas where children expect to find them and place them away from normal running areas.
11. Teach children to use play equipment safely. Supervise children continuously.

Comfort

Teachers are responsible for ensuring that children can use work and play areas easily and comfortably enough to engage in meaningful activities. Children work best when the temperature is comfortable, the air is fresh, and light is adequate. Children tend to be quieter and more socially interactive in less than full-intensity light, but they need the latter for close work. To diminish heat or light, dim lighting that is full intensity by turning off some of the lighting fixtures. Easy access to water inside and out is also essential for both health and comfort. In addition, young children should have a shaded play area protected from wind and weather for comfortable activity year round.

Space

Early childhood professionals are responsible for planning the effective use of classroom space. Ideally, floor space is at least 35 square feet per child, not counting closets, hallways, and immovable storage units. Outdoor space should be two to three times this number (70–105 square feet per child). Greater densities (more children or less space) in the classroom are linked to increased aggression, decreased social interaction, and noninvolvement with tasks (Maxwell, 2000). Sometimes facilities that at first glance appear limited can be adapted. For example, in high-ceiling classrooms, a loft can be used to increase the total space available. Activity centers that are fairly stable, such as the listening center, could be placed on the top level of the loft, with another center, such as the pretend-play center, underneath. This arrangement would make effective use of the vertical space.

The organization of physical space is an effective predictor of program quality because it affects what children can do, determines the ease with which they can carry out their plans, and affects the ways in which they use materials. Vertical space provided by walls, the backs of storage units, bulletin boards, and even windows may be used to support children's learning (Readdick & Bartlett, 1994). For example, an interactive word or picture activity could be secured to a window shade mounted on the wall and the shade returned to the rolled-up position when it is not in use.

When teachers arrange space in the classroom, they must consider how this arrangement will influence children's behavior. First, children need private space where they can work independently or gain control of their thoughts and feelings. A study carrel, secluded chair, or pile of pillows can meet this need. The coat storage area, the cubby, and children's school bags are private places where children might store their work and private possessions. Landscaped areas where children can sit near bushes, under trees, or well away from equipment provide private spaces outdoors.

Second, a small-group space for two to six children encourages quiet interaction with one another. They are likely to exhibit cooperative and helping behaviors when they are in close personal space (2 feet) and when the task set for the group is noncompetitive. Small-group spaces should vary in size, with secluded spaces for a pair of children as well as for four to six children. Often a small table with the appropriate number of chairs can meet this need. When areas are designed for small groups rather than only for individuals or large groups, behaviors such as wandering, running, fighting over materials, and repeating the same activity many times can be minimized (Kostelnik, Whiren, Soderman, Stein, & Gregory, 2002).

Often the outdoor play equipment determines the configuration of individual and small-group spaces outdoors. Swings may accommodate individuals or two to three children. Usually climbers accommodate three to five children at a time, depending on the size and the complexity of the climbing structure. Likewise, depending on how it is used, mobile equipment such as tricycles, ladders, and crates may be used by two or more children.

The third kind of space is for a large group in which children listen to stories, sing, engage in games or other movement activities, and share whole-group instruction. Although some common whole-group activities can be carried out while children are seated at desks or tables, having a separate area where children can sit on the floor is preferable. They are closer together, can see pictures or demonstrations better, and often feel more like a cohesive group when seated on the floor.

Most outdoor large-group areas are very large, spaced so that children may engage in ball games and other whole-group motor activities. Ideally, a second large outdoor space exists where children can gather comfortably in the shade for demonstrations and instruction.

To structure all three types of space, teachers must separate them by clear, physical boundaries. Storage units, pathways, equipment, low dividers, and even the arrangement of materials on a table can delineate boundaries. As one second-grade teacher indicated, "I painted an old bathtub red, filled it with pillows, and placed it near the window. When a child wishes to be alone, he or she gets a book and sits in the tub. The other children do not bother him or her and neither do I. When ready, the child returns to the ongoing activity." Imaginary boundaries, such as a pretend line between two children sitting side by side at a table, are not effective. Children naturally expect to interact with neighbors. However, they can determine the appropriate number of participants for a specific space by the number of chairs or the amount of floor space within the boundaries. Teachers can also use signs to indicate to children the number of people that an area can accommodate.

Fences, paved surfaces, curbs, sandpits, grass, and other structural features usually establish the boundaries in outdoor areas. Adults may add movable features such as tents, blankets, or orange cones to mark other areas for specific planned events.

Pathways between activity areas allow children to move readily from one activity to another without interfering with the ongoing learning of other children. These pathways must be planned so that the flow of children in the classroom or outdoors is smooth and efficient.

Sound

Sound control is an ongoing challenge in programs that encourage independent work, cooperative work, and learning center work. A generally noisy environment from which children cannot get relief is not conducive to overall cognitive development, academic achievement, or health (Maxwell, 2000). Hard surfaces in the classroom are easy to keep clean but tend to increase noise, and softer surfaces that absorb noise provide a warmer, more resilient surface to touch but are more difficult to maintain. Hard-surface floors are best where there are messy activities or children are likely to track in dirt from outdoors. Carpeted floors are best in areas in which children will be sitting on the floor and playing actively.

With soft, sound-absorbing materials in the classroom, normal noise is diminished. For example, large pillows, instead of chairs, placed on a small carpet can be used in the independent reading area so that children can read aloud without disturbing others nearby. Draperies, carpet, pillows, stuffed animals, and upholstered furniture are all sound absorbent. Rooms with large expanses of bulletin boards are quieter than those with plain hard-wall surfaces. Another strategy to control sound environmentally is to increase the secluded spaces for one or two children and decrease the number of spaces for six or more children. Such control can be accomplished by using furniture or mobile screens for barriers between activity areas or by decreasing the floor area of some of the centers.

Some children are noisier in highly complex environments. If a particular center seems to be noisy, unproductive, congested, or disruptive, carefully observe what is occurring. Sometimes the activity needs to be redesigned or reorganized, separated into two activities, or possibly eliminated. Sometimes simply adjusting the amount of table or floor space will correct the difficulty.

One of the main advantages of outdoor learning is that children may be as quiet or as noisy as they like. Often activities that generate a lot of purposeful noise, such as exploring the use of musical instruments, are better offered in the outdoor setting, where others are much less likely to be disturbed. However, even outdoors, children must be considerate of other children in classrooms if nearby windows are open. When this is the case, you should move noisy activities far enough away from the building to minimize disturbing others rather than eliminating such fruitful learning opportunities.

Equipment and Material Size

Furnishings, tools, and equipment should be appropriate for the size of the children using them. Children experience serious discomfort if their feet do not touch the floor while they are seated and conversely if their knees bump into the table. Small scissors are easier to manage than adult-size scissors. Outdoor climbers have rungs closer together for 3- to 5-year-olds than would be appropriately challenging for their larger and older counterparts. The rate at which preschool children enter into complex play also appears to be related to the size of the space and the child-sized structures and equipment in the space (Tegano, 1996). When children have sufficient space to move without interfering with others and experience challenge matched with their current size and ability, they engage comfortably with one another and the materials that support play and learning.

Mobility

Teachers are responsible for planning programs that actively involve children and allow them to move from place to place in an orderly manner. Pathways should be wide enough for children to walk on without bumping into other children or interfering with the work and play of others. Avoid long, empty spaces because they invite running or hurrying. Instead, break up the space by carefully arranging the centers. When children must move around a diagonally placed table or walk around a pair of easels, they slow down. Some teachers use the center of the room as open space, with learning areas arranged on large tables or clusters of small tables placed so that traffic must move around them.

Attractiveness

An attractive environment is one that appeals to the senses. Texture, color, pattern, design, scent, and sound all contribute to the sense of beauty and place. An attractive environment communicates to everyone, but especially to the children and adults who work and play there.

Meaning emerges as emotions are associated with a place. People shape an environment and are shaped by it (Greenman, 1995). An attractive learning environment is child centered, serene, and exciting. It invites children to engage and provides privacy for reflection.

Early childhood educators are responsible for providing children with a clean and orderly environment free of unpleasant odors. When adults demonstrate their respect for cleanliness and attractiveness, children are more likely to imitate this desirable behavior. Organize the classroom so that it is uncluttered, clean, and visually appealing. An orderly environment is more interesting, and children can see the materials that are intended to attract their attention. Sit on the floor and look around to gain a keener perspective of the room from the child's viewpoint. Sometimes a room that appears attractive at an adult level may give a different impression when it is seen from the child's height.

Teachers also help children care for their learning and living environment. As a part of learning responsibility, children should be encouraged to put materials back where they belong. This activity is also an opportunity for children to learn classifying, matching, and reading skills if the storage areas are adequately labeled. Keeping working surfaces clean is also a reasonable expectation of children. Before children leave a messy area, encourage them to wipe the surfaces and clean up for the next child's use. Pictographs or written instructions for cleaning and storage also contribute to children's emerging literacy skills because the information is practical, useful, and meaningful to them.

Ultimately, adults must arrange the physical environment to contribute to the ongoing instructional program. Materials, bulletin boards, and pictures should be rotated to reflect various topical themes. Bright touches attract children to the centers where the teacher intends them to become engaged. Both the elements added to attract children and the substance of the learning centers should be changed regularly and reflect the children's changing needs and interests.

Overall, simplicity is the key to the entire physical setting. Remove extraneous materials. Each object visible in the room should have a purpose and meaning for the children. When you ask yourself, "Is this contributing to the goal I had in mind?" or "What am I trying to accomplish with this?" you should have a clear, immediate answer. In addition, avoid leaving children's work displayed longer than 1 week; take it down and display other, newer work.

The elements of the physical environment fit together in a comprehensible way and should be designed to make life in that place a rich experience. The effective use of light and children's art displays, plants, art from around the world, and animals adds to the beauty and livability of the classroom. A classroom that is more homelike and less institutional helps children feel secure and ready to learn. The aesthetic qualities of the classroom provide the children with a code for behavior and for feeling that contributes to their sense of beauty as well (Tarr, 2001).

The natural environment is unparalleled in opportunities to enhance children's experiences of beauty, interesting scents, and wildlife in all forms. Tiny gardens or clustered plantings, vegetation permitted to grow on fencing, scented herbs and shrubs, and flowers in a playground stimulate young children's senses and curiosity. If such vegetation is combined with birdbaths and feeders, the attractiveness and opportunities for children to learn about the natural environment will be enhanced. Children also have a role to play in maintaining the outdoor play–learning environment by watering plants, filling feeders and baths, and picking up paper and other bits of materials that blow into the area (L. Frost, Talbot, & Monroe, 1990).

Storage

Teachers are responsible for the selection, storage, and display of materials. Objects should be stored near the area where they will be used. Ideally, materials will be in open shelving if children are to have ready access to them and in closed cupboards or on high shelves if the teacher needs to maintain control of the materials. For example, pencils, paper, scissors, and paste are used daily and should be readily accessible near the tables where they are used. In contrast, finger paint or a microscope might be put away and retrieved as needed. Materials that are small and have many pieces, such as counters, small plastic building blocks, and fabric scraps, should be stored in plastic containers. Usually the cardboard boxes in which the materials are sold do not hold up well with long-term use. Transparent plastic boxes are a good alternative. Teachers should also consider safety in storage, especially when stacking containers or placing heavy items on high shelves.

Children have ready access to materials that are stored near the area where they will use them.

Easily accessible storage for outdoor learning materials is as essential as for indoor materials. Wheeled toys, tools, containers, sleds, and other materials essential for the optimal use of outdoor learning should be securely stored in a large outdoor shed or a closet opening to the outdoor areas. Teachers and children alike will find such storage convenient and will use the contents more frequently than if they must carry mobile equipment some distance.

Safety, comfort, space, noise control, mobility, attractiveness, and storage are elements that must be considered in any arrangement of the learning environment. One of the most effective ways to organize for developmentally appropriate programs is to plan for learning centers. A *learning center,* or *activity area,* as it is sometimes called, is a space within the setting, prepared with a careful selection of materials and structured to promote specific goals.

WHY USE LEARNING CENTERS?

Mrs. Lakashul visited a kindergarten group near her home the spring before her child would enter kindergarten. Coming in midmorning, she saw small groups of children busily engaged in a variety of activities. Occasionally one child would leave an area and begin another activity elsewhere. Conversations and the clink of materials could be heard, although the room was not noisy. The teacher stayed with a small group of children for several minutes until she finished showing them how to use the materials and then moved on to another group. Children's writing samples and labeled drawings were displayed on the wall. Children were intensely engaged and obviously enjoying the activity. At the end of the session, Mrs. Lakashul said, "Children love it here, don't they? How do you ever manage to have so many children so busy at the same time?" "Oh, children enjoy learning centers. I plan activities for each area, and children accomplish their goals at their own pace," replied Ms. Green.

Learning centers in early childhood settings have proven to be an apt and responsive vehicle for meeting young children's needs. Centers are carefully designed areas that contain planned learning activities and materials drawn from the program's basic skills curriculum and from the themes being taught. Because learning centers offer choices to children, the difficulties usually connected with developmental and experiential differences are minimized. Children with special needs fit well within a learning center approach because coaching and support from the teacher and assistance from one child to another are normal for all children (Genisio & Drecktrah,

2000–2001). When well constructed and carefully thought out, learning centers resemble an effective blend between a workshop and a library setting. Youngsters take charge of their own work.

Because children are free to move about the room, centers allow for different attention spans and children's need for movement, as well as the wide range of developmental differences usually found in young children. Used in collaboration with thematic or project-based planning, such centers provide a setting in which children can explore concepts in an in-depth and integrated manner. When adults use guided-discovery approaches and children are encouraged to experiment, both divergent thought and convergent thought are promoted (Clayton, 1989). Cooperative learning, which teaches both leadership and following skills to children, is easily implemented in a center-based classroom. Direct, meaningful learning experiences also influence the development of young children's brains (Rushton, 2001).

Benefits to teachers are also numerous. Early childhood teachers are expected to prepare and monitor the environment, evaluate both children and programming, and bring about responsive and needed changes to support children's learning. With the use of learning centers, they are free to walk around the room and spontaneously evaluate the children's use of materials and learning experiences. Teachers introduce new materials and centers and then move among the children, providing support and instruction. Adults can watch to see which kinds of activities actively engage individual children and which promote only cursory interest. They can note when children are able to integrate and transfer concepts developed in one area to their work and play in other areas with different materials.

Because children in learning centers are active and busy, the teacher can also take brief periods to work with selected individuals or small groups of children on various aspects of knowledge and skill building. Evaluation of children's progress, which should take place in the natural setting by the teacher, is also more easily accomplished.

CHARACTERISTICS OF EFFECTIVE EARLY CHILDHOOD LEARNING CENTERS

Establishing learning centers is not a guarantee that optimal knowledge and skill building will occur. Much thought must go into the use of the physical space available; the number and kinds of centers; the materials, supplies, and resources; the children's interest levels, talents, and abilities; and the overseeing of activity, evaluation, and feedback to children by knowledgeable and capable adults. Children must be taught the skills necessary to effectively use the centers, including the purposes of the centers, ways to exercise self-discipline, and strategies for self-appraisal related to what they are learning. To do this, construct centers with attention to the following six key points:

1. Organize and implement centers on the basis of your knowledge about the children and their abilities. For every activity and experience that occurs in a classroom, ask yourself the following questions:

❑ How does this activity center contribute to long-range outcome goals?
❑ What domain-related objectives are the basis for this activity or experience? What do I hope the children will gain from this?
❑ How does this activity build on most of the children's past knowledge?
❑ Is this the best possible way to present such an idea or concept?
❑ Is this the best possible use of the children's time?
❑ Are the activities, experiences, and materials well matched to the children's developmental levels and interests?
❑ Does this activity provide an opportunity for children to explore ideas or be creative with the materials?
❑ How will I evaluate the effectiveness of this activity or experience?

2. Keep center activities flexible and adaptable rather than rigid and static. Although you may have in mind a particular outcome following children's use of materials in a center, you will want to be alert for paths children want to take in their exploration. Children often have good ideas about creative and divergent ways to use available materials. In a well-designed learning center, children can work on domain-related goals established by the teacher while still fulfilling their needs in that or another domain. This flexibility can be accomplished by using basic open-ended materials stored and available in each area in addition to newly introduced materials.

3. Provide an array of learning centers to children daily—and with time—that are well diversified and provide for a balance across all developmental domains (Brewer, 2001) to provide a comprehensive curriculum adjusted for the children's age. In addition, the amount of space needed for a specific center might be altered as children develop. For instance, a language arts center for 3-year-olds might be enlarged and enhanced to provide separate reading, writing, and listening centers for the 5- or 6-year-old.

4. Take time to introduce children to new activities and materials before children encounter them by themselves. Some teachers prefer to give children "previews of coming attractions" by letting them know, just before

they prepare to leave, what to expect the next day. Other instructors plan an opening or greeting time in their schedules. During this time, discuss what may be new or unusual, any safety information children need, and any limits on the number of children who can be involved. Demonstrate the use of particular materials or unfamiliar equipment.

After children have had opportunities to explore the materials, teachers may want to assign certain tasks to be completed. For example, as part of a thematic unit on clothing, one teacher set up a center as a "shoe shop." One of the children's tasks was to weigh one of their shoes with nonstandard weights, record the number on a paper shoe the teacher had provided, and place their work in a shoe box positioned in the area. The teacher demonstrated the activity from start to finish by weighing one of her shoes and having the children count the numbers of weights used. She then recorded the number on one of the paper shoes and placed it in the designated shoe box. The teacher reminded the children that, for this particular activity, they must keep the container of nonstandard weights in the shoe-shop area and limit the use of them that day to the children who were involved in weighing. However, the children were allowed to use the weights to weigh other objects in the shoe-shop area. Besides serving the purpose of knowledge and skill building about use of the materials, such introductions activate children's curiosity and encourage them to visit a particular center.

The focus of a learning center may also be made evident to children by the placement of materials within it. For instance, after children have had experience with rubbings of objects, the teacher may highlight a leaf-rubbing activity by putting all the relevant materials in the middle of the art table. Doing so would draw children's attention to the leaves, crayons, and paper, which would make the activity appear inviting. Yet, children could still have access to other art supplies stored on shelves nearby. Written directions in the form of pictographs or words (see Figure 5.1) and periodic participation by the teacher are other ways the goals and procedures of an activity could be made clear to children.

5. Use the area or center space to address different domains with time. Depending on how teachers structure a learning center and how they set goals, the same materials (e.g., art materials, blocks) could be used to address the cognitive domain one day, the language domain another day, and the social domain yet another.

6. Interact spontaneously with children engaged in center activities. Enhance, extend, and evaluate learning experiences and developmental outcomes. Hold brief conferences with children about processes and products as children act on the materials in the room. Teachers who choose to be active with the children during this

FIGURE 5.1 Painting-at-the-Easel Pictograph

Source: Drawing by Barbara Rohde. Used with permission.

time can also ward off potential difficulties as children work and play together in the chosen context.

Keep the following questions in mind as you read the next section.

❏ Have you wondered how to construct the centers you have seen in classrooms?

❏ Do you know where to put various types of centers in the space available?

❏ Could you organize a learning center if you had the equipment, furnishings, and materials?

EXAMPLES OF CENTERS

The kinds of centers found in any early childhood setting vary dramatically in terms of number, materials and equipment available, and creative ideas generated by both teachers and children. Most of the typical learning centers described in this section may be used either indoors or outdoors if climate and weather permit. The age of the children involved as well as the length of the program day or program year will determine to a large extent the numbers and types of centers to develop.

Some centers that are typically part of an early childhood program may vary from one classroom to the next in the materials that are added or subtracted but not in their particular type. Some key centers are the language arts center; the creative arts and construction center (two- and three-dimensional art or modeling); the science and collections center; the math, manipulative materials, and table games center; a dramatic play area; and a large space for blocks. Frequently, a large, open space has several centers (e.g., blocks; gross-motor activities; music, dance, or games; or group storytelling) set in it during one day, but not at the same time. Some centers may be broken down further into subcenters. For example, a book corner and a listening center may be established separately from a writing center, although content areas such as these naturally lend themselves to integration so that children will have easier access to equipment and materials needed to carry out their ideas.

Special-interest centers may be set up for shorter periods (1 day to a few weeks), on the basis of the interests of the children and teacher. For example, large motor-skill equipment such as a climber or a balance beam may be added, particularly when weather limits outdoor use of such equipment. Music, woodworking, and cooking centers, and special collections of one kind or another, are introduced, removed, and then reintroduced periodically. Such centers may require the use of additional adults to monitor and support children's use of materials or space, as might be the case when cooking or tie-dyeing is planned.

All centers share some characteristics regardless of the children's age or the nature of the program. Guidelines for setting up any center are as follows:

❑ Provide furnishings of appropriate type and size to make the center comfortable.

❑ Provide open shelving and clear plastic containers to promote independence and for easy access, display, and storage.

❑ In so far as possible, store materials used in a regular center either in or near it. Doing so supports the children's independence and sense of responsibility.

❑ Provide a variety of writing or drawing utensils appropriate for the center (pencils, pens, markers, etc.) in every center.

❑ Provide paper of many shapes, sizes, and purposes, such as Post-it note pads, old envelopes, lined paper, small pads, and so on, as appropriate for each center.

❑ Display books, magazines, cookbooks, telephone books, clothing patterns, or other sources of written material prominently in all centers so that children can easily see what they are about. For example, an enlarged floor plan from a housekeeping magazine can stimulate construction in the block area as children read and interpret it.

❑ Provide the tools and materials needed for cleanup, such as sponges in areas where art materials or water is used or brooms and dustpans where play dough or sand is used.

❑ Consider the electricity and water sources and the placement of doors, windows, and pathways throughout the room, as well as potential hazards, when placing specific centers in a room.

❑ Introduce new materials and tasks to all the children, and include pictographs, tape-recorded directions, or other clues so that children can use the center independently. Include directions for the care of materials and for cleanup as appropriate.

❑ Include theme-related activities in three to four centers each day, and periodically change all centers in a planned way. Every center will need a variation within a 2- to 4-week period, but rarely (if ever) should all centers be changed at once.

❑ Some centers should be self-sustaining, requiring only initial guidance from the teacher. The number of such centers should vary with the children's age and experience.

Language Arts Center

The most important rationale for providing language experiences to children through a center-based approach is that doing so supports children's emerging language skills and abilities. A special part of the classroom becomes an arena for children's active discovery of language through quality, age-appropriate experiences in listening, reading, writing, drawing, and reenacting stories. In such settings, children can collaborate and compare their products, both with one another and against the rich and diverse literature sources.

Some teachers interact personally with each child daily in this center through the use of brief "mailbox" messages. Children eagerly look forward to checking each day to see what special messages the teacher has left and frequently respond by writing a message to the teacher. At first, the message may be only a word or the child's name and a picture. Children also begin to write notes to one another and answer messages received. Mailbox "messaging" in the language arts center is a highly motivating activity; children enjoy the surprise element of finding and leaving messages and are writing for real purposes (Soderman, Gregory, & O'Neill, 1999b). Having a real purpose is a powerful factor in children's wanting to develop literacy skills.

Story reenactment may be a part of the language arts center for younger children, but it is frequently an independent center for children in kindergarten and the primary grades. A well-read book and props related to the story that define the characters and the action are essential for the children to enact the story successfully. Sometimes stories are retold with puppets, flannel boards, or other similar strategies.

Listening centers with story tapes and books may be either a periodic addition for younger children or a regular part of the kindergarten and primary classrooms. Overall, the five general guidelines for organizing a language arts center are as follows:

1. Provide materials for all areas of language development: listening, speaking, reading, writing, and viewing.
2. Display the front covers of books rather than the spines.
3. Make a sheet-covered mattress or large pillows available as a comfortable spot for book reading and viewing.
4. Display the alphabet and written messages at the children's eye level when they are seated in the area.
5. Provide books that remain in the area so that children may reread them.

Creative Arts and Construction Center

Young children are naturally drawn to creative arts and construction materials with which they can produce two- and three-dimensional products representing their perceptions, feelings, and ideas about their world. You can often hear children expressing these thoughts aloud as they tactically manipulate a variety of textures, patterns, shapes, and products in the creative arts and construction center. In this center, children's cognitive perceptions are revealed as they represent their world in simple to more complex forms. Cows can be any color; the sky is something over their heads, not coming down in a distance to meet a horizon; adults tower over children; and suns are reserved only for happy, warm pictures, not for every picture. In construction activity, children develop increasingly sophisticated skills in manipulating materials, arranging and rearranging them to represent aspects of their world. The teacher's role is (a) to demonstrate the skills that children need to use the materials, (b) to stimulate thinking, and (c) to encourage children's explorations (see chapter 9). Instructors should provide explicit valuing and reinforcement of children's personal expression and private interpretations. Five guidelines for organizing the space and materials follow:

1. Arrange storage units and furnishings near a water source; ensure that traffic does not flow through the center. A corner is desirable.

2. Provide a rack or a table on which wet products may dry.
3. Provide a space in which children's work may be displayed and a system by which work is sent home regularly.
4. Provide materials for maintaining the area, such as sponges, paper towels, and paint smocks to cover clothing.
5. Arrange easels side by side or provide materials at a large table so that children may work alone or together.

Science and Collections Center

Basically, children who are engaged in science discovery observe and manipulate a variety of constructed and natural objects in ways that help them to recognize similarities, differences, and relationships among the objects and phenomena. They sniff, look at, listen to, feel, pinch, and, if possible, taste a variety of materials to develop and extend their ability to make careful and accurate observations.

Encouraging children's investigation of natural and constructed phenomena in their world is the primary focus of the science and collections center. Teachers guide children toward an understanding of scientific processes as they have children scan, explore, attend, observe, sort, classify, vary conditions, compare, predict, describe, label, and evaluate outcomes. In addition to learning the scientific method, children begin to value the role that their own sensory perceptions, imaginations, and intuition play in understanding these phenomena.

To prepare the science and collections center adequately, teachers must become efficient in gathering, taking inventory of, and replacing science resources; protecting children's safety; organizing interesting indoor and outdoor experiences; and arranging the environment. Teachers also need to be alert to the quality of the science experiences they are providing and ensure that such experiences contribute to conceptual growth rather than fostering "magical" thinking. Effective science and collections centers always have something active for the child to do, not just objects or media to view.

Although young scientists benefit most from exploring and working with real materials, many good electronic teaching aids are now available and can be stocked near a video or compact disk player for the children's independent use. Exciting full-color, realistic photographs can be selectively displayed in the center. Teachers who want to attract children, rather than dust, to a science center will work diligently at setting up attractive, attention-getting displays, using novelty, humor, simplicity, and suspense to draw children (Holt, 1989).

The following three guidelines indicate how to set up a science and collections center:

1. Locate the science center according to the nature of the science content. Growing plants require either sunlight or a grow light. Studies of water volume and pressure require a water source. Collections may be placed anywhere.
2. Demonstrate the use, care, and storage of the tools.
3. Provide cameras, writing or drawing paper, and pencils for recording observations, and a variety of reference materials with pictures and drawings.

Math and Manipulative Materials Center

For children to acquire mathematical concepts, attach language and symbols to these concepts, and grow in their ability to learn new concepts, they need a lot of hands-on experience with diverse materials designed to challenge their abilities to perceive similarity and difference in many dimensions. The activities and gaming experiences children encounter in the math and manipulative materials center guide them toward an increasingly complex organization of motor behavior, perceptual development, and mathematical concepts.

The teacher's role is to provide stimulating materials and to structure sequential experiences that will move the children from a concrete, intuitive level of thinking to higher, reflective, and autonomous thought. In the beginnings of concept development, abstract symbolization interferes with children's understanding. No matter how carefully adults design or simplify the presentation of abstract symbols to young children, they inevitably understand only what they can concretely discern from direct sensory experience. The numeral *III* or *3* does not have meaning in and of itself until the child has counted three objects several times and then associated the numeral with the quantity of three. The most viable arena in which to give children time for such exploration and application is in a center that highlights activity revolving around patterning, sorting, classifying, varying, comparing, graphing, and connecting quantities and symbols. The objectives and activities outlined in the mathematics section of chapter 11 can be carried out most successfully through organized center activity. In addition, this center might focus on fine-motor skills, problem-solving activities, or enhancement of memory skills. To organize this center, refer to the following four guidelines:

1. Provide ample materials of varying difficulty levels on the shelves, well spaced for younger children. Cluster similar toys. Materials for all aspects of mathematics and quantitative thinking should be available.
2. Provide a balance of open-ended materials (pegs, Legos, sewing cards), self-correcting materials (wooden cylinders, puzzles, nesting boxes), collectibles (bottle caps, buttons, seashells, baby food jar tops), and games (lotto, concentration, and cards).
3. Refrain from storing all manipulative materials on the display shelves. Rotate items from the storage area to the display area regularly.
4. To keep interest high, rotate some materials between mornings and afternoons for children in full-day programs.

Blocks Center

Many skills and abilities are fostered in the blocks center because this relatively open-ended material is readily adapted to all developmental domains. For example, fine-motor and gross-motor coordination develop from children's bending, lifting, stacking, balancing, pushing, pulling, and reaching. In addition, increased understanding of directionality, manual dexterity, eye–hand coordination, the ability to configure, problem-solving skills, socialization, and conceptualization of patterns, symmetry, and balance are gained. When appropriate literacy materials are included in the setting, the block center may also provide reading and writing experiences (Stroud, 1995). Photographs and sketches of block structures allow the children's constructions to be saved and are an excellent starting point for either taking dictation about the children's work or their writing about their building (Stritzel, 1995).

Unit blocks and large hollow blocks are critical to an effective block center. They may be supplemented with theme-related materials such as trucks and trains or with other dramatic play props such as hats or hoses. Children frequently make signs to communicate the meaning of their structures. Seven suggestions for organizing the block center are given next. A more comprehensive discussion of using blocks is provided by Wellhousen and Kieff (2001).

1. Arrange storage units around a large space that may be used at other times for whole-group instruction, enclosing three sides of the area to diminish the traffic flow.
2. Locate the area in the noisy part of the room on a firm area rug or a carpet.
3. Label the storage areas with silhouettes of the blocks that should go on each shelf, and provide bins for storing other props that are changed regularly to create interest and stimulate desired play.

4. Establish rules for treating the blocks with care, and encourage safety. Children should take only the blocks they plan to use and construct at least 1 foot from the storage shelves to allow others access. The blocks should remain clean and unmarked.

5. For older children, provide materials for making signs and use floor tape to mark areas for individual play.

6. Provide a variety of other materials for children to use in their constructions, such as sheets, cotton, bottle caps, vehicles, and animal and human figures, appropriately stored on nearby shelving.

7. If the area is also used for large-group instruction, attach fabric (use Velcro fasteners) over the blocks displayed on shelves. Doing so allows the area to be closed and creates a visual boundary, which enables children to focus on the activities in whole-group experiences.

Pretend-Play Center

In the pretend-play center, children interact with one another to reenact their life experiences and play any number of imagined roles. In this center, they have a chance to be in charge. They can pretend to be an authority figure (doctor, teacher, big brother, police officer, mother, or father); someone who has a dangerous or risky profession (soldier, boxer, or race car driver); or even someone who does bad things (robber or monster). They can experiment with cause and effect with only pretend consequences. They integrate and extend their understanding about what happens in particular settings (pizza place, beauty shop, or post office) and build varying perspectives about social, family, and gender roles. In addition to these benefits, children gain self-expression, vocabulary development, a sense of belonging and cooperating, and various modes of social exchanges that require the development of physical, logical, and social knowledge.

The ages and interests of children in the group are important considerations when you are promoting certain activities and experiences in the pretend-play center. For example, younger children may have a need to use the center for housekeeping. They will want relevant props, such as dolls, doll furniture, and dress-up clothes. Older children will also enjoy using housekeeping materials occasionally. However, they may be more interested in using the center when it is equipped to simulate other contexts they are learning about in their ever-widening world: stores, a space command center, a television station, an auto repair clinic, a restaurant, a formal school setting, a post office, or a hospital. Such equipment is especially necessary for encouraging boys to use the center. Older and younger

children may use the same props but enact portrayals in different ways. Care should be taken so that the diversity and scope of the roles children have available are not restrictive, as may happen in a series of theme-related, pretend-play sets (Petrakos & Howe, 1996). As children mature, their play may become more realistic. Instead of merely playing at pizza making, they will want to make the real thing and "sell" it to classmates who come in, sit down, order, eat, and pay before leaving.

If space and other resources are available, two pretend-play centers are desirable. The interaction between a theme-related center and a housekeeping center often brings together boys and girls who do not usually choose to work or play together. Opportunities for being creative, interacting socially, and understanding complex relationships (such as that between work and family) are often fostered.

Older primary-aged children often use pretend-play props to stage plays, and they spend much time and energy planning and producing these events. The following six suggestions will assist you in setting up a pretend-play center:

1. Enclose the center with furnishings so that children may easily determine when they are in or out of the center. Avoid lining up the equipment against a wall. A wall may be one boundary, and the equipment may be placed to form a corner or an opposite wall. Placement near the block center often encourages extensions of the play.

2. Add new props and remove others once or twice a week to expand understandings and maintain interest. Younger children may need the same setup for a longer time than will older children.

3. Adjust the pretend-play center to coordinate with thematic units and projects as necessary.

4. Store prop boxes for theme-related pretend play in a closet or on a high shelf. Do not allow clutter to accumulate in the pretend-play center.

5. Encourage primary-age children to bring items to school to use to construct appropriate pretend-play environments for themselves.

6. Include books and material that are relevant to the theme that is typically found in the setting, such as a shopping list pad in a housekeeping center or a menu in a restaurant center.

Large-Group Center

Perhaps the large-group center is the center that most develops a spirit of unity within the classroom. In this center, children come together with the teacher as a group for a number of purposes: singing, listening to a story, discussing what will occur or what has happened during the day, writing a group letter to someone, participating in a choral reading or a musical activity, attending to entertainment or information from visitors, or engaging in finger plays. Lots of enjoyable, safe experiences occur in this center. For instance, whether a child knows every word in the song or in the story being read is not noticeable. In addition, because many stories, songs, poems, and rhymes are shared repeatedly, eventually children do learn every word and are proud of it. To develop a space for whole-group instruction, use the following four suggestions:

1. Provide sufficient space to seat children and adults comfortably. Such seating is usually on the floor, so a rug or a carpet is desirable.
2. Close open cupboards or cover other materials to diminish distractions.
3. For young children, create seating spots with floor tape to designate individual places in the group.
4. Arrange a focal point where the teacher and specialized materials are located. Big Books, music players or instruments, and easels for experience stories are typical materials. Bulletin boards with songs and poetry posted on them are also helpful in this center.

Sand and Water Centers

Sand and water have been used for many years in early childhood programs because these materials are so versatile. Children have complete control of the materials and, when accessories are carefully selected, they learn about the flow of fluids, volume, measurement, comparison, observation, and evaluation. Children develop eye–hand coordination during pouring, scrubbing, grasping, and squeezing activities and strengthen small muscles when they are digging, ladling, carrying, and controlling the materials. Usually children share the area, engaging in conversation and cooperatively using materials. The process is soothing and relaxing as well. This center is often an area where children with special needs prosper because most of them are eager to participate and are successful in doing so. Ideal for children aged 3 to 5 years for exploratory and sensory experiences, the sand and water centers are exceptionally useful for teaching principles of numeric operations when standard measures are used and concepts such as conservation of volume when containers of various shapes but the same volume are provided. In addition, children's social and language skills may be promoted and other concepts supported when sand and water centers are properly facilitated (Crosser, 1994). Usually, such other concepts are

related to a theme. For example, when the topic is dinosaurs, children learn about paleontologists' role in digging the bones out of the earth by digging up (cleaned and prepared) bones in the sand center. Teachers facilitate learning by preparing the environment, offering information, and gently probing children's thinking about the topic. Conversely, teachers facilitate children's understanding when they listen, comment, and inquire about topics related to activities generated by the children, such as where rivers would flow and where streets would be needed in a sandbox city. Often sand and water centers are provided both indoors and outdoors. The following four guidelines indicate how to set up these centers:

1. Place a covered sand or water table near the source of water and on hard-surface flooring. If a hard surface is not available, place the table on a large, heavy plastic sheet in a carpeted room. Large pans can be used and hung on the walls when not in use if covered tables are not available.
2. Provide a 5- to 10-gallon, plastic, covered pail for storing the sand when water is in the table.
3. If space and resources allow, offer both a sand table and a water table.
4. Rotate accessories used with sand and water regularly in accordance with program goals.

Outdoor Nature Center

Plants and small animals such as insects, reptiles, birds, and mice may live in an undisturbed section of the playground. Usually at the back of the property, this land may remain uncultivated, unplanted, and unmowed so that the natural wild flora and fauna may grow. Not much land is required to provide a place where children might discover worms, insects, and butterflies. The natural environment fascinates children, and much is to be learned from it (Rivkin, 1995). Many cognitive and aesthetic activities may be developed for use in this naturalized setting (S. Cohen, 1994; Wilson, 1995). The Cooperative Extension Service in each region of the United States has written materials related to naturalized gardens and can identify poisonous plants. The five guidelines for developing this type of center are very general:

1. Select an outdoor area away from traffic. Such areas are usually in the back of the schoolyard or lot.
2. If the area is covered with gravel or hard-packed or otherwise inhospitable soil, cultivate the earth and add compost. Worms, dry leaves, and other vegetable materials may also be added to the area.

3. If the area is large enough, transplant shrubs and other plants native to the region that attract butterflies and other insects.

4. Wait. With time, this area will become an interesting place for children to explore and participate in guided-learning experiences related to the natural environment.

5. Hang and maintain bird feeders.

Commercial Playground Centers

Many playgrounds have commercially constructed climbing units and other equipment to encourage physical and pretend play. Such equipment should meet established safety guidelines for playgrounds. In traditional playgrounds, the equipment is freestanding, and in contemporary playgrounds, pieces are combined in more architecturally pleasing configurations, although there is no great difference in children's use of such equipment.

Children's play outdoors differs from that indoors. Outdoor play is more social for both boys and girls; it supports gross-motor skill development, and, for boys, it may be a primary environment for language development. Interestingly, children of working class parents appear to excel in many developmental areas during outdoor play rather than during indoor play, perhaps because of having more experience playing outdoors (Dempsey & Frost, 1993).

Professional staff may or may not have input when playground equipment is purchased but are always responsible for supervising children in the safe use of equipment (Hudson, Thompson, & Mack, 1997). Eight guidelines for using playground equipment as a learning center follow:

1. Know first aid and have appropriate materials on hand to clean and care for minor injuries. Know the procedure to implement in case of serious injury.

2. Examine the playground with other staff members, and establish written guidelines on how children are to use equipment.

3. Avoid allowing too many children on the same piece of equipment at the same time. Encourage turn taking, and direct children's attention to other activities.

4. Demonstrate the proper use of equipment to children and other adults. For example, children should use three-point climbing on structures. This means that only one foot or hand should move at a time, and the other three extremities should be in contact with the equipment.

5. Avoid lifting young children up to trees, slides, or climbers. If they cannot climb by themselves, they are probably unsafe there. Children who are not "pushed" by adults or teased by other children into trying activities beyond their capabilities tend to remain on equipment for which their skills are best suited.

6. Constantly observe play patterns to note possible hazards, and suggest appropriate equipment or use changes.

7. Construct and maintain a schedule for using the playground with other class groups. Avoid overcrowding.

8. Prepare written accident reports with special attention to surface conditions, type and extent of the injury, child's age, and a summary of how the accident happened. Also note weather conditions. Periodically review these reports, looking for patterns of injuries and needs for supervisory changes.

Other Centers

The scope and variety of learning centers outdoors may complement or duplicate that of learning centers indoors. In addition, numerous other centers are common either indoors or outdoors, such as those for woodworking, music, mathematics, construction, and sensory exploration and those related to specific themes such as grocery stores or spaceships. A center devised specifically to support cooperative activity may be desirable if space permits. Examples might be group parachute activities outdoors or specific tasks in any indoor center that cannot be completed alone, such as constructing a museum in the classroom.

DEALING WITH IMPLEMENTATION ISSUES

Parents, teachers, and administrators often have a number of questions about classrooms that include large segments of time devoted to center activity:

"How can you tell what they're learning?"

"How do you know what children are participating in since they're all over the room?"

"What if a child never visits the language arts center and spends all her time playing with blocks?"

"There are so many materials needed. Where can I get them all?"

"I'm uncomfortable not having any structured time. Do I have to use centers all day long?"

Getting Started

Construction of learning centers depends on (a) the program philosophy; (b) resources such as the number of staff, the materials, and the space available; and (c) any constraints such as a program's established curricular and evaluation requirements. Preplanning involves deciding on the room arrangement, the organization of materials, the number of centers to be used, the amount of time to be allotted to center participation, and the way to introduce the process to children. Early childhood educators beginning to use centers should set up the number and kinds of centers they think they can manage, choosing and maintaining those that need the least direction and contact from the teacher, using familiar materials, and having a clear purpose. Once begun, centers can be changed or elaborated on, or new centers can be developed. Depending on the children's age, they require 2 to 4 weeks to learn the routines and classroom expectations. Once children have been taught appropriate interaction strategies, centers are fun, safe, and stimulating (Ford, 1993). Later, adults can add to or expand established centers to be more responsive to the children's interests and needs and an expanded curricular framework.

Structuring Self-Sustaining Centers

Although the presence of aides and volunteers in an early childhood classroom can enhance learning center activity, additional adult support is not always possible, particularly in the primary grades. Many classroom teachers find themselves the only adult overseeing everything that goes on in the classroom. When this is the case, teachers must become skillful at setting up centers that are self-sustaining. The following five guidelines are for enhancing learning center activity that requires initial guidance only or that allows completely independent action on the part of the children:

1. Introduce the activity, explaining its purpose and demonstrating proper use of the materials. Give children the opportunity to ask questions. Tell children where and for how long materials will be available and give necessary reminders about using them cooperatively with others, such as keeping resources only in the learning center so that others can find them.

2. Introduce new centers and more complex activities only after general center activity has begun. Work closely with an initial, smaller group of children who can then assist other children who subsequently want to participate. Polaroid pictures of children going through each step in an activity can be taken, with sequential steps numbered and labeled. Doing so contributes not only to children's autonomy in the classroom but also to their understanding of the sequential nature of product development.

3. Use a variety of direction-giving strategies, such as pictographs for very young children and written instructions or oral instructions on the tape recorder for older children.

Some centers should be self-sustaining, requiring only initial guidance from the teacher.

4. Provide center activities that support the need to practice skills previously taught. Such practice is particularly useful for youngsters who have missed school or for those who need more repetition to learn new skills.

5. Structure activities in which children can complete a project independently. One teacher had planned to make fruit salad with her preschoolers and considered eliminating the activity after she learned that a parent volunteer was ill and would not be able to help. Instead, she altered her original plans slightly. She brought in only soft fruit, put it all in the water table, and provided plastic knives. She put footprints on the floor around the sides of the water table to indicate how many children were allowed to participate at any given time and explained these guidelines to the children in large group before learning center activities were made available. Thus, she was able to move ahead with the activity, which went well, with only periodic guidance required on her part.

Deciding How Many Centers to Make Available

The number of centers to operate at any particular time will depend on physical space and the teacher's desire to limit or expand learning options for children. In general, at least one and one-half center activity "slots" should be made available per child; for example, 20 children would require at least 30 activity spaces. When there are four chairs at a table and enough materials for four children to work at a time, that activity has four slots. Each puzzle provides one slot unless it is large, then two or three children may work on it at the same time. Blocks usually provide four slots for younger children and six slots for older youngsters if space is available. Teachers frequently use pictographs or numerals to indicate the number of children who can successfully be accommodated at once in a learning center.

TABLE 5.1 "Have-To" Centers

Painting	Listening	Computer	Reading	Games	Math	Journals	Cooperative Project
Tara	Megan	David	Leroy	Anne	Jerry	Carol	Beth
Lisa	Tom N.	Barry	Leslie	Sam	Ian	Cal	Sarah
Viola	Mark	Tom W.	Mara	Andy	Tara	Leroy	Ian
	Barry	Sarah	Cal	Carol	Beth	Sam	Lisa
	Jerry	Beth	Anne	Tom N.	Barry	Leslie	David
	Lisa		Megan	Viola	Andy	Mara	
			Mark			Sarah	

Monitoring Children's Use of Centers

Record keeping and evaluation are important if the teacher is to have a clear idea of each child's accomplishments. Useful evaluation can take place through observation when children have complete freedom of choice, which is most often the case with very young children. Participation by older children may include teacher-assigned tasks to complete or choices from a few options so that specific processes or skills can be observed and documented.

Several approaches have been useful to professionals using centers. One approach is to keep careful records of the activities available to children daily. Once the overall goals and program objectives have been clearly developed and listed, activities planned to support them are briefly described and dated. Some teachers leave space for comments on the success of the activity. This written information becomes a record of program presentations, but it does not provide information about individual involvement and performance.

Two approaches that can be used to determine which activities children are selecting work fairly well. First, on participation charts, children's names are listed vertically on a page and the centers horizontally to form a checklist. This checklist can be used quickly several times a week at different times during center activity to provide a reasonable sample of children's involvement (see chapter 7 for a more explicit example of this). The second strategy is to provide each child with a set of "tickets" with his or her name written on them. The children then deposit tickets in a box or an envelope in each center as they enter the activity. The number of tickets is related to the amount of time needed for activity choice and the amount of time teachers think children will need to spend engaged in particular activities, and this number may vary from child to child. This approach was highly successful for a group of children who had difficulty making choices and sticking to the choices they made. After the children went home, the teacher then recorded which children had been in which centers by checking their names off on a participation chart as she picked up the tickets.

This approach is sometimes modified for older children by having two colors of tickets—one color representing the centers in which the teacher expects all the children to participate during the day or week, and a different-colored ticket that may be used anywhere. Each center is clearly labeled with the color of ticket that may be used there. Although children may choose the teacher-indicated center at other times, they must choose it at least once during the day or week.

In one first-grade classroom in Fort Wayne, Indiana, when the children arrive each morning they first check the "learning center guide" written on the blackboard. This guide lets them know which centers will be available during the day. It also identifies the centers in which each child must participate—"have-to" centers—which vary from child to child. A sample of the learning center guide is provided in Table 5.1.

Children are free to choose any of the available centers. However, they must be sure to visit and complete the tasks in the centers under which their names appear. When they have completed an activity that is listed as a "have to," the children cross out their names on the board.

In another class with a similar schedule, children keep track of their have-to centers on a form that includes the week's activities (see Figures 5.2 and 5.3). Each child then keeps these forms in a folder from which he or she will select portfolio materials at the end of the week. The teacher determines have-to centers on the basis of children's interests and learning needs, changing the children's names daily so that youngsters have different have-to assignments each day.

Evaluating Skill Development

To check on children's development of basic skills, some teachers select small groups of children with whom to

FIGURE 5.2 Sample Activity Report

Activity Report	Week of
ART TABLE	PRETEND PLAY
BLOCKS/CONSTRUCTION	PUZZLES
BOOKS	SNACK
COMPUTER	WOODWORKING
EASEL	WRITING
MATH	

This is how I felt about the day:	Terrible	Sad	O.K.	Good	Terrific!
Monday	1	2	3	4	5
Tuesday	1	2	3	4	5
Wednesday	1	2	3	4	5
Thursday	1	2	3	4	5
Friday	1	2	3	4	5

Source: From Donna Howe, Child Development Laboratories, Department of Family and Child Ecology, College of Human Ecology, Michigan State University. Adapted with permission.

FIGURE 5.3 Sample Evaluation Form

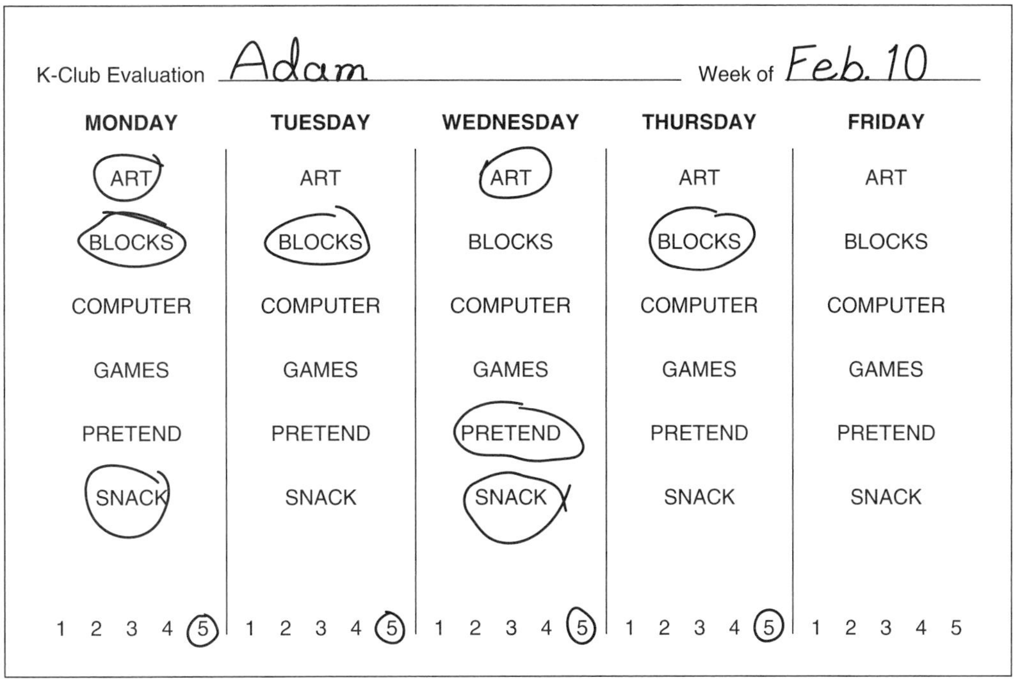
K-Club Evaluation Adam Week of Feb. 10

MONDAY	TUESDAY	WEDNESDAY	THURSDAY	FRIDAY
ART	ART	ART	ART	ART
BLOCKS	BLOCKS	BLOCKS	BLOCKS	BLOCKS
COMPUTER	COMPUTER	COMPUTER	COMPUTER	COMPUTER
GAMES	GAMES	GAMES	GAMES	GAMES
PRETEND	PRETEND	PRETEND	PRETEND	PRETEND
SNACK	SNACK	SNACK	SNACK	SNACK
1 2 3 4 5	1 2 3 4 5	1 2 3 4 5	1 2 3 4 5	1 2 3 4 5

Source: From Donna Howe, Child Development Laboratories, Department of Family and Child Ecology, College of Human Ecology, Michigan State University. Adapted with permission.

work on specific tasks. These small-group activities are in operation during center activity, and the group of children selected will vary, depending on the teacher's objective and the children's needs. For example, one teacher noticed that four children were having difficulty leaving spaces between words in their journal writing. During center activity, she asked the four of them to come together to discuss the need for a strategy to help them remember and asked them what could be done. It was interesting that the children offered different solutions. One child suggested putting periods between each word to indicate a space. Another thought that hyphens would be helpful until she remembered simply to leave a space. The important point is that the children were involved in solving the problem rather than relying on the teacher to do so or being told the "correct" way to improve their writing. Before long, the four children began leaving spaces between their words, and the temporary aids they had devised—periods and hyphens—soon disappeared.

Similarly, a teacher of a group of 3- and 4-year-olds noted that a few of the children were having great difficulty using scissors. She invited them to a table on which strips of construction paper and quality scissors were lying and showed them how to cut. By observing each child carefully, she could assist the child with the way he or she held the paper and scissors as needed for the child to acquire the skill.

Teacher-made checklists are helpful in looking at individual and general class progress in any domain of interest. For example, a preschool teacher wanting to document evidence of social interaction listed each of the children's names across the top of an observation form and variables down the left-hand side such as "developing friendship skills," "initiating play/work with others," "cooperating with others," "helpful to others," and so forth. A clipboard containing the developed checklist was kept readily available during the next week, and when certain behaviors were observed, they were documented and dated. A second-grade teacher interested in whether children were acquiring phonics skills made a listing of those he had been introducing in large and small groups through a variety of literature experiences. From this list, he developed a checklist with spaces on it so that he could record when a child had been introduced to the particular skill, when the child had participated in activities that supported development of the skill, and when the child demonstrated mastery of the skill. Additional strategies for assessing children's learning are discussed in chapter 7.

To this point, learning centers have been discussed individually. However, as a functional matter, centers must be combined into one cohesive whole and carefully placed in a classroom.

Organizing Physical Space in the Classroom

Few classrooms are ideal. Consider the organization of the space in the following classrooms. The preschool or kindergarten classroom (Figure 5.4) has the advantage of a large adjacent storage area but has numerous corners. When setting up the classroom, the teacher carefully selected the size of the centers located in difficult-to-see spots and the nature of the activities going on in them. The first-grade classroom (Figure 5.5) has a more traditional shape and was arranged to accommodate center-based instruction for most of the day. Whole-group instruction occurs in the block area with the children sitting on the floor. Subject-matter labels are used to denote the activities that are usually located in the various areas of the room, but these designations are not rigid. For example, social studies activities are often located at the center labeled "Spelling," and many science activities are moved to the art table when more space is needed or when more children are at work in the center. A summary of questions to answer about room arrangement is suggested in Figure 5.6 (Dodge, 1995; Gullo, 1994).

Organizing Outdoor Environments

The principles of using the indoor environment to influence development also apply to outdoor environments. The playgrounds illustrated in Figures 5.7 and 5.8 support several learning centers. Note that many features such as play structures, water sources, hard surfaces, trees, fences, hills, and plantings are fixed.

Playground 1 (Figure 5.7), nearest the building, is for the youngest children. Sand is used under the climbing structure to absorb the force of falls but is also available in the curbed sandbox nearby. The climbing and slide structure is bounded by a hard surface used for wheeled toys. Designed for children younger than age 6 years, the structure has short risers, a stair, an arched climbing structure, and a chain climber, all leading to various heights of the structure for a variety of challenges for younger children. Both a single-person slide and a lower two-person slide provide differences in comfort in high places. A tire swing structure is adjacent to the climbing apparatus and is large enough for three small children. A pretend playhouse at the far end of the yard features a doorway, windows, shelves, and seats. The floor is composed of a force-absorbent material that absorbs heat and light, which makes it free of snow and ice earlier than the turf or sand-covered areas. A picnic table shaded by a large tree is convenient for snacks or table activities. Between Playgrounds 1 and 2 and opening into both is a sizable shed for storing snow shovels, sand and water toys, wheeled vehicles, water tables, tables, chairs, and other occasionally used equipment.

Playground 2 (Figure 5.8) features a turf-covered hill encircled by a track with a canvas-covered tunnel for wheeled toys. An open, grassy lawn supports games. The drinking fountain near the storage shed is accessible from both gated playgrounds. Nearby is a basket-like hoop where balls shoot out in three directions. Tucked into corners are herb gardens where children are encouraged to touch, smell, and taste these pungent plants. A variety of insects and worms are usually seen there. Birds are encouraged through the selection of flowering, seed-bearing trees and shrubs along the drive and by bird feeders in Playground 1. The hilltop in Playground 2 has shade trees suitable for climbing. Bushes at the one end and corner of this playground provide spaces for children to play hide-and-seek, make "camps," and engage in various pretend-play experiences. Teachers have noticed that children act as if they cannot be seen in these places, even during the winter when the trees and shrubs have no leaves. Near the walk are two other pieces of equipment, one in which children may lift themselves up and that is similar to parallel bars and another with a roller on which youngsters may climb up and run in place. During the heat of summer, children play under hoses that are strung across Playground 1 to the open grassy area. A gated, hard-surface walk connects the parking lot and the walkway to the building, along which children draw with chalk or play hopscotch. Children of any age are safe in this more naturalized setting.

ADJUSTING THE PHYSICAL ENVIRONMENT

When the physical environment is managed so that children are receiving clear cues as to their expected behavior with materials or in a specific place, the teacher is providing an indirect approach to guidance (Eliason & Jenkins, 2003; Hildebrand & Hearron, 1999). The goals of this strategy are to do the following (Crosser, 1992, p. 27):

❏ Stimulate learning possibilities
❏ Protect children
❏ Protect equipment
❏ Maintain a peaceful learning environment

Children respond in predictable ways to environmental changes. There are three fundamental ways of changing the environment: The teacher may add something to or remove something from the environment or may alter something to make it safer and easier to use correctly.

Adding to the Environment

To improve children's abilities to maintain a clean and orderly classroom, the teacher may do several things. Putting a colored cube in a plastic bag outside the bin

FIGURE 5.4 Preschool or Kindergarten Classroom

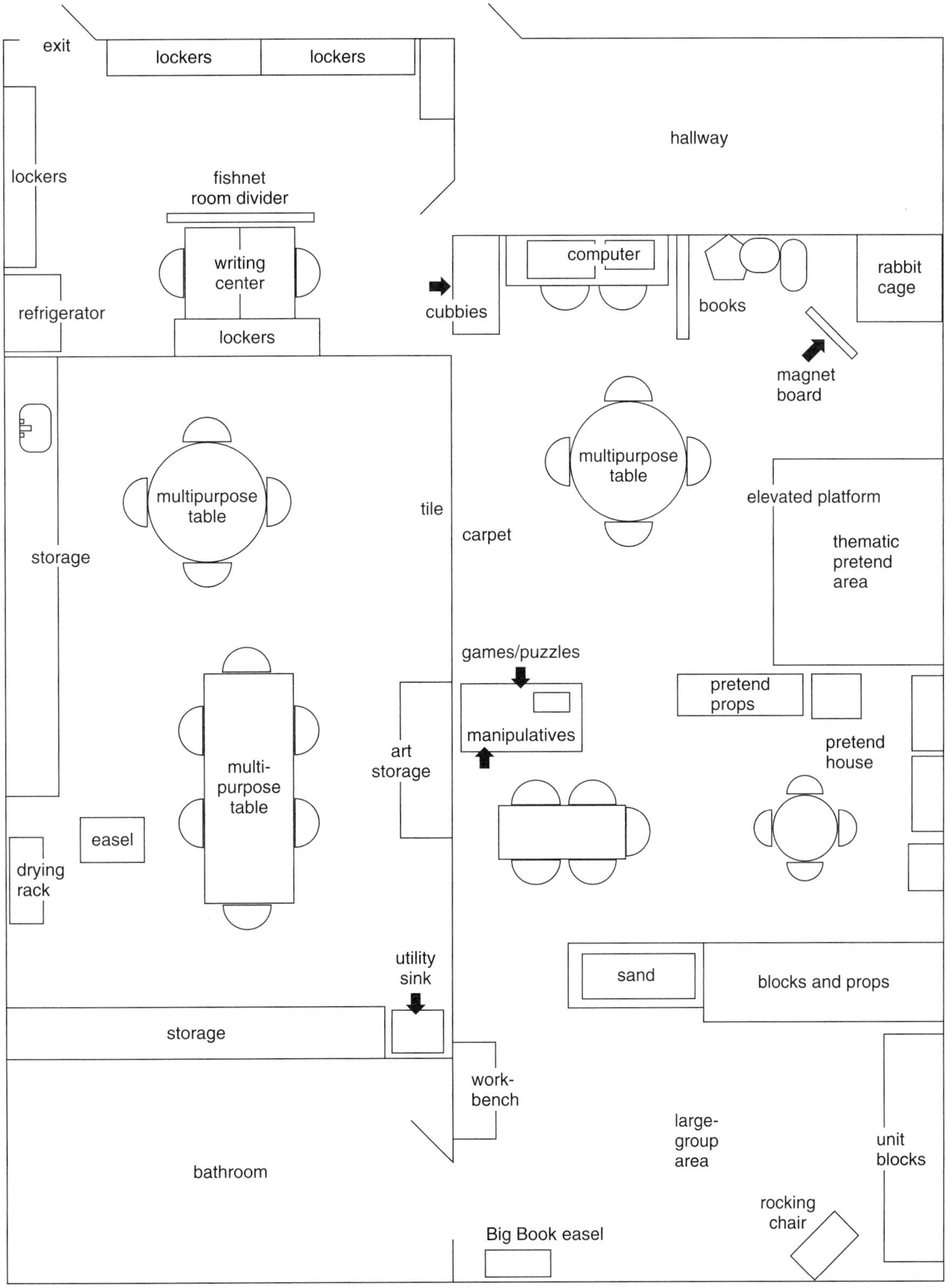

exit

lockers | lockers

lockers

hallway

fishnet room divider

writing center

refrigerator

lockers

cubbies

computer

books

rabbit cage

magnet board

multipurpose table

multipurpose table

storage

tile

carpet

elevated platform

thematic pretend area

games/puzzles

manipulatives

pretend props

pretend house

multi-purpose table

art storage

easel

drying rack

utility sink

storage

work-bench

sand

blocks and props

bathroom

large-group area

unit blocks

rocking chair

Big Book easel

FIGURE 5.5 First-Grade Classroom

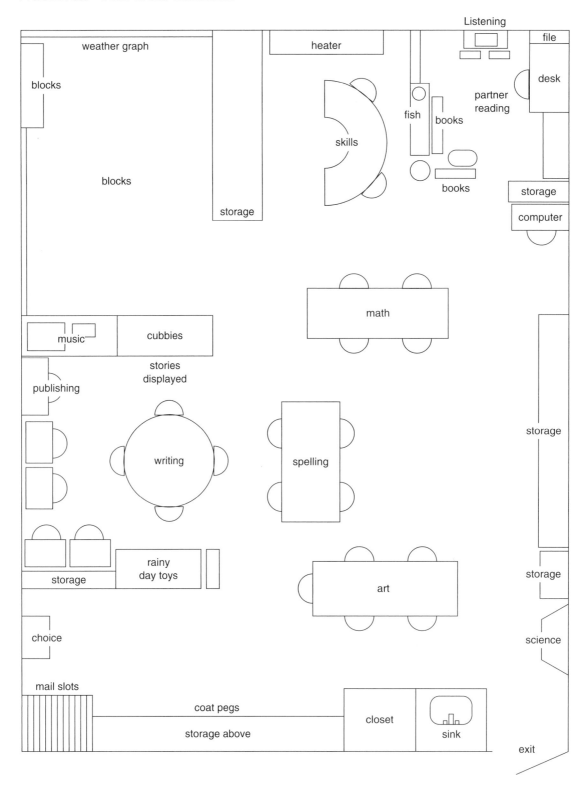

FIGURE 5.6 Questions to Ask to Assess the Physical Arrangement of the Room

1. Can children move from one part of the room to another without interfering with other children?
2. Are the boundaries between learning centers clear?
3. Are areas arranged to encourage active child choice?
4. Are pathways arranged so that children do not interrupt each other?
5. Is storage nearby and labeled so that children can put things away?
6. Are centers placed so that quiet areas are clustered away from more active, noisy areas?
7. Are there places where children may work alone? with a small group? with a large group?
8. Are temporary centers adjacent to core centers to which they are related?
9. Can adults see the children all the time?
10. Is the space large enough for adults and children to gather with comfort?
11. Has the classroom been checked for safety?
12. Are furnishings child sized?
13. Do the decorations reflect the children's specific backgrounds, experiences, and identities?
14. Is the environment filled with words, books, and symbols?
15. Is there a convenient place for children to keep their personal belongings?
16. Are adult areas separated from child areas?

where the inch cubes should be stored helps children locate the bin easily. Adding drawings for children 3 to 5 years old and labels to shelves for the 6- to 8-year-olds also works well.

To make a learning center more successful, the teacher might add a sorting tray or a muffin tin to a classification task or provide a hula hoop for a youngster trying to count out 10 sets of seven different objects on the floor. A simple practice such as giving children inexpensive meat trays or paper plates to place colored cubes in while they are constructing a pattern enables them to use the same bin of materials without inadvertently taking someone else's selection.

Adding reference books and writing materials to various learning centers in the room supports literacy goals. For example, one teacher placed a telephone book in the housekeeping pretend-play area and a children's encyclopedia with the section on hamsters marked and displayed near the hamster cage. Children are basically curious and will use these reference materials, given appropriate support and instruction. One group of first-grade youngsters learned the principle of alphabetical order when a homemade telephone listing of children in the program, paper, and pencils were placed as props in a housekeeping center. They required only occasional assistance in locating desired numbers of friends.

Guidance by manipulating the physical environment is the least intrusive and sometimes the most effective approach to achieving an orderly classroom. When a few 4-year-olds seemed to be grabbing one another's play dough, the adult gave each a plastic placemat on which to work. In one classroom in which the teacher was continuously admonishing a group of 6-year-olds to play cooperatively with the blocks, she introduced a sign that said, "6 Children." Once children's attention was focused on the sign, they agreed to monitor the overcrowding in the center themselves. In a second-grade classroom where children were having difficulty with story reenactment, the teacher added a few distinctive props and a name tag for each character. These materials were sufficient to help the children keep track of the story line and the identity of each story character.

Removing Something from the Environment

Occasionally, simply removing chairs from an area is sufficient to let children know that fewer than the usual number of children may work in that center at the same time. In a Head Start classroom, the teacher removed 10 pairs of scissors from the basket because she was unable to assist more than six inexperienced children at once. When several youngsters persistently became unruly as they drove their large-wheeled trucks through a kindergarten classroom, the teacher temporarily placed the trucks in storage at the end of the day. In a suburban school, a first-grade teacher removed toys children had brought from home that distracted them from their work. When materials distract children from engaging in profitable experiences, when they pose hazards, or when teachers need to streamline centers to provide behavioral cues, the teachers should remove or reduce such materials so that appropriate behavior is most likely to occur.

Altering the Environment

Indirect child guidance through managing the physical environment sometimes requires ingenuity. A first-grade teacher substituted an electric pencil sharpener for the traditional variety so that children would not grind their pencils to nubs. A kindergarten teacher provided a simple wooden bootjack so that children would no longer use the edge of their lockers to pull off their boots. A teacher of 4-year-olds used a baby cupboard safety device to ensure that the cabinet where plant fertilizers were kept remained closed. Sometimes these adjustments are even simpler: adding detergent to drippy

FIGURE 5.7 Playground 1

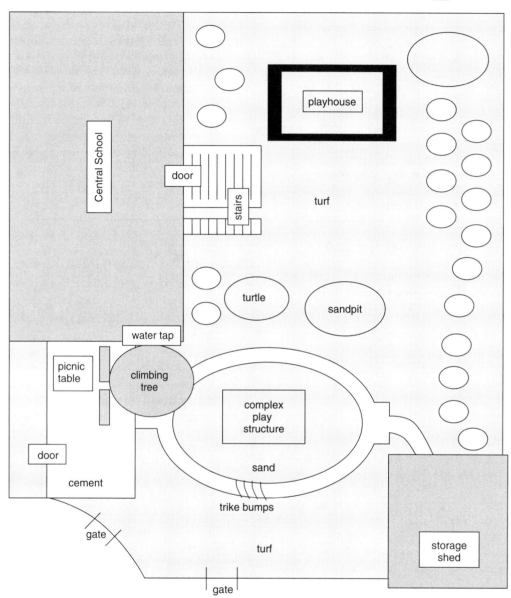

paint to thicken it and make it easier to wash out, placing floor tape on the floor to designate an area in which primary-age children may build with blocks, adding flour to the play dough that second graders made with incorrect amounts of ingredients.

Teachers must also accommodate children with special needs. Children in wheelchairs or walkers need wider pathways than do children who walk unaided. Some of these children may need trays attached to their chairs so that they can work, whereas others may be able to work successfully at a table with a cutout por-

tion. Children who have vision impairments need predictable pathways kept clear. Children with hearing aids often experience excessive background noise, so teachers may need to adjust the locations of centers or the amount of soft surfaces in the environment. Children who are emotionally vulnerable may profit from having a private place where they may go when under stress. Teachers can also assist typically developing children to become aware of potential hazards to their peers with special needs and to make the appropriate accommodations.

FIGURE 5.8   Playground 2

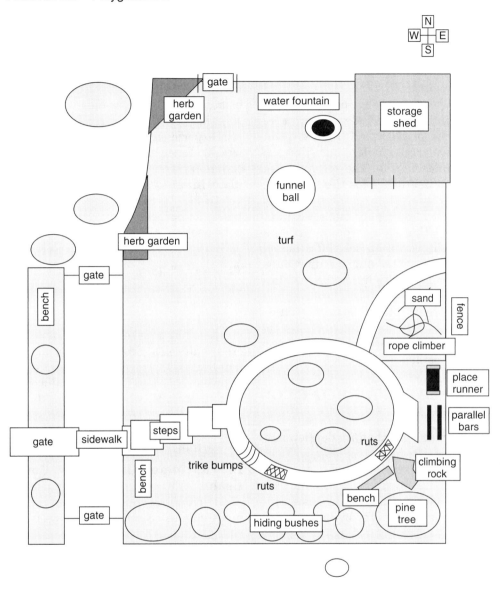

Teachers must observe their students carefully in the environments they have created and adjust the physical environment first if children are failing to engage in productive activities as desired. Play and work can be facilitated in this way without complete reliance on admonitions and oral directions, which can be wearing on children and adults alike. When these strategies are used consistently with children aged 3 to 5 years, as they get older, they learn to apply the strategies to new situations that emerge.

Center-based learning occurs best in a well-ordered environment in which ample storage is available for each core center, in which children learn to put away materials and use them safely and appropriately, and that is clean, pleasant, and designed for action. All this

is feasible by providing the appropriate furnishings, equipment, and materials and by teaching children how to use and care for them.

SELECTING MATERIALS FOR EACH CURRICULAR DOMAIN

Because hands-on learning is a fundamental premise of developmentally appropriate practice, variety in materials is necessary to provide a balanced program. Materials to support center learning typically need to be acquired for 3 to 5 years before a classroom is supplied adequately. Materials that support literacy, numeric understanding, science, art, music, and other centers last much longer than the workbooks often promoted by publishers. With continuous use, all materials should be added to or replaced as they become lost or broken. In addition, nearly all classrooms have insufficient storage space built in for these materials, so mobile storage, additional shelving high in the room for long-term storage, and plastic containers, bins, or baskets to contain multipiece manipulative items should be obtained early in the acquisition plan.

Programs for 3- to 5-year-olds often begin with appropriate equipment but must include plans for replacement and expansion of choices. Child care centers have the particularly challenging task of providing interesting materials for the morning and different but appropriate materials for the late afternoon so that children's interest is maintained while their learning progresses. Fortunately, many excellent alternatives are available that address similar competencies. For example, the seriation task of stacking containers can be met with stacking circular cups, hexagon cups, octagon cups, kitty in the keg, square boxes, and Russian nesting dolls. For the preschool child, the perceptually new material is viewed as novel even though the task of ordering remains the same. Children approach and use such playthings with interest and enjoyment.

GENERAL GUIDELINES FOR THE SELECTION AND USE OF MATERIALS

Teachers must provide materials that are developmentally and age appropriate (Bredekamp & Copple, 1997) and that support hands-on experiences. For example, children learn about plants by growing them. They learn about culture by sharing family traditions within the class. They learn about geography by using a map to find something in the classroom. They learn about reading and writing by participating in functional written communications. In chapters 1, 3, and 4, you reviewed principles of development and how to apply these concepts to adult-planned activities. When a book such as this one is directed to programs serving a wide range of ages—3 to 8 years—the specific selections are important at each age level. For example, simple balance scales are adequate for 4-year-olds to understand the concepts *heavy* and *light,* but a more accurate scale with weights or a calibrated spring scale is more appropriate for 7- or 8-year-olds who must learn to add and subtract accurately by using it. Both scales provide direct experience with the concepts of mass, volume, and weight. Regardless of the children's age, teachers have common goals: to facilitate curricular learning, to stimulate interest and curiosity, and to facilitate appropriate social behavior. So that you can implement these goals, some general guides have been developed for your use.

Provide for Firsthand Experiences with Real Things Children vary greatly in their abilities to handle abstract concepts. Begin instruction by using concrete materials, then use increasingly abstract materials to encourage children to reconstruct their experiences. The presentation in Table 5.2 illustrates concrete materials, bridging materials, and more abstract materials that can be used for this purpose. Three- to five-year-olds and younger children need mostly concrete materials, whereas 7- and 8-year-olds may use a mixture of concrete and a few more abstract materials as a basis for learning. All children profit from hands-on learning regardless of age.

Provide Materials That Are Complete, Safe, and Usable Puzzles with missing pieces, dull scissors, unstable climbing equipment, and broken tools or equipment should be removed, repaired, or replaced. Materials that do not work do not contribute to the learning experience but instead engender frustration and distress. For instance, commercial or homemade learning center props should be sturdy so that many children

TABLE 5.2 Examples of Materials Varying From Concrete to Abstract

Concrete	Increasingly Abstract	Abstract
Bulb planted in soil for observation	Photographs of bulb growth	Discussion or graph of plant growth
Parquetry blocks and corresponding colored pattern cards outlining each shape	Parquetry blocks and black-and-white pattern cards outlining each shape	Parquetry blocks and pattern cards outlining a general shape rather than individual shapes
Unit blocks	Graph paper	Numerals
Field trip	Film or pictures	Letters or words
Cooking activity	Pretend-play kitchen	Picture book recipe

can profit from using them. Laminating the pieces to a matching game that are constructed of railroad or poster board rather than construction paper, which tears easily, is initially more expensive, but the material lasts throughout the activity and may be used often in subsequent years.

Provide Literacy-Related Materials in All Centers Children of all ages will use functional literacy materials consistently if they are available: cookbooks and paper to make grocery lists for the housekeeping center; drawing paper and pens to record plant growth; and markers and music-score paper when children are trying out instruments. Books may go anywhere (Goldhaber, 1997). When resources are available, children try to use them, asking questions and seeking information, thus the teachable moment is generated from the skillful use of materials.

Provide Materials That Represent the Diversity of the United States and Most Particularly the Diversity of the Local Community Music, art, games, play materials, and photos are available that do the following:

❏ Depict men and women in a variety of work roles as well as in the traditional roles

❏ Illustrate families of various compositions and ages

❏ Show workers in agriculture, business, education, health, and service occupations

❏ Portray all races and religions of the world respectfully

❏ Represent the variety of lifestyles and family incomes honorably

❏ Display images and objects that allow all children to feel welcome in the classroom community

When positive images and experiences are included in the day-to-day classroom practices, teachers can help enrich children's understandings of diverse populations (Elgas, Prendeville, Moomaw, & Kretschmer, 2002).

Demonstrate the Proper Use of Materials and Equipment A simple, direct demonstration of materials and equipment at the time of first use increases the probability of safety and materials conservation. Avoid assuming that children know how to use materials properly. Because the children who come into the learning environment are diverse in their experiences and family resources, such assumptions are not practical. For example, the 5-year-old who may know how to use cellophane tape may not understand the use and function of paste and may have never seen glue. Rarely do young children know how to conserve these products. In addition, the appropriate use of a material such as blocks

changes as children learn and mature. Three-year-olds need much space because they generate horizontal structures such as roads or sprawling buildings that are simple enclosures. Seven-year-olds may build successfully in smaller spaces that are about 3 feet square. Children of all ages need stimulation for their ideas and direction in appropriate behavior while using the center independently or with other children.

Purchase Sturdy, High-Quality Equipment A set of hardwood blocks is expensive as an initial purchase, but because they are almost indestructible, they can be used for decades. Housekeeping furnishings made of hardwood and carefully crafted last more than a decade, in contrast with products designed for home use, which last only 3 or 4 years. High-quality materials are also necessary for effective instruction. For example, a toy xylophone, compared with a quality instrument, is lacking in tone and is often off pitch. Administrators and teachers who make long-range plans and purchase high-quality equipment find that durability offsets the initial cost.

Demonstrate the Proper Care and Storage of Materials and Supervise Children as They Take on Organizational Tasks Show children how to wash brushes, wipe tables, roll dough into balls and place it into containers, sort small items into appropriate storage containers, dust if necessary, and wash and wax blocks occasionally. Label shelves or containers with words, symbols, or pictures, depending on the children's age, so that children may put items away. Cleanup and maintenance work is worthy of respect, and children can be taught to take pride in the care and maintenance of their work space.

Give Reasons for the Standards You Set for Children's Use of Materials One first-grade teacher indicated that if she saw someone being careless with materials once, she demonstrated again and reminded the child what should be occurring. She explained that everyone wanted a turn to use the materials, and if they were destroyed, no one else could use them. The children in her group learned that continued misuse of materials led to loss of the privilege of using them. Giving children reasons for the standards helps them understand the principles involved. Individual responsibility and group responsibility are also learned as children develop a work ethic and standards for the care and use of material.

Using the Same Materials for Many Purposes

Some materials (blocks, sand, water, clay, and computers with software) are extremely flexible in their use. The same items may be used to meet goals across the curriculum. In the developmentally appropriate classroom, children are often free to use such materials to meet their personal needs, which may be related to any domain. On other occasions, the teacher guides children's use of materials to address particular curricular goals. For example, collage materials, which have traditionally been associated with aesthetics, can be adapted for use in other domains as well because the material is content free. This concept is illustrated by the sample activities cited in Figure 5.9.

Each activity described in Figure 5.9 is designed for center use in which children may choose to engage in the activity. Naturally, when the collage materials are being used for one domain, activities with other materials must be planned for the remaining domains. Notice that the difference in domains is apparent in the strategies and guidance provided by the teacher. This example demonstrates the potential for adults to consider materials flexibly and broadly.

ORGANIZING TIME INTO A SCHEDULE

Grandmother Herb came to visit Nathan's nursery school. Happy and eager for her to see his school, he entered the play yard, where he was greeted by a teacher, and moved quickly to the climbing equipment. He climbed, slid, rode tricycles, walked a balance beam, and dug in the sand during this outdoor period. When the teachers began to sing a song, he moved quickly to the stairway where the group gathered before entering the building.

Taking off his own coat, he walked into the room and sat in a large area where others were gathering and looking at picture books. Soon Ms. Eppinger led the children in a finger play, read a short story, and told the children what was in store for the day. Dismissing the youngsters in small groups, the teacher moved through the centers to see that all the children were immersed in their chosen task.

FIGURE 5.9 Collage Materials in Several Domains

Affective

Activity: 1-2-3-4-5 Collage
Purpose: To work through a task from beginning to completion
Procedure: Select several items for a collage. Make your collage, show it to a friend, and talk about it. Put your extra materials away, and announce "The end."

Aesthetic

Activity: Color Collage
Purpose: To contribute to the aesthetic environment of the school
Procedure: Make a collage in colors you like best. When you are finished, hang up your work for everyone to see and enjoy.

Physical

Activity: Snip or Tear Collage
Purpose: To practice fine-motor skills
Procedure: Choose some large paper. Either cut or tear it into little pieces to make your collage.

Language

Activity: Texture Collage
Purpose: To increase children's descriptive vocabulary
Procedure: Choose some materials from the box that feel different. Create a collage of many varied textures. Tell someone else as many words as you can think of to describe the textures.

Social

Activity: Buddy-up Collage
Purpose: To practice negotiation skills
Procedure: Each of you will receive a bag containing different collage materials. If you need or want something from someone else's bag, find a way to ask, trade, or share to get what you want.

Cognitive

Activity: Number Collage
Purpose: To practice number skills
Procedure: There are four pans of materials for you to choose from. Select four items from each pan and glue them onto your paper. You will then have four sets of four.

Grandmother Herb watched as Nathan moved independently from one area of the room to another during the center time. She sat next to him while he was working with the play dough; another child came by with a sign that announced that the children had 5 minutes left. Nathan explained that it was time to put away the materials as he continued to roll out the play dough and cut it. When his grandmother asked if there was anything she should do, this group of 3-year-olds explained exactly what to do and how as they put the play dough in a covered container, carried their tools to the sink, wiped off the table, and moved to the large-group area.

Grandmother Herb was astonished that children who had just turned 3 years old could move through the day with such ease, take care of themselves and their materials, and be so independent.

How does a child know what to do and when to do it? What makes the movements from one place to the next smooth? Are there principles of planning the day's schedule that can be applied to any group of children? You will understand the answers to these and other questions as you peruse the following sections.

The ultimate goal of preparing a schedule for the day is to provide a social context in which children feel comfortable and secure. Such a schedule allows time for children to begin a task, engage in it, and complete it without hurry or interruption. Routines are predictable so that children feel continuity from one day to the next and from one week to the next. In developing the fundamental plan or daily routines, teachers must consider the pace at which children work, the variety that children need in the mode of instruction and in the groupings of children that work together, and the overall balance of the program.

In some classrooms, regular instructional time outdoors is an important part of the daily schedule.

Routines

Routines are patterns of behavior that, once learned, are incorporated automatically into the daily life of children and adults. Age of children, length of day, and type of program determine the selection of the routine events. In Figure 5.10 some sample routines are defined. In the Sample Schedules section that follows, fitting the routines together into a daily schedule for different program types and age groups is illustrated.

Pace

The *pace,* or speed, of daily activities is often determined by the overall schedule of events. Teachers must decide who is to set the pace. When adults set the pace, children change activities when told to do so. Some children may be finished ahead of schedule, and others may be just beginning an activity. Adults generally set the times in the schedule when children must be in a specific place at a specific time, such as mealtimes or times for outdoor play.

In other instances, allowing children to set their own pace is appropriate. For example, when some tasks are required and others are optional within a long time segment, children may set their own speed of moving through the planned experiences. One child may complete only the assigned tasks, another child may complete one or two additional activities without feeling any pressure or need to hurry, and a third child may not be able to complete the assigned tasks on a specific day and may need more than 1 day to accomplish the educational goals successfully. Children vary considerably in their learning pace, task completion, need for repetition, and attention and intensity that they bring to each learning experience. Such individual differences in style or pace can best be managed by encouraging self-regulation. However, teachers are responsible for guiding and encouraging children who appear to be disengaged, distracted, or otherwise uninvolved in the program.

Usually 3- to 5-year-olds thrive in an open setting in which most of their program day has child-paced activities. Many youngsters of this age are just beginning to attain the self-control necessary to pursue a task in depth. Older children respond well to a balanced program of child- and adult-directed activities.

Variety

You will need to provide learning experiences in a variety of group compositions. The size of the group of children engaging in a learning experience affects the nature of children's and adults' interpersonal interaction as well as the instruction methods. Listening to music or stories and making plans for the day are generally done with the whole class. Specific skills are often learned in small

FIGURE 5.10 Typical Routines in Early Childhood Programs

Arrival: Children enter the program from family automobiles, neighborhood streets, or buses. They remove and store outer clothing and move into the classroom.

Morning exercises: Taking attendance, discussing the weather, identifying the date on a calendar, assigning daily tasks such as watering plants or collecting milk or lunch money.

Greeting time: Teachers greet children individually or in a group, introduce the centers available, give assignments, or otherwise convey the plan of the day to the children.

Center time/Free choice/Free play: Children engage in activities designed by the teacher. Often the activities represent all domains of learning.

Limited free choice: A restricted array of choices. This may be used in child care programs during the long arrival time. Sometimes, particularly with primary grades, a particular domain has many activities from which children choose, such as language arts.

Five-minute warning: This may be a spoken or an unspoken signal given near the end of center time so that children know that projects will soon be put away.

Cleanup: Children put away materials, wipe tables, and attend to room maintenance tasks.

Group time: A planned agenda of whole-group instruction. For younger children, thematic instruction music, a literature experience, or a group motor experience is typical. Any subject matter may be presented to older youngsters.

Transitions: The movement between major time segments when all the children are changing activities. Transitions occur between all major routine segments.

Toileting: This routine is determined mostly by the location of plumbing and the children's age. It always includes getting children to and from the toilet, assisting with clothing if necessary, using the toilet, and hand washing. It may include toilet learning and diapering for younger children or children with special needs.

Meals: Breakfast, snacks, and lunch may be served in either family-style or cafeteria settings. Some children also carry lunches. Hand washing, moving to the lunch area, eating, and cleanup are included.

Naps: Setting up cots; getting comforters such as favored toys, blankets, or sheets; and getting children settled in a quiet darkened area for rest are typical. Some children need to be patted, listen to music, or engage in other forms of comforting to fall asleep.

Journals: Children communicate graphically, initially through drawing, then a combination of words and drawings, and eventually through written communications.

Drop Everything and Read (D.E.A.R.): Adults and children engage in individual silent reading.

groups determined by the teacher. Usually the groups are pulled together on the basis of either the observed needs of the children or a balance between more and less skillful children. Once the children have been shown how to do the tasks and all groups are started, the teacher may focus on one or more groups for more-intensive instruction. The teacher must monitor the ongoing activity of all the groups when this strategy is being used. During free-choice time, children select both the task and the group. Individual activities may be initiated by either the child or the adult but are carried out by one child working alone. Developmentally appropriate classrooms have daily opportunities for children to work alone, with small groups, and with the whole group.

Variety may also be achieved by changing the purpose, size, composition, and duration of the group. The purpose that a group of children may have for working in a small group may vary, with one group working to-

gether to clean an area of the room, a second group working on a common mural, and a third group meeting with the teacher for reading instruction. Children work in pairs, groups of three or four, or casual groupings at centers where the group size varies as children move in and out of the specific center.

The teacher may determine the composition of groups according to the common interests of the children, friendships, or chance. Knowing that some children share a common interest, such as baseball, may provide the perfect vehicle for learning about players, reading scores, or figuring averages. Other small groups may be based on a common skill they have or need to practice. Teachers are also familiar with friendship groups as they form and re-form throughout the year and can take advantage of the established leadership patterns within them. Chance groupings are usually the outgrowth of other factors such as the speed with which children finish a task. Another format is small coaching groups of children in which their abilities are deliberately mixed so that the more capable students may assist their peers in learning. Each type of grouping has specific strengths that allow it to contribute to the total program. The formation and the use of all these groups vary throughout the year as the class needs change.

Variety in the activities and materials used in centers is also important for maintaining interest and enthusiasm in the program. For example, in child care settings, the selection of clothing in the dress-up area of pretend play can add interest even if the choice of hats and shoes is different during the morning play period than during the afternoon play period.

Balance

A group of kindergarten, first-grade, and second-grade teachers representing a variety of communities identified the following characteristics of a balanced schedule (Kostelnik, 1990):

❏ Short and long time segments

❏ Active and quiet periods

❏ Self-directed and teacher-directed activities

A balance between self-selected activities and small-group, teacher-led activities must be maintained (Hendrick, 2003). Children need opportunities to make decisions and develop their unique interests and competencies. Such development is nurtured when they are allowed choices within the curriculum. If all the alternatives are well-planned, wholesome choices consistent with the overall curricular goals, teachers can feel confident that children are learning from the materials and one another as well as from the adults in the program.

The schedule must take into account the balance between physically active tasks and passive tasks. Usually children function best when vigorous and quiet activities are alternated. For example, outdoor play or gym should follow or precede periods of whole-group instruction. Most young children cannot be physically passive for prolonged periods. Movement that is embedded within a longer period, such as moving to another center or substantial handling of materials, allows for moderate physical involvement.

Children need balance in the amount of time indoors and outdoors. Teachers must provide for outdoor play to promote children's health and fitness. Opportunities to learn desired habits and skills outdoors abound. For example, teachers may take children outside as a component of instruction related to the natural environment. Expectations for appropriate learning and behavior should be consistent inside and outside regardless of who is supervising in either space.

Within time periods, children should have opportunities to explore, acquire skills and information, and practice emerging competencies. Children need chances to focus on materials, interact with their peers, and engage in teacher–child interactions. A rule of thumb is that one third of the time children should engage in large-group activities, one third of the time they should engage in small-group experiences, and one third of the time they should be involved in individual activities (L. G. Katz, 1987). Considering how difficult sitting still is even for adults, this guideline is probably reasonable for structuring time allotments in any learning environment if good learning involvement and positive outcomes are desired. When children are given less than 30 minutes to play outdoors, they are unable to attain the higher levels of social and cognitive play (Dempsey & Frost, 1993). The balance of these many dimensions varies across age levels and throughout the school year.

Adaptation of the Schedule

Schedules will vary depending on the specific characteristics of the individuals within the group. Some children have less self-control and fewer skills in regulating their behavior than do others. Groups of children are thus likely to vary considerably in their ability to engage in a responsive learning environment. Therefore, even within programs, schedules are likely to vary from classroom to classroom. Also, the time allotments within the daily schedule will change during the year as the children's maturity changes. Variations in the daily schedule are also appropriate as seasons and weather alter. Likewise, experienced teachers who know their children well make small adaptations regularly as a result of the children's interest or inability to attend (Ratcliff, 2001).

Integration

In developmentally appropriate classrooms, teachers attempt to integrate topics in science, health, and social studies, and other important segments of information in various ways. Teachers provide reading experiences from information books, set up centers with related activities, and develop full study units on specific topics, such as trees, families, and dental health, that incorporate all the developmental domains. Therefore, separate time segments with these labels generally do not appear in the daily schedule.

Schedule Preparation: A Guide

Following are 11 guidelines for preparing a schedule:

1. Prepare a form that designates space in 15-minute intervals beginning a half hour before the start of the session and ending a half hour after the session and that is divided by the days of the week.

2. Block in time segments that are established for your group at the building or center level. These segments may include meals, playground time, and access to library or other specialty teachers.

3. Choose whole-group instruction time segments to facilitate (a) planning groups, (b) giving directions on the use of centers, or (c) sharing experiences with music, literature, and games. A short whole-group activity before center time helps children focus on alternatives and reminds them of their learning goals and responsibilities.

Keep whole-group sessions short. These activities should not exceed 15 minutes of sedentary time or 20 minutes of active time for 3-year-olds. Whole-group, teacher-directed instruction for 7-year-olds should not exceed 20 to 30 minutes. However, when an activity alternates between hands-on activity and teacher direction, it may be longer and still be successful.

4. Schedule center time so that children have a minimum of 1 hour in which to engage in self-directed learning. Three- and four-year-olds may need less time at the beginning of the year, and 8-year-olds may be profitably engaged for 2 hours or more. Some teachers schedule independent work by pairs of children at one time of the day and more openly flowing small groups in centers at another time.

5. Indicate when and where teacher-directed, small-group instruction will occur. If it is embedded in the center time, carefully consider how to bring children into the small group and supervise the centers. Several sets of small groups working cooperatively on projects may also be planned. Teacher-directed small-group sessions usually last 10 to 15 minutes for the youngest children and 15 to 20 minutes for older children.

6. Minimize transitions of the whole group. Confusion, noise, and interpersonal conflicts are common when all children are moving at the same time. The fewer of these transitions, the fewer instances of disruption.

7. On all occasions children must know which activity occurs next, where to go, and what to do. Schedules should be discussed with the children and clear communication signals given. Signal 5 minutes before center or independent work is to be set aside so that children have an opportunity to bring their work to a close.

8. Clearly indicate times of cleaning up, putting on and taking off outdoor clothing, performing classroom chores and maintenance tasks, collecting lunch money, taking attendance, and tending to other responsibilities that the teacher and children share. Although these activities are seldom seen as part of the curriculum, many of them can become important opportunities for children to develop in the affective and social domains.

9. Allow for flexibility. If children are to respect their work and the learning of others, they must have an opportunity to complete their tasks. Some small groups will become so interested in their learning activity that they will pursue it much longer if allowed to do so. In general, child-generated learning about topics that truly interest the children lasts much longer than the guides suggested in this chapter. Teacher-controlled learning in which children have less interest may be much shorter in duration.

10. Prepare children for changes in routines. If the schedule must be altered to respond to the children's needs, follow these steps:

a. Identify the goal to be met by the change in the schedule.
b. Consider more than one alternative change. Can the change be accommodated without altering the whole schedule? Can an addition be made within free-choice or center time and not change the duration or sequence of events?
c. Discuss the changes with the children. Usually telling them briefly the day before and reminding them early on the day of the change are sufficient. Write the change on a poster or the chalkboard for older children, posting the new schedule. An alternative would be to write the current schedule on sentence strips and then rearrange them with the children.
d. If new or more-independent behavior will be required of the children, discuss this change with them. Schedule changes are opportunities for addressing affective and social learning goals.
e. Allow time for children to accommodate to the alterations. Three- and four-year-olds usually require 3 weeks to become comfortable with a new schedule; 6- and 7-year-olds may adapt in half this time.

If possible, plan major schedule changes after holidays or school vacations. Every time children are out of school longer than the weekend, they are experiencing a schedule change. Three- and four-year-olds may repeat their separation behaviors; 5- and 6-year-olds will take several days to readapt to school. If teachers modify their schedules when children must go through an adjustment period anyway, the number of adjustment times is reduced.

11. Schedule a closing with the children at the end of each day. Various strategies for doing so are presented in chapter 4. Regardless of how the closing exercise is handled, children find a routine pattern at the end of the day a satisfying finish.

SAMPLE SCHEDULES

Preprimary Schedule

Presented next are two schedules that are fairly typical for 3- to 5-year-old children (Tables 5.3 and 5.4). Most noticeable are the long time segments within the schedule. Many activities would occur within each of

TABLE 5.3 Half-Day Program for 3- to-5-Year-Olds

Minutes	Activity
5–10	Arrival, individual greeting
45–60	Indoor free choice
10	Cleanup, toileting
10–15	Snack
15–20	Group time
30–45	Outdoor play/Indoor gross-motor play
5–10	Review of day/Dismissal

these segments, some of which would be self-selected and others teacher initiated or directed. All choices would be planned according to the curricular goals in this book.

TABLE 5.4 Full-Day Program for 3 and- 4-Year-Olds

Minutes	Activity
60	Arrival and limited choice
15	Greeting time; morning exercises
15	Toileting/Hand washing
30–45	Breakfast/Snack
45–60	Free choice: centers
10–15	Cleanup
15–20	Group time
10–20	Transition outdoors, getting wraps
35–45	Outdoor free choice
10	Cleanup outdoors
10–20	Transition indoors/Undressing
10–15	Toileting/Washing hands/Quiet music and looking at picture books
45	Lunch
15	Toileting; getting settled on cots
15	Quiet transition: story record, teacher reading or telling a story, quiet music
45–60	Naps: provisions made for children who wake early or cannot sleep
30	Wake-up time, fold and put away blankets, put on shoes, toileting
45	Indoor free play; open snack as a center
10–15	Cleanup
15–20	Small-group instruction
10–20	Transition outdoors/Getting dressed
60	Outdoor free play: Dismissal occurs gradually as parents arrive to get children.

Two sample schedules are provided, each from a different program. Note that some variations occur. These plans were in use at varying times of the year and in rural, suburban, and urban schools. The teachers using them necessarily adapted their program to fit the children's needs, the school schedule, and the curriculum of the program.

The full-day schedule does not have a precise time for beginning and ending because children arrive according to parental work schedules and leave gradually. Toileting is normally by demand, with adult reminders. Also, meals are handled both as a part of center time and as a whole-group experience. During the winter months, in many programs the schedules are adjusted so that outdoor play is at the beginning and end of the day to prevent the time-consuming process of helping children with snowsuits and boots more than once.

Kindergarten Schedule

Each of the kindergarten schedules shown in Tables 5.5 through 5.7 was designed in response to the children's behavioral skills and needs. The literacy skill development and mathematical-thinking activities are incorporated into the free-choice time. All centers have materials for recording by drawing, writing, or graphing, or other materials are available for children to use to represent an idea, such as a hardboard thermometer whose given temperature can be adjusted with string. In kindergartens that meet for a half day and include whole-group instruction, the length of the group time is about 5 to 10 minutes more than that in the preschool group schedule. Schedule A (Table 5.5) is for kindergartners with no whole-group activity, and Schedule B (Table 5.6) is from an all-day, alternate-day program. In this case, *all day* means a morning session and an afternoon session with lunch between and is not as long as the full-day child care schedule. Schedule C (Table 5.7) is from a classroom in which children had limited entry skills. The children were experiencing

TABLE 5.5 Kindergarten Schedule A: Program Without Whole-Group Instruction

Minutes	Activity
10–15	Arrival/Morning exercises
60–80	Centers
10	Cleanup
10–15	Small-group time
10	Snack
30	Outdoor play/Gym or special instruction
5–10	Closing exercises/Dismissal

TABLE 5.6 Kindergarten Schedule B: Double Session or "Full Day"

Minutes	Activity
20	Limited choice, lunch count, attendance
15	Morning exercises, planning the day
150	Center time
10	Cleanup
25	Group time
10	Toileting/Transition to lunch
40	Lunch
30	Toileting/Quiet individual activities, films
25	Materials-based math experiences
30	Gym
15	Sharing/Evaluation/Closing
20	Outdoor play dismissal

center-based instruction for the first time and were beginning to develop skills for participating in a group.

First-Grade Schedule

Considerable variation in schedules is common. The first-grade schedule given in Table 5.8 incorporates a number of special, once-a-week activities common in all first-grade classrooms in the district. It uses a materials-based math program and the whole-language approach. A clear attempt to minimize whole-group transitions has been made.

The last schedule, shown in Figure 5.11, demonstrates the combination of group reading instruction and center-based instruction. Centers are set up by goal area such as math or social studies or by activities,

TABLE 5.7 Kindergarten Schedule C: Inexperienced Children in a Group Setting

Minutes	Activity
15	Morning exercises; whole-group greeting
30–45	Limited choice: multiple centers in one domain
5–10	Cleanup and preparation to go outdoors
15–25	Outdoor play/Transition indoors
20–30	Group time: theme related, music, alphabet
45–60	Free choice of centers in all domains
5–10	Cleanup
10–15	Individual evaluation/Dismissal

TABLE 5.8 First-Grade Schedule With Whole-Group Language Instruction and Hands-On Mathematics, Some Traditional Content Separations

Minutes	Activity
25	Arrival, morning exercises, collecting folders on Monday, journals
25	Whole group: discussion, songs, movement, thematic instruction, common writing experiences, explanation of small-group activities and demonstrations if appropriate. Directions written on board.
65	Small groups of children rotating among reading group with the teacher, reading and writing with a "study buddy," center choice as available in other domains
15–20	Transition, toileting, recess
20	Snack and story from a chapter book read by the teacher
MWF 20	Spelling: rules, finger spelling, and individual chalkboard practice
TTh 20	Gym
20	Sharing, author's chair, readers' circle. Each day one child writes clues for a guessing game and places it in a mystery box.
70	Lunch, outdoor play
M 40	Whole-group mathematics
TWTH 15	Drop Everything and Read (D.E.A.R.)
TW 25	Process writing. Children engage in creative writing, have a peer conference before signing up for a teacher conference, editing, and publishing
TH 25	Library
MTWF 45	Centers: some new each week, some "must do," teacher circulates
TH 45	Music with specialty teacher
15	Recess
M 30	Music
T	Projects related to themes or to health, social studies, or science
W	Math activities
TH	Math and spelling review
F	Science or social studies
5–10	Cleanup and dismissal

yet children also have opportunities for teacher-directed instruction in language. Other activities are used instead of workbooks (see Figure 5.12). The schedules for other primary grades may be constructed similarly.

FIGURE 5.11 Sample Schedule for First Grade

9:05–9:15		Daily business: attendance, pledge of allegiance		
9:15–9:30		Large group: explain schedule for morning and give directions for how to do independent work		
9:30–10:00		Small group: focus on any content or skill that the teacher deems appropriate		
10:00–10:30		Large group: motor skills in the gym		
10:30–11:45		Children are divided into groups of four to seven		

Language Art Centers

Start:	9:35	10:35	11:00	11:25	
Group:	1	2	3	4	Creative writing
	2	3	4	1	Listening
	3	4	1	2	Reading
	4	1	2	3	Independent work

11:45–12:40	Recess and lunch
12:40–12:45	Attendance; go over schedule for afternoon
12:45–1:05	Large group: calendar (skills: counting, days of week, months, time, etc.), story time
1:05–1:45	Math Their Way: individual or small-group instruction with activities
1:45–2:00	Music (large group): always involves movement

Free-choice learning centers or separate time periods, depending on the project, from 2:00–3:20

2:00–2:20	Science or social studies: varies in form depending on the project
2:20–2:45	"Author's chair": children share their stories in large group
2:45–3:20	Free-choice activity: often based on some type of theme
3:20–3:30	Cleanup and dismissal

ORGANIZING THE CHILDREN

Harry is an outgoing youngster who has just turned 6 years old. Only yesterday, he wanted to count the days left in the school year by 13s. Most of the children in his class are just learning to count to 100 by ones, but Harry has little difficulty with skip counting. He also enjoys simple math operations and is usually accurate in deriving the answers.

Miriam, also age 6 years, is very quiet. Although it is nearly the end of the year, she has made little progress in working out the simplest number combinations. Her counting has improved, but she still finds going beyond 20 confusing.

Dustin, who is 6 years old as well, is cheerful and friendly. He can sing a counting song, although he has difficulty counting groups greater than five. Born with Down's syndrome, Dustin has just achieved independence in using the toilet and can take care of his personal needs. His vocabulary is functional, and he is making slow but steady progress in a variety of domains.

Do these children belong in the same classroom or in different classrooms? Should children who are similar be grouped? The classroom teacher generally does not make this decision. Instead, this decision is a function of the program as a whole, although classroom teachers often have a voice in organizational strategies.

Homogeneous Groups

When children are organized so that they are as similar as possible, the grouping is called a *homogeneous group*. For many years, adults have grouped children by using easily distinguishable criteria including age, gender, religion, race, and ability. In turn, each of these arbitrary means for grouping youngsters has been criticized as being biased. Two arbitrary classifications—ability and age—are still used in some public programs. Ability tracking by IQ or level of demonstrated skill in a prescribed area of the curriculum, generally reading or math, has been common practice.

Long-term ability grouping fails to improve children's academic achievement and simultaneously damages many children's self-concepts. For instance, higher achieving children do not do better when together, and lower achieving children do much worse in homogeneous classrooms, partly as a result of unequal treatment (Glickman, 1991). Only age grouping along with all other arbitrary means of separating children appears to have widespread support.

Heterogeneous Groups

When children are organized so that there are no arbitrary criteria for putting them together, they are in a *heterogeneous group*. Groupings in which children are

FIGURE 5.12 Center Selections from a "Penguin" Unit Over a Week

Centers

_____Name

_____ Scale—Measure 56 each of two things.
* _____ Water table—Measure and compare foam to measuring birdseed to water.
_____ Find these places on the pull-down world map *and* globe:

Antarctica   New Zealand   Australia   South Africa
Falkland Islands   Galapagos Islands

_____ Tell the four directions on a compass and where the needle points.
_____ Measure the height of the penguins on the penguin cards and arrange little to big.
* _____ Read "Penguins" quietly to yourself.
_____ Basic "Bear Facts": M _____ T_____ W _____ Th _____ F _____
_____ Fill in the overlapping shapes.
* _____ Put a note on your television at home to watch the "Trans-Antarctica Expeditions," Dec. 14 (Sunday) on ABC.
* _____ Write the names of *all* Mr. Popper's penguins.
_____ Make a "Super Dad Penguin Poem" poster.
_____ Walk like a penguin (*carefully!*) across room.
* _____ Tell Fred why penguins like to "toboggan."
* _____ Compare how you stay warm in cold weather with the way penguins do.
* _____ Write real facts from "Mr. Popper's Penguins."
* _____ "Mr. Popper's Penguins" activities 1 _____ 2 _____ 3 _____ 4 _____ 5 _____ 6 _____
Penguin Book _____ Popper's Worksheet _____
_____ Color the "Follow the Directions" paper.
_____ Read and color "The Anxious Snowman."
_____ Spelling M _____ T _____ W _____ Th _____ F _____

Sunday   Monday   Tuesday   Wednesday   month
Thursday   Friday   Saturday   week   year

*means *write about it.*

mixed in terms of ability, cultural differences, gender, race, and socioeconomic background offer many benefits. Children representing diversity in rates of learning, styles, abilities, and talents work comfortably together in a developmentally appropriate program, and their achievement is enhanced (Barbour, 1990). The inclusion of children with special needs into early childhood classrooms has been effectively implemented for a number of years.

Another way in which groups with even greater heterogeneity are achieved is by mixed-age grouping, in which children as much as 2 years apart in age are in classrooms together. A strong case has been made for multiage classrooms as a component of developmentally appropriate practice (L. G. Katz, Evangelou, & Hartman, 1990) because the younger children develop social skills from older child models and the older children have the opportunity to learn leadership skills. In addition, in mixed-age groups, comparison with age mates occurs much less often than in traditionally graded groups (L. G. Katz, 1995). Other research indicates that prosocial behavior among preschool children is related to the length of time they have attended a mixed-age group in their child care setting (Derscheid, 1997). Still other researchers (Ong, Allison, & Haladyna, 2000) found that children in multiage classrooms exhibited higher achievement in reading, writing, and mathematics than that of their third-grade counterparts in a single-age classroom. Finally, when single-age groups and multiage groups are compared, the multiage groups often have numerous organizational characteristics typical of those of developmentally appropriate classrooms: learning centers, a focus on hands-on learning, a child-centered curriculum, and authentic assessment.

Such positive outcomes hold true for children and programs throughout the preprimary and primary years. However, strong evidence indicates that the impact of heterogeneous groupings of children 6 years old and younger is especially beneficial (L. G. Katz et al., 1990).

SUMMARY

The organizational responsibilities of the teacher using developmentally appropriate practices are considerable. Classrooms must be arranged to facilitate quiet movement and to help children maintain a focus on their work. Learning centers must be carefully designed, indoors and outdoors, to meet a variety of goals. Equipment and materials must be chosen to meet the specific curricular goals. Time needs to be organized in the daily schedule, which is generally divided into long blocks with children moving among carefully selected centers for at least part of every day. Children should be grouped heterogeneously as classrooms with small, focused instructional groupings to meet the children's specific educational needs. The purpose of all organizational work is to prepare the physical, cognitive, aesthetic, and social environment so that opportunities exist for learning and growth-producing interaction among the people in this context. Fortunately, once the basic plans are made and implemented, teachers can concentrate on fine-tuning them to suit particular children and to meet individual needs.

Applying What You Read in This Chapter

1. **Discuss**
   a. What are the advantages and disadvantages of learning centers as an important part of the early childhood classroom?
   b. Imagine that you are in an established program. Discuss the advantages and disadvantages of having cross-age grouping in all classrooms rather than graded classrooms.
   c. Refer to the section on scheduling children's days. Discuss the principles that you can derive for organizing the schedule and that can be applied to any group.
   d. How will literacy be properly supported if children participate in center time during the primary grades? Explain how this will be done.
   e. Describe the teacher's role in keeping children safe and healthy by means of the physical environment.

2. **Observe**
   a. Observe children in a classroom for at least a half day and record the schedule they are currently using. Note the number of whole-group transitions and describe the children's behavior. Also note individual transitions as a child completes one task and goes to another during center time.
   b. Scan a playground in a city park or a schoolyard. Identify features that provide safe activity and features that might pose a hazard. List what should be done to eliminate hazards.
   c. Observe empty classrooms at more than one location. Sketch sample layouts of furnishings and materials and describe how you think the experiences in the various classrooms would differ for the children therein. Discuss your observations with others.

3. **Carry out an activity**
   a. While you are participating as a volunteer or a student in a particular setting, alter the structure of materials or furnishings in some way to influence the children's behavior. Review this chapter to help you decide what you might do.
   b. Carry out the classroom assessment given in Figure 5.6.
   c. Use a floor plan provided in this text or that of the classroom where you have had experience. Rearrange the furnishings and explain how this rearrangement would affect the children's behavior. Then try rearranging furnishings to achieve one of the following potential goals:

      ❏ More cooperative behavior
      ❏ More helping and sharing
      ❏ A quieter environment
      ❏ More creativity

4. **Create something for your portfolio**
   a. Develop at least one pictograph to use with young children for a basic routine that you would expect them to implement independently after some initial guidance.

5. **Add to your journal**
   a. Reflect on the experience you have had in organizing for learning and compare it with what you read in this chapter.

CHAPTER
6
Promoting Self-Discipline in Children

You may wonder:

How do children learn which behaviors are acceptable and which are not?

How do children's development and life experiences influence their behavior?

Why do children seem to obey some adults better than others?

What strategies are most effective for teaching children how to get along?

In this chapter on promoting self-discipline in children, we present information to help you answer the preceding questions.

The following incidents occur in a kindergarten during one session:

Samantha interrupts the story "Caps for Sale," saying, "I like the checked cap best." Other children declare their favorites as well. Soon everyone is talking at once.

Teacher 1 says:	*I'll never get this story done if you keep interrupting. Shh.*
Teacher 2 says:	*You're excited to tell me which cap you like best. It's hard to hear with everyone talking at once. Talk one at a time. Samantha, what color did you say you liked best?*

Leonard continues painting during cleanup time.

Teacher 1 thinks:	*Leonard is so uncooperative. Why can't he listen to directions?*
Teacher 2 thinks:	*Leonard needs some physical assistance to stop what he's doing and make the transition to cleanup.*

Two children get into a fierce shoving match over who will be the line leader on the way to the gym.

Teacher 1 thinks:	*This is unacceptable behavior. I'd better get over there. No gym time today.*

Teacher 2 thinks:	*This is unacceptable behavior. I'd better get over there. They need help using words to settle this argument.*

Both these teachers are tired at the end of a busy day with children. Both find the children's behavior demanding and anticipate having to put a great deal of energy into socializing children to act properly in their classrooms. However, Teacher 1 assumes the children are deliberately disobedient. She foresees having to spend her time "keeping on top of" the children and making sure they behave. This teacher views incidents of misbehavior as interruptions. In contrast, Teacher 2 assumes the children are just learning how to conduct themselves in group settings and that they will make mistakes in the process. She anticipates having to spend a lot of time teaching children the skills they will need to get along in the classroom and to be successful learners. She views incidents of misbehavior as teachable moments.

These teachers illustrate differing attitudes about children's classroom behavior and the teacher's role in maintaining classroom discipline. Teacher 2 exemplifies attitudes and roles compatible with developmentally appropriate practices. Teacher 1 does not.

WHAT CHILDREN NEED TO KNOW

For children to become truly engaged in the learning process, they must have a sense of how to behave in their center, school, or family child care home. Following is a description of some of the fundamental skills that they need so that they can thrive in group environments (Damon, 1995). Children are most successful when they know how to express their needs and wants constructively, respond with compassion to others' needs, act with civility, take proper care of materials, act safely, constructively engage in learning activities, attend to instruction, distinguish acceptable from unacceptable classroom behavior, help, and cooperate. Children do not automatically know how to engage in these behaviors. Consequently, early childhood professionals do not expect children to come to their programs understanding what constitutes appropriate classroom behavior, nor do they simply demand that children act in certain ways (Gartrell, 2003; Read, Gardner, & Mahler, 1993). Instead, adults teach children what is expected and how to conduct themselves appropriately. These educational aims require the same kind of planning and teaching that other aspects of the curriculum demand. Just as teachers provide opportunities for children to learn about science, math, and literacy, they also provide opportunities for children to learn how to interact with others and manage their behavior independently and in groups. When children make mistakes or demonstrate ignorance, early childhood professionals do more than simply correct children. They teach children appropriate alternative strategies that they can eventually apply on their own. Thus, in developmentally appropriate classrooms, professionals focus their efforts on helping children develop self-discipline (Bredekamp & Copple, 1997).

WHAT SELF-DISCIPLINE IS

The after-school kids bound off the buses. They jostle, bump into each other, head for the hall, drop their backpacks, hurry into the lavatories, and race to the snack bar. Some head for the gym to hear the rules for a kickball game–eight-year-old Matt is among them. He listens attentive and eager, for about five minutes. Then he begins to squirm, look around, and elbow the children next to him. . . . Jeremy, the teacher's aide, steps quietly in behind Matt. "Remember, Matt, be calm. You know how to wait," he whispers. Matt says to himself, "I can wait, I can wait." He gets himself under control and waits for the game to begin. *(Steiner & Whelan, 1995)*

In this example, Matt, with the help of a supportive adult, managed to control his natural impulses to move about. He also resisted the temptation to continue poking at his peers. Both are signs that he is developing skills associated with self-discipline. *Self-discipline* is the voluntary, internal regulation of behavior (Marion, 1999). It involves acting in socially acceptable ways based on reasoning, concern for others, and an under-

standing of acceptable and unacceptable behavior. Self-disciplined people do not need others to make them do the right thing or to forbid them from engaging in antisocial conduct. Neither are they dependent on external rewards or punishments to guide their actions. Instead, they consider other people's needs and feelings while simultaneously adapting their actions to fit the rules of the society in which they live. Self-disciplined children control negative impulses, resist temptation, and delay gratification independent of supervision. They also initiate positive social interactions and undertake constructive social plans without having to be told to do so (Bukatko & Daehler, 2001; Knapczyk & Rodes, 1996). Refer to Table 6.1 for examples of how these behaviors are enacted in children's lives.

HOW SELF-DISCIPLINE EVOLVES

Self-discipline evolves gradually in an "outside" to "inside" developmental process (Marion, 1999). That is, children proceed from relying on others to control their behavior for them to eventually achieving greater self-regulation. This gradual shift in control from others to self is a significant developmental task that begins in infancy and continues throughout the teenage years.

The Earliest Days (No Regulation)

Infants have no sense of right or wrong. They also have no skills to regulate their behavior in accordance with other people's needs or expectations. Thus, they lack self-discipline of any kind. Gradually, through experience and maturation, toddlers and young preschoolers become capable of responding to external controls applied by parents and teachers as a means for behaving in certain ways. This form of regulation is called *adherence.*

Adherence (External Regulation)

Children motivated by adherence rely on adults to control their actions for them. The most basic form of external control involves physical assistance. Following are some examples:

The parent volunteer holds Melanie on her lap during group time to help her focus on the story. Melanie attends to the story.

The teacher physically separates two children who are fighting on the playground. The children stop pushing each other.

The after-school aide puts her hand over Michael's to keep him from waving the saw around at the workbench. Michael keeps the saw low.

TABLE 6.1   Components of Self-Discipline as Exhibited by Young Children

Behavior	Examples
Control negative impulses	Anthony suppresses the urge to strike out in anger when someone accidentally trips him. Hessa refrains from laughing aloud when Anthony falls.
Resisting temptation	Jerome walks all the way over to the trash bin to deposit his gum wrapper, even though he is tempted to drop the crumpled paper onto the playground.
Delaying gratification	Rachel waits for Marla to finish telling her story before blurting out her own exciting news.
	Steven postpones taking another fruit kabob until everyone else gets one.
Initiating positive social acts	Shannon comforts Latosha, who is sad about a ruined project.
	Jason shares his glue with a newcomer to the art center.
Making and carrying out social plans	Vinny wants a turn with the magnifying glass. He devises a strategy for getting one, such as trading, and then tries bargaining with another child.
	Ashley recognizes that Marcus is having difficulty carrying several balls out to the playground. She helps him by holding the door open.

Gradually, children also learn to respond to oral cues as a means of knowing what to do and what not to do. For instance,

The teacher reminds Diego to wash his hands before sitting down for lunch. Diego washes his hands.

Sandra's dad talks her through the steps involved in feeding the iguana. Sandra feeds the iguana correctly.

The teacher's aide provides Joshua with a script of what to say during an argument with Michael. Joshua tells Michael, "I wasn't done yet."

In each of these situations, adults provided controls that children were not able to exercise on their own.

Another form of adherence occurs when children act in certain ways either to gain rewards or to avoid negative consequences (Bukatko & Daehler, 2001; Kostelnik, Whiren, Soderman, Stein, & Gregory, 2002). You can see adherence in operation when a child who has been scolded for dumping all the puzzles on the floor eventually refrains from dumping them again to avoid additional correction. Likewise, children's desire to receive adult praise, or approval from a peer, may prompt them to use the paints properly or share a toy with another child. In each case, rewards and negative consequences have contributed to children's early differentiations of acceptable and unacceptable actions. Relying on these kinds of external controls is a step beyond having no control. It is also a necessary first phase in moving from no self-discipline to internal regulation. However, adherence has drawbacks that make it an undesirable end in itself.

Consider the following situation. The children are lining up at the door to go outside. Mr. Martin, their teacher, has promised a smiley face sticker to children who get in line and do not cut ahead. Adrianne, who is near the end of the line, wants to be first but quietly stands in place because she wants the sticker. Her behavior is regulated by the promise of the reward, not by concern for her classmates' rights. Under these circumstances, Adrianne will probably follow the teacher's directions but only when he is present. Because the child has no internal basis for following the rule, she may resort to cutting in front of others if she thinks the teacher is not looking.

Adrianne illustrates the basic problem with adherence. Children who depend on external controls must be monitored constantly. They behave appropriately only in situations in which physical or oral assistance is readily available and in instances in which the threat of punishment or the promise of a reward is obvious. When such controls are missing, the possibility of misbehavior is great. Having no other means for understanding right and wrong, children lack the self-direction necessary to act appropriately on their own.

Identification (Shared Regulation)

A more advanced degree of self-regulation occurs when children follow a rule in imitation of someone they admire. Children's positive actions become their way of emulating the conduct and values of important people in their lives (Berk, 2003; Hoffman, 1970). This type of self-regulation is called *identification*. Because children identify with nurturing, powerful figures, teachers are often the focus of identification. This case is especially true when children and teachers enjoy positive relations with one another.

Children who rely on identification adopt another person's code of conduct to guide their actions but have little understanding of the reasons behind such behaviors. For instance, influenced by identification, Jacob may wait his turn in line because a teacher he especially likes advocates such conduct. However, Jacob does not grasp the concept of fairness that waiting represents. In addition, identification requires children to second-guess how another person might behave under certain conditions. If Jacob encounters a situation to which he has never seen the teacher respond, he may not know what to do himself.

Identification represents shared behavior regulation. Children remain dependent on an outside source to help them control their actions but are beginning to use internal thought processes as well. They do not need constant monitoring. Yet, they still have no way to determine what to do in unfamiliar circumstances. Consequently, although identification is more advanced than adherence, it does not represent the highest form of self-discipline.

Internalization (Self Regulation)

When children construct a personal sense of right and wrong and act in ways consistent with what they believe to be right, we say they have *internalized* that behavior (Hoffman, 1970; Shaffer, 2002). In other words, children act in certain ways because they think it is the right thing to do, not to gain a reward or the approval of others (Kohn, 1996). Children in this phase of behavior regulation feel concern and a sense of responsibility for the welfare and rights of others as well as for themselves. They also comprehend moral concepts such as justice, truth, and honor (Shapiro, 1997). For these reasons, internalization represents the ultimate form of self-discipline.

Sophie demonstrates internalization when she waits her turn in line even though she is tempted to push ahead. The reasoning that guides her behavior is that cutting in front of others would interfere with their rights. Such interference violates her sense of honor, which prompts Sophie to remain where she is in the line.

Children who have internalized certain standards of behavior understand the reasons behind acceptable and unacceptable actions. This understanding gives them a reference point for determining how to behave appropriately in all kinds of situations, even those that are unfamiliar. These understandings eliminate the need for constant supervision. Children can be depended on to regulate their behavior. Moreover, internalized behaviors are long lasting. Children who internalize notions of fair play or honesty will abide by these ideals long after their contacts with certain adults have ended

and despite the temptation or opportunity to act otherwise (Kostelnik, Whiren, et al., 2002; P. R. Newman & Newman, 1997).

WHEN THE ROOTS OF SELF-DISCIPLINE FORM

In general we can assume that the younger and less experienced the child, the more likely his or her behavior will be regulated by adherence. As children engage in relationships with nurturing adults, identification becomes a more significant factor in the way children behave. With time (there is no way to predict exactly how much), increasing numbers of children demonstrate internalization of common rules, such as walking indoors or handling the gerbil gently. With each new adult and each change of setting, the process begins somewhat anew. However, as children mature and gain experience, their reliance on external controls lessens, especially for expectations that are commonly held from one setting to another.

As you can ascertain, the foundations for self-regulation are laid early in life. With suitable adult support, 3-, 4-, and 5-year-olds can distinguish appropriate actions from inappropriate actions in a variety of situations and develop an understanding of the reasoning behind these categories. They can also become more aware of others' feelings, recognize the impact of their actions on people and things, and acquire alternative strategies for achieving their aims. Children who do not learn these behaviors in early childhood have more difficulty achieving internalization later (Berk, 2003; Magid & McKelvey, 1990).

DEGREES OF SELF-DISCIPLINE AMONG CHILDREN AND WITHIN THE SAME CHILD

Children achieve self-discipline at rates and in degrees that vary from child to child (Bukatko & Daehler, 2001). Within any group of children, the variations in social competence will be great. For instance, Noelle may take only a few weeks to learn how to behave appropriately at group time. LaRene may take much longer to grasp this notion. Giovanni may respond easily to gentle reminders to share, whereas Sam may need physical assistance to accomplish this task. In addition, the same child may respond to different motivations in different circumstances (Turiel, 1998). That is, Juanita may stay out of the mud to avoid a warning. She may adopt attitudes toward cheating that are similar to those held by an admired teacher. In addition, when she accidentally receives too many lunch tokens, she may return some because keeping them would not feel right. What all this means is that children will vary widely in their

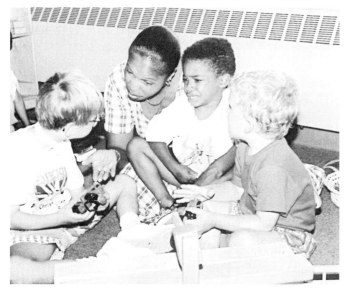

Children need adult support as they develop the emotional and cognitive skills necessary to follow rules on their own.

progress toward self-regulation. These variations are a result of development and experience.

DEVELOPMENTAL INFLUENCES ON SELF-DISCIPLINE

Children's capacity for self-discipline increases with maturity. Although 4- and 5-year-olds can generally regulate themselves in some situations, they do not have the same degree of self-control as that of children who are 8 and 9 years old. Several developmental factors contribute to these age differences, including factors related to children's emotional, cognitive, and language development and their memory skills. In each of these areas, children's increasing understanding and skills emerge according to the principles of developmental direction: simple to complex, concrete to abstract, and inaccurate to more accurate.

Emotional Development

Emotions provide children with strong internal signals regarding the appropriateness or inappropriateness of their behavior. As children learn to pay attention to these signals, their self-control increases. Two important emotional regulators are guilt and empathy (R. A. Thompson, 1998; Hoffman, 1990). Guilt warns children that current, past, or planned actions are inappropriate. It serves as a brake, causing children to reconsider or stop their actions. Empathy (understanding others' feelings and reacting with complimentary affect) conveys the opposite message. It prompts children to engage in positive actions in response to other people's emotions. Children as young

as 2 years old are capable of both guilt and empathy (Emde, Biringen, Clyman, & Oppenheim, 1991; Goleman, 1995). However, what induces these emotions in preschoolers is different from what prompts them in second and third graders.

Empathy Empathy is what prompts children to comfort a victim, offer to share, or willingly take turns. Empathy is the driving force behind Alice's response to Lucinda, a 4-year-old who was crying after her mother left. Alice, her classmate, rubbed Lucinda's back gently and said, "That's okay. I'll be your mommy 'til your mommy comes back" (Zavitkovsky, 1986). Alice recognized Lucinda's distress, empathized with her predicament, and offered a plan to help. All these behaviors are related to self-discipline.

At first, infants and toddlers simply duplicate the overt signals of distress they witness in others. This is why a 2-year-old might cry upon seeing or hearing another child's sobs. By the time they are 3 years old, children recognize that another person's distress calls for relevant action on their part, such as soothing a peer who has fallen down. However, their responses tend to be limited to only one or two strategies. As children progress through the later preschool and early elementary years, they become more adept at responding in a variety of ways to offer encouragement, comfort, and support (D. F. Miller, 2004).

Guilt Initially, children experience guilt only when they violate a known rule or fail to meet the expectations of the important adults in their lives. For instance, 4-year-old Carl slaps Selma in a struggle over the cookie cutters. Selma begins to cry. Triumphant about having gained a desired possession, Carl is unmoved by Selma's distress. He experiences no guilt until the teacher reminds him that the rule is "Hitting is not allowed." Once he becomes aware of the contradiction between his behavior and the rule, Carl may feel guilty about breaking it and disappointing the teacher. Conversely, if he were 7 or 8 years old, Carl might empathize with Selma's unhappy response and feel remorse and guilt at being the source of it (Williams & Bybee, 1994). This combination of empathy and guilt could even prompt him to do something to make up for his earlier actions. Violation of a formal rule would not figure as prominently in his feelings as it had during the preschool years. Instead, Carl would be more focused on the internal distress his actions had caused another person and, as a consequence, himself. Eventually, during middle childhood, children feel guilt and empathy even when they are not the cause but perceive that they could have done something to prevent a problem (Kostelnik, Whiren, et al., 2002). Hence, a 10-year-old seeing an argument between Carl and Selma might intercede out of empathy toward two persons in distress and to avoid feeling guilty over not helping. In this way, children gradually respond to guilt and empathy as a way to support their personal notions of right and wrong. This gradual shift from external prompts to internal prompts contributes to the inner control that children need to achieve self-discipline. Although it has its beginnings early in life, such complex and "other-oriented" motivation does not fully emerge until adolescence.

What all this means for early childhood educators is that on some occasions they will witness children offering help or comfort to their peers and on other occasions the same children seeming to be oblivious to people's reactions or concerns. In either case, children's emotional development is enhanced when adults point out how their actions affect those around them ("You shared the play dough with Sheree. She looks happy" or "When you pushed Mark, he got angry"). Likewise, children follow rules better when they are taught how these rules protect people's feelings ("Those are William's cars. He doesn't like it when you grab. Ask him to share"). Finally, when children demonstrate that they have responded out of empathy or guilt, their efforts need to be recognized and reinforced ("You're trying to help Sandra feel better. That's a kind thing to do" or "You didn't mean to step on Leon's fingers").

Cognitive Development

Children's notions of what constitutes "good" and "bad" behavior change with age (Kohlberg, 1964; Tisak & Block, 1990). Whether they judge an action as right or wrong is influenced by their reasoning powers and the extent to which they comprehend another person's perspective. The cognitive processes of centration and irreversibility, and the extent to which children can associate one behavior with another further affect how well they conduct themselves.

Children's Reasoning About Right and Wrong

Four- to six-year-olds make judgments about right and wrong based mainly on whether behaviors are immediately rewarded or punished. Children interpret actions that result in social rewards (e.g., a smile, positive words, getting what they want) as good and those that incur social costs (e.g., a frown, negative words, having their goals blocked) as negative. For instance, children conclude that taking turns is good because adults praise them or that pushing and shoving over who goes first is bad because adults correct them. The link between goodness–rewards and badness–punishments remains constant even if society views the behavior differently. For this reason, young children who observe a class-

mate's gaining attention by clowning around may interpret silliness as "good" because it is reinforced. They might also conclude that comforting a classmate is "bad" if the victim rejects their efforts or other children make fun of their attempts.

Another way children of this age decide that actions are bad is if such actions result in physical harm to people or property or if they violate people's rights (Tisak & Block, 1990). Actions that do, such as hitting, breaking, or calling names, are readily identified by children as unacceptable. Children do not interpret behaviors that disrupt the social order of the group, such as not putting toys away, and those that violate interpersonal trust, such as telling a secret, as inappropriate until middle childhood.

Because younger children's moral reasoning is still immature, they need a lot of support in knowing what is expected and why. Adults who state their expectations clearly and offer reasons for these expectations help children progress toward self-discipline. The reasons that make the most sense to children aged 3 to 8 years are those that focus on harmful effects to people ("Tell him you're angry; don't hit. Hitting hurts"), property ("Wear a smock so that you don't get paint on your clothes"), and human rights ("It's important that everyone get a turn").

Children's Perspective-Taking Abilities To interact effectively with others and make accurate judgments about which actions would be right or wrong in particular situations, children must understand what other people think, feel, or know (Kostelnik, Whiren, et al., 2002). This understanding is called *perspective taking*. Because this skill is just emerging in young children, youngsters 8 years old and younger often have difficulty putting themselves in another person's shoes. This dilemma is a result of being unable, rather than unwilling, to comprehend or predict other people's thoughts (Waite-Stupiansky, 1997). Thus, children have trouble recognizing other people's viewpoints, especially when such views conflict with theirs. They erroneously assume that everyone interprets each situation just as they do. Not until such differences are brought to children's attention do they begin to recognize that their perspective is not shared. At this age children benefit from hearing that there is more than one way to view a situation. This information could be supplied as relevant situations arise ("You want a turn on the tricycle. Harry wants a turn, too" or "You're having fun painting. I'm worried that the paint is getting on your sleeves") or through planned activities, such as reading a story in which different characters see the same situation differently.

Sometime between their 6th and 8th years, children start realizing that their interpretation of a situation and that of another person might not match (Bukatko & Daehler, 2001). Still, they do not always know what the differences are, or they may conclude that variations are a result of the other person's having access to incorrect or incomplete information. As a result, second and third graders often go to great lengths trying to convince others that their view is the logical view. This trait sometimes makes them appear argumentative or lacking in sensitivity. On these occasions, adults must remind themselves that such behaviors are an outgrowth of children's immature reasoning, not simple obstinacy. When this happens, children need adults to listen carefully, without interruption, and then acknowledge their perspective. Children also need to hear the facts of the situation repeated more than once and in varying ways.

The Impact of Centration   Throughout early childhood, children tend to focus their attention on a single aspect of a situation, neglecting other important features that might help them approach the situation more accurately or effectively (Peterson & Felton-Collins, 1991). This phenomenon, known as *centration,* results in children's having a limited rather than a comprehensive perception of social events. For instance, centration causes children to overlook important details regarding their actions and others' behavior. This situation is exemplified when Rayanne focuses so intently on using the glitter paint for her project that she does not realize that other children are waiting for some or that she is using it all. Centration also prompts children to focus on only one way to achieve their aims. Caleb demonstrates centration when he repeatedly says "Please" to try to get a chance to play with another child's toy from home, even though he is refused several times. Even when youngsters recognize that their actions are inappropriate, they may be unable to generate suitable alternative behaviors without adult support. The younger the child, the more this is so. The ability to see an event from more than one angle and to consider several ways to respond accrues only gradually, during many years. This ability is enhanced when early childhood professionals point out options to children and help youngsters brainstorm suitable alternatives in problem situations.

The Effects of Irreversible Thinking   Young children's behavior is further influenced by the irreversible nature of their thinking. Evidence suggests that children have difficulty mentally reversing a physical action that they are in the process of carrying out (Flavell, 1977; Waite-Stupiansky, 1997). As a result, children are not adept at contemplating opposite actions, and they have difficulty interrupting ongoing behaviors. This inability in turn influences their ability to regulate personal actions and respond to adult directions that are

stated in negative terms. For instance, when Kyley pushes on the door of the toy stove to open it, the words "Don't push" called out by the parent volunteer hold little meaning for her. She is unable mentally to transpose the physical act of pushing into its opposite action of pulling or stopping. Neither can she interrupt her pushing simply by thinking about what to do. She needs assistance to reverse her behavior. Such assistance could be an oral direction from the adult to *pull* on the door or adult modeling of the desired behavior. With maturation, children improve in their ability to mentally reverse physical actions, but the influence of irreversible thinking remains evident throughout the preschool and early elementary years. Because irreversibility is such a powerful force in children's thinking, adults must remember to state directions and expectations in positive terms. Modeling the desired behavior also helps children understand what the adult wants him or her to do or stop doing.

Associating Behaviors in Meaningful Ways   Younger children view social behaviors as self-contained events. They have difficulty seeing how a current action (e.g., calling a peer derogatory names) relates to what has gone on before or what might happen in the future (e.g., child will avoid the name-caller from then on). They also have difficulty comprehending how one action (e.g., hitting) is much like another one (e.g., kicking). This is especially true when associating these behaviors requires abstract thinking (e.g., the notion of hurting someone). Adults who offer children reasons for what is and what is not acceptable help children recognize these connections (e.g., "I can't let you hit; hitting hurts" and "It's not okay to kick. Kicking hurts"). With maturity and experience, 7- and 8-year-olds become more proficient at making such generalizations on their own (Berk, 2003). Also, they become better able to mentally categorize like behaviors and comprehend the similarities among potential outcomes (i.e., hitting, kicking, pinching, and biting are all potentially hurtful behaviors, which makes them unacceptable). However, these understandings are still forming even during the adolescent years, and not until that point do children make accurate connections entirely on their own.

Recognizing Changes in What Is Acceptable Behavior at Different Ages   One noteworthy point is that as children's thinking becomes more complex, they must continually readjust their notions of desirable and undesirable categories of behavior. For instance, throughout the preschool years children learn to seek help from adults when they see trouble and to work cooperatively to accomplish tasks. Many preschoolers learn these lessons well. However, as they move into first and second grade, such formerly desirable behaviors take on negative connotations. Labeled "tattling" and "cheating" by adults, such actions are often discouraged. At first, these new interpretations confuse children, which causes them to persist with old concepts or to become immobilized by uncertainty. Through trial and error, they eventually incorporate new definitions into their thinking and act accordingly. This reprocessing of information occurs repeatedly throughout the grade school years. It is enhanced when adults provide concrete rationales to children for classroom expectations and when teachers exercise patience as children develop more-comprehensive, sophisticated understandings.

Language Development

As children acquire greater and more-complex language skills, their capacity for self-control also increases. This increased self-control occurs because language contributes to their understanding of why rules are made and gives them more tools for attaining their goals in socially acceptable ways.

Interpersonal Speech   Children as young as 3 and 4 years old come to early childhood programs with command of a well-developed receptive vocabulary and the ability to express their basic needs (Berk, 2003). Yet, they are not always successful at telling others what they want or responding to oral directions. As a result, young children often resort to physical actions to communicate. They may grab, dash away, refuse to answer, push, or strike out rather than use words to express themselves. At such times, children need teacher assistance in determining what to say ("You seem upset. Say to Martha, 'I'm using this now'" or "You don't want Jonathan to chase you. Say, 'Stop'"). As the elementary years progress, children become more proficient in both receiving and giving oral messages. They find words a more satisfactory and precise way to communicate. However, second and third graders may still need support in determining the best words to use in emotionally charged circumstances or situations that are new to them.

Private Speech   In addition to the words they direct toward others, young children use private speech (self-talk) as a means of exercising self-control (Berk & Winsler, 1995; Vygotsky, 1978). That is, they reduce frustration, postpone rewards, or remind themselves of what to do by talking aloud to themselves. We hear this when a preschooler says to herself, "Blue shoes, blue shoes" as a reminder of what she is looking for and when a second grader outlines his approach to an assignment in a mumbled tone as a way to help himself plan. The self-talk Matt used to help himself wait through the directions to the kickball game (described previously) is another good example of children's use of private speech to gain control of their actions. Consequently, when adults hear children talking to themselves, they should allow them to continue rather than asking them to hush. Offering children sample self-talk scripts is another way to help children move toward greater self-regulation.

Memory Skills

Closely related to language are skills associated with memory. As children grow older, their memory does not necessarily increase: They just become better able to use stored data as a resource for determining future behavior (Maccoby, 1984). Preschool children and children in the lower elementary grades are still very dependent on having others show or tell them how to behave in new situations. In addition, they periodically "forget" expectations from one day to the next or from one setting to another. To be successful, they need frequent reminders about rules and procedures and clear explanations about what to expect when routines change or new activities are introduced. As children reach second and third grade, they will be better able to remember appropriate ways to act without continual adult support (Kostelnik, Whiren, et al., 2002). At this age, children benefit when adults talk with them about strategies that they can use to remember what is acceptable and what is not.

HOW EXPERIENCE INFLUENCES SELF-DISCIPLINE

As you now know, development plays a vital role in how well children eventually regulate their behavior. Children's day-to-day experiences with peers and adults are other factors that influence the degree to which children achieve self-discipline. The most frequent modes of experience include modeling, attribution, instruction, and consequences.

Modeling

One way children learn what is expected of them is by imitating the actions of powerful adults with whom they have strong, affectionate associations (Bandura, 1991). Early childhood professionals serve as such models who, through their behavior, demonstrate compliance or lack of compliance with certain standards of conduct. Young children learn potent lessons regarding desirable attitudes and behaviors as well as how to enact them when they see their teachers treat others with kindness, tell the truth, use reasoning as a way to solve problems, or assist someone in need. Alternatively, because youngsters also follow negative models, they sometimes imitate the aggressive or thoughtless acts committed by those around them.

Attribution

Attribution is an oral strategy that adults use to influence children's images of themselves and therefore their behavior (Moore, 1986). Teachers use attributions unconsciously or deliberately to direct children's attention to positive traits ("brave," "smart," or "kind") or negative traits ("stupid," "lazy," or "good-for-nothing"). For instance, teachers may characterize children as "patient" or "good at waiting." When this occurs, children gradually become even more patient and better able to delay gratification. Conversely, when adults tell children they are naughty or irresponsible, children not only incorporate these negative labels into their self-image but also adapt in greater measure the corresponding behaviors to support them (Dreikurs & Soltz, 1991). Attribution induces children to think of themselves in the terms described and to behave in corresponding ways to live up to the adult's image of them.

Instruction

Instruction may be carried out indirectly, in response to an ongoing interaction, or in planned lessons.

Indirect Instruction Indirect instruction involves all the behind-the-scenes work and planning that ultimately influences young children's behavior (Hildebrand, 1997). These teaching methods tend to be aimed at creating a classroom atmosphere in which self-control is enhanced. We already focused in this text on positive methods of indirect instruction. For instance, the use of environmental cues, as described in chapters 3 and 4, signals children about the expectations for tasks or learning areas that may not be specified by oral or written instruction. Similarly, the strategies that you read about in chapter 5 were designed to help children manage their behavior and get along with peers. How adults organize space, equipment, materials, and the daily schedule affects the degree to which children develop the skills they need to be self-regulating. For example, warning children about upcoming transitions allows them to anticipate a change in routine and adjust their behavior accordingly. Simply expecting children to shift quickly from one activity to the next without warning fails to supply the tools children need to regulate their behavior well.

On-the-Spot Coaching In contrast with the indirect methods just described, on-the-spot coaching involves physical or oral intervention aimed at influencing the behavior of particular children at a particular time. What is right, what is wrong, which behaviors are expected, which are restricted, how behavioral standards are to be met, and how children's behavior appears to others are directly conveyed to children through words and actions. This assistance is provided as relevant situations arise, which allows early childhood professionals to take advantage of teachable moments throughout the day. In doing so, teachers not only remind children of appropriate behavioral standards, but also supply children with information they can use to regulate their future behavior. This instruction occurs within a relevant context and in a way that is supportive, not punitive. Thus, early childhood professionals teach children self-control directly by using oral strategies such as informing, suggesting, advising, explaining, reasoning, encouraging, and clarifying (Weinstein & Mignano, 2003). Typical remarks include "Cover your mouth when you cough," "Maybe you could take turns," "Tell him you're angry—don't hit," "Mr. Ramirez really appreciated when you helped him carry those boxes," and "When you didn't say 'Hi' back, she thought you didn't like her." Physical assistance, demonstrations, redirection, distraction, substitution, removal, and physical restraint are additional techniques associated with direct instruction (Gartrell, 2003; Wolfgang, 1996).

Planned Lessons On-the-spot coaching occurs at various times throughout the day as children's behavior warrants it. However, planned lessons are thought out by the teacher in advance and may constitute part or all of an activity. Such lessons may be carried out at any time of the day by using one or more of the teaching strategies described in chapter 3. The following examples illustrate this kind of instruction.

Mr. Wilson wants children to learn the words please *and* thank you. *He plans to teach his class the following rhyme: "Two little magic words open any door with ease. One little word is 'Thanks.' The other little word is 'Please.'" He carries out this minilesson during the circle time at the end of the day.*

In Ms. Carson's multiage primary class the children are planning and carrying out a group project—building a rocket out of an old refrigerator box. Their teacher gathers materials in advance and prepares a large open space in which they can work. She also leads the children in a discussion of the steps they think they might use to implement their project from start to finish. As the children proceed, Ms. Carson helps them refer to their plan to see how well they are following it.

Consequences

Other instructional tools that early childhood professionals use are *consequences*. Consequences come in two varieties—positive and negative—and are aimed at rewarding desirable behaviors or penalizing negative behaviors. For example, practitioners reward children for following rules by using praise ("You remembered your pictures from home; now you're ready for today's work on animals") and tangible rewards ("Here's a star sticker for remembering to return your library book" or "You did such a good job cleaning up, you may have 10 more minutes of recess"). Such strategies are aimed at increasing the likelihood that children will repeat their positive acts in the future and are examples of positive consequences.

Teachers use negative consequences to reduce the probability that undesirable behaviors will be repeated (Dinkmeyer, McKay, Dinkmeyer, Dinkmeyer, & McKay, 1997; Vasta, Haith, & Miller, 1998). The way in which negative consequences are enacted influences how effective they are in promoting self-discipline. Negative consequences that are harsh, unreasonable, and shameful cause children to feel demeaned or fearful. Neither of these reactions leads to guilt or empathy, both of which are emotions necessary for the emergence of self-discipline. Nevertheless, some negative consequences are constructive actions that help children learn alternative ways to achieve their aims through the process of being corrected. They enable children to approximate desirable conduct and remind them of the impact that their actions have on themselves and others (Charney, 1998). Corrective action taken in this manner provides children with valuable information they can use to guide their actions on their own in the future.

HOW ADULT DISCIPLINE STYLES INFLUENCE CHILDREN'S SELF-DISCIPLINE

Instruction, modeling, attribution, and consequences are practices all early childhood professionals use in one way or another. Such strategies can be combined differently, which results in distinct adult discipline styles. These variations in style have been the subject of research since the late 1970s. Although we still have much to learn, we can safely say that most adults approach child guidance in one of four ways: from an uninvolved approach, a permissive standpoint, an authoritarian viewpoint, or an authoritative perspective (Baumrind, 1967, 1973, 1995). Each of these discipline styles is characterized by certain adult attitudes and strategies related to the four social dimensions of control, communication, maturity demands, and nurturance:

1. *Control* is the way and extent to which parents and teachers enforce compliance with their expectations.
2. *Communication* involves how much information adults provide children throughout the guidance process.

3. *Maturity demands* describes the level at which adults set their expectations for children's behavior and compliance.
4. *Nurturance* refers to how much caring and concern is expressed toward children.

Differences among the uninvolved, permissive, authoritarian, and authoritative styles result from varying combinations of these four dimensions (see Figure 6.1; Bukatko & Daehler, 2001; Shaffer, 2002):

Uninvolved adults are low in all four dimensions.

Permissive adults are high in nurturance, but low in control; make few maturity demands; and engage in minimal communication with children.

Adults employing an *authoritarian* style are high in control and maturity demands and low in communication and nurturance.

Early childhood professionals who are high in all four dimensions demonstrate an *authoritative* style.

Few people personify a "pure" style regardless of which one they adopt. In fact, from time to time adults may demonstrate behaviors characteristic of all four. However, adults also commonly gravitate more toward one style than the others. Recognizing the characteristics of each and their impact on children helps us to understand the relationship between adult behavior and child outcomes. Knowing this, early childhood professionals can make deliberate choices regarding their approach to child guidance. Such information also helps us to better appreciate the goals parents have for their children's behavior and the strategies they use to achieve their aims.

The Uninvolved Teaching Style

Teachers who demonstrate an uninvolved style put little effort into developing relationships with children or guiding their behavior (Hetherington & Clingempeel, 1992). Such adults are egocentric, focusing on their personal needs and agendas before the children's. This self-absorption may arise for various reasons, including stress, depression, or ill health. Whatever the cause, the outcomes for children are poor. Youngsters lack the security that comes with positive relationships and the comprehension that comes through reasoning. They have no way to determine right from wrong and no opportunity to develop relevant social skills. Such youngsters get a clear message that they are unimportant and that the adult has little hope for their future. None of these circumstances promotes self-regulation. Instead, youngsters whose lives are dominated by uninvolved adults display feelings of insecurity and alienation as well as detached and disruptive behaviors early in life. Truancy, delinquency, and precocious sexuality

FIGURE 6.1 Differences in Attitudes and Practices Among the Uninvolved, Permissive, Authoritarian, and Authoritative Discipline Styles

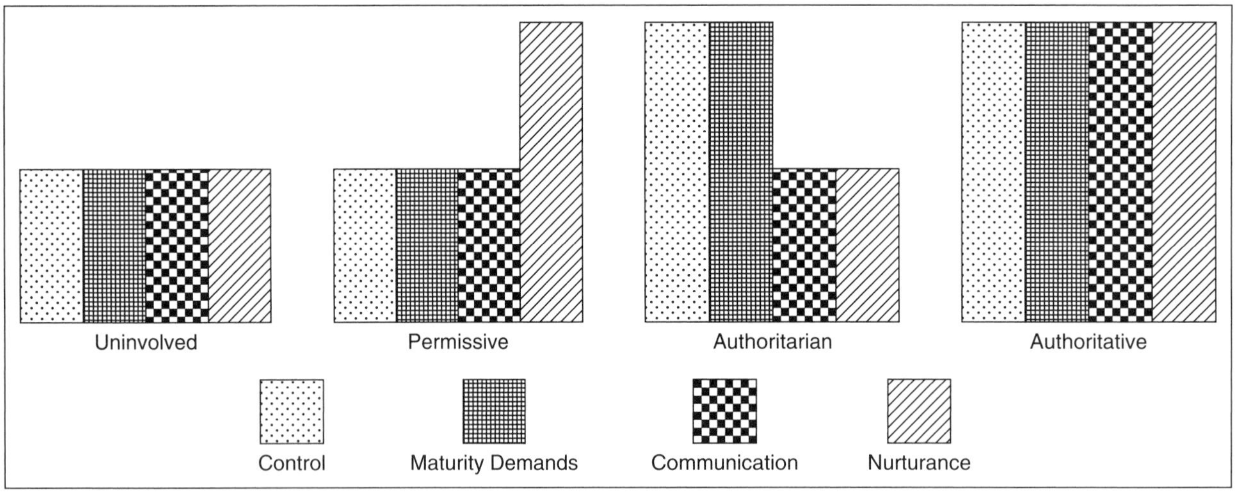

The bars labeled: Uninvolved, Permissive, Authoritarian, Authoritative. Legend: Control, Maturity Demands, Communication, Nurturance.

are common behaviors of such children during adolescence (Baumrind, 1991).

The Permissive Teaching Style

Permissive teachers treat children with warmth and affection. However, they pay little attention to shaping children's present or future behavior. Some teachers do this because they believe that having positive relationships with children is sufficient to get youngsters to behave in socially acceptable ways. Other adults believe that behavior controls stifle children's development. Still others drift into this approach simply because they do not know how to get children to "listen." Whatever the reason, permissive adults provide little instruction to children about what is acceptable behavior and what is not. They do not talk with children about how their behavior affects others or help children recognize other people's needs. Because these instructors have low expectations for children's conduct, they give children minimal responsibility and ignore most negative behaviors. If a child engages in gross misconduct, permissive adults use love withdrawal as their primary means of discipline ("I don't like children who hit"; Baumrind, 1978; Shaffer, 2002). This response temporarily denies children the one social support permissive adults are usually willing to provide—nurturance.

Unfortunately, children subjected to a permissive approach show few signs of self-discipline (Baumrind, 1995; Berk, 2003). This lack of control occurs for several reasons. First, because the impact of their behavior on others is not explained, children fail to develop feelings of guilt and empathy, the necessary ingredients for self-regulation. Second, the fact that youngsters receive few cues about which behaviors are

socially acceptable and which are not also means children do not develop the backlog of experience they need to make appropriate decisions in the future. Third, to make matters worse, peers and other adults tend to view these children's unrestricted conduct as immature, inconsiderate, and unacceptable. This negative perception contributes to children's feelings of anxiety and low self-esteem. As a result, children who interact mainly with permissive adults tend to be withdrawn, unproductive, and dissatisfied with their lives. By adolescence, the permissive style is correlated with delinquent behavior and poor academic performance (Patterson & Stouthamer-Loeber, 1984; Pulkkinen, 1982). These negative outcomes are similar to those associated with the style that is its direct opposite: the authoritarian style.

The Authoritarian Teaching Style

Unlike permissive educators, authoritarian teachers have high standards for children's behavior and exert strong control over children's actions. To achieve these standards and control, they act as strict taskmasters who value children's unquestioning obedience above all else. Theirs is the philosophy of "I say and you obey" and "Do it because I said so!" Failure to meet their expectations is dealt with swiftly and forcefully, most often through shaming techniques or physical punishment. In either case, their chief aim is to show children who is boss as opposed to helping children consider how their behavior affects others or how to determine better strategies to use in the future. Not too surprisingly, authoritarian adults have cold, distant relationships with young children. Youngsters view them as harsh disciplinarians who focus more on finding mistakes than on recognizing their efforts to behave appropriately (Shaffer, 2000).

The coercive discipline strategies characteristic of the authoritarian style cause children to maintain an external orientation to behavior regulation. In the short term, youngsters act in required ways out of fear or unreasoned obedience, not out of empathy or concern for others (P. R. Newman & Newman, 1997). This behavior impedes their ability to develop the reasoning and caring necessary for self-discipline. In the long run, children whose primary experiences are with authoritarian adults tend to become unfriendly, suspicious, resentful, and unhappy in the classroom. They are often underachievers and exhibit increased incidents of misconduct as well as extreme antisocial behaviors (Baumrind, 1983, 1995). These outcomes add up to a dismal prognosis for children who are the product of this teaching style. A more positive outcome results from the authoritative approach, which we consider next.

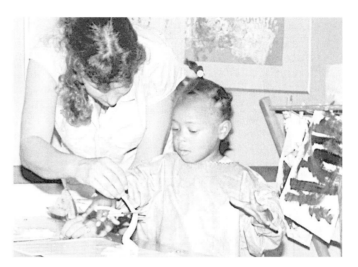

Authoritative teaching begins with positive teacher–child relationships.

The Authoritative Teaching Style

Authoritative teachers combine the positive dimensions of permissiveness (nurturance) and authoritarianism (maturity demands and control) while avoiding the negative aspects (Bukatko & Daehler, 2001). In addition, such teachers rely on some strategies that permissive and authoritarian adults fail to use, such as clear communication and other-oriented reasoning. Early childhood professionals who adopt an authoritative style encourage children to assume appropriate responsibility and get what they need in socially acceptable ways. When children attempt a new skill, adults acknowledge their accomplishments; when children face challenges, teachers help them develop new approaches. These methods contribute to children's feelings of competence and worth. Simultaneously, authoritative teachers establish high standards for children's behavior and are quick to take action to teach them how to strive toward these standards. Explanations, demonstrations, suggestions, and reasoning are the primary instructional strategies they use (Hendrick, 2001; Lefrançois, 2001). When children behave inappropriately, authoritative adults take advantage of the opportunity to discuss guilt, empathy, and the perspectives of others. They also provide on-the-spot coaching to help children recognize acceptable and unacceptable behaviors as well as potential alternatives. This nonpunitive form of child guidance is sometimes called *inductive discipline* because adults induce children to regulate their behavior on the basis of the impact their actions will have on themselves and others (Kostelnik, Whiren, et al., 2002).

The authoritative approach to child guidance is the style most strongly related to the development of self-discipline (Franz, McClelland, & Weinberger, 1991; Vasta et al., 1998). Children know what is expected of them.

They also develop the skills necessary to behave in accordance with that knowledge. Such youngsters tend to be sensitive to others' needs, happy, and cooperative. They are well equipped to resist temptation, delay gratification, and control their negative impulses. They are also better able to initiate and maintain constructive social plans on their own (Baumrind, 1983, 1995). Consequently, their behavior is the most internalized of the four patterns described in this text. For all these reasons, children benefit when early childhood professionals adopt an authoritative approach to child guidance.

Adoption of an Authoritative Approach to Child Guidance

Because authoritative teaching is the most effective way to promote self-discipline in children, it is strongly aligned with developmentally appropriate practice. Permissive, neglectful strategies and authoritarian methods are categorized as inappropriate (Bredekamp & Copple, 1997). Many people formerly believed that teachers' discipline styles were directly related to their personalities or temperaments. Such individuals further assumed that not much could be done to change a person's natural style (Lewin, Lippitt, & White, 1939). We now know that, although early childhood educators do have personality traits and abilities that seem more in keeping with one style or another, through training and practice any early childhood professional can learn to be more authoritative (Kostelnik, Whiren, et al., 2002). The following strategies in combination exemplify an authoritative approach. They are listed sequentially so that preventive strategies precede remedial strategies.

❑ *Authoritative teachers build positive relationships with children*   (Gartrell, 2003; Kontos & Wilcox-Herzog,

1997). Establishing emotionally supportive relationships with children is the cornerstone on which authoritative teaching rests. In the classrooms of authoritative teachers, children are treated with warmth, caring, empathy, and respect. Adults interact with each child each day in ways children interpret as supportive, attentive, and enjoyable. Teachers enhance their relationships with children when they do the following:

Greet children by name

Get down to the children's eye level when talking with them

Smile at children often

Listen carefully to what children have to say

Speak politely to children

Invite children to talk or interact with them

Comfort children who are unhappy or afraid

Laugh with children at their jokes

Talk with children about their (the children's) feelings

Assist children in finding constructive ways to express their emotions to others

Never coerce, shame, taunt, or physically hurt children for any reason

❑ *Authoritative teachers model behaviors they hope children will imitate* (Bandura, 1991; Reynolds, 2001). Setting a good example is an effective way to teach children right from wrong because it proves to them that certain behaviors are desirable. However, simply observing appropriate actions does not necessarily teach children how to enact them. To move to this level of learning, children's attention must be drawn to the specifics of the model's behavior. Teachers provide such guidance when they point out the model's actions and talk children through what they are seeing. Doing so helps youngsters identify the critical facets of an interaction that they might otherwise miss. Therefore, if a teacher wants children to copy his or her gentle handling of the class gerbil, he or she could say, "Watch how I pick up the gerbil. First, I'll put both hands under her tummy so I don't drop her. See how I'm holding my fingers? This way I don't squeeze her too hard." Showing children the procedure without direct explanation or hoping that they will figure it out themselves simply by watching is less likely to result in accurate imitation. Moreover, modeling is most potent when the teacher behaves in ways consistent with his or her words. Mrs. Lopez, who emphasizes the value of polite behaviors and remembers to say "Please" and "Excuse me" when talking to the children, illustrates such congruence. She is more likely to achieve compliance with her expectations than will Mrs. Kelly, who preaches good manners but frequently interrupts children or orders them to do things without the customary social graces.

❑ *Authoritative teachers use positive attribution to support children's favorable self-perceptions* (Wittmer & Honig, 1994). Teachers help children become tidier, less impulsive, more generous, or more cooperative by referring to them in these terms and espousing their belief that the child in question can act in these ways. For instance, when the children are standing at the door, Mrs. Martine notices their efforts to wait and makes remarks such as "Corey, you're waiting very patiently," "Janice, you really know how to wait—you're standing with your arms down and your feet still," and "Keiko, you're showing a lot of patience standing there." Children hear remarks such as these frequently. The teacher does not wait for full compliance but recognizes approximations toward the desired end. In this way, children gradually perceive themselves as capable of exercising patience and become more patient with time. Likewise, before starting a small-group activity, Mr. Noor prefaces his directions by stating, "This project will require a lot of cooperation, and I know you can do it." In both examples, teachers have deliberately used positive attribution to promote children's positive self-image and increase their repertoire of socially acceptable behaviors.

❑ *Authoritative teachers emphasize cooperation rather than competition to promote empathy among children and increase children's social skills.* Such teachers encourage all children to do their best but never at one another's expense (Marion, 1999). Thus, they avoid pitting one child or group of children against another (e.g., "Let's see who will get the most problems right, the boys or the girls") and refrain from using competition to motivate children to get things done (e.g., "Let's see who can put the most blocks away" or "Whoever gets the most problems right can pick the game for recess"). Similarly, they do not reinforce one child at the expense of another (e.g., "Cathleen, your paper is so very neat, I wish the rest of the class would try hard like you"). Such competitive strategies cause children to conclude there can be only one winner and that helping or cooperating with others will sabotage their chances to come out on top. To counteract self-centered thinking, teachers focus on individual progress and group accomplishments instead (e.g., "You got more problems right today than you did yesterday" or "Let's see how quickly we can all put the blocks away"). Remarks like these clear the way for students to come to one another's aid and work together as appropriate. In addition, group rewards encourage children to work as a team to accomplish common aims. Putting up a star for each book read by the class or each act of kindness shown is one way to help children keep track of their progress as a whole and direct their attention to the positive outcomes an entire group can achieve.

❑ *Authoritative teachers help children learn prosocial skills as a way to promote empathy and social competence* (L. G. Katz & McClellan, 1997). These teachers
plan activities such as inviting children to create a
mural cooperatively or assigning "buddies" to help one
another with a project as a way to accomplish this aim.
Such teachers read books that focus on helpful or cooperative behaviors and lead class discussions about these
concepts. They also demonstrate kindness through skits
and role-playing activities. In chapter 14, we provide examples of this type of instruction. Teachers also use on-
the-spot instruction to help children learn the basics of
kindness—what it looks like and how it feels. Inviting
children to comfort an injured classmate and giving children information about how their teasing hurt another
child's feelings are typical situations in which such on-
the-spot teaching could be used.

❑ *Authoritative teachers help children learn to negotiate as a way to achieve their aims nonaggressively*
(Weinstein & Mignano, 2003). Teachers use three approaches to help children learn to negotiate. One is to
create natural opportunities for children to practice negotiation skills. For instance, rather than putting the
same color of paint on two easels to avoid arguments,
the teacher makes different colors available at each. He
or she then urges the children to find ways to share
their resources. Children are allowed to work things out
for themselves with on-the-spot coaching provided by
peers or the adult.

A second approach is for teachers to use puppets,
flannel board stories, storybooks, or skits to illustrate
relevant negotiation skills such as sharing, turns taking, and bargaining (Crary, 1996). Children have
chances to see both appropriate and inappropriate skill
use, evaluate the tactics chosen, and generate ideas for
alternative resolutions.

A third strategy is to turn children's everyday arguments into opportunities for them to learn conflict resolution techniques in real-life situations. This method is
particularly important because even youngsters who can
rationally discuss the value of negotiation within the
context of a planned activity may forget and resort to
aggressive strategies in the heat of actual confrontations.
At times like these, children benefit from having a mediator assist them through the steps necessary for recon-
ciliation to occur. Mediators are often adults, but they
may also be other children in the program (DeVogue,
1996; High/Scope Curriculum, 1998). In chapter 14, we
provide a step-by-step model of conflict mediation and
describe how to teach children effective mediation skills.

❑ *Authoritative teachers encourage children to participate in the rule-making process* (Bickart, Dodge, &
Jablon, 1997; Weinstein & Mignano, 2003). Early child-

hood professionals hold class meetings and open-ended
discussions in which they invite children to help create
the broad rules by which everyone in the class will live.
Such a discussion might begin with the teacher's
asking, "How can we make our classroom a safe, comfortable, and happy place to learn?" Children's ideas are
written on a chart and then posted for all to see. Sample
rules might be the following:

Be helpful to others.

Solve problems with words.

Treat others the way you want to be treated.

Respect people's property.

Act in ways that are safe.

Similar discussions are carried on throughout the year
so that youngsters may consider the value of their rules
with time and revise them as necessary. In this way children and teachers share responsibility for typical classroom rules and for making sure such rules are followed.

❑ *Authoritative teachers intervene and redirect children's behavior when children's actions could hurt
someone, damage property, or interfere with the rights of
others* (Bredekamp & Copple, 1997). When authoritative teachers see a potential problem brewing, they ask
themselves the following three questions: (a) Is the
child's behavior potentially or currently unsafe for the
child or others? (b) Does the child's behavior threaten to

*Even very young children can help create meaningful
rules for the classroom.*

damage property? (c) Does the child's behavior interfere with the rights of others? If the answer to any of these questions is yes, the teacher intervenes by setting a limit on the child's behavior. Doing so involves explaining why the behavior is unacceptable and redirecting the child to engage in a more appropriate action. This alternative behavior becomes a rule for the situation at hand (Kostelnik, Whiren, et al., 2002). For instance, Mr. Woodson observes that Mallory is squeezing the guinea pig until it squeals. Knowing that the animal is frightened, he intervenes. Placing his hand lightly on Mallory's, he says, "You're having fun with the guinea pig. He sounds like you might be squeezing too hard. That hurts. Hold him gently like this." If Mallory cannot loosen her grip, Mr. Woodson will physically assist her in holding the animal more appropriately or put the frightened creature back in its cage for a while. Although individual teachers vary in their interpretation of what makes a situation potentially dangerous or threatening, considering the preceding three questions is a consistent, dependable means for deciding when to set limits on children's behavior.

❑ *Authoritative teachers address problem behaviors that are important enough to deal with each time that they occur and ignore those that are not* (Bredekamp & Copple, 1997). Authoritative teachers set only limits that are important enough to enforce each time the problem behavior arises. They realize that not every minor infraction requires intervention. For instance, when Ms. Williams sees a child deliberately ruin another child's artwork, she intervenes immediately, reminding children of the rule about respecting people's property. Also, she continues to enforce the rule, day after day, no matter how tired or otherwise occupied she might be. However, although she sometimes finds children's smacking their lips loudly while they eat irritating, many days she does not want to be bothered with restricting this behavior. Because "on again, off again" limits do not provide the consistent enforcement children need to learn them, Ms. Williams tolerates this minor annoyance in order to address more important issues for the time being. Later, if she determines that children's lip smacking truly interferes with their ability to eat safely, she will make "quiet lips" a limit and enforce this rule each day. Thus, the criterion of *importance* helps authoritative teachers order their priorities and focus on only a few guidelines for behavior at a time. This approach increases the likelihood that children will be able to follow the guidelines successfully.

❑ *Authoritative teachers state their expectations in reasonable, definable, and positive ways* (Clarizio, 1980; Kostelnik, Whiren, et al., 2002). *Reasonable* means children can actually do the required behavior; that is, youngsters have both the knowledge and the

ability to meet the expectation. For instance, if children are expected to work on their journals independently, the teacher must first determine whether they already possess the necessary skills—knowledge of where the journals are kept, previous practice with paper and writing tools, the ability to distinguish their property from that of others, and the skills to write in a focused way for a period of time. If children lack know-how about any of these, the teacher might revise the rule to match their abilities or spend time teaching them the required actions.

Definable expectations are those in which both the adult and the child have the same understanding of the expectation. Effective statements identify the exact behaviors the adult wants the child to perform. Specific expectations such as "Walk; don't run" and "Only knock down your own blocks" are easier for children to follow than are vague statements such as "Act nice" and "Behave yourself."

Finally, children are more successful at meeting expectations that tell them what to do instead of what not to do. "Put your hands in your pockets" is less difficult for children to respond to than "Don't fidget" or "No pushing." Likewise, "Sing softly; don't shout" is more apt to lead to compliance than the statement "Don't shout" all by itself. Therefore, how expectations are stated has much to do with how well children can follow them. Teachers who state *positive* rules are more likely to help children move toward internalization than teachers who do not.

❑ *Authoritative teachers offer children reasons, explaining why certain behaviors are acceptable or unacceptable* (Bugental & Goodnow, 1998; Faber & Mazlish, 1995). Reasons help expectations and limits make sense. The reasons that make the most sense to children aged 3 to 8 years are those that are specific, that help them associate one behavior with another, and that match their developmental understandings. Mr. Ramirez is addressing these three criteria when he tells Dana, who is shouting across the room to a friend, "Walk over and tell her what you found so other people can concentrate on their work." In this way, he has linked the desired action to the rights of others in the class. In other situations, he might refer to safety issues or the protection of property because these are the reasons children this age find most credible. Simply forbidding Dana to talk "Because I said so" or "Because that's the rule in our room" would be too general and therefore inappropriate. Reasons are essential to the critical thinking necessary for self-discipline to develop. Therefore, authoritative teachers provide reasons every time they make a rule or intervene to correct a child's mistaken behavior (e.g., "I'm worried you'll fall if you run. Please walk" or "There are only enough cupcakes for everyone to have one. Put one back").

❏ *Authoritative teachers remind children of the rules often* (Bickart et al., 1997). Such teachers know that children may forget what constitutes appropriate behavior from one day to the next or from one situation to another. They also realize that although children may understand that certain behaviors such as running in the classroom are not allowed, youngsters may not be able to substitute a more acceptable action without coaching. Teachers' reminders take two forms. First, they talk with children about desirable behaviors at times when infractions are not an issue. Such discussions allow children to calmly explore the value and reasons for certain expectations without the added pressure of conflict between their needs or desires and those of others. Second, early childhood professionals remind children of the rules at the moment when the rules are needed. For example, teachers say, "Remember to walk in the classroom" when children are caught running. They avoid accusatory statements such as "How many times have I told you about running inside?" or "You know better than to run inside." Such statements fail to teach children the appropriate alternative behavior and do not help them remember what to do the next time. The former reminder serves as a minilesson from which children can extract meaningful information for the future.

❏ *Authoritative teachers use substitution to channel children's inappropriate behaviors in more positive directions* (Bredekamp & Copple, 1997). If a child is making jokes during the Author's Chair group time, the early childhood professional substitutes another time of the day for this behavior ("You may tell jokes *after* group is over, not now"). If a child is pounding on a fragile toy, the adult substitutes pounding at the workbench. If a child is washing the table with dirty water, the adult asks the child to substitute clean water instead. When several children are talking and therefore blocking the entrance to the classroom, the adult asks them to move to a better spot. In each case, the children's actions are rechanneled by substituting a more appropriate time, object, or place.

❏ *Authoritative teachers use positive consequences to maintain children's desirable behaviors* (Wolfgang, 1996). Authoritative teachers recognize the effort required by children to display positive behaviors or compliance, and they take the time to acknowledge these productive outcomes. One way they do this is by using effective praise. As you may remember from chapter 3, such praise means giving children specific feedback about the appropriate behaviors they display and why such actions are desirable. Thus, Ms. Tanimoto reinforces Bert's efforts to remember to raise his hand by saying, "Bert, you remembered to raise your hand. That shows you have something to tell us." She does not simply say, "Good job, Bert." The former comment highlights Bert's appropriate behavior in a way that

makes sense to him and acknowledges that he has followed a classroom rule. Conversely, the perfunctory "Good job" gives Bert little information and may lose its meaning with time.

Sometimes positive consequences are implemented in the form of earned privileges. For instance, if the rule is "Push the keys on the computer one at a time," children might be told that when they demonstrate this skill they can use the computer on their own. By granting increased independence, the teacher rewards children for carrying out the desired action.

❏ *Authoritative teachers stop children's unsafe behavior first and then work on resolving the problem that prompted it* (Reynolds, 2001). When children's actions are potentially harmful to themselves or others, authoritative teachers step in immediately to halt the dangerous actions. At times doing so requires physical intervention such as positioning themselves between two angry children or using mild physical restraint. Once the dangerous situation has been neutralized and children can focus on what is being said, the adult begins to help children work through the difficulty. Such instruction may be accomplished by holding a conversation, redirecting, offering children choices, removing the child from the situation for a brief time, or modifying the environment in some way to allow children to meet their needs more easily and get along.

❏ *Authoritative teachers use logical consequences to help children learn acceptable conduct from the experience of being corrected* (Eaton, 1997). *Logical consequences* teach children alternative behaviors to replace the inappropriate strategies they may be using to satisfy their needs and desires. As these substitute means are strengthened through practice and positive consequences, children gradually incorporate them into their behavioral repertoire, which facilitates their acting appropriately in the future.

Logical consequences make an obvious connection between the child's behavior and the resulting intervention (Wolfgang, 1996). Consequences of this type help children either rehearse the desired behavior or, in some way, restore a problem situation to a more positive state. For example, if the rule is "Walk; don't run" and Louise runs down the hall, a logical consequence would be to have her retrace her steps and walk. The act of walking approximates the rule and allows Louise to enact it physically. This consequence provides her with a better reminder than simply scolding her. Children who practice rules in this way increase their chances for future compliance.

At times, such approximations are not feasible, so restitution is an alternative. For instance, if Julie draws on the wall, the logical consequence would be to insist that she wash off the marks. This action would return the wall to a more acceptable state and show Julie that the unacceptable act of defacing the classroom will not be tolerated. This type of adult intervention is a better solution than simply forbidding her to participate in a favorite activity or making her sit away from the group for a while. Although the latter acts demonstrate adult displeasure, they do not teach Julie responsibility toward school property. Used too often, such unrelated consequences keep children at the adherence level of compliance rather than providing them with the tools needed for internalization.

❏ *Authoritative teachers warn children of the logical consequences for breaking rules before applying them.* Such warnings are given through an either–or statement that repeats the rule and describes to the child what will happen if the rule is broken (Kostelnik, Whiren, et al., 2002). For example, if the rule is "Push your sleeves up before you paint," the warning could be "Either push your sleeves up yourself, or I will help you." If the rule is "Wait your turn in line," the warning might be "Either wait your turn, or go to the end of the line." In both cases, the warning gives children the opportunity and incentive to change their behavior themselves. It also serves as a signal that if they do not comply, the adult will take steps to ensure their compliance. Maintaining a calm demeanor is essential so that the warning becomes a plain statement of fact rather than a threat. Its purpose is to provide maximum guidance to children before adult enforcement.

❏ *Authoritative teachers follow through on their warnings when children fail to comply.* Following through is essential because it helps children make a connection between the broken rule and a more desirable, alternative behavior. Because logical consequences are educational, following through gives children valuable information about how to redirect their behavior (Curwin & Mendler, 1999). It also shows them that adults mean what they say, which makes the classroom a more predictable place in which to learn.

The follow-through procedure consists of first acknowledging the child's desire within the situation. This acknowledgment is a nonevaluative summary of the event from the child's viewpoint. The next step is to repeat the warning briefly and then declare that the consequence will take place. A sample script follows: "Ralph, you're eager to get a drink. Remember I said either wait your turn or go to the end of the line. Now go to the end of the line." The teacher waits a moment to see if Ralph can do so himself. If not, the teacher might have to escort Ralph to the designated spot as a way to maintain enforcement.

Following through in this way must be consistent. Every time the rule is broken, the consequence must be enforced. Rules enforced erratically, varying from situation to situation or from child to child, are rules that children ignore. Authoritative teachers thus insist on only a few rules as a way to maintain consistency.

Rule enforcement must be immediate. Once the teacher gives the warning and a short time for the child to comply, he or she must follow through if compliance does not occur. Long delays between when the child breaks the rule and when the follow-through takes place diminish the educational impact of the consequence.

When warnings are consistently followed by enactment of logical consequences, teachers' actions become predictable to children. Youngsters learn that if they do not comply at the warning stage, a follow-through will take place. This strategy encourages them to respond to the warning without having to experience a consequence directly. Behavior change at this point shows some self-regulation by children, although at the adherence level. Gradually, children learn to use rules and their accompanying reasons as a behavioral guide. In this way, they begin to exercise more control over their conduct while teachers exert less. Thus, children gradually make the transition from external to internal behavior controls.

❏ *Authoritative teachers collaborate with family members to promote children's self-discipline* (Gartrell, 2003; Kostelnik, Whiren, et al., 2002). Children benefit when all the significant adults in their lives communicate and work together toward mutual goals. With this fact in mind, teachers talk with family members about their expectations for their children and the guidance strategies they use at home. In turn, teachers acquaint families with expectations held for children in the early childhood setting, answering family members' questions honestly and openly. In addition, early childhood staff talk with family members about mutual ways to help children achieve self-control. These conversations are held in a spirit of shared learning and support.

THE RELATIONSHIP BETWEEN AUTHORITATIVE TEACHING AND DEVELOPMENTALLY APPROPRIATE PRACTICE

Although the strategies associated with authoritative teaching are strongly associated with developmentally appropriate practice, they alone are not sufficient to equal it. As with all other aspects of early childhood education, early childhood professionals must ask themselves if their expectations and the methods they use to maintain them are age appropriate, individually appropriate, and socially and culturally appropriate for the children. With these queries in mind, let us consider the following expectation, which is typical in many early childhood classrooms:

At group time, children must raise their hands to speak.

Question: Is this expectation age appropriate?

Answer: This is not an age-appropriate expectation for 3-year-olds, who are just learning to converse in groups. On the basis of what we know about young children's need for sensory involvement and movement, group-time activities should not be dominated by oral turn taking and waiting. A better strategy would be to practice such skills in small groups of two or three children. In either case, hand raising is not a particularly useful way to help young children learn to talk together.

Children 7 and 8 years old will be better equipped to respond to this rule. They have both the oral and physical skills necessary to wait and to signal with a raised hand that they desire to talk.

Question: Is this expectation individually appropriate?

Answer: This might be an appropriate expectation for Dan, who has had many opportunities to participate in circle-time conversations and who is feeling relaxed and comfortable in the group. It may be less appropriate for Duwana, who is new to the classroom and is feeling apprehensive about participating in the group conversation.

Question: Is this expectation socially and culturally appropriate?

Answer: This expectation may fit some children's cultural experience. However, it may be less relevant to children whose family and community experiences include a strong emphasis on group response and spontaneous affirmations of things that are being said. Program setting and activity type are other sociocultural factors to consider. Raising your hand to speak may make sense as part of a demonstration, but it may be irrelevant if brainstorming is the group activity under way.

This example illustrates the complexity of guiding children's behavior. There are no "one size fits all" answers. Instead, early childhood professionals continually make judgments about the standards they set and the strategies they use. Adults gear their guidance strategies to match and respect children's current capabilities, simultaneously recognizing that what may work best for one group of children may not be suitable for a second group and that what is effective for one child may not be best for another (Bredekamp & Copple, 1997). In deciding which strategies to use and when, authoritative teachers also consider less intru-

sive alternatives before engaging in those that require more intervention. This approach is illustrated in Figure 6.2, the authoritative teaching continuum (Gordon & Browne, 1996). The initial strategies in the continuum give children maximum control of the situation; the latter strategies put more control in the adult's hands.

AUTHORITATIVE TEACHING AND THE IMPORTANCE OF TEAMWORK AMONG STAFF

Individual teachers who adopt authoritative methods report increased satisfaction with their teaching and more confidence in working with children. They also report better harmony in the classroom and more frequent incidents of positive behaviors among their students (Kontos & Wilcox-Herzog, 1997). These positive results are multiplied when all personnel in the early childhood setting (full time, part time, paid, and volunteer) collectively and consciously set out to adopt an authoritative approach (Bernero, 2003; Gartrell, 2003). The more successful the adults are in creating an authoritative environment, the more easily children develop the relationships and skills they need to achieve self-discipline.

The essential element in creating an authoritative environment, whether in a single early childhood classroom or in a multiclassroom program, is communication. Communication is fostered when the program includes the following:

❏ A written policy describing how discipline will be addressed in the early childhood setting. This document describes how discipline problems will be prevented, how staff will support children's positive behaviors, and what to do if children engage in inappropriate behavior (J. A. Taylor & Baker, 2002). A copy of the policy is provided to every staff member, volunteer, and parent or other relevant family member. Such policies usually include a brief statement of beliefs regarding the importance of self-discipline and the conditions that foster it; a small number of critical rules children and adults have helped to create; and a statement of how the rules will be established and maintained.

❏ Opportunities for staff members and family members to share ideas and work together to promote self-discipline among children. Regular communication occurs between home and the program, including formal and informal interactions.

❏ In-service training that addresses the skills associated with authoritative teaching. Such training involves everyone who works with children in the

FIGURE 6.2 The Authoritative Teaching Continuum

1	2	3	4	5	6	7	8	9	10	11	12

1. **Observe and listen.** Keep children in view from a short distance. Become aware of what the situation entails. Make yourself available if children want to come to you, but let them work things out if they can.
2. **Add or take something away** to make a situation easier for children to manage on their own. For instance, too few objects for children to use in the water table could lead to squabbles. Adding a few more might be all that is needed for children to share more successfully. In contrast, too many objects in the water table might make pouring and playing without splashing one another difficult for children. Removing a few items could make using the materials cooperatively easier for them.
3. **State your observations.** "It looks like two people want to use the funnel at the same time." "It looks like there's a problem here." "I heard some shouting. What's happening here?" "You found a way to share the water wheel. That was a friendly thing to do."
4. **Provide information.** "You thought he was splashing you on purpose. He was trying to get all that water into that little hole and a lot splashed out. It was an accident." "Sometimes when two people want the same thing at the same time, they decide to share or take turns." "You could get another container and fill it together."
5. **Pose questions and make plans.** "What could you do to solve this problem?" "What could you do instead of hitting her to show you're angry?" "Let's make a plan so this won't happen again."
6. **Give choices.** "John is using the funnel right now. You may use the strainer or the green plastic tubing." "It's cleanup time. You may put away the smocks or drain the water out of the table."
7. **Physically intervene.** Stop hurtful actions such as hitting by catching the child's hands. Hold onto a wiggling child to help him or her hear what you are saying. Separate two children who are pushing.
8. **Help children negotiate problems.** Serve as a translator in the situation. "Did you like it when he scratched you? What could you say to him about that?" "What did you want?" "James, you think it would be okay to take turns. What do you think, Robert?"
9. **Remind children of limits.** "You really wanted the water wheel. It bothers me when you grab to get what you want. Ask Jerome for a turn next." "Remember, we have a rule that everyone must share the toys at the center." "I can't let you hit him. Hitting hurts. Say, 'I'm next.'"
10. **Connect actions to consequences.** "Either take turns with the water wheel or you'll have to choose something else to do." "If you hit again, you'll have to leave the water table." "You found a way to get everyone's container in the water table. That solved the problem."
11. **Take action in conjunction with the child.** "You're having a hard time remembering to share the things at the water table. Let's look around for another activity for you to do." "You splashed water all over Jenny. Let's get some towels and help her dry off."
12. **Enforce consequences.** "You hit. Now you must leave the water table."

program, including teachers, bus drivers, cooks, aides, and so forth.

❏ Regularly scheduled times during which team members brainstorm solutions to typical behavioral problems, discuss ways to promote positive child behaviors, and reach a consensus about how certain rules will be interpreted and enforced.

❏ Program policies that are reviewed and revised periodically.

In addition to these strategies, team members might agree to adopt the authoritative strategies outlined in this chapter a few at a time. Colleagues may practice as well as observe and listen to one another and provide supportive feedback regarding successes and ways to improve their skills. The checklist provided in Figure 6.3 is a simple tool that team members could use to guide their observations.

QUESTIONS ADULTS ASK ABOUT PROMOTING SELF-DISCIPLINE IN CHILDREN

Promoting self-discipline among children is a challenging task. This subject prompts many questions from teachers, administrators, and family members regarding philosophy and implementation. Following are discussions about some of the most common issues they think about.

Why Can't I Just Say "No" and Be Done with It?

When children engage in inappropriate behavior, we are tempted to simply say "No" or "We don't do that here." Occasionally these oral shortcuts have the desired effect; children stop misbehaving. Unfortunately, such success is usually short lived, and children repeat the same infractions later. Moreover, children tend to comply only under direct supervision. The moment the

FIGURE 6.3   Authoritative Teaching Skills Checklist

Most of the time 2	Sometimes 1	Seldom 0

❑ Demonstrates interest in children: Greets children individually, says good-bye to each child, invites children to interact, gets down to the children's level when talking to them.

❑ Demonstrates respect for children: Listens to children, allows children to finish what they are saying, picks up on children's interests as the subject of conversation, acknowledges children's comments and questions.

❑ Offers children choices.

❑ Includes children in classroom decisions.

❑ States rules that promote safety, protect property, or protect others' rights.

❑ States expectations in a positive manner: "Ride on the cement" *not* "Don't ride on the grass."

❑ Suggests alternatives to unacceptable behaviors: "Ask for a turn" or "Walk" instead of "No running inside."

❑ Acknowledges children's positive behaviors.

❑ Offers reasons for expectations.

❑ States consequences that are immediate.

❑ States consequences that are consistent.

❑ States consequences that are logical.

❑ Uses an appropriate warning prior to enacting a consequence: States the warning as an either–or statement linking the rule to a logical consequence.

❑ Follows through on the stated consequence if the child does not comply.

❑ Acknowledges the child's viewpoint in problem situations.

❑ Intervenes when children are aggressive by stopping the hurtful actions and setting a limit.

❑ Uses proximity control: Moves near children to survey the situation and gives children cues to change behavior.

❑ Uses gentle restraint: The adult holds one child back from hitting another child.

adult's back is turned, problem behaviors resume. Such lapses occur because admonitions alone do not lead to children's internalization of the rules but to adherence instead. Authoritative teaching yields a different result; children become more self-disciplined with time. Although following through on a logical consequence or mediating a conflict may take several minutes, children gain skills from these interactions that help them become independent problem solvers and more self-disciplined. These outcomes are well worth the initial investment of time required to achieve them.

What If I Am the Only Teacher in the Room?

Being on your own in the classroom requires you to maintain a global outlook while interacting with children individually and in small groups. As you work with youngsters in one part of the room, glance around to see what else is happening. Sometimes a smile, a nod, a "thumbs up" sign, or eye contact with children in other parts of the room is sufficient to keep the class running smoothly until you can make your way to an area. In addition, when you use authoritative strategies such as acknowledging children's positive behavior, offering reasons for rules, and enforcing consequences, you provide minilessons both for the children directly involved

and for other children nearby. Such modeling and direct instruction benefit everyone and help children gain the skills they need to work more independently and to settle some issues themselves. In addition, some teachers develop a buddy system, in which teachers periodically check on each other to make sure things are running smoothly. Having a reciprocal arrangement in which a child who needs a change of scene can visit another teacher's classroom also works well in some elementary or after-school settings.

Shouldn't Children Already Know How to Behave by the Time They Get to Kindergarten and First and Second Grade?

Children do not enter kindergarten, first grade, or second grade having mastered the social domain. Even youngsters who have attended nursery school or child care find that elementary school expectations are more structured and elaborate than those they encountered in the past. Many children have never eaten in a lunchroom, walked down a long hallway, or gone to a gym. They may never have sat at a desk, worked with only one teacher, or been in a group of 20 children. All these new situations call for new behaviors. Thus, the first 3 years of elementary education mark a transitional period during which children redefine themselves within the context of an institution more formal than the family, neighborhood, or child care center (Bickart et al., 1997). Throughout this time children learn the boundaries of the student role and ways to function successfully within it. As a result, children in the early grades continually experiment with assorted social strategies, discovering what works and what does not and what is permitted and what is not allowed.

Not only does this learning take time, but it cannot be hurried. Children are not just memorizing school rules; they are constructing an understanding of what each rule means and applying this concept to their behavior. Consequently, knowing the rules and being able to follow them independently are two important but very different tasks, and the latter is much more challenging than the first. It is unrealistic for school personnel or families to expect children to achieve self-discipline before they enter school or soon thereafter. Years, not days or weeks, are necessary for mastery to develop. For these reasons, child guidance deserves special consideration in the early elementary curriculum. Adults cannot simply demand that children engage in socially acceptable behaviors; instead, they must focus on teaching children how to do so.

How Can We Promote Consistency Between the Way Guidance Is Handled in the Early Childhood Setting and How It Is Addressed at Home?

The key to achieving some measure of consistency between home and program is to establish open channels of communication in which all parties feel valued and respected. The first step is for each party to share basic information. Parents need to know how children will be socialized in the early childhood setting and the rationale for particular goals and strategies. They also need to receive accurate information about their role in the process. Practitioners in turn need to know about parents' aspirations for their children and the measures used at home to promote these aims. This kind of information could be exchanged during a home visit, at a program orientation, or through written materials.

Consistency is further enhanced when parents, teachers, and administrators get together to explore values and philosophies. Workshops, parent–teacher conferences, and informal discussions at the classroom or program level are effective ways for school staff and parents to share ideas and problem-solving techniques related to child socialization (Bickart et al., 1997; National Association of Elementary School Principals, 1990). These times are most productive when the emphasis is on mutual understanding and collaboration.

What Can Be Done When Conflicts Exist Between the Teacher's and Parents' Approaches to Discipline?

Many times the influential people in children's lives have different ideas about how children should behave. Consequently, they may advocate conflicting codes of conduct. For instance, in the interest of group harmony, program personnel may require children to respond to bullying from peers by using nonviolent strategies. Family members, more focused on children's self-defense skills, may encourage them to "fight it out" when threatened. Both ideas—harmonious living and personal safety—have merit, but they are different and seem to call for incompatible responses from children. This conflict puts children in a dilemma: To obey one set of expectations, they have to violate another.

Whenever contradictory situations such as these arise, they might be handled in three ways. The first is for teachers and parents to discuss their differences honestly and directly, searching for common ground. In the preceding situation, both teachers and parents most likely want children to be safe. They agree on the goal, but their means for achieving it differ. If they recognize their mutual aim, they will have a compatible base from which to explore potential resolutions to the child's predicament.

On other occasions, conflicts arise from differences in style. Teachers sometimes believe they have little in common with parents who hold nonauthoritative attitudes toward discipline. Likewise, parents who espouse authoritarian or permissive philosophies may question the authoritative techniques used in the program. Thus, the second approach is to emphasize the similarities between philosophies rather than concentrating on the discrepancies (Bollin, 1989). Authoritarian and authoritative styles both advocate firm control and high standards; permissive and authoritative styles promote warm, accepting relationships between children and adults. Discussing authoritative strategies in terms of how they support these overarching principles provides some common ground between philosophies.

For instance, parents with authoritarian attitudes may believe that offering children choices is unnecessary or undesirable because youngsters should simply do as they are told. To help such parents feel more comfortable with providing choices for children, the teacher could recommend that the adult first establish boundaries on the child's behavior (such as getting dressed now) and then offer the child a choice (the color of the shirt to wear). This explanation combines an authoritative value (helping children achieve independence) with an authoritarian value (achieving compliance) and builds a bridge between the two.

A third strategy for reducing children's confusion about contradictory home–program expectations is to help children realize that adults have differing reactions to their behavior. This enables teachers to stress that certain standards may be situation specific: "You're upset. At home you don't have to pick up. That may be, but it bothers me when the puzzles are all over the floor. Pieces could be lost. Here at the center everybody is expected to help. Find a puzzle to put away."

On the rare occasions when no mutually satisfactory resolution seems possible, acknowledge that differences exist and make clear to parents how and why authoritative strategies will be used at school. Children benefit from exposure to authoritative models, even when other adults in their lives are more authoritarian or more permissive. Teachers and administrators who reason with children provide alternative models of interaction and problem solving for children to evaluate and try.

What About Sending Rule Violators to the Administrator's Office?

The old standby of sending children to see the principal or the director when they are disruptive actually undermines the classroom teacher's authority and makes subsequent confrontations between adult and child more likely. Although teachers may want to impress on children the seriousness of their misdeeds by banishing them from the classroom, the message conveyed by doing so is "I give up" or "I don't know how to handle your behavior." A better alternative is to use logical consequences consistently within the classroom each time children act in unacceptable ways. Such an approach familiarizes them with appropriate alternative behaviors and shows them that early childhood professionals mean what they say. Early in the year, teachers may have to sacrifice instructional time with the group to follow through on stated consequences with an individual child. For example, the story may be set aside for the day or the math activity shortened. However, these immediate liabilities will be offset in the future because fewer such incidents will occur (Kostelnik, Whiren, et al., 2002). Children will come to recognize the predictability of the adult's response and discover that corrective action is always taken without the adult's losing patience or giving in. Trips to the office will occur rarely and only in the most serious circumstances. When a child does go to the office, he or she will be accompanied by the teacher, who, with the principal or director, will participate in a team-oriented approach to problem solving with the child.

SUMMARY

The guidance strategies that early childhood professionals use when children are young influence the attitudes and dispositions children will carry with them into later life (L. G. Katz & Chard, 1989; Turiel, 1998). Likewise, the strategies they use early in the year affect how well children behave as the year goes on. If self-discipline is our ultimate aim, we must, from the start, consciously use the authoritative strategies that fit this goal. Initially, such strategies will be more time consuming than will authoritarian or permissive techniques. However, as the weeks and months pass, children will gradually grow in their ability to monitor their behavior. As children's skills increase, not only will they refrain from inappropriate actions, but they will also initiate greater numbers of positive actions. When these conditions prevail, time spent on corrective action becomes less and less, which makes the initial investment of teacher time worth the effort.

Young children are not born knowing the rules of society or the settings in which they participate. How to achieve their goals in socially acceptable ways, get along with others, and adjust their personal behavior within the bounds of societal expectations are concepts that children have to learn how to do. This learning begins at birth and continues throughout the school years. Parents, teachers, other significant adults in children's lives, and peers all contribute to the lessons children experience during this time. Initially, young children depend on others to direct their behavior for them. However, with time, they learn to respond to rewards and punishments or the moral codes of admired adults as clues about how to behave. These guides are useful and necessary but do not represent the most self-disciplined form of social behavior, which occurs only if children treat certain standards of conduct as logical extensions of their beliefs and personal values. Whenever children think about their behavior in this way, they are said to have reached *internalization*. Internalization equals self-discipline. Self-disciplined children do not simply comply with adult standards minus adult supervision. They grow into ethical, compassionate people who do what they think is right to support their internally constructed perceptions of right and wrong.

The extent to which children exhibit self-discipline is affected by developmental factors such as emotional maturity, cognition, language, and memory. Another major influence is children's daily experiences with people. Throughout early childhood, parents and teachers in particular have a tremendous impact on which social behaviors children adopt. These grownups use a variety of socialization strategies such as modeling, attribution, instruction, and consequences to help children learn acceptable codes of behavior. However, not all adults use or combine these strategies in the same way. Four of the most common variations—uninvolved, permissive, authoritarian, and authoritative—have been the subject of much research. The uninvolved, permissive, and authoritarian styles yield negative results that undermine self-regulation and positive social adjustment in children. The authoritative style has been most strongly linked to the development of self-discipline. Consequently, much of this chapter is devoted to describing techniques associated with authoritative teaching. Such strategies can be applied in a single classroom or on a programwide basis.

Applying What You Read in This Chapter

1. **Discuss**
   a. On the basis of your reading and your experiences with young children, discuss each of the questions that open this chapter.
   b. On the basis of the ideas and strategies outlined in this chapter, discuss what you might do in the following situations:
      - Jennifer and Marlene each want to use a rolling pin at the dough table. Only one rolling pin is available.
      - The pretend-play area is set up for four children. You notice seven children playing there.
      - A parent calls to report that children are rowdy at the bus stop each day. She is worried that some of the younger children will get hurt as a result of the older children's chasing and shoving.
      - Sharon slams her book on the table. "I can't read this. I'll never read this. It's too hard," she screams.

2. **Observe**
   a. Observe a group of children in a classroom or outdoors. What are some of the positive behaviors you notice among the children? What are some of the problems they encounter in getting along? How do the children respond to one another in these situations? What implications do your observations have for your approach to child guidance?
   b. Observe a classroom of teachers and children. What are some of the strategies adults use to guide children's behavior? Do these strategies support or detract from the long-range goal of helping children achieve self-discipline?

3. **Carry out an activity**
   a. Interview two early childhood educators who work with children of different ages. Ask them to describe the most common discipline problems they face. How do they solve such problems when they arise?
   b. Attend a community presentation or workshop related to child guidance. What was the presenter's main message? What kinds of questions did people in the audience have about the topic? What is your reaction to what you heard?

4. **Create something for your portfolio**
   a. Describe a situation in which you guided a child's behavior. What was the child doing? What did you do? How effective was your approach? What might you do if the same situation arose again?
   b. Ask a supervisor to identify three strengths that you demonstrate by using an authoritative style with children. Also ask him or her to identify one aspect that you need to work on in the future. Develop a plan to maintain your strengths and improve in the area identified.

5. **Add to your journal**
   a. What is the most significant concept that you learned about promoting self-discipline in children from your readings and your experience with children?
   b. Describe what you would have to do to become more authoritative in your approach to child guidance.

Evaluating and Guiding Children's Progress by Using Authentic Assessment

You may wonder:

How do I keep track of what children are learning in my classroom?

What is meant by "authentic" assessment and how can it be implemented in early childhood classrooms?

What part should standardized tests play in evaluating children's development?

How can information about children's development and learning be organized to give an accurate picture of children's progress?

How can information related to assessment be shared effectively with parents?

In this chapter on the assessment and evaluation of young children, we present information to help you answer the preceding questions.

Gavin Williams knows how important oral language development is for the 3- and 4-year-olds in his classroom. He takes periodic samples of each child's communication, and today, while the children are at free play, he is recording some of the conversation he hears. He notes the oral turn taking going on, the fact that the children are able to sustain a conversational theme, and some of the vocabulary they are using, such as "quart" and "engineer." Marking down Kendra's use of alliteration— "buttery, buttery bundles of corn"—he makes a note to himself to showcase this in large group tomorrow and to invite other children to invent some phrases.

While the children in Ms. McAfee's room are busy at their centers this morning, she is spending a few minutes with each of them, going over their self-appraisal checklists. She helps each child review the emerging literacy skills they are working on and to color in those that the child has achieved and that she has observed. "Good for you," she tells Juana. "You've learned 2 new skills this month. You have only 3 left, and then you'll have all 10 skills checked. Which one is going to be your special target for the next time we visit about this?"

Mary Descharne is listening as a small group of children practice presenting their portfolios to one another. With her help, they have chosen five of their best pieces of work for the past 3 months, have designed a showcase folder, and will share their work with their family members at a special celebration on Thursday night. The pride they feel is reflected in their faces as they describe why they chose a particular piece and the meaning it has for them.

Each of these teachers is involved in ongoing, strategic, and purposeful assessment and evaluation. Daily, they are active in documenting what the children in their classrooms know and will need to know, the progress being made toward learning and developmental goals, and whether or not various aspects of their program are supporting each child's growth. For them, assessment is not something that is contrived or something they do in addition to their teaching; it has become an integral and useful component of each day.

THE CHANGING FACE OF EARLY CHILDHOOD ASSESSMENT

Appreciation of the need for well-designed assessment and evaluation to help professionals make well-informed decisions in early childhood education is growing. In addition to learning more about how individual children think, learn, develop, and behave across time, educators need to collect and document information to inform instruction, to identify children who might benefit from special help or additional health services, and to report children's progress to their families. All this constitutes what is known as *assessment,* which takes place primarily through observation, administration of commercial and teacher-constructed tools, and examination of the products that young children create (Morrison, 2001).

Other professionals, funding or regulatory agencies, boards of directors, school boards, legislators, and citizen groups may also require early childhood educators to collect information about the children they are teaching. Social and educational factors that are contributing to the changing landscape of assessment include differing ideas about the purposes of assessment. Some of these differing ideas have to do with

❏ how children develop and learn;
❏ the changing nature of the population in schools and centers;
❏ changing educational outcomes, curricula, and teaching strategies;
❏ the development of state-wide standards and mandated testing;
❏ and the limitations and inadequacies of traditional testing. (O. McAfee & Leong, 2002, pp. 2–3)

Assessment in education is never a value-neutral enterprise but instead reflects a society's commitments and ideology (Archbald & Newmann, 1988). In the United States, commitment has been renewed to "leave no child behind," to revitalize public school education, and to place a more intense focus on preprimary and early primary education to ward off later school failure. As billions more of federal dollars are being spent to fund special programs in early childhood education, educators are being held more accountable for successful outcomes; in turn, this accountability is creating a more rigorous assessment and evaluation system.

Some scholars believe that connecting assessment to real learning and school improvement in meaningful ways will require our looking at it with new eyes. For us to be able to do so, the National Research Council's Committee on the Foundations of Assessment recommended in 2001 that

> instruction in how students learn and how learning can be assessed will need to be a major component of teacher preservice and professional development programs. This training should be linked to actual experience in classrooms in assessing and interpreting the development of student competence. To ensure that this occurs, state and national standards for teacher

licensure and program accreditation should include specific requirements focused on the proper integration of learning and assessment in teachers' educational experience. (Stiggins, 2002, p. 763)

In addition, we must become more skillful in designing classroom assessments that will be useful not only to adults for all their purposes, but primarily to the children who are being evaluated. Even very young children need to better understand expectations and to have some understanding of what is needed to reach each of these targets.

RESPONSIBLE EARLY CHILDHOOD ASSESSMENT AND EVALUATION

A truly effective assessment system is more than just a collection of separate observations, tests, and formal or informal assessments performed by various professionals at different stages in a child's life. However, in most school systems and communities, such a collection is currently the norm. Often, no connection exists between preprimary screening and assessment and later school entry, other than ensuring that children have had their immunizations. Frequently, any information that was gained during well-child screenings or from nursery school, child care, or Head Start attendance is lost. Such information may include anecdotal records, health histories and records of special needs, records of home visits, checklists relative to oral language development and social skills acquisition, and notations about the emergence of motor skills.

Following entry into kindergarten, there may be little understanding from grade to grade about a child's development other than the general information that is reported in permanent school records or on a child's report cards. Many teachers "start all over" at each grade level in terms of understanding the child's strengths or learning limitations, and sometimes this approach is even purposeful. Ms. Stibble, a second-grade teacher, is adamant about not looking at previous information about children coming into her room: "I don't want to be biased before they even start!" she exclaims. As a result, valuable time in understanding the children's needs may be wasted.

Because a system is interactive by definition, it must be cohesive; all the various components included must be related, including a defined scope and sequence of the curricular skills and concepts children are expected to develop as they move from learning context to learning context. Coladarci (2002) made this point when he suggested that a local assessment system should demonstrate the following five features:

1. The assessments collectively are relevant to announced learning (or developmental) targets.

2. The system is made up of assessments that are initiated at the classroom, school, district, and state levels. Classroom-level assessments reflect the day-to-day evaluation practices of teachers and draw on multiple formats, such as running records, unit exams, papers, projects, performances, and portfolios of work samples.

3. The assessments are conducted across age groups, including the preschool years and early primary grades.

4. The system allows for multiple opportunities for the child to demonstrate knowledge, understanding, and skill development. A single administration of an assessment, whatever its form, typically provides an insufficient basis for making inferences about student proficiency.

5. Each assessment in the system has an announced rationale. The assessment's purpose, audience (ex. children, parents), and articulation with other assessments in the system (for example, a phonological awareness assessment for a four-year-old, a 2nd grade reading test, and a 4th grade state-wide literacy test) should be clearly stated. (pp. 773–774)

Individuals who are implementing evaluation procedures greatly affect the outcome, by design or by default. That is, assessment and evaluation will be effective only to the extent that attention is paid to (a) the evaluator's relative subjectivity–objectivity and skills, (b) the state of the child at the time of evaluation, (c) the properties of the evaluation setting, (d) the timing of the evaluation, (e) the appropriate selection of data collection tools and strategies, and (f) the thoughtful application of outcomes. Assessment and evaluation findings should never become conversational fodder for the teacher's lounge or other public gatherings, and negative comments about a child (i.e., points of weakness) should be considered only in light of how corresponding strengths or modifications in instructional strategies can help minimize the limitations discovered.

Examining the Evaluator's Subjectivity–Objectivity and Skills

Perhaps nothing is as dangerous in the evaluation setting as evaluators who (a) are unaware of their personal traits, values, and expectations and (b) lack evaluation know-how. The latter would include a lack of knowledge about child development as well as a lack of the ability to structure and apply appropriate evaluation strategies. Because we are advocating that evaluation in early childhood settings be carried out primarily by the classroom teacher, we have little control over any effects related to differences in the teacher's and child's gender, race, ethnic background, and personality other than to ensure that the evaluating teacher is aware that establishing good rapport with individual children is a prerequisite to good evaluation. Teachers must also examine as objectively as possible the

expectations they bring into the situation and avoid providing spoken and unspoken reinforcement to one child that is not given just as freely to other children.

Obtaining the Child's Best Response

Young children are notoriously difficult to test. They have no concept of the importance attached to an assessment and are inexperienced with paper-and-pencil formats. They tire easily, are easily distracted, may have little interest in doing well, may be wary of the evaluator if he or she is unfamiliar, and may simply refuse to cooperate. English may be a second language for some children, and their cultural background can also affect their performance. Every effort should be made to obtain several samples of the child's best work—performed when the child is at ease, healthy, and motivated—which will then be evaluated. Many of these problems can be almost completely eliminated in early childhood classrooms in which evaluation procedures become a normal and less intrusive part of everyday activity.

Choosing an Evaluation Setting

Ideally, early childhood classrooms, where evaluation should take place, are pleasant environments with adequate ventilation, light, and space; pleasing aesthetic qualities; minimal distractions; and modified noise levels. Realistically, these factors are not always optimal. When they are not, both children's learning and their evaluation may be negatively affected. These factors should be considered when educators are planning classroom activities that will serve as a basis for evaluation. Children should not be removed from the classroom to unfamiliar settings for evaluation of activities and events that normally occur in the classroom. However, every effort should be made to ensure that the classroom setting and the ongoing activity in the room at evaluation time do not distract from the children's best efforts.

Determining the Timing of the Evaluation

Teachers need to consider two aspects of timing. One is the consistency in the scheduling of skill and behavior sampling. The other is the assessment itself. Some forms of assessment, such as vision and hearing testing and obtaining health records and family profiles, are most helpful when secured as early as possible before interaction with the child begins. Evaluation should be both formative (i.e., ongoing) and summative. Teachers should build into their programs not only ongoing methods of collecting daily work samples, but also opportunities for planned observation and discussion with children; educators must also use more formal measures such as scoring oral reading tapes at specified periods during the year. Assessment of skills and behaviors should not be attempted until the teacher has established rapport with children and children have had adequate opportunity to practice the skills and behaviors to be assessed. Assessment should also not be undertaken at certain times of the school year and on school days when children are more likely to be distracted, are less able to concentrate, or are likely to feel rushed (e.g., directly before recess, on the day of a Halloween party, or after returning from vacation).

Selecting Data Collection Strategies and Tools

When we think of testing situations, we usually envision people sitting quietly taking paper-and-pencil tests in group situations. This scenario in early education spells disaster and is developmentally inappropriate. Errors on such a test would most likely result from a lack of skill in recording rather than from lack of knowledge in the content area being evaluated. Moreover, young children are developing their ability to respond to direction and may, in a group setting, become confused about what they need to do. Their confidence in alerting an adult to problems they are having in the situation will depend on the rapport established with the attending adult. Such a methodology does not match children's everyday integrated experiences in good early childhood classrooms and lends itself more to the testing of isolated skills.

Before deciding what kinds of strategies or tools are needed, teachers should determine the purpose of the assessment. What do they want to know about this child and how specifically? Is diagnostic information needed? How will the data be used? Who else will need to see and use the data? If a federal or state granting or funding agency will be involved, will it accept only standardized test results, or are teacher-constructed measures considered as valid? What factors about the child or the testing situation should affect the teacher's decision? How much time can be spared for the evaluation, and when and where should it take place? Will just one child be evaluated, or a group of children? Should a direct strategy be used that involves the child, or can an unobtrusive measure work just as well so that the child is unaware of being tested? Once the basic purpose and related details have been considered, teachers can select a number of good evaluation methods.

STANDARDIZED TESTING: WHAT PART SHOULD IT PLAY IN EVALUATING CHILDREN'S PROGRESS?

Eight-year-old Lamont is taking a standardized reading test, and it's clear that he's having trouble. With his head bobbing and nose pointing to each word in the passage, he scans back and forth, whispering aloud each of the words. When finished, he moves on to the questions. Slumping down in his chair after a brief time, he throws his pencil down on the test booklet and folds his arms, a defiant look on his face. Only two answers have been bubbled in, but he's had enough. (Soderman, 2001, p. 55)

In every U.S. community today, a great deal rests on positive test outcomes, and the stakes are high to have outcomes skewed toward high-achieving children. Even though standardized tests are constructed so that 50 percent of children test above the mean and 50 percent below, no community finds having too many children (even 50 percent) in the bottom category as acceptable. U.S. children are now being tested to an extent that is "unprecedented in our history and unparalleled anywhere else in the world" (Kohn, 2000, p. 2). Not surprisingly, concern abounds about the growing mismatch between instruction and children's experiential backgrounds and developmental levels. Educators complain about greater pressure to alter the curriculum and instruction to fit assessment, rather than assessment's being used as a tool to measure learning. Perhaps worst is the possibility that we are growing so accustomed to what has become an acceptable status quo relative to high-pressure assessment that we rarely question whether what we are doing constitutes reasonable and appropriate assessment. As a result, children's well-being in some of our centers, schools, and communities is being disregarded in the drive toward greater accountability.

Standardized testing continues to be a big business in the United States. According to reports, approximately 93 to 105 million standardized tests of achievement, competency, and basic skills are currently administered each year to fulfill local and state mandates, to identify or qualify children for compensatory or special education programs, to be used for screening and placement for prekindergarten and kindergarten, to provide graduate equivalency degree (GED) tests, to determine college admission, and to fulfill the National Assessment of Educational Progress testing requirements (Neill & Medina, 1989). Think about how many standardized tests you have taken in your educational career so far. This continued growth in testing has been costly to already financially burdened school districts, and more than $423 million per year is now being spent on testing in the United States. In addition to being costly, standardized and criterion-referenced testing is time consuming, and one estimate indicates that children in second grade now spend a total of 1 month on test preparation and standardized testing per year (O. McAfee & Leong, 2002, p. 185).

Prior to 1950, standardized testing as we know it today was rare in school systems and, before 1965, even less frequently seen in preschools and the early elementary grades. Because of an influx of federal dollars during the 1960s to stem poverty and the accountability requirements that accompanied these dollars, standardized testing became an accepted and increasingly prominent feature of public education. Mainly, it was a quick and easy method of documenting that programs were "working." However, eventually these tests took on a life of their own, shaping the very programs, educators, and children they were designed to evaluate. In large measure, they continue to do so today.

Pressure to achieve greater "educational accountability" has gradually spawned widespread approval of such practices as "teaching to the test" (if not the actual test) and placing heavy emphasis on worksheets, drills, and other inappropriate teaching strategies in early childhood classrooms. All these practices have been designed to raise scores because of the erroneous assumption that high scores on standardized tests equal high rates of learning by the children taking the tests. Harvard University's Howard Gardner (2001) labeled this movement a social "frenzy" and said that it is an inappropriate response to a perceived problem of failing schools.

Alfie Kohn, author of *The Schools Our Children Deserve: Moving Beyond Traditional Classrooms and Tougher Schools,* noted:

> Don't let anyone tell you that standardized tests are not accurate measures. The truth of the matter is that they offer a remarkably precise method for gauging the size of the homes near the school where the test was administered. (Kohn, 2000, p. 349)

He based this account on a number of studies documenting that socioeconomic status accounts for an overwhelming proportion of the variance in test scores and that four variables explain 89 percent of the difference between students who do well and those who do not: (a) number of parents living at home, (b) parents' educational background, (c) type of community, and (d) state poverty rates. Of these four factors, 74 percent of the variance is derived from only one of the factors: whether or not two parents are in the home.

In addition to the problems already described, weaknesses and limitations of standardized tests may include cultural bias in those selected; limited test content; inaccurate or inadequate norms; and inappropriate use of results. Although most of these tests are published by commercial testing companies, we cannot assume that they have all gone through the rigorous statistical and psychometric process recommended by the American Educational Research Association (AERA), American Psychological Association (APA), and National Council on Measurement in Education (NCME; O. McAfee & Leong, 2002). Each professional who is involved in selecting or administering a standardized test must take the responsibility of ensuring that the test has proven technical and educational adequacy and is suitable for the population of children being tested. Such individuals should ask themselves, "Is the test fair for children from all income levels, normed for all racial and ethnic backgrounds represented in the classroom, and suitable for children whose primary language is not English? Does the format call for skills children are unlikely to have, such as bubbling in responses? Is it group administered, which makes following directions difficult for young children? Does it call for teaching children in developmentally inappropriate ways so that they are successful on the test but unable to use the information in other ways? Is it a one-shot-only test that would be insensitive to a young child's learning spurts and regressions?" If the test is inappropriate, teachers must be vocal about such inappropriateness and be able to suggest alternatives.

Nevertheless, not all standardized screening and assessment of young children need be scrapped. Standardized testing is reasonable for both research purposes and diagnostic purposes when it is conducted with the preceding cautions in mind. It can tell us how children in one school compare with those across a school district or across the nation, help school districts identify curriculum strengths and weaknesses, and be used to evaluate subsequent efforts to ameliorate these weaknesses (Sattler, 2001).

Diagnostic assessment intended to determine conclusively whether a child has special needs requires multiple types of data and sources (Meisels & Provence, 1989). Thus, carefully constructed standardized tests are legitimate tools to consider. They should be *valid;* that is, they should measure what they are intended to measure so that reasonable inferences can be made on the basis of the results. They also need to be *reliable;* consistency within the instrument should be built in—consistency with time so that a retest within an appropriate time frame would yield the same results and consistency when it is used by more than one person (interrater or interobserver reliability). Such tools may provide a more complete understanding of a child's strengths and weaknesses by allowing teachers to compare the child's performance with an established standard. This procedure can help educators document the pre- and postintervention status of groups of children who may be considered at risk because of socioeconomic factors or the geographic context in which they are reared. The tests are not intended to provide in-depth information about the ways children learn or to ameliorate learning disabilities (Sattler, 2001). However, in a relatively limited amount of time, a sample of behavior can be obtained and used to measure developmental status and changes or effects of remediation. The challenge is to find reliable and valid measures, obtain a typical response from the child, and then use the data only in conjunction with other relevant information to evaluate a child's physical, intellectual, social, or psychological abilities and functioning.

PLACEMENT OF YOUNG CHILDREN ON THE BASIS OF TEST RESULTS

The technical aspects of standardized testing are only one consideration. Another is that faulty decisions affecting children's futures are made when too much importance is attached to a particular test or score, even though the test is valid and reliable. For example, if we were to interrupt your reading of this chapter right now, have you take a test on what you have read so far, score the test, and then compare your performance with that of a group of people much like yourself (placing you somewhere on a normal curve), you might react in one of two ways. If your performance was better than average, you might come away from the experience feeling pleased. Furthermore, if decisions about your professional life or future were based on your performance, you might feel relieved that your score was at or above the norm. However, if your performance on the test rated below average, your reaction would be different. You might try to explain: "But I didn't take the test seriously. . . . I didn't realize what was hinging on the results. . . . I didn't feel well. . . . I know I'm better than the test indicates; in fact, I'm considered excellent in the classroom with children because I'm rather creative, and the test didn't measure any of that. The material we were tested on was presented in a boring way—I couldn't relate to it."

Fortunately, this situation is only hypothetical, and your performance on such a test would not affect your job or your future. Moreover, because you are an adult and can interpret your performance in light of your actual strengths and weaknesses, you would probably be fairly assertive in articulating your concerns if any attempt were made to use the score inappropriately. Young children do not yet have this ability, and many of their parents may not be confident enough to question decisions made by professionals, particularly when "real numbers" and evidence from a standardized test are available to back up such decisions. Therefore, consideration about placing children in special entry programs, resource rooms, and learning groups should be made only after comprehensive data have been gathered and evaluated.

THE CONCEPT OF AUTHENTIC ASSESSMENT

Because standardized tests have limited use with young children other than for diagnostic or research purposes, the focus in this section of the chapter is on more authentic or alternative measures that the classroom teacher can use in natural settings where children work and play. Such measures include the "innumerable and complex ways in which teachers appraise children's learning in the classroom . . . almost any type of assessment other than standardized tests and similar developmental inventories and achievement tests" (O. McAfee & Leong, 2002, p. 2). Characteristics of authentic assessment include the following:

A variety of data is collected across time. Unlike standardized tests, which provide a "snapshot in time," authentic assessment gauges a child's developmental progress at particular checkpoints against an expected range of maturational behaviors, skills, readiness levels, and concept formation.

All developmental domains are of interest and are evaluated, rather than just a child's academic productivity and performance.

It takes place in the natural learning context and is conducted by persons familiar to the child.

It is functional and curriculum embedded (i.e., it is an integral part of what goes on in the regular classroom and involves children working with everyday objects and materials on everyday performance tasks and in a purposeful pursuit of learning).

It is based on discovering children's best performance rather than on documenting what they do not know or cannot do well.

It is useful for planning classroom instruction to organize and move children's learning forward.

It is a shared responsibility among teachers, children, parents, and other professionals involved in the child's overall development, and effective communication is ongoing among these partners.

Early childhood professionals can accrue important advantages when they systematically and professionally document children's progress with authentic-based assessment as a way to facilitate learning and development. The National Association for the Education of Young Children (NAEYC, 1996a) has indicated that to provide an accurate picture of children's capabilities, teachers must observe children across time and use their findings to adjust their curriculum and instruction. In addition, assessment should not be used to recommend that children be eliminated from particular programs, retained, or assigned to segregated groups on the basis of ability or developmental maturity. Eighteen principles set out by the NAEYC to guide practitioners in assessment procedures for children aged 3 through 8 years are as follows:

1. Curriculum and assessment are integrated throughout the program; assessment is congruent with and relevant to the goals, objectives, and content of the program.

2. Assessment results in benefits to the child, such as needed adjustments in the curriculum or more individualized instruction and improvements in the program.

3. Children's development and learning in all the domains—physical, social, emotional, and cognitive—and their dispositions and feelings are informally and routinely assessed by teachers' observing children's activities and interactions, listening to them as they talk, and using children's constructive errors to understand their learning.

4. Assessment provides teachers with useful information to successfully fulfill their responsibilities: to support children's learning and development, to plan for individuals and groups, and to communicate with parents.

5. Assessment involves regular and periodic observation of the child in a wide variety of circumstances that are representative of the child's behavior in the program over time.

6. Assessment relies primarily on procedures that reflect the ongoing life of the classroom and typical activities of the children. Assessment avoids approaches that place children in artificial situations, impede the usual learning and developmental experiences in the classroom, or divert children from their natural learning processes.

7. Assessment relies on demonstrated performance during real, not contrived, activities, for example, real reading and writing activities rather than only skills testing.

8. Assessment utilizes an array of tools and a variety of processes including, but not limited to, collections of representative work by children (artwork, stories they write, tape recordings of their reading), records of systematic observations by teachers, records of conversations and interviews with children, teachers' summaries of children's progress as individuals and as groups.

9. Assessment recognizes individual diversity of learners and allows for differences in styles and rates of learning. Assessment takes into consideration children's ability in English, their stage of language acquisition, and whether they have been given the time and opportunity to develop proficiency in their native language as well as in English.

10. Assessment supports children's development and learning; it does *not* threaten children's psychological safety or feelings of self-esteem.

11. Assessment supports parents' relationships with their children and does not undermine parents' confidence in their children's or their own ability, nor does it devalue the language and culture of the family.

12. Assessment demonstrates children's overall strengths and progress, what children can do, not just their wrong answers or what they cannot do or do not know.

13. Assessment is an essential component of the teacher's role. Because teachers can make maximal use of assessment results, the teacher is the *primary* assessor.

14. Assessment is a collaborative process involving children and teachers, teachers and parents, school and community. Information from parents about each child's experiences at home is used in planning instruction and evaluating children's learning. Information obtained from assessment is shared with parents in language they can understand.

15. Assessment encourages children to participate in self-evaluation.

16. Assessment addresses what children can do independently and what they can demonstrate with assistance, because the latter shows the direction of their growth.

17. Information about each child's growth, development, and learning is systematically collected and recorded at regular intervals. Information such as samples of children's work, descriptions of their performance, and anecdotal records is used for planning instruction and communicating with parents.

18. A regular process exists for periodic information sharing between teachers and parents about children's growth and development and performance. The method of reporting to parents does not rely on letter or numerical grades but rather provides more meaningful, descriptive information in narrative form. *(NAEYC, 1996a, pp. 15–16)*

STRATEGIES FOR AUTHENTIC ASSESSMENT IN THE EARLY CHILDHOOD CLASSROOM

In keeping with the concept and principles of authentic assessment, we as educators can employ a number of useful strategies to gather the information we need to determine whether children will need special services and whether they are benefiting from the kinds of learning activities we have planned for them. O. McAfee and Leong (2002) differentiated between two interrelated processes in documentation: collecting and recording. They described "multiple windows" for capturing information about children; such windows involve a variety of sources, methods, and contexts. For example, one source could be the child; other sources could be parents, other adults working with the child, and previous records that are available. Methods might include observing the child systematically or informally, obtaining responses from the child (work samples or oral interactions), and eliciting information from others. Contexts in which we collect the information about a child may also vary and include the classroom or any other situational context in which behaviors of interest occur, including the playground, the child's home during a home visit, field trips, or even walks around the neighborhood. Recording what we observe or hear about children can also take a number of forms. Following are a number of strategies for documenting detailed information about young children.

Screening and Readiness Procedures

The terms *screening* and *readiness* are not synonymous. Screening tools provide a method for sorting out children who may need diagnostic assessment and intervention; readiness measures help us evaluate whether or not children have acquired characteristics that equip them to come to elementary school with knowledge of how to learn, including confidence, curiosity, intentionality, self-control, and the ability to relate, communicate, and cooperate (Meisels, 2001, p. 8).

Developmental screening tests are not as in-depth as diagnostic tests; instead, screening tests have fewer items and assess a broader number of areas. Included may be abilities in large- and small-muscle coordination, perception, language, and cognitive ability. Commonly used and well-constructed examples of such tests include Ages and Stages (AGS), the Early Screening Inventory—Revised (ESI-R), the Denver Developmental Screening Test—II (DDST-II), the McCarthy Screening Test (MST), and Developmental Indicators for the Assessment of Learning—Third Edition (DIAL-3; O. McAfee & Leong, 2002).

One area in which some early childhood educators struggle is the effective assessment of incoming kindergarten children to determine whether they are "ready." Currently, many school districts are reassessing earlier scrambles to identify weaknesses in children and are instead turning their energy toward structuring "readiness roundups." These events serve a number of purposes: provide authentic assessment of incoming children (observation and documentation are the primary methods); identify children who may have special needs; allow sharing of necessary information with parents; allow educators to answer parents' questions; help educators determine the number of incoming kindergarteners; and provide a friendly, welcoming orientation for both parents and children (Thelen & Soderman, 2002). The roundups are held in a regular kindergarten classroom during the spring or summer, and experienced teachers are on hand to observe the children interacting with one another and with materials. Of special interest is how they naturally handle such activities as large-group time and transition times. As a result, children in districts who offer readiness roundups are having a more positive first experience with school. Instead of taking a test, they are able to enjoy engaging activities planned for them. Parents can

meet with the school principal and other professionals during this time to become better acquainted with school policy and the ways in which they can work with educators to support their child's successful orientation to school.

In addition to providing a more positive experience for children, the process just described allows seasoned professionals—preprimary and kindergarten teachers, Chapter 1 supervisors, elementary counselors and principals, speech teachers, school social workers, and psychologists—to observe the children at work and play. For instance, in some districts the speech teacher is required to interact purposefully with each child for a brief time during this period to obtain a speech/language sample. Visual and auditory screening are also scheduled to ensure that these primary learning modalities are intact.

Spotting the child who may have problems working with other children, adults, or materials is rarely difficult. For these children, additional assessment is structured, and a private meeting is scheduled with the child's parents so that educators can learn more about the child's history and present strengths and limitations.

Structured and Nonstructured Observation

One of the most underrated evaluation tools for use with the young child is observational assessment. In observational assessment, the objective and experienced eye of someone who is knowledgeable about child development is invaluable. Observational assessment has much to offer: It is nonintrusive for the child; it yields instant, credible information that has on-the-spot utility for improving interactional and instructional strategies with children; it has important value for formulating hypotheses to evaluate at a later date; it can be used virtually anywhere where people are behaving; and it allows the professional to capture, in natural settings, important data that could not be obtained by other methods.

Behavioral observation serves a number of valuable functions in the assessment process by providing a more personalized picture of a child's spontaneous behavior in everyday life settings (classroom, playground, hospital ward, or clinic playroom) than can be obtained from more-formal methods (Sattler, 2001). Information about the child's interpersonal behavior and learning style and a systematic record of child behaviors can be used for planning intervention or classroom instruction. In addition, behavioral observation allows for verification of others' reports regarding the child's behavior and for comparisons between behavior in formal settings and that in more naturalistic settings. Such observation also affords us an opportunity to study the behaviors of children who are developmentally disabled and are not easily evaluated by other methods.

Young children are particularly good subjects for observations because they have not yet learned to mask their feelings, thoughts, and behaviors very well. The technique also has great utility because it avoids the limitations of paper-and-pencil methods and, being fairly unobtrusive, requires no cooperation on the child's part. One 4-year-old who was moving through a screening process for kindergarten entry had everyone believing her name was Melissa (her name was Kate, but she preferred the name Melissa). She refused to answer any of the questions until her mother noted what was occurring and intervened, telling her that she had "better take things seriously and quit fooling around!" The teacher who was relating the story said, "She might have been one of our kids tagged for further diagnosis if her mother hadn't clued us in." As it was, Kate turned out to be an exceptionally bright kindergartner.

Observation of children can be seriously flawed when bias or misinterpretation by the evaluator results in the *halo effect* or the *leniency factor*. For example, if a teacher observing Kate's earlier performance interpreted the behavior as a tendency to lie, the teacher might allow this interpretation to negatively color his or her future observations of Kate. However, if the teacher viewed Kate's performance as the funny stunt of a highly creative child, he or she might see Kate *more* positively in subsequent situations than may be warranted (halo effect). The leniency phenomenon distorts observation differently. The observer would rate not only Kate more highly than would be indicated but *all* subjects more highly; we see this phenomenon in grade inflation in secondary and postsecondary education in which entire classes of students receive a 4.0 despite distinct differences in performance.

Early childhood educators will also want to step back occasionally and observe their program in action

(Morrison, 2001) to watch the way their classroom arrangement and organization are affecting children's learning. Educators will benefit by noting how children interact with other children, materials, and equipment; the comfort level children have in working together and how they express their emotions; and whether the current structure and planning support active, engaged learning.

Informal observation methods most useful to early childhood educators include the use of anecdotal records, frequency counts and charts, checklists, rating scales, and participation charts.

Anecdotal Records   Anecdotal records (see Figure 7.1) are also sometimes called *narrative records, descriptive narratives, specimen records, continuous narratives,* and *jottings*. They are on-the-spot, story-like descriptions of both typical and unusual behaviors of a child (O. McAfee & Leong, 2002). However, what distinguishes the anecdotal record from the rest, is that the anecdotal record is usually a briefer account of a single event and the method used by busy and involved classroom teachers. Conversely, narratives usually contain a great deal more information, a continuous written stream of everything said or done during the observation as well as more in-depth notes about environmental aspects surrounding the behavior; narratives are more often used by clinicians and researchers.

Anecdotal records are most conveniently written on stick-on notes or index cards to be filed and contain sufficiently detailed descriptions of a particular behavioral event that can then be used with subsequent observations to formulate hypotheses or conclusions about a child's behavioral functioning. Included is necessary information about the event, any known stimulus, persons involved, direct quotations if important to understanding the situation, and the child's behavioral responses. Unusual behaviors of any kind are noted. Any subjective inferences or interpretations

FIGURE 7.1   Anecdotal Record

Child's Name: Gary Denzell
Date: 10/16/03
Time: 10:17 A.M.

Observer: B. Miller
Setting: Kindergarten Classroom

Children were asked by Ms. Sharpe to complete a worksheet identifying like and dissimilar objects. Gary continued to play with unit blocks until reminded by Ms. Sharpe to take his place at the table and begin working. He looked up but still did not move. When she moved toward him to get him to comply, he kicked down the block structure he had been making and walked to the table. Ms. Sharpe noted, "That's better." Gary did not respond.

Interpretation: Gary balked when asked to do seatwork. He clearly preferred playing with blocks/trucks. Would there be a better way to "teach" logicomathematical concepts than having him complete a paper-pencil task, which he continues to have difficulty with?

may be noted but must be kept separate from the observation.

Preschool classrooms and primary classrooms that are structured to include at least an hour of free play per day are excellent environments in which to observe children in this way. To ensure that every child receives a weekly structured observation, some teachers prepare a grid on which all the children's names are listed. Putting the grid on a clipboard, the teacher then spends 15 minutes to one-half hour circulating in the classroom during center time, directly focusing on four or five children per day and noting behaviors of interest. Teachers may also elect to draw certain children aside during this period to have a brief miniconference about a particular skill or concept and make a note of the interaction. The grid is then cut into individual sections, with the notes on each child dated and stored in the teacher's portfolios for future reference.

Frequency Counts Frequency counts are simply tallies of specified behaviors as they occur (see Figure 7.2). Sometimes we have a feeling that a particular behavior is either increasing or decreasing on a day-to-day basis with a child. Occasionally, we may want to collect baseline information before beginning purposeful intervention to alter behavior. Frequency counts can help us document whether our intuitions about a situation are correct and can then be charted to display the effects of instituted treatment (see Figure 7.3). For example, a behavior of interest might be a child's aggressive interaction with other children, and a frequency count could document maintenance of, an increase in, or a decrease in the number of incidents of the behavior following intervention.

FIGURE 7.2 Tally of Aggressive Interactions

Child's Name:	Gary Denzell
Behavior:	Aggressive interaction with other children—biting, hitting, spitting, kicking
When:	During center activity (9:10–10:15)
Where:	Ms. Johnson's room
Observer:	B. Miller
Dates:	November 17–November 21, 2003

Days	Tally	Total
1	//////	6
2	////	4
3	///	3
4	/	1
5	//	2

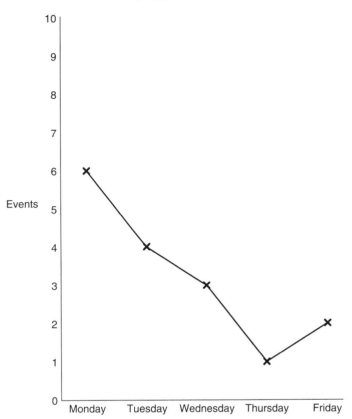

FIGURE 7.3 Charting Aggressive Interactions

Checklists and Inventories Checklists can range from formal criterion-referenced lists of developmental behaviors and skills to teacher-constructed inventories listing behaviors of interest to the educator. Checklists allow educators to note both individual achievement and group achievement and usually require a simple check mark (✓) to indicate that the skill or behavior has been noted (see Figure 7.4). Teachers interested in documenting observation of a skill more than once may note the first observation by making a horizontal mark (−), the second with an added vertical mark (+), and additional diagonal lines for subsequent observations of the skill (✳, ✳).

Rating Scales and Rubrics Rating scales are similar to checklists in that lists of behavioral variables are made. They differ in that an evaluative component is attached that qualifies behavior or skill acquisition (see Figure 7.5). When a rating scale is used, objectivity can become a problem, and evaluators need to keep objectivity uppermost in mind when rating the child's behaviors. Such scales can be color coded for easier interpretation (e.g., 1 = green; 2 = blue; 3 = yellow; 4 = red). Evaluators may choose from a variety of predetermined categories or ranges of behavior, extremes, or opposites. These may be represented by a numbered continuum attached to a

FIGURE 7.4   Example of Self-Help Checklist

CHILDREN'S SELF-HELP CHECKLIST

Date: 11/28/03

Teacher: Mrs. Gonzalez

	Robert	Joanna	Jerry	Larue	Donna	Gavin	Laura	Paul	Rosalie	William
Knows telephone number	✓			✓	✓	✓		✓	✓	
Can give full address	✓				✓	✓				
Buttons with no help	✓	✓		✓	✓	✓	✓	✓	✓	✓
Zips	✓			✓	✓		✓			✓
Can tie shoes	✓			✓		✓				
Puts materials away without being reminded	✓		✓	✓					✓	
Follows directions	✓		✓	✓	✓	✓			✓	
Cleans up after self	✓				✓				✓	
Asks for help when needed	✓				✓					

specified criterion (e.g., choosing from 0–10, in which 0 = low and 10 = high) or an open continuum (e.g., Extroversion ☐ ☐ ☐ ☐ ☐ ☐ ☐ Introversion).

To increase their objectivity in rating a product, behavior, or skill, individuals can develop *rubrics*. Rubrics are scoring tools that list clearly defined criteria to articulate gradations of quality from excellent to poor, high to low, and so on. The criterion to be evaluated is given at the left, and gradations of quality are then listed. For example, a rubric for evaluating the quality of a student-led conference by second graders could be written so that a child could self-evaluate his or her performance (see Figure 7.6). The rubric is shared with and explained to children before the project is implemented, which serves a double purpose: (a) It is a performance guide, letting children know what is expected prior to the event, and (b) it is a device they can use afterward to appraise their performance.

Participation Charts Time-sample participation charts are useful for recording where children are at a particular time during the school day and whom they interact with most often. Following the preparation of a coded form for documentation purposes, an observer simply notes the location of each child at a designated time. For example, in Figure 7.7, all areas of the classroom have been coded (A–J). Areas assigned to the two supervising adults in the room (Mr. Tanamato is the teacher, and Mrs. Gross is his aide) are identified. The children's names have been recorded down the left side of the form, and designated times when observations are to be made are recorded across the top. In a matter of seconds, the observer can document each child's location at that particular time. After a number of observations have been made, educators can examine these charts to look for patterns in children's interactions with other children and adults, as well as their involvement or noninvolvement in certain activities. For example, using the participation chart in Figure 7.7, a 1-week time sample that documents where 15 children are at five times during the morning's scheduled center

FIGURE 7.5 Example of Rating Scale

SOCIAL SKILLS RATINGS SCALE

Date: ____4/11/03____

Teacher: _Mr. Lofy_____

1 = Skill well developed; color code green
2 = Practiced often but not always; color code blue
3 = Working on; color code yellow
4 = Rarely observed; color code red

	Juan	Jim	Sandra	Jason	Kelly	Amy	Diedra	Eric	Taylor	Regina	Elizabeth	Kerry	Ervin
Developing friendship skills	3	3	1	3	3	1	1	1	3	1	1	3	4
Initiates play/work with others	4	1	1	2	4	2	2	2	4	1	1	3	4
Makes suggestions	4	1	1	3	1	1	2	1	1	1	1	1	4
Takes suggestions	1	3	2	2	3	1	1	2	3	2	2	2	3
Negotiates conflicts (compromises)	3	3	2	3	2	1	2	1	3	2	1	2	4
Is cooperative and helpful	2	2	1	2	3	2	2	1	4	2	2	2	3
Shares materials	2	3	2	2	1	2	1	1	4	2	2	2	3
Gives assistance to others	3	4	2	2	1	2	3	2	4	2	1	2	3
Respects others and their property	2	2	1	2	2	1	2	2	3	2	1	1	3
Conforms to reasonable limits	1	2	1	1	3	2	1	1	2	1	1	1	2
Demonstrates self-control	1	2	1	2	2	2	1	2	2	1	1	2	3
Adapts to new situations	3	3	2	2	3	1	1	2	3	1	2	2	3
Terminates interactions in socially acceptable ways	2	3	1	2	1	1	2	1	3	2	1	3	3
Interacts with new people	3	3	2	3	4	1	1	1	4	1	1	2	4

activity, a teacher could obtain answers to the following 10 points of interest:

1. You have had the feeling that too many children (more than five at one time) are in the art area. Do you need to structure a rule about this?

2. You suspect that the boys rarely visit the language arts center. Is this true?

3. The children seem to avoid Brian (or vice versa). Is this happening?

4. Mr. Tanamato reports that Sam spends too much time in the bathroom. Does he?

FIGURE 7.6   Rubric for Evaluating My Performance in the Student-Led Conference

Criterion	Quality		
I shared the important features of my work with my parents.	Yes, I shared enough to give them a good sense of my work in all subject areas.	Yes, I shared some but left out other key work samples.	I shared few samples of my work.

5. You suspect that a few children may be coming to school without breakfast. Who are they?

6. What percentage of the children are visiting the science area each day?

7. The children appear to be avoiding one of the adults. What can you learn about the situation?

8. Some of the children are being dropped off late; you think that you need to document this tardiness so that you can talk to the appropriate parents. Which children are noticeably tardy and not arriving by 8:00?

9. Three boys are best friends. Who?

10. You found whole rolls of toilet paper in a toilet in the bathroom on Tuesday and Friday. Who may need to be watched more closely?

By examining the data collected during the 5 days listed in Figure 7.7, you might draw the following conclusions in response to the preceding questions:

1. No rule seems to be needed about too many children in the art area. Only one incident was recorded.

2. Yes, few boys appear to be working in the language arts center—only Brian every day and Michael on Monday. What can be done to stimulate their interest?

3. Yes, observation indicated that Brian and the other children are not interacting—he is often at lockers or in the bathroom or language arts center, where there are few other children. This situation needs to be observed more carefully so that a cause can be established.

4. We cannot tell whether Sam is spending too much time in the bathroom from this set of observations. Try event sampling for an answer to this question.

5. Jenny and Julio may be coming to school without breakfast. This situation needs to be followed up immediately by talking to the children.

6. Only 20 percent (3) of the children visited the science area last week.

7. Boys are avoiding areas where Mr. Tanamato is stationed, even M, W, and F snack (also science on M,

W, F and blocks and large motor on T, Th). Need to follow up.

8. Kevin was tardy on M, T, W, Th, F. Joey was tardy on M, T, F. Michael was tardy on T, W.

9. Bill, Sam, and Julio appear to be best friends and travel from activity to activity together.

10. Kevin and Sam are the only boys who were in the boys' bathroom on both T and F. This situation bears closer watching.

Oral Reading Tests: Running Records

As educators in some school districts move to a literature-based approach to reading in the primary grades as an alternative to basal texts, many of them are looking for a quantitative method for documenting that children are making progress in reading accuracy and in their ability to recognize and correct mistakes without help. One literature-based method for obtaining samples of children's reading accuracy at several times during the year is for the teacher to conduct an individual oral reading test and running record with individual children. The teacher, using a photocopied or typed version of the age-appropriate story, then listens to evaluate the quality of the child's reading, noting mistakes, number of words read, self-corrections, words omitted, words added, and words reversed (see Figure 7.8). Notes are made on comprehension, fluency and expressiveness in reading, and the nature of the child's mistakes. These assessments can also be tape-recorded for future reference across time by the teacher and the child or to demonstrate the child's ability to a parent or another professional.

Scoring the oral reading sample (see Figure 7.9) consists of establishing an accuracy rate, a meaningful mistake rate (mistakes that do not destroy syntax or meaning; e.g., *house* for *home*), a self-correction rate, and a comprehension score that ranges from fragmentary understanding (1) to full and complete understanding of the story (4). Such scores, across time, indicate whether the child is improving in accuracy and the ability to self-correct and whether more- or less-difficult material would be more appropriate. A summary of the process appears in Figure 7.10.

FIGURE 7.7 Time-Sample Participation Chart

	Monday					Tuesday					Wednesday					Thursday					Friday				
	8:15	8:30	9:00	9:15	9:30	8:15	8:30	9:00	9:15	9:30	8:15	8:30	9:00	9:15	9:30	8:15	8:30	9:00	9:15	9:30	8:15	8:30	9:00	9:15	9:30
Brian	A	B	F	J	I	B	A	I	J	J	I	J	J	B	I	H	A	H	I	B	I	J	J	A	I
Amy	C	A	H	D	G	H	A	D	C	C	A	B	H	D	D	D	C	C	A	—	C	C	A	B	D
Kevin	—	—	I	E	E	—	A	I	B	D	—	—	F	E	E	—	—	B	A	D	—	—	B	E	E
Amanda	C	B	D	A	C	C	C	D	E	E	A	F	F	D	D	C	C	C	D	D	D	D	D	F	A
Jenny	A	I	H	D	D	A	H	D	D	F	G	A	C	C	C	A	—	D	D	C	A	G	G	G	E
Joey	—	E	D	D	E	—	—	—	A	F	F	E	E	D	—	H	A	D	F	D	—	—		F	D
Bill	D	D	C	C	G	D	B	F	A	C	D	D	B	G	G	A	D	—	F	F	G	G	G	H	D
Sam	D	B	C	C	G	D	B	F	A	C	D	D	B	G	G	A	D	—	F	F	B	G	G	H	D
Sarah	G	G	A	D	D	D	D	C	C	H	D	—	A	F	F	C	C	G	C	C	D	C	C	C	A
Erin	G	A	D	H	B	F	F	D	A	B	A	D	—	H	B	D	D	F	E	—	B	A	D	D	C
Tamera	G	A	D	D	C	D	A	C	C	C	—	A	C	C	C	E	F	F	G	D	A	C	C	D	G
Julio	A	D	C	B	G	A	B	F	A	C	D	D	B	G	G	A	D	—	F	F	A	G	G	H	D
Ahmad	G	G	D	E	E	F	F	A	B	D	—	—		B	F	D	D	A	D	G	E	E	E
Randi	D	I	A	G	G	G	G	D	D	A	A	C	H	C	D	F	F	C	D	A	D	A	B	C	C
Michael	B	J	D	E	E	—	—	I	A	F	—	—		D	D	A	F	F	B	F	D	F	F

A = snack*
B = bathroom
C = dramatic play
D = art center
E = blocks/trucks**
F = manipulatives
G = large motor**
H = science*
I = lockers
J = language arts center

*Mr. Tanamato, MWF; Mrs. Gross, TTh
**Mrs. Gross, MWF; Mr. Tanamato, TTh

FIGURE 7.8 Analysis of an Oral Reading Sample

```
Name: Juana Perez
Date: April 4, 2003
Evaluator: Mr. Lofy
                         Fish Is Fish
                              ʕ                        Word Total
AT THE EDGE OF THE WOODS THERE WAS A BIG              10  / X
POND, AND THERE A MINNOW AND A TADPOLE                18  X
SWAM AMONG THE WEEDS. THEY WERE INSEPARABLE           25  X
FRIENDS.                                              26

ONE MORNING THE TADPOLE DISCOVERED THAT              32  X
DURING THE NIGHT HE HAD GROWN TWO LITTLE LEGS.       41  X
"LOOK," he said triumphantly. "LOOK, I AM A FROG!"   50  / X
"NONSENSE," SAID THE MINNOW. "HOW COULD YOU BE A     59  X
FROG IF ONLY LAST NIGHT YOU WERE A LITTLE TINY FISH, 70  / /
JUST LIKE ME!"                                        73

THEY ARGUED AND ARGUED UNTIL FINALLY THE             80  X
TADPOLE SAID, "FROGS ARE FROGS AND FISH IS FISH      89
AND THAT'S THAT!"          ʕ                          92

IN THE WEEKS THAT FOLLOWED, THE TADPOLE GREW         100  /
TINY FRONT LEGS AND HIS TAIL GOT SMALLER AND         109
SMALLER.                                             110
```

Teacher–Child Miniconferences

Holding brief, one-on-one conferencing sessions between teacher and child about particular aspects of the child's work is an evaluation method that can be used to further follow up on any of the methods described to this point. The teacher may ask questions to probe the child's thinking about the products, clarify concepts that are still fuzzy in the child's mind, and learn more about what the child is interested in working on in the future. Information gathering is most effective when teachers offer open-ended requests such as "Tell me how you figured this out" or "This part is especially interesting. Tell me how you thought of that." Discussions that take place in small- and large-group meetings between children and the teacher also yield information about children's conceptualization that can be useful for more in-depth planning and assessment.

The Ecomap

Finding out about the child's world outside the classroom can enhance assessment, particularly when this is done early in the year, perhaps in preparation for the initial fall conference between teachers and children's parents. The ecomap (see Figure 7.11) is a paper-and-pencil exercise designed to provide a simple, visual overview of the child's experience in the family and community. The teacher invites the parent(s) to sketch out the child's ecomap and to begin by drawing a circle in the middle of the paper and placing the child's name in the center. Other circles representing the most salient systems in the child's life (e.g., immediate family members living both in and outside the household, as well as extended family—grandparents, influential aunts, uncles, etc.) are then placed around the center circle and connected by lines. Other connections related to health care, recreation, extracurricular activities, parents' workplaces, the child's best friends outside school, child care, and so forth can be added to provide more information. As the connections are drawn, the teacher may elicit additional information about any connections that seem to be highly problematic or supportive for either the child or the parent. In this way, the teacher becomes acquainted with the way children spend their time and energy outside the classroom. Also revealed is the qualitative nature of the various contexts, which provides a better understanding of a child's special needs or of life events that may be affecting the child's classroom performance. Parents who have participated in the exercise have reported that it allowed them to establish better rapport and feelings of collaboration. Others have said the process made them more aware that even a very young child's world can be fairly complex.

FIGURE 7.9   Scoring the Oral Reading Sample in Figure 7.8

Name: Juana Perez

Date: April 4, 2003

Evaluator: Mr. Lofy

Literature Category: Level 3

A. Words read: 110
B. Mistakes (X): 8
C. Self-Corrections (/): 5
D. Meaningful mistakes (/): 0
E. Total corrected/meaningful mistakes (B + C + D)

Accuracy Score: (A – B) ÷ A
              (110 – 8 ÷ 110) = .93

Self-Correction Rate: C ÷ E
              5 ÷ 13 = .38

Comprehension (1 = fragmentary to 4 = full)**:** 3

Comments: Juana's self-correction abilities are increasing (score
          on 2/27/03 = .22, score on 4/4/03 = .38). Compre-
          hension was good, and she enjoyed reading to me.
          According to accuracy rate, literature category is still
          too difficult. Retest in May.

Self-Appraisal by the Child

Children are rarely challenged to evaluate their own progress, yet doing so is important. Besides conferencing with the teacher periodically about their work, they can learn to document involvement in the classroom by using checklists that have been developed in many of the domains. For example, skills in a certain area (e.g., physical development, social-emotional development, or emergent writing) may be listed (see Figure 7.12), with spaces that can be dated by the teacher or student and then colored in by the child as a skill is achieved. As the year progresses, children are reminded about maintaining the skill every time they make entries and are reinforced as they see the number of skills adding up on the checklist.

Teachers will want to produce self-evaluation checklists that list a range and number of skills so that every child will be able to check or color in at least a few skill blocks at the beginning. Skills to be acquired should be reasonably within a child's reach, given more time and practice. For children who are progressing more slowly, a checklist that breaks the skills down more finely and recognizes smaller gains in development should be devised. For younger children, pictographs and a rebus are helpful.

Tabita is indicating how he spent his time at school and will evaluate whether his day was terrific, good, OK, sad, or terrible.

FIGURE 7.10 Analyzing and Scoring Oral Reading Tapes

Analysis

1. Listen to the tape the child has made.
2. Underline *all* mistakes, writing above printed word what reader actually said.
3. Do not count the same mistake twice.
4. Indicate self-corrections by putting a *C* above the word and underlining it.
5. Circle any words omitted.
6. Put a caret (^) in the space if an extra word is added, and write the extra word above.
7. If letters or words are reversed, mark with horizontal *S* (~).
8. Make notes on retelling, comprehension, particular qualities of reading, or problems.
9. In the right margin
   a. indicate a meaningful mistake (does not destroy syntax or meaning) by a slash (/).
   b. indicate a self-corrected mistake by underlining a slash (/).
   c. indicate a mistake not corrected or that destroys meaning or syntax by a crossed slash (x).

Scoring

1. *Use the following designators:*
   A = Count total number of words read.
   B = Add total number of uncorrected mistakes (X).
   C = Add number of self-corrections (/).
   D = Add number of meaningful mistakes (/).
   E = Total number of all mistakes (B + C + D).

2. *Obtain accuracy score.* From total number of words read, subtract number of uncorrected and nonmeaningful mistakes. Divide the resulting number by the total number of words read. Thus, use the following formula: [(A − B) ÷ A].

Note: If accuracy rate is less than 95 percent, the child is likely to flounder and lose ability to use strategies ordinarily at his or her disposal. Try an easier text. If 100 percent accuracy, suggest a more difficult text to child.

3. *Obtain self-correction rate.* Divide number of self-corrections (C) by total number of all mistakes (E). Thus, use the following formula: [C ÷ E].

Note: The self-correction rate assesses a child's determination to make sense of what is being read. The higher the percentage, the more the child is gaining meaning from reading.

4. Determine comprehension or retelling score, using the following criteria:
   1 = fragmentary understanding
   2 = partial understanding
   3 = fairly complete understanding
   4 = full and complete understanding; ability to make inferences from what is read

Note: Oral reading tapes may be passed on from a teacher in one grade to a teacher in another so that the teachers can assess a child's reading progress with time. It is important to use only one tape for each child, date each entry, and use the same scoring criteria across a school district so that interpretation of children's scores will be valid. Also, a school district should establish a "literature difficulty index" or category by using suggested lists such as that published in Routman and Butler's (1991) *Transitions*. It should be noted when a child is moving to a more difficult level of reading material, for it is expected that a child's accuracy and self-correction scores will temporarily decrease until the child increases skills at the new level.

ORGANIZATION AND USE OF AUTHENTIC ASSESSMENT AND EVALUATION DATA: PORTFOLIOS AND STUDENT-LED CONFERENCES

In a local school district, an early childhood education committee has been given the task of structuring a districtwide portfolio and student-led conferencing process. Maggie Williams, a first-grade teacher, is serving as the facilitator and summarizing a list of concerns that committee members have raised: Will parents accept the new process? Should standardized and unit testing be continued? Should all teachers be required to implement the process? How involved should the children be? What products should be saved and included?

FIGURE 7.11 Ecomap: The Child's Developmental Contexts

*AFDC, Aid to Families with Dependent Children.

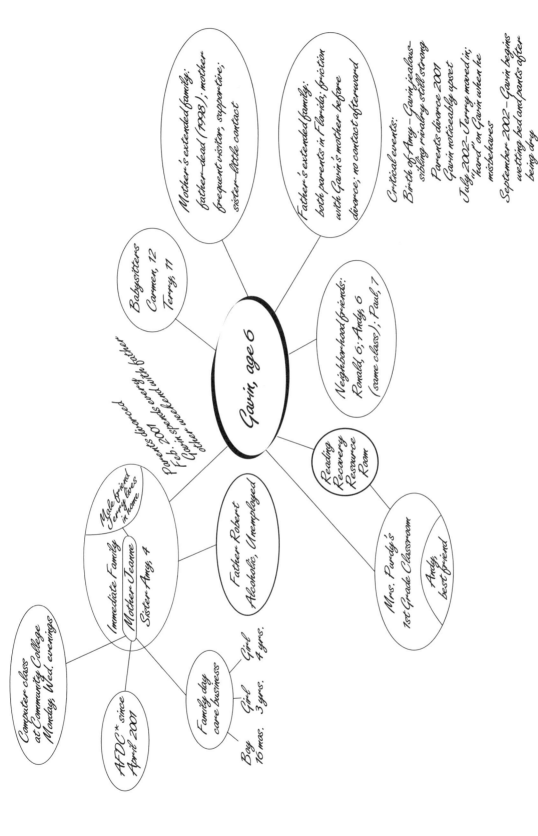

Computer class at Community College Monday, Wed. evenings

AFDC* since April 2001

Family day care business
Boy 16 mos.
Girl 3 yrs.
Girl 4 yrs.

Immediate Family
Male friend Jerry "lives in home"
Mother-Jeanne
Sister-Amy, 4

Father Robert Alcoholic, Unemployed

Parents divorced Feb. 2001 spends every other weekend with father Gavin spends every other weekend with father

Babysitters Carmen, 12 Terry, 11

Gavin, age 6

Mother's extended family: father-dead (1998); mother frequent visitor, supportive; sister-little contact

Father's extended family: both parents in Florida; friction with Gavin's mother before divorce; no contact afterward

Neighborhood friends: Ronald, 6; Andy, 6 (same class); Paul, 7

Reading Recovery Resource Room

Mrs. Purdy's 1st Grade Classroom
Andy, best friend

Critical events:

Birth of Amy—Gavin jealous-sibling rivalry still strong

Parents divorce 2001
Gavin noticeably upset

July 2002—Jerry moved in; "hard" on Gavin when he misbehaves

September 2002—Gavin begins wetting bed and pants after being dry

January 2003 chicken pox

June 2003 Because of health and family problems, missed 42 days of school during 2002/03 school year

199

FIGURE 7.12   A Form for Child's Self-Appraisal

Date:	9/27	12/5	2/14	4/12	5/10	6/12
I can zip.						
I play and work with others.						
I share with others.						
I help clean up.						
I put materials away after using them.						
I try new things.						
I am helpful to others.						

Portfolios: Matching Assessment with How Children Learn

Children are delighted when they see for themselves how they have grown, and there is no better way to allow them to do so than by keeping their work samples and other artifacts that they produce so that they can compare today's work with yesterday's. When children show their dossier, portfolio, or process folios of work to others, teachers can share in their obvious mixture of pure delight and heavy seriousness as children select their personal best.

The purpose of structuring portfolios is threefold: (a) to make sense of children's work, (b) to let others know about their work, and (c) to relate the work to a larger context (Grace & Shores, 1991). Samples may include a child's drawings, paintings, video- or audiotapes, maps, graphs, descriptions and photographs of projects and friends, charts, webs, and written work—in short, anything that meaningfully depicts their progress. The process promotes developmentally appropriate instruction in that it requires professionals to plan performance-based evaluation activities from which products can be collected intermittently during the school year and to allow children adequate time and guidance to work on relevant artifacts for their portfolios.

The most compelling feature of portfolios is that they focus more on what children *can* do, whereas traditional assessment focuses primarily on what they *cannot* do or cannot do well. Beginning as general collections of their work, portfolios are then reduced to selections that the children think are representative of their progress. Coexisting portfolios at any one time include the following four (Tierney, 1991):

1. An *individual portfolio* in which the child stores dated work samples from his or her daily work as artist, reader, writer, problem solver, and scientist (Stone, 1997). When introducing the process, teachers may consider bringing in professionals who keep some sort of portfolio (e.g., photographers, models, architects, artists, journalists, or educators) to lead a discussion with children about what can be developed in each area of the curriculum. Because a sense of ownership will be important, children should brainstorm about the kinds of representative samples to save and have input into subsequent decisions. When children are working on pieces for the portfolio, the teacher will want to remind

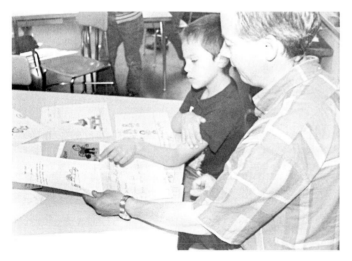

Portfolios are useful for noting development across time in various domains.

them about qualitative aspects of the work and the importance of their best effort.

Storage for easy access is important. Some teachers have obtained large, individual pizza boxes in which children store their work. Other educators have had children make portfolios out of large pieces of sturdy tagboard. With large classes of children, two or three places can be established in the room for folder storage so that children do not have to wait in long lines to place daily work in their portfolios.

2. A *showcase portfolio* intended to be shared with others. It contains a specified number of carefully selected pieces that the child believes are the best examples of his or her work. The selection of these pieces may be negotiated with the teacher or remain wholly the child's choice. At the time of selection, the child communicates to the teacher the reasons that he or she considers a particular piece a good choice. The pieces should always be arranged chronologically so that they indicate growth. For very young children, maybe only three to five pieces will be included. Primary-age children can be helped to select samples of work from each curriculum area and to categorize the material for the viewer. If able, children may also construct a preface, a table of contents, or labels to tell the reader how the materials were developed or organized.

Decorated or personalized showcase portfolios can be simple or elaborate, depending on the children's skill and motivation. Teachers can encourage children to customize them as creatively as possible and to take pride in the uniqueness of their personality or work style. As soon as children can write, they can include a statement of purpose for or an introduction to the portfolio. One child wrote, "Dear reader: My portfolio contains art work, journals, center work, writing pieces, and spelling sheets. This is work I adore, so please try not to rip it" (Soderman, Gregory, & O'Neill, 1999a).

3. A *teacher portfolio,* usually a manila folder, with selections or copies of work from the student portfolio, as well as checklists and inventories of skill development, anecdotal notes, and any other data that the teacher believes are particularly illustrative of the child's academic and personal growth. The teacher may want to include items that children may not have selected for their showcase portfolios but that depict particular strengths or limitations of the child's work. These portfolios are not shared at student-led conferences but may be useful if parents want to confer later with the teacher or if the teacher needs to confer with other professionals who are involved in educational planning for a child.

4. An *institutional portfolio* that contains a specified collection of the child's work during the time the child is in the school. The contents are a few particular items agreed on by the staff that are to be collected at each grade level for all children at consistent times during each year. For example, at the preschool and kindergarten level, children may be asked to draw a self-portrait at the beginning and end of the year. Also included may be a social skills checklist, a self-appraisal checklist, and an ecomap. In first grade, the child's self-portraits at the beginning and end of the year are again included, along with two samples of the child's best writing (the spring sample might be a simple math story problem), and K–5 inventories of literacy and math progress are begun and entered. A picture of the child at each level, perhaps with special friends, should be included. These portfolios are collected at year's end (unless the child will be staying with the same teacher) and sent on to next year's teacher. Some elementary schools hold a celebration evening for children who will be going on the next year to a middle school and present the children and their families with these longitudinal, comprehensive collections of their work. Such collections are highly valued because they paint a picture of significant growth by children as they move through the elementary years. One child who was looking back at some of the earliest entries grinned broadly and remarked, "I was such a baby then!" When schools are implementing new instructional practices, the portfolios help determine whether children's skills are improving with time.

Student-Led Conferences: Bringing Parents and Others into the Process

Producing a good piece of work is enormously satisfying, yet our satisfaction is expanded considerably when we share it with others. Sharing it with others is what student-led conferencing is all about. Such conferencing encourages children to reflect on what they have produced and to think about their goals. It is a celebration in which parents and interested others can view a child's accomplishments firsthand, make supportive comments and suggestions, exchange information, and be actively involved in the child's work world (Stone, 1997). Instead of being cut out of the process (as in traditional parent–teacher conferencing), the child is not only brought into the process but, appropriately, takes center stage. Instead of the teacher's relating simple scores or grades to parents and telling about work that was not produced, the onus is put on the child to present evidence of growth and achievement during a specific time period. It is the children's celebration.

Student-led conferencing comprises three stages: (a) a preparatory period, (b) implementation of the conference, and (c) a debriefing period.

Getting Ready for the Big Event At specific times during the school year, anywhere from once to quarterly, teachers and children plan for a portfolio conference. The teacher sets a convenient time for parents to attend (one that does not conflict with other community events or with parents' work schedules), helps children to select and organize materials, sends out written invitations, plans for pictures to be taken, organizes child care and transportation if necessary, and informs the parents about the process. Schedules can be drawn up to ensure that the teacher has adequate time to meet each family. An optimal structure is to have four or five families in the room at one time for 20 to 30 minutes, depending on the class size. Preprimary and kindergarten teachers who have two classes per day will want to schedule two separate evenings to accommodate parents comfortably.

The teacher will want to stress the importance of parents' remembering to be only positive because the work they will be viewing is their child's personal best at that particular time. If parents are inexperienced with the process, professionals can provide examples of questions parents may ask children during the conference (e.g., "Which piece is your favorite? Why?" "What are your goals for the next work period?" "What do you think is the most important thing you've learned this year?" "What do you enjoy most about school this year? What do you find most difficult?").

In addition to selecting pieces for their showcase portfolio, children may practice communicating about their work by showing their portfolios to a classmate (a portfolio buddy) and to someone else in another class before the conference. They may role-play introducing their family members to the teacher, write invitations, and plan with the teacher how to restructure the classroom environment for the evening. For example, children can make posters celebrating the event, table decorations, and decorated paper tablecloths. They can make a parent guest book for written feedback, make refreshments, make a welcome sign for the door, and help select soft, instrumental music to be played in the background. They may also help clean and organize the classroom for the event. Children also discuss with their teacher the activities that might be of special interest to their parents: sharing their favorite books (and showing off their improving reading skills), including their parents in their classroom center experiences, reviewing their journals, participating in group projects, and viewing videos showing them at work in the classroom.

These events are perfect venues for displaying documentation boards. At the Child Development Laboratories at Michigan State University, these three-sided boards, with panels approximately 2 × 5 feet, line the hallways outside the early childhood classrooms during student-conferencing days. They contain documentation of the exciting learning that has transpired during particular projects. Although each board is unique, it contains a description of the curricular goals and objectives that received special attention during the project. Also included are pictures of the children involved in working on included activities, narratives by the children about certain concepts and skills they were learning, and brief written perspectives by the teacher. Three-dimensional artifacts produced by the children during the project are also labeled and arranged on the table near the boards, providing additional documentation of completed work for parents and others to view. Family members spend a great deal of time examining the boards prior to and following their conference time. The boards are also available for viewing by university faculty coming into the school for research and by members of the public who might be visiting the laboratories, creating interest in the school's approach to early education. The boards are then archived and may be brought out to share with other classes of children or adults who are involved in similar projects.

Celebrating Because of their extensive involvement in the preparatory phase, children are very excited about the celebration—perhaps even a little nervous. As in the case of the artist, photographer, architect, writer, and scientist, the work in which they have so much personal investment is about to be viewed and evaluated by others. Even very young children can be encouraged to introduce their parents to the teacher and then to read a favorite book with their parents, engage a parent in a favorite classroom activity or game, share their journal, and look through the portfolio. As children mature, student-led conferencing can become more sophisticated. However, the evening should maintain an air of celebration and be as enjoyable as possible for all.

In many school districts where attendance at parent–teacher conferences has been extremely low, administrators report that nearly 100 percent of parents attend student-led conferencing because they find it so enjoyable. Moreover, because their children are the presenters, non-English-speaking parents do not experience the extreme language barriers that keep them away from parent–teacher conferences. Because the focus is on what the children *did* accomplish and they feel grown up in taking on the role of presenter, most children share the feelings of one second grader who exclaimed to her teacher the next morning, "That was fun! When are we going to do it again?"

Debriefing: How Was It? A written follow-up to thank parents for attending and to find out what they enjoyed or did not enjoy about the conference is important so that future portfolio celebrations can be improved. A brief survey sheet can be included in the thank-you note, including such questions as What did you like about the conference? Is there anything you would like to see changed? How has your child responded to the student-led conference? Would you like to see this type of conference format continue in the future? Why or why not? A place for comments and suggestions can also be included (Soderman et al., 1999a).

The teacher will want to schedule time with individual or small groups of children to discuss their reactions to the conference and even have children who can write fill out evaluation forms. Eric, a first grader, drew a picture of himself playing a board game with his parents, all three with huge smiles on their faces, which said a lot about his experience. He titled his page "CONNFORNS [CONFERENCE]" and wrote, "I like when I plad games. I like when I sode (showed) my Mom & Dad my fobler (folder). I like when I sode them the room." Children may discuss their favorite aspect of the conferences and what they will do differently the next time, and they may suggest changes to make for the next conference during the preparatory or implementation phases.

Portfolios and student-led conferencing empower children, teachers, and parents. In organizing their work and articulating to others what they have done to produce this work, children grow in their ability to make decisions and to take responsibility for their achievements (Batzle, 1992). Portfolios help them connect schoolwork with real purposes for learning skills, help them recognize their strengths and weaknesses, and help them see learning as sequential and connected with effort—life skills that are just as important as the academic skills being evaluated.

Teachers take on a different role, one that rids them of a "boss mentality" and instead equips them to become facilitators, consultants, and more knowledgeable guides in children's learning. They gain greater expertise in a wide range of developmental skills and become creative rather than prescriptive in structuring classroom learning experiences (Tierney, 1991). Parents are brought intimately into an interactive evaluative process that is more meaningful, more pleasurable, and more productive in terms of understanding and appreciating their child's growing abilities. The portfolio process is more effective when it includes student-led conferencing and when schools and school systems have institutionalized the practice across the entire period of children's school careers.

SUMMARY

Developmentally appropriate early childhood evaluation is necessary for documenting young children's growth and for providing sound information for program planning in the primary grades. Formulating an effective evaluation strategy to measure children's progress requires the following:

Early childhood educators with a solid understanding of the many facets of child development

Formulation of developmental objectives in all learning domains of interest, on the basis of child development research and theories

A planned range of appropriate performance-based activities and experiences for children that are keyed directly to developmental objectives and children's abilities and interests

Appropriate and authentic evaluation strategies for measuring children's engagement in activities and developmental progress with time

Thoughtful timing of individual, small-group, and large-group evaluation (time of day, spacing during school year)

Effective use of evaluation data to improve the quality of each child's educational experiences and growth

A useful structure for organizing and sharing obtained formative and summative information with relevant others (i.e., the children, parents, other educational staff working currently or in the future with the child and administration)

Although standardized tests can help us understand and plan for the child with special needs, information gained from them should be used only along with other equally valid sources. Single scores on standardized tests should never be used in isolation to direct or redirect the lives of young children; nor should they be used to structure children into homogeneous settings when the children could be better served in regular programs and with their peers. In general, standardized testing in preschool through second grade is largely unnecessary. Alternative evaluation methods are preferred, including observation of the children and collection of a variety of valid work samples.

Findings from evaluating children's work should be used. Although this may seem obvious, testing and evaluation often do not go beyond collecting scores to assign grades or make comparisons across classes or schools. The process should always culminate in a plan by the teacher to structure learning experiences for the child. Results may also help the professional to note the strengths and weaknesses of classroom instruction and guidance. Findings should be considered in the context of the teacher's knowledge of the child and influence the timing and nature of the next evaluation.

All assessment findings should be carefully cataloged for future use, and information should be kept confidential except when it is used to support the young child's educational experience. In the hands of professionals knowledgeable about child development, curriculum planning, and early childhood assessment, effective evaluation can become one of the tools needed to plan advantageous beginnings for children and the kinds of classroom experiences that will lead to sustained curiosity and a desire for lifelong learning.

Applying What You Read in This Chapter

1. Discuss

a. Return to the questions that opened this chapter. On the basis of your reading and your experiences, discuss your response to each question in detail.

b. If you were interviewing for an early childhood teaching position and a member of the interviewing team asked you what you know about authentic assessment and how you would implement it, how would you answer?

2. Observe

a. Arrange to view the portfolios of a class of first graders and a class of third graders in a local elementary school in which student-led conferencing is used. Ask for permission to observe implementation of the process. Determine the following:

(1) What products were kept in the portfolios? How does this differ between the first graders and the third graders?

(2) During the conferencing, what role do the children play? What role does the teacher play? In what ways is the process an effective way to share information? In what ways could it be improved?

3. Carry out an activity

a. Carry out a reading accuracy test with a second grader, using the process described in this chapter. Use Leo Leonni's *Fish Is Fish* as the text. What is the child's accuracy score? self-correction rate? How would you score the child's comprehension?

Summarize what you learned about the child's literacy skills.

b. Using the information you gained about ecomaps in the subsection The Ecomap, ask the parents of one or more children in a nearby early childhood education setting if you may interview them. What can you discover about the child that might be helpful in working with that child in an educational context?

4. Create something for your portfolio

a. Develop a position statement about the need for more authentic assessment of children in the early childhood classroom. Give reasons why it supports developmentally appropriate educational practices.

b. Create a subsection on your ability to assess and evaluate the progress of young children. Include a listing and brief description of a number of authentic methods. Carry out as many of these methods as you can with a child of the appropriate age. Summarize the results of each assessment procedure and attach a copy of the child's work.

5. Add to your journal

a. What are your earliest memories of taking tests? How well do you do today when you are taking tests? What are your strengths and limitations?

b. How confident do you feel about implementing authentic assessment and evaluation strategies? In what area do you need more information or practice?

CHAPTER

8

Strengthening Developmentally Appropriate Programs Through Family Involvement

You may wonder:

What does *family involvement* really mean?

Why are people so interested in involving parents or other significant family members in early childhood programs?

Why do some parents get so caught up in their children's education while other parents do not?

How should I respond to family members who seem unable or unwilling to become involved in the early childhood program?

What are some effective strategies for working with family members as partners in children's education?

In this chapter on building family partnerships in early childhood education, we present information to help you answer the preceding questions.

A tear trickled down Tish Kelley's cheek. The mother of a 3-year-old, she thought that on the first day of preschool, her daughter would cling to her at least a little. However, Joelle Kelley entered the classroom happily, eager to play with the toys and the other children. "'Bye, mom; you can go now," she said. Tish sighed, "Only 3 years old and already she doesn't need me."

During a home visit with the kindergarten teacher, Patrick's father explains that Patrick has been diagnosed as showing signs of attention deficit disorder. He stresses that Patrick is a loving child who needs plenty of affection, simple directions, and clear boundaries.

At a school-sponsored curriculum night, Kathy Hale, a parent of a first grader, mentions that she is a weaver. She says, "My daughter loves to watch the loom in action. Would you like me to come in sometime and show the children how to weave?"

Mrs. Salari wonders whether or not her 8-year-old son is showing signs of a learning disability. Her best friend says yes, her mother-in-law says no, and now she is asking your opinion as an early childhood professional.

Imagine that you are the teacher in each of these scenarios. Take a moment to consider the family members

you have just met. They are all different. Yet, they are also alike in many ways:

- ❑ Each of them is a significant person in a young child's life.
- ❑ Each has an emotional investment in that child.
- ❑ All have ideas and opinions about raising and educating young children.
- ❑ Each family member has the potential to become more actively involved in the early childhood program in which his or her child participates.

What you do and say in situations such as those that were just described will influence the degree to which families will feel welcome in your classroom and the extent to which they will become active in their children's education. For this reason, you must think carefully about your relationships with children's families and about how you might encourage them to become involved in the early childhood program.

THE CHANGING NATURE OF FAMILY INVOLVEMENT IN EARLY CHILDHOOD EDUCATION

The notion of involving parents or other significant family members in children's early education is not new. For years, connecting home and school has been a fundamental aim of parent cooperative nursery schools, Head Start, and other early intervention programs (Unger, Jones, & Park, 2001). These efforts have had such promising outcomes that now, when we talk about creating or maintaining developmentally appropriate education programs, we always include family involvement as an essential component (Larsen & Haupt, 1997). In fact, the National Association of State Boards of Education (NASBE, 1988) recommends that all education programs serving children aged 3 through 8 years do the following:

❏ Promote an environment in which family members are valued as primary influences in their children's lives and as essential partners in the education of their children.

❏ Recognize that the self-esteem of parents/significant family members is integral to the development of the child and should be enhanced by the family's positive interaction with the program.

❏ Include family members in decision making about their own child and the overall early childhood program.

❏ Assure opportunities and access for family members to observe and volunteer in the classroom.

❏ Promote an exchange of information and ideas between family members and teachers which will benefit the child.

❏ Provide a gradual and supportive transition process from home to school for those young children entering school for the first time. *(p. 19)*

Current professional practice goes beyond focusing solely on the biological parents to including *any* person who has responsibility for making decisions about the well-being of each child—stepparents, adult partners of biological parents, grandparents, and foster parents either informally or formally fostering children—specifically including both men and women. Opportunities for family inclusion in the life of the program are numerous and varied. The role of educators in the early childhood program now encompasses more than merely sponsoring a fall open house or periodically rounding up experts to speak to family members about current issues in education. Today, a clear emphasis is placed on two-way communication and on families and professionals' working together to enhance children's learning (Briggs, Jalongo, & Brown, 1997).

As you can probably ascertain, the concept of family involvement within a developmentally appropriate framework is much more comprehensive, interactive, and collaborative. Involving family members in chil-

dren's education is a continuous process that incorporates parents and other extended family members in various phases of the total educational program, including the planning, implementation, and assessment phases (Bredekamp & Copple, 1997). Family members and early childhood professionals form an alliance in which they develop a common understanding of what children are like—how children develop, how they behave, the challenges they face, and how they can be helped to meet these challenges. The adults also come to a shared conception of what good education is—what it looks like, how it operates, what it strives to achieve, what it requires, and what it precludes. When such alliances occur, family members and teachers learn together, mutually supporting each other in their efforts to make life more meaningful for the children and themselves (Goldberg, 1997). In this way, professionals and families become partners in the educational process.

The coalition between family members and teachers can take place in several ways and with varying degrees of participation by both groups. Joyce Epstein, a leading researcher on the subject, identified five categories of family partnering that range from lesser to greater ties between children's homes and early education programs (see Table 8.1).

The desirability of all five types of family involvement is currently so well accepted that the federal government now mandates inclusion of parents and other significant family members as participants, advisers, and knowledgeable consumers of services in all phases of Project Head Start, in the education of children with disabilities (Public Laws 94–142 and 99–457), and in federally administered child care. Increasingly, state governments have followed suit. As a result, in early childhood programs across the United States, family members are involved in children's education at all levels—from tutors at home to classroom participants, from volunteers to paid employees, from advisers to program decision makers. Those involved include first-time parents, teenage parents, older parents, single parents, dual-career parents, stepparents, parents of children with disabilities, grandparents, foster parents, aunts, uncles, and sometimes older brothers and sisters (Chang, Salazar, & DeLeong, 1994). Moreover, although originally targeted at programs for very young children, family participation efforts have reached beyond such programs, into elementary, middle, and high schools (Weinstein & Mignano, 2003). All this has transpired because we as educators have discovered that children, parents, and programs benefit immensely when family members take an active part in young children's educational experiences.

TABLE 8.1 Five Types of Family Involvement with Examples

Type 1: Child Rearing	Type 2: Communicating	Type 3: Volunteering	Type 4: Learning at Home	Type 5: Representing Other Families
Professional staff member facilitates the development of skills leading to improved learning at home. Adults in the family acquire knowledge and skills that enable them to supervise, teach, and guide their children.	Professional staff member communicates effectively with family members. Family members receive and respond to the messages from the program.	Professional staff member solicits assistance from family members and organizes the work they are to do. Family members participate in the classrooms with the children and attend workshops or other programs for their own benefit.	Professional staff member provides family members with strategies to assist their children's learning at home. Adults in the home respond to the children's request for assistance, monitor homework activities, and coordinate family learning opportunities with program-based experiences.	Professional staff member recruits and prepares family members for decision-making roles at all levels: program, district, and state. Family members become active in community or advocacy activities that monitor or advise programs. They work for educational improvement for all children.
Examples Provide suggestions that older children and adult family members can use that support the children's learning, such as make-and-take workshops to construct learning games, written materials regarding discipline or other common challenges, or information about television programming. This material may be delivered through the Web, videotapes, and telephone messages or in groups.	**Examples** Hold regular conferences with family members once or twice a year and follow through. Prepare documentation boards or notebooks of children's learning and leave them in places accessible to parents. Send home "happy notes" about the child's progress in school. Be accessible to family members so that they can communicate informally about their needs and interests as well as about family concerns. Organize a variety of events that facilitate communication between families and staff, such as open houses, coffees, and potluck meals. Create a library around the needs and interests of the families in the program.	**Examples** Survey the interests, skills, and talents of the family members who can be invited to volunteer. Structure a well-organized program for volunteers that taps their skills, is interesting to the adults, and is valuable to the children. Invite family members to participate regularly in the program.	**Examples** Give information to family members regarding children's learning and appropriate skill and concept acquisition—for example, how to form manuscript lowercase letters correctly so that children can learn to write their names. Calendars of simple activities that provide for daily learning at home or newsletters that tell parents what children are working on in school that can be supported by home conversation are also effective. Make a library of toys, activity packets, and children's books accessible to family members, or cooperate with a local library to do so. Create opportunities to teach parents how to deliver learning experiences across all domains in the home.	**Examples** Conduct leadership workshops for family members. Ask specific persons if they would like to participate on advisory groups or committees. Refrain from "taking over" such activities or ignoring the decisions that are rightfully the families'. Support family members when they become involved in advocacy groups or represent citizens or families in independent organizations.

Source: Adapted from Five Types of Parent Involvement: Linking Practices and Outcomes. In J. L. Epstein, *School and Family Partnerships: Preparing Educators and Improving Schools.* (1998). Boulder, CO: Westview Press.

CHILDREN BENEFIT FROM FAMILY INVOLVEMENT

It is not possible to "grow" people unless you nurture their roots.
—Martin Luther King, Jr. (King & King, 1984)

Most of what each child learns has its roots in the home. There, children first develop emotions and values, and there they learn to walk, talk, and make sense of their everyday surroundings. Parents teach not only directly but also indirectly by approving or disapproving and supporting or negating what children learn elsewhere. Therefore, including family members in early childhood programs provides continuity between home and school and enhances children's learning in both environments. It also provides an opportunity for better cultural understanding among both teachers and family members (S. Kagan, 2000). For instance, family participation has been linked to greater awareness and responsiveness, more-complex child language skills, better problem-solving abilities, increased academic performance, and significant gains in cognitive and physical skill development in children (Larsen & Haupt, 1997). For older children, family participation has also been linked to improved attendance and better attitudes toward school, better homework habits, and better overall achievement (Feuerstein, 2000).

Although mothers have traditionally been the focus of parental involvement, recent research indicates that fathers have a unique role to play regardless of whether they live with their children (Viadero, 1997). Children whose fathers are involved in the programs that their children attend generally have enhanced achievement above and beyond that of children whose mothers are the only engaged parent.

FAMILY MEMBERS BENEFIT FROM FAMILY INVOLVEMENT

The two women met by chance at the grocery store—one a former "co-op" mom; the other, the cooperative nursery school teacher. "You'd never recognize Damon. He's 5 foot 6 and still growing," gushed the mom. Parent and teacher talked for several minutes about Damon's current accomplishments at the middle school. The teacher was pleased. She remembered a time when this mother found her son's challenging behavior almost too much to bear. As they were about to part, the mother caught the teacher by the hand and whispered, "I never thanked you, you know. You were a lifesaver. You really helped me to appreciate my son. I've never forgotten it."

Although every family is not affected as dramatically as this mother was, the results of parents' involvement in their children's education are often very encouraging. Parents who become involved in their children's education gain greater understanding of their children's development and needs, exhibit more acceptance of children's individual differences, find more enjoyment in their children, and develop more-flexible child-rearing attitudes (Brewer, 2001). Parents have also reported increased feelings of competence and self-worth as a result of involvement (R. Powell, 1989). In addition, involved parents are more likely to understand what the child is being taught and to believe that they should help at home and encourage and support the child's learning at school (Eldridge, 2001).

PROGRAM BENEFITS FROM FAMILY INVOLVEMENT

The Community Calendar
Local Items of Interest:

This week the children and teachers in Mrs. Waters' room will be conducting child-led family conferences. The purpose of these conferences is for children, families, and teachers to work together to review each child's progress and to plan future goals.

Families and staff at the Glencairn Elementary School planned, raised funds, and helped build a new playground for the children during the past year. Called the "Field of Dreams," this playground is a real dream come true.

Family and community members provided 1,600 volunteer hours for the Reading First program at Allen Street School.

Clearly, children and families benefit when families are closely involved in the life of the center or school. The same is true for early childhood programs overall. For instance, active participation by family members has been found to provide them with more accurate and timely information regarding program aims and strategies. Closer contact between home and school gives both family members and teachers a more complete picture of children's abilities and improves their consistency in working toward desired goals. In turn, this seems to promote family identification with the program and heightens family members' satisfaction with and appreciation of teachers' efforts (Eldridge, 2001; Revicki, 1982). In addition, as family members become more influential in program decision making and increasingly active in program activities, they are more likely to communicate to children the importance of the programs in which they are both involved (U.S. Department of Education, 1986).

Involved family members also serve as additional human resources to early childhood programs, extending the reach of the program, allowing children to receive more individual attention, and making additional knowledge and skills available to teachers and administrators (Berger, 1999). Finally, we know that highly involved parents and grandparents are more likely to support program policies, offer financial assistance, and rally community efforts to promote or maintain the early childhood programs with which they are affiliated.

BARRIERS TO FAMILY INVOLVEMENT

With all the benefits that result from family involvement, you might expect that both teachers and families would be eager to engage in the process. Yet, frequently families and professionals have certain misperceptions about each other that hinder the development of effective home–school relations. For instance, the two groups sometimes believe that they are working at cross-purposes (see Table 8.2; Gonzalez-Mena & Widmeyer Eyer, 2001).

With so many demands on their attention and so many hopes wrapped up in the children, families and professionals often find understanding each other's viewpoint difficult. They may interpret different ways of doing things as wrong or as subtle criticisms of their approaches or as deliberate attempts to undermine their goals. None of these perceptions foster feelings of trust and cooperation.

Another dilemma occurs when family members and teachers both feel unwelcome (the family member in the program and the teacher in the home) or ill suited to function in a collegial capacity (the parent as teacher and the teacher as peer). The teacher may be viewed as less helpful and less interested in the family than he or

Family members need to feel welcome in the program so that they will become involved in their child's learning.

she actually is, and teachers are likely to underestimate family members' strong desire to be included in their children's education (Weinstein & Mignano, 2003). For example, researchers report that of the 21,000 teachers they were in contact with, 90 percent considered the level of parental involvement in their classrooms inadequate (Carnegie Foundation for the Advancement of Teaching, 1988). Yet, fewer than half the teachers responding to a subsequent survey gave family involvement a high priority in their classrooms. They believed that such efforts would prove fruitless (Brandt & Epstein, 1989). Convinced that today's parents (especially those from low-income, single-parent, and dual-career families) would be unwilling or unable to participate in program-related activities, many teachers chose not to involve them. However, many parents (as many as

TABLE 8.2 Mutual Misperceptions of Teachers and Families

Teachers Wonder Why Family Members	Families Wonder Why Teachers
Tend to linger after saying good-bye to their child. (Don't families know this makes the separation process more difficult?)	Are in such a rush to get them out of the room. (Don't teachers know this makes the separation process more difficult?)
Push for academics too soon. (Don't families know how children learn?)	Do not make the program more like "real" school. (Don't teachers know I want my child to learn?)
Get upset when their child gets dirty. (Can't families see this is a sign of learning?)	Do not keep their children cleaner. (Can't teachers see this is a sign of learning?)
Do not do a better job teaching children to behave. (They can't control him at home but want us to control him in the program.)	Do not do a better job teaching children to behave. (They can't control him in the program but want us to control him at home.)
Always criticize them. (Can't families see we're doing our best?)	Always criticize them. (Can't teachers see we're doing our best?)

90 percent) reported caring a great deal about their children's performance in school and being interested in learning effective ways to support children's learning on the home front (Epstein, 1986). Approximately 20 percent of the parents surveyed were already successfully involved. Another 70 percent wanted to become more active in their child's schooling but did not know how to do so (Brandt & Epstein, 1989). In particular, inner-city parents, single parents who worked outside the home, immigrant parents, and parents of children beyond the preschool years reported the fewest opportunities for contact with teachers and other program personnel (Berger, 1999).

With this huge discrepancy between family members' stated desires and the degree to which they actually participate, an examination of why such differences occur is appropriate. Family participation poses challenges from both the parents' viewpoint and that of educators. Families usually do not know what is meant by *family involvement* or why it is important. Some family members believe that because they lack professional teaching skills, they are unsuitable partners in the educational process. Others hold back because they are unsure of what to do—how to offer support at home or what strategies to use. Still others feel rebuffed because, at their child's school or center, family involvement is confined to menial tasks, is limited to fundraising, or is so ill timed (last-minute, inconvenient hours) or so poorly conceived (disorganized, irrelevant, and uninteresting) that only a few family members have the means or desire to come forward. In other cases, family members answer requests for volunteering but receive no follow-up contact or acknowledgment of their interest. Also, often family members are treated as intruders at school. Rebuffed, ignored, or patronized, many family members conclude that they have little to contribute (Greenberg, 1989; Rosenthal & Sawyers, 1996). In addition, the level of parental involvement in the home frequently goes unrecognized by professional staff, even though regular family discussions of children's learning and school experiences are known to be effective in supporting children's achievement.

These obstacles to family involvement are intensified among low-income families, many of whom have had unfavorable school experiences of their own. They may relive those unhappy times when their offspring enter programs outside the home. Unfortunately, family members' initial negative perceptions are often reinforced as teachers and administrators appear to be insensitive to the family's incredible financial and work constraints and operate from the perception of deficits rather than the perception of family strengths. Matters may become worse with time if teachers or administrators get in contact with low-income families only when

their children are having problems. These kinds of encounters contribute to families' feelings of shame, anger, distrust, and hopelessness, all of which detract from their motivation to become involved in the formal educational process.

Some barriers involve practical considerations. For instance, schedule conflicts arise when the involvement activities are at times when parents are unavailable to participate. Poor working families frequently have much less time for involvement than do middle-class families (Bracey, 2001). Likewise, immigrant families and others whose primary language is not English often encounter communication challenges, as do English-speaking families when teachers use jargon (Eldridge, 2001). In addition, families raised in other cultures do not always know that they might be receiving teachers' messages in their children's book bags and do not look for them because the practice is atypical for their cultural group.

Besides these practical considerations, educators at schools and centers are sometimes resistant to full parental inclusion. Parental involvement requires a lot of the teacher's time, and teachers are already busy. Teachers and administrators are educated in the professional practice of teaching children but often do not know how to effectively design a parental involvement program. In addition, a "culture of blame" may pervade some programs so that the barrier of lack of trust between families, and administrators and teachers may occur. Another problem is that a level of risk is involved as parents participate in policy decisions and become better consumers of educational services, which increases administrators' wariness (Pena, 2000). Fathers who indicate that they desire involvement in their children's schooling and believe that they have a responsibility to be involved also report that they are obstructed in their efforts to participate (Baker & McMurray, 1998).

Both a readjustment of the attitudes of educators and family members and more-concerted efforts to emphasize the partnership aspects of family involvement are needed if these obstacles to family involvement are to be overcome. Evidence currently indicates that the early years are the optimal period in which to address such problems (Briggs et al., 1997).

CHARACTERISTICS OF EFFECTIVE FAMILY INVOLVEMENT

As educators have become increasingly aware of the benefits of family involvement and the obstacles that sometimes hinder its development, their attention has shifted from answering the query "Why?" to exploring the question "How?" Consequently, much of the research since 1990 has focused on discovering the variables that characterize effective family involvement efforts. From these studies, four key elements have been identified: collaboration, variety, intensity, and individuation. A brief overview of each follows.

Collaboration

> Parents and teachers are more similar than different—they have many goals in common and a need to share information. *(Brewer, 2001, p. 204)*

Collaborative relations between early childhood personnel and families yield fruitful results for adults as well as for children. Such relations are most apt to develop when families and teachers recognize each other's importance in the child's life. Because neither school nor family has the resources to take on the entire job of educating the young, it is not in the best interests of either to attempt to duplicate each other's efforts. Rather, children's education is enhanced when home and school see themselves as distinct entities, performing complementary, interconnected functions (Griffore & Bubolz, 1986). One interpretation of how family members and teachers might function in a mutually supportive relationship is offered in Table 8.3.

Collaboration is enhanced when open channels of communication exist between professionals and families and when they both work together to enhance children's learning (Brewer, 2001; Epstein, 1998). Thus, family involvement represents a balance of power between families and teachers—a partnership. In this partnership each member is valued and recognized as a "child expert." Families know their own child better than anyone else does. Teachers know many different children and have specialized knowledge of child development, program content, and educational strategies. When family members and teachers combine their areas of expertise, collaboration becomes a reality.

Variety

Lisa Digby is the room mother for her son's second-grade classroom. She belongs to the PTO and the library committee. Whenever a job needs doing at school, Mrs. Digby can be counted on to help.

Carole Wilson has been to school once, the day she enrolled her daughter for kindergarten. She works an 8-hour shift at a shirt factory and has a part-time job at Red's, a local convenience store. She has little time to spend at school volunteering.

If you were to talk to these mothers, you would find that both are keenly interested in their child's early education, and both want to be included in some way. However, what works for one will not necessarily suit the other.

Family members differ in the extent to which they are willing or able to take part in educational programs and in how they want to be included. Consequently, effective family involvement encompasses a variety of means by which family members can participate and does not

TABLE 8.3 The Home–School Alliance

10 Things Family Members Wish Teachers Would Do	10 Things Teachers Wish Family Members Would Do
Help build children's self-esteem	Provide the resources at home for reading and learning
Get to know each child	Set a good example
Communicate often and openly with families	Encourage children to try to do their best in school
Give family members direction about how to work with children at home	Emphasize academics
Maintain high academic and behavioral standards	Support the program's rules and goals
Welcome and encourage family involvement	Call teachers more often and earlier if there is a problem
Be active in and support family council or PTA activities and projects	Take responsibility as parents
Provide enrichment activities	View drinking alcoholic beverages by underage youth and excessive partying as a serious matter, not a joke
Expect and encourage respect for other children, classroom visitors, and yourself	Be aware of what is going on in the early childhood program and become more involved in program activities
Remember that family members are allies and want to help	

Source: From *PTA Today,* November 1984. Complete article available from the National PTA, 700 N. Rush St., Chicago, IL 60611-2571. © 1988 National PTA School Is What WE Make It! planning kit. Adapted with permission.

require all parents to be involved in the same ways, at the same time, or to the same degree (Epstein, 1998). Variety can be considered in terms of the kinds of contacts that occur between home and program, the format they take, the purpose for which exchanges are made, who initiates them, where they occur, how frequently they occur, the type of parental response necessary for success to be achieved, and the resources required for participation. These variations are outlined in Figure 8.1.

More variety within a single home–program interchange and across the whole array of contacts is better. When a broad mixture of family involvement opportunities is created, educators demonstrate their interest in and acceptance of many kinds of families. Also, families receive visible proof that they may contribute according to their preferences, talents, resources, and degree of comfort with the interface between home and early childhood program (Berger, 1999).

Intensity

The more *we get together, together, together,*
The more *we get together, the happier we'll be.*

This familiar children's song makes an important point that can be applied to family involvement. Parental participation outcomes are more likely to be positive if contacts are more frequent (R. Powell, 1989). Regular, focused contact is necessary to promote the development of trusting relationships between parents and practitioners. Also, when opportunities for involvement are numerous, families can more easily find entrées to programs that better suit their needs and interests. In

FIGURE 8.1 Variable Characteristics of Parental Involvement

Kind of Contact
Predetermined agenda – – – informal structure
Scheduled – – – spontaneous
Face-to-face – – – indirect

Format
Written – – – spoken
Goal directed – – – open ended
Presentation or discussion – – – hands-on experience
Large group – – – small group – – – individual

Purpose
Provide input – – – elicit input – – – collaborate
Build – – – establish – – – maintain – – – change relationships,
  goals, strategies

Initiator
Child – – – family member – – – program personnel

Location
Home – – – program – – – community

Frequency
One-time event – – – several times – – – continuous

Role of Parent
Receiver of information – – – program supporter – – – audience – – –
home tutor – – – classroom participant – – – colearner – – – decision
maker – – – advocate

Resources Required
Time and energy (ranges from little to much) – – – skills (ranges
from few to many, general to specialized)

It is possible to combine variables within each characteristic as well
as to create combinations among them.

addition, family members generally do not feel as though they are a part of their child's education unless educators at the school or center place particular emphasis on involving them (Eldridge, 2001). Frequent, varied contact across time conveys the message that the educators value parents and that parental inclusion is not simply tolerated but welcomed and expected.

Individuation

Every shoe fits not every foot.
—Anonymous

Educational programs are most likely to elicit a positive response from families when opportunities for participation are tailored to meet families' particular needs and perceptions (Epstein, 1998). There is no one formula for family involvement, and no single program can be generalized successfully to every population. Instead, the best outcomes emerge when a match exists between what early childhood programs set out to do and what families want, when congruence exists between the strategies implemented and those to which family members feel receptive, and when program designers take into account family constraints such as child care and transportation needs, employment obligations, and economic or physical stress, such as fatigue from coping. Once this process is under way, the chances for collaboration improve; as collaboration becomes greater, so do opportunities for individuation.

As you might assume, families are more likely to become partners in their children's education when practitioners take into account collaboration, variety, intensity, and individuation. Because these dimensions of family involvement are so important, they provide the backdrop for the rest of this chapter. In the text that follows, you will read about specific strategies for creating partnerships with families around children's early education.

EFFECTIVE FAMILY INVOLVEMENT TECHNIQUES

All the strategies suggested in this section may be used in individual classrooms or generalized to whole programs. We have listed about 50 ideas to give you a wide array of options to consider. However, note that no single educator would institute every strategy. A more likely approach would be to adapt one or two ideas from each of several categories to create a comprehensive family involvement plan. Such plans would be individualized to meet the needs of the children, families, and staff members within your program. Regardless of how simple or elaborate a family involvement plan might be, the goal is always the same—to reach out to families and help them

feel included and an integral part of their child's education (Kendall, 1995). The first step is always the same, too—to establish positive relationships with families.

Establishing Relationships with Families

It's important to me that families know as much as they can about me so that they can feel comfortable leaving their child with me. It's not easy leaving your child with a stranger.
—Texia Thorne, teacher

I think they're terrific. The teachers seem to care not only for my children, but they care about me. When I come in looking tired, they ask me, "How are you doing? What can I do to help you? How are you feeling?"
—Debbie King, Kristine's mom

No matter what your position in an early childhood program—practitioner-in-training, teacher, or administrator—you can begin to establish positive relationships with the families of the children in your group. The following simple guidelines will help you to forge closer ties with the most significant people in children's lives.

Show that you truly care about each child. An old Danish proverb states, "Who takes the child by the hand takes the mother by the heart." Keep this message constantly in mind and recognize that, first and foremost, families want early childhood professionals to pay attention to their children and treat them as special (Reisman, 1996). To show families that you care, treat each child as an important, valued human being by your words and deeds each day. Recognize, also, that a loving education includes ensuring that children go outdoors with all the clothing their family sent that day, that children's noses get wiped, that children's tear-stained faces get washed, and that notes from home are read and answered. Oversights of these "details" speak volumes to families and may give the unintended impression that you are too busy or uninterested.

Make personal contact with families. No substitute exists for face-to-face communication between people. If you are fortunate enough to work in an early childhood program in which families come into the building to drop off or retrieve their children, take advantage of these times to greet family members, inquire about their day, and have a friendly word. This means making yourself available at these times rather than rushing around making last-minute preparations or focusing solely on getting the children into their coats to go home. If you do not see families regularly, take advantage of the times when you do see them. Mingle with family members at program events rather than chatting with your colleagues. Greet family members and see that they have activities to do or people with whom to talk.

Treat parents and other significant family members as individuals. Communicate with them on a one-to-one basis, not only in groups. Use an adult interpreter with families whose primary language is not English. Periodically, provide time for family members to talk with you privately. Interact with them as interesting adults, not simply as Felicia's mom or Pedro's dad.

Show genuine interest in family members by listening carefully and responding. A real barrier to family involvement occurs when family members form the impression that early childhood personnel are too busy or too distant to give much thought to what family members are thinking or feeling. Dispel this notion by doing the following:

❏ *Provide openings for family members to share their concerns or inquire about their child's program experience.* "What changes have you seen in Jack recently?" "What are Anne's favorite play activities at home?" "Do you have anything you're wondering about regarding Suman's development?"

❏ *Listen attentively when family members talk to you.* Maintain appropriate eye contact and provide other nonverbal cues such as nodding or matching the person's mood with congruent affect to show that you are grasping his or her message. (For instance, if a family member is telling you something humorous, respond with smiles. If the tenor is serious, respond in kind.)

❏ *Ask questions relevant to family comments. Invite family members to elaborate on what they are saying.* Reply "Tell me more about that" or "Then what happened?" Such comments help family members to feel heard and valued.

❏ *Remain silent long enough for family members to gather their thoughts.* Once you ask a question or make a remark in response to something a family member has said, pause. Avoid rushing on with additional talk simply because you are unsure of what to do next.

❏ *Respond to family members' queries honestly and directly.* If you do not know the answer to something, say so. Promise to find out. Then do it.

Be courteous to family members. Treat family members with consideration and respect. Pay attention to nonverbal behaviors (e.g., facial expressions, posture, and gestures) and words. Implement the following strategies daily:

❏ *Greet family members when you see them.* Address them by their proper names, using Mr., Ms., Mrs., or Dr. Pronounce family names correctly. Use the correct surname for each adult. Adult surnames may differ from the child's surname.

❏ *Avoid using professional jargon unnecessarily.* Using terminology that people do not understand implies an unequal relationship and sometimes makes families feel unwelcome or uncomfortable talking with you. Use familiar words to explain what you mean (e.g., talk about "children working together" instead of "cooperative learning"; "pretend play" instead of "imitation and symbolic play"; "acknowledging the child's point of view" instead of "reflective listening"; and so on).

❏ *Avoid addressing notices and newsletters to be sent home with the words "Dear Parents."* Doing so implies that all children in the program are living in two-parent families. A more inclusive salutation would be "Dear Family Members."

❏ *Arrange to have relevant program materials translated in the home languages of the families in your classroom.* Provide a translator (perhaps a family member from another family) to facilitate conversations between you and new families whose home language you do not speak. Learn a few words in each family's home language. If family members feel embarrassed about their English skills, one strategy that is sometimes helpful is to share how frustrated you "feel at not being able to communicate in the parents' language. This helps to break down any tinge of superior/inferior perceptions from the relationship, and keeps both of you on the same level as human beings" (Lee, 1997, p. 58).

Honor family confidentiality. Mrs. LaRosa's husband left her this morning. Shannon O'Malley is thinking about going back to school. Vincent Kaminski has been diagnosed with a serious illness. Family members trust you to keep private information to yourself. Remember that personal information should never be shared with anyone not directly involved in the problem, including coworkers, members of other families, and outside friends. Not only is violating this trust unethical, but doing so could ruin your relationship with the family and that family member's relationship with educators in the program forever.

Focus on family strengths. Early childhood professionals enhance the possibilities for relationship building when they look for family strengths rather than focusing solely on what appear to be family faults (Rosenthal & Sawyers, 1996). You can achieve this in several ways:

❏ *Concentrate on what family members can do, not only on what they have difficulty accomplishing.* Identify at least one strength for each family in your class. Find ways to build on these strengths during the year.

❏ *Catch yourself using judgmental labels in reference to families.* When this happens, try to think of the families in alternative ways. For instance, initially you might think, "Sarah comes from a 'broken' home." Shift to a more positive perspective: "Sarah comes from a family in which her grandmother is tremendously supportive." You need not totally ignore family problems or concerns, but you should avoid labeling families and thinking of them in a deficit mode.

❏ *Listen respectfully when children share information about their family with you.* Be careful to avoid making judgmental comments such as "How awful" or "I wouldn't boast about that." Instead, reflect children's feelings about what they have shared (e.g., "You sound excited" or "That worried you").

❏ *Make sure classroom materials reflect the cultural groups and family compositions of the families in your group.* Taking this approach provides a visible sign that you value each child's family.

❏ *Try to look at situations from the family's viewpoint.* For instance, a parent who is having difficulty separating from his or her child at nursery school is not simply being uncooperative. Rather, the parent may be feeling guilty about leaving the child or worried that the child is not getting the attention he or she would receive at home. Likewise, a parent who fails to respond to a telephone call from the educator may be overwhelmed by work demands, not simply uninterested in his or her child. Trying to see things from each family member's perspective will help you to appreciate family circumstances and find alternative, more-effective means of communicating.

❏ *Provide positive feedback to families about their children's progress and their child-rearing successes.* Offer family members information illustrating children's increasing abilities. For instance, knowing that Ruby's mother was concerned about Ruby's skills in relating to other children, the teacher sent home a note saying the following: "Today, Ruby offered her turn at the computer to a child who was eager to get involved before time ran out. She did this all on her own. I thought you'd enjoy hearing about her growing awareness of the needs of others." Comments or brief notes about issues that you and the family are working on together go a long way toward helping families feel like partners in the educational process.

Share control with families. If family members are to become truly involved, we must be willing to include

them as partners in the educational process (Hohmann & Weikart, 1995). You can communicate this desire to families in several ways:

❏ *Take your cues from family members.* If they indicate a desire to communicate in certain ways, follow through. If the message seems to be, "I'm not ready," avoid pushing too hard. Wait a while and then try again. Interact with families in ways that seem to feel most comfortable to them. Some family members will appreciate a telephone call, others would prefer that you communicate in writing, and still others would like an in-person conference. Try to accommodate these preferences as best you can.

❏ *Learn from family members.* Watch how a mother interacts with her child: What words does she use, and what nonverbal behaviors do you see that seem to be effective? Imitate these in your behavior with the child. Ask family members about their children. How do they help the child make transitions at home? What are the child's special interests? This kind of information could be a tremendous help in facilitating your communication with each child and indicates to families that you value their knowledge and skills.

❏ *Collaborate with family members on decisions regarding their child's educational experience.* Be honest and clear about the child's achievement and behavior. Deciding together on certain goals for children and strategies for achieving these goals is an important component of shared control, as is including family members in finding solutions to problems. Avoid announcing what you plan to do to address certain issues in the classroom. Instead, if you see a problem developing in which help from home would be useful (e.g., Samantha is having difficulty separating from her mother; Doug is not paying attention to directions in class; Marcel is getting into fights with children on the playground), initiate a dialogue with the appropriate family members and invite them to work with you to find a solution (Gonzalez-Mena & Widmeyer Eyer, 2001). When you engage in these practices, shared control clearly translates into shared decision making.

Make frequent attempts to include families in children's early education. Begin by planning several simple contacts throughout the year rather than depending on one elaborate event. Offer some one-time involvement opportunities (such as an orientation or a hands-on workshop) as well as a few that encourage sustained participation (such as issuing a weekly newsletter, inviting family members to volunteer in the classroom each month, or asking for periodic help with materials at home).

Offer many ways for families to become involved in their children's education. Remember to diversify the kinds of contacts you make, the format they take, their purpose, and their location. Invite specific family members to participate in specific activities such as sharing their hobby or work. Also, vary the role that family members assume as well as the time, energy, and physical resources required. Make sure to create involvement opportunities related to all five types of family involvement (see Table 8.1).

Tailor the involvement strategies you select to meet the needs of the families with whom you are working now. Avoid relying on the same approaches every year without considering how family needs might differ. For instance, last year a Saturday morning pancake breakfast was just the event to stimulate family interest and enjoyment of the program. However, this year the children have been creating a classroom museum. A visit by family members to take a tour of the project might be a better match between the children's interests and their desire to include their families in their investigations. In addition to avoiding habitual approaches, be cautious of commercially prepared parental involvement programs. These programs do not always match the interests and requirements of a particular group of families. If your school or center has adopted such a program, review it carefully. Carry out only the segments that are suitable for your group.

Gathering Information from Families

Vivian Paley, a former kindergarten teacher and noted author, told the story of a father who came to school to share with the children memories of his childhood. Inviting family members to tell family stories was one way she found to gather family information that was comfortable for adults and valuable for children:

"I was born in a small village near Calcutta in India," Vijay's father tells the class. "We had a sliver of a stream that ran along between our village and the forest. From the moment our summer holidays began, all the children played in the stream. We built dams out of stones to make the water tumble faster and we sailed pieces of wood, pretending they were ships on the ocean. One day my cousin Kishore screamed that he saw a bear in the woods and we all ran home. Then he said it was a joke and we were all angry with him. However, we didn't want to waste time being angry because soon it would be time to return to school. And, so, every day, if our mothers wanted to find us, they knew we would be playing in the stream."

We stare at Mr. Shah as we had never seen him before. Then we look at Vijay, our shy Vijay, and he is grinning. "There!" his smile seems to be saying. "Now you see how much there is to know about me." *(Paley, 1995, p. 46)*

Information may be gathered from families informally (e.g., chatting with families at drop-off time and pick-up time or making conversation at program events) as well as in more formal ways. A few basic strategies are outlined next.

Use enrollment or intake information as a way to learn more about the families of the children in your classroom. When families first enroll their children in an early childhood program, they are often asked to supply information about their child in writing on an enrollment form or orally through an initial intake interview. Typical questions that families are asked are presented in Figure 8.2.

Throughout the program year, invite family members to share anecdotes and information about their child. This information might be used as the basis for classroom activities and to increase your knowledge of the child and his or her family. Word such requests as invitations to share information, not as commands to meet your expectations. Figure 8.3 offers an example.

Ask for input from family members about their learning goals for their children. Talk with parents and grandparents about the children's activities at home as well as the skills or behaviors that they would like to see further developed. Give them a short list of program-related goals for children. Ask them to indicate which of these goals they deem most important for their child. Collect the information and use it in designing classroom activities. Refer to family members' lists periodically, and use them as the basis for some of your communications with families throughout the year.

Find out about family interests and discover ways in which family members might like to become involved in the early childhood program. Recently, a mother asked if she could visit her child's kindergarten class for the morning. The teacher, very pleased, said yes and assigned the parent to the art table. Several weeks later, by happenstance, the teacher learned that the mother was an accomplished cabinetmaker. Although the mother had enjoyed the art area, the teacher regretted missing an opportunity to have this mother help the children with some real woodworking skills. This oversight was not a major problem; however, it points out the importance of knowing each family member's talents and interests and making plans with these interests in mind. One way to discover such interests is to use a family interest survey such as that shown in Figure 8.4.

Seek out cultural information. Read about the cultural heritage of the families you serve and then check with them to see if what you learned through reading accurately reflects their practices and beliefs (Mangione, Lally, & Signer, 1993). A very honest, open approach would be to ask parents if what you read was true and if their family held a particular belief. Ask

FIGURE 8.2 Family Information of Interest to Educators

Family Structure

❏ How many children are in your family?
❏ Who lives in your household?
❏ Who else takes care of your child during the day or on weekends?
❏ How are decisions made in your family?

Child Rearing

❏ What words does your child use for urination? Bowel movement? Private body parts?
❏ Describe your child's eating schedule.
❏ What foods does your child like or dislike? Are there any foods to which your child is allergic?
❏ Describe your child's sleeping schedule.
❏ How do you put your child to sleep?
❏ How does your child react when he or she is angry or unhappy? Excited or confused?
❏ How does your child relax or comfort himself or herself?
❏ What are your child's favorite activities?
❏ How do you handle the following situations?

   Toilet training
   Sharing
   Messy play (paints, sand, water)
   Sex roles
   Racial concerns

❏ Who does your child play with at home?
❏ What rules do you have for your child at home?
❏ What do you do to teach your child to behave?
❏ What are your child's responsibilities at home?
❏ Are there other things you think we should know about your child?

Family Culture

❏ What is your ethnic or cultural background?
❏ What languages are spoken in your home?
❏ What traditions, objects, or foods symbolize your family?

Source: Adapted from *Parents as Partners in Education,* by E. H. Berger. (1999). Upper Saddle River, NJ: Merrill/Prentice Hall; *The Anti-Bias Curriculum: Tools for Empowering Young Children,* by L. Derman-Sparks and the ABC Task Force. (1989). Washington, DC: National Association for the Education of Young Children; *Roots and Wings: Affirming Culture in Early Childhood Settings,* by S. York. (1991). St. Paul, MN: Toys 'n Things Press; and Michigan State University Child Development Laboratories enrollment forms.

more and assume less (File, 2001). If you are genuinely attempting to understand the culture and to bridge the inevitable gaps, family members are usually pleased to help and support your efforts.

Ask for evaluative feedback from families throughout the year. Let families know that their opinions count by providing numerous opportunities for them to provide feedback about their child's experiences in the early childhood program as well as their own. Suggestion boxes near the program entrance, short questionnaires sent home that can be returned anonymously in a postage-paid envelope, written or oral evaluations administered at the end of workshops or other school events, and telephone surveys conducted by staff or parents are some methods that prompt family input. Another effective strategy is to hold family–teacher forums once or twice a year at school. These regularly scheduled, informal gatherings give family members and teachers a

FIGURE 8.3   Example of a Request for Information About a Child

Dear Families:
Soon we will begin a unit on how people are born and grow. We need some pictures and information about your child as a baby. Please fill out this form and use this plastic bag to send in one or two baby pictures of your child or your child's "baby book" if you have one. We will be sure to keep things clean and safe and will return them by the end of next week.

Our Child as an Infant
Our child, _____, was _____ inches long at birth and weighed _____ pounds. Our child liked to eat _____ when he/she was a baby. He/she didn't like _____. His/her first word was _____. His/her hair was _____. (Please share any information that would tell us about the child as a baby such as habits, sleeping patterns, favorite toys, etc.)

Source: Adapted from *Teaching Young Children Using Themes,* by M. J. Kostelnik (Ed.). (1991). Glenview, IL: Good Year Books.

chance to evaluate the program together. Loosely structured around a broad topic, such as children's personal safety issues or promoting children's problem-solving skills, they provide for mutual exploration of educational ideas and strategies. Moreover, family members may ask questions and make suggestions for changes or additions to early childhood programs in an atmosphere in which such communication is clearly welcome.

As a follow-up to these evaluation efforts, let family members know that you intend to act on some of their

FIGURE 8.4   Family Interest Survey

FAMILY INTEREST SURVEY

Your Name _____

Child's Name _____

We are delighted that you and your child are enrolled at Central School this year. We look forward to working with you. As you know, we encourage family members to be involved in our program as much as possible. To give us an idea of ways you would like to become a partner in the educational process, please check your areas of interest below. Thank you. We look forward to partnering with you.

Potential Family Interests
_____ Working with my child at home
_____ Sending in materials from home
_____ Translating materials for families in the program
_____ Reviewing materials for the program
_____ Building or making materials for the program
_____ Helping with the family toy-lending library
_____ Helping to find potential field trip sites or community visitors
_____ Helping with community trips
_____ Working with the teaching team to develop ideas for the classroom
_____ Planning special events in the community
_____ Planning special events at the center
_____ Attending events for parents
_____ Serving as a family "mentor"
_____ Attending a family-to-family support group
_____ Serving on the parent advisory council

Provide family members with the information that they need to become partners in the educational process.

suggestions. Later, inform them (through a program newsletter or at a group meeting) of changes that have resulted from family input.

Keeping Families Informed

Is my child happy? Is my child learning?

How are you addressing reading in the classroom?

I don't understand my child's new report card. Where are the letter grades we used to get in school?

The preceding questions are typical of those that family members have about early childhood education in general and their child's current setting in particular. Anticipating such questions and communicating relevant information to families is an important part of being an early childhood professional. How you respond to unanticipated queries or demands for information will also be important.

Develop written materials for your classroom in which you make clear your desire to include families in their children's early education. Identify benefits to children, families, and the program as a whole when families become involved in the program in some way. Provide specific guidelines for the form that family involvement could take and how home–school contacts might evolve. For example, let families know they are welcome to visit the classroom or that jobs will be available that they can do at home if they choose. Send these materials home to families and review them during a home visit or a program orientation at the school or center.

Acquaint family members with your educational philosophy, the content of the curriculum, program goals, and the expectations you have for children in your classroom. Integrate this content into a beginning-of-the-year family orientation as well as into any written materials (e.g., handbook, program brochure, written bulletins, or videotape of program activities) sent home describing the curriculum. Discuss child development and program goals for children, offering examples of related classroom activities that family members might see or hear about. Use hands-on activities to help family members better understand the materials in the classroom and their relationship to children's learning.

Familiarize families with a typical day for children in the program. Family members feel more comfortable with the program if they can envision how their child spends his or her time there. At the least, families should receive a copy of your daily schedule that outlines the timing of classroom events and explains the general purpose of each segment. Some teachers also utilize a slide or video presentation, held early in the year, that illustrates how children in their class move through the day. Motivated to attend by seeing pictures of their child, parents leave having learned more about the early childhood program and its philosophy. A similar outcome occurs when educators put on a "miniday," in the evening or on the weekend, during which parents proceed through an abbreviated but total schedule in their child's company. Children are proud to lead their mom, dad, or grandparent through the routine, and family members gain insights into their child's classroom participation.

Periodically write one- or two-line notes regarding children's positive program experiences. Send these "happy notes" home with the child to demonstrate your interest in both the child and the parent (Berger, 1999). A child's first journey to the top of the climber, an enthusiastic creative writing experience, or the child's pride in knowing many new facts about insects is a good occasion for a short handwritten note from you. If you write one note every other day, the families in a class of 30 children could receive three or four such contacts in a year. Once or twice, include an instant snapshot of the child happily engaged in a classroom activity as a keepsake for families.

Create a weekly or monthly newsletter to inform families about the program and the children's experiences away from home. This simple form of communication can familiarize families with what is happening in the classroom, provide family members with ideas for subjects to talk about with their youngsters at home, and stimulate family members to engage in home-based learning with their children.

Preschool-level teachers usually write the newsletters themselves. Newsletters designed for the early elementary grades may include contributions from the children (Berger, 1999). In either case, make newsletters short and visually interesting by using subheadings and graphics. Avoid overcrowding. Divide the content into sections in which items are highlighted, by outlining, indenting, using boldface, capitalizing, or changing typeface.

The newsletter content may include one or more of the following items:

- A review of the children's experiences at the center or school since the last newsletter
- A description of activities children will take part in throughout the next several days or weeks
- Specific, practical examples of how family members could address or reinforce children's learning at home
- A brief discussion of the theme (if you engage in theme teaching) and the facets of it children will be exploring
- Relevant classroom, family, or community news
- Invitations to family members to participate in the classroom, donate materials, or suggest upcoming classroom events

Stay in touch with family members who seem unresponsive. Avoid stereotyping family members as uncaring or impossible to work with. Remain pleasant when you see them. Periodically send notes home to let families know about their children's positive participation in program-based activities. Continue to offer simple,

easy-to-do suggestions for home-based participation. Keep the input from the program as positive as possible, and make few demands. You might not see immediate results; however, as a representative of the educational program, you could be making a favorable impression on the unresponsive family member. In turn, your groundwork could serve as the foundation for his or her greater participation later in the child's education.

Establishing Two-Way Communication Between Families and the Program

Everyone wants to feel that he or she has something to offer. The most depressing feeling in the world is the feeling of having nothing to offer—nothing that's acceptable.
—Fred Rogers (1997)

Both teachers and families have valuable contributions to offer each other: insights, information, ideas, and support. The back-and-forth flow of communication helps both of them develop a more complete picture of the child and their role in that child's early education. Thus, the concept of two-way communication between persons at home and those in the formal group setting is a critical element of developmentally appropriate practice. Following are some ways to begin establishing reciprocal relations with families.

Vary the communication strategies you use rather than relying on a single method. Be sure to exchange information with families regarding the program in general and their children in particular. Both kinds of communication are necessary if family members and practitioners are to know and understand each other (Brewer, 2001). Table 8.4 provides a summary of communication strategies by type (general vs. specific).

Take advantage of arrival and departure routines as a time to establish two-way communication with families. As one child care provider stated,

> It's great to have family conferences, but those happen only once in a while. Most of my communicating with parents goes on in the five minutes I see them at 8:00 A.M. or the 5 minutes at 5:30 P.M. That's when I develop rapport with them, get in tidbits about child development in, and try to problem-solve because parents are always in a hurry. Yet those five minutes add up. Before you know it we've been having weeks of mini-contacts, day after day, and we have come to know a lot about one another and about the child as well. (Sciarra & Dorsey, 1998, p. 355)

Establish telephone hours during which you and family members may call each other or the time and day that you usually answer e-mail. Set aside 1 or 2 hours each week for this purpose, varying and dividing the time between 2 or more days. In a note sent home to

TABLE 8.4 Home–Program Communication

Ways to Convey General Program Information	Ways to Convey Specific Information About Individual Children
A program handbook	Enrollment forms
A videotape of program activities	Telephone calls
Orientation meetings	Home visits
Home visits	Greeting and pickup routines
Newsletters	"Happy notes"
Bulletin boards	Photos of children engaged in activities
Program visits and program observation by family members	Family–teacher notebooks kept for individual children
Educational programs for families	Regular and special conferences
Social events for families	
Articles sent home to families	
Family–teacher forums	

families, notify them of your availability as well as the telephone number where you can be reached (at home or at the program). Also ask family members to indicate which time might be the most convenient for a call from you. Obtain the telephone numbers of relatives or other persons because immediate families may move abruptly.

Early in the year, establish a positive basis for communication by calling each family to briefly introduce yourself and share a short, happy anecdote about the child. This practice does much to dispel some family members' dread that a call from a teacher always means trouble. It also enables parents to get in contact with you more easily as needs arise. Make it a goal to touch base in this way with each child's family two or three times a year.

Create a notebook for an individual child through which family members and staff communicate as it is sent back and forth between the child's home and the program. This notebook can serve as an alternative to the "happy notes" described previously. Write brief anecdotes to the parent regarding the child's school experience. Encourage family members to write about home events (e.g., visitors, changes in routine, illness, disruptions, accomplishments, and interests) that might influence the child's performance in the program. A line or two conveyed once or twice a week between the home and school settings can do much to expand family members' and the teacher's knowledge about the child and each other. This strategy is particularly effective when children participate in multiple educational settings outside the home, such as after-school child care or a special education program. Passing the notebook among all these settings increases communication and the likeli-

hood that the child will receive a coordinated program. Sample entries are provided in Figure 8.5 for Sarah, a 5-year-old child with cerebral palsy who attends a special education class in the morning and an after-school child care program in the afternoon.

Carry out home visits as a way to get to know children and family members in surroundings familiar to them. Although time consuming, such contacts are a powerful means of demonstrating interest in the child and his or her family as well as your willingness to move out of the formal educational setting into a setting in which parents are in charge (Weinstein & Mignano, 2003). Visiting children at home also enables you to meet other family members or persons living there and to observe the child in this context.

Home visits benefit family members by giving them a chance to talk to the teacher privately and exclusively. Parents or other important adults in the child's life may feel more comfortable voicing certain concerns in the confines of their home than they would at school. When these visits are conducted early in the child's participation in the program, children have the advantage of meeting their teacher in the setting in which they are most confident. When they arrive at the center or school, the teacher is already familiar to them.

Despite all these potentially favorable outcomes, some family members are uneasy with home visits. They may be ashamed of where they live, fear that their child will misbehave, or suspect that the teacher is merely prying into their private affairs. To avoid aggravating such negative perceptions, give families the option of holding the visit at another place (e.g., coffee

FIGURE 8.5 Example of Family–Teacher Communication Through Notebook Entries

---

Jan. 6, 2003

Sarah had a wonderful Christmas vacation. We spent the last week in Miami—temps 80–84 degrees, sunny, swimming every day. She is *not* eager to be back, I'm afraid. We tried to tell her that kids who live in Florida have to go to school and don't get to swim all day and go out every night to dinner with Grandma & Grandpa. She's not convinced.

Mrs. G. (Mom)

1-6-03

Hi. Welcome back. Sarah is "stacking" in her wheelchair—is there a change in seating? Just curious. She ate a good lunch.

Leslie (special ed. teacher)

1-6-03

I hate to be out of it—please define *stacking*. Sarah spent today at a tea party with Michelle and Kelly and Lara. They discussed vacations, served "milkshakes" and muffins. Ryan asked Sarah several times to come and see his block structure. She finally agreed.

Dana (child care teacher)

1-7-03

Dana, "stacking" is a postural problem where the head is tilted back and her shoulders are flopped forward. Sarah will sit up if we say "Can you pick your shoulders up better?" or anything similar, and she's very proud that she's able to do so.

Leslie

1-14-03

Sarah is bringing dinosaur stickers for sharing—the other kids can have one to take home.

Mrs. G.

1-14-03

Stickers were a hit! Sarah would also like to share with her Adams School friends. Sarah enjoyed reaching for and grasping scarves in the gym. She chose pink ones (we didn't have purple). She elected to "supervise" the art area, where Michelle and Kyle asked her for choices for the Boxosaurus decorations.

Dana

---

shop, playground, church, or community center) or postpone your visit until you have established a relationship in other ways and the family is more receptive to your coming (Berger, 1999).

Teachers, too, may have qualms about visiting children's homes. They may feel unsafe in certain neighborhoods or believe that the hours invested will prove too many. In addition, administrators of some programs discourage home visits because of liability concerns or unavailable compensation. Yet, home visit programs are part of many early childhood programs. Once used mostly by educators in preschool programs, home visits are now sometimes scheduled by K–2 teachers during district "record days" or when the upper grades are having conference days. For instance, K–2 teachers at the Mary Harrison Elementary School in Toledo, Oregon, requested that the board of education provide a small remuneration per family for home visits that was equal to that allowed for middle and high school teacher participation in extracurricular activities. Altogether, the K–2 teachers visited 97 percent of the families at home or in other public locations in the evenings and on Saturdays. Teachers and parents were both enthusiastic about the visits and agreed to continue the practice in coming years. Parents felt genuine interest from teachers, and teachers found the insights and relationship enhancement that occurred well worth their time and energy (C. Cummings, personal communication, 1991). Suggestions

FIGURE 8.6 Home Visit Hints

Before getting in contact with families, determine the purpose of your visit. Some teachers choose to focus primarily on meeting and working with the child; others prefer to make the adult family member their major focus. Still others decide to split their attention somewhat evenly between the two.

Create a format for your time in the home that supports your purpose in going there. A sample agenda for the third option cited above might be as follows:

1. Arrive.
2. Greet family member and child.
3. Chat with family member a few moments. Give him or her program forms to fill out and a short description of how children spend the day at the center or school. Usually these are written materials, but some programs offer information on audiocassette for parents who cannot read.
4. Explain that next you would like to get acquainted with the child and that you will have a chance to talk to the family member in about 15 minutes.
5. Play and talk with the child while family member is writing, reading, or listening. Use modeling dough you brought with you as a play material.
6. Give the child markers and paper brought with you and ask him or her to draw a picture that you can take back to school to hang up in the room.
7. While the child draws, talk with family member(s) about concerns, interests, and questions.
8. Close by taking a photograph of the child and family member(s) to put in the child's cubby or in a school album.

Supplies needed:

Map with directions to child's residence
Markers
Paper
Modeling dough
Camera
Film
Audiocassette tape player

In a letter, inform families of your intention to carry out home visits. Explain the purpose of the visit, how long it will last (not more than an hour), and potential home visit dates from which they might choose.

Follow up on the letter with a telephone call a few days later to arrange a mutually convenient time for your visit and to obtain directions.

Carry out each home visit at the appointed time.

Follow the visit with a short note of thanks to the family for allowing you to come, and include a positive comment regarding the time you spent together.

for conducting successful home visits are offered in Figure 8.6.

Structure family conferences to emphasize collaboration between family members and teachers. Consider the following points as you plan each conference (Berger, 1999; Gonzalez-Mena & Widmeyer Eyer, 2001):

❏ Create a cordial written invitation in which family members have options for scheduling times and you express a genuine desire to meet them.

❏ Provide family members with sample questions that they might ask you as well as examples of questions that you might ask them (see Figure 8.7). When providing these, assure parents that they are just samples and do not preclude any other inquiries parents may have.

❏ Confirm each appointment with a brief, personal telephone call to clarify family members' questions or a short note to let them know you are looking forward to meeting with them.

FIGURE 8.7 Potential Family Conference Questions

Sample Teacher Questions

1. How does your child seem to feel about school?
2. Which activities or parts of the day does your child talk about at home?
3. Which children does your child talk about at home?
4. How does your child spend his or her free time?
5. Is there anything that your child dreads?
6. What are your child's interests and favorite activities outside school?

Sample Family Questions

1. How has my child adjusted to school routines?
2. How well does my child get along with other children? Who seems to be his or her best friends?
3. How does my child react to discipline? What methods do you use to promote self-discipline and cooperation?
4. Are there any skills you are working on at school that I/we might support at home?
5. Are there any areas in which my child needs special help?
6. Does my child display any special interests or talents at school that we might support at home?
7. Does my child seem to be self-confident, happy, and secure? If not, what do you think the home or program can do to increase his or her feelings of self-worth?

- Allow enough time for each conference to ensure a genuine exchange of ideas and information.
- Secure a private, comfortable place in which to conduct the conference.
- Greet family members and thank them for coming. Take time to engage in welcoming social rituals such as offering a cup of tea or chatting for a few moments about the weather or inquiring about a member of the extended family before beginning the more factual content of the conference.
- Begin on a positive note by conveying a pleasant anecdote about the child.
- Briefly outline the major areas you hope to cover. Ask family members if they have items they would like to add. Mention that the purpose of this conference is to exchange ideas. Urge family members to ask questions or interject their comments as you go.
- Throughout the conference, refer to the goals the family members signified as most important on the personalized goal sheet they filled out at the beginning of the year. Provide evidence of the child's progress in these areas. Add other goals you may also be focusing on.
- Keep the conference as conversational as possible, eliciting comments from family members as you go.
- Answer family members' questions directly, honestly, and tactfully. Avoid using jargon and judgmental terms to describe the child. Deal in specifics rather than generalities, and base your discussion on objective observations and concrete examples of work.
- End on a positive note.
- Collaborate on future goals and strategies.
- Clarify and summarize the discussion.
- Make plans to continue talking in the future.
- Follow up on any agreed-on strategies such as sending spelling words home.

Collaborate with families to support linguistically diverse children at home and in the program. Ask family members to teach you some words and phrases that could be useful for interacting with the child. Invite family members to the program to tell stories, sing songs in their home language, and share other oral traditions typical of their family. Encourage families to bring music, objects, or foods into the classroom to share and talk about. Ask them to provide storybooks, newspapers, and magazines printed in their home language for use in the classroom. When working with older children, provide ways in which family members can use their primary language to help their children with program-related assignments or activities at home. Create a home library that includes a variety of print materials written in families' home languages for children to borrow. Make the importance of the child's home language clear to the child and therefore to you. Stress that although children will be learning English in the formal group setting, such learning does not require children to abandon or reject the language of the home (Kostelnik, Whiren, Soderman, Stein, & Gregory, 2002).

Make contact with noncustodial parents. Provide opportunities for noncustodial parents to participate in home visits, open houses, and other school activities whenever possible. Mail newsletters to those who live elsewhere.

Work with family members to support the development and learning of children with special needs. All family members have the potential to learn and grow with their children. More than most families, families of children with disabilities are forced to confront similarities and differences and to reexamine their assumptions and values. One crucial aspect of your job is to support such families as they become contributing members of the educational team (Deiner, 1993). To do this, use the techniques you have learned so far as well as the strategies described next:

❑ *Gather and share information regarding all aspects of the child's development and learning.* Children with disabilities are whole beings. They cannot be summed up by a single label such as "hearing impaired" or "language delayed." When you talk to families, avoid focusing on only the child's disability. Talk about the whole child.

❑ *Treat families with respect, not pity.* Families are families first and the family of a child with a disability second (Deiner, 1993). They will have many of the same strengths, needs, concerns, hopes, and dreams expressed by other families in your class. Keep these in mind as you communicate with them.

❑ *Listen empathically as families express their feelings about their child.* Family members have many reactions to their child's disability. Some deny the reality of the situation. Others feel angry, helpless, or depressed. Others are proud of their child and his or her accomplishments. In every case, the best approach is to listen without giving a lot of advice or telling families how to feel. Paraphrase reflections (described in chapter 3) are an excellent tool that shows your interest and effort to understand.

❑ *Expect families to vary in their expectations for their child.* Some families may believe the child has enough problems already. Such families often have low expectations for children's performance in the early childhood program. Other families view a disability as something to be overcome. They may expect their child to excel beyond normal development and learning for any child that age. Many families fall somewhere between those extremes (Kostelnik, Onaga, Rohde, &

Whiren 2002). Respond with sensitivity to these variations. There is no one "right" attitude. Accept families as they are and help them, as you would any other family, to determine reasonable expectations for their children.

❑ *Learn about the child's disability.* You do not need to be an expert on every form of disability, but you do need to know how to obtain relevant information. Ask family members to tell you about their children and how they work with them at home. Read articles and books about various disabling conditions. Locate human resources in your community to support children and families in educational settings if a child has a disability.

❑ *Work cooperatively with other professionals involved in the child's life.* Often children with disabilities take part in a wide array of services involving professionals from varying agencies and backgrounds. You will be one member of this team. You may participate in a formal planning process with other team members and the family. However, many times coordination may become difficult or communication may break down. Make an effort to communicate with the other helping professionals in children's lives. The traveling notebook described in Figure 8.5 was one means of doing so.

Integrating Families into the Program

Hanging at the top of the stairs at the Cesar Chavez School is a large quilt containing more than 100 fabric squares—each one different. Some are colored with fabric crayons, others are stitched or sewn, and still others have been embroidered or quilted. This quilt came about through a cooperative effort of families, staff, and children. Each family and staff member received a plain cloth square on which he or she could sew, cut and paste, or draw a picture or some other symbol that captured his or her feelings about the Cesar Chavez School. Families could work on the squares at home or at workshops in which family members, along with the children, were given materials and guidance about how to create a square of their choosing. Emphasis was placed on participation by many people rather than on achievement of a perfect final product. As a result, even children and adults who believed they lacked arts and crafts talent were enticed into participating in the project. The quilt required several months to complete. Today it hangs as a warm and loving tribute to the community spirit of the Cesar Chavez School. It is also visible proof that families, children, and staff are partners in the educational process.

The quilt at the Cesar Chavez School is a good example of how educators in one early childhood setting integrated families into the ongoing life of the program. Following are additional strategies that you can use.

Institute an open-door policy in which family members are welcome to come to the classroom or program unannounced. Invite family members to watch or participate in some aspect of the children's day. Provide simple guidelines so that family guests will know what to expect from you and the children while they are on site. For instance, make them aware of locations from which they can observe unobtrusively. Clearly indicate the times when you are available to chat and the times when your attention must be focused on the children. Offer suggestions of typical times during the day when parents might drop in for a short while to interact with the children without arranging in advance to do so. Snack time, the story time before recess or nap, and outdoor times are periods of the day when parent visitors might easily be accommodated.

Invite family members to visit the classroom for particular occasions. These times might be incorporated into a whole-group social affair such as a family–child breakfast or a Sunday afternoon open house. Fathers attend family activities more frequently than any other type of program activity (Turbiville, Umbarger, & Guthrie, 2000). Family members might also be invited to share in a certain classroom activity such as making applesauce or planting seeds. Consider asking individual parents to become involved in a specific project (e.g., making bread, supervising the children's creation of a "Boxosaurus," or listening to children read). In every case, let families know they are welcome and that their presence will enrich the program. Issue your invitations far enough in advance for family members to arrange to be there. Follow up each visit by asking family members to fill out a reaction sheet. Provide a simple form on which they can briefly record their impressions, suggestions, and questions. This evaluation lets families know that their opinions are valued.

Encourage family members to participate in the classroom as volunteer teachers for part or all of a day. Issue an invitation in which you describe the volunteer role. Clearly indicate that family members, by virtue of their life experiences, have the skills necessary to do the job. Follow up by speaking to individual family members about how they might become involved. Fathers are more likely to respond to a specific, personal invitation than to a more global invitation (Turbiville et al., 2000). Support your volunteers by using the suggestions outlined in Figure 8.8.

Involve family members in making classroom collections or materials either for their use or for children to use at school. Ask parents or grandparents to donate a song, story, or recipe that is a family favorite. Collect these items from family members individually (in writing or in person), or plan a program event in which such items are shared. A potluck dinner or a family songfest in which children also participate may pave the

way for beginning such a collection. Likewise, stories can be obtained by inviting family members one at a time to spend a portion of their day in the classroom telling their child's favorite bedtime story. During the telling, the teacher can note the book used or tape-record the parent's rendition and later transcribe it and add it to a class anthology. In each case, these collections are tangible evidence of parents' contributions to the program. They can be assembled with time with minimum hardship to either families or staff. Moreover, such collections signal to family members that their cultural traditions are valued by educators and are worth sharing with others.

Create home-based alternatives to on-site volunteering. For instance, ask family members to volunteer to prepare materials at home, make arrangements for field trips and with resource people, coordinate parent discussion groups, find resource materials at the library, compare prices of certain types of materials or equipment at local stores, or react to activity plans that will eventually be used in the classroom.

Provide home-based learning activities for family members and children to do together. This strategy is appropriate for all families but especially for those whose time is limited because of employment and family constraints. In fact, evidence suggests that for these families, home-based learning is the single most effective means of parental involvement (Epstein, 1984).

However, to achieve positive outcomes, families require clear expectations and guidelines about what to do. With this in mind, let parents know early in the program that home-based activities are essential for helping children to learn. Ask them to carry out activities at home for which you provide specific, yet brief, written or audiotaped directions. Provide these directions regularly (e.g., weekly). For each activity, invite family members to also tell you how easy it was to do and how much they and their children enjoyed it. Offer feedback to families about how their assistance at home is affecting their child's learning.

Invite interested family members to participate in policy-making decisions. For instance, ask family members to help create program–playground rules, develop snack guidelines, or generate ideas for specific classroom practices. Collaborating with parents to evaluate classroom materials as well as commercially available equipment or programs is another appropriate way of giving family members decision-making powers in early childhood education. If your program has a governing body such as a family council or governing board, encourage families in your group to consider participating as attendees and as decision makers.

Show genuine pleasure in every family member's attempts, no matter how large or small, to support the children's education. Continually let families know how

FIGURE 8.8 Guidelines for Working With Family Members as Teachers in the Classroom

❏ *Establish clear guidelines for family volunteers regarding their responsibilities in the classroom.* Offer specific suggestions as to what volunteers are to do and a rationale for delegated responsibilities. An activity card with this information could be prepared and then handed to a different parent day after day. Read the card aloud, or prepare an illustrated chart if the parent is an uncertain reader. An example of such a card is offered below.

> Welcome! Today please:
> 1. greet children and help them find name tags. Goal: to make them feel welcome and learn how their name looks.
> 2. supervise matching game. Goal: for children to notice similarities and differences.
> 3. join the children at lunch. Encourage them to pour and serve themselves. Goal: to model trying new foods.

❏ *Take time to demonstrate some of the activities family members are to supervise that day.*
❏ *Help family members feel welcome in the classroom.* Introduce them to the children, and provide youngsters with name tags so that parents can interact with them more comfortably.
❏ *Inform family members that when they volunteer in the classroom, all children in the group will view them as a teacher.* Remind the child that Mom, Dad, or Grandma will be helping many children and will have special responsibilities throughout the day. This helps clarify the adult's role for both Mom, Dad, or Grandma and the child (K. Payne, 1991).
❏ *Talk with family members about how to handle some potentially disruptive situations in the classroom.* Also discuss what to do if their child is involved. When this latter issue is ignored until it happens, some family members may fail to act or may overreact out of embarrassment. Neither response is conducive to the family members' feeling comfortable at school.
❏ *Give family volunteers in the classroom meaningful tasks to carry out:* helping children in the pretend-play area, engaging children in conversation, assisting children at the snack table. Avoid requesting them to do only busywork like washing the easel and brushes or cutting straws for a future fine-motor activity. If family members are to become partners in the educational process, they must be given real responsibilities from which they can derive genuine satisfaction.
❏ *Notice family members' successes in the classroom and comment on family members' helpfulness and effectiveness.* Describe their work in terms of better class functioning and individual child learning. This will underscore their value to the educational process.

much you appreciate the time and effort they put into their child's education, not just because their help allows you to do a better job but also because the children benefit so greatly. Extend your personal thank-you often. In addition, in classroom newsletters or community newspapers, acknowledge family contributions. Families may also be officially recognized at program events or with tangible tokens of appreciation such as certificates, plaques, or thank-you notes from the children.

Involving Men in Early Childhood Programs

Mr. Wasserman had just returned home with his 4-year-old daughter and told his wife, "I don't want to pick Gwennie up at the child care center anymore."

Mrs. Wasserman inquired, "Why not?"

"I went in and got her, put on her coat, looked for her bag, and none of the teachers even said hello or looked at me. They said hi to all the mothers and told them

about their kid's day. If we ever want to know what is happening, you will have to go yourself."

Michael begged his father to go to the parent conference with his mother. When his parents both agreed to go, he was extremely pleased. On their way home, Michael's dad said, "I don't know why Michael wanted me to go. I was the only father there."

The desire to include men in the early education program has arisen fairly recently. Although women have joined the workforce, no corresponding increase has been found in men's involvement in tasks traditionally associated with women. However, the essential roles of both men and women in the development and education of children are now more fully understood. Male involvement in children's education is associated with higher achievement and with social competence (Bernstein, 1998; Fagen, 2000).

In general, the barriers to involvement by men are similar to those for women. However, men face even more barriers and more-formidable barriers. For instance, are men actually welcome in programs? The experience reported by Mr. Wasserman is unfortunately all too common. There appears to be ambivalence between the desire that teachers express and their behavior. Fathers are also ambivalent, as Michael's dad expressed. When neither the teachers nor the fathers (men) are confident that they know what to do and why they are doing it, the fact that fewer men than women are involved, except at home, is not surprising.

Furthermore, men and women have different interaction styles. Most men are individualistic and competitive, whereas most women focus more on relationship building. The issue of male power is a considerable part of teachers' hesitancy to involve men in their programs (Turbiville et al., 2000).

Because women compose the largest portion of early childhood educators, these professionals in the field must overcome such barriers. Fortunately, when early childhood professionals are committed to including men in their programs and have the support and training necessary to plan and implement appropriate strategies, male participation increases (McBride, Rane, & Bae, 2001).

The principles of collaboration, variety, intensity, and individuation are valid for both men and women. However, men are much more likely to respond to a direct request for assistance than for a general request for parental participation. Requests for participation must be compatible with work schedules or tasks that can be completed in the father's home.

Establishing relationships, gathering information, and keeping families informed are also important if the fathers' involvement is to be optimal. Thus, educators

may have to institute dual parental contact for children whose parents do not share a household. Men report a desire for school involvement, believe that they have some responsibility to be involved, and find the loss of contact with and on behalf of children to be one of the most difficult aspects of parental separation (Baker & McMurray, 1998). Therefore, information should be gathered for noncustodial parents as well as for the parents who are the primary caregivers. Sending notices of meetings, scheduling conferences, and asking for participation all support the connection between the child and the parent.

Activities planned specifically for men or with men's interests in mind have been successful in some programs. For example, educators in one program held a special workshop on motor skills on a Saturday morning (Figure 8.9). Both men and women attended, although more men attended than had ever attended any other event. Similarly, at Edgewood Primary School, educators held a special celebration for children and the important men in their lives. Children invited grandfathers, fathers, stepfathers, and other males who were special to them. This event was held in the evening and was planned to engage adults and children in lively, beneficial activities.

Involving men in early childhood programs continues to be a challenge, even in programs in which some success has been achieved. However, when the early childhood educators are committed and follow through to the implementation stage, progress is made toward achieving this goal.

Providing Family Education

At a recent get-together for the families in her room, Consuelo Montoya invited the participants to give her ideas about topics they would like to explore in the coming months. Families brainstormed five ideas. Next, Consuelo put up a sign at the entrance to her room, asking family members to put a mark by the idea they most wanted to have a chance to talk about. Families who could not come to the room in person were invited to telephone in their preferences. Following are the results:

Consuelo Montoya's Classroom—Family Topics Wish List

> *Sibling Rivalry = /////////////*
> *Healthy Snacks Kids Will Eat = /////*
> *Celebrating Family Traditions = ////////*
> *How to Help Children Make Friends = ////////////////*
> *Taming the TV Monster = ////////*

On the basis of these outcomes, Consuelo plans to organize a workshop entitled "How to Help Children Make

Friends." She and another teacher will gather ideas and information for families and then share it during a family education evening at the center. A workshop on sibling rivalry could come next. For that workshop, Consuelo is thinking of inviting family members to talk about what they do at home when the bickering starts.

This example was one teacher's approach to developing family education opportunities for families of children enrolled in her classroom. Many other ways are available for educators to carry out this important facet of family involvement. Following are some guidelines for how to begin.

Conduct a simple needs assessment of family member concerns and interests related to child rearing and other family issues. This process could be carried out for only your classroom, among several classes, or on a programwide basis.

You can proceed in several ways. One way is to invite family members to a brainstorming session in which mutual concerns are generated. A second approach is to conduct a brief written or telephone survey in which family members identify the issues that are most important to them. A third technique is to provide family members with a broad range of potential issues that could be addressed and then ask them to indicate which are most important to them. The summary of the results can then be used to provide direction for future parental education efforts.

Deal with the most pressing needs for the group early. However, a word of caution is advisable: Avoid simply going with the notion of majority rule. Instead, look at the concerns in terms of various demographic subgroupings such as low-income families or single-parent households. For example, a workshop on sibling rivalry or children and television would be of interest to a broad range of families in your class, whereas blended families might find the following two topics pertinent: (a) living with other people's children and (b) dealing with stepparent stereotypes. Addressing both general and specific concerns in your plan will give it the widest possible appeal and will be more sensitive to all families served by the program.

Invite family members to educational workshops that involve both them and the child. Consider using a format in which children receive child care half the time while their family members discuss program-related information with other family members and staff. The second half of the session could be devoted to parents and children's working together, practicing skills, or creating make-it-and-take-it items for use at home. A sample agenda for one such workshop is offered in Figure 8.9.

Help family members anticipate typical developmental changes throughout the early childhood period.

FIGURE 8.9 Saturday Morning Family–Child Motor Skills Workshop

9:00–9:15	*Arrival*	Children are taken to supervised child care rooms.
9:15–10:15	*Discussion*	Ms. Iamfit talks with family members about the development of motor skills such as throwing, catching, and skipping.
10:15–10:30		Family members pick up preschool-aged children from child care rooms, receive name tags, and go to first activity station.
10:30–11:30	*Activity stations*	Family members rotate from station to station every 10 minutes, approximately six families per station. 1. Make it/take it: Family members and children choose to make one or more gross-motor items for use at home— nylon paddles, milk jug scoops, newspaper balls; also provided are instructions and activity ideas for jump ropes, suspended balls, streamers, and pillow balls. 2. Throw and catch 3. Striking 4. Gallop and skip 5. Balance 6. Nutritional awareness and snack
11:30–11:40	*Closing*	All participants gather in the rainy day room for a large-group song with movement.

This workshop will be repeated next Friday from 6:30 to 9:00 P.M.

Knowing what to expect empowers family members to respond appropriately when such changes occur and makes them more confident teachers of their children. A note home to families, a brief discussion in the classroom newsletter, a small-group discussion, and an organized workshop on a related topic are a few ways to get this kind of information home. Chatting informally with family members individually and frequently is another valuable way to convey developmental information to parents. These personal contacts are especially useful because teachers can provide appropriate information and answer questions with a specific child in mind.

Provide general information about child development and learning, in take-home form, to family members. Books, pamphlets, cassettes, and videotapes can be made available through a parent lending library. In a box easily accessible to parents, file articles culled from magazines, newsletters, and early childhood journals such as *Young Children, Day Care and Early Education,* and *Childhood Education* (Bundy, 1991). Provide more than one copy of each article so that you can recommend relevant readings and parents can take them home with no obligation to return them. Periodically send home a note highlighting new material available for parents to borrow or keep. Organize family discussions around one or more of these reading topics or give family members a checklist on which they can indicate whether they would like a particular article sent home with their child.

Facilitating Family-to-Family Support

A group of parents was seated at a picnic table for the Sugar Hill Child Development Center end-of-year potluck dinner. Eventually the conversation turned to what they liked best about the program. In addition to the satisfaction many of the parents derived from watching their children develop and learn in a happy, safe, and stimulating program, they most appreciated having a chance to talk with members of other families who were coping with some of the same child-rearing challenges.

"I just want to talk with a grown-up sometimes. Not about the office or my work, but about how they get their kid to take vitamins or what if she doesn't want to kiss grandma."

"It's easy to feel like you're the only one whose child is or isn't doing something. (Remember Tim and the shoes?) But here there are other parents I can talk to. . . . Makes you feel less alone."

These families voiced one of the most significant benefits of family involvement: the opportunity to get to know and interact with the members of other families

responsible for raising a child. Such positive outcomes are more likely to occur when educators in early childhood programs take deliberate steps to help families make these contacts.

Arrange opportunities for family members to talk with one another informally. Plan some casual get-togethers whose primary aim is to provide family members with an opportunity to build their social networks and communicate with their peers. Make sure to include an unstructured break to facilitate family-to-family conversation during more formally scheduled events. Strong evidence indicates that these informal exchanges are just as valuable to family members as the regularly scheduled program is (R. Powell, 1989). In fact, for single parents, strengthening informal social networks may be the most effective means of eliciting their involvement in their children's education (Cochran & Henderson, 1986). The same is true for families whose home language is not English. Linking parents who speak the same language and encouraging informal support networks helps create a sense of belonging that families appreciate (Lee, 1997).

Work with other teachers, parents, and administrators to organize a family-to-family mentoring program. Pairing new families with family members already familiar with program philosophy and practices helps ease the entrée of newcomers and gives established families a responsible, important means of involvement. Give the mentors guidelines about how to fulfill their role. Some of their duties might include the following:

❏ Calling new family members to welcome them and answer their initial questions

❏ Arranging to meet new families prior to their involvement in the program and provide a tour of the facility

❏ Inviting new families to accompany them to open houses or orientation sessions held early in the year

❏ Translating relevant program materials or serving as translators during family conferences or other program-related gatherings

❏ Checking in periodically to answer questions and provide information as needed.

Talk to your program administrator about creating peer support groups for teen parents, single parents, working parents, families of children with disabilities, and noncustodial parents. Suggest that your program promote support groups by providing not only the location for group meetings, but also child care during the time such groups meet. If such groups are already part of your program, make sure individual parents in your class know about them.

Suggest that a place in the school or center be set aside as a family lounge. This space could serve as a headquarters for program-related family projects. A living-room-type atmosphere seems welcoming to family members, as does a pot of coffee and a family reference library. Family members also appreciate a large bulletin board on which announcements, community news, and parent requests for child care, toys, clothing, or transportation are posted. Updating information often, removing out-of-date material, keeping the board neat and organized, and placing it in a prominent location will prompt family members to check it frequently.

SUMMARY

Practitioners and family members who work together create a strong foundation for developmentally appropriate programs for young children. This chapter describes the aims and benefits of family involvement in early childhood education. The principles of collaboration, variety, intensity, and individuation provide a framework for thinking about successful approaches to including families. On the basis of these principles, various strategies for increasing family involvement are suggested. The guidelines we selected highlight the broad repertoire of skills you will need to work more effectively with families. However, you will not use all of these strategies in any single year. Although many questions remain as to how to reach and involve *all* families, the inclusion of the child's family will continue to remain a high priority among educators of young children. Our job as early childhood professionals is to continue investigating alternative methods of fostering family involvement and to welcome family members as full-fledged partners in the educational process.

This chapter is the last in part 2. You now have a wide array of tools to use to design a developmentally appropriate curriculum for young children, including small- and whole-group planning and implementation skills, organizational and time-management skills, guidance strategies, and techniques for including family members in children's early education. Part 3, which follows, focuses on the curriculum.

Applying What You Read in This Chapter

1. **Discuss**
   a. On the basis of your reading and your experiences with families, discuss each of the questions that open this chapter.
   b. Assume that you are a teacher of 4-year-olds. Leon's grandmother will be volunteering in your classroom today. What will you do to ensure that the experience is positive for Leon, his grandmother, and yourself?
   c. Describe how you would apply the principles of age appropriateness, individual appropriateness, and sociocultural appropriateness to the concept of family involvement.

2. **Observe**
   a. Observe a program in which family members volunteer in the classroom. What does the head teacher do to make the experience a success for families, children, and staff?
   b. Arrange to accompany an early childhood professional on a home visit. What is the purpose of the visit from the practitioner's perspective? Describe what the practitioner does to address this purpose. Explain how the family responded and whether the original purpose was achieved. Were any additional outcomes accomplished? What were they?
   c. Observe a family involvement event at an early childhood program. Describe the purpose of the event, how families learned about it, and the support strategies designed to facilitate family involvement. Use Figure 8.1 to guide your description. Describe what occurred during the event and family reactions to it.

3. **Carry out an activity**
   a. Think about an early childhood setting in which you are or have been involved. Create a comprehensive family involvement plan for this program by choosing one or two strategies from at least three categories listed in this chapter. Provide reasons for your choices.
   b. Interview an early childhood educator about his or her work with families. Ask the practitioner to describe some of the methods he or she uses to help families feel welcome and involved in their child's education.
   c. Identify the cultural background of one or several families in your program that varies from yours. Find a community event or resource through which you might learn more about this cultural group. Participate and describe what you discovered about the culture and about yourself.

4. Create something for your portfolio
   a. Take pictures and record families' reactions to a family involvement activity you planned.
   b. Create a family newsletter for a specific group of children. Provide a written rationale for why you developed your newsletter as you did.

5. Add to your journal
   a. What is the most significant concept that you learned about family involvement from your read-

ings and your experience with children and families?
   b. Make a list of the most pressing concerns you have about family involvement. Describe what you will do to address your concerns.
   c. Describe a positive interaction you had with a family. What made it work? Describe a less successful interaction. What went awry, and how might you avoid a poor outcome in the future?

Part 3

The Curriculum

As a prospective parent is being shown around the center, she asks the director, "What kind of curriculum do you follow?"

The first-, second-, and third-grade teachers have been called together to reexamine the social studies curriculum for the lower elementary grades. There is much talk about how this curriculum should look in comparison with that adopted by the upper elementary committee.

Mrs. Cohen, a new kindergarten teacher, asks whether she will be expected to teach children to "write on the lines." She is told, "Oh, no. We dropped that from the curriculum 2 years ago."

The program staff have spent an exciting day learning about children's self-esteem. The question they want answered is, How can we best address self-esteem within our curriculum?

As part of the accreditation process for the school, the early childhood coordinator is asked to submit a copy of the curriculum for review.

Curriculum is something everyone connected with education talks about, yet it can mean different things to different people. When some individuals discuss curriculum, they are simply referring to the goals and objectives of the program. Others have in mind a written plan for student learning or a syllabus that lists topics of study and how these topics will be taught (Brewer, 2001). Still other persons equate curriculum with certain materials or types of activities commonly associated with a particular center or school. The form the curriculum takes can also vary from detailed written descriptions to sets of beliefs and experiences that can be grasped only by observing the program in action. Because so many interpretations of the term *curriculum* exist, we will clarify how this term relates to the curriculum detailed in the next six chapters.

DEFINING THE CURRICULUM

Curriculum is all the organized educational experiences provided for children by the early childhood program. These experiences can take place inside the classroom or beyond, involving educators, family members, and other people in the community. In its written form, curriculum includes stated goals and objectives, strategies and activities aimed at supporting all aspects of children's development and learning, and methods of assessing children's progress and program effectiveness.

Formulated within a framework of developmental appropriateness, the curriculum described in the chapters that follow represents one interpretation of how to educate children aged 3 through 8 years. Hereafter, it is referred to as the *Children's Comprehensive Curriculum*. The Children's Comprehensive Curriculum has a two-fold purpose: (a) to help children develop the knowledge, skills, attitudes, and dispositions essential to becoming happy, contributing members of society and (b) to give educators the tools necessary to facilitate such learning. Developed in its original form by faculty in the

Department of Family and Child Ecology at Michigan State University, the Children's Comprehensive Curriculum has been implemented and evaluated in the Child Development Laboratories on campus since 1988. Variations of it have been adopted by nursery school, child care, Head Start, Chapter 1, and preprimary special education programs throughout the Midwest. Educators in numerous school districts have also used this curriculum as the basis for redesigning their goals, objectives, and methods for teaching children in kindergarten through fifth grade. The version offered in this book represents an amalgamation of these adaptations.

Why Use the Children's Comprehensive Curriculum?

The Children's Comprehensive Curriculum is divided into six domains: aesthetic, affective, cognitive, language, physical, and social. Considered individually, the six domains represent major facets of child development. Although we realize that no one aspect of development can be isolated from the rest, we have found that purposeful planning for each domain results in a more comprehensive approach to instruction. Thus, taken altogether, the entire array represents a "whole-child" approach to teaching. It unites an understanding of what is (i.e., how children develop and learn) with value statements of what ought to be (i.e., goals and objectives for children's development and learning now and in the future), with methods for achieving these aims (i.e., teaching strategies and activities). A brief overview of each domain within the Children's Comprehensive Curriculum is presented in Table 1.

Why Emphasize Developmental Domains Over Subjects?

Practitioners more accustomed to the traditional subject-matter designations of art, math, science, reading, social studies, physical education, and the like may question the

TABLE 1   Curricular Domains Within the Children's Comprehensive Curriculum

Domain	Developmental Focus
Aesthetic	Appreciation of the arts and enjoyment of sensory experiences
Affective	Trust, autonomy, initiative, industry, self-awareness, self-esteem
Cognitive	Perception, physical knowledge, logical-mathematical knowledge, social-conventional knowledge, scientific understanding, critical thinking skills
Language	Receptive language, listening skills, expressive language, reading, and writing
Physical	Fine- and gross-motor skills, body awareness, physical health
Social	Social skills, socialization, social studies

child-oriented categories of developmental domains. They may wonder whether the material included within the following chapters will meet their needs and to what extent domains relate to their work with children.

Although standard curriculum divisions are comfortable because they are familiar, subject matter alone is not a sufficient source of curriculum (Spodek, 1973). Too often it leads to fragmented, isolated skill development or the exclusion of other kinds of knowledge and skills essential to children's ultimate success in society. Consequently, a subject-matter orientation is not comprehensive enough to suit our purposes. We prefer to emphasize a broader range of perceptions, dispositions, knowledge, and skills. For instance, art and music are covered under aesthetics, but so too are dance and other sensory experiences. The affective domain includes not only learning processes related to self-awareness and self-esteem, but also the development of independence and a sense of industry. Science and math are components of the cognitive domain but do not constitute the whole of it. This domain also includes problem solving, critical thinking, and perception. Reading is found within the language domain, and so are listening, speaking, and writing. The physical domain encompasses gross- and fine-motor skills, health, and body image. Incorporated within the social domain are social studies content, and processes and skills fundamental to children's increased social competence.

As children participate in the six developmental domains, they experience a comprehensive educational curriculum that goes beyond the subject-oriented programs characteristic of many primary schools. The domain-focused curriculum also transcends the traditional materials-based programs associated with numerous preprimary settings.

Why Emphasize Developmental Domains Over Materials?

Several philosophers throughout the history of early childhood education have advocated including certain materials to enhance particular learning goals for children. Froebel's gifts; Montessori's pink tower; and Hartley, Frank, and Goldenson's emphasis on blocks, water, and clay are typical examples. In each case the teacher's role was closely tied to facilitating children's use of these items. However, in the 1940s and 1950s, many teachers began to take a more passive role, treating the curriculum as inherent in the materials. This notion stemmed from maturational and psychoanalytic perspectives that assumed development merely unfolded in a benign environment or children needed certain materials to use in cathartic ways (Hartley, Frank, & Goldenson, 1952; Read, 1966). This viewpoint has given way to the more interactive approach designated in chapters 1 and 2.

Nevertheless, the idea that materials do the teaching is still prevalent. Many practitioners assume that if they have the proper equipment, the instructional aspects of the program will take care of themselves (Kostelnik, 1990). When teachers make this assumption, goals for children's learning are often unspecified or ambiguous, and teachers may neglect to challenge children sufficiently. Instead, their main focus becomes one of monitoring children for appropriate materials use. Although having carefully selected materials and equipment is a necessary ingredient of quality children's programs, it is not a sufficient foundation for the early childhood curriculum (Bredekamp & Copple, 1997). Materials supplement the curriculum; they do not equal it. Moreover, the same materials can be used to support learning across domains. This broader view distinguishes a domain-focused curriculum from a materials-based approach.

DESCRIBING THE STRUCTURE OF CHAPTERS 9 THROUGH 14

Each of the next six chapters focuses on a single curricular domain. Each chapter includes these segments:

I. Introduction—This part of the chapter describes the importance of the domain to children and its relevance to early childhood education.

II. Issues—A brief discussion of current educational issues related to the domain and how they might be addressed in early childhood programs is offered next.

III. Goals and Objectives—For each domain an ultimate goal and a list of intermediate objectives are presented. The ultimate goal is a global statement about the idealized long-range educational purpose of the domain. Ultimate goals are lifelong in intent, spanning an individual's entire educational experience. They are equally applicable to children in preprimary programs, elementary school, and middle or high school and beyond. Knowing the ultimate goal for each domain helps educators keep sight of "the big picture," giving them a focus that goes beyond any one particular skill or bit of knowledge. Ultimate goals are guideposts educators can use to gauge how well their instructional practices support long-term aims as well as immediate outcomes.

Each ultimate goal is further subdivided into several intermediate objectives. Intermediate objectives identify distinctive categories of behavior relative to children's development and learning within the domain. They help educators recognize domain-related skill patterns and concepts and outline the content and processes around which practitioners should plan classroom instruction. In this guide these objectives are listed in sequence from most fundamental to most complex. Consequently, the intermediate objectives can be used as a guide for sequencing learning experiences for each domain. Their purpose is to give teachers needed direction in planning while simultaneously allowing them the autonomy to decide how best to address each objective in light of children's interests and capabilities. Thus, teachers can use the intermediate objectives as a source of activity ideas. Such activities could include classroom routines, children's use of classroom materials to explore objects and concepts, and teacher-initiated lessons. A diagram depicting the relationship among the ultimate goal, the intermediate objectives, and activities for a sample domain is offered in Table 2.

Once teachers have settled on activities that address the intermediate objectives they have chosen,

TABLE 2 The Relationship Among the Ultimate Goal, Selected Intermediate Objectives, and Sample Activities for the Physical Domain

Ultimate Goal	Intermediate Objectives	Sample Activities
	Children will	
For children to achieve physical competence and develop knowledge, attitudes, skills, and behaviors related to a healthy lifestyle	1. develop awareness of the location of their body parts.	a. sing and act out the "Head, Shoulders, Knees, and Toes" song. b. make body tracings, labeling external body parts. c. play the Hokey Pokey game, emphasizing left and right. d. make body tracings, labeling internal body parts.
	2. engage in activities that require balance.	a. walk the balance beam. b. play the Statue game. c. use stilts. d. ride a two-wheel bicycle.
	3. practice fine-motor skills.	a. move small objects with kitchen tongs. b. string beads. c. make letters in sand on trays. d. cut out snowflakes.
	4. learn health and safety procedures.	a. brush their teeth each day. b. sing "This is the way we wash our face" to the tune of "Here We Go 'Round the Mulberry Bush." c. play the Red Light, Green Light game. d. read a story about "good touch and bad touch."

they can identify more-specific instructional objectives (e.g., behavioral objectives) suited to the learning needs of children in their class. We believe that these latter objectives are best created by individuals who know the children well. For this reason, we have not attempted to identify these objectives in this guide.

IV. Teaching Strategies—This segment offers practical, pervasive strategies teachers can use to address the domain in their classrooms. The suggested techniques were developed by practitioners in the field and represent concrete ways to operationalize the goals and objectives.

V. Activity Suggestions—Each of the curriculum-focused chapters ends with a selection of sample activities that support the domain. All activities include the following components:

A. Activity name

B. Intermediate objective to which the activity relates

C. Recommended materials

D. General procedure for carrying out the activity with 5- to 6-year-old children

E. Suggestions for simplifying the activity for 3- to 4-year-old children

F. Suggestions for extending the activity for 7- to 8-year-old children

These activity suggestions are illustrative, not exhaustive, examples of the types of activities and lessons teachers can plan for use inside and outside the classroom. However, we have striven to present a broad array of activities that cover the range of intermediate objectives within the domain.

RECONCILING THE USE OF DOMAINS WITH OTHER CURRICULAR APPROACHES

Some practitioners work in programs in which the curricular focus is established on a programwide or even a statewide basis. Teachers faced with having to reconcile a more traditional subject-based or materials-based curriculum with domains have two options. First, they can advocate for a domain-focused orientation within their organization. Second, they can look for ways to integrate their current curricular approach with that suggested in this book. Most often this involves subsuming subjects or materials under the broader construct of domains. For instance, some school districts have adopted the six curricular domains along with the ultimate goals and intermediate objectives for each. Next, committees have examined current subject-related instructional objectives (often found in a district-adopted curriculum guide) to determine their appropriateness and the extent to which they support a particular domain. On the basis of the committees' recommendations, suitable revisions in objectives, classroom practices, and assessment tools are enacted. Individual practitioners can pursue a similar path, clustering subjects under domains and then evaluating their instructional practices in terms of the ultimate goals for each.

Likewise, practitioners accustomed to thinking of curriculum as materials have begun by taking equipment standard to their program and generating ideas for using the material to support intermediate objectives within various domains. For instance, blocks can be used to address objectives in any of the six curricular domains. This process can be repeated with other objects such as art materials, puzzles, small manipulative items, sand, and water. An example of this method of integration was provided in chapter 5.

In conclusion, as educators in more and more programs consider adopting policies and procedures to support developmentally appropriate practice, the notion of curricular domains will become increasingly common. One purpose of this text is to help educators better understand this approach to curriculum planning and implementation. The best way to begin is to examine what each domain entails, starting with the aesthetic domain.

The Aesthetic Domain

You may wonder:

What is meant by the word *aesthetics?*

What are *the arts?*

Why is aesthetic education important for children's learning?

What can I do to enhance children's aesthetic development?

In this chapter on stimulating children's aesthetic interests and participation, we present information to help you answer the preceding questions.

The children have created a "tent" in the preschool room by using a blanket draped over a folding table. Maggie and Joy decide to take the xylophone, the bells, and a drum into the tent. "We're making a tent band, Mr. Jordan!" they say as they crawl under the edge of the blanket. He smiles as he hears their creative musical play and listens to their laughter. He makes a mental note to ask the children to tell about their band at sharing time.

Mrs. Gerhard carefully uncovers a large print of the painting An Afternoon at La Grande Jatte, *by George Seurat. "Tell me what you see in this painting," she says. The 5-year-olds seated on the floor kneel to look more closely. Luke announces, "This is good work. I like it." Gillian says, "It's a happy earth." Antonio agrees, "I like this. Lots of color and a cat." The teacher nods and asks, "Where is this place?" DaJuan points to the corner, "I see boats." Shawnna notices, "There's a lady trying to catch a fish." Kyle leans in and says, "I see a monkey and a dog. I think it's South America or Africa." Their teacher smiles and says, "You're looking very carefully; I wonder what you think the artist was trying to tell us in this painting." Tiara shouts, "It's about a wedding! There's the wedding girl!"*

Four-year-old Caleb looks from rock to rock on the tray, searching for his favorite. He notices that the rocks are different colors, some are smooth, and some sparkle when water is poured over them. Picking one up, he announces, "Here it is. This is my best." Teacher assistant Mr. Rey says, "You chose rock number 14, Caleb. Tell me what you like about this rock and I'll write it on our chart."

Dora and Rachel stand in front of their teacher's aide, Mrs. Oppenheimer, as she strums chords softly on the guitar. The children listen and watch intently. Dora's head and shoulders begin to sway from side to side. She moves slowly to the music, responding to the gentle rhythms.

Amber's preschool group is dramatizing the story "The Three Billy Goats Gruff." She decides to be one of the goats going across the bridge. She practices using her best billy goat voice to say, "It is I, Big Billy Goat Gruff."

The first graders in Ms. Fernandez's class have been working in small groups for 15 minutes. Izayah's group is responsible for making trees for the class mural. The children are busy discussing what trees look like and cutting, arranging, and gluing paper shapes they have produced. Izayah decides his tree needs more leaves; he searches through the scrap box for the colors he wants. "Mine will be very leafy," he says with pride.

Each youngster just described is involved in aesthetic activities appropriate for early childhood educational settings. In this chapter, we explore the idea that involvement in the arts is important for every child and should be a vital part of the curriculum.

AESTHETICS DEFINED

The word *aesthetics* comes from the Greek word *aisthetikos*, which refers to the ability to perceive through the senses. Aesthetics deals with artistic sensibilities and focuses on determining what is beautiful and good, as well as on appreciation (Jalongo & Stamp, 1997). *Aesthetics* is defined by the Consortium of National Arts Education Associations ([Consortium], 1994) as "a branch of philosophy that focuses on the nature of beauty, the nature and value of art, and the inquiry process and human responses associated with these topics" (p. 82). In simple terms, aesthetics is a person's capacity to perceive, be sensitive to, and respond to human creations in the arts and to beauty in nature.

THE ARTS DEFINED

The term *the arts* is defined as both "the creative work" and "the process of producing the creative work." In the broadest sense, this term refers to all the creative forms that have been produced throughout human history. The arts fall into four broad categories: visual arts, performing arts, usable arts, and literary arts. *Visual arts* include painting, drawing, sculpting, making prints, carving wood, making mosaics or collages, designing, and so forth. *Performing arts* include singing, dancing, playing instruments, performing dramas, engaging in storytelling, using creative movement, creating puppets and puppet shows, and many others. *Usable arts* (crafts) include weaving, making ceramics, making pottery, knitting, making baskets, making jewelry, making furniture, and countless others. *Literary arts* include creating original stories, poems, plays, commercials, jokes, skits, essays, and novels, and many other written forms of expression.

SCOPE OF THIS CHAPTER

As you might ascertain, aesthetic learning encompasses a broad spectrum of experiences related to different art forms and appreciation of natural beauty. To make this chapter manageable, we use the term *the arts* to refer to four basic categories: music, dance, drama, and visual arts. Although this chapter provides a variety of examples, other activities involving the natural world, the performing arts, storytelling, poetry, movement, and dance can be found in other chapters throughout the book. For example, activities related to nature are found in chapter 11, The Cognitive Domain; storytelling activities are located in chapter 15, Integrating Curriculum Through Pretend and Construction Play; movement and dance activities are found in chapter 13, The Physical Domain. In addition, for our purposes, literary arts are included in chapter 12, The Language Domain. Teachers can also transform many activities into aesthetic experiences for children by selecting an aesthetic goal (such as "to gain pleasure from a variety of sensory experiences" or "to contribute to the school's aesthetic environment").

AESTHETIC EDUCATION FOR YOUNG CHILDREN

Aesthetic education in early childhood is a deliberate effort by teachers to provide experiences in the arts, nurture awareness of the arts, foster appreciation of the arts, and develop skills in evaluating art forms (Jalongo & Stamp, 1997). Children learn about the arts by responding to them and by making their own art. Therefore, aesthetic experiences may be either responsive or productive (Figure 9.1). Table 9.1 provides an overview of both these types of aesthetic experiences and the types of activities that are included in each.

Responsive aesthetic experiences involve the child in recognizing the beauty in nature, appreciating art and nature, and forming related judgments and preferences. In the activities described at the beginning of this chapter, Joy and Maggie are playing with and responding

TABLE 9.1 Responsive and Productive Aesthetic Experiences

Type of Activities	Goal and Examples
RESPONSIVE AESTHETIC EXPERIENCES	
Discovery activities	*Goal:* To develop appreciation of natural beauty *Examples:* ❏ Observing beautiful fish ❏ Examining interesting rocks ❏ Watching cloud formations in the sky ❏ Discovering beauty in spiderwebs ❏ Smelling flowers, grass, or spices
Exposure activities	*Goal:* To develop appreciation of the arts *Examples:* ❏ Looking at details in paintings or photographs ❏ Touching a sculpture ❏ Watching a dance ❏ Listening to a choir ❏ Watching a dramatic performance
Evaluation activities	*Goal:* To form judgments and preferences *Examples:* ❏ Comparing several baskets ❏ Selecting the best collage for a portfolio ❏ Choosing a favorite song ❏ Telling characteristics liked about a dance
PRODUCTIVE AESTHETIC EXPERIENCES	
Creative activities	*Goal:* To develop creative expression *Examples:* ❏ Playing an instrument ❏ Dancing ❏ Finger painting ❏ Singing a song ❏ Making a pipe-cleaner flower ❏ Playing a role in a drama

FIGURE 9.1 Aesthetic Development Model

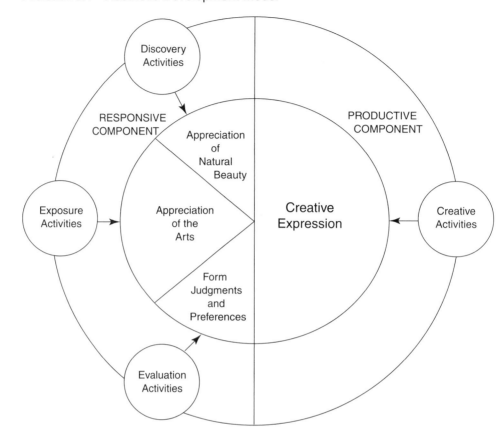

to musical sounds. The 5-year-olds exploring the painting are learning to appreciate the visual arts. Caleb, looking at rocks, is learning appreciation of beauty in nature and preference formation. Dora and Rachel are learning to appreciate the performing art of guitar playing. All these children are involved in responsive aesthetic learning. Responsive aesthetic experiences include discovery, exposure, and evaluation activities.

Discovery activities, such as Caleb's examining the rocks, give children opportunities to respond to natural beauty. Youngsters may explore details of natural objects by using all their senses in the form of looking, listening, smelling, touching, and sometimes tasting, which thus enhances their appreciation of nature.

Exposure activities, such as Dora and Rachel's exposure to the guitar, broaden children's familiarity with the arts. These activities provide opportunities for children, as observers and consumers of art, to listen to a variety of music, view dance or dramatic performances, or view the visual arts in many forms. For ideas on ways to bring the arts to children, see the Appendix to this chapter.

Evaluation activities, such as the 5-year-olds' examining the painting, encourage children to discuss and evaluate a variety of visual art, music, dance, and drama forms. Students may decide on criteria for evaluating

the art (such as "It uses color in a pleasing way" or "It delivers a message") and express their preferences on the basis of these criteria.

Productive aesthetic experiences involve the child in *creative art activities,* which engage the child actively with materials, props, instruments, and tools useful for making art, music, drama, or dance. These activities stimulate creativity and provide opportunities for self-expression. Painting a self-portrait, gluing felt pieces into a pleasing design, and experimenting with movement to music are examples of creative art activities. At the beginning of this chapter, Joy and Maggie were creating a band through their play, Amber was participating in a simple drama, and Izayah was working on a paper mural; all these children were engaged in creative expression.

Many times, children create their own aesthetic activities through play, although sometimes teachers guide their learning. Often teachers combine activities to achieve several goals. Following is an example of how one teacher used three aesthetic activities to teach children to become familiar with, evaluate, and create their own art.

Mrs. Gonzalez's first graders are studying about air. This week their focus is on things that move in the air. The teacher asks if anyone has seen art that moves in the air. Children suggest kites and hot-air balloons. She hangs several examples of mobiles (a seashell mobile, a wooden bird mobile from Mexico, and a baby's nursery mobile made of stuffed cloth shapes) in the classroom. The children examine the mobiles and talk about their individual experiences with mobiles. They notice the shapes, colors, and effects of air movement (exposure activity).

The next day, Mrs. Gonzalez shows the class a picture of a famous mobile, Lobster Trap and Fish Tail, *by Alexander Calder (Abrams, 1985). She asks them to imagine how it was made and to tell what they like about it (evaluation activity). During independent reading, Mrs. Gonzalez encourages the class to look at books showing other mobiles.*

On the third afternoon, Mrs. G. displays a collection of materials, and the class discusses ways they could use them to make their own mobiles. She provides scissors, a variety of paper, hole punches, markers, thin wooden dowels, and string. By now students have many ideas for their mobiles; some ask for assistance in attaching and suspending the shapes, but most work independently (creative activity). As the students finish, they hang their unique mobiles throughout the classroom and examine one another's work.

IMPORTANCE OF AESTHETIC LEARNING

There are many reasons to engage children in aesthetic learning. An emphasis on beauty and the wonder of nature helps children respond emotionally and make connections to the natural environment. These early affective connections can form a foundation for social consciousness, care, and knowledge (Kemple & Johnson, 2002). Learning through the arts also fosters the development of many skills, including eye–hand coordination and good work habits, and provides children with opportunities to experience success (Alvino, 2000).

The arts have also been attributed with playing a vital role in establishing a bond among the generations that technology sometimes drives apart. This important link contributes to shared experiences for people of all ages. One educational expert described the role of early childhood art education as having three important aims: (a) personal fulfillment, (b) awareness of art in society, and (c) transmission of a cultural heritage (Nikoltsos, 2000). Successful art experiences stimulate youngsters to respect themselves, communicate their ideas and feelings, discover their own point of view, and appreciate different viewpoints and cultures.

Involving youngsters in creative visual art, music, dance, and drama contributes to and enhances a prosocial climate in the group. Children who sing together, create puppets together, play instruments together, and dance together are more likely to behave cooperatively in other circumstances. Activities such as these build group cohesion and social solidarity.

In addition, learning in other domains is greatly enhanced through the arts. Respected developmental psychologist Howard Gardner, through his theory of multiple intelligences, said that many children learn best in ways other than the linguistic, mathematical, or logical approach (Gardner, 1985, 1991, 1993b). Youngsters frequently make connections to learning more readily through kinesthetic, tactile, auditory, interpersonal, and spatial experiences. Howard Gardner's work helps us expand our view of nonverbal forms of knowledge to include musical, bodily-kinesthetic, spatial, and visual forms (Wright, 1997). In other words, aesthetic activities provide ways to explore these forms of knowing and play a tremendous role in developing perception.

Gardner suggested that the well-documented differences in children challenge an educational system that assumes everyone can learn the same way. When the arts are not part of the curriculum, teaching and learning quickly become monotonous, spiritless, and routine.

RELATIONSHIP BETWEEN AESTHETIC LEARNING AND KNOWING

Connections between the arts and thinking are well established. We have only to look at the communication of thought and ideas in the work by young children attending the schools of Reggio Emilia, Italy, to see how important this connection is. Children in these schools engage in the creative arts process; they gather information, reformulate it, and express their cognitive knowledge through original representations. The process of creativity involves learning to see relationships, redefining the elements, and reorganizing the parts into something new (a synthesis). For children, creative experiences that stimulate thinking are critical to cognitive development. According to art education researcher Viktor Lowenfeld, "The greater the opportunity to develop an increased sensitivity and the greater the awareness of all the senses, the greater the opportunity for learning" (Lowenfeld & Brittain, 1965, p. 5).

When children engage in aesthetic experiences, they encounter five subgroups of knowledge. Four of these are physical, logical-mathematical, representational, and social-conventional knowledge. Children also have chances to consider how and why they think as they do. This fifth type of knowledge is known as *metacognition.* Each of these is described further in chapter 11, The Cognitive Domain. For now, let us explore how aesthetic experiences foster all types of learning.

Physical Knowledge in Aesthetic Learning

Construction of aesthetic "physical knowledge" involves discovery of the physical characteristics of materials in art, music, dance, and drama. For example, by using musical instruments, students learn about the variety of sounds instruments make, how instruments produce sounds, and what instruments can do musically. Through playing with movement, children become aware of body positions, gestures, the feel of movement, control of their limbs, and the physical characteristics of dance. Through play with materials, such as clay, children learn what the medium feels like, what it will do when it is combined with water, how the clay can be transformed with fingers and tools, and the limitations clay has because it dries hard if it is not kept moist. Through experimenting with blocks and other construction materials, children learn characteristics of design and balance (Kolodziej, 1999).

Logical-Mathematical Knowledge in Aesthetic Learning

Through productive and responsive experiences, children physically or mentally construct or recognize relationships. Concepts of size, shape, area, placement, distance, timing, loudness, and other characteristics can be learned through art, music, dance, and drama. These understandings are the fundamentals of logical-mathematical knowledge. Therefore, when a kindergartner adds blue scribbles above a self-portrait, the child uses logical-mathematical knowledge to express his or her relationship to the sky. Playing instruments or singing songs involves the use of rhythm, beat, long and short tones, and loud and quiet sounds—all mathematically based. Similarly, when a child engages in tap dance, the child practices slower and faster taps, and higher and lower movements, and matches his or her motions to the teacher's movements. All these involve logical-mathematical understandings.

As teachers use the vocabulary of the arts (Figure 9.2), they give children richer language to use for describing, comparing, evaluating, and expressing preferences in the arts. Using terms such as *color* and *line,* or *tone* and *rhythm,* helps children understand the elements of art or music. With older children teachers can more specifically focus activities on the elements. One innovative art specialist, featured in the journal *Young Children,* described the way she uses the elements of line, shape, texture, and color as themes for kindergarten take-home art appreciation kits (Mulcahey, 2002). Parents and children together look at simple reproductions of an artist's work, consider questions about a particular art element, then use the materials in the kit to create their own art, incorporating that element. Kits such as those just described help both children and parents become aware of art elements and actively look for them in their everyday world.

Representational Knowledge in Aesthetic Learning

Producing original visual art, music, drama, or dance requires the person to think of an experience, an idea, or a feeling and express it by manipulating the elements of the medium. In other words, learning within the arts involves representing something by something else. This activity is highly symbolic and involves the learner in focused representational thought. Being able to imagine something that is not present and then find ways to express this thinking concretely to others is a major cognitive accomplishment (C. Seefeldt, 1995).

Social-Conventional Knowledge in Aesthetic Learning

Through social-conventional knowledge in the arts, we teach understanding and respect for cultural traditions, history, and heritage. Experiences with music, visual arts, dance, and dramatics serve as symbols of cultural identity for children. An important role of aesthetic learning is to lay the groundwork for strong links to the achievements from the past. Children's understanding of their heritage can begin in preschool with the awareness that people—artists—made the pictures in their favorite books, the sculpture in the park, and the woven hanging in their living room (Bredekamp & Rosegrant, 1995).

Social-conventional knowledge is part of aesthetics when the learner acquires concepts and understandings related to the arts in society. For example, the names and characteristics of cultural dances (such as ballet, the polka, the hula, the waltz, the tango, or square dance) are passed from generation to generation as social-conventional knowledge. Moreover, when teachers expose children to art forms by using words such as *portrait, landscape, still life, print, watercolor, sand painting, mosaic, appliqué,* and *collage,* they utilize social-conventional knowledge. The art of drama has many conventions, such as monologue, dialogue, skit, and rehearsal, and many dramatic techniques to learn. When children learn acceptable, respectful audience behavior for musical performances or learn what is expected when they visit an art museum or an art gallery, they are learning social-conventional knowledge.

Metacognition in Aesthetic Learning

A simple way to define *metacognition* is "thinking about thinking." Teachers help children think about their own

FIGURE 9.2 Commonly Used Terms in the Arts

Teachers use descriptive words that refer to various aspects or characteristics of the arts. Through repeated use, children learn to recognize and appreciate these characteristics. Following are some common terms used to describe the visual and musical arts, and examples of their usage.

Visual Arts Terms

Line
A mark that continues a dot made by a tool on a surface
"Look at the way that fork makes zigzag *lines* in the clay."
"Josh, you decided to paint curvy *lines* with the green paint."

Color
A characteristic or visual sensation of light
"What *colors* do you see in this picture?"
"How do you think these bright *colors* would look on black paper?"

Shape
Form; the outside edge of an object or an enclosed space
"Can you find the curved *shapes* in this design?"
"Angie is making her own abstract *shapes* with tissue paper."

Texture
The surface quality or how an object feels or looks
"Which wallpaper has a rough *texture*?"
"You made the grass in your picture look really *soft*."

Design
Composition; the overall combined elements
"You filled your paper with a busy *design*."
"How did you make your collage look so *happy*?"

Balance
Forms or spaces appearing to be in equilibrium
"The dark areas *balance* the light areas of this painting."
"Monica used symmetrical *balance* in her design."

Pattern
Recurring sequence of elements
"Look for the *pattern* in this picture."
"You're making *patterns* with that sponge."

Musical Arts Terms

Beat
The steady pulse of music
"Notice how the *beat* changes from fast to slow."
"Clap to the steady *beat* of this march."

Volume
The loudness or quietness of the music
"Please turn up the *volume* so that we can hear the music."
"When the *volume* goes down, make your arms go down."

Tone
Individual sounds or notes in music
"You're making lots of *tones* on that horn."
"This song starts with high *tones*, then has middle *tones*, and ends with low *tones*."

Melody
The tune or how tones move up and down in music
"You made up your own *melody*."
"When I hummed the tune, you recognized the *melody*."

Harmony
Combinations of tones sounded at the same time
"I love the *harmony* in that song."
"You and Andrew are making *harmony* together on the xylophone."

Rhythm
Groupings of long and short musical sounds
"Listen and clap to the *rhythm*."
"You're drumming a simple *rhythm*."

Tempo
Relative rate of speed of the musical piece
"This march has a fast *tempo*."
"Let's slow the *tempo* to a walk."

thought processes by asking carefully chosen questions at the appropriate times. In aesthetic learning, metacognitive processing is valuable for organizing thinking, making decisions about a sequence of steps, and helping students to develop greater insight into their self-expressive work. When a teacher responds to a child's unique idea by asking, "How did you figure that out?" the teacher encourages the student to consider the process that he or she used to arrive at a particular solution. Other questions that stimulate similar thinking are "How did you know?" "What clues are you using to help find your answer?" "What steps did you use to make your creation?" and "What made you choose that instead of this?"

CHILDREN'S ACQUISITION OF A FUNDAMENTAL KNOWLEDGE BASE FOR AESTHETIC DEVELOPMENT

Young children are naturally curious; because of this curiosity, the aesthetic domain is particularly relevant to them. Youngsters enjoy exploring nature, are motivated to create art and music, delight in the movement of dance, and spend hours in meaningful dramatic play. At first, the process of manipulating materials is more important to them than the product created. A youngster's early art, music, dance, or drama is made without regard to the effect of their work on others. Later, a greater need to communicate ideas and meaning becomes important to the child, and he or she begins to evaluate his or her work according to emerging aesthetic standards based on developing tastes and combined with messages received from the environment. Aesthetic milestones in the development of aesthetic preferences, musical interests, vocal music, instrumental music, creative movement, visual representations, and drama are described in this section.

Development of Aesthetic Preferences

Children's early aesthetic responses begin with sensory exploration of objects and sounds. A child may demonstrate preferences for a particular texture or smell, such as the soft edge on a blanket or a particular beloved toy. By age 5 years, children's preferences for certain kinds of music begin to surface. Many children as young as 3 or 4 years old begin to make choices from their environment, gathering and exploring collections of particular objects such as stones, seashells, or buttons. At a later stage, these collections become more sophisticated and must be acquired by deliberate searches. For some children the treasured objects may be bottle caps, coins, or baseball cards. Other children are fascinated by special dolls, models of horses, and so forth. In addition,

children are likely to enjoy spontaneous conversations about these special objects and demonstrate beginning levels of adult aesthetic evaluative behaviors—describing, analyzing, interpreting, and judging—but they often need help organizing their comments and applying criteria.

Development of Musical Interests

In infancy the appeal of music is usually the quality of sound. Babies often show interest when adults sing to them, in the sound of bells, and in soft music. As children grow and are exposed to various musical experiences, their interests broaden to include the element of melody. They learn to prefer what they become familiar with, particularly enjoying songs with repetition, in which the same melody is heard repeatedly. Examples of such songs are "Twinkle, Twinkle, Little Star" and "Old MacDonald Had a Farm." Later, children develop a keener interest in pitch—recognizing when sounds go up or down and discriminating when sounds have changed. Very young children have difficulty attending to more than one musical dimension (such as volume, rhythm, beat, or tempo) simultaneously, and when asked to make decisions about what they hear, they do not respond with any degree of accuracy. By age 5 or 6 years, many children demonstrate understanding of sound contrasts such as high–low, loud–soft, and up–down. Likewise, 6-year-olds can identify pairs of chords as same or different. Although educators understand that within any group of children of a given age, a wide range of musical abilities will be found, educators also know that musical interest and appreciation can be enhanced through a variety of regular musical experiences.

Development of Vocal Music (Singing) Behaviors

Infants explore musical sounds through vocal play and experimentation. Two-year-olds may produce "phrase songs," which consist of rhythmic repetition of a word or a phrase with pitch inflection close to that of speech. Much of their singing is self-generated and spontaneous, occurring as they explore sounds or "voice inflection play" (Bredekamp & Rosegrant, 1995, p. 102). By 3 years of age, many youngsters, if encouraged to express themselves musically, begin to impose structure on their improvisations by repeating selected patterns. Young children's pitch range of their spontaneous singing can be extensive. However, when children are learning songs by imitation, a more limited range seems to be most comfortable. Many 3-year-olds can sing whole songs and develop a large repertoire. As their vocal control is gained, boys and girls expand their range of usable pitches and can produce melodies more accurately. Later, they are able to fit together diverse rhythm patterns and appear to sense the function of form. By age 5 years, many children can use a steady, accurate beat; melody; and rhythm repetitions in their singing. The process of learning to sing in tune depends on opportunities, encouragement, and positive feedback so that they know they are matching pitches. Children in the early primary grades can learn songs that are reasonably complex. Songs with greater demands on memory and sequencing skills are not beyond most 6- to 8-year-old children.

Development of Instrumental Music Interests

Early in life, infants begin to intentionally make sounds by kicking or hitting objects. Their fascination with making sounds expands as they become more mobile. Young children do not initially use rhythm or melody instruments as a way to produce tunes, but rather to experience sound, such as the ring of a bell (Bredekamp & Rosegrant, 1995, p. 102). By age 3 years, children are creating patterns by repetitions, and by age 5 years, they can make a steady beat. Four- to six-year-olds are ready for more group experiences involving exploration of rhythm and melody instruments. Soon after, they become interested in the "right way" to play simple instruments. By age 6 years, some children begin to imitate conventional music patterns, and unfortunately they may lose some creative spontaneity. Youngsters at this stage benefit not only from plenty of opportunities to freely explore instruments, but also from encouragement to improvise melodies and create their own music.

Development of Creative Movement and Dance Interests

From the earliest days of life, babies respond to music through body movement. Even newborns become more active when lively music is played and calmer when slower, quieter music is played (Wilcox, 1994). Infants sway and bounce, and by age 18 months, they clap, tap, and spin in larger spaces. Two-year-olds tend to respond actively to rhythmic music, but each at his or her tempo. By 3 years old, children have gained greater coordination in movement; they enjoy moving and dancing creatively with others and participating in singing games that involve movement. From age 4 years to age 6 years, children increase in their ability to clap and march in response to a steady beat, and they enjoy participating in action songs such as "Shake My Sillies Out," "Here We Go Looby-Loo," and "The Hokey Pokey." They are becoming more skilled at synchronizing movement with the rhythmic beat of music. By age 6 to 8 years, children have mastered basic move-ments and can match these movements to music. They can also invent their own movements to music and are better able to follow more-complex directions in simple folk dances (Jalongo & Stamp, 1997).

Development of Creative Visual Art Expression

Children's artistic representations change and develop new characteristics as the children mature and have more experiences. Studies have shown that this change occurs in all cultures. Children go through a similar pattern of artistic growth everywhere in the world, but individual children go through the sequences at different rates and have unique outcomes (Koster, 1997). Toddlers take pleasure in the physical movement of a crayon, pencil, or marker and gradually notice the resulting marks they make on paper. The way these uncontrolled marks change was the subject of an enormous research project by Rhonda Kellogg from the 1950s through the 1970s. She collected and studied more than 1 million examples of children's drawings from around the world. In her unparalleled work, she analyzed the patterns in children's drawings and showed that marks made by youngsters the world over were similar. She identified and categorized 20 kinds of basic scribbles, studied various placement patterns, and investigated ways young children combined shapes (Kellogg, 1969, 1979). In Lowenfeld

The scribble stage

The preschematic stage

and Brittain's (1965) classic work, these researchers described developmental stages of creative representation from toddlerhood to adolescence (Table 9.2).

Children's drawings gradually change from random scribbling to controlled scribbles by the time the chil-

The schematic stage

dren reach age 4 years. Between age 4 years and age 7 years, youngsters develop a set of visual symbols of their own invention to represent familiar concepts that they apply to various media. They learn that their creations communicate messages to other people and begin to value the product. By age 8 years, a youngster can create drawings that are more complex and involve multiple views and details. These children are interested in many forms of artistic expression, and with encouragement they continue to refine their visual perceptions as they mature.

Descriptions of artistic stages are useful as guides for expectations at various ages and stages of development. However, many children reach these milestones much more quickly (C. M. Thompson, 1995a). Variations in development and children's previous experiences with the visual arts make a difference in artistic progress among children.

Development of Enactment or Dramatic Behaviors

Infants enjoy beginning enactment in such games as This Little Piggy and Peek-a-Boo. By age 1 year, most children can enact simple gestures meaning "eat" or "sleep" or can pretend to touch a forbidden object. By age 2 years, children are attempting to enact simple finger plays such as "The Eency Weency Spider" and are using real-life objects to take on familiar caregiving roles such as feeding or rocking a baby. Children from age 3 years to age 5 years become capable of *deferred imitation;* that is, they imitate movements of objects they have experienced in the past, even when the model is not present (Inhelder & Piaget, 1964). The amounts of pretend play and imaginative role-playing greatly increase during this period. Children 6 to 8 years old demonstrate continued interest in fantasy, but they demonstrate an emerging emphasis on nonfiction accounts of experiences in their play. As children learn to read and write, they may write and perform their own creative dramas, if they are encouraged. They also seek more elaborate props and begin to participate in more-formal types of drama. Development affects the kinds of aesthetic activities (Table 9.3) that children are likely to engage in.

AESTHETIC LEARNING AND THE TEACHER'S ROLE

The way in which teachers relate to aesthetics and the arts can greatly affect children's aesthetic development. When teachers nurture the arts in their classrooms, build on children's interests and abilities, encourage

TABLE 9.2 Stages of Creative Representation

Age range (yr)	Stage[a]	Description
	SCRIBBLING	**BEGINNINGS OF SELF-EXPRESSION**
2–4	Early scribbling	Disordered scribbles. Purely kinesthetic. Child is establishing motor coordination.
	Middle scribbling	Controlled scribbles. Child notices a connection between motions and resulting marks. Variety of motions increases. Color becomes useful to distinguish marks from background.
	Late scribbling	Child begins naming scribbles. Child's thinking changes from kinesthetic responding to having mental pictures. Child connects marks with world around him or her. Choice of color begins to have some meaning to child.
	PRESCHEMATIC	**FIRST REPRESENTATIONAL ATTEMPTS**
4–7	Early preschematic	Child controls motions to produce simple symbols that relate to his or her visual world (e.g., circles, vertical and horizontal lines). Symbols change often. Objects are randomly placed. Color choice relates to emotional reactions. Child produces a "person" symbol.
	Late preschematic	Child gains better motor control, which allows for experimentation with a variety of symbols. Exaggeration of certain symbols indicates importance. Color choices continue to relate to emotional reactions.
	SCHEMATIC	**ACHIEVEMENT OF FORM CONCEPTS**
7–9	Schematic	Child arrives at highly individualized visual symbols (or schemata) that satisfy him or her and are used repeatedly. Schemata represent child's active knowledge of objects; schemata change only when meaningful experiences influence child's thinking. Spatial relationships are not random.

[a]For descriptions of later stages—Dawning Realism: The Gang Age (9–11 yr.), The Pseudo-Naturalistic Stage (11–13 yr.), and Adolescence Art (13–17 yr.)—see *Creative and Mental Growth* (Lowenfeld & Brittain, 1965).

individual expression, and praise children's work, an enthusiasm for learning grows (Colbert, 1997). In addition, teachers can commit more time to this valuable part of the curriculum. We have only to look at the environment and the children's artwork from the Reggio Emilia schools to see that making art the heart of the curriculum has a strong impact on children's self-expression and learning. Teachers influence the extent to which students value the arts and provide a rich background of experiences that free children to become creative producers and tasteful consumers of the arts as adults.

How do teachers do this? Teachers who are the most effective in providing high-quality art experiences for young children know how to share their enthusiasm for the arts, focus on developing children's creativity, and strive to become more creative themselves.

CURRENT EDUCATIONAL ISSUES

Teachers and administrators are faced with many issues that affect their thinking, planning, and implementation of educational programs for young children. Some of the current concerns dealing with aesthetic development are discussed in this section.

Teaching the Arts Without Special Training

I have to teach art and music in my kindergarten classroom but I don't have the training. Isn't it best to leave those things to the specialists?

Teachers need not be artists or musicians to teach children to appreciate the arts and be aware of beauty

TABLE 9.3 Examples of Aesthetic Activities for Growing Children

Aesthetic component	Activities by age group		
	1- TO 3-YEAR-OLDS	3- TO 5-YEAR-OLDS	6- TO 8-YEAR-OLDS
Aesthetic preferences	Exploring natural objects, music, child-appropriate art objects (wood toys, dolls, bells).	Exploring and collecting objects. Describing what they like about valued objects and own work.	Exploring, collecting, describing, analyzing, interpreting, and evaluating objects, own work, and others' work.
Musical interests	Lullabies; musical toys; songs with repetitions; simple melodies (e.g., "Ring Around the Rosie").	Repetitive and cumulative songs; more-complex melodies. Guided music listening.	Wide variety of song types. Beginning to relate music to moods. Interest in musical notation.
Vocal music interests	Songs with simple tunes that repeat (e.g., "Twinkle, Twinkle, Little Star"); songs that use child's name ("Hello, Everybody").	Improvising; singing while swinging; songs with repetitions; substituting words (e.g., "Mary Wore a Red Dress").	Singing more-complex songs (e.g., "Swingin' on a Star"); silly songs (e.g., "A Peanut Sat on a Railroad Track"); rounds (e.g., "Make New Friends"). Musical notation.
Instrumental music interests	Manipulating objects with sounds (e.g., bell, xylophone, tambourine, triangle).	Simple instruments; music with defined beat and rhythm; cooperative instruments. Improvising.	Imitation of established melodies and rhythms. Some improvisation; using instruments with own songs.
Creative movement and dance behaviors	Spontaneous movement to music using arms and legs.	Singing and dancing games (e.g., "The Farmer in the Dell"); action songs (e.g., "Bingo"; "Head, Shoulders, Knees, and Toes"). Using props.	Improvising. Simple folk dances. Organized dance instruction.

Source: Adapted from *The arts in children's lives: Aesthetic education in early childhood,* by M. R. Jalongo & L. N. Stamp. (1997). Needham Heights, MA: Allyn & Bacon.

in their natural surroundings. Any personally productive experiences that teachers have had, whether writing a paper in college, decorating a home, or planning a vegetable garden, can help them identify with the act of creating.

> Every teacher does not have to be practiced in all media in order to think creatively. It is rather the intense experience accompanying any creative occupation that is important for keeping alive the teacher's appreciation and understanding of creative experiences of their students. (Lowenfeld & Brittain, 1965, p. 11)

Teachers who believe that the arts and a love of natural beauty are important, who openly demonstrate these attitudes, and who encourage children to involve themselves in creative endeavors do much to influence children's positive attitudes and aesthetic development, regardless of the teacher's specialized background or training.

Teachers are wise to utilize specialists if they are available, to observe strategies for motivating children and responding to their work, and to ask for advice concerning materials and techniques unfamiliar to them. However, teachers should avoid relying on specialists to provide the bulk of aesthetic experiences they offer. Instead, weekly plans should include activities for their particular group of youngsters, based on knowledge of individual and group needs and the unique understanding of the children that only classroom teachers can achieve. Children should have frequent opportunities for singing, making their own art, dancing, and enacting drama, in both planned and spontaneous activities each week.

Teaching the Arts by Using Adult-Designed Products

I have a number of art projects I do. The parents love it when the kids bring home their paper turkey all decorated the way I do. What's the harm?

Sometimes teachers fall into the trap of presenting art activities with a particular product in mind, one either designed by the teacher or found in a book. They may believe they are providing creative art, but nothing could be further from the truth. Listen as well-meaning Ms. Karley introduces the activity: "Today we're all going to make turkeys just like this one (holding up a completed brown paper tracing of a hand, with four fingers colored as feathers, and a head indicated with an eye colored on the thumb). First, you trace your hand on the paper I'll pass out, then take your red crayon and . . ." Some children enjoy following the directions but may think that the art project is not theirs. Many children find they cannot meet the adult standard that is set. When children are expected to follow step-by-step directions, severely limited to the teacher's ideas, choice of materials, and techniques, the child is forced to produce something that most likely holds no meaning for him or her. This situation can cause frustration and feelings of inadequacy as the child recognizes that the finished product does not look just like the teacher's.

Ms. Karley's good intentions for a fun activity result in children with negative attitudes about art and convince children that they are incapable. Moreover, activities such as this can be destructive to whatever creative thinking children bring to the activity, because all the finished work is intended to look alike and children are not reinforced for imaginative approaches to the task planned by the teacher.

Now consider how this activity could be presented in a way that encourages more creative thinking and results: "Does anyone know the name of this bird?" Mr. Tiehl holds up a large photograph of a real turkey. He asks, "What do you notice about it? Look carefully at the neck; did you notice that reddish-orange piece of skin? Has anyone ever seen a turkey? Where do you think you would find a turkey? Where else? What would that look like?" He listens, responding to children's thinking. "Ok, you had really good ideas. Today during work time you may go to the art table and make your own kind of turkey if you want. Remember, everyone's will be different because we all have our own ideas. There are some materials on the shelf nearby to use (pointing to baskets and trays holding a variety of paper, crayons, scissors, glue sticks, markers, yarn, real feathers, pipe cleaners, and scrap paper). If you want to use something that is not on the shelf, just ask me. I will come back and see how you are doing in a while. Your turkey could be big or little, fat or thin, whatever you want. Now who will be the first four at the center?" Children who are interested and motivated readily move to the art table. Those who want to make something different that day are also encouraged to take a turn. Finished works are hung or put aside to dry. The children produce a flock of unique creations that are personally satisfying. Children watch one another work, notice new things, and learn from one another. Mr. Tiehl has used the photograph as the only model for the children to follow and has facilitated children's learning instead of limiting it to an adult-designed stereotype.

Responding to Children's Creative Products

I don't know what to say to children when they show me their artwork. I don't want to say the wrong thing.

Traditionally, adults respond in a variety of ways to children's creations. Researchers have analyzed the impact of six kinds of adult responses: complimentary, judgmental, valuing, questioning, probing, and correcting. Each response affects the child, some in positive ways, but many in negative ways (Schirrmacher, 1986). Table 9.4 provides a summary of the impact of traditional adult responses to young children's creative work (Schirrmacher, 1986).

Frequently adults think children want an oral response to their work, when an unspoken signal such as a smile or a nod would be sufficient. However, when an oral response is requested—such as when the child asks, "Teacher, how do you like my picture?"—adults should avoid looking for representation (adult realism) and use a more effective approach. By focusing on one of the elements of the arts (e.g., line, color, texture), we encourage aesthetic awareness and open a dialogue if the child is comfortable discussing his or her work. Probing responses used occasionally also encourage children to talk about their work from their perspective. Listen to what the child says, and respond in terms of what is said, remaining interested but nonjudgmental. When children use obviously recognizable symbols, teachers should still remain as objective as possible. Indicate understanding of the meaning, but avoid showing preference for realism over abstract art. Table 9.5 provides examples of effective adult responses to children's art.

GOALS AND OBJECTIVES

Planning aesthetic activities is easier when teachers consider specific goals and objectives. Through the National

TABLE 9.4 Impact of Traditional Adult Responses to Children's Art

Response	Example	Impact on Child
Complimentary	"Very nice."	Cuts off discussion.
Judgmental	"Great work, Joey."	Empty comment with overuse. Child thinks anything he or she does is terrific, no matter how little effort is put forth.
Valuing	"I like that very much."	Puts emphasis on the product, not on the process. Too often rewards what is recognizable by adults; ignores personal expression that is not.
Questioning	"What is it?"	Insists it be something; disregards abstract expression. Disappoints the artist, who thinks its identity is obvious.
Probing	"Tell me all about your picture."	Encourages child to discuss; avoids passing judgment on child's work. Assumes that the child will enjoy and learn from verbalizing his or her ideas.
Correcting	"Very good, but the grass should be green."	Assumes that the child must copy reality. Discourages creative expression.

Standards for Arts Education (Consortium, 1994) and the Music Education Standards (Music Educators National Conference [MENC], 1994), music educators and arts educators have provided a set of useful goals and objectives for teachers to use.

The ultimate goal of education in the aesthetic domain is for children to become aware of, appreciate, and participate in creative processes that integrate feelings, thoughts, perceptions, and actions within the arts and other sensory experiences, as a way to achieve pleasurable, personally meaningful ends.

Intermediate Objectives

As children progress toward the ultimate goal, they will demonstrate the following 15 competencies:

1. Gain pleasure from natural beauty and other sensory experiences with no other goal in mind
2. Become familiar with various forms of the arts (visual art, music, dance, and drama)
3. Become familiar with various styles within a particular art form (e.g., in dance: ballet, tap, folk, and square)

TABLE 9.5 Effective Responses to Children's Aesthetic Products

Response	Examples	Impact on Child
Acknowledge effort.	"You worked a long time on it."	My hard work is noticed.
Recognize use of aesthetic elements.	"You used lots of different shapes." "The bright yellow areas look even brighter next to the dark gray ones."	Yes, I did. I didn't notice that. That looks good to me.
Indicate understanding of symbols.	"I noticed your tree has lots of fruit." "The people in your picture are standing in the rain."	Good; you know what I mean.
Acknowledge child's feelings.	"You're pretty proud of your collage. You're disappointed with your painting."	I don't have to feel the same way about all my art.
Ask for information.	"Show me a part you like." "Tell me something about your picture."	I can tell things about my art that only I know.
Broaden child's self-concept.	"You really like animals."	Yes, I guess I do.
Recognize progress.	"This is the third drawing you've made about our field trip."	I've accomplished a lot.

4. Use various materials, tools, techniques, and processes in the arts

5. Recognize and respond to basic elements of visual art (line, color, shape or form, texture, composition, balance, pattern, and space)

6. Recognize and respond to basic elements of music (beat, pitch, melody, rhythm, harmony, dynamics, tempo, timbre, texture, and form)

7. Recognize, reflect on, and discuss aesthetic experiences

8. Work collaboratively with others to create art, music, dance, or drama

9. Appreciate the arts as a means of communication

10. Recognize their own strengths as creative and performing artists

11. Engage in art and music criticism (describe, analyze, interpret, and judge)

12. Contribute to the aesthetic environment of the school

13. Develop a concept of the arts as a lifelong pursuit

14. Begin to understand and appreciate the arts in relation to history and culture, both their own and others'

15. Recognize and respond to connections between the arts and other disciplines

TEACHING STRATEGIES

Following are 20 teaching strategies that can be used to create meaningful aesthetic experiences for children:

1. *Model aesthetic awareness and enthusiasm.* Respond to the aesthetic qualities of the world around you. Point out the beauty you see in the sky, trees, clouds, rocks, and other natural objects. Talk about discoveries you have made and the enthusiasm you have about works of art or music you enjoy. Demonstrate a positive attitude about opportunities to be involved in the arts both in and out of this setting. Be a role model for how to be engaged in the arts. For example, tell children ways you are a participant or an observer (saw a theater performance, listened to music, played an instrument, or attended a recital).

2. *Prepare an aesthetics-friendly classroom environment.* Use the physical environment of the classroom to provide examples of aesthetic experiences. Mount and display children's artwork at their eye level. Occasionally play music for pure enjoyment during other activities. Encourage children to sing for pleasure at various times of the day, such as transition or departure times. Remove clutter and use low shelf tops as places for displaying plants, sculptures, and items of natural beauty such as seashells, flower arrangements, and beautiful rocks. Display reproductions of artists' work in the classroom as decorations or use them in art appreciation activities.

3. *Organize a creative arts center or a "creation station."* Maintain basic supplies in labeled containers, allowing easy access to them by the children. Store the more-specialized supplies for occasional use. Basic materials (see the following list) should be available for regular use by the children. Some early childhood educators favor the use of a great variety of materials, constantly introducing new and different materials to youngsters. These teachers are reluctant to offer the same materials 2 days in a row, perhaps for fear children will become bored. However, as Dr. Carol Seefeldt, Professor of Early Childhood and Child Development at the University of Maryland, warned,

> Children continually faced with new media are never able to gain control over, or develop skill in the use of, any one medium. Unless children have the opportunity to gain experience with basic media over time, they will find it difficult to achieve the skills required to use that medium as a means of artistic expression. *(C. Seefeldt, 1987).*

With this is mind, teachers should provide young children with frequent opportunities to use basic art materials so that they can develop this sense of mastery. Teachers can introduce basic materials, such as those listed next, and make them available regularly. For example, painting at the easel should be offered almost daily. Finger painting should be offered several times a month. Materials for drawing (crayons, pencils, or markers) on paper, as well as construction paper and scissors, should be provided daily.

Basic Art Materials for Young Children (see Figure 9.3)

- ❏ Tempera paints (primary colors [red, yellow, blue], white, and black)
- ❏ Watercolor paints (paint boxes with refillable colors, or larger paint cakes)
- ❏ Finger paints (primary colors) with finger-paint paper
- ❏ Drawing materials (crayons, pencils, markers)
- ❏ Paper (manila paper, newsprint, construction paper—white and a variety of colors)
- ❏ Art chalk (like pastels, softer than blackboard and sidewalk chalk)
- ❏ Glue (white, nontoxic), paste, glue sticks
- ❏ Modeling clay
- ❏ Modeling dough (homemade is easy; see Figure 9.4)

Basic Tools for Art

- ❏ Paintbrushes—various sizes and shapes
- ❏ Paint containers (cups with covers)
- ❏ Rollers, sponges, other objects used to apply paint

FIGURE 9.3 Inappropriate Art Materials for Young Children

> Some art materials are not appropriate for young children to use because they are unsafe or contain ingredients that can pose a threat to children if the materials are used without strict adult supervision:
> ❑ Oil-based paints
> ❑ Inks that are not water soluble
> ❑ Leaded paints of any kind
> ❑ Turpentine, paint thinners
> ❑ Asbestos products
> ❑ Chemically treated wood
> ❑ Toxic products or products that create toxic fumes, such as some adhesives
> ❑ Permanent markers

❑ Tape (transparent, masking)
❑ Scissors
❑ Staplers
❑ Paper fasteners
❑ Hole punches
❑ Recycled plastic containers of various sizes
❑ Tongue depressors or craft sticks
❑ Rulers
❑ Supply of newspapers

The following adhesives and materials can add variety and inspire creativity in art activities. Make these materials available when they are needed or requested.

Variety or Occasional Materials and Tools for Art

❑ Craft sticks
❑ Wood glue
❑ Glue sticks

❑ Glue–paste mixture (white school glue and white paste combined 1 : 1)
❑ Variety papers (paper towels, tissue paper, waxed paper, crepe paper, tinfoil, cellophane, etc.)
❑ Pipe cleaners
❑ Straws (plastic or paper)
❑ Thread, yarn, ribbon, string
❑ Wire
❑ Cardboard scraps
❑ Liquid starch (apply to manila paper for wet-chalk drawings)
❑ Wood scraps
❑ Glitter
❑ Recycled clean socks, T-shirts, gloves
❑ Cardboard boxes (salt, oatmeal, gift, shoe, milk, toothpaste)
❑ New or sanitized plastic foam meat trays
❑ Colored sand (mix powdered paint into play sand)

FIGURE 9.4 Recipes for Modeling Dough

Soft Dough
2 c. flour
1/2 c. salt
2 T. alum
3–5 drops food coloring
2 T. cooking oil
2 c. water

Boil water. Add salt and food coloring. Mix in oil, alum, and flour. Knead. Store in airtight container.

Baker's Clay Dough
1 1/2 c. salt
4 c. flour
1 1/2 c. water
1 tsp. alum

Mix dry ingredients; add water gradually. When a ball forms, knead dough well: add water if too crumbly. Shape. Bake at 325° F until hard.

Hardening Dough
1 c. water
3 c. salt
1 c. cornstarch

Mix water and salt; place pan over medium heat. Gradually mix in cornstarch; heat until mixture thickens into a mass. Cool on aluminum foil before kneading.

- Natural objects (leaves, stones, seeds, seashells, acorns, gourds, etc.)
- Paper cups, paper plates, paper napkins
- Paper tubes (paper towel, toilet paper)
- Magazines, wallpaper pieces
- Squeeze bottles
- Egg cartons
- Spray can tops, jar lids, milk jug lids, other plastic lids
- Old, clean toothbrushes
- Other small bits (buttons, sequins, beads, feathers, lace)

4. *Provide a variety of music-supporting materials.* Young children need a rich musical environment in which to grow (MENC, 1994). When children have many opportunities to explore and create with basic rhythm instruments, experiment with a variety of pitched instruments, and listen to many kinds of music, their enjoyment of and participation in musical experiences are greatly enhanced. The following music materials are recommended for early childhood programs.

Basic Rhythm Instruments

- Rhythm sticks (wooden dowels, lengths of broom handles, heavy straws, or heavy paper towel rolls)
- Maracas
- Triangles
- Jingle bells
- Sand blocks
- Tambourines
- Cymbals
- Drums

Basic Pitched Instruments

- Xylophones
- Tone bells

Children learn from exploring a variety of musical sounds.

- Simple wooden or plastic recorders
- Kazoos

Other Music Materials

- Record player with a variety of records
- Tape recorder with speakers and a collection of taped music
- Compact disk (CD) player with a collection of musical CDs
- Simple cassette tape recorder that can be used by children
- Chord instruments (such as guitar, autoharp, piano, keyboard)—these add interest and variety to children's singing but are not necessary for musical success in the classroom

5. *Provide a variety of creative movement props.* Movement is an important musical response because it is unspoken and allows the teacher to better understand the aspects of the music that the child is sensing (Bredekamp & Rosegrant, 1995). Simple props can motivate creative movement exploration:

Props for Creative Movement and Dance

- Plastic hoops
- Scarves of various colors
- Streamers or flags (e.g., crepe paper or strips of tissue paper attached to short, safe handles such as wide craft sticks or straws)
- Rhythm sticks
- Tambourines
- Paper towel rolls
- Pom-poms
- Batons

6. *Provide props for creative dramatics.* Supply the children with simple items to stimulate role-playing and creative dramatics:

- Props that suggest roles: fire helmets, short hoses, paper towel rolls, maps, boots, badges; cash register, play money, empty food containers, menus, plastic dishes, apron, play money, trays; steering wheel, earphones, board with knobs and dials
- Props related to familiar stories: "The Three Little Pigs": sticks tied together, cardboard bricks, ears, pot; "The Three Bears": three different-sized bowls, spoon, three chairs, three pillows; "Caps for Sale": felt rounds in various colors, monkey tails, chairs
- Props that stimulate imaginative stories: wand, top hat, cloak, crown, skirts, vests, purses, wallets, telephones, wigs, microphone, animal noses, masks, stuffed animals, hand puppets, and finger puppets

7. *Value all aspects of the creative expression process.* No matter what stage of development the child is in, teachers should recognize and value that level. Individual developmental differences are expected in any group of children. The way teachers and other supportive adults respond to the child's aesthetic products (e.g., the drawing, the dance, the song, or the dramatic production) will have lasting effects on the individual. Adult responses to children's attempts at creative expression either help establish an environment of acceptance and encouragement or clearly indicate to children that their own ideas will not be tolerated. In general, teachers should use praise judiciously. Be flexible and prepared for unique actions and products, such as when Anthony uses the props intended for "The Three Billy Goats Gruff" to create his own story about the planet Mars. Observe; engage the child in dialogue about his or her creation, showing interest and asking questions such as "Do your people from Mars have names?" or "How will they solve their problem of no food on Mars?" Show children you value their creative experimentation. Let children know you like when they use their own ideas in aesthetic activities, especially if these ideas are different from others' or yours. Use words such as "Your picture doesn't have to look like Matthew's. I like it when everyone's looks different; everyone has his own different ideas, and that's good."

8. *Teach children to respect and care for materials.* Teachers should demonstrate how to clean and store materials properly. For example, rhythm instruments should be carefully placed into storage containers at the end of the activity. Paintbrushes should be washed carefully and laid flat or handle down to dry. Watercolor paint boxes or paint cakes should be rinsed with clear water and left open to dry. Teach children to replace caps on markers to preserve their moisture for longer use. Paper scraps large enough to be used another day should be kept in a scrap collection box and recycled.

9. *Involve children in daily musical experiences.* All children sing; they begin as soon as they gain sufficient control over their voice to talk. Even teachers with little musical training, or those who believe they have a less than adequate singing ability, can share the joy of music with youngsters. At various times throughout the day, such as at transition times, during cleanup, at the opening of group meetings, or at the end of the day, teachers should sing songs with the class, play a recorded piece of music as background, or encourage children to clap along as they tap out rhythms with a tambourine.

10. *Motivate children's creativity in a variety of ways.*

❑ Demonstrate techniques that are new to children. Using the same materials that children will use,

Demonstrating new techniques motivates interest and creative thinking.

show ways to manipulate the tools and substances to achieve particular effects. Do not demonstrate how to make a picture or a recognizable product. Allow children to create their own ideas by using the techniques you demonstrate. For example, show the children how to use a glue stick or how to bend and add pieces of pipe cleaners together.

❑ Use motivational talk. Following demonstrations, engage children in discussions that encourage children to suggest ideas using the technique or material demonstrated. For example, say, "Using this way to flatten and roll the clay, think about what you might make; who has an idea?" or "Now that you know how to use the tape player, what songs will you record onto your tape?" Write their ideas on a list.

❑ Role-play ideas. One of the best ways young children learn about something is to experience the concept with their whole body. Children's artwork increases in creativity and detail following role-playing experiences. Using children's ideas, suggest they move like tall trees blowing in the wind, be a wave crashing to the shore, or crouch like tiny mice in the grass. Afterward, children can apply these ideas to making pictures, performing a drama, or creating a dance.

❑ Show photographs or actual objects and talk about them. This kind of motivation can help children make connections to prior knowledge, notice more detail, enhance the appeal of expressing their perceptions, and break down simplistic ideas they may have formulated through other experiences. For example, shown a picture of a thunderstorm, children can use the rhythm instruments to create their own storm with great gusto.

❑ Encourage imagining. Suggest that children close their eyes and imagine something that is very different from here and now; for example, ask them what they might see, hear, and smell if they were standing at the seashore or walking deep in a forest. For older children, suggest that they change their perspective, such as imagining what they could see when looking down from a very tall tree or while flying over the rooftops, or what it would be like walking on a distant planet. Ask them to describe what they are picturing in their minds and encourage them to listen to one another's ideas. Suggest that they express their ideas in a story, drawing, or creative dance.

11. *Use unspoken signals.* Rather than giving oral praise directed at their work, respond positively to children's efforts, enthusiasm, and concentration by using smiles, a nod, an occasional pat on the back, or a thumbs-up as they create. This strategy can be extremely reinforcing, but use it sparingly to avoid imposing your judgement.

12. *Connect creative experiences to concepts children are exploring.* Mrs. Martin's kindergartners are learning about opposites (such as high–low, fast–slow, big–small, warm–cool). After brainstorming examples, she challenges them to use creative movement or art materials to express two opposite words they select. After they have practiced, she videotapes their movement efforts. Some students draw pictures illustrating the concepts, and others use play dough.

13. *Explore materials before asking children to use them.* Spend a few minutes with materials that are new to children before the children use them. Become familiar with what these materials can do and discover problems children may encounter. For example, if the paint is too runny, add thick paint or detergent to avoid drips and disappointed artists. If the autoharp is out of tune, take time to tune it to make the sounds more appealing.

14. *Avoid making a product when you are demonstrating a technique.* Be sure to introduce the class to any new technique or process (e.g., cutting, gluing, sanding, pouring, rolling) that may need explanation. For example, show children how to hold down the buttons on the autoharp to create different chords, while strumming lightly across the strings. Show ways to apply glue to Styrofoam—where it is most needed and the appropriate amounts to use. However, keep in mind the importance of focusing on the technique (or process) instead of any subject matter during a demonstration. When demonstrating techniques, avoid making a recognizable object. The reason for this practice is simple:

Whatever the teacher makes will establish an extremely strong model; children will feel the need to copy it. Children will believe that this is the product the teacher wants and abandon their ideas. Even very creative individuals have difficulty thinking beyond what their teacher shows them as "the correct way." For example, Mr. Sanders demonstrates the techniques of crayon resist to his kindergartners. He stresses pressing hard with the crayons so that the drawing will show through the paint. He uses crayons on white paper to show some light lines and some heavy lines instead of making shapes (such as flowers or a house) with the crayons. Afterward, as he paints over the lines, he guides the children to notice which lines showed up the best, instead of focusing on what a beautiful picture he made. After the demonstration, he asks children to tell what kinds of pictures they might make by using these techniques. The children are motivated to engage their own creative thinking.

A different way of focusing on the technique instead of the subject matter is to make an imaginary product during the demonstration; that is, present the steps of the process, gesturing with the tools, without actually making anything and without showing a finished product. For example, to demonstrate making paper bag puppets, put your hand inside a small plain paper lunch sack and show how it might become a creature, gesturing where the mouth might be, where ears might go, and possible positions of other features children suggest.

15. *Give children the gift of time.* Support children's aesthetic development by giving them time for the essentials—to become familiar with materials in an unhurried, uninterrupted, and unstructured way without insisting that they "make something." Children need time to repeat aesthetic experiences, including time to watch others who are engaged. Do not waste children's time by filling it with coloring sheets and other adult-designed activities aimed at making specific objects. These activities rob children of valuable time for developing skills and using marks to create meaning (Kolbe & Smyth, 2000).

16. *Accept children's ideas for creative movement, art expression, music, and drama.* Avoid overdirecting; remember that creative activities should provide opportunities for self-expression; expect students to individually respond to suggestions from you or to the music or materials. Encourage children to look at one another's creative responses occasionally. Allow individuals to volunteer to share their ideas, but avoid requiring them to perform.

17. *Discover and use picture book illustrations as works of art.* Every year, new and wonderful children's books are published that contain perfect examples of visual artistic expression. Teachers should share at least one beautiful book with their students each day. Help

children (a) discover the joy of art available to hold in your hand, (b) explore and recognize techniques, and (c) open doors to insights. Before (or after) reading the story each day, take time to introduce each picture as a painting, discussing the visual qualities. What child has ever read Maurice Sendak's *Where the Wild Things Are* (Sendak, 1963), Lois Ehlert's *Eating the Alphabet: Fruits and Vegetables from A to Z* (Ehlert, 1989), or Rylant's *The Relatives Came* (Rylant, 1985) without pausing to look at the incredible pictures? Teachers should treat books as priceless gifts and each illustration as a gem to be treasured. This demonstration of appreciation can influence children to develop a lifelong interest in collecting good art and owning beautiful books.

Other activities using book illustrations for various purposes are the following:

❑ Find a selected artistic technique, such as Eric Carle's painted papers, in a collection of books.
❑ Explore the various ways in which a particular subject is depicted by different artists—for example, grandmothers, as portrayed in picture books such as *Charlie and Grandma,* by Sally Ward (1986); *Gifts,* by JoEllen Bogart (1994); *My Grammy,* by Marsha Kibbey (1988); and *Bigmama's,* by Donald Crews (1991).
❑ Study and imitate an illustrator's use of materials (technique), such as collage, in any book by Ezra Jack Keats; use of colored clays, as in *Gifts,* by Jo Ellen Bogart (1994); or use of a mixed media technique, as in pictures by Leo Lionni.

18. *Use different kinds of questions to help children describe, analyze, interpret, and judge works in the arts.* Questions can extend children's ability to respond to the arts. Using various kinds of questions regarding the arts, elicit a variety of kinds of thinking from children:

❑ *Cognitive memory questions* motivate thinking about facts (e.g., "What do you see (or hear)?" "What are some words to describe this?")
❑ *Convergent questions,* or *closed questions,* have expected answers (e.g., "What is the largest thing in this painting?" "What's the slowest part?")
❑ *Divergent questions,* or *open-ended questions,* have many possible answers (e.g., "Why do you think the artist used black in this picture?" "How does this music make you feel? Why?")
❑ *Evaluative questions* ask for children's values (e.g., "What part of that dance did you like the best?" "Which shell is your favorite? Why?")

19. *Avoid reinforcing only a realistic approach to the arts.* Children recognize when teachers truly value individual differences. Teachers who reward (in spoken or unspoken ways) only work that contains naturalistic symbols of real objects, and ignore more-abstract expressions, severely limit young children's creative expression of thoughts, feelings, and events. Young children often experiment with materials without intending to relate their finished product to reality, or their inner thoughts. They may be fascinated by the way the colors change when they touch each other, or how the sand sticks to the glue and not to the paper. Adults who insist that they "see something" in children's pictures impose the value of realism that can force children into this singular mode of expression and the frustration of such limits. If, instead, we focus on the artistic elements of the work (such as color, lines, arrangement of shapes), or the effort expended by the artist, children see that they are free to use whatever means of expression they want, without worrying that their work will be devalued.

20. *Involve all the children in the arts.* The arts provide opportunities for success for all students, regardless

FIGURE 9.5 Example of Involving a Child with Special Needs in the Arts

Paul

Paul is a child who demonstrates giftedness in many areas. At age 6 years, he is surprisingly perceptive, has extensive general knowledge, learns basic skills quickly, and, when interested, becomes deeply absorbed for long periods (Kostelnik, Onaga, Rohde, & Whiren, 2002). He is fascinated by all kinds of ships, collects models and pictures of ships, and often spends time drawing ships. He enjoys telling adults about what he knows, but he finds that other children are not as interested in ships as he is. His teacher believes that Paul's strong interest is important and should be nurtured. She offers library books on the subject, takes time to discuss what he has discovered, and encourages Paul to use art materials to create his own ships. She recently introduced Paul to papier-mâché, suggesting that he might design a ship with craft sticks. As this new project takes shape, Paul is learning new techniques with materials and the value of planning to achieve a goal. Several children in the class are taking an interest in Paul, asking him about his ship.

Note: Papier-mâché is an advanced technique that may be difficult for children who lack experience with other three-dimensional construction materials (e.g., clay, wood, or pipe-cleaner sculpture); it also requires controlled eye–hand coordination, and more-advanced skills in planning.

All children benefit from aesthetic experiences.

of their abilities or disabling conditions. Activities with various visual art media and music should be adapted to allow as much participation as possible according to the child's individual needs. Creative dramatics and movement should be approached in an open-ended manner to provide success on many levels for all children, including students with special needs (such as giftedness; see Figure 9.5).

APPROACHES TO TEACHING THE ARTS

As you learned in chapter 3, different approaches can be taken to teaching anything. Some approaches are more teacher controlled, some are more child controlled, and others share the control between teacher and child. Just as these approaches can be applied to teaching in general, they also apply to teaching in the arts. The various approaches can be thought of as a continuum from closed to open approaches. The more aspects of the activity the teacher controls, the more closed it is. The fewer aspects of the activity the teacher chooses, and the more the child selects for him- or herself, the more child controlled, or open, the experience is. Figure 9.6 shows this continuum of teaching approaches and how it relates to the arts. Notice the variety of dimensions of the art activity that can be more or less controlled by the teacher: *Materials* include all physical objects and tools needed for the activity—for example, paint, wood, glue, or salt. *Techniques* are how the materials are manipulated—for example, gluing sand on paper, cutting cloth strips, applying tissue paper, and so forth. The *subject* is the topic or theme of the activity—for example, birds, ocean, family, germs, and so forth. The *product* is what the finished work will look or sound like—for example, a map, a list, a picture, an ornament, and so forth.

Consider examples of the three teaching approaches. For our purposes, the examples will relate to visual art; however, teaching any of the arts (music, creative movement, drama, dance) applies.

Mr. Stein plans a finger-painting activity that is completely *teacher controlled*. He chooses the paper, cuts it to 8 × 11 in., and selects blue paint (the materials). He describes the technique of applying blue paint with a spoon and using fingers to spread it on the paper. He tells the children they will all be making pictures of the sky (the subject) and that their paintings (the product) will be hung on the wall when they are dry. As the children paint, he reminds them of the way they are supposed to work, pointing out that they should stop "messing around" with the paint and make their sky pictures. All the children produce similar blue paintings, which pleases Mr. Stein because he plans to glue one die-cut bird to each painting to go along with their theme—birds. After their paintings dry, most children have difficulty differentiating which painting belongs to whom. Some children toss their paintings into the trash. Children react negatively to the experience.

Ms. Porter's approach to art is completely *child controlled*. Children are free to work with any materials they want, using whatever techniques they devise. They may select any subject and produce any product they want. Ms. Porter does not enter the art area, assuming

FIGURE 9.6 Continuum of Teaching Approaches

Teacher Controlled ————————	Shared Control ————————	Child Controlled
Teacher chooses all materials		Child chooses materials
Teacher chooses techniques		Child chooses techniques
Teacher chooses subject		Child chooses subject
Teacher's product		Child's product

that doing so would interfere with children's creativity. Today, during free-choice time, a few children enter the art area, look around, then leave. One child spends her whole free-choice time in the area, using markers, scissors, yarn, and glue to make a picture for her mom. Ms. Porter notices that few children use the art area, even though they have many choices, and she wonders why.

Mrs. Alvarez's approach to teaching art is *shared control*. She plans some aspects of the activity but leaves many aspects open for children to choose. She arranges newspaper on one end of the art table and lays smocks on three chairs. She prepares plastic containers of red, blue, yellow, and white finger paint, placing them on the newspaper with a plastic spoon in each. She wets a clean sponge and puts it on a dish near the paint. She also lays a pencil and one piece of finger-paint paper in front of each chair. As children arrive, she gathers them together and demonstrates how to use the materials if they choose to finger paint today. As she moves the red paint on her paper, she asks them to tell her what she could paint. She listens to their ideas and makes observations such as "Rachel, you're thinking about making handprints with the paint" and "Jose, you want to make your dog." She purposely does not make a recognizable picture but instead focuses on a variety of ways to move her fingers in the paint, hoping that doing so will inspire additional thinking. She asks open-ended questions such as "What if I used two colors of paint?" and "How could I make my picture look as if the wind is blowing?" Afterward, as she demonstrates washing her hands in a bucket, she suggests that they begin a waiting list because only three children can finger paint at a time. During the morning, she checks in to see how the painting is progressing. She notes that most of the children have signed up to paint. She comments on how well the children are taking turns and remembering to wear smocks. She points out that Michelle found her own way to use her fingers in the paint. She remarks that each painting is unique. David chooses to use the other end of the table to make his creation out of crepe paper, construction paper, and glue that he finds in labeled containers on the art shelf. Mrs. Alvarez smiles and gives them a thumbs-up. When their creations are dry, the children easily find their own and are eager to tell about them. Later, many of the children write or dictate a story about their experience. Mrs. Alvarez facilitates learning through the physical setup, demonstration, discussion, and choices. Her teaching approach provides a balance of teacher control and child control as well as independence and sensitive intervention without her monopolizing the activity. She has motivated children to think and solve problems; has taught them about technique, sharing, and cooperation; and has given them new insights into themselves as artists.

ACTIVITY SUGGESTIONS

As described in chapter 3, six generic activity types form the basis for planning and teaching. Following are examples of some of these activity types as they apply to the aesthetic domain.

✎ Oh Up! Oh Down! (For Children of All Ages)

Objective 4 For children to use various materials, tools, techniques, and processes in the arts.

Materials Book

Procedure After reading or hearing a story that the children particularly enjoyed, suggest that the group stand up and form a circle or stand facing each other. Tell children that they are going to use their bodies to become people, animals, or objects in the story. Teach them signals to use to begin and end their dramatic interpretations: "Oh-up" means to stand up and begin; "Oh-down" means to stop and crouch down. Have everyone go down into a crouch; then say, "When we come up, we're all going to be (e.g., the papa bear tasting his porridge). Oh-up! . . . (do it with them) . . . Oh-down!" Orally reinforce creative ideas that children use. Repeat the procedure, using other ideas. Encourage children to participate, but do not force them. If some children insist on watching, select a place nearby where they may easily join in if they change their mind.

To simplify Select ideas that are obvious and easy to visualize (e.g., "Be the baby bear crying over his broken chair" or "Be Goldilocks going to sleep in the bed"). Do this for a short time and end before the children become tired.

To extend After the obvious ideas, select some ideas that are more subtle (e.g., "Be the chair that breaks when Goldilocks sits down" or "Be the door that opens when she knocks"). Let children take turns being the leader, suggesting ideas. Alternatively, use this as a warm-up exercise before having the children act out the whole story as a class.

✎ Pitch Play (For Older or More Experienced Children)

Objective 6 For children to recognize and respond to basic elements of music (pitch).

Materials Pitched instruments

Procedure Teach children how to have musical "conversations" that involve matching pitches, with one person leading and the other responding like an echo. Demonstrate with another adult or a competent child. Suggest that the child listen to what you sing, then repeat your words using the same sounds (matching pitches). For example, the leader sings, "Hel-lo," using two pitches, one for each syllable. Response: "Hel-lo." Practice this strategy, using various words, until doing so becomes easier.

Next, have the child lead, and you reply with different words but matched pitches. The leader sings, "Hel-lo." Response: "Hi-there."

Finally, switch roles again and have the student make up his or her response to your lead, still matching your pitches.

To simplify   Start simple, using one-pitch conversations.

To extend   Use two sets of pitched instruments, such as bells or xylophones, using the same procedure: One leads, the other echoes. Be sure to start with two pitches that are very different (high–low) and gradually use those that are more difficult to distinguish (high–middle) or (middle–low).

✎ Listen to This! (For Older or More Experienced Children)

Objective 3   For children to become familiar with various styles within a particular art form.

Materials   Tape recorder, collection of short passages of various kinds of music

Procedure   Arrange a tape recorder or record player and a collection of musical pieces in a quiet corner of the room. Encourage children to take turns listening to the music selections alone or with a friend. To focus attention on appreciation of the range of styles, select music that varies greatly, such as folk, rock, classical piano, catchy tunes from commercials, television theme songs, marching band music, part of a symphony, chamber music, and jazz. If you are making your own tape, organize the selections with blank spaces between them so that children can easily distinguish beginnings and endings.

To simplify   Limit the number of music styles to two or three.

To extend   Ask children to bring in samples of various music that they enjoy at home. Encourage parents to contribute to a collection of samples, especially requesting music from various cultures.

✎ Let's Stick Together (For Older or More Experienced Children)

Objective 4   For children to use various materials, tools, techniques, and processes in the arts.

Materials   Clay, cutting tools, water

Procedure   Potter's clay offers opportunities for three-dimensional sculpture and ceramic design. However, occasionally in the drying process, attached pieces fall off. Discuss this fact with the children, and demonstrate a process in which clay pieces are attached so that this will not happen. Prepare two pieces of clay to attach. Using a tool that makes shallow cuts (such as a table knife, fork, or wooden ceramic tool), score crosshatching lines into the surfaces to be joined. Then apply plain water with a finger to wet both scored surfaces and produce a slippery "glue." Press the pieces together and blend the clay to completely cover the line of attachment. Give children clay, tools, and water, and encourage them to practice attaching pieces.

To simplify   Offer children large (fist-sized) pieces to attach; set these aside to dry.

To extend   Invite children to think of things that have parts (e.g., animals have legs, a head, and a tail) to attach. Brainstorm ideas. Encourage them to work on their own creations, using the technique demonstrated.

✎ Art Talk (For Children of All Ages)

Objective 7   For children to recognize, reflect on, and discuss aesthetic experiences.

Materials   None

Procedure   Plan an aesthetic experience for the class, such as experimenting with watercolor paints on wet paper or listening to the music of "Fantasia" on tape. Afterward, gather children together to discuss what they remember, know, think, and value about the experience. Ask questions such as "What did you see or hear? What do you remember about that?" (cognitive memory questions), "What colors of paint were we using today?" (convergent question), "What words can we use to describe different parts of this music?" (divergent question), and "How did you like this activity?" (evaluative question).

To simplify   Ask only one or two questions. Keep the discussion short but listen to everyone's reply.

To extend   Follow up the discussion by having children draw, write, or dictate their feelings and thoughts about the experience.

✎ What Does It Mean? (For Older or More Experienced Children)

Objective 9   For children to appreciate the arts as a means of communication.

Materials   A sign, reproductions of paintings, crayons or markers, paper

Procedure   Point to a written sign or message in your classroom. Read it aloud and ask what the message tells us. Discuss the fact that some art, music, and dance communicate ideas to an audience without using words. Show children a print of a painting that has an appropriate and understandable message, such as Degas' *Dancers With Fans* (Abrams, 1985), depicting ballet dancers on a stage, or Homer's *Snap the Whip* (Abrams, 1985), showing young boys playing in a schoolyard. Do *not* tell children the title. Ask the children to look carefully, notice details about the picture, and tell what they think the artist was communicating. Let students know that there are no "right" answers, that anyone's ideas can be valid, and that sometimes the same work has many messages. Accept all ideas. Later, tell children about how each piece of art has a title, which helps us to understand the message of the picture. Tell the children the title of the picture and listen to children's comments. Follow this by providing familiar drawing materials (crayons or markers, and paper) and suggest that children make a picture with a message. Display the pictures and give students time to look at and speculate about what message each might be communicating. Ask each artist to tell what the message is and to give the work a title. Display titles with their pictures.

To simplify   Relate the concept of artistic messages to other unspoken messages such as gestures, facial expressions, and body language. Use the obvious messages, and use examples that communicate more obviously.

To extend   Show an example of a painting in which the message is less obvious, more abstract, and nonrepresentational, such as Mondrian's *Broadway Boogie Woogie* (Abrams, 1985), a composition of geometric shapes, or Miro's *Hirondelle/Amour* (Abrams, 1985), a colorful work with lively shapes open to many interpretations. Encourage children to offer opinions about what the artist is communicating.

✎ Object Prints (For Younger or Less Experienced Children)

Objective 4   For children to use various materials, tools, techniques, and processes in the arts.

Materials   Paint, pans, sponges, paper towels, collection of interesting objects, paper

Procedure   Introduce object printing by demonstrating the down–up motion used to make prints on paper with various objects. Prepare several shallow pans of paint in a variety of colors. Pour the paint onto flat sponges or layers of paper towels, and offer a selection of interesting objects (wooden spools or other wooden shapes, small pieces of sponge, dowels, potato

mashers, corrugated cardboard pieces, cotton swabs, forks, plastic cups, a small pine tree bough, pine cones, etc.) to print with. Provide large-sized paper to print on, giving children a selection of color. Encourage children to experiment with the various objects and to fill their paper with interesting printed shapes.

To simplify   Limit the number of objects or the number of paint colors. Hammer a nail into wooden shapes to make them easier to manipulate.

To extend   When the prints are dry, ask children to try to recall which object they used to make an individual shape on the print. Another time, have children make their own collections of objects to print.

✎ Name That Tune (For Younger or Less Experienced Children)

Objective 6   For children to recognize and respond to basic elements of music (melody).

Materials   None

Procedure   Teach and practice singing a number of simple children's songs with the children, such as "The Eency Weency Spider," "She'll Be Comin' 'Round the Mountain," "Mary Had a Little Lamb," "Yankee Doodle," "Old MacDonald Had A Farm," and so on. After the tunes have become familiar to the children, explain that you are going to play a game with the class. Hum without using the words (or use a kazoo) to create the melodies, asking children to listen and name each song.

To simplify   Use short, simple songs that children know well.

To extend   Teach the class some new songs and try this exercise. Try it again the following day, without singing them with words first.

✎ Feel the Beat (For Younger or Less Experienced Children)

Objective 6   For children to recognize and respond to basic elements of music (beat and tempo).

Materials   Recorded music with a strong beat, rhythm sticks or tubes, tambourine

Procedure   Play a number of recorded instrumental selections with an obvious beat (a steady pulse) and a variety of tempos (relative speed of the beat). An audiotape demonstrating different kinds of music can be made with pauses between short musical segments. Play the tape and respond to the beat with your hands (clap hands, slap thighs). Have the children begin in a sitting position, and say, "Listen to the music. Feel the beat. Clap on the beat with me." Do not expect young children to match the beat exactly. Next, suggest that children move their hands a different way to the beat (punch the air, point a finger, wave, etc.). Suggest that the children move more of their body to the beat (nod their head, shrug their shoulders, sway their hips, step in place, walk to the beat).

To simplify For children who do not feel the beat, help them by placing their hands over yours as you clap. Then switch, having your hands cover theirs. Try using an oral cue on the beat to help children become more aware. Say, "Beat-beat-beat-beat-beat" or "Clap-clap-clap-clap." Younger children are better able to keep time with a moderate tempo than with a slower tempo.

To extend Offer children simple rhythm instruments on which to tap the beat of the music, such as rhythm sticks or empty paper towel tubes. Demonstrate tapping on the floor, softly on a shoe, or on the thigh. Explain the terms *beat* and *tempo;* play a game in which children take turns demonstrating a fast tempo, a slow tempo, and a medium tempo by hitting a tambourine as everyone else moves in time to the beat.

✎ **My Own Song (For Children of All Ages)**

Objective 10 For children to recognize their own strengths as creative and performing artists.

Materials None

Procedure Model and encourage children to select familiar tunes and sing their own words to them. For example, to the tune of "Frère Jacques," or "Are You Sleeping?" sing, "Going home now, going home now, going home, going home, going going home, going going home, going home, going home."

To simplify Suggest that children sing their name using the melody of a familiar, simple song, such as "Mary, Mary, Mary, Mary, Mary, Mary, Mary, Mary, . . ."

To extend Encourage children to use more-extensive personal descriptions with the melody. "Frère Jacques" can sound like "My name's Sandy, my name's Sandy, how are you, how are you, I live in a yellow house with a dog named Patches, I like school, I like school."

SUMMARY

Teaching through the arts is a satisfying process. When children engage in arts that are truly meaningful to them, so-called art from the heart, teachers share the excitement of these creative experiences. Seeing children express wonder at the beauty of butterfly wings gives us hope for future adults who appreciate nature. Encouraging children to respectfully handle a wooden sculpture or to listen to the "March of the Toy Soldiers" with their eyes closed inspires imagination and creative thinking. Supporting children as they examine samples of wallpaper to decide what they like and do not like focuses children on the notion that art is all around them and that they can have preferences that are worthwhile. Recognizing that a child has grown in his or her ability to create music, art, dance, or drama helps teachers realize the power of the arts to enrich lives.

Applying What You Read in This Chapter

1. Discuss
  a. After considering the value of creative art, think about how you feel about using coloring books and coloring pages with young children. Discuss your thinking with a partner, giving a rational argument for your stance.
  b. Obtain an example of a child's artwork. Consider several ways in which you, as his or her teacher, could respond appropriately to the child's work. Tell how each response may affect the child.
  c. Talk about the ways in which teachers can use music in the classroom. List as many ways as you can think of.

2. Observe
  a. Locate a program or a school that has an arts (art, music, dance, creative movement, or drama) specialist working with the children. Arrange to observe as the specialist works with a group. Take notes on the strategies, techniques, and content of the lesson. Discuss your observations. How does what you observed relate to the goals and objectives for the arts in this chapter?

3. Carry out an activity
  a. Plan a music activity using musical instruments to teach two of the following musical concepts: beat, rhythm, tempo, and pitch. Carry out the activity with a group of children. Consider how the children responded. Evaluate your results.
  b. Select a familiar story for children to enact. Make, or encourage children to make, a collection of props that will stimulate them to act out the story. Plan how you will introduce the story and props to

the children and how you will motivate them to participate in the activity. Help children think of the gestures, movement, and dialogue that would help tell the story.

4. Create something for your portfolio

a. Review the three teaching approaches described in this chapter. Think about which approach you will primarily use with the arts and why. Create a statement describing your choice and tell how it fits with your philosophy of education.

5. Add to your journal

a. Consider your background in the arts. What formal and informal experiences did you have as a child? Were they positive or negative? Think about your current participation in the arts. What experiences influenced this participation? Consider how this affects your disposition toward teaching the arts.

APPENDIX

✎ Field Trip to Art Musem

Take the class to an art gallery. Visit ahead of time, taking note of which pieces would interest the group. Purchase postcard prints of some of the artwork. Distribute these to small-group leaders, along with suggestions for things to point out. Encourage the groups to move slowly through the exhibits, looking for the artwork depicted on the postcards. Move among the small groups, asking questions to motivate children to notice variety in the use of materials, subject matter, and kinds of art (paintings, drawings, sculpture; carved designs, etc.) represented.

To simplify Go for a short time. Arrange for very small groups or pairs of children assigned to each adult. Prepare adults to look at things in general, stopping to analyze the pieces that children show interest in.

To extend Plan a longer visit. Prepare children for some particular pieces of artwork that they will see. Analyze these pieces carefully as the children discover them. Plan follow-up activities of drawing or painting something they remember.

✎ Artists in Our Town

Invite a visual artist, a musician, a dancer, or an actor (one of the parents or a community person) to visit the class. Ask this person to bring samples of his or her work and the tools necessary to perform the work. Ask your guest to demonstrate the art form and discuss how he or she became interested in this type of art. Encourage children to ask questions.

To simplify Keep the presentation short (10 minutes). Arrange the artist and his or her tools in an area of the classroom where children can talk with him or her during free-choice time.

To extend Send a note home to parents asking them to help their child find someone they know (in their family or neighborhood) who is an artist, a musician, a dancer, or an actor. Explain that your objective is to help children understand more about art in the culture. Ask them to help their child talk to this person and find out information about him or her (e.g., what kind of artist are you? How did you get interested in that? How old were you when you started?). Provide time for children to report to the class about the artist they found, or invite the artists to come as visitors.

The Affective Domain

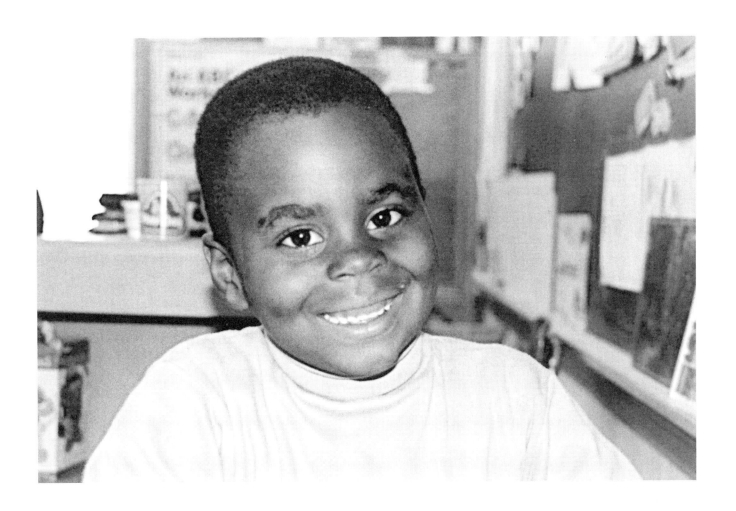

You may wonder:

How do children develop self-awareness and a secure sense of self?

What is *intrapersonal intelligence*? How does it relate to a child's sense of self? Is it different from emotional intelligence?

How do variations in children's personality development influence their self-esteem?

How can I help children who are not coping well with stress to develop greater resilience?

How can I actively foster healthy self-esteem in young children?

In this chapter on the affective domain, we present information to help you answer the preceding questions.

Before continuing to read this chapter, take another look at the child pictured on the previous page. You might describe him as relaxed and happy. People who know him would add that he is friendly to others, emotionally healthy, and highly competent. At 6 years of age, he has a secure sense of self. The emotional repertoire that we all need in order to contend with everyday life challenges— self-awareness, self-esteem, self-respect, belief in ourselves and in our future, and feelings of competency—is forged in childhood. It depends heavily on how well each of these various aspects is nurtured in our earliest years.

In early childhood settings in which professionals take an active role in supporting children's affective development, we can see numerous examples of their efforts: a teacher comforting a preschooler who is distressed that his mother has left; a teacher conducting a group discussion with the class about a beloved guinea pig who has died; a teacher offering genuine praise to a child who has worked carefully through a challenging math story problem; and a teacher helping a child develop an oral script that might assist the child in entering a play group of peers. These teachers recognize that facilitating emotional health and resilience in young children begins with establishing a warm and supportive classroom environment. In addition, such teachers know they must actively build components into the everyday curriculum that promote children's growth in becoming self-aware, making personal decisions, managing intense feelings and emotions, and handling stress. Children must also be given guidance about taking others' feelings and concerns into account, communicating with others, developing personal insight and assertiveness, learning self-acceptance, and taking personal responsibility (Goleman, 1997).

CHILDREN'S DEVELOPING SELF-AWARENESS AND SENSE OF COMPETENCE

Newborns have no sense of self as apart from their immediate caregiver. However, by the time they are a year and a half old, they are clearly beginning to understand the differences between themselves and others. We see this understanding in their frequent use of the word *mine*, their delight in identifying themselves in pictures and mirrors, and their increasingly correct usage of pronouns when they are referring to others. During the preschool years, children use physical attributes to describe their uniqueness ("I'm a boy. I'm three. I live in a blue house!"). Somewhat later, they begin to compare themselves with others ("I can run faster than my little brother!"), and by early elementary school, they are defining themselves in terms of psychological traits ("I turn my work in on time") and internal states and beliefs ("I hate it when I can't stay up to watch TV!"; Kostelnik, Whiren, Soderman, Stein, & Gregory, 2002).

Fully in tandem with growing self-awareness is the child's emotional development. Learning appropriate ways to express every aspect of their personality is one of the most difficult jobs young children have. Children struggle daily with refining self-help and social skills, mastering unfamiliar tasks, and coping with their emotions and tensions. The stage for their being able to develop these skills is set in early infancy as children learn that adults caring for them can be counted on to behave either affectionately and predictably most of the time or insensitively and neglectfully in response to their children's distress and needs.

As young children move into the 2nd and 3rd years of life, the trust or mistrust that they have developed has an impact on their achievement of subsequent developmental tasks. At this stage, children begin to exercise increasing autonomy as physical, cognitive, and social abilities also develop. For children experiencing day-to-day encouragement to actively explore in a safe, supportive, high-quality environment, increased confidence and competence are likely to be the outcome. In contrast, children who live in chaotic environments with overly critical and controlling adults are more likely to develop a sense of doubt about themselves and their ability to deal with an enlarging life space. Predictably, these children move less competently into the preschool years.

By the time they are ready for kindergarten, many 5-year-olds have developed a sense of how others value their efforts to explore ideas, carry out plans, gain information, and master new skills. Children who have developed a strong sense of initiative enjoy gaining increased competence. They seek ways to use their energy in appropriate and constructive ways and take pride in cooperating with others in skill-building activities. Conversely, children who have experienced less nurturing care in the early stages of development are less likely to initiate activity on their own or be successful in ventures to do so. They may have problems related to task completion, and these children often demonstrate less ability in problem solving or decision making. They may hang back in play or act so aggressively that they fail to establish meaningful friendships. For example, a 4-year-old boy who had grown bored watching his mother try on eyeglass frames in an optometrist's office began teasing a little girl standing by her mother, who was also trying on frames. Even though his behavior became highly inappropriate and annoying to others, his mother ignored what he was doing. At one point, the small girl said to the child, "You're bad!" Surprisingly, the tone of her voice brought an abrupt stop to his teasing. He looked confused for a minute and then went to his mother to report the affront.

"She said I'm bad," he complained.

"Well, you *are* bad," said his mother, not even looking at him. The long-term effect of this kind of response on a child's self-image is unfortunately predictable, especially when it is combined with little or no effort to provide him with more-appropriate behavioral skills.

Each day of a child's life is filled with events and successful and unsuccessful interactions with others. One infant's cries are responded to promptly with nurturing warmth and concern; another is left for long periods without adult attention or contact. One 2-year-old's parent views his child's frequent "no" as an expression of her growing autonomy; another's parent sees it as the beginning of a power struggle and something that must be curbed. Five-year-old Brian's reluctance to join in with other children is seen by his teacher as a need to build social strategies; to his father, it is a source of irritation and "sissiness." The second graders in Mrs. Milan's class learn mostly in silence when she is not speaking and by waiting to respond to her directions; those in the second-grade classroom down the hall are encouraged by their teacher to be independent, to be self-reliant, and to rely on their own thinking as much as possible (Gestwicki, 1998). Cumulatively, these isolated but potent and cumulative forces result in children's building an internal picture of themselves as capable and valued—or inept and relatively unimportant.

Like everything else in an organism, an individual's concept of self develops and changes during the life span; however, evidence indicates that a person's *global self-concept*—all the beliefs a person has about him- or herself—is structured fairly early in life and appears to be well developed by the time a child is 8 or 9 years old. Components of the self—your perceptions about how competent you are intellectually, physically, emotionally, and so forth—are known as *self-esteem*. These perceptions are affected by how worthwhile a person feels in any particular situation and are either enhanced or hampered by the large and small events children experience every day, their interactions with others, the demands that are placed on them, and the emotions that result from these experiences.

At first, very young children think of their emotions as simply happy, mad, sad, and afraid. These core emotions form the foundations from which all other emotions emerge. This emergence is a gradual process occurring during the first 5 years of life. Children younger than 5 years old are generally unaware that people can experience more than one emotion at a time. For example, if a parent expresses anger toward them, they believe that the parent is *completely* angry and, therefore, not holding other emotions at the same time, such as love, fear, sadness, or disappointment. In contrast, 5- and 6-year-olds develop the recognition that people can feel more than one emotion at a time but still believe that contrasting emotions such as feeling angry and loving, smart and stupid, or happy and sad about the same *event* are not possible. For example, on learning that the family would be moving to another state, 6-year-old Kevin expressed his profound sadness about leaving his friends, his favorite tree swing in his backyard, and his school. As well as acknowledging his feelings, his first-grade teacher discussed with him some possibilities he had not considered about the town that he was moving to and that it would be fun to send e-mail back and forth to each other. She underscored the fact that changes we encounter can cause both unhappy and happy feelings and that she understood that his current feelings were mostly sad. She encouraged him to write to her and tell her about the fun things he was finding after he moved to his new town.

Not until middle elementary school do children begin to understand that such events as their parents' divorce or moving to another town can cause both positive emotions and negative emotions and that people can hold contrasting feelings simultaneously about other persons, objects, or situations. However, even with this understanding, children may experience considerable confusion and a sense of anxiety about not having a clear-cut response (Kostelnik, Whiren, et al., 2002). Children younger than 10 years old generally do not associate the source of their emotions with what happens in their minds. Rather, there is a more simplistic and direct linking of their emotional state to their physical state of being. If they miss a parent or are hungry, tired, or injured, they perceive emotions such as sadness, irritability, anger, or fearfulness as directly resulting from the situation rather than from what they *think* about the situation or how they interpret it. They are also unaware that a person can feel certain emotions internally and mask them externally. Thus, these children may not be alert for subtle cues in others' responses to them when their social behavior is inappropriate or "thoughtless."

As primary-age children develop a more sophisticated intellectual capacity, they become better equipped to evaluate their social skills and status in light of others' behavior and expectations. In developing a consolidated sense of themselves, children watch others' compliance and transgressions and the consequential approval or disapproval of such behavior. They listen to evaluations of their actions and others' actions and begin to formulate a rudimentary understanding of others' desires, beliefs, and emotions.

Thus, from the preschool years until preadolescence, children struggle with developing responsibility and living up to the reasonable expectations of people they come into contact with. They learn that doing so requires effort on their part and that making poor choices about following through on such tasks as homework and household chores results in others' disappointment or disdain. To the extent that children feel free to assert themselves in everyday interactions with peers, teachers, parents, and others and are reinforced for efforts at skill building and successful accomplishments, they develop a positive attitude about learning. When their efforts are discouraged, ignored, or short-circuited by others, a sense of inferiority results, which causes them to veer away from challenges and responsibilities or to behave in a hostile and socially inappropriate manner. These behaviors, although frustrating to professionals working with these children, are simply natural defensive mechanisms in youngsters who have experienced significant contact with others who are largely insensitive to and unsupportive of their developmental needs. Although most educators empathically recognize the root cause of such behavior, the conduct of poorly nurtured children is often disruptive and time consuming. It has a negative impact on their progress and interferes with other children's progress. As a result, professionals frequently find themselves feeling some ambivalence toward these children who are so difficult to manage on a day-to-day basis.

CHILDREN'S ACQUISITION OF A FUNDAMENTAL KNOWLEDGE BASE FOR AFFECTIVE DEVELOPMENT

Daniel Goleman (1997), author of *Emotional Intelligence,* suggested that operationalizing *intrapersonal intelligence*—that is, becoming emotionally "smart"— involves five components of behavior:

1. *Developing self-awareness:* Becoming aware of your emotions as they happen and monitoring them
2. *Managing your emotions so that they are appropriate:* Being able to calm yourself under stressful conditions and being able to shake off problems that occur
3. *Motivating yourself toward goal accomplishment:* Being able to stifle impulsive behavior
4. *Recognizing emotions in others and having empathy for others*
5. *Effectively handling relationships with others:* Having social competence, which undergirds popularity, leadership ability, and interpersonal effectiveness

As in every other developmental domain, children are active in constructing a knowledge base they will use in every internal and external operation related to their emerging emotional structures. With respect to *physical knowledge,* they become increasingly aware of their tendencies to react and behave under certain conditions and gain awareness about their dispositions, capabilities, and abilities. Their *logical-mathematical knowledge* is enhanced as they develop the logical organization to deal with incoming affective information (How am I like others? How am I different than others?) and recognize and contrast the distinct and recurrent patterns in their behavior and that of others. *Representational knowledge* increases as they learn new ways to express their inner emotional thoughts and feelings through the increased use of speech as language develops, through the refined use of body language, and through written expression as literacy skills emerge. In the *social-conventional* arena, they are intensely interested in learning more about how others view them, what the rules are for socially acceptable ways of behaving, and more about gender, ethnicity, and interpersonal applications.

Children exercise their increasingly sophisticated *metacognitive abilities* by putting their sensory channel modalities to work to investigate emotional cause and effect. As they do so, they grow in their conscious conceptualization of their emotional strength and limitations (self-awareness, self-esteem, self-concept), develop better instincts about themselves and others, and acquire strategies to affect their emotions and those of others. In the earlier example of the 4-year-old who had been told by his mother, "You *are* bad!" this experience and many others add daily to his emotional knowledge base. Physically, he sees himself as able to get away with outrageous behavior and still be ignored by his parent. Logically, he comes to know that he is perceived in the situation as "bad" rather than "good," and he chooses to represent this "badness" by continuing to tease his peer, despite the negative feedback given to him by everyone else in the context. All this and the labels that are pinned on—"bad boy"—are part of his growing social-conventional knowledge about himself. Metacognitively, he is learning that his behavior can cause irritation to others (a confusing mix of positive and negative emotions). However, his behavior is also an attention-getting mechanism (a highly positive emotion), and attention is something that he craves and can actively elicit without undue consequence in the form of punishment. Conversely, a child who receives authentic messages that he or she is fun, capable, or intelligent can be observed to represent these concepts in play and other interpersonal behaviors.

CHILDREN'S STRESS REACTIONS IN RESPONSE TO OVERWHELMING EMOTIONAL DEMANDS

All the aspects of affective development discussed, in combination with the quality of care the child experiences, result in a child's ability to cope with perceived demands in the environment. Some children have little

Stress can overwhelm children as well as adults.

ability to bounce back from negative experiences, whereas others seem to have tremendous resilience.

Children experience emotional demands from any number of sources. These sources range from individual stressors (disabling conditions, inadequate or imbalanced diet, difficult personality) and intrafamilial stressors (birth of a sibling, death of a loved one or pet, a parent's getting a more important job, moving to a new house, marital transition of parents, poverty, abuse, or neglect) to those outside the family. Extrafamilial sources may include unsatisfactory child care; a poor match between developmental levels and classroom expectations in the school setting; a lack of appreciation of cultural differences by others; negative peer relationships in the neighborhood, at birthday parties, or at sleepovers at someone else's home; and unsafe factors in the community. Other potential challenges may include the fast-paced society children live in, the push to grow up and be independent of adult support, high-fat diets, a lack of exercise to release tension, too many extracurricular activities, and heavy exposure to television.

Evidence indicates that children who are most effective in coping with *normal* stressors (e.g., getting up and dressed in time for the school bus, being disappointed once in a while, being left out of a play opportunity) learn how to cope with larger issues. Also, children who can find or generate more alternatives for coping usually do much better and build confidence in managing stressful situations. In coping with stressors, children use the same sorts of strategies that many adults use, including such defense mechanisms as denial, regression, withdrawal, and impulsive acting out. However, as is true for adults, these behaviors in children are clear-cut signs that they need additional or different skills in perceiving or dealing adequately with a situation.

How can we determine whether a child is emotionally healthy? Hendrick (1996) suggested that teachers consider the following questions about a child who seems troubled, noting that if most of the questions can be answered affirmatively, the chance is good that the child *is* functioning in a healthy manner:

Is the child working on emotional tasks that are appropriate for his or her age?

Is the child learning to separate from his or her family without undue stress and able to form an attachment with at least one other adult in the setting?

Is the child learning to conform to routines without undue fuss?

Is the child able to become deeply involved in play?

Does the child have the ability to settle down and concentrate?

Does the child usually interact with others in an appropriate and nonaggressive way?

Does the child have access to the full range of feelings, and is he or she learning to deal with them in an age-appropriate way? (pp. 118–119)

When stressful situations persist for long periods and the child is unable to experience relief, other symptoms may appear, such as increased irritability, depression, anxiety, sleep disturbances, somatic problems, or a dramatic increase or decrease in appetite. Highly stressed children *look* stressed. Significant and long-standing tension may manifest in the quality of speech, as dark circles under the eyes, in the child's posture, and occasionally in compulsive behaviors. When the child's developed resources are unequal to the demands experienced, behavioral disorders and increased psychological vulnerability also frequently result. We see this in mental and conduct disorders, school failure, psychosomatic illness, and early involvement in criminal behavior, drug use, sexual activity, and alcohol use.

Without additional help, children who are unable to cope effectively will barely be able to benefit from what is going on in the classroom academically and socially. Nor do children necessarily benefit from the teacher's offering quick fixes, dictating "appropriate" responses, or pushing them to talk when they are not ready to do so. Helping the child to replace ineffective strategies calls for a patient and carefully planned approach from the teacher that utilizes many of the guidelines suggested subsequently in this chapter. When additional focused attention and support are not helpful, other professionals may need to be drawn in to help the child modify his or her emotional upset and responses.

PROMOTION OF HEALTHY SELF-ESTEEM IN THE EARLY LEARNING ENVIRONMENT

Praise more and criticize less.
Notice them.
Ask them about themselves.
Look into their eyes when you talk with them.
Tell them their feelings are okay.
Giggle together.
Set boundaries that keep them safe.
Listen to their stories.
Delight in their discoveries.
Keep the promises you make.
Let them solve most of their own problems.
—Roehlkepartain (1998)

In a first-grade classroom, an educational consultant observed a group of children who had viewed a digital video disk (DVD) on space rockets and then been invited by their teacher to draw a picture of a rocket. The teacher reminded the children to put their names on their pictures and to date the pictures so that the work could be entered into their writing portfolios. As the consultant drew near to watch Michael, who was drawing an especially creative rocket, he glanced up at her and then quickly covered the poorly scrawled name he had written in the upper left corner. When the adult smiled and complimented him on his beautiful rocket, he smiled back but kept his printing covered, covertly watching until she moved on and only then withdrawing his hand. Six-year-old Michael had already learned to be ashamed of his efforts to print.

In another classroom, a troubled child told his teacher, "I'm no good!" She responded emphatically, "No, no, no—you *are* good. We aren't going to talk like that. I don't want to hear anyone in this room putting himself down!" The child, who for some time had been experiencing alcoholic and abusive parents' arguing and moving toward divorce, had trusted the teacher enough to bring his pain openly to her. He was being truthful about his feelings about himself. No matter how undeserved, he felt worthless. Wanting to help him think better of himself, the teacher had unwittingly denied both his emotions and his pain.

Resulting feelings of self-worth are reflected in a child's overt behavior in the classroom, in the peer group, and on the playground. Clues and patterns that indicate whether a child is experiencing low self-esteem are substantiated in children's negative self-statements ("I'm rotten at this!" "I can never get anything right"); elaborate defenses to protect a fragile ego; problematic behavior (unrealistic fear, unjustified anger, continued lying, conceit, overconcern with past or future); avoidance of play, projects, or working with others; or lack of interest in appearance, cleanliness, and care of possessions.

Because young children are still malleable, those who come to school with positive self-perceptions and those who come with somewhat damaged selves because of unsupportive situations will each continue to modify this most basic building block of emotional life. However, professionals must be careful to be positive and confirming for *all* children, not just those who are having emotional difficulties. Children who arrive at the school door with apparently high self-esteem may experience difficulty when academic tasks become overly challenging or ethnic and racial biases are at work among children, despite the teacher's best effort to rid the classroom of them. In such cases, teachers must be active in insulating children from a negative view of themselves and provide strategies for coping. Poorly nurtured children also need a great deal of support from a patient, caring, and knowledgeable teacher so that they can move in a more positive direction. Such support will call for a professional's using constructive disciplinary strategies consistently in tandem with genuine reinforcement every time these children choose prosocial behavior. It calls for focusing daily attention on each of them, providing opportunities for them to work out their feelings through play, and teaching them to practice positive self-talk in difficult situations ("This is hard, but if I keep trying, I'll learn how to do it"). Positive behavioral changes can be facilitated by offering encouraging statements that express positive aspects of a difficult situation without denying children's feelings (Kostelnik, Whiren, et al., 2002). For example, the teacher who responded to the child who said "I'm no good" by saying "No, no, no—you *are* good" might have said instead, "It sounds as if you're having a rough morning. In spite of that, you've managed to complete all of that project. Let's look at what you still have left to do."

Ultimately, children's self-understanding is the result of the diverse and cumulative experiences with significant others in their world, both adults and peers. Urie Bronfenbrenner, Professor of Human Development at Cornell University, maintains that not only do children need nurturing adults in their world who "are crazy about them," but there must also be times when the same adults are cool and capable of delivering authentic, corrective feedback to a child who has stepped outside appropriate behavioral boundaries. N. E. Curry and Johnson (1998) suggested that children develop senses of re-

silience, power, competence, trust, and optimism from repeated experiences in which they transform negative states into positive states. These researchers added that children may be at risk when they experience persistently positive self-feelings or persistently negative self-feelings; the former situation results in narcissistic self-absorption and an inability to deal adequately with social challenges.

Primary-age children seem to have no qualms about rejecting children who are self-absorbed, uncooperative, disruptive, and inappropriately hostile. Unless intervention occurs in such cases to provide and reinforce more-appropriate skills and behaviors, such children learn to accept the negative identity others ascribe to them. Later, they often isolate themselves from others or gang up with other aggressive and hostile children who have also experienced rejection, and we have witnessed the most horrendous long-term outcomes of such rejection in cases such as that at Columbine High School in Colorado and other secondary schools in the United States. Clearly, fostering effective social skills needed to work and play well with others is worth spending time on in the classroom. The constructed early childhood learning ethos that promotes in young children shared ownership, a sense of community, and responsible participation in turn motivates further positive development of cooperation, control, connectedness, and mastery.

Evidence suggests that we can build better resilience in young children by using the following six strategies in our early childhood classrooms:

1. *Building in more opportunities for play.* Increasingly, adult agendas are diminishing this powerful resource for developing resilience. Children appreciate teachers who take both a serious approach and a playful approach to learning. Play provides children with opportunities to problem solve, socialize, exercise leadership and following skills, build communication skills and engage in give-and-take with their peers, and reduce tensions they are feeling. It also provides them with a chance to experiment with controlling people and objects. All these abilities are key in whether or not a child builds the capacity to recover from conditions that might be predictive of failure.

2. *Modifying children's difficult behavior without sending a message that the child is not okay;* working with children to develop ways in which they can regulate their behavior and emotions, and acknowledging their efforts and successes.

3. *Teaching them to become effective problem solvers,* which translates into the power of independence; finding a way to have conversations with them about what they want to accomplish and building steps they need to take to get there, whether the target is social interaction or academic success.

4. *Teaching them ways to better express their thoughts, ideas, and feelings;* discussing ways in which each child is unique and strong; helping them document these characteristics and then referring to such characteristics at times when the child needs additional support.

5. *Building rapport and connectedness in the classroom.* As much as possible, we need to build within each child a spirit of being a special and valued member of the team. Along with this, we must help each child to increase his or her capacity for appreciating, caring for, and empathizing with others.

6. *Knowing what goes on in children's lives outside the classroom* (i.e., knowing which supports they have and which are missing); being willing to advocate for the kinds of interventions they need to reduce risk factors and providing more protective factors to ameliorate or buffer these risks.

Children in the primary grades want to be competent and recognized by others as competent. Educators can take advantage of this "optimal period" and natural motivation of children by guiding them toward more fully integrated intrapersonal and interpersonal strengths. Doing so calls for including in the early childhood program an adequate focus on the development of self-awareness, cooperative relationships, mutual respect, and a climate of fairness, caring, and participation. In addition, educators in truly effective schools must work closely with families and the community before children enter the formal system. These linkages with families must then be maintained and strengthened as children move through the developmental tasks of early childhood and into adolescence and young adulthood.

VARIATIONS IN PERSONALITY DEVELOPMENT

Even when teachers and parents are fairly sensitive about factors influencing the self-esteem of growing children, negative interaction styles can develop when children are perceived to be difficult and consistently difficult to manage. Children exhibit extremely different personality attributes that may be inherited characteristics. Included are such traits as these:

❑ *Activity level*—motor activity and inactivity
❑ *Rhythmicity*—predictability in bodily function
❑ *Approach–withdrawal*—child's initial responses to new objects, people, foods, and so forth
❑ *Adaptability*—response to change
❑ *Intensity of reaction*—energy level in response to stimuli and impulse control

❑ *Responsiveness threshold*—level of stimulation necessary to evoke a response
❑ *Attention span and persistence*—time spent in pursuit of activity
❑ *Distractibility*—vulnerability to interference during pursuit of an activity

In a series of longitudinal studies conducted to examine individual temperaments in young children on the basis of the preceding traits (McDevitt & Carey, 1978; Thomas & Chess, 1977, 1980, 1984; Thomas, Chess, Birch, Hartzig, & Korn, 1963), researchers documented three basic types: easy (40 percent of the children studied), difficult (10 percent), and slow to warm up (about 15 percent). About 35 percent of the children studied could not be classified into one of these categories. "Difficult" and "slow-to-warm-up" children react more negatively to change or seem to march to a slightly different drummer than most children do. Teachers often stay awake at night thinking about more-effective ways to deal with these children. Fortunately, temperament is not necessarily destiny and what makes a difference are the emotional experiences the child will have while growing up (Goleman, 1997).

Often when adults look on these differences in personality as stubbornness on the child's part, a power struggle is set into motion. Altering a difficult child's behavior and still having both adult and child maintain a healthy sense of autonomy and power can be a fragile undertaking. Doing so calls for respecting such differences as legitimate but helping the child to see and appreciate how some changes might be personally advantageous—for example, in getting along better with others and forming friendships. Jerome Kagan (1997/1998, pp. 55–56) warned practitioners not to become so caught up in the "new romance with biology" that they award temperament *too* strong a voice in responding to children. What is critical to remember, he noted, is that no human psychological profile is a product of genetic influences or environmental influences alone. Instead, it is a fabric consisting of both kinds of threads. Inherited characteristics are always modified by the child's experiences with others.

Adults wanting or attempting to modify children's interactive styles will need to examine what part *their* personality is playing in the situation. The child's behavior may be perfectly appropriate but simply irritating because of personality differences between child and adult. Legitimately, such a situation may call for compromise. For example, perhaps the slow-to-warm-up child would not balk at schedule changes so much if the teacher would take more care to warn the child about them. Perhaps the more active child is unable to sit still in large-group presentations but the large-group sessions are longer than necessary because they are a favorite part of the adult's teaching day. Shortening them somewhat, at least for a period, and having the child adapt to increasingly longer sessions may be a workable compromise.

CURRENT EDUCATIONAL ISSUES

Although everyone agrees that good emotional health is necessary for effective functioning and a positive quality of life, not everyone agrees that classroom teachers should be actively involved in guiding the development of children in this arena. Several issues form the basis of this opposition.

Including Affective Education in the Curriculum

One issue, raised by persons who oppose teacher involvement in affective education, is the belief that academic achievement should be the primary and only concern in an educational context and that affective development should be left as the legitimate province of the family. This sort of attitude goes against not only a philosophical concern for the overall development of young children, but also the principles of developmentally appropriate practice.

In addition, children are moving out of the family's care and into the extrafamilial arena earlier and earlier, with professionals in child care centers and educational settings assuming increasing responsibility for nurturing children as well as educating and keeping them safe. Increasing numbers of children are coming into the school setting with poorly formed attachments and in need of both emotional resources and a warm, trusting relationship with an adult to correct the direction of their affective development. The school performance of children with weak affective ties is predictably poor. They are less independent and more noncompliant, have poorer social interactional skills, and lack confidence and assertiveness. Such children are more at risk for harboring hostility, negative self-esteem, a sense of negative self-adequacy, emotional instability, emotional unresponsiveness, and a negative world view (Currie, 1988). Richard Weissbourd, author of *The Vulnerable Child* (1996), identified school conditions necessary for children to find a capacity for work, love, and play. They need protection from destruction and prejudice, a continuous relationship with a consistently attentive and caring adult, opportunities in school and in the community for real achievement, and strong friendships with adults and other children (Scherer, 1997).

Having Professional Competence

Another issue, also raised by individuals opposing teacher involvement in affective education, is related to

the perceived lack of training by professionals to be competent, sensitive, and effective in this area. In the past and in particular institutions of higher learning, much of teacher training was focused on academic content and methods, and only cursory attention was paid to the affective and social domains. More attention was given to structuring consequences for negative behavior than to developing children's self-esteem or establishing a positive classroom climate in which to nurture emotional development. As a result, many beginning teachers found themselves ill equipped to deal with children's affective and social problems and relied heavily on artificial methods for keeping children "under control."

Currently, program standards in early childhood education maintain that preservice teachers be trained to understand developmental sequences and to work with all children in a sensitive and supportive way (National Association for the Education of Young Children, 1996b). Teachers also learn strategies for intervention when children lack emotional stability and social skills and are made aware of the need to design an atmosphere of trust and experiences for children that will actively enhance positive development. Similarly, effective public school systems are providing in-service aid to teachers so that they can help children develop more-positive self-esteem, find appropriate outlets for strong feelings, deal with natural and acquired fears, and learn conflict management. In short, affective development is not left purely to chance. In good early childhood programs, it is considered as important as academic aspects, and well-trained and sensitive teachers are viewed as critical.

Debating About Touch in Early Childhood Settings

One issue frequently raised by educators about providing nurturance to children and satisfying their affective needs is the concern that hugging children, patting them on the back, or letting a young child sit on the teacher's lap could result in allegations of inappropriate contact. A number of wrongful accusations have caused administrators of many early childhood programs to take a defensive posture, which has led to taboos against any hugging, patting, or touching and has thereby shortchanged the children. As a way to avoid cutting out this essential aspect of a school program and to protect educators from precarious positions, some researchers have suggested that the need for a warm, caring relationship between the teacher and the children be fully communicated to parents and the community; that children be instructed about "good touch, bad touch"; and that the hugs, touches, and short personal conversations that are so necessary in a nurturing climate be delivered only when other people are visible (Currie, 1988, p. 90).

Meeting the Needs of Children with Special Needs

The inclusion of children with special needs in early childhood programs was initially met with mixed reactions by professionals unfamiliar with children who have disabilities. However, with respect to supporting their emotional development, these children are similar in many respects to children without disabilities. They need and want affiliations with others, nurturing relationships, and stimulating and enjoyable classroom experiences.

Any number of childhood disorders may hamper affective development. Included are conditions in the category of pervasive developmental disorders (PDDs), which are characterized not only by marked impairments in social reciprocity and communication, but also by behavioral abnormalities. These disorders are neurogenetic and may coexist with other disabilities, such as mental retardation, inattention, hyperactivity, and epilepsy. Autism is the most widely known PDD. Children with autism may exhibit such behaviors as repetitive motor mannerisms (e.g., hand or finger flapping), persistent preoccupation with parts of objects, a delay in language development or repetitive use of language, lack of make-believe or socially initiated play, lack of eye contact, and failure to develop peer relationships (American Psychiatric Association [*DSM-IV-TR*], 2000). One critical goal is to teach skills that extend the child's ability to interact well with others and adapt in social situations. Most important in this arena, children with autistic disorders need to understand that behavior carries meaning. They require help in modifying socially inappropriate gestures, building communication skills, establishing daily routines, and extinguishing negative, destructive, or aggressive behaviors. Finally, they need teachers who are willing to gain access to information and the increasing numbers of helpful materials being developed for teachers dealing with behavioral difficulties in young children.

Attention-deficit disorder (ADD) and attention-deficit/hyperactivity disorder (ADHD), additional neurobiological syndromes that appear in early childhood, can also have pervasive and long-lasting negative effects on affective and social development. Researchers believe that in 80% of the cases of ADHD, the disorder results from heredity rather than negative parenting or poverty (although these factors may further complicate the condition). These impairments often lead to academic underachievement and problems with adaptive skills in daily living, with communication, and with the social skills necessary for self-sufficiency. These children are more vulnerable to peer rejection and are at increased risk for physical abuse because of their difficult behaviors. So that their chances for success are increased, they need to be in classrooms in which teachers are knowledgeable about behavior management strategies (see Figure 10.1) and coaching—and can deliver such help sensitively and in age-appropriate ways to help these children build self-confidence and self-management skills. Close communication and coordination with the child's family is also critical (Batshaw, 2002).

FIGURE 10.1   Example of a Behavior Management Strategy for a Child with Attention-Deficit/Hyperactivity Disorder

Phillip

Seven-year-old Phillip has a history of poor school performance. His second-grade teacher, Mrs. Emmons, is aware of his history of being disruptive, not following directions, blurting out silly comments, and moving from activity to activity without any focus. This year, he was diagnosed with ADHD, combined type, which is characterized by a short attention span, hyperactivity, and impulsivity. A reading disability further complicates the situation.

Mrs. Emmons realizes that she cannot completely erase Phillip's low frustration tolerance, inability to recognize the consequences of his behavior, and tendency to become bored easily. However, she is committed to stemming further social and academic failure as much as possible.

With the help of professionals knowledgeable about ADHD effects and by learning more about Phillip's strengths both inside and outside school, she and Phillip both believe that he has made considerable progress this year. She knows that one effective strategy is to provide immediate and consistent positive consequences when he behaves appropriately and negative consequences when he chooses not to. She is carefully noting his frustration level for handling new material. She has also helped him focus on his organizational skills and has found ways to help him consistently increase his ability to stay on task. Sitting near positive role models in the classroom and having a second set of books at home for homework assignments have been helpful. She has also increased the number of hands-on activities in her classroom, something she believes that all the children have benefited from. Mrs. Emmons notes, "Both Phillip and I have learned a lot about ADHD this year. It's not always easy, but it's not big enough to lick either one of us, either."

Acquiring Self-Esteem: Can It Be Taught or Must It Be Developed?

Another major issue regarding the affective domain is the misconception that self-esteem is something that is provided for children—that simply giving children everything they want, frequently telling them how special they are, and engaging them in 15-minute sessions of self-esteem building endows them with healthy dollops of self-esteem that they can then draw on when it is needed during future challenges. This approach does not work. In fact, such an approach may negate children's understanding the relationship among hard work, true accomplishment, and feelings of self-worth. Nongenuine praise and ignoring a lack of effort can diminish motivation in children. Young children are in the process of developing an internalized sense of others' values, and they will eventually compare or evaluate their worth against this standard. To create a context in which good self-esteem is nurtured, adults must take the time each day to observe children's real accomplishments and comment on them. They need to provide the guidance children need to develop internal control and make healthy choices. All this must take place in an atmosphere in which adults demonstrate warmth, respect, acceptance, authority, and empathy (Kostelnik, Whiren, et al., 2002).

Evaluating Emotional Growth

Measuring and evaluating affective development also seem to be problems for many classroom teachers. However, both can be accomplished by using a variety of strategies. Criterion-referenced checklists can be developed directly from the curricular objectives that follow. Teachers can also use these checklists as a reminder about the need to structure a growth-producing environment and activities in the classroom. Other data sources might include a series of anecdotal records of particular behaviors such as offering assistance to another child, documentation through participation charts, notations about unstructured play and work partnerships formed, and structured and informal observations of the child's affective statements and behaviors. More-specific strategies related to assessment and evaluation can be found in chapter 7.

GOALS AND OBJECTIVES

The ultimate goal of education in the affective domain is for children to regard themselves as valued and capable persons. For children to make progress toward this goal, they must perceive the classroom as a psychologically safe and supportive environment and have a variety of experiences that promote the growth of emotional health, self-awareness, and positive self-esteem.

Intermediate Objectives

As children progress toward the ultimate goal, they will demonstrate the following 34 competencies:

1. Learn that school is safe, supportive, predictable, interesting, and enjoyable
2. Demonstrate that they have a feeling of belonging in the school environment
3. Engage in affectionate relationships beyond the family
4. Demonstrate a growing ability to care for themselves and to meet their own needs
5. Begin and pursue a task independently
6. Control their behavior without external reminders
7. Gain experience and demonstrate independence in using age-appropriate materials and tools
8. Complete a task they have begun
9. Assume responsibility for caring for their personal belongings and classroom materials
10. Contribute to classroom maintenance (e.g., caring for classroom pets, watering plants)
11. Experience the pleasure of work
12. Recognize factors that contribute to quality work (e.g., time, care, effort, responsibility)
13. Make reasonable attempts to master situations that are difficult for them
14. Become aware that criticism should be about ideas, not persons
15. Learn to give criticism constructively
16. Value their gender, family, culture, and race
17. Engage in a full range of experiences, not just those limited to stereotypes related to gender or background
18. Increase their knowledge, understanding, and appreciation of their cultural heritage
19. Develop cross-gender competencies of various kinds
20. Identify the characteristics and qualities that make each of them unique
21. Identify their emotions
22. Explore similarities and differences among people as a way to gain personal insight
23. Make choices and experience the consequences of personal decisions
24. Demonstrate increasing awareness of and an ability to evaluate their accomplishments and to set new standards and goals
25. Understand the concepts of *possession* and *ownership*
26. Evaluate and describe their competencies

27. Experience success

28. Learn how to effectively express and clarify thoughts and feelings about emotionally charged situations, problems, and crises

29. Learn satisfying and effective strategies for coping with personal emotions and tensions

30. Learn to accept both positive emotions and negative emotions as a natural part of living

31. Become familiar with the situational circumstances that influence personal emotions

32. Learn how to act deliberately to affect their emotions

33. Learn how to recover from setbacks

34. Imagine and speak of future potential for themselves

TEACHING STRATEGIES

Following are 12 strategies that educators can use to help children develop a healthy emotional repertoire:

1. *Create a positive classroom climate.* Structuring a positive classroom climate is essential for educators to create learning contexts in which children build a strong sense of feeling valued, confident, and competent. Doing so requires that teachers be knowledgeable about and sensitive to variations in personality, as well as children's successes and failures in forming attachments to others. We as educators need to assess and determine whether children are achieving competency or mastery, inner control and assertiveness, and prosocial behaviors to minimize developmental risk (Brendtro, Brokenleg, & Van Bockern, 1997).

Today's lack of civility is seen as a serious and worsening problem that is contributing to the growing social aggression and violence in the United States. Such incivility can be remedied in part if professionals at every educational level create a climate of classroom civility, which involves having civic responsibility and determining the proper ways to view and treat one another (Kauffman & Burbach, 1997). In such contexts, children have opportunities to develop personal insight into appropriate and inappropriate responses when they are involved in emotionally charged situations with others.

As an educator, use a variety of strategies to build a sense of community and promote children's development away from egocentrism and excessive individualism. To foster cooperative relationships and mutual respect, actively build rapport and team spirit. Impress on children that they need others in order to feel a sense of belonging, liked, valued, cared for, and in union with others. To develop a sense of community in the classroom, begin on the first day of school to develop social bonds

and a sense of being a team among the children, using cooperative learning strategies. Encourage children to reinforce one another's efforts and to support one another in a respectful way. Provide activities that will sensitize them about the fact that we feel worthwhile not only when we achieve something, but also when we display positive behaviors toward others and behave with kindness, courtesy, trustworthiness, and responsibility.

2. *Establish a low-stress and emotionally supportive environment.* As an early childhood professional, you are a key person in helping young children make a smooth and comfortable transition into the program and in developing and maintaining their enthusiasm for working and playing with others. Establish a predictable schedule, and provide a daily overview of the day's activities, including any changes in routine, notice of visitors, and so forth. Monitor the pace at which the program moves and decide whether a distinction is being made that work is dull and play is the only activity to look forward to. Evaluate whether your sense of humor is alive and making the classroom a pleasurable place in which to spend time. Familiarize yourself with information about children's fears, and provide a safe and supportive context in which children can gradually work through them. Examine your self-esteem and how you model stress and conflict management to children when you are under pressure.

3. *Assess the physical makeup of the room and the use of space and materials.* Establish a stimulus-reduced area in which children who are seeking quiet can work. Balance quiet and active experiences so that children are not emotionally or physically overloaded. Evaluate the room for visual and auditory overstimulation, as well as noise levels, lighting, and temperature. Make space available where children can store their individual

Give children adequate time and encouragement to finish tasks themselves.

belongings and where their work can be prominently displayed at their eye level. Make some materials available that children can select for themselves, and take time at the beginning of the year to ensure that the children understand how to use them. Follow through to see that the children return the materials to their proper storage areas.

4. *Work collaboratively with parents, building effective, continuing home–school partnerships.* Handle the separation process from home to school with sensitivity and respect for children's individual needs. If possible, provide opportunities for a gradual introduction to the school setting. Comfort anxious children and parents, and provide information to parents about how to ease children's transitions from home to school. Develop a system with parents to share knowledge about events at home or school that may be emotionally upsetting to a child.

5. *Monitor school materials and routines to avoid reinforcing stereotypes, and create activities that challenge stereotypes and prejudice.* An important first step for professionals is to evaluate the content and source of our prejudices and to determine how these prejudices might influence our beliefs about children and their families (Haberman, 1994). We also need to survey the kinds of activities and materials used in the classroom. Provide children with opportunities to interact with adult members and other children of their culture and other cultures. Plan visits to various work sites, and invite people to explain a variety of occupations, including those that are nontraditional.

6. *Promote children's emotional development and sense of worth.* Talk with children about their emotions, and structure activities and experiences specifically to build awareness of situations and events that influence emotions. Brewer (2001) suggested some general ideas for such activities:

Have children dramatize situations in which anger or frustration is handled appropriately.

Use puppets to model appropriate responses to emotions. For example, with younger children, use puppets to model using language rather than hitting to express anger. With older children, model different responses to frustrations, such as not winning a race or a game.

Help children learn to acknowledge and label their feelings as they participate in classroom activities.

Choose literature in which the characters respond to emotions appropriately, and discuss how they felt and acted.

Provide empathy for children's fears and concerns. These fears and concerns may be imagined (fear of

Provide opportunities for children to describe their emotions.

monsters), realistic (fear that someone will make fun of them), or learned (apprehension about visiting the doctor). Because they are all real to the child, adults can help by acknowledging the child's discomfort and offering physical or spoken consolation (Kostelnik, Whiren, et al., 2002).

Allow children to share their humor: Appreciate the growth of their sense of humor.

Primary-age children may be helped to express their feelings through writing. Select examples of literature that illustrate how children have written about their frustrations or stresses and learned to cope more effectively with them through writing.

Praise children's accomplishments, and, to build self-esteem, use genuine praise and more reinforcement than negative criticism. Give children adequate time and encouragement to finish tasks for themselves.

7. *Refrain from shaming or comparing children with others or labeling them with derogatory words.* In classrooms with a lack of basic respect, children will not engage intellectually or emotionally, no matter how well developed the curriculum (Wagner, 1996). Develop a ready bank of reinforcing and encouraging phrases, such as the following (remember to be specific so that praise does not become meaningless):

You worked so hard to figure that out. I'm proud of you!

I'm happy to see you cooperating like that.

It's such a pleasure working with you because you try so hard.

That's really an improvement!

Hey, I can see that you've been practicing and that it's paying off.

You are really burning those old neurons today!

Now that's what I call a terrific job. You've remembered to leave spaces between every word.

You've completed your homework every day this week. Good for you!

That was a friendly and very caring thing to do.

Wow! You have it figured out, don't you?

You have to feel really proud of. . . . It took meeting the problem head on, and you did it!

Accept and respect temperamental idiosyncrasies, providing support when it is needed for children who adapt more slowly to change. Do not say children's names in a tone that means "No," "Stop," or "Don't!"

Never ignore difficult behaviors or problems such as lying, stealing, or cruelty to self or others (see chapter 6). When children demonstrate a pattern of difficult behaviors and are unresponsive to your attempts to modify them, seek help by working with other professionals who have more-specific expertise.

Develop a sense of belonging and connectedness for each member of the class. Have the class send cards to children who are sick. Model and let children know that your motto is "We're a team; we respect and take care of one another."

8. *Promote children's competence.* Competence is the ability to meet age-appropriate expectations at a reasonably high standard. Be patient when you are helping children modify their behavior. View children's inappropriate behavior as a gap in their knowledge or skills. Rather than expecting immediate change, identify steps in progress, giving children reinforcement when you see them trying to correct a particular behavior.

Use subtle cues to remind children that their behavior is close to exceeding limits. Whenever possible, allow children opportunities to assess the situation, determine what should be done, experience consequences, and modify their behavior in a positive direction.

Set effective limits with clearly defined expectations. Involve children in structuring classroom rules, and apply natural and logical consequences consistently when rules are not observed. (Refer to chapter 6 for further information regarding rules and consequences.)

Protect children's growing sense of autonomy by giving them frequent choices. Offer such choices only when you are willing to accept children's decisions. Be careful about providing too many choices or overloading children with decision-making "opportunities" that are meaningless or are better made by adults.

9. *Help children find satisfying ways to express their emotions to others.* When an emotion has been expressed inappropriately, recognize a child's feelings about the situation before moving ahead with helping the child correct the situation or learn new skills. Instead of stepping into a conflict situation and acting on their behalf, provide them with a sample script to help them express their emotions and needs (e.g., when a child needs to learn to express feelings to another child, he or she might be advised: "Tell Gemil, 'I don't like it when you grab things from me. I wasn't finished with the puppet. Please give it back to me'").

10. *Provide support for children with special needs.* For children who have difficulty controlling impulsivity because of neurological disorders that manifest behaviorally (e.g., ADD, autistic-like disorders), use such approaches as nonpunitive separation to remove the child from an overstimulating situation. Use scaffolding and work-completion strategies to help such children better organize their day. Provide reinforcement for staying on task and provide frequent goal-setting sessions and helpful, concrete suggestions for more-appropriate behavior.

When children focus on the negative, accept their statements and then ask, "How do you wish it were different? What could you do to change it?" Help students set goals for what they can change and be more accepting of what they cannot.

11. *Teach children to be competent and responsible workers.* Involve children in planning, implementing, and evaluating some class activities and decisions. Set aside a portion of each day in which children may engage in free-choice, self-initiated activities. Design activities in which the primary purpose is to teach children to use various classroom tools. Give children opportunities to carry out classroom jobs. Encourage them to clean up after themselves whenever possible and to assist others who need help.

Encourage children to evaluate the decisions they have made by reflecting on how well they defined the problem, whether they thought about all the alternatives, whether they persisted long enough, what turned out well, and what they might do differently the next time. Also, invite children to evaluate their accomplishments. Conference with them and provide task-specific feedback and questions to help them focus on what they have learned and the next steps to enhance their learning. Guide them toward self-examination of their growth and work rather than relying on only the teacher's or their parents' evaluation. Involve them in producing self-appraisal reports prior to parent conferences (see chapter 8).

Support children in their efforts to try new or uncomfortable tasks. Talk about their efforts, and praise their courage and determination to try, not just the results. Include scaffolding strategies; gauge the amount of support and challenge necessary for optimal growth, slowly decreasing support as the child moves toward increasing autonomy (Bodrova & Leong, 1996).

12. *When working with children with disabilities avoid tendencies to overprotect them so that they can develop autonomy as much as possible.* Assist children only when assistance is needed. Whenever possible, encourage children who are not disabled to seek help from children with disabilities. Doing so helps both the child with the disability and the child who is not disabled to build the perception that an existing disability should not be the central focus when an individual is evaluating another person's abilities.

ACTIVITY SUGGESTIONS

✎ I Can Get There All by Myself (For Older or More Experienced Children)

Objective 11 For children to experience the pleasure of work.

Materials Paper, markers, scissors, glue

Procedure Demonstrate to children how to draw a simple map from your home to the school. As you draw it, talk about several landmarks on the way. Draw them in and label them. Draw a clock by the house, noting the time (on the hour or half hour) that you usually leave for school. After drawing the school, add a clock by it indicating (again, on the hour or half hour) what time you usually arrive. Tell the children, "This is a map of the way I come to school every day. The clocks indicate the time I leave for school and the time I arrive. Each of you gets to school each day by walking or riding in a car or bus. That means you have to get ready to leave by a certain time and then get to this classroom by the time school is ready to start." Invite each child to construct a simple map showing their home, the school, and a route between.

To simplify Tell the children that you would like to construct a classroom map showing the school and the way to each of their homes and that you need their help in drawing their houses. Have them make just a picture of their homes on individual pieces of paper and cut around them. Construct a simple mural showing just larger cross streets, and help the children paste their homes east, west, south, or north of the cross streets.

To extend Have the children also indicate the approximate time (half hour or hour) that they leave their homes and arrive at school. Have them draw a more elaborate route between home and school on an individual basis. Have them take part in constructing the classroom mural that integrates all their homes in relation to the school.

✎ All About Me Book (For Children of All Ages)

Objective 20 For children to identify the characteristics and qualities that make each of them unique.

Materials Paper, scissors, magazines, writing tools

Procedure Have the children describe themselves on paper, then bind the pages together in a book. Pages that could be included may contain the following:

"This is me"—a self portrait
"This is my family"—a family portrait
"Here is my hand"—a hand tracing
"Some things that I can do"—a dictated or written list of skills
"My favorite foods"
"My favorite animals"—magazine picture cutouts

To simplify Have the child dictate words to teachers or classroom aides. Create fewer pages.

To extend Have the children decide what should go on each page. Have the children write in narrative form for each page to extend the information provided about themselves. Have them further illustrate each page.

✎ Happy Faces (For Younger or Less Experienced Children)

Objective 21 For children to identify their emotions and become more aware of facial expressions of happiness.

Materials Paper plates with tongue depressor handles attached to them, yarn for hair, markers, crayons, glue, construction paper, facial features cut out of magazines (be sure to use magazines with pictures of many differnt races of children and adults)

Procedure In the art center, spread out materials. Help the children use the materials to make puppets with happy faces, providing suggestions but not giving them a model to copy. Encourage them to talk about how they feel inside when they are wearing a happy face or how they feel when someone else looks at them with a happy face.

To simplify With extremely young children, provide prepared puppets and encourage them to discuss feelings that go along with happy faces.

To extend Have older children write and stage a puppet show about an especially joyous situation. Extend children's ability to identify body language expressions of happiness. Have them hold the stick puppets in front of their faces as they march up and down, repeating this chant in happy voices (to the tune of "Here We Go 'Round the Mulberry Bush"):

This is my happy face, happy face, happy face. This is my happy face being worn at school today.

This is my happy march, happy march, happy march. This is my happy march taking place at school today.

✎ Match Mate (For Younger or Less Experienced Children)

Objective 22 For children to explore similarities and differences among people as a way to gain personal insight.

Materials None

Procedure Play this as a circle game. Pick one child to be in the center. Teach the children the following song, to the tune of "Ring Around the Rosie":

Match Mate, Match Mate,
Looking for a Match Mate,
Match Mate,
Match Mate,
You are it!

As the children sing and hold hands, the "Center" child moves around the circle, stopping in front of someone on the words, "You are it!" The other children then guess in what way the two children match. The child who was chosen as the "mate" will then become "it" for the next round.

To simplify Teacher chooses child to be "it" and just chants the words with the other children while the "it" child chooses a mate.

To extend The "Center" child selects a mate on the basis of two or three matching characteristics.

✎ I Can! (For Older or More Experienced Children)

Objective 26 For children to evaluate and describe their competencies.

Materials Large empty juice cans, colored paper strips, markers, blank booklets, paste or glue

Procedure Provide or have children each bring in a large empty juice can that has been washed and checked for any sharp edges. Have them place a label around the can that says "I CAN!" and then decorate the can so that each is individual. As they learn and demonstrate a new skill, have them fill out a special colored paper strip, dictating or writing the skill and dating it. Have them put the strips in the can.

To simplify Watch for children who fail to recognize their accomplishments. Remind these children that small gains also need to be recorded, and help them identify some of these gains or set goals that can be accomplished.

To extend At the end of each month, have the children transfer their "I CAN!" slips into an ongoing booklet, denoting the beginning of each month (e.g., "In November, I learned to do these things") and pasting in the strips following the heading. The pages could also be illustrated in some way. The booklets become a vehicle for children's self-assessment. They can also become one piece of a portfolio, shared with a portfolio buddy or the entire group, and shared with parents at conferences or open houses.

✎ We're Learning to Do So Many Things (For Younger or Less Experienced Children)

Objective 26 For children to evaluate and describe their competencies.

Materials Large precut hand on easel, markers, blank booklets

Procedure Tell the children, "Just think of how many things you do every day from the time you get up in the morning until you go to bed." Place a large precut hand on the easel. Tell the children, "Sometimes when someone is able to do a lot of different things, we say they are 'pretty handy.'" Ask them what they think the expression means, and discuss the many ways we use our hands to accomplish what we need to. Label the precut hand, "We Are Pretty Handy." Encourage the children to think of skills they have developed, print them on the hand, and then have the group decide where to place it in the classroom.

To simplify For children who have difficulty thinking of things they do, have the group suggest something they can probably do.

To extend Have the children construct an individual booklet that contains about 10 pages, titled "Learning to Be Handy." Have them work on completing the pages by drawing their hands on each page and then listing a separate skill they have learned on each of the fingers (e.g., "I brush my teeth," "I can count to 25," "I fix my own cereal," "I make my bed," "I feed my dog").

✎ Toy Land Relaxation (For Younger or Less Experienced Children)

Objective 29 For children to learn satisfying and effective strategies for coping with personal emotions and tensions.

Materials   Hinged toy figure, flexible cloth figures, taped musical selections for marching and relaxing, tape player

Procedure   To help children become familiar with and contrast feelings of bodily relaxation and tension, talk with them about how our bodies are hinged together. Help them discover where these "hinges" are located (neck, wrist, fingers, ankles, toes, and waist) and how stiff and tight their bodies feel when the hinges are all "locked up." Contrast this with what happens when these same hinges are loose by having the children relax each locked body hinge, starting with the neck, then the waist, wrists, and so on, reminding them to sit down carefully as their body becomes increasingly limp.

To simplify   Demonstrate the process of locking up and loosening up with toys, such as stiff, inflexible robots and limp cloth dolls or animals.

To extend   To increase children's sense of contrast, use marching music and practice being stiff robots; then switch to some peaceful, relaxing music, and encourage children to slow everything down and become completely limp and relaxed. Discuss with children other states they have experienced and how their bodies felt at the time, what their facial expressions may have been, what they may have said, or how they may have behaved (e.g., being angry vs. being happy and relaxed). For a follow-up activity, have children choose pictures from magazines that depict faces of people who seem "tight," angry, and hurried and those in which people seem "loose," happy, and relaxed.

✎ **Relaxing Our Bodies (For Children of All Ages)**

Objective 29   For children to learn satisfying and effective strategies for coping with personal emotions and tensions.

Materials   Compact disk (CD) of relaxing music, CD player

Procedure   One way to relax is through deep breathing. Even very young children can learn to do this with guidance. Have the children learn to assume a relaxed, comfortable position and be very quiet so that each of them can just listen to their breathing as they breathe in and out through their noses. As they relax, help them breathe more deeply and deepen their feeling of relaxation by having them try some of the following exercises:

❑   Imagine the air that comes to you is a cloud. The cloud comes to you, fills you, and then leaves you.

❑   Imagine your chest (or lungs) as a balloon. You may want to demonstrate this by putting your hand on your chest and then having them feel their chests as they breathe in deeply. Tell them, "As you breathe in, or inhale, your lungs expand like a balloon; don't

they? As you exhale, or breathe out, your lungs deflate like a balloon."

❑   As you inhale, say the word "in" to yourself. As you exhale, say the word "out."

To simplify   Have the children learn to assume a comfortable, relaxed position. Put on some relaxing music, and have them stretch slowly to the music, and then just lie quietly and listen to it. Use the words *relax* and *relaxing* to acquaint them with relaxation terminology.

To extend   Have the children experience tensing specific muscle groups and then relaxing them. First, be sure that they are familiar with all the body parts that follow, and demonstrate any unfamiliar terminology used, such as *clench* and *shrug*. Then talk them through the exercise as follows:

Muscle	Tensing Method
Forehead	Wrinkle your forehead. Try to make your eyebrows touch your hair. Count to five. Relax.
Eyes, nose	Close your eyes as tightly as you can. Keep them closed and count to five. Open your eyes and relax.
Lips, cheeks, jaw	Keeping your mouth closed, make as big a smile as you can. Keep the smile on your face and count to five. Relax. Feel how warm your face is.
Hands	Hold your arms in front of you. Make a tight fist with your hands. Squeeze them as tightly as you can while you count to five. Relax. Feel the warmth and calmness in your hands.
Forearms	Extend your arms out. Pretend you are pushing against a wall. Push forward with your hands and keep them against the invisible wall. Hold them there and count to five. Relax.
Shoulders	Shrug your shoulders up to your ears. Keep them there while you count to five. Relax.
Thighs	Tighten your thigh muscles by pressing your legs together as tightly as you can. Count to five. Relax your legs.
Feet	Bend your ankles toward your body as far as you can. Hold them there and count to five. Relax.
Toes	Curl your toes under as tightly as you can. Hold them there. Count to five. Relax.

Afterward, encourage the children to talk about how their bodies felt while they were doing the exercise. Tell them that some people like to relax their muscles when they go to bed by doing this exercise.

✎ We Get Angry . . . (For Children of All Ages)

Objective 31 For children to become familiar with the situational circumstances that influence personal emotions.

Materials Children's books about anger

Procedure After you discuss the feeling of anger with children in a large- or small-group situation and read some books about anger (e.g., *When I'm Angry,* by Barbara Gardiner and Jane Aaron; *Alexander and the Terrible, Horrible, No Good, Very Bad Day,* by Judith Viorst; *Attila the Angry,* by Marjorie Weinman Sharmat; *Let's Be Enemies,* by Janice May Udry; *The Sorely Trying Day,* by Russell Hoban; *The Hating Book,* by Charlotte Zolotow), have the children share examples of moments when they feel or have felt angry. Discuss ways in which the characters deal with the situations to help them get rid of the angry feelings. Talk about positive and negative strategies people use when they are trying to get rid of angry feelings.

To simplify After reading the stories, talk about what made the main character angry or upset.

To extend Write the title "We Get Angry When . . ." at the top of a large sheet of paper on the easel. List examples or write a class experience story as the children share their ideas. Older children could write and illustrate individual "I Get Angry When . . ." booklets.

SUMMARY

Young children have much to learn about themselves and the effect they have on others. What they learn in the early years from significant others in their lives—particularly from parents, teachers, and peers—becomes vitally important in their later ability to form and maintain relationships, work and play well with others, and feel valued, confident, and competent in any number of situations.

The development of emotional strength and stability, a lifelong task, is interdependent with children's cognitive, physical, and social development. Because children spend major amounts of time in extrafamilial settings and because they are moving into these contexts earlier and earlier, good learning environments are those in which affective, physical, and social development are valued as highly as academic aspects of learning. Caring professionals who are able to structure positive learning climates, actively promote children's emotional development and sense of self-worth, and foster children's competence are key players in facilitating positive affective outcomes for young children. Also critical is the sensitivity of caring adults to differences in personality, gender, ethnicity, and race in the children and families with whom they work.

✋ Applying What You Read in This Chapter

1. **Discuss**
   a. Review each of the opening questions in this chapter.
   b. In what way does the acquisition of self-esteem depend more on internal factors than on external factors?

2. **Observe**
   a. Arrange to visit an early childhood classroom and observe the following:
      (1) The overall affective climate in the classroom. What contributes most noticeably to it? What detracts from it?
      (2) Evidence that the teacher supports children on an individual basis as well as a cohort group. Cite specific examples of how he or she does this.

3. **Carry out an activity**
   a. Read Daniel Goleman's book *Emotional Intelligence* (1997). Find out what he believes is the cost of emotional illiteracy.
   b. Interview one or more principals of an elementary school. Ask to see how affective development is planned for in the curriculum. Ask, "How is this translated into everyday instruction? Could you give me some specific examples?"
   c. Survey 10 parents about character or moral education and whether they believe that it should be part of the school curriculum or left for families to provide for their children. What are their reasons for their preference?
   d. Survey one child at each level, preschool through third grade, to find out how involved each is in

terms of extracurricular activities. How much television does each child watch? How much leisure time does each have, and how do they spend it?

4. **Create something for your portfolio**
   a. Develop a lesson plan for the affective domain.
   b. Write a brief position paper outlining your beliefs about the importance of planning for affective development in the early childhood classroom.

5. **Add to your journal**
   a. How well is your emotional intelligence or intrapersonal intelligence developed? Because this is a lifelong process, are there areas that need attention? How can you address needed skill building?
   b. When you feel overly stressed or overwhelmed, what strategies do you use to reduce stress for the short term? for the long term? How do you react physically to undue stress? psychologically? behaviorally?
   c. In what temperament category would you place yourself: easy, slow to warm up, difficult, none of the three? What are some characteristics that make you believe that this conclusion is appropriate?

The Cognitive Domain

You may wonder:

How does the current emphasis on children's brain development contribute to our understanding of children's cognitive development?

What was the process of cognitive maturation that brought me to this point in my development? How "smart" am I, and in what ways am I "smart"?

What exactly is meant by the term *scaffolding,* and how does scaffolding take place most effectively in the early childhood classroom?

What should our goals be for science and mathematics education in the early years? Is hands-on activity alone sufficient to accomplish these goals?

How much emphasis should be placed on involving children with technology in the early childhood classroom? Does such involvement enhance or deter early learning?

In this chapter on the cognitive domain, we present information to help you answer the preceding questions.

In a discussion with a group of kindergartners after reading It Looked Like Spilt Milk *(by Charles Shaw; Harper Collins), Ms. Linscott asks the children, "How do you think clouds stay up in the sky?"*

"They're stuck up there 'cause they're made out of white stuff . . . out of lots of white glue and stuff!" offers Kiley.

"And sometimes they fall down at night and the next day it's all sun and no clouds in the sky . . . just all sun!" adds Latonya helpfully.

Young children's thinking is dramatically different from that of older children and adults, and this fact is illustrated repeatedly by young children's "cute" but inaccurate statements. They literally see the world from an entirely different perspective. Their fascinating journey toward more-mature thinking comprises a combination of inherent capacities, accumulated experiences, and the quality of their relationships with others who accompany them on this journey.

Development in the cognitive domain—that is, the maturation of processes and products of the human mind that lead to "knowing" (Berk, 2002a)—is a complex process that has a significant and continuous impact on all other domains of development. Likewise, growth and increasing competence in other domains influence the qualitative development of intellectual capacities. For example, a young child's ability to imagine or fantasize what being another member of the family—mommy, daddy, or baby—is like, equips the child to take on such a role in a group of children playing "house." In turn, interacting with other children as they play out their concept of "house" increases the child's knowledge and skill base in a variety of areas. In this case, vocabulary, understanding of social do's and don't's, one-to-one correspondence, and a sense of number as the children divide and combine materials are all enhanced. Also advanced is the children's ability to manage conflict as they sort out roles and goal-directed behaviors. In addition, their understanding of cause and effect grows as they operate on objects, challenge and cooperate with one another, and devise alternative ways to accomplish a variety of intended outcomes.

Because of the roundabout fashion in which the intellect evolves, promising new directions in early childhood education that support the integration of various learning domains and experiential learning have enormous potential. They are made even more effective when each child's cognitive levels are matched carefully with classroom learning experiences and when professionals are sensitive to the negative effects of overchallenging or underchallenging the children in their care.

COGNITIVE MATURATION

Contributions of Neuroscience to Understanding Children's Cognitive Development

A father comforts a crying newborn. A mother plays peekaboo with her ten-month-old. A child care provider reads to a toddler. And in a matter of seconds, thousands of cells in these children's growing brains respond. Some brain cells are "turned on," triggered by this particular experience. Many existing connections among brain cells are strengthened. At the same time, new connections are formed, adding a bit more definition and complexity to the intricate circuitry that will remain largely in place for the rest of these children's lives. *(Shore, 1997, p. ix)*

Neurodevelopment Since the 1970s, when anatomic study of the brain began in earnest, we have learned more about the human brain than in all of recorded history prior to then (Gardner, Kornhaber, & Wake, 1996). Much of the knowledge that had been learned about brain development before the 1970s had remained generally in the realm of medicine. Except for a brief mention in courses that educators may have taken in developmental and educational psychology, this information was not viewed as essential for preservice teachers. This is no longer true. Information about brain development, the potentially negative effects of risky environments on young children, and links between brain research findings and children's cognitive development are now hot topics in the field of early childhood education.

New evidence in the field of neurobiology provides valuable insights into planning for young children. For instance, we now know that the human brain contains some 50 billion neurons at birth and that at least 10 billion of these neural cells continue a process of connecting with one another in a series of plateau and acceleration periods. Because of a gene called *CREB*, which stimulates the number of connections made by each axon (see Figure 11.1), each of these cells has the

FIGURE 11.1 Neuronal Growth

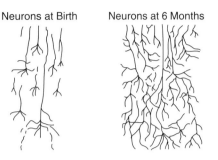

Neurons at Birth   Neurons at 6 Months   Neurons at 2 Years

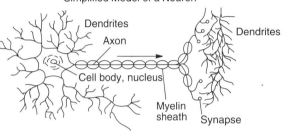

Simplified Model of a Neuron

Dendrites
Axon
Cell body, nucleus
Myelin sheath
Synapse
Dendrites

capacity to connect with a thousand others and lay out the complex neural pathways for developing language, logical-mathematical understanding, social interaction, affective growth, and aesthetic intelligence. By 2 years of age, children have developed half of all the neural connections that will be made during their lifetime. Then begins a process of pruning, or "weeding out," less used synapses while other connections continue to build and strengthen. The fatty myelin sheath that covers the nerves is fully formed in most children at about age 6 years, which allows for smoother electrochemical impulse transmission and the beginning of more-sophisticated thinking patterns.

During acceleration periods of brain growth, myelinization and axon and dendrite growth in the brain are significant, which enables millions of new connections to form. Following each acceleration period, children are able to experience more-complex levels of learning. In the early childhood classroom, we see this result in a child's excitement over finally "getting it"—finally understanding a concept or mastering a skill that has been difficult in the past, such as managing to tie a paint apron without help, writing first words independently, or regrouping in math without assistance.

Although we still have little understanding about gender differences in brain development, available findings have implications for early childhood education. In the preschool and early primary years, young males move into the brain growth acceleration stages generally 6 to 18 months later than females do (see Figure 11.2). Other researchers have documented significant male lags in emerging literacy through the first grade that

FIGURE 11.2 Plateau and Acceleration of Brain Growth According to Epstein (1978)

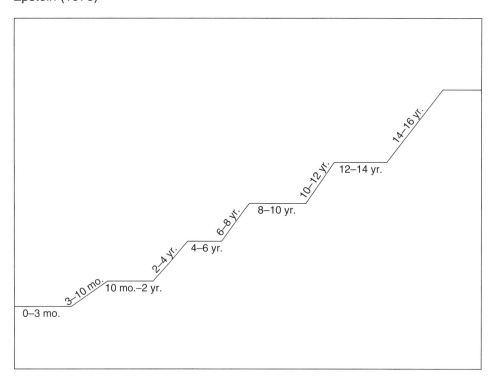

result from differences in visual memory and saccadic development (movement of the eye across the page during reading; Soderman, Gregory, & O'Neill, 1999a). Moreover, as children move toward adolescence, the female brain is fully formed about 2 years before the male brain.

In forging new frontiers into how the mind works, neuroscientists have begun to document particular areas of brain activity in relation to environmental stimulation. As a result, we know that a brain does not simply grow larger as our toes and fingers do; instead, it forms particular connections that are unique to each individual, depending on the quality and repetition of stimulating multisensory experiences encountered in the early years (Begley, 1997). These repeated experiences strengthen specific *synapses* (brain connections) with time. In turn, such experiences exert a critical influence on the kinds of pruning and neural connections (synaptogenesis) that ultimately produce the mature brain and corresponding abilities and capabilities in the child.

Evidence also suggests that particular sensory experiences in the early years may have a dramatic influence on brain wiring. For example, if a child has a particularly "chatty" and nurturing mother, oral language is increased. Children exposed to music (particularly classical music because of the repetitive patterns) experi-

ence more neural circuitry in the areas controlling spatial-temporal reasoning and later connected to mathematics and engineering. The peak learning years for human beings appear to be between the ages of 4 and 10 years, a time when children make huge leaps in language, logical-mathematical, and social discoveries (Viadero, 1996). Ultimately, the pruning, which becomes most aggressive around age 10 years, destroys the individual's weakest synapses, which results in a more specifically patterned, efficient, and powerful brain (Begley, 1997; Courtney, Ungerleider, Keil, & Haxby, 1997; Nash, 1997).

Challenges to Optimal Development Just as we know that high-quality early environments set in motion positive trajectories for development, a number of factors have a negative influence on brain development. Some of these may occur genetically as life begins, setting off any number of disorders that can influence later cognition; in addition, poor prenatal nutrition, maternal drug and alcohol use, and several maternal chronic illnesses can result in problematic fetal brain development and loss of cognitive potential. Children diagnosed with mental retardation generally have substantially subaverage intellectual functioning that ranges from mild to severe, as well as adaptive impairments (their ability to function

FIGURE 11.3 Example of Teaching a Child with a Cognitive Domain Challenge

---

Colin

Colin, a 7-year-old in first grade, was diagnosed with fragile X syndrome at age 4 years. Early in his development, his parents had suspected a problem because of speech, language, and motor delays. A diagnostic examination revealed that a genetic defect had resulted in decreased production of FMRP, a protein that is highly important for neurological development and functioning. Colin's parents were warned that although mental retardation was a likelihood in fragile X cases, his IQ scores indicated that the retardation was mild. Accordingly, he would likely require special education services at some time but could probably do fairly well in regular classes.

As Colin grew older, his speech was halting or sometimes echolaic (parrot-like), particularly when he became stressed or anxious. Now, at age 7 years, his somewhat enlarged head, extremely narrow face, and long, protruding ears, which are characteristic of the disorder, are more pronounced. Although only mild retardation had been predicted, Colin is beginning to have difficulty with any task requiring memorization. This is particularly true with math. Colin's teacher has observed that he seems to have more difficulty when tasks are broken into parts than when he is presented with all parts of the task at once. This seems odd to her, but Colin appears to be better at simultaneously processing what needs to be done. She notes to his parents, "Despite his learning problems in math, he's doing especially well in reading. Also, because of his wonderful sense of humor, he's pretty popular with the other children. Colin and I are working on strategies for the difficulties he's having in math. All in all, he's having a pretty good year and making a lot of progress."

---

in daily life; see Figure 11.3). Cases of severe mental retardation can usually be attributed to a biological origin. In most cases of mild mental retardation, the causes remain unclear. However, both genetic components and socioeconomic factors, such as poverty and undernutrition, often contribute to the prevalence (Batshaw, 2002).

Strong evidence indicates that traumatic and chaotic environments also negatively affect neural connections and cognitive growth in young children being reared in risky situations. Elevated stress hormones such as cortisol result in diminished brain growth in regions of the brain related to memory, learning, and emotional attachment; simultaneously, arousal is increased in other regions related to hyperactivity, anxiety, impulsive behavior, attention regulation, and self-control (Gunnar, Brodersen, Krueger, & Rigatuso, 1996; Shore, 1997).

Even if a child's environment does not contain overt abuse or serious neglect, it may be one in which the child is simply deprived of the kind of stimulating experiences that produce the most fertile minds. Previously, we had suspected that human development hinges strongly on the interplay between nature and nurture (Shore, 1997). However, convincing professionals who believed that intelligence, school success, and the way we interact with the world are primarily the result of fixed brain structures at birth—with environmental experiences considerably less influential—was difficult (Newberger, 1997). Research results now remove any doubt about the effect of inadequate early experiences; such results yield serious implications for parents, policy makers, and early childhood educators. Ironically, parents are more

pressed for time than ever (Nash, 1997, p. 51), and quality child care for working parents remains a problem in terms of both availability and cost. Likewise, although we as educators have made inroads into providing a better match between children's cognitive levels and primary classroom experiences, many children are still sitting in classrooms in which a serious gap exists between professional knowledge and instructional practice. Susan Kovalik (1997), a well-known educator and advocate for developmentally appropriate practice, termed this gap a *breach of morality* in the profession. She reminded us, "[We] are the only species that creates the environment that creates us," and she challenged all educators to provide the rich and flexible learning context that every child deserves.

A New View of Intelligence   Howard Gardner's (1997) theoretical perspective of intelligence, discussed previously in this text, suggests the possibility that strengths and outcomes in brain connections may also be heavily influenced by a child's natural inclinations. Gardner thinks that the neurobiology just described results in "core information processing mechanisms" associated with particular intelligences or talents. Making the claim for relatively autonomous intelligences, he defined *intelligence* as "the ability to solve problems or fashion products that are of consequence in a particular cultural setting or community" (Gardner, 1993a, p. 15). As was outlined in chapter 2, he offered at least eight intelligences that account for the many variations seen in human beings within and across all cultures. He cited evidence for his theory from the many studies of breakdowns in specific mental functioning in persons who are brain damaged and from the intellectual profiles of special populations (e.g., prodigies and savants) who demonstrate extraordinary development in one area but only minimal or even diminished capability in other areas. At the heart of his theory is his belief that humans come equipped with certain intelligences that are genetically programmed to be activated or "triggered" (e.g., syntactic ordering in language or pitch in music), but he noted that not everyone progresses to an expert end state in all areas (e.g., mathematics or music).

So far, the greatest influence of his theory has been felt in educational circles in which children are challenged to round out their range of talents, encouraged to use a special strength to shore up a weaker area, and allowed to demonstrate performance competence in ways other than through traditional paper-and-pencil tests. He noted that some of the diverse ways in which educators have applied his theory have been "brilliant," whereas others have been "idiotic" (Gardner, 1994, p. 581). The message is that intelligence manifests in human beings in diverse ways. Instead of asking how intelligent a child is, we need to ask, "In what way does this child demonstrate intelligence? What does the child's interests tell me that may be useful in planning for instruction? How can the child's intellectual strengths be used to balance minimal or diminished capabilities in other areas of development?" (Hatch, 1997).

THEORETICAL CONTRIBUTIONS OF JEAN PIAGET AND LEV VYGOTSKY

Piaget is important not because he got it all right, but because he was the first person to portray children's intellectual development in detail and because people continue to address the questions that Piaget himself first addressed.
—Howard Gardner

Although the theoretical conclusions of Swiss epistemologist Jean Piaget are being reexamined in light of current research in the field, his contributions continue to be highly useful in understanding the qualitative cognitive changes that occur in the young child. Piaget perceived that maturation evolves from a human organism's self-motivated efforts to adapt to and make sense of day-to-day experiences. His theoretical views fit well with current neurobiological findings about cognition, as do the approximate ages of children at which Piaget observed significant changes in their thinking capabilities.

In developing useful concepts, or schemes, children purposefully repeat certain acts (e.g., dropping an object from the high chair, rhyming certain sounds or

words, observing how someone ties shoelaces, drawing or scribbling, listening to a story, riding a tricycle, working a puzzle, or writing at school in a daily journal). These acts result in their "bumping into" new information that is either simply assimilated or produces a need for accommodation in terms of current functioning. When human beings cognitively *assimilate* experiential knowledge, they do so without feeling any particular need to adapt the way they think about a phenomenon or situation. However, other times they become *disequilibrated,* or thrown out of balance cognitively; this imbalance occurs because they have begun to notice something about a situation or phenomenon that no longer fits comfortably into their old way of thinking about it. Then, to reequilibrate, or rid themselves of their confusion, they have to adapt their thinking in some new way.

For example, at 2 years of age, Kevin had only one concept for all wheeled vehicles, and he referred to them all as "cars." He persisted in doing so, no matter how many times someone corrected him. However, subsequently, as a result of new experiences with a number of wheeled objects and structural maturation of the brain, he began to realize that some vehicles *were* different from one another. His growing *interest* (according to Piaget, an element critical for mental action) in his wheeled toys caused him to zero in on the various characteristics of the toys. This interest also spilled over to include the real cars, trucks, and other vehicles he came across in his everyday experiences. Kevin seemed especially motivated to investigate these differences and, as he approached age 3 years, his parents were amazed at the quick rate of growth in his ability to identify differences in the toy vehicles he owned and saw in magazines and books. He remembered their names, and he put his wheeled toys into categories as he played, making one garage for cars, another for his trucks, and still another for all the others. As Kevin neared 7 years of age, his keen interest in wheeled toys and real vehicles continued. He often drew vehicles and could demonstrate that within the category of cars, he knew there were Fords and Volvos, sedans and coupes, convertibles and hardtops, and sports cars and family cars. During a span of 5 years, his inaccurate, one-card mental file for vehicles had expanded into a more mature scheme for understanding wheeled phenomena and for interacting with his environment. According to Piaget, these higher order schemes are an outcome of both genetic, biological unfolding and experiences that catch a person's attention and interest and create the internal motivation to mentally try a task repeatedly to "figure it out."

According to Piaget, children experience four stages of mental operations as they make sense of their world and the people and objects in it. These stages include (a) a sensorimotor period from birth to approximately age 2 years, in which infants learn primarily through their senses and by manipulating objects; (b) a preoperational stage between ages 2 and 7 years, in which children classify in rudimentary and intuitive ways and see simple relationships, even though they do not understand why or how something works; (c) a concrete operational period from approximately age 7 years to age 11 years, in which children grow in their abilities to understand and use mathematical operations; and (d) a formal operational period, in which they develop abstract concepts and become able to understand cause-and-effect relationships, think about the future, and become more competent at testing ideas they have. Although these stages are age related, the specific years of age connected to them are approximate. Children are continuously moving toward acquisition of higher level processes while still showing evidence of characteristic limitations identified with particular stages. Early childhood educators working with young children can benefit greatly by understanding and respecting the characteristic modes of thinking within certain stages so that activities and experiences match cognitive levels and neither underestimate nor exceed a child's ability to gain from them.

Piagetian Characteristics of Preoperational and Concrete Operational Thought

Because this text focuses on constructing effective learning environments for children aged 3 to 8 years, characteristics specific to children in Piaget's preoperational and concrete operational periods deserve a closer look.

The Preoperational Child *Centration,* children's tendency to center on only one aspect of a stimulus rather than processing all available information and holding changes in two dimensions at the same time, is an important aspect of preoperational thinking. As children move toward the end of the period, they are not as easily fooled and are more able to decenter in situations or with materials familiar to them. Although their thought is perhaps still not as logical as that of the average 8- to 11-year-old, they are relying less on intuition and the appearance of things when they explain why things happen. Their understanding of cause and effect becomes clearer, and more-mature preoperational children are also beginning to move away from the egocentrism that limits them from seeing other people's viewpoints.

Closely related to centration is a lack of ability to think in more than one direction (irreversibility). *Reversibility,* the concept that objects or actions can be

structured, restructured, and then rearranged as originally structured, is limited in the preoperational child. Children younger than 5 years old are influenced by perceptual salience; that is, their perceptions dominate their understandings, and seeing is believing. Thus, they do not automatically know what older children are coming to know—that number, mass, distance, volume, and area remain constant despite changes in appearance and that you can also undo operations. For example, at a summer camp craft class, 9-year-old Juana and her 3-year-old brother Carl had each created a sculpture from toothpicks and marshmallows. Each child had been given 20 marshmallows and 10 toothpicks to create whatever he or she wanted. Carl, after completing a "spaceship" with his materials, began pestering Juana for more toothpicks and marshmallows to make a different spaceship because he did not like the one he had created. "Just use the ones you have!" she responded testily. Carl looked down in a confused way at the unwanted creation, thought again about the other one he had in mind, and cried, "But they're all gone! I don't have no more!" From Juana's viewpoint, it was possible to construct a new product from the materials available; from Carl's, it was not.

Children in the Concrete Operational Stage Children who have moved into the concrete operational stage still benefit from using real objects when they are problem solving but are now better equipped to deal with symbolic forms. Because their ability to decenter is more highly developed, they can focus on details while keeping the whole in mind, a skill necessary for understanding part–whole relationships involved in place value in mathematics or phonics in literacy. Like Juana in the preceding example, children in the concrete stage can be more reflective about such operations and what would be required to undo an action.

Researchers have documented that, with coaching, children may be able to perform such operations somewhat earlier than Piaget believed they could. With the preoperational child, physical action and concrete materials are prerequisites to developing their understanding of particular phenomena. They are often better able to express their feelings, thoughts, and conceptualizations through symbolic play than through speech. However, when they are able to use varied strategies and trial and error to test possibilities and solutions, they become capable of more-complex thinking and can use knowledge in increasingly sophisticated ways. Thus, effective early childhood teachers are always looking for opportunities to help children refine their ideas, to inspire them to do the difficult work required to figure something out, to focus their thinking, and to search for information; such teachers also model a higher level of reasoning for the young children who are learning in their classrooms (DeVries, Zan, Hildebrandt, Edmiaston, & Sales, 2002).

In contrast to Piaget, Lev Vygotsky (1962), a Russian-born psychologist and contemporary of Piaget, differed in his perspectives about mental activity and resulting learning. Whereas Piaget believed that development leads to learning, Vygotsky believed that development is the result of social learning. He believed that mental activity is uniquely human and is the internalization of social signs, culture, and social relationships. Although Vygotsky died prematurely in 1934 at the age of 37 from tuberculosis, he was an astoundingly prolific writer; he turned out almost 50 impressive pieces of psychological literature. A Stalinist persecution of Russian intellectuals a year after his death resulted in a 20-year ban on his writings; however, in 1956 they were reissued and have become one of the most dominant influences on constructivist thinking and educational practice today (Moll, 1996).

Vygotskian Perspectives

Lev Vygotsky's concept of the *zone of proximal development* (ZPD) is important to us as educators in terms of children's optimal learning. He believed that development should not be viewed as a fixed entity. Instead, he saw it as a dynamic and constantly changing continuum of behavior, degree of maturation, or zone that is limited by behaviors that appear close to developing in the near future. He described two levels that form the parameters of development at any particular time: (a) the lower level of performance, designated as *independent performance* (i.e., what the child knows and can currently do without the help of someone more knowledgeable—an adult, a peer, an imaginary partner, or older children at higher developmental levels), and (b) a higher level, designated as *maximally assisted performance,* which the child can achieve with support or scaffolding (i.e., clues, hints, rephrasing, demonstrations, explanations, specifically structured practice activities). Adults or more-knowledgeable peers provide the scaffolding that allows the child to move forward and continue to build new competencies (see Figure 11.4). The adult's involvement is then reduced as the child grows in his or her ability to handle the problem or skill independently. Once skill independence becomes established, more-challenging tasks may be introduced, which form a new ZPD in this area for the child. Subsequently, with assistance and practice, the assisted level becomes part of the child's independent performance. In this way, continuous, advanced maturation occurs. This concept of the ZPD means that effective teachers should be aiming toward the higher level of the child's ZPD, while remembering that there are limits to how far a child can be challenged cognitively at any particular time. When skills or concepts that are too far beyond a child's ZPD are introduced, children will "tune out," ignore, fail to use, or use incorrectly that which is being pushed inappropriately (Leong & Bodrova, 1995).

FIGURE 11.4 Scaffolding Children's Performance in Reading

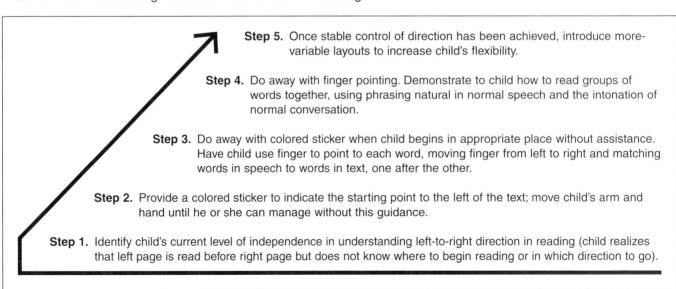

Step 5. Once stable control of direction has been achieved, introduce more-variable layouts to increase child's flexibility.

Step 4. Do away with finger pointing. Demonstrate to child how to read groups of words together, using phrasing natural in normal speech and the intonation of normal conversation.

Step 3. Do away with colored sticker when child begins in appropriate place without assistance. Have child use finger to point to each word, moving finger from left to right and matching words in speech to words in text, one after the other.

Step 2. Provide a colored sticker to indicate the starting point to the left of the text; move child's arm and hand until he or she can manage without this guidance.

Step 1. Identify child's current level of independence in understanding left-to-right direction in reading (child realizes that left page is read before right page but does not know where to begin reading or in which direction to go).

Source: Adapted from Clay (1995).

Adults can facilitate children's higher order thinking through scaffolding.

Also critical for educators to understand is Vygotsky's belief that "all higher mental functions are internalized social relationships." He thought that children continually make sense of and are drawn to learn more about concepts, skills, and processes because of their interactions with others. They learn what they are interested in learning or what they perceive as rewarding to learn.

The bottom line is that knowledge cannot come in neatly packaged sets of understandings that can be passively given to children. When such packaging is attempted, we risk short-circuiting in-depth or true understanding of phenomena in children because we cut them off from the intriguing and engaging work of concept formation.

CHILDREN'S ACQUISITION OF A FUNDAMENTAL KNOWLEDGE BASE FOR COGNITIVE DEVELOPMENT

To this point, we focused on how children come to know things; now let us concentrate on what they *need* to know. A necessary knowledge base comprises primarily five subgroups (DeVries & Kohlberg, 1990):

1. *Physical knowledge*—observable attributes of objects and physical phenomena: size, color, shape, weight, texture, tendencies under varying conditions (e.g., objects roll downhill; snow is cold; sugar is sweet; spiders have eight legs).

2. *Logical-mathematical knowledge*—relationships between objects, and phenomena deriving from obser-

vation; developing a logical organization to deal more effectively with incoming knowledge, including classifying, patterning, seriating, numbering (counting, one-to-one correspondence, equivalence of groups of numbers, invariance of number), using space in relationship to the body (vertical and horizontal coordinates; right and left, in-front and behind coordinates; depth and distance coordinates; topological—closed or open shapes, inclusion–exclusion, proximity, order—and Euclidean geometric—lines, angles, equalities, parallelism, distance perspectives), and using time (order of events and length of events). Development in this arena is critical to the child's ability to organize a complex and confusing world.

3. *Representational knowledge*—imaginative expression of symbolic thought that represents the child's mental world; manipulation of images, art, symbols, and language to stand for objects, events, and concepts (Steinberg & Belsky, 1991); competence in restructuring an experience in another way through symbolic representation (dramatic and creative play, rhythmic movement, imitation, construction of two- and three-dimensional models) and sign representation—which evolves through spoken language and then written language as follows:

Using names for objects in the environment

Using words to identify the properties and functions of objects

Using words to denote location in space and time

Using words that describe relationships (comparing, describing differences and similarities, enumerating, measuring, and ordering)

Using words to relate physical knowledge

Using words to relate social knowledge

Using words to tell events and stories

Using words to relate personal feelings and thoughts

4. *Social-conventional knowledge*—cultural and societal conventions, rules, and viewpoints transmitted to children by family, society, school, and peers to guide behavior related to other individuals, institutions, and the use of goods and services (e.g., 911 is a number to call if someone is in danger; some families have more than one mother and father; many Jewish families celebrate Hanukkah; most people finish high school; farmers produce most of our food).

5. *Metacognition*—proficient strategies for monitoring your thinking processes. Becoming an effective problem solver requires that children develop this unique cognitive quality. It is activated and enhanced when we help them develop the requisite skills needed for critical and fair thinking, mental flexibility, organization of their ideas, and application of the many essential

components of learning (O. McAfee & Leong, 2002). The use of Socratic or open-ended questioning can move children away from fragmented, fuzzy, and inconsistent thinking by challenging them as appropriate: "How do you know that? "Where did you find that out?" "Why do you think someone would do that?" "When would that not be true?" "Is there another way to think about that?" "How would you explain that to someone else who wanted to learn it?"

Children are the best source of topics that interest them, and skillful teachers mobilize children's enthusiasm for learning when they design interdisciplinary "anchors." These anchors are complex problems that children think are worth solving and that capture their desire to learn a set of relevant skills and concepts. Such anchors can be invented or natural, as long as they fulfill the following requirements (Barab & Landa, 1997, p. 53): capture children's imagination; are perceived as important by learners; legitimize the disciplinary content they integrate; accommodate a variety of learning approaches, styles, and cultural experiences; require children to draw on concepts and skills associated with more than one discipline; and generate developmentally appropriate activities.

The Reggio Emilia and project approaches to early childhood education, which have been gaining popularity in the United States, are just two examples of instructional approaches used to teach children rather than teaching to a curriculum. Both use children's interests as worthwhile catalysts for skill and concept development. For example, a primary-school teacher asked children to bring in articles of interest from their local newspapers. The class showed more than a passing interest in an article about the community's concern about an increase in roving packs of dogs. The children were guided toward thinking about the problem from a number of hypothetical perspectives and asked to create a web of ideas that might be investigated. Included in their subsequent research was finding out about rabies and rabies treatment, the origin of humane societies, the cost of keeping dogs and other animals, and the duties and training of dog-catchers. The children wrote stories about the situation from the dogs' perspective, investigated varieties of dogs and their histories and uses, drew pictures of dogs, and read stories about dogs. All during their study, children's interest remained high, as did their academic skill building and understanding of methods of finding information and organizing and communicating it to one another and to their teacher and parents.

Researchers have suggested that each child's brain is a "rich, layered, messy, unplanned jungle ecosystem"

that probably thrives best in a learning context that includes many sensory, cultural, and problem layers closely related to the real-world environment in which children live—the environment that best stimulates the neural networks that are genetically linked to it (Sylwester, 1995, p. 23). This finding speaks to one of the most important questions being asked in early childhood education. Is the teachers' role to directly teach children, or is their role only to support children as they construct knowledge? A recent observation in an Oakland County, Michigan, kindergarten class at math time provides some insight into this dilemma. In this case, the teacher missed a great opportunity to extend children's understanding through scaffolding and reflective discussion:

Many of the children were actively involved with manipulatives while the teacher worked on sorting with a small group of youngsters. She passed a container filled with interesting objects around the group and asked each child to select two that were similar in some way. She then asked each child to tell the others how his or her objects were the same. Although every child was successful in choosing two objects that were similar in some way, not one child could tell her the similar feature. Clearly, though, some children had an understanding of the salient characteristic because they attempted to show it nonorally. For example, one child, who had selected a quarter and a plate, used his finger to trace a circle in the air. However, he did not have a name for this characteristic. The teacher then complimented the children on their selections and excused them from the group.

Effective teaching requires the early childhood educator to play many roles in the classroom, as described previously in chapter 3. In addition to being a facilitator and learning guide, the teacher must also be active in transferring existing knowledge that children cannot discover on their own. In this case, children needed vocabulary (social-conventional knowledge) to help them articulate what they were trying so hard to describe. Although many thoughtful, well-meaning early childhood teachers are struggling with this issue, direct instruction is an appropriate and necessary component in early childhood classrooms as we help children work on problems they find interesting to study.

The Young Child as Scientist

Children are full of questions and expend a great deal of their energy on discovering how things work, what people do, and how they can become more-competent players in the general scheme of life. They have a driving need to learn: how electric outlets work, how toilets flush, how things open and close, where bubbles go, how seashore waves "melt" sand castles, and how whales can stay underwater so long without breathing.

Preschool children act on their intense curiosity by observing, trying out simple operations, and questioning adults, repeatedly. For these children, events simply happen or happen by magic. They turn on the television and Barney appears. They ride with their family in the car at night, and the moon follows them—amazing! Later, as neural pathways mature and primary-age children gain experience and information, their understanding of cause and effect is more often correct, although still limited. So that children can build a consistent picture of the physical world, educators must consider children's prior knowledge base, relate new learning experiences to this base, and modify the presentation of new and subsequent experiences on an individual and small-group basis if children are to expand conceptually. Doing so calls for evaluating any misconceptions children have about a particular phenomenon, and young children have a lot of them. To develop the concepts and skills needed to comprehend their world from an accurate and scientific perspective, preschoolers and elementary children need teachers who have a basic understanding about scientific concepts that children need to explore and a view of science as a dynamic process that must involve science inquiry. Children also need access to thoughtfully selected materials and many opportunities to work with and observe scientific phenomena. Finally, they benefit enormously from teachers who structure time for them to revisit, represent, discuss, and demonstrate the experiences they have with the specially selected materials (Moriarty, 2002, pp. 20–21).

Science is a "process of finding out and a system for organizing and reporting discoveries" (Lind, 1997, p. 75). Children who are in the process of observing, thinking, and reflecting on actions and events are doing science. When they are organizing factual information into more meaningful concepts, problem solving, and acting on their curiosity, they are doing science. In trying to understand how the work of scientists is related to their lives and investigations, they are doing science. They are *not* doing science when they are merely listening to someone talk about science, reading about it in a textbook, or learning facts and memorizing formulas. As we provide opportunities for them to be actively involved in the scientific process by forming hypotheses, collecting data, and formulating and testing their conclusions, we provide for them the basic skills they will need for lifelong "sciencing"—multisensory observing, questioning, comparing, organizing, measuring, communicating, experimenting, relating (drawing ab-

stractions from concrete data), inferring, and applying. In the early childhood classroom, we can increase the effectiveness of these opportunities by making sure that we respect children's current abilities and potential capabilities.

Debriefing after each science activity to evaluate the kinds of concepts children are forming is a necessary strategy for building integrity into our instructional planning and for helping children realize that science is more than a collection of activities and already-known facts. They need to know that the solution to problems or new discoveries can sometimes spring from intuitive feelings about a particular phenomenon, as well as from already-documented laws, theories, and principles. Thus, children should be encouraged to think divergently (in many directions) and creatively as well as convergently (centered on already-known facts) in their problem finding, problem solving, and articulation about what their findings mean. These cognitive skills are those that the American Association for the Advancement of Science believes are critical for living in a complex world.

Nowhere is Piaget's view of children's developing intellectual capacities more useful than in understanding where we often go wrong in early science education. Because conceptualization in the early years is unsystematic and intuitive, helpful adults want to guide children toward more complex, integrated modes of thinking and capability in organizing knowledge. The primary strategy for doing so is usually to supply manipulative materials and activities that allow children to "mess around"—observing, comparing, classifying, and measuring—with the belief that concepts will be learned in the process and that children can then easily move on to semiconcrete (iconic) and then abstract learning experiences. Unfortunately, we often move too quickly, trying to teach concepts that are too far beyond the child's level of understanding (or ZPD). A good example of this can be found in study themes in early science education that Kovalik and Olsen (1997) call "wildly age inappropriate." These study themes center on concepts that are too highly abstract and not experienceable in any way, which sets up a serious mismatch between content and cognitive capacity. The solar system as a subject for second or third graders is one of the most common: "The ground on which we stand is spinning at hundreds of miles an hour, and the distances between planets are computed in millions of miles or even light years, a measurement that most adults can't relate to" (p. 6). The problematic result of these mismatches is that children are unable to apply or interpret deeper meanings of the content, lose interest in science, and develop more-negative attitudes toward it (Lind, 1997). Nonetheless, we should not ignore the young child's interest in understanding some *basic* solar system concepts: "Where does the sun go at night?" "What are stars?" "Why does the moon change?" Allowing children to construct coherent ideas about abstract themes can be facilitated by structuring long-term investigations in which we teach them to observe a phenomenon of interest across time, to document their findings, to revisit these findings, to build a knowledge base, and to use knowledge "gained on one day as the foundation for the next day's exploration" (Conezio & French, 2002, p. 15). For example, they can build more-sophisticated concepts about day and night by noting changes in the weather and seasons, playing with and recording the length of shadows at various times of the day, and having access to a number of delightful books about how shadows are made, how light travels, and the cycle of day and night.

Age-appropriate math and science concepts are those that we would typically expect children to understand at particular ages, according to our knowledge of child development norms and our experience with young children. Preschoolers probably function best when we spontaneously provide science experiences related to their outdoor play (spiders, insects, plants, soil, sand, and water) and natural interest in animals and animal homes.

As children move into the primary grades and progress in conceptual depth and complexity, teachers can engage them in doing a great deal more of the recording and written communication of their findings, building collections of natural materials, constructing dioramas, and using information books for guided study, focused reading, and vocabulary building. Science should continue to be primarily a hands-on activity, which can include gardening, hatching eggs, studying pond life, and so forth. Science curricula are available that provide age-appropriate activity suggestions for elementary children, notably those that came out of such projects as the Elementary Science Study (ESS), the Science Curriculum Improvement Study (SCIS), the Science-A-Process Approach (SAPA), and the American Association for the Advancement of Science's *Benchmarks for Science Literacy*.

Teaching children about basic concepts in science is a natural catalyst for curriculum integration. For example, when the children in Mr. Mishler's room became interested in the dandelions cropping up in a field near the school, their investigations led them to drawing and writing about their magnifications and dissections of the plants and plant roots, measuring and graphing lengths of stems they found, estimating and counting the numbers of emerging plants, and painting the fascinating yellows and greens of the new plants and the plants that had already gone to seed. The children classified the leaves of dandelions and other plants,

discussed and formulated a definition of what constitutes a weed and what constitutes a flower, read and constructed poems about flowers and fauna, and performed for another class the silly song that Mr. Mishler wrote about dandelions. They began using the correct term for the yellow substance that came off on their fingers and chins when they were handling the dandelions and discovered the purpose of the substance in the life cycle of plants. They experimented with creating a yellow dye and methods for removing it from swatches of material. Clearly, all curricular activity could spring from science; at the least, good sciencing requires integration of activities and experiences from all other learning domains. The depth and breadth of children's learning will depend on hands-on opportunities to collect a wide variety of information and guidance in integrating this knowledge through reflective discussion about what they discover.

Using a more in-depth, theme-repetitive approach toward science education that can lead to higher order problem-solving skills rather than rote memorization should be a priority in good science teaching. Another priority should be to help children make connections between science and real-world issues. Once children have developed the basic skills of observing, inferring, and experimenting, they should be encouraged to engage in scientific inquiry, a process that requires them to think about and interpret what they are gaining through the many sensory-experience activities in the early childhood classroom. According to Lind (1997), inquiry serves five essential functions:

1. It assists in the development of understanding of science concepts.
2. It helps students "know how we know" in science.
3. It develops an understanding of the nature of science.
4. It develops the skills necessary to become independent inquirers about the natural world.
5. It develops the dispositions to use the skills, abilities, and habits of the mind associated with science. (pp. 83–84)

Remember that teaching with a hands-on approach to science does not automatically teach problem solving and inquiry. Also necessary is the teacher's ability to ask good, open-ended questions and to provide well-planned activities involving guided discovery, problem solving, and social inquiry. For example, when Ms. Villareal asks children to use the paper bear tracks she has developed to measure the distance between the "bear den" and the dramatic play center, she is simply using a hands-on approach. However, when she tells them, "Find some way to measure the distance from the bear den to the dramatic play center and then report to the group on how you did this and what you found out," she is engaging the children in inquiry. The first approach simply has children carrying out a process she designed. The second encourages children to develop scientific skills that will become enormously useful to them—discovering a way to gather data when they need to problem solve, mentally organizing the information, and effectively articulating it to someone else.

The Young Child as Mathematician

Today, mathematics instruction is less about teaching basic computation and more about helping students become flexible thinkers who are comfortable with all areas of mathematics and are able to apply mathematical ideas and skills to a range of problem-solving situations. *(Burns, 2000, p. 28)*

For young children, mathematics is everywhere. It is a natural and integral part of their world. They see numerals everywhere—on their house, on the clock, on the cereal box, on their play telephone, on the car and in books. Many of their favorite finger plays, songs, and rhymes, which are used to encourage language, also develop math vocabulary and concepts: "Ten Little Monkeys Jumping on the Bed"; "One, Two, Buckle My Shoe"; "Eency Weency Spider"; "The Grand Old Duke of York" (S. S. Smith, 2001). Favorite books, such as Jon Scieszka and Lane Smith's *Math Curse,* Eric Carle's *Rooster's Off to See the World,* and Pat Hutchins' *The Doorbell Rang,* help shape children's early perspectives about the relationships among different components of mathematics and their connection to every aspect of children's lives. At home, in preschools, and in elementary schools, young children sit at the computer, interacting with such characters as Zack the cabdriver and Chester the lazy raccoon, who take them through a variety of math activities in Infinity City or into fractions and decimals in a program called *Math Keys* (Minnesota Educational Computing Corporation [MECC]; Macintosh/Windows).

Diversity in race, ethnicity, social class, gender, out-of-school experiences, and modality-related learning styles is critical to consider when we are designing developmentally appropriate classrooms (Charlesworth, 2000). Even prior to kindergarten, some children understand that a counting sequence indicates increasingly larger quantities; others can also identify objects to 10, recognize some numerals, and identify coins and geometric shapes. Some kindergartners may even solve simple addition and subtraction problems in their heads. Other children in the same classroom may never have seen a computer, and their math vocabulary may be limited to the words *big* and *little.*

Even though wide differences can be found in any one classroom of children, preschoolers and early primary-age children do share one characteristic: As pointed out previously, their conceptualization is limited by thinking parameters common to the preoperational period (i.e., centration, egocentrism, and irreversibility). Thus, most children have a considerable amount of work to do before they will truly understand what "fiveness" is all about, as well as other logical-mathematical concepts. For example, although a child may be able to demonstrate "counting," he or she may have no true understanding of the hierarchical nature of counting. As with other mathematical concepts, children's understanding of counting moves through a sequence governed by a set of principles. As described by Hohmann and Weikart (1997), these principles include the following five:

1. *The one-to-one principle.* Using one and only one number name (such as "one, two, three") for each number counted.
2. *The stable-order principle.* Using the number names in a stable order, such as "one, two, three" even though the order may be unconventional, such as "six, eleven, fifteen."
3. *The cardinal principle.* Using the last number name spoken to describe the number of objects in the set, "One, two, three . . . Three snakes!"
4. *The abstraction principle.* Counting part of a mixed set of items, for example, counting the red blocks in a building made of multicolored blocks.
5. *The order-irrelevance principle.* Recognizing that the order in which objects are counted is irrelevant. Six balls are always six balls no matter which one you count first. (p. 482)

Moreover, the child's logic may not yet be developed enough to know that a rearrangement of the same objects leaves the number or amount unchanged. For example, 4-year-old Chelsey was presented with two rows of five pennies each and asked to count each row. She did so, counting the pennies one at a time, and said there were five pennies in each row. When asked, "Are there the same number in each row, or does one row have more?" she methodically counted again and responded, "They're the same." As she watched, the pennies in the second row were spread farther apart from one another. When asked, "Now is there the same number in each row, or does one row have more?" she quickly pointed to the second row and said with confidence, "This one has more!" Chelsey was obviously centering on the length of the two rows and was unable to think about the difference in spacing at the same time. With this kind of understanding, Chelsey did not yet have an anchor for making decisions about the use of number.

Young children are eager to build on their basic concepts of logical-mathematical knowledge. Many of these concepts, such as comparing, classifying, and measuring, are needed as the child grows conceptually in other developmental domains, including the affective, social, and aesthetic arenas. Similarly, concepts the child is developing in other areas, such as science (observing, communicating, inferring, predicting, hypothesizing, defining, and controlling variables) and language (higher, slower, warm, hardest, longest, and juicier), will be important for logical-mathematical extensions (Charlesworth & Lind, 1995).

At first, a child's mathematical knowledge is gained through naturalistic experiences completely controlled by the child; these experiences are complemented by informal, exploratory activity in which adults offer comments or ask questions. Eventually, this type of activity is replaced by primarily structured acquisition, which consists mostly of preplanned activities conceived by the teacher (Ginsberg & Baron, 1993). Young children need a prolonged period of informal exploration before they can form basic concepts about shape, one-to-one correspondence, size, weight, texture, and amount. For the preschooler, this exploration occurs through such natural activities as building with blocks; pouring water; working with sand, puzzles, and play dough; cooking; and matching, sorting, and seriating objects. In interacting with adults and one another during such activities, they also extend their foundational math vocabulary, picking up words used for comparison, position, direction, sequence, shape, time, and number (S. S. Smith, 2001).

NATIONAL EXPECTATIONS AND STANDARDS

Since the 1990s, much of the momentum for moving toward a more comprehensive, useful, and meaningful instructional approach has been provided by the leadership of the National Council of Teachers of Mathematics (NCTM), which formulated the 1989 *Curriculum and Evaluation Standards for School Mathematics* for grades K–4, 5–8, and 9–12. Together with the National Association for the Education of Young Children (NAEYC), the NCTM has published a position statement that includes preschool-age children for the first time (NCTM, 2000). The overall goals of the Standards (see the Intermediate Objectives for Mathematics subsection later in this chapter) are for children to learn to value mathematics, become confident in their ability to perform mathematics, become mathematical problem solvers, learn to communicate mathematically, and learn to reason mathematically. This document clearly stated that rote memorization is obsolete. Students are to process information more actively,

Pairing children in cooperative learning situations enhances concept building.

develop the kind of skills and understandings that will allow broad application in a number of fields, and learn to use tools such as calculators and computers for problem solving. Instruction should grow out of genuine problems of interest to children, and teachers are to engage children in small-group and paired activities. Educators are also mandated to follow up on classroom activity, discussing with children the methodologies the children have developed for their problem solving and what they have learned (Kennedy & Tipps, 1999). Ongoing authentic assessment is the primary strategy suggested for documenting children's conceptual understanding and includes anecdotal records taken during observation and interviews and from work samples (drawings, graphs, sketches, and written work), inventories, and the child's self-appraisals collected in a portfolio. Assessment and evaluation should include strategies to determine a child's conceptual understanding of operations as well as his or her ability to work through problems by applying the "rules."

To promote optimal development of these concepts, effective teachers equip their classrooms with a wide variety of well-chosen, interesting manipulative materials that invite exploring, sorting, combining, and experimenting. Minimally, these include interlocking counting cubes, linking materials in a variety of colors and shapes, measuring instruments, play money, geoboards, tangrams, geometric models, attribute blocks, collections (keys, buttons, seashells, plastic animals, and bottle tops), beads, timers and clocks, base 10 materials, and probability devices (dice, spinners, etc.).

Effective teachers also structure many opportunities for children to hear the correct names for conventional tags again and again, especially those that cause children problems (e.g., in 11, there is no "teen" sound; in 20, there is no "2" sound), which promotes understanding, proficiency, and the language needed to describe operations. Such teachers involve children in activities especially contrived to promote a framework for mathematical thinking and problem solving. Teachers monitor and nurture this understanding by posing good questions to help children notice discrepancies and come closer and closer to the correct answer. They encourage children to think about the relevant pieces of information needed to solve problems and challenge them to think of other ways to find an answer or defend their proposed solutions. Many of the experiences the children have are gamelike, including board games, dice, cards, bingo games, lotto, and measurement of real aspects of the near environment. Other experiences come naturally out of the everyday operation of the classroom, which helps children perceive mathematics as relevant and useful rather than as something to memorize and repeat (Brewer, 2001).

As with science, every aspect of the curriculum can and should be used to promote logical-mathematical conceptualization. The integration of linguistic and mathematical thinking—having children write about mathematics—is an especially good technique for encouraging children to examine their ideas and reflect on what they have learned (Burns, 2000). Children should be challenged to think mathematically, rather than just arithmetically, and inquiry and discussion about why a fact is so should replace the practice of just "getting the right answer." In this way, children develop internal rules and principles to help them understand number and number relationships in our base 10 system of numbers. This internalized comprehension can then be used in other situations, such as those requiring understanding of multiple digits or place value. Children who are given the correct answer repeatedly do not necessarily discover why a fact is so. Thus, they are left with little ability to make use of the information without a helping adult to continue to do the headwork. Teachers who encourage memorization of math facts without teaching some simple but helpful rules or "tricks" to remember produce children who "learn arithmetic at the expense of learning mathematics" (Baroody, 1987, p. 44).

CURRENT EDUCATIONAL ISSUES

Making sense of all the information we currently have about cognitive development and experiential considerations is a complex but critical task for early childhood educators to tackle if children are to become effective, lifelong learners. Despite the extensive work to reform early learning contexts and ensure qualitatively better

outcomes for children, a number of controversial issues persist. These issues include the following four:

1. *The use of a Piagetian constructivist approach versus the use of a Vygotskian approach to instruction.* Educators continue to argue about how much focus should be placed on the child's own construction of knowledge versus emphasis on a sociocultural approach in which the teacher takes a more active role in guiding children toward increasingly higher levels of understanding. The two views are complementary. We can and should provide children with both kinds of experiences. The introduction of new information should always be accompanied initially by children's opportunity to construct their own relationships and share these with their peers and their teacher (Charlesworth, 2000). However, this approach takes place best in a social context that allows children to work with others on real projects and problems in which they share a personal investment. Children should be encouraged to talk with one another and the teacher about their work to foster the development of conceptual understandings as well as their ability to calculate correct answers.

Some children, because of personality traits or cultural differences, may be less apt to try new experiences or to take risks without encouragement to do so. Others, because of negative past experiences with failure, may avoid activity that calls for higher order thinking and skills—even when they are relatively ready for it. Instead, they persevere in areas in which success is ensured. The teacher's role in moving such children along may include breaking more sophisticated tasks into manageable parts and helping children recognize how their past success and experiences can be used to tackle new challenges. Although all children benefit from genuine reinforcement for efforts to attempt more-demanding tasks, those who noticeably avoid learning challenges must receive such attention and support in order to modify their attitudes toward approaching a more rigorous learning experience.

2. *An emphasis on conceptual knowledge to understand concepts versus the development of precise skills and procedural knowledge.* We make a mistake when we construct programs in which one emphasis is favored over another. Evidence indicates that young children can develop highly efficient skills to solve math or science problems without ever understanding what lies behind the process they have used. Although they can demonstrate expertise in getting the "right answer," they are often hard pressed to explain the procedure to someone else or to transfer the discrete skills to other situations or problems. Because the brain requires a great deal of repetition so that it can detect patterns, concept formation is better ensured when children

experience both variety and repetition in not only logical-mathematical activities, but also the follow-up discussion that has been recommended for making sense of their findings. Thus, professionals must develop classroom experiences that help children make meaningful connections through enriched, thematic, and real-life experiences rather than cutting off such connections by "bits and pieces" instruction (Association for Supervision and Curriculum Development, 1998).

3. *The use of technology in the early childhood classroom.* Becoming knowledgeable about the growing number of technological tools available must be a requirement for today's learner. The questions related to their use include how early children should be introduced to them, how much time should be allocated to their use at the expense of other learning, and whether they should be allowed in "testing" situations or only in follow-up practice once conceptualization has been fixed.

Despite the widespread use of calculators, teachers and parents continue to resist their use in school. Many people believe that children who are allowed to use them will fail to develop a conceptual understanding of mathematics operations. The results of more than 80 studies on this issue firmly dispute this idea. These results indicate that using calculators in instruction and testing sharpens children's performance, problem-solving ability, and affective attitudes about mathematics (Kennedy & Tipps, 1999).

Although young children need to learn to estimate and calculate problems mentally (mental math), they must eventually learn to do paper-and-pencil math and to use a calculator. Each of them should have access to a calculator, and the calculators they are given should have easy-to-read numbers found directly on the keys, easy-to-depress keys that move distinctly when depressed, four functions with an automatic constant for addition, and solar power (S. S. Smith, 2001). Even very young children can use such calculators in the dramatic play center and the math and science centers. Just as they are taught other skills with tools, they should be allowed to explore and practice with calculators, which are sure to become an increasingly important and helpful tool in their understanding number operation.

Similarly, computers can enhance learning and should be considered a necessary piece of equipment in the early childhood classroom, providing games and simulations that aid problem solving, and allowing students to use some fairly engaging tutorial programs for skill building and practice. Teachers need to be astute with respect to selecting software that is operationally easy to use. Not only should it be entertaining, but it also should teach a skill, process, or concept. Professionals

also need to observe the children carefully to ensure that they can understand the task involved and are not just pushing buttons. Kennedy and Tipps (1999) provided a guide to software selection:

Where does it fit into the instructional design?
Can it be used for informal introduction of a concept, for directed learning, or for investigation of math or science concepts?
Will it add something unique to the program?
Can it be used for independent, small-group, or whole-group instruction?
How does its cost stack up against the need for other math learning aids?

These researchers also suggested a number of publications that offer technical, instructional, and practical aspects of computer programming with young children, including *Arithmetic Teacher, Child Care Information Exchange, School Science and Mathematics, Journal of Computers in Mathematics and Science Teaching,* and *Instructor Magazine*'s monthly feature on technology.

4. *The use of heterogeneous or homogeneous groups.* All evidence points to the value of structuring heterogeneous groups that are changed often enough to keep them dynamic, useful, and energetic. Children, like adults, are continuously scanning the environment to pick up information that will help them make sense of it. They watch what others do who are more or less skilled in accomplishing a task and then imitate, expand on, or modify what they see for use in their own problem solving, decision making, and leisure pursuits. Children on all points of a developmental continuum benefit from interacting with others who either need or can provide information about or strategies for accomplishing a task. Children who are grouped narrowly in homogeneous settings grow and develop but not at the rate they would if they were in a supportive, heterogeneous setting. In heterogeneous settings, teachers can then structure one-on-one or small-group sessions as miniworkshops on skill building or scaffolding. In this way, they can zero in on specific learning difficulties experienced by one or more children without denying these children the chance to learn from others.

Effective early childhood classrooms are those in which children have many opportunities to express their thoughts, wishes, and ideas to one another as well as to adults. The best early childhood classroom exists in an active, well-prepared, workshop-like environment. A truly effective early childhood classroom must be carefully constructed by a professional who understands that young children are eager to learn and will respond responsibly when they are given the freedom, resources, and guidance necessary. Efforts should be made to match what happens in the classroom as nearly as possible to what happens in the child's head and to provide both familiar and slightly discrepant logical-mathematical problems that relate to children's experience and engage their interest. Moreover, to be able to act effectively on a full range of later problems, children must maintain an appreciation of their ability to think divergently, creatively, and imaginatively in addition to developing convergent modes of thinking. This kind of approach to information seeking and problem solving cannot result from learning a narrow set of learning strategies for information processing (Gardner et al., 1996).

GOALS AND OBJECTIVES

The ultimate goal of education in the cognitive domain is for children to acquire, apply, adapt, integrate, and evaluate knowledge as they construct new or expanded logical-mathematical and scientific concepts. To help identify ways in which cognitive activities fit into the early childhood curriculum, we divided the selected intermediate objectives for this domain into three areas: (a) general cognition, including problem-solving, critical thinking, and perception processes; (b) science; and (c) mathematics. Because cognitive processes pervade all aspects of learning, teachers should address certain universal objectives daily. These objectives are described in the general cognition section. More-specific objectives traditionally associated with the subject areas of mathematics and science are listed separately.

Intermediate Objectives for General Cognition

As children progress toward the ultimate goal, they will demonstrate the following 13 competencies:

1. Explore the observable properties of objects and the relationships among objects
2. Discriminate similarities and differences among objects
3. Organize objects, events, and information by means of matching, classifying (subclasses and supraclasses), sequencing, and patterning
4. Attach meaning to symbols in the environment (e.g., signs and numerals)
5. Develop and refine their attending skills and their ability to ignore irrelevant information
6. Develop strategies for remembering (e.g., recording, creating personal rules, making associations)
7. Develop and refine their investigative and problem-solving skills by observing attentively; posing questions or problems to solve; exercising divergent and convergent thinking; using estimation, concepts of chance, and sampling to make better predictions; gathering information (questioning, experimenting, observing, and consulting); analyzing information, objects, and events; applying prior knowledge; and making inferences
8. Develop and refine their reporting skills by connecting and combining information in an integrative manner; evaluating predictions; drawing conclusions; reviewing or summarizing experiences; generating alternative approaches to problems; and communicating findings
9. Generalize knowledge and skills from one situation to another and across subject areas
10. Become aware of their thought processes
11. Build more accurate, complete, and complex concepts with time
12. Recognize and make use of diverse sources of knowledge
13. Recognize that data come in many forms and can be organized and displayed in diverse ways

Intermediate Objectives for Science

As children progress toward the ultimate goal, they will demonstrate the following 11 competencies:

1. Examine natural objects, using their multisensory abilities
2. Learn the scientific process by predicting what they think will happen on the basis of a hypothesis, guessing why certain things happen, carrying out experiments, talking about the result of their experiments, and formulating conclusions
3. Explore firsthand a variety of cause-and-effect relationships
4. Demonstrate an awareness of the interdependence of all things in the world
5. Acquire scientific knowledge related to the life sciences (characteristics of plants and animals, life cycles and basic needs, habitats, and relationships)
6. Acquire scientific knowledge related to the physical sciences (change in matter; forces affecting motion, direction, speed, light, heat, and sound; physical properties and characteristics of phenomena)
7. Acquire scientific knowledge related to the earth sciences (weather, space, ecology, and major features of the earth)
8. Explore a variety of scientific equipment, such as simple machines, magnets, and measuring instruments
9. Use scientific equipment appropriately and safely

10. Develop and use an accurate vocabulary to describe, name, and measure scientific events, objects, and processes

11. Participate in recording scientific data

Intermediate Objectives for Mathematics

As children progress toward the ultimate goal, they will demonstrate the following 17 competencies (Adopted from National Council of Teachers of Mathematics, 2000).

Number and Operations Standard

1. Understand numbers, ways of representing numbers, relationships among numbers, and number systems

   a. Count with understanding and recognize "how many" in sets of objects
   b. Use multiple models to develop initial understandings of place value and the base 10 number system
   c. Develop understanding of the relative position and magnitude of whole numbers and of ordinal and cardinal numbers and their connections
   d. Develop a sense of whole numbers and represent and use them in flexible ways, including relating, composing, and decomposing numbers
   e. Connect number words and numerals to the quantities they represent, using various physical models and representations
   f. Understand and represent commonly used fractions, such as 1/4, 1/3, and 1/2

2. Understand meanings of operations and how operations relate to one another

   a. Understand various meanings of addition and subtraction of whole numbers and the relationship between the two operations
   b. Understand the effects of adding and subtracting whole numbers
   c. Understand situations that entail multiplication and division, such as equal groups of objects and sharing equally

3. Compute fluently and make reasonable estimates

   a. Develop and use strategies for whole-number computations, with a focus on addition and subtraction
   b. Develop fluency with basic number combinations for addition and subtraction
   c. Use a variety of methods and tools to compute with, including objects, mental computation, estimation, paper and pencil, and calculators

Patterns, Functions, and Algebra Standard

4. Understand patterns, relations, and functions

   a. Sort, classify, and order objects by size, number, and other properties
   b. Recognize, describe, and extend patterns such as sequences of sounds and shapes or simple numeric patterns and translate from one representation to another
   c. Analyze how both repeating and growing patterns are generated

5. Represent and analyze mathematical situations and structures, using algebraic symbols

   a. Illustrate general principles and properties of operations, such as commutativity, using specific numbers
   b. Use concrete, pictorial, and oral representations to develop an understanding of invented and conventional symbolic notations

6. Use mathematical models to represent and understand quantitative relationships; model situations that involve the addition and subtraction of whole numbers, using objects, pictures, and symbols

7. Analyze change in various contexts; describe qualitative change, such as a student's growing taller; describe quantitative change, such as a student's growing 2 inches in 1 year

Geometry Standard

8. Analyze characteristics and properties of two- and three-dimensional geometric shapes and develop mathematical arguments about geometric relationships

   a. Recognize, name, build, draw, compare, and sort two- and three-dimensional shapes
   b. Describe attributes and parts of two- and three-dimensional shapes
   c. Investigate and predict the results of putting together and taking apart two- and three-dimensional shapes

9. Specify locations and describe spatial relationships, using coordinate geometry and other representational systems

   a. Describe, name, and interpret relative positions in space and apply ideas about relative position
   b. Describe, name, and interpret direction and distance in navigating space and apply ideas about direction and distance
   c. Find and make locations with simple relationships such as "near to" and in coordinate systems such as maps

10. Apply transformations and use symmetry to analyze mathematical situations

    a. Recognize and apply slides, flips, and turns
    b. Recognize and create shapes that have symmetry

11. Use visualization, spatial reasoning, and geometric modeling to solve problems

    a. Create mental images of geometric shapes by using spatial memory and spatial visualization
    b. Recognize and represent shapes from different perspectives
    c. Relate ideas in geometry to ideas in number and measurement
    d. Recognize geometric shapes and structures in the environment and specify their location

Measurement Standard
12. Understand measurable attributes of objects and the units, systems, and processes of measurement

    a. Recognize the attributes of length, volume, weight, area, and time
    b. Compare and order objects according to these attributes
    c. Understand how to measure, using nonstandard and standard units
    d. Select an appropriate unit and tool for the attribute being measured

13. Apply appropriate techniques, tools, and formulas to determine measurements

    a. Measure with multiple copies of units of the same size, such as paper clips laid end to end
    b. Use repetition of a single unit to measure something larger than the unit, for instance, measuring the length of a room with a single meterstick
    c. Use tools to measure
    d. Develop common referents for measures so that comparisons and estimates can be made

Data Analysis and Probability Standard
14. Formulate questions that can be addressed with data, and collect, organize, and display relevant data to answer them

    a. Pose questions and gather data about themselves and their surroundings
    b. Sort and classify objects according to their attributes and organize data about the objects
    c. Represent data by using concrete objects, pictures, and graphs

15. Select and use appropriate statistical methods to analyze data; describe parts of the data and the set of data as a whole to determine what the data show

16. Develop and evaluate inferences and predictions that are based on data; discuss events related to students' experiences as likely or unlikely
17. Understand and apply basic concepts of probability

TEACHING STRATEGIES

The most important fact to keep in mind when you are teaching preprimary- and primary-age children is that the minds of these children are evolving—and if they are to build a solid and reliable cognitive base, we cannot do all the thinking for them. Teachers who fail to appreciate the young child's need to construct knowledge may diminish his or her potential development. Conversely, teachers who go overboard in minimizing their role in the child's developing intellect, morality, and personality also err. A teacher does not promote understanding by permitting students' constructions to stand even though they clash with experts' constructions. Rather than waiting for correct scientific entities and ideas to be constructed and validated, teachers need to find a way to provide developmentally appropriate experiences to challenge misconceptions (Zahorik, 1997).

In the early years, children need to be taught by professionals who are knowledgeable about constructing environments conducive to learning. Instead of imposing their predetermined goals, these teachers provide materials, activities, and suggestions that encourage initiative and independent pursuit. Such teachers allow children adequate time to explore, investigate, reflect, and ask questions. They differentiate effectively between teaching strategies that promote logical-mathematical and physical knowledge and those needed to extend social-conventional knowledge in young children (Kamii & DeVries, 1977). This approach calls for, in the former case, refraining from providing the correct answer, challenging children to think about what it might be, and having them follow through by investigating and evaluating their ideas. In the latter case, when extending social-conventional knowledge, good teachers respond to a child's inquiries with correct information; if they are not sure what the answer is, they are honest about not knowing and then work with the child to obtain the information needed. Following are eight additional ideas for structuring a fertile climate for learning:

1. *Encourage intellectual autonomy when expanding children's general cognitive skills.* Use "long-term, multifaceted projects and themes that offer a broad and integrative framework for interaction" to effectively set the scene (Berk & Winsler, 1995, p. 145). The concept of using hands-on experiences and activity for developing the young child's conceptual thinking will be especially

important. Introduce every concept with real objects first, and plan several related experiences to reinforce a given concept rather than presenting isolated activities at random. Emphasize the process rather than solely the products of children's thinking.

Questioning used to stimulate their thinking or to discover why children have categorized, sequenced, or solved a problem in a certain way should be open ended. Allow children to reach their own conclusions regarding cause-and-effect relationships, and the answers they offer should be accepted. When children make errors, plan further experiences or suggest other approaches that might help the children discover the correct answer or have more success with individual tasks. However, when children are having difficulty with a concept or with demonstrating proficiency, help them break a task into more manageable parts and introduce them to the next step in the sequence when doing so would be helpful. Teach particular skills and facts in contexts relevant to children.

2. *Develop children's ability to move out of a comfort zone with respect to inaccurate concepts.* Cardellichio and Field (1997) underscored the teacher's role in closing the gaps between children's "spontaneous constructs" and scientific constructs by providing the child with enough data to force them to challenge misconceptions and create strong, accurate conceptualizations. Such gap closing can be accomplished through well-constructed activities used along with information books, resource persons, field trips, and provocative questioning. These researchers also suggested the following seven strategies for encouraging cognitive development and divergent thinking:

a. *Hypothetical thinking:* a powerful technique to create new information. Einstein developed his theory of relativity by asking, "What would it look like to ride on a beam of light?" For example, a teacher might ask, "What would happen if you . . . ?" "What if . . . ?" The key is not in asking the organized question but in the follow-up questions such as "What if this had happened?" "What if this had not occurred?" "What if this were not true?" "What if I could find out how to do something I can't do right now?"

b. *Reversal:* turning the current perspective upside down. For example, say, "What if you had your mother's role and she had yours?" "What if we slept during the day and stayed awake at night?" "What if we always ate our dessert before we ate the rest of our dinner?" "What if children ran the schools and teachers were students? What would it be like?" "What if we had only summer clothes to wear in the winter and winter clothes to wear in the summer?"

c. *Application of different symbol systems.* Instead of using words to tell something, ask children to create a song, act it out, or develop another set of symbols to use in place of a current set.

d. *Analogy.* Look for correspondences to create new insight about both elements in an analogy. Say, "What is like this?" "How is this like _____?"

e. *Analysis of point of view:* determining why someone holds a particular opinion or belief. Say, "What harm might occur if we . . . ?" "What do you think one of your parents might think about that?" "Who would love it if . . . ?" "What if the wolf turned out to be . . . ?"

f. *Completion.* Give the beginning of a story and ask children to form the ending; give the ending of a story and ask children to form the beginning or the middle.

g. *Use of graphic organizers (charts, tables, information webs, Venn diagrams, and flowcharts).* These organizers promote children's comprehension and vocabulary development, eliminate oversimplification, and extend children's understanding of the complexity of relationships, events, and so forth. They help to make relationships among concepts concrete and explicit.

3. *Place more emphasis on children's understanding of concepts than on rote learning.* Keep in mind that children's development of logical-mathematical concepts follows a predictable pattern. Always begin teaching new concepts by using concrete experiences. Provide a variety of manipulatives (real objects) to be used for sorting, classifying, comparing, estimating, predicting, patterning, graphing, measuring, counting, adding and subtracting, understanding parts and wholes, and gaining concepts of number, conservation of number, quantity, shapes, mass, and volume. When involving children in making mathematical equations, provide sets of real objects in addition to materials such as number stamps and number cards before paper-and-pencil tasks are introduced. Circulate among children, observing how they are approaching tasks, and structuring brief miniconferences to check their understanding of the targeted concept.

After children have had numerous concrete experiences, introduce representational concepts (e.g., pictures or drawn figures). Introduce abstract experiences last (e.g., abstract symbols such as $2 + ? = 5$). Allow children ample opportunities to explore a given material before asking them to use it in a prescribed way. Present the same mathematical concepts and skills on many occasions and in many ways (e.g., drawing numerals in the air, in sand, in salt, in finger paint, on the chalkboard, and on paper). Involve them in playing a variety of games using cards and dice.

4. *Integrate science and mathematical concepts and skills throughout all areas of the early childhood curriculum.* Link logical-mathematical activities with social studies and language arts as well as with pretend-play, affective, aesthetic, physical, and construction activities as often as possible.

5. *Extend children's science and mathematical vocabulary.* Use a wide variety of accurate terms when talking with children about their day-to-day experiences (e.g., number, mass, size, shape, position of objects in space, relations among objects, and changes in the functioning, position, or characteristics of objects).

6. *Use everyday experiences in the classroom to help children connect science and mathematics to daily living and see it as useful and necessary.* Capitalize on problems that occur naturally in the classroom, school, or community that can capture children's curiosity.

Incorporate mathematical tools into classroom routines (e.g., calendars, clocks, rulers, coins, scales, measuring cups, graphs). Practice addition and subtraction in natural settings without symbols, encouraging children to use headwork to solve problems. Draw children's attention to aspects of daily work and play in the classroom that utilize mathematical concepts (e.g., durations of time—5 minutes until cleanup, 15 minutes for recess, and 2 weeks off for spring vacation).

Introduce scientific concepts by building on the everyday experiences in the lives of the children in your class. Make available a wide array of natural materials through which children can explore the physical world. Examples include collections of natural objects (seashells, rocks, and bird nests), live animals (fish, guinea pigs, and insects), plants, and scientific tools (scales, magnifiers, and magnets). Take advantage of spontaneous events to highlight scientific ideas. Emphasize children's discovery of principles of cause and effect by allowing them to draw conclusions based on their experiences with real objects. Select scientific themes that include both first-time experiences for children and experiences with which children are familiar.

7. *Develop positive learning attitudes and practices in the classroom.* Model an interested, curious, enthusiastic attitude toward science, and encourage children's curiosity by providing them with numerous hands-on scientific experiences and relevant demonstrations. Carry out scientific demonstrations with groups small enough that children can become actively involved and can feel free to ask questions about what they are observing. Help children to observe more carefully by first directing their attention to a particular aspect of an object or a phenomenon and then asking them to describe what they see (e.g., "Look up at the sky. Tell me what you see"). Encourage children to make predictions by asking them, "What will happen next?" and hypothe-

size and draw conclusions by asking them, "Why do you think that happened?" Convey only accurate scientific terms, facts, and principles to children, checking out any information about which you or the children are unsure. Help children recognize many sources of scientific information, such as books, their experiences, and resource people.

8. *Use collections as a way to extend and assess children's ability to categorize, classify, and display information.* Give children individual or group opportunities to create collections of natural objects. Offer them guidance on collecting objects and what may be appropriate or inappropriate to collect. Provide opportunities for children to display and tell about their collections.

ACTIVITY SUGGESTIONS

General Cognition Activities

✎ Sniff Test (For Younger or Less Experienced Children)

General Cognition Objective 1 For children to explore the observable properties of objects and the relationships among objects.

Materials One set of small vials, each with a particular and unique smell (e.g., flower, perfume, lemon, orange, garlic, coffee, extracts, and a second set of vials with the same scents); blindfold; magazines

Procedure Have the children form a circle. Choose one child to be blindfolded in the center. Distribute one set of vials among children in outer circle. The blindfolded child is given one vial from the second set and must move around the circle, using his or her sense of smell to find the matching vial and identify what he or she is smelling.

To simplify Have children individually match each container to magazine pictures of the source of the scent.

To extend Enlarge the variety of scents. Choose scents within categories (e.g., all flower scents, all fruit scents, or all coffee scents). Design a similar activity to test sense of taste.

✎ Mystery Box (For Younger or Less Experienced Children)

General Cognition Objective 5 For children to develop and refine their attending skills and their ability to ignore irrelevant information.

Materials Box; set of related objects

Procedure "Hide" several objects in a box. Provide oral clues to the children about the identities of the objects. Invite the children to ask you questions about the objects to discover what is in the box.

To simplify Place only one object in the box. Select an object with which all the children are familiar.

To extend Place several objects in the box that are different but have one characteristic in common (e.g., all are articles of clothing). Have one of the children take on the role of "clue giver."

✎ Housing Costs (For Older or More Experienced Children)

General Cognition Objective 11 For children to build more accurate, complete, and complex concepts with time.

Materials *This Is My House*, by Arthur Dorros (Scholastic); catalogs and newspaper ads of housing items (furniture, appliances, etc.); paper; pencils; magazines

Procedure After reading the book, guide a discussion with the children about what their "ideal house" would be like and the items it would contain. With the children's help, make a webbing of categories of items (e.g., appliances, furniture, plumbing items, kitchen items, bedding and towels, accessories). Have children form pairs or small groups, and ask them to estimate what each webbed list of items might cost. Using catalogs and other pricing information, have children locate the actual costs and determine the differences between their estimates and the real prices.

To simplify In large group, have children list the items they think are necessary in an ideal house. Encourage them to stretch their thinking by asking questions to elicit important items they have forgotten to include. Very young children could cut pictures from magazines to make a "room." Other children may draw pictures of their ideal house.

To extend Have children individually list items they would include in their house. Divide children into "research" groups to determine the exact cost of each category of items by taking a trip to local stores to check prices of the items and reporting back to the large group.

Science Activities

✎ Balloon Race (For Children of All Ages)

Science Objective 2 For children to learn the scientific process.

Materials Balloons, straws, masking tape, easel, easel paper, markers

Procedure Before beginning the activity, tell the children the object is to find out how to use their straws to blow air onto the balloons and move them as quickly as possible from the starting line to a designated wall. Ask the children to develop hypotheses and to make predictions about directing the balloons. Write these on an easel. Give five different-colored inflated balloons and five straws to a group of five children. Have other children observe, telling them they will also have a chance to do the activity. Establish a starting line that has been marked off with masking tape. Have teams of children participate in the activity. After each time, return to the original hypotheses and predictions and adapt them on the basis of what happened. When all the teams have participated, have the children draw conclusions.

To simplify Have the children participate in the activity and then discuss what they think made the balloons go faster. Accept their answers. Prompt them to think about any differences that may have contributed to speed or direction of movement.

To extend Invite the children who are observers to watch carefully to determine whether they will do something differently when they participate in the activity. Prior to each "team event," have children offer ideas about what they think contributes to speed and managing direction. Afterward, have them evaluate their ideas and generate new ideas. After every child has had a chance to participate, ask the children to produce an "advice sheet" related to the activity, listing tips (conclusions; e.g., blowing in the middle of the balloon, not blowing down on or on the side of the balloon, or blowing steadily) that they would provide to other teams of children who might want to try the activity in the future.

✎ Soil Samples (For Younger or Less Experienced Children)

Science Objective 1 For children to examine natural objects, using their multisensory abilities.

Materials Containers for gathering soil samples, trowels for digging, plastic wrap, magnifying glasses, pots and molds, water glasses, water pitcher, quickly sprouting seeds, paper, markers

Procedure Help children gather a number of kinds of soil samples—such as sand, gravel, clay, and loam—placing each sample in a different container and covering with plastic wrap to retain moisture. Before the soil samples have time to dry out, place them on separate sheets of paper for examination. (*Note:* Working with small groups of children is recommended so that subtle changes can easily be observed.)

To simplify Invite the children to use magnifying glasses to observe differences in the samples. Have the children rub the samples between their thumb and forefinger to note differences in texture. Ask them to smell the samples to detect any differences in smell. Provide a number of pots and molds and suggest that they try to mold the samples. Discuss with them which samples seem to hold together better than others and why this might be so.

To extend Examine the various samples to determine how much air they contain by filling separate water glasses with each of the soil samples and leaving some room at the top to add water. Slowly pour in water from the water pitcher, and watch as it soaks in and displaces any air, helping the children to note the size and frequency of bubbles. Assign a team of children to each soil sample and have them carefully examine the pile for organic components, such as stones, insects, and leaves. Have each team note the kinds of components they find, decide how to record their findings, and then report their findings to other teams. Place samples of each kind of soil in pots. Water to see if any weeds will sprout. Record findings. Place quickly sprouting seeds (one variety) in various samples and have children note which kinds of soil promote the best growth. In another experiment, have children test different growing conditions by altering light, water, and heat (Nickelsburg, 1976).

✎ What's the Solution? (For Younger or Less Experienced Children)*

Science Objective 3 For children to explore firsthand a variety of cause-and-effect relationships.

Materials Sand, salt, water, two clear jars, coffee filters, teaspoon measure, spoon for stirring, other materials (e.g., sugar, baking soda, coffee, corn starch, dirt, gravel, beans, tempera paint), paper, pencils

Procedure Explain to the children that sometimes things mix together without changing. Sometimes the things being mixed turn into something new, which is then called a *solution*. Have children fill one of the jars with very warm water, add 1 teaspoon of sand, and stir for 30 seconds. What happens to the sand? Then have them hold the filter over the mouth of the empty jar. Empty the first jar into the filter. What is left in the filter? What is left in the jar? Ask whether they have created a solution, reminding them of the definition of the term. Next, have them empty and clean both jars and repeat their experiment, this time using a teaspoon of salt instead of sand. What is left in the filter? What is

in the jar? Where is the salt? What happens to the salt? Have they created a solution or not?

To simplify Carry out the experiment using only the salt.

To extend Have them experiment with other materials such as sugar, baking soda, coffee, corn starch (use 1/2-cup cornstarch and 1/2-cup water to produce an interesting goo), dirt, gravel, beans, and tempera paint. Have children who are able record their findings in their science journals. Have children construct a chart on which they differentiate materials that dissolve from those that do not.

✎ In and Out of Balance (For Younger or Less Experienced Children)

Science Objective 11 For children to participate in recording scientific data.

Materials Balance scale, wooden blocks, spoon, Ping-Pong ball, pencils or pens, other objects

Procedure Ask the children to carry out a series of experiments to see which weighs more: (a) a wooden block or a Ping-Pong ball, (b) a Ping-Pong ball or a spoon, (c) a spoon or a wooden block. Have them draw the results of each experiment in their science journals, numbering and dating each experiment.

To simplify Have them discriminate between only two objects.

To extend* Have them choose other objects that are more difficult to discriminate visually, recording their predictions prior to the experiment, then their findings.

✎ Me and My Shadow (For Older or More Experienced Children)†

Science Objective 6 For children to acquire scientific knowledge related to the physical sciences.

Materials *Me and My Shadow,* by Arthur Dorros (Scholastic); one of the following for each child: piece of cardboard or stiff paper from which to make a cutout of a shape or figure, pencil, thread spool, adhesive tape, large piece of white paper, crayons or markers; assorted materials (e.g., construction paper, waxed paper); pens or pencils

Procedure After reading *Me and My Shadow,* have children make a cutout figure (person, bear, horse, etc.), use the tape to attach the cutout figure to the eraser end of the pencil, and then stick the pointed end of the

Source: Adapted from Scholastic's *The Magic Schoolbus.*

Source: Adapted from Hein and Price (1994).
†*Source:* Adapted from Brainard and Wrubel (1993).

pencil in their thread spool. Ask them to predict what will happen when the figure is placed in the sun. On a sunny morning, have them go outside and place the figure in the center of a large piece of paper. Have them use different-colored markers or crayons to trace the shadow on their paper at approximately 10:00 A.M., noon, and 2:00 P.M. Discuss with them how the shadows changed during the day.

To simplify   Supply cutout figures.

To extend   Have the children determine how to block the shadow made by the figure by using assorted materials (construction paper, waxed paper, plastic wrap, tissue paper, etc.). Have them describe what happens with each type of material. Have children measure the length of the shadows made at 10:00 A.M., noon, and 2:00 P.M. and describe what happens. Older children can write about the outcomes in their science journals. Provide information books about shadows and have children look up information about how shadows are formed. Have children construct drawings of the shadows formed at particular times of the day.

✎ Plants or Animals (For Older or More Experienced Children)

Science Objective 5   For children to acquire scientific knowledge related to the life sciences.

Materials   A variety of laminated pictures of foods (e.g., milk, fruit, vegetables, hot dogs, bread, cheese, hamburger, beans); two boxes, one labeled "Plants" and another labeled "Animals"; paper; pencils or pens

Procedure   Discuss with the children that all living things need food and that some food comes from plants and some from animals. Have the children sort the food according to their sources. Once the foods are sorted, have the children make a list of the foods in each category.

To simplify   Sort the foods without listing them.

To extend   Have the children find out how green plants get their food. How is this different from the way animals get their food? Ask children if they can think of foods they eat that are a combination of plant and animal (e.g., spaghetti).

Mathematics Activities

✎ Grouping and Sorting (For Younger or Less Experienced Children)

Math Objective 4a   For children to sort, classify, and order objects by size, number, and other properties.

Materials   Sets of objects that can be grouped on the basis of size, shape, color, pattern, or position

Procedure   Give children daily opportunities to classify a variety of objects. Remember that there are no right or wrong ways for children to classify. Instead, emphasize the process by which children reach their conclusions. Use the following script to guide your instruction:

"Show me a way to put these into groups that are alike."
"Good. You found a way to sort the objects."
"Tell me why these things [point to one grouping] go together." (Repeat for each grouping and accept the children's answer for each.)
"Show another way to sort the objects into piles."

To simplify   Use fewer objects with more obvious grouping possibilities.

To extend   Provide greater numbers of objects and those with more than one common characteristic so that children will discover more-sophisticated combinations (e.g., grouping all yellow objects that have something to do with transportation).

✎ Pictorial Story Problems (For Younger or Less Experienced Children)

Math Objective 2b   For children to understand the effects of adding and subtracting whole numbers.

Materials   Pictorial scenes and sets of related objects, blank number strips, markers

Procedure   Give children individual pictorial scenes, such as an apple tree or a field, a barn and corral, or a seashore. Invite children to place selected objects on a particular scene and to tell an arithmetic story problem about what they have just depicted (e.g., "There were five apples on the tree, and three fell on the ground. How many apples were there in all?").

To simplify   Use only a few objects. Demonstrate a simple addition problem.

To extend   Use more objects. Invite children to think of as many combinations as possible. Have children develop written number strips for each combination after it is concretely constructed (e.g., $2 + 5 = 7$; $3 + 4 = 7$; $1 + 6 = 7$; $10 - 3 = 7$). Children may also work with partners, with one child thinking of and constructing the problem and the other child checking the work and developing a written number strip.

✎ Count and Match (For Younger or Less Experienced Children)

Math Objective 1e   For children to connect number words and numerals to the quantities they represent.

Materials Magazines, scissors, magnifying glasses, cards with numerals and representative symbols, blank cards, glue or paste

Procedure Have the children gather pictures that clearly display a certain number of objects (e.g., number of teeth in a smiling face, number of birds flying in a flock, or number of boats sailing on a river). Have children pair up, and tell them to look at the picture, count the objects, and then match the picture to a card with the numeral identifying the number of objects. Magnifying glasses can be supplied to help children distinguish the numbers of objects more clearly.

To simplify Use cards displaying only the numerals 1 to 5 and including matching round circles or other graphics to represent the number indicated.

To extend Provide materials for matching numbers of objects beyond five. Have children search through magazines for pictures that can be matched with particular numeral cards. These can be pasted on cards, mixed up, and then sorted by children into appropriate piles coordinated with the appropriate numeral cards.

✎ Fraction Fun (For Older or More Experienced Children)

Math Objective 1f For children to understand and represent commonly used fractions.

Materials Unifix cubes or bear counters in two colors, graph paper, markers in same two colors as cubes or counters

Procedure Have children line up six same-color cubes or bears. Ask them to make additional rows, substituting one more cube of the opposite color in each additional row until they get down to a seventh row made up entirely of the opposite color. Ask children what they notice (e.g., the colors look like stairs). Ask, "How many cubes are in the first row? What fractional part of our whole is the different-colored cube in the second row (1/6)? In the third row?" and so on.

To simplify Begin with only four blocks in the first row, asking questions appropriate for the children's current understanding.

To extend For older children, ask, "What fractional part of our whole is the different-colored cube in the first row (0/6)?" Use 10 blocks as a starter row. Have children make up fraction word problems to go along with their display (e.g., "If there were 10 apples, and Mother used 8 of them to make a pie, what fraction of the apples is left?"). Have children represent their two-color fractions on graph paper. Have children show and write their fractions. Ask, "What fraction is more of the bar, 2/10 or 8/10?" Note, "8/10 is bigger than 2/10. We show this as 8/10 > 2/10."

✎ Place-Value Pocket Game (For Older or More Experienced Children)

Math Objective 1b For children to use multiple models to develop initial understandings of place value and the base 10 number system.

Materials A series of laminated cards on which individual numerals 1–9 are written; pocket charts with six slots labeled (from right to left): ones, tens, hundreds, thousands, ten thousands, and hundred thousands

Procedure In small or large groups, choose individual children to play the game. Hand a child two or three numeral cards (fewer cards for a child with a less developed understanding) to form a two- or three-digit number. For example, hand the child the numerals 2, 3, and 6. Say, "Form a number that has 6 hundreds, 3 tens, and 2 ones [632]. Now tell us the number you have made." Have children suggest any corrections if needed and tell why they are needed. Have the child select another card and play the game again. Vary the number of cards given to a child by matching it to individual performance level. Children will build skills by watching higher degrees of performance demonstrated by other children.

To simplify Demonstrate the game before asking children to play. Use only one or two places. Place numeral cards, noting the place for each, then ask the children to tell the number you have made. Once they understand place value, place two or three numeral cards, and then ask whether the cards represent a number you say to them.

To extend When the children are ready, challenge them to play up to the hundred thousands place.

✎ Bull's Eye! (For Older or More Experienced Children)*

Math Objective 3c For children to use a variety of methods and tools to compute with, including objects, mental computation, estimation, paper and pencil, and calculators.

Materials A set of laminated cards with a numeral between 1 and 100 on each card, a set of cards with a numeral between 100 and 1,000 on each card, a set with a numeral between 1,000 and 10,000 on each card, calculators, paper, pencils or markers

Procedure Using a set of cards selected according to children's abilities, group three or four children together

_____

Source: Adapted from Kennedy and Tipps (1999).

to play the game. Each child draws two to four cards (as agreed on by the group) and mentally estimates the sum of the numbers, which is written down. Each student then uses a calculator to find the sum and checks with the others. If correct (Bull's Eye!), the child receives a point. The child with the most points at the end of the time or after five rounds is the winner.

To simplify Limit numerals to 1–50.

To extend Have children use calculators to determine the difference between each sum and each estimate. The difference between the two numbers becomes a score. After five rounds, the group sums the scores for each player, and the player with the lowest sum is the winner.

SUMMARY

Cognitive development in the young child is a complex process. Outcomes depend on the quality of children's experiences both inside and outside the formal classroom as they move through a series of psychosocial and neurobiological changes.

Children's ability to acquire knowledge and then use it effectively to plan, monitor, and evaluate their capabilities is better ensured when they have developed and can maintain a measure of confidence in themselves and in others. This type of confidence results when they are nurtured by adults who understand the critical interrelationship between cognition and all other areas of development.

Learning environments that stimulate optimal cognitive growth are those in which curricular construction is guided by sensitivity to variations in development, in which children are encouraged to be both independent and collaborative learners, and in which high task involvement is motivated through the presentation of diverse and engaging activities that young thinkers and doers perceive to be personally useful.

Applying What You Read in This Chapter

1. **Discuss**
   a. How does Piagetian theory influence our use of manipulative materials to introduce math and science concepts in the early childhood classroom?
   b. What are the differences in the way Piaget and Vygotsky thought about early learning contexts?
   c. How does inquiry go beyond process learning? What are some strategies that encourage inquiry?

2. **Observe**
   a. Make an appointment to observe the classroom of an experienced early childhood teacher. What is the instructional approach for the cognitive domain? What logical-mathematical materials are present in the classroom? How does the teacher use the outdoor environment? Are children encouraged to discuss their findings and how they arrived at their answers or to simply be involved in activities?

3. **Carry out an activity**
   a. Identify upcoming specialized trainings or courses in manipulative math or hands-on science. Plan to attend one this year and try at least five of the ideas with a group of young children.
   b. Keep a journal for 1 week. What kinds of problem solving were you called on to do that involved the use of the math or science concepts described in this chapter?
   c. With a small group of school-age children, ask, "Can you prove at least three things that happen or don't happen when water freezes?" How do they react? What do they say they will do to find the answer? Discuss how this approach might yield different results than those obtained by simply asking the children to fill a container with water, freeze it, and then explain what happens.

4. **Create something to put in your portfolio**
   a. Develop a math-based lesson plan based on the format provided in this text.
   b. Develop a cognitive- or science-based lesson plan based on the format provided in this text.

5. **Add to your journal**
   a. Think about your early experiences with math and science. Did you take higher level courses in secondary school and college? Were you encouraged to do so? Do you think your strengths or limitations in this area have had an effect on your professional development?
   b. How aware are you of the way you approach problem solving on an everyday basis? How adept are you at analyzing problems? How rational or logical are you in problem solving? How adaptable are you in your thinking? How fair-minded are you in judging others? Think of a specific example of your behavior when you answer each of these questions.

The Language Domain

You may wonder:

How does oral language develop in young children?

What is the connection between oral language and reading and writing?

How can I enhance young children's phonological awareness in developmentally appropriate ways?

What is meant by *balanced literacy?*

How can I integrate language experiences across the curriculum?

In this chapter on the language domain, we present information to help you answer the preceding questions.

Three-year-old John listens intently at his Head Start center as the dental hygienist explains why brushing our teeth is necessary to prevent tartar from forming. He watches as she shows pictures of brownish tartar that has collected on some teeth. Later, he is playing with the family cat and exclaims, "Mom, look! Snowball has tartar sauce on his teeth!"

Five-year-old Nancy draws a picture of herself as a ballet dancer. When her teacher asks her to write a story about the picture, she does so by drawing a series of round shapes next to the picture, but no letters or words. She explains, "I can write, but it takes too long, so I make these."

Eight-year-old Eugene looks critically at a folder of written work he has produced during the past 12 weeks, looking for three of his best pieces to place in his "showcase" portfolio. He is proud of the work he has done and is looking forward to sharing it with his parents at the upcoming student-led conferences.

All these children are in varying stages of language and literacy development. The quality of this development hinges on early and subsequent experiences in language exposure, interactions with others that focus on the use of print, and engaging opportunities to apply newly developing and higher level understandings in a variety of situations. Development of language and development of literacy are continuous processes. Both depend on neural

structures and on culturally mediated learning experiences that drive children from rudimentary understandings to independent sophistication with language.

Critical components of emergent literacy include the development of reading, writing, speaking, listening, and viewing. All these components must be made meaningful and useful to children if they are to become fully literate. Listening and viewing require paying attention to communication that is heard or visually represented; writing requires learning a writing system to communicate with others across time and space; and reading involves making meaning from texts through the use of semantics, syntax, and visual, aural, and tactile clues and connecting it with prior knowledge. All this communication occurs within a child's social environment in transactions with others. Most influential are the important adults in a young child's life; from them, the child learns how language structure is modeled and begins to discover the purposes for communicating with others (Soderman, Gregory, & O'Neill, 1999b).

ORAL LANGUAGE DEVELOPMENT

Alexander, at age 2 years, is already attuned to three languages. His maternal grandmother has come to the United States from Hungary to live with the family and care for him while his parents work. Because she speaks little English, the language she and Alexander have begun to share is Hungarian. His favorite playmate is a slightly older toddler who lives next door, Sarah Ho, whose primary language is Chinese. When crossing the

Communication and language building occur in the sandbox.

street on the way to the playground with his grandmother, his friend Sarah, and her mother, he remembers and repeats his grandmother's warning of, "Vigyázz . . . kocsi! (Careful . . . car!)." At the playground, when he shares a sand toy with Sarah, her mother reminds Sarah to tell him, "Xiè-xie (Thank you)." He looks thoughtful for a moment and then repeats the words over and over to himself softly as he fills his pail with sand, "Xiè-xie, Xiè-xie." That evening, when asked by his grandmother, "Megfürdik? (take a bath?)," he shakes his head and responds, "Nem (No)" and then looks at his English-speaking father and says, "No!" just to be sure everyone understands that he is not yet ready to begin his bedtime ritual.

Even with a variety of multicultural influences, Alexander's English language development at age 24 months is on target. His *receptive vocabulary* (i.e., the number of words he understands) contains about 300 words. His *expressive vocabulary* (i.e., words he uses to express himself) is clearly not as large but seems to be exploding as he demonstrates a few new words each day. He is learning that he can use language for various purposes: to satisfy his needs and wants (instrumental), to control others (regulatory), to create interactions with others (interactional), to express his personal thoughts and opinions (personal), to create imaginary worlds (imaginative), to seek information (heuristic), and to communicate information to others (informative; Stewig & Jett-Simpson, 1995).

By the time Alexander is 6 or 7 years old, he will have a remarkable, adult-like grasp of the grammar, syntax, vocabulary, noun phrases, meaning, and pronunciation that make up his primary languages. He will accomplish all this without ever being wholly aware of language forms and structures. His creative ability to imitate and pick up on the patterns, rhythms, and meanings of language is believed to be primarily the result of innate tendencies.

Solid research documents human language as a built-in, *genetic* predisposition that is hardwired into the brain. As far as we know, only human beings can acquire language, although many other species develop strategies for communication (M. Cole & Cole, 2000). In chapter 11, we discussed that some human developmental processes are *experience expected* and others are *experience dependent*. Early speech and language appear to be both. However, they are largely experience expected; that is, they develop even if there is deprivation or overstimulation in the child's environment, and they seem impervious to both. If children are not exposed to linguistic experience by puberty, they would likely fail to acquire language; however, such cases are extremely rare. However, even in normal situations, the eventual quantity (vocabulary development) and quality (syntax and ability to elaborate) of the child's language development depend on exposure and stimulation. Thus, we talk, sing, and read to young children to *save* synapses from elimination, not to cause synapses to form (Bruer, 1999, p. 95).

Red Flags in Speech and Early Language Development

By age 2 years, some children, mostly boys, are noticeably lagging in language development. Seventy-five percent of all expressive language delays resolve by the time children enter school. A quarter of them do not (Kalb & Namuth, 1997). These latter delays often signal more-serious and long-lasting problems (Figure 12.1), such as those resulting from congenital or acquired hearing impairments or problems in the cognitive, sensorimotor, psychological, emotional, or environmental systems (e.g., poverty, nonverbal family, bilingual home, or repeated and untreated ear infections). Parents and caregivers of young children who are not keeping up with their peers in language development frequently take a wait-and-see approach rather than seeking intervention.

Mispronunciations are common in the preschool years, primarily because of a lack of auditory discrimination. A quarter of all children have difficulty untangling consonant sounds in their primary language even as late as 7 years of age, and this difficulty is often reflected in their spelling and articulation blunders. Thus, children pronounce *then* as "ven" (see Figure 12.2) and *birthday* as "birfvay." *And* is often pronounced as "ad," *spaghetti* is more frequently than not labeled "busketti," and words such as *trouble* and *tree* are heard and spelled as "chrubel" and "chree." Problems in dysfluency that frequently occur in 3- and 4-year-olds, such as primary stuttering, are often labeled *hesitant speech*. This type of speech results from children's having to focus

FIGURE 12.1 Teaching Language Skills to a Child with Special Needs

---

Theresa

Theresa, a 4-year-old, has been blind since birth. Because of a severe case of respiratory distress syndrome, she had required high levels of oxygen for many weeks as a premature infant. By the time she was 4 months old, she had been diagnosed with retrolental fibroplasia. Subsequent lags in development resulted in delayed speech, although her performance on the Peabody Picture Vocabulary Test—III (PPVT-III) for receptive language appeared normal. By age 4 years, her behavior had become difficult. She reacted strongly against change and, when frustrated, she would hold her breath, scream, rock, and bang her head.

When Theresa was enrolled in a school program with children who could see, her teacher, Ms. Wing, was unsure about whether *she,* not Theresa, could cope. The blindness was less of a problem than the temper tantrums. Ms. Wing found that the best resource she had for trying to turn the situation around was Theresa's parents, who had begun to attend some classes to help them with training Theresa at home. Strategies that the parents and the teacher agreed to implement involved removing Theresa to a quiet place when she began screaming and telling her that she would have to stay there until she could rejoin the group without frightening the other children. When she began rocking or banging behaviors, Ms. Wing and Theresa's parents quickly involved her in other tasks. Gradually, with all the adults in her life reacting consistently and helpfully, Theresa's behavior both at school and at home began to improve, and she became more independent.

Knowing that Theresa would have to rely on Braille for reading and heavily on her auditory strengths for vocabulary, Ms. Wing introduced a larger number of tactile activities in her classroom. She has worked not only with Theresa, but also with the other children on becoming especially astute listeners. "This is a skill that all the children in my classroom need in order to become good communicators and more highly successful readers and writers later on," notes Ms. Wing.

---

cognitively on *how* they are communicating something rather than on *what* they want to say. Listening patiently for them to speak usually gives them the time they need to communicate.

Many speech/language pathologists agree that speech or language therapy is unwarranted prior to kinder-

FIGURE 12.2 Auditory Discrimination That Is Not Yet Fully Developed: "One day my daddy came home with a baby bunny. Then (Ven) it was time for my mommy and my daddy to leave."

garten, especially if the child is showing good comprehension and using gestures to communicate. However, children who are clearly frustrated at being unable to communicate their feelings and needs may be in danger of developing behavioral problems (Kalb & Namuth, 1997). Also, children progress through a *speech readiness period,* beginning at approximately age 9 months and extending until age 2 years, in which they appear to be most receptive to learning language. Although apparent problems may seem to resolve later, some experts believe that too much developing cognition may be lost in the interim because language and developing cognition are so closely intertwined. Moreover, children who are not speaking effectively by school entry often lack the ability to interact successfully with others in the learning context. Behaviors of a preschool child that may signal more-serious long-term outcomes include the following:

Does not turn when spoken to, recognize words for common items, or use sounds other than crying to get attention

Does not respond to changes in tone of voice or look around for sources of sound, such as a ringing doorbell

Cannot point to pictures in a book that are named or understand simple questions

Cannot understand differences in meaning (e.g., *up* and *down*), follow two requests, string together two or more words, or name common objects

Does not answer simple "who," "what," and "where" questions

Cannot be understood by people outside the family

Cannot use four-word sentences or pronounce most individual sounds in words correctly

The bottom line in determining the seriousness of abnormal speech and language development in children prior to age 5 years seems to lie in ensuring that from early infancy on, a child's receptive language is intact and that the child is demonstrating comprehension reasonably appropriate for his or her age level, good intelligibility, and a willingness to be engaged with others in his or her daily activities. If delays persist until kindergarten, most pediatricians recommend speech therapy (Cowley, 1997, p. 21).

CHILDREN'S ACQUISITION OF LITERACY: CONNECTIONS AMONG ORAL LANGUAGE, PHONOLOGICAL AWARENESS, AND EMERGING READING

Before continuing to read this chapter, take a moment to reflect. Can you remember learning to read and write? What specific memories and mental pictures are you *immediately* aware of related to the process?

When we are asked to reflect on our earliest literacy experiences, many of us think about sitting in a formal reading group at approximately 5 to 6 years of age. A basal text (early reader) is being used, and individual children in the group are being called on to read brief portions of the text. The teacher is there to correct mistakes and help the reader along.

How closely does this description match what flashed through *your* mind when you were considering the preceding questions? Usually forgotten or discounted are the many other experiences that we had in infancy and early childhood—the many listening, pictorial representation, letter, word, and text experiences we had before formal reading instruction. Most important was the extent to which our parents and others communicated with us, elaborated on our efforts to communicate with them, encouraged our practicing language, and modeled correct grammar usage, moving us along a continuum of oral language development (C. E. Snow, Tabors, & Dickinson, 2001; Watson, 2001).

In infancy, children become increasingly sensitive to the sounds, rhythm, and intonation of language around them. With their built-in cognitive mechanisms, they move from initially making just throaty sounds to babbling at 4 months of age and then imitating a broader range of sounds by age 8 months. Around this time, they are already beginning to narrow their "ear" to the distinctive set of *phonemes* (the individual sounds) constituting our primary language. By age 1 year, children proudly show off with several words and babbled sentences that mean something to them but not necessarily to anyone else. Then, because of a heady growth of neural connections prior to age 18 months, an explosion of receptive language occurs, during which they may learn as many as 12 words a day (Lach, 1997). At about 20 months old, they realize that everything in their world has a name, and "What's that?" becomes a favorite question.

Those of us who reached the upper limits of early language development were fortunate enough to have had a multitude of rich literacy experiences. Such experiences may have included leafing through cardboard picture books as infants, nestling into a lap and being read favorite stories, watching television programs such as *Sesame Street,* and observing others while they were reading and writing. We played "school" with other children, perhaps being challenged by an older sibling to name all the "B–buh" words we could think of; drew pictures and scribbled with chalk on the sidewalk; excitedly sighted a favorite place to eat because we knew its name started with a huge *M* or *B*; and looked at newspapers, magazines, and other print around our homes. We had many other experiences: making our names and other words in finger paint or sand, deciphering secret codes from friends, looking at comic books, rhyming silly words, being fascinated with the sound and corresponding written version of certain words (even "naughty" words), picking out specific letters on license plates while riding in the car, and identifying our first few sight words correctly without anyone else's help.

As young children mature, their interactions with others support the growth of oral language and early *phonological awareness* (sensitivity to any size unit of sound), as well as *phonemic awareness* (awareness that the speech stream consists of a sequence of sounds or phonemes; Yopp & Yopp, 2000). This knowledge of sounds in speech is a critical skill that must be addressed with young children because it becomes the most powerful influence on their eventual success in learning to read and to spell.

Developing phonological awareness depends on how well children develop their listening skills prior to age 4 years. Enjoyable listening activities can be built into the day to enhance auditory skills through listening and response interactions (Machado, 1998). Such activities include the following:

❑ Oral or musical signals given to children to alert them to a change in activities

❑ Auditory memory games

❑ Sound cans from which children match similar sounds

❏ Activities to determine whether children can follow one-, two-, and three-step directions or oral commands

❏ Games that challenge children to imitate sounds (such as imitating the teacher's changes in voice [loud–soft], speed, and pitch [high–low]; holding their nose; and so forth)

❏ Times when children listen to the sounds of crunchy foods that are chewed or broken in half

❏ Songs, such as "Pop Goes the Weasel," or games, such as Simon Says, in which children must listen to and respond to a signal

❏ Matching games in which pictures of animals must be matched to the sounds they make

❏ Hidden-sound activities in which children must identify and discriminate certain sounds (e.g., baby rattle, tambourine, toilet flushing, stapler) that are made behind a screen or on a recorded message

❏ Play telephone activities

❏ Sound stories—stories during which children make a related sound every time a particular word is mentioned in the story (e.g., making the sound *yum yum* whenever the word *spinach* appears)

❏ Games that provide clues that children must listen to so that they can identify a particular object in the room

Children with little phonological awareness before elementary school become severely disadvantaged; strong evidence indicates that children who are at the bottom of their class in phonemic awareness remain at the bottom of their class in reading in later elementary school (Busink, 1997; Juel, Griffith, & Gough, 1986). For example, children who enter school with little or no knowledge of nursery rhymes or print awareness perform significantly poorer in reading, even through Grade 3 (Soderman, 1995).

The skill of detecting sounds in language depends wholly on the child's developing good listening skills. It is supported when children have ample opportunities to engage in meaningful conversations with adults, have interesting books read to them to enlarge their vocabularies, and play with other children in ways that require speech to be used to express their ideas. Alliteration activities, in which all the words used begin with the same sound, and rhyming activities that involve *onsets* (beginning sounds of words) and *rimes* (word families that begin with a vowel and share the same spelling ending) help children develop phonological awareness. For instance, when Ellis is listening to his mother read his favorite nursery rhymes and rhyming picture books—and when he and the other children are participating in songs and finger plays in the classroom—his ears and

brain are being trained to pick up the individual sounds in spoken words.

Adults can enhance children's listening skills and phonological awareness when they do the following:

1. Include activities in which children hear, say, and see language simultaneously. This can help children at all stages of literacy development to see some of the connections between oral and written language. For example, when Ms. Gregory chooses big books that have rhymes in them, points to the words as she reads, and invites children to clap or snap each time they hear the rhyming, and to tell her the rhyming pair, she is building their phonological awareness.

2. Encourage word play by planning for rhyming activities using stories, games, and songs so that children can hear the sounds of language and manipulate them orally.

3. Design segmentation activities. With very young children, teachers can have them just count the number of words in a single sentence. For older children, a teacher can segment the words into discrete sounds.

4. Use alliteration activities often, by making up or writing silly poems and reading alliteration books.

5. Encourage children to use temporary spelling (writing the sounds they hear, which may or may not include all the letters in the conventional spelling of the word). *(Soderman, Gregory, & O'Neill, 1999b, p. 32)*

Phonological awareness not only has an impact on the beginning reader, but also greatly affects readers in all other stages. Children who have a strong foundation in phonological awareness and an ability to segment and manipulate onsets and rimes (e.g., *band, sand, gland, hand*) in words are better able to sound out new words or even nonsense words. Such children also develop greater automaticity, which allows reading to become much more fluent (Stanovich, West, & Cunningham, 1991). Given the impact that phonological awareness has on later reading and spelling abilities, waiting for it to happen "naturally" would be unfair. It belongs in every classroom, preschool through Grade 3.

Training in phonological awareness alone is not sufficient for children to develop full literacy skills. The training must then be directly connected with a working knowledge of the alphabet as well as an accurate understanding of the correspondence between *graphemes* (the letter symbols) and phonemes (discrete sounds in language). *Phonics,* the relationship between the sounds and the letters in written language, allows children with well-developed auditory discrimination to make a clear and concrete connection between phonemes and graphemes so that their phonological processing skills can become engaged in decoding; otherwise, visual strategies may take precedence (McGuinness, Olson & Chaplin, 1990; Soderman, Gregory, & O'Neill, 1999b).

We know that children's knowledge about the alphabet as they enter kindergarten is one of the single best predictors of eventual reading achievement. Using our alphabetic writing system to decode text requires the child to translate units of print (graphemes) into units of sound (phonemes); writing requires them to translate units of sound into units of print. "At the most basic level, this task requires the ability to distinguish letters. A beginning reader who cannot recognize and distinguish the individual letters of the alphabet will have difficulty learning the sounds those letters represent" (Whitehurst & Lonigan, 2001, p. 16). Initially, children may find the alphabet confusing, because letter groups such as *b, d, p,* and *q* are rotations of the same visual pattern in different positions. Similarities of other combinations such as *v* and *n,* or *m* and *w,* are also a challenge; *s* is a letter in one position, but the rotated symbol is not a letter. This is a stage at which playfulness with language can enhance early literacy learning. Many games and songs, as well as a treasure trove of lovely alphabet books, can introduce children to letters.

The Internet is also a fertile source of alphabet activities that can be used to increase children's ability and fluency in identifying letters. Duffelmeyer (2002, pp. 632–633) reported that the following alphabet Web sites have highly appealing graphics, animation, gamelike conditions, and audio support that children will find motivating (most, but not all, of these sites have sound effects):

ABC Order (Macromedia Shockwave): http://www.learningplanet.com/act/abcorder.htm

Alphabet Letters: http://www.literacyhour.co.uk/kids/alph_char2.html

Animated ABC's: http://www.enfamil.com/guides/childdevelopment/language7.html#animated%20ABCs [scroll down page and click on lowercase letters at bottom]

Haunted Alphabet (Macromedia Shockwave): http://funschool.com/games.php?section=g1 [click on Kindergarten icon and scroll down list]

These Are the Letters of the Alphabet: http://pacificnet.net/~cmoore/alphabet/index.htm

Hidden Letters (Shockwave Flash): http://www.sesameworkshop.org/sesamestreet

Other principles children must internalize related to writing are as follows:

Letters must be in a certain order to spell a word.

In English, writing goes from left to right, and top to bottom.

Capitalization rules require changes in the size and the shape of letters.

Spaces are used to denote words and ends of sentences.

The preschool period is a time when children are eager to learn about the "purposes and mechanics of the reading enterprise" (Bowman, Donovan, & Burns, 2001, p. 65). However, by the time many young children enter school, any number of sociocultural influences have begun to set the trajectory for success or failure. Many children from low-income populations struggle with literacy development. Because research now documents persuasively that more-aggressive attention to early language and literacy contexts for these children can reduce this risk (Dickinson & Tabors, 2001; V. R. Snow, Burns, & Griffin, 1998), more effective preschool and parental education must be made available and carefully coordinated within a seamless preschool–elementary program of well-designed curriculum, instruction, and assessment. Effective assessment of what children know (and in which language they know it) is a critical element in developing good early literacy programs. Such assessment calls for a careful evaluation of children's earliest learning experiences prior to kindergarten in both home and school contexts, because these contexts serve as a foundation for and are predictive of later literacy development. Professionals working with young children must also have a keen understanding of how pre-literacy- and literacy-related skills, such as alphabet knowledge, phonological awareness, and concepts of print, develop and the part they play in structuring effective learning environments (Tabors & Snow, 2001).

Theoretical Perspectives About "Readiness"

Even before children can read a word, they perceive reading experiences as delightful ways to learn about story characters, fantasy and reality, problems, turning points and solutions, settings, points of view, and styles of authors and illustrators. With adult assistance, they learn that common elements exist among stories and that "those funny marks" indicate dialogue or what the characters "say." When teachers provide the opportunity, children can retell stories that have been read to them, outlining the details and main ideas with enough clarity to document that the children are deriving meaning from print.

Despite an intensive campaign started in the 1980s by reading association professionals to broaden perspectives about literacy, its beginnings, and its complex, culturally interactive aspects, literacy continues to be equated primarily with formal reading ability—and formal reading ability with skill in decoding words. Also persisting are fairly rigid ideas that a "readiness" factor determines when a child is ready to read or write (at approximately age 5 or 6 years) and that a "deficiency" factor (at about the end of first grade) exists when children have not yet learned to read. Given the documented variability in the development and experience of young children, these two factors wedge children into a narrow and unrealistic window for acquiring literacy.

Two major perspectives about early reading acquisition currently exist: (a) a reading readiness perspective—an "all-or-nothing" approach in which maturation is seen as a precondition of the child's ability to read and reading is seen narrowly as an ability to decode words, and (b) an emergent literacy perspective (Clay, 1979), which challenges not only the maturation theory inherent in the readiness perspective, but also the behaviorist theory for teaching reading skills.

Vygotskian theory provides a highly useful framework for understanding how literacy is acquired. This theory is friendly to both readiness *and* emerging literacy perspectives, in that Vygotsky (1929) differentiated between *natural development* and *cultural development*. The first involves organic growth and maturation of the child, and the latter, the child's literacy learning through the use of symbolic and abstract tools (Mason & Sinha, 1993). The proposition of adopting Vygotskian theory in a developmentally appropriate approach to literacy in the classroom is exciting. Doing so allows for the differences we find in the young children with whom we are working. It also advocates an interactive process for supporting the child's developmental progress rather than simply waiting for "readiness" to occur. As mentioned in chapter 11, this process is called *scaffolding* and involves determining what a child can currently do independently and then moving the child forward to a new level with assistance.

Kay Clevenger, a superb teacher at Miller Early Childhood Center in Brighton, Michigan, uses the scaffolding approach in her teaching. Recognizing that one of the children doing a fair amount of good writing was ready for the next step—leaving spaces between his words—she challenged him to find a strategy. He decided he would put dots between each word to help him remember (see Figure 12.3). Before long, he recognized that putting dots between the words took longer than just leaving spaces, and he quickly moved to a new level of understanding and capability in his writing.

In another setting, Mr. Hewlett scaffolds a small-group reading experience. Prior to beginning an unfamiliar story with new vocabulary, he leafs through the book, showing the children the pictures and challenging them to guess what the story is about. Mr. Hewlett usually takes time to ask the children about their experiences with the subject matter. Then, after writing some of the vocabulary words on a white board and asking the children to watch for the words in the story, he leads into the book, saying, "Let's find out how this situation turned out differently!" The emotional climate in any

FIGURE 12.3 Scaffolding to a Higher Level of Emerging Writing: No spaces between words to placing dots between words as a reminder

scaffolding situation should be not only warm and supportive, but also one in which the tutor constantly adjusts the amount of intervention to the child's needs and abilities. Most of all, the instructional nature of scaffolding should not be allowed to overtake the active engagement of the child in moving to a higher level of understanding (Berk & Winsler, 1995).

For adults to be most effective at scaffolding literacy tasks, they must have expertise with respect to child development and knowledge about the sequence in which literacy skills emerge. For example, in emerging writing, children progress through the following stages:

Stage 1—Emergent

Writes preletter marks, followed by differentiation of marks (see Figure 12.4)

Uses letter-like forms

Writes letters and letter strings: BuTERToWGlpR

Writes words with fixed quantities (e.g., uses three to five letters, no matter how long or short the word is)

Uses single letters for words

FIGURE 12.4 Stage 1 in Emerging Writing: Lauren, age 4, trying to write a thank-you note to her grandmother, complained to her mother, "I don't know grown-up writing!" "Just write like a 4-year-old," suggested her mother. Lauren drew lines on the page to make it "writing paper" and scribbled her message. When asked to read it back, she said, "I don't know what it says. I wrote it in French!"

Enters consonant stage: Initial consonants appear (e.g., VKn for vacation)

Skips endings

Does not use spaces between words

Uses correct directional movement

Learns letter names and letter sounds

Uses approximations and invented spelling

Uses some known words in correct positions

Can select own topic to write about

Stage 2—Early

Uses end sounds of most words correctly

Knows letter names and letter sounds

Enters alphabetic stage: Vowels appear (e.g., *vacashun* for *vacation*)

Overcompensates for vowels (e.g., *moashun* for *motion; ideeus* for *ideas*)

Can spell many difficult words correctly

Uses more correct spellings than approximations

Uses initial blends

Uses editing skills

Underlines approximations

Uses word sources to correct approximations

Uses capital letters in correct places

Writes a title

Varies topic choice

Stage 3—Fluency

Uses final blends

Uses suffixes correctly (e.g., *-s, -ing, -ed, -ly*)

Uses syllables

Uses editing skills

Compares own work with print in books and elsewhere

Correctly places quotation marks, question marks, apostrophes, and commas

Correctly divides story into paragraphs

Publishes correct articles of work

Varies sentence beginnings

Can sequence ideas

Writes in a variety of styles: friendly letters, factual reports, imaginative pieces, retellings, and poems

Developmentally Appropriate Enhancement of Children's Phonological Awareness

We know that a number of factors *predict* or, when not well developed, *deter* literacy success. Many of these factors are developed naturally by the young child in the preschool years but can also be enhanced by activities structured for the early childhood classroom. For example, when parents or teachers take young children on a shape hunt to find as many triangles, squares, circles, and rectangles as they can, children are developing visual discrimination, awareness of whole–part relationships, memory to recall images and configuration, the ability to differentiate and discriminate, the ability to follow directions, and receptive and expressive vocabulary. With block and puzzle play, children increase visual discrimination, eye coordination, awareness of whole–part relationships, awareness of spatial relationships, memory to recall sequences and placement, and the ability to attend to detail. Listening games in which children must attend closely to discover the secret object enhance memory, auditory discrimination, and the ability to attend to detail and vocabulary. Watching Big Books as the stories are read or sitting in an adult's lap to listen to a favorite book heightens children's awareness of literacy conventions (left to right, top to bottom, page to page), vocabulary, reading for meaning, and eye coordination; subsequent games with familiar text increase the child's sight knowledge of words and the growing knowledge of the internal structures of words (syllables, orthographic shapes of graphemes, grapheme–phoneme connections, visual discrimination, memory of configuration, and speed in differentiating between mirror images, such as *b/d, p/q, m/w*, and *91/19*). All these skills serve as precursors for and enhance growing literacy.

The development of literacy skills follows a definite sequence. This sequence is a highly interactive process. The child first begins to attend to the symbols and tools and then, with the continued help of adults or older children in a second stage, gains more experience with the symbols and begins to remember them. For example, the child may practice reading-like behavior or write out a "menu" in the pretend-play area. In the third stage, the child discovers how to put the symbols into practice but still depends heavily on external aids (the child may write a story by using invented spelling and words from the classroom word wall or by asking a peer for help). Finally, in the most sophisticated stage, the child has acquired literacy to the extent that he or she has internalized the constructs necessary to be independent and confident in carrying out literacy tasks.

In a jointly published position statement relative to developmentally appropriate practices for teaching young children how to read and write, the International Reading Association (IRA) and the National Association for the Education of Young Children (NAEYC) stated their belief that achieving high standards of literacy for every child in the United States is a shared responsibility of schools, early childhood programs, families, and communities (IRA & NAEYC, 1998). However, research indicates that teachers have a unique responsibility to promote children's literacy development. This perspective is also that taken by the U.S. Department of Education in its "No Child Left Behind" approach to teaching about the complex, multifaceted processes of reading and writing. Developmentally appropriate literacy practices need to be challenging but achievable, with sufficient adult support and with the understanding that children do not progress along developmental continuums in a rigid manner; instead, each child is unique in the way he or she acquires concepts and skills related to reading and writing. Teaching practices recommended by these two groups as essential for providing developmentally appropriate literacy experiences during both preschool and the primary grades are included in the Teaching Strategies section near the end of this chapter.

A Balanced Literacy Program

Ideas abound about how to teach reading and writing to young children. Incorporating a *balanced literacy ap-* *proach* simply means ensuring that effective components of oral language, reading strategies, and writing experiences are included daily in the preprimary and primary classrooms (Coleman, 2001). Doing so requires including activities that are sometimes teacher directed and modeled, sometimes wholly exploratory and independent on the child's part, and sometimes interactive between child and teacher. For example, an oral language component would include speaking *with* the child and *to* the child and providing opportunities for children to do the talking. Similarly, daily reading and writing activities must be provided that involve children's watching others read and write, interacting with a more experienced person (teacher, parent, peer) in literacy activities, and working alone to practice skill building. To gauge whether children are making sufficient progress in each of the three areas, the teacher must also use coordinated assessment strategies.

Sometimes, teachers are not sure how to include all these aspects daily. A system called *literacy rotations* (Soderman, Gregory, & O'Neill, 1999b, pp. 98–99) is one example of how some teachers structure adequate time for such activity:

Mrs. Steinmetz allows 80 minutes each morning for daily literacy rotations in her classroom. For the first 20 minutes, she calls together the entire group of children into large group, where she explains to them the activities that will occur in the three 20-minute, rotated minigroups that will follow large group. During this time, she also demonstrates procedures and strategies for the activities they will be carrying out independently. This approach is especially useful in multiage classrooms and takes advantage of the children's varying skill levels (the minigroups are always heterogenously constructed); it is also effective for breaking a class into smaller groups so that she can work intensively with a smaller group while other children gain independence in reading and writing activities.

Today, she begins with a group starter that immediately engages their interest: a secret message they are to decode with her help. She then launches into a brief "Morning Message," in which she works interactively with them on both reading skills and writing skills. After reading with them a familiar poem they have read at the start of each day's session, she then does a quick activity with some enjoyable phonics work connected to the poem. She reminds them about ways they can take responsibility for their independent learning and designates a person in each group who will act as a "traveler," the child who will bring any questions to her that someone in the small working group cannot answer. She explains carefully what the red group will be doing as they start in the independent writing center and demonstrates the process to them. They will be using the materials provided on the table to form as many contractions as they can and to write the contractions in their reading journals, listing the two separate words and then the contraction that can be made. They may work with a partner or independently, and if they have additional time, they may make up other contractions.

The blue group will begin with silent or buddy reading work, choosing from a selection of books she has gathered. After reading one of the books independently or with a partner, these children are then to go back, look for all the contractions they can find, and list them in their reading journals.

The green group will begin their rotations with Mrs. Steinmetz. For them, she begins a shared reading experience with a book they have already enjoyed, Dr. Seuss's Oh, the Places You'll Go! *and challenges them to hold up their index fingers silently anytime they spot a contraction during the reading. Following the reading, she asks the travelers in the other small groups if they have any questions and then does some additional work with the text for phonological and print awareness. A follow-up activity for material comprehension completes the session. Today, she provides the group with copied pages of the text and invites them to discuss the order in which they appeared in the book, to work together to hang them on a clothesline in that order, and then to determine how well they remembered the sequence by using the book as a check.*

Mrs. Steinmetz observes the transmission of learning that occurs as children answer questions she has about the text and pose their own. She likes that the children have learned to be fairly autonomous about the independent work they have been given to do, so that they do not interrupt her focus with the shared reading group. She can assess differences in the children's understanding, skills, and concepts because she is working with them on a small-group basis; she then addresses these needs more intensively during the day by working with children individually or in small, homogeneous groups of two or three as needed. As she enthusiastically describes the process, "I win and they win!"

INTEGRATION OF LANGUAGE EXPERIENCES ACROSS THE CURRICULUM

Remember some of your favorite activities when you were a young child, such as playing jump rope to chants such as "I'm a little Dutch girl" ("dressed in blue. Here are the things I like to do . . .") or the science report you created in elementary school about different trees (complete with leaf samples pasted to the pages) or the globe you constructed from a balloon and collage and then meticulously labeled for social studies? All these activities served multiple purposes relative to skill development—and all of them enhanced your language development. The strength of the language domain is that it reaches naturally across the curriculum into every other domain.

Literature of all kinds should be used to introduce "big ideas" to children, including such ideas in science, mathematics, history, and social studies (Routman, 1996). Children should become as familiar with *expository text* (factual or informative literature) as they are with *narrative text* (fictional stories), and they should be encouraged after the reading of a narrative text to do some follow-up work from expository texts when they have questions. For example, Ms. Rinker was sharing Eric Carle's *The Very Hungry Caterpillar* with her class when DeMarco questioned the author's use of the term *cocoon*. "My dad says that should be called a *chrysalis*," he challenged.

Knowing that DeMarco's father had probably used the term *chrysalis*, Ms. Rinker said, "I think DeMarco's father is correct. How do you think your father knew that, DeMarco? Where do you think *we* can find out about that word?" An ensuing and very appealing "science lesson" took place, with a group of interested children taking a trip to the school library on a fact-finding mission. Later, they looked at differences between varieties of moths and butterflies, which led to their classifying, labeling, painting, and drawing a number of them. Along with an interested parent, another group of children looked on the Internet and discovered that Eric Carle had addressed the discrepancy and had provided an explanation about continuing to use the word *cocoon*. A discussion followed about whether Mr. Carle should change the word, and the children wrote a class letter to Mr. Carle, letting him know that they agreed with his decision and why they did so.

To reach across the curriculum, many teachers create what they call *literacy spin-offs*—that is, activities in other curricular domains that seem to evolve naturally from reading a favorite narrative text. The book provides the children with a shared basis of understanding for the subsequent activities, which may occur during the span of a day, a week, or longer, and the teacher makes an effort to structure activities in all developmental domains. For instance, a group of early childhood teachers met to develop a set of spin-off activities that could be used with the text *This Is My House*, by Arthur Dorros, a favorite book for many of the children in their classrooms. In the book, children from many countries tell about their houses, which are typical of the kind found in their country. The diversity of homes is depicted, as well as how each is constructed, and a sample of the different languages people speak is provided as each child in the book proudly proclaims, "This is my house!"

As a connected reading experience, the teachers discussed with the children whether their lives would be similar or different if they lived in the other cultures depicted in the book. The children were assigned the task of interviewing an older family member or friend to discover what that person's house looked like when he or she was young and if the house had changed while the person lived there or afterward. The children worked together to construct a salt dough globe and labeled it to show the seven continents that were connected with the houses depicted in the book. They also constructed dioramas of the different homes to depict the climate and living conditions particular to each home and learned such terms as *continent, equator, compass rose, hemisphere, foundation, adobe, thatch, yurt, houseboat,* and *shelter*. Next, they graphed the kinds of dwellings they and their families lived in and, with their parents' help, developed scaled floor maps of their homes' layouts. They found out about the various materials their homes were made of and researched how the materials were made. Inviting a local contractor to visit school, they developed a descriptive listing of the cost of constructing a home of a particular size and estimated the cost of equipping and furnishing such a home, depending on the items selected. Small groups were assigned to take trips to a furniture store, an appliance shop, and a plumbing shop to check out their estimates and report back. After singing, "There was a crooked man who bought a crooked house," and after a discussion of the importance of measuring correctly when you are building a house and what would happen if the walls were not the same height, they drew crooked houses, constructed crooked houses from popsicle sticks, and made up poems about their creations to share with one another. When asked what would happen if the floor were slanted, they constructed inclined planes and watched and recorded the results when various items were rolled down them. Individually, the children created essays about what houses and furniture might say if they could talk and shared their writing with one another during Author's Chair sessions (described in chapter 4). They made rubbings from the outsides of their homes and brought them to school for comparison and for discussion with their classmates. The spin-off naturally swung in the direction of animals' homes and, after studying animal habitats and listing some questions they had, the classes took a joint field trip to the zoo to look at various animals in habitats that simulated the animals' natural homes. From these activities, the children greatly increased their overall vocabulary, their

fund of knowledge, and their conceptual understandings across the entire curriculum.

Including print materials throughout the room, not just in the library corner, also increases children's attention to written language as it relates to learning in other domains (McGee & Richgels, 2000). For instance, one preschool teacher included books in every learning center in her classroom—books on machines, transportation, and building in the block area; cookbooks, telephone book, magazines, an address book, and home construction books in the housekeeping area; books about artists, color, and design in the art area; and number books and books about nature in the math and science area.

Using literature to reach across the curriculum is natural, and many ways exist for doing so. However, to do so in the most effective way, professionals must (a) discard rigid ideas about time blocks that segment the day or week, (b) think creatively about how all curricular components relate to one another, and (c) involve the children, their families, and the community in the activities that take place inside and outside the classroom. Good planning is required to ensure a balance of activities, and thoughtful evaluation strategies are necessary to provide the documentation needed to ensure that children are making progress.

A number of publishers have developed resources specifically for integrating emergent literacy with dramatic play, science, math, art, music, motor skills, and social studies. Good sources include McGraw-Hill/Good Apple, Scholastic, Pearson Learning, Dale Seymour, Carson-Dellosa, Evan-Moor/Monday Morning, Creative Teaching Press, Milliken, and The Education Center/Mailbox. Web sites for these publishers and the titles they offer are easily accessible.

CURRENT EDUCATIONAL ISSUES

As many new teachers enter the field of early childhood education, they are often confused when they discover that colleagues in the same learning community are at opposite ends of a philosophical continuum about guiding young children's emerging literacy. Some educators have no established philosophy, which leaves them at the whim of any new idea that comes along or believing that "nothing is ever new . . . only recycled." When such individuals discuss issues related to curriculum, literacy instruction, or assessment, they have difficulty agreeing about a consolidated direction and, as a result, rarely effect productive change that supports a strong language arts approach for young children.

In other learning communities, staff form ongoing study groups around targeted issues to determine whether existing programmatic practice is still the best practice or whether change is warranted because of new understandings in the field. Following a recent in-service workshop to talk about new directions in early literacy, the early childhood professionals attending were invited to develop a list of questions that continued to bother them. The following questions represent the issues that surfaced quickly and seemed to arouse the most heated discussion:

Question: I teach in a program that increasingly serves families from very diverse populations. A number of children entering the program do not speak English. Do you have any hints about including these children, particularly about how to support their language and literacy acquisition?

Answer: The NAEYC has developed a position statement for responding to linguistic and cultural diversity (NAEYC, 1996a). Children enrolled in educational programs who are ELL (English-language learners), NEP (non–English proficient), or LEP (limited-English proficient) need the respect and active support of professionals and peers who will be helping them add English to their primary language. However, more than this, these children need a teacher who considers bilingualism as a positive attribute rather than a linguistic, cognitive, and academic liability. These children come into the classroom already knowing a lot about language (their own) and, while acquiring a second language, will be driven to higher levels of cognitive flexibility, metalinguistic awareness, concept formation, and creativity than is required of unilinguistic children in the setting (E. Garcia, 1993).

Professionals will want to examine the entire classroom structure: Is it a community of learners with an environment that promotes children's interaction with adults and peers? Are the opportunities for all children to speak, listen, read, and write (even in their native language) rich and varied? Are learning goals ("Let's see how much we can find out about this!") rather than performance goals and drill ("How much do you know about this?") emphasized? Is the active role the student brings to learning recognized and valued? How creative are instructional strategies? Is there sufficient repetition of activities and predictability so that the child can begin to develop a comfort level? Are visual aids, toys, photographs, and books from the child's culture included, as well as tapes, stories, rhymes, and songs? Do opportunities exist for the child or the child's family members to share with others experiences such as a song or counting from the primary language? Are authentic strategies available for evaluating the child's progress?

Because the rate of acquisition of a second language (including reading and writing abilities) is highly related to proficiency levels in the child's primary language, every effort should be made to have the child continue gaining proficiency in his or her home language. Doing so calls for encouraging parents to continue speaking and reading frequently to the child in their native language and recruiting someone familiar with the child's home language to participate in the classroom for at least a portion of the day if possible. This person can be a parent, family member (perhaps a sibling), or person in the community who not only can translate in "sticky" situations, but also can scaffold language and literacy experiences for the child both in the home language and in the language being acquired. *Code switching* (the child's switching from one language to the other even within the same sentence) should be accepted without comment (Zentella, 1981).

Young children can acquire a second language quickly. Within about 3 months in a supportive, secure environment, most will begin to demonstrate that they are making gains in second-language acquisition. For children whose primary language is developing typically, a second language is usually not a challenge.

Question: People disagree about the best way to teach beginning readers about phonics. Some professionals advocate that direct, systematic teaching of phonics *hampers* learning to read, whereas others believe that trying to teach it in the context of a literature-based approach leaves too much to chance. I'm confused! Which camp is correct?

Answer: Patricia Cunningham, a recognized expert in early literacy and author of *Phonics They Use* (2000), concluded the following:

The answer to the question of whether phonics should be taught in a synthetic or analytic manner seems to be neither. Synthetic approaches generally teach children to go letter-by-letter, assigning a pronunciation to each letter and then blending the individual letters together. Analytic approaches teach rules and are usually filled with confusing jargon. Brain research, however, suggests that the brain is a *pattern detector,* not a rule applier and that, while we look at single letters, we are looking at them considering all the letter patterns we know. Successfully decoding a word occurs when the brain recognizes a familiar spelling pattern or, if the pattern itself is not familiar, searches through its store of words with similar patterns. . . . The kind of phonics instruction we need and for which we should advocate is not the "old phonics." It is not rules and jargon and worksheets. *(pp. 185–186, 192)*

Regie Routman (1996) also had much to say on this subject, noting that children rely on sound sequences, visual patterns, graphophonic relationships, and meaning (i.e., familiar patterns) for their invented spelling (see Figure 12.5) and construct their own knowledge of phonics. In turn, teachers can rely on children's invented spelling to indicate what children are picking up relative to phonological awareness.

As pointed out previously, phonological awareness activities connected with words children are familiar with are extremely valuable when such activities are used along with frequent experience with good literature. For novice readers, the child's name and other sight words are a good beginning, as are familiar songs, nursery rhymes, finger plays, and poems. All these aids can help children learn letter names, match the names to the corresponding shapes, and then match the names and shapes to the corresponding sounds. Children need to learn print conventions, that words can be categorized according to their beginning sounds (onsets) and rimes, that phonemes have corresponding graphemes, that patterns exist within words, and that words have particular endings—and they can

learn all this in the context of engaging activities with the print they love. Children also enjoy the fun of exchanging phonemes in word families and the many other awareness-raising activities that make learning to read and write as natural as speaking.

Fewer than 5 percent of children have neurological difficulty with reading unless they undergo intensive remediation. A synthetic phonics approach may enhance the abilities of children who are visually dyslexic and need to focus more specifically on word parts as a decoding strategy. Conversely, for children who have auditory dyslexia, such a teaching strategy would make matters *worse* because breaking an unknown word into letters and then trying to put it back together into a recognizable entity is nearly impossible for them.

Question: The principal at my institution insists that every time I display children's work in the hallway or in my classroom, it must be fully edited and correct. These children are only first graders and are doing their best at invented spelling. Shouldn't that be good enough to celebrate?

Answer: We think so, and so do a number of researchers who think that temporary or invented spelling is the

FIGURE 12.5 Example of Invented Spelling, Which Children Use to Construct Their Own Knowledge of Phonics

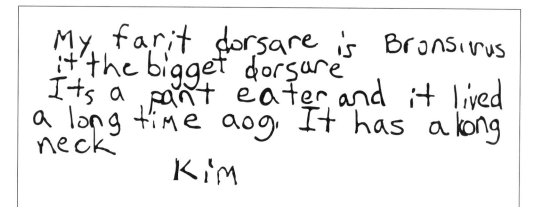

My favorite dinosaur is brontosaurus.

It [is] the biggest dinosaur.

It's a plant eater and it lived

a long time ago. It has a long

neck.

Kim

Grade 1

FIGURE 12.6 Temporary Spelling of "I'm in the ballet class."

I'm in the ballet class.

Susan

Kindergarten

most significant change in preschool and primary-grade practice since the 1970s. Richgels (2001) said, "Before invented spelling, there was little or no writing in preschool, and primary-grade writing was largely a wasteland of penmanship drill, assigned copying, and fill-in-the-blanks work" (p. 142). Proponents of temporary spelling claim that it allows teachers a way to measure and assess children's phonemic awareness. Well-conducted research (Dahl, Scharer, Lawson, & Grogan, 1999; McGee & Purcell-Gates, 1997) indicates that allowing children to use invented spelling along with instruction in phonological awareness increases children's phonics knowledge. Children can think about how words are formed . . . and push their

developing abilities rather than simply raising their hand and having a teacher spell the word correctly for them. Research indicates that when children are allowed to write freely in preschool through Grade 2, they take more risks with their writing and are inclined to draw more-sophisticated words from their receptive vocabulary (see Figure 12.6). When they are not allowed to use invented spelling, children are hampered by having to use only the words they know how to spell or those that they can ask someone else to spell for them. Consequently, their writing content may be spelled correctly, but of necessity it may be dull and basic; even though they may have rich words in their receptive vocabularies, they are unable to use them because they have little experience seeing these words in print and cannot yet use reference materials efficiently.

Children's progress in moving toward conventional spelling will depend on their developing knowledge of phoneme–grapheme connections, their visual memory, the amount of daily practice they have in seeing and forming words in print, and the quality of minilessons and writing activities that professionals or parents structure or model for them. We need to clearly inform parents that temporary spelling *is* only a temporary tool. Children's writing progresses toward adult standards in stages in much the same way as they learned to speak, and parents need to be assured that we *are* guiding children toward this end. The best way to do so is to keep dated work samples of children's work to show parents how children are gaining in their ability to spell words conventionally (see chapter 8). Increasing numbers of primary teachers are using the technique of having children write the same familiar nursery rhyme (e.g., "Humpty Dumpty") once a month to demonstrate the children's progress.

Question: Should we be correcting children's writing in their journals?

Answer: No, but you *may* have *them* edit their writing. On an individual basis and after children have begun to write a number of words and sentences by using invented spelling, have them begin to edit for targeted errors. For example, prior to their making their journal entry on Tuesday, ask them to go back to Monday's entry and underline just one word that was difficult to spell or reread and then look it up on the word wall or in the classroom dictionary. Children who still do not know the alphabetic sequence or are unfamiliar with the use of reference materials will need scaffolded assistance until they can use them independently. Another day, you can have children go back for two or three entries and make sure they have a capital letter on each of their sentences. This approach is an effective way of teaching composition with a contextual approach, as long as the child is developmentally ready for this next step. *Remember:* The more *you* do the correcting, the slower the child will be in internalizing the error.

Question: What about the child who is not yet writing? Should I take dictation from individual children?

Answer: The answer depends on what your objective is. If the child is still at a stage in which he or she does not yet know that speech can be captured with symbols on a page, then writing what the child dictates, reading it back to the child, and

Developmentally appropriate classrooms are joyful places in which children commit their ideas to paper with confidence.

having the child read it back again is a valuable learning experience for the child. Once the child knows that combinations of letters represent words, that spaces must be left between words, and that print communicates to others what we want to tell them, we need to back away from taking dictation from individual children so that their motivation to learn is not hampered. However, you do need to write in front of children daily, taking time to name the letters for emerging readers and writers and to point out configurations of particular words. Words that children need to use frequently in their writing can be placed on the classroom word wall and walked through daily so that they become internalized. Once words are put on the word wall, children should be encouraged to refer to them and expected to spell the words correctly. Classroom dictionaries can be made for each child, with copies updated regularly with the children's help. Concept charts on display in the classroom that contain a number of words that the children have dictated to the teacher about an ongoing theme or project are also helpful as children write about their experiences.

GOALS AND OBJECTIVES

The ultimate goal of education in the language domain is to help children develop their innate capacities to share their thoughts and feelings with others and to accurately interpret communications they receive. The curriculum should include the following experiences.

Intermediate Objectives for Listening and Viewing

As children progress toward the ultimate goal, they will demonstrate the following 10 competencies:

1. Participate in experiences that help them interpret unspoken messages, including tone of voice and facial expression
2. Enhance their listening skills
3. Demonstrate courteous listening behaviors by
   a. Looking at the speaker
   b. Sitting relatively still
   c. Waiting for a turn to speak
   d. Responding to oral cues
4. Increase their receptive vocabulary
5. Identify and discriminate similarities and differences among sounds (e.g., environmental sounds, letter–sound associations, words)
6. Improve their ability to focus on relevant oral content and ignore distractions
7. Develop their understanding of contemporary media (e.g., television, videos, compact disks [CDs], digital video disks [DVDs], and computer technology) and the impact of media on learning and values; discriminate which aspects are likely true and which are fantasy
8. Demonstrate auditory memory by repeating in correct detail and sequence the messages they hear
9. Demonstrate auditory comprehension and critical listening skills by
   a. Retelling, in their words, the messages or stories they hear
   b. Responding to oral language with relevant comments or questions
   c. Orally linking personal experience to what they have heard
   d. Responding accurately to single- and multistep directions
   e. Drawing logical conclusions
   f. Distinguishing facts
   g. Listening selectively for main ideas
   h. Experimenting with and discussing different ways to express the same idea

10. Identify and use resources—including knowledgeable people, field trips, reference materials, and electronic media—to investigate a particular question or topic

Intermediate Objectives for Speaking

As children progress toward the ultimate goal, they will demonstrate the following eight competencies:

1. Experiment with language sounds, rhythm, volume, pitch, and words
2. Expand their abilities to
   a. Articulate intents, emotions, and desires
   b. Describe events from the past, present, or future
   c. Generate questions and demonstrate understanding of the answers
   d. Maintain a conversation with another person about an object or an event experienced
   e. Demonstrate their level of comprehension of concepts and situations
   f. Tell stories about pictures
   g. Create and describe original imaginative situations
   h. Persuade others appropriately
   i. Rephrase or clarify their messages to others
   j. Present information with clarity, becoming more fluent and coherent
   k. Present conclusions based on the investigation of an issue or a problem
3. Use appropriate body language (eye contact, body position, and gestures) to alert a listener to their intent and to convey emotion
4. Note how their use of inflections, articulation, volume, intonation, and speed aids or hampers the listener in understanding their messages
5. Increase their expressive vocabulary in size and precision
6. Participate in conversations with others
7. Participate in group conversations with others, with and without teacher guidance
8. Demonstrate self-confidence and poise during group speaking and creative dramatics activities

Intermediate Objectives for Writing

As children progress toward the ultimate goal, they will demonstrate the following 17 competencies:

1. Observe others' purposeful writing, thus extending their awareness that writing transforms thoughts, ideas, and feelings into print symbols to communicate meaning
2. Put their thoughts on paper, first through simple pictures and then progressing through the developmental stages of writing

3. Use their own temporary versions of writing, working gradually toward conventional spelling, handwriting, punctuation, and format

4. Write for a variety of purposes (e.g., to list, inform, narrate, describe, and persuade), increasing the amount and quality of their writing with time

5. Expand their writing vocabulary

6. Increase their ability to select topics to write about

7. Learn to organize their ideas in a logical sequence

8. Begin to use writing strategies such as mapping, webbing, and clustering to organize and plan writing

9. Express their ideas in complete thoughts

10. Improve their ability to evaluate and edit their writing, prepare rough and final drafts, and publish narrative, expository, and other text forms

11. Describe their goals and challenges in writing to others

12. Use reference materials, including electronic sources, to help them improve their writing

13. Explore and discuss differences in words, phrases, and language patterns used in spoken and written contexts, both within their environment and from other cultures

14. Identify and use correct formats for certain types of writing (e.g., personal letters, business letters, stories, and scripts)

15. Use the writing process to create original stories, poems, and informational pieces

16. Use aspects of the writer's craft—including dialogue, characterization, conflict, and logic—to formulate and express ideas

17. Use word-processing programs on the computer

Intermediate Objectives for Reading

As children progress toward the ultimate goal, they will demonstrate the following 23 competencies:

1. Enjoy shared reading experiences with varied genres of literature, including classic and contemporary literature

2. Acquire an adequate reading vocabulary

3. Practice reading-like behavior, moving from "pretend" reading to attempting to match the flow of their language with book illustrations and with print

4. Respond to written symbols in the environment (e.g., their name and others' names, signs, advertisements, labels)

5. Predict, on the basis of the information in the text and their personal life experiences, what will come next in stories that are being read

6. Discuss or demonstrate, either for listening or for independent reading, how the characteristics of various narrative genre and story elements convey ideas and perspectives through
   a. Story sequence (first, next, last; beginning, middle, end; before, after)
   b. Main ideas both at the literal level and at the inferential level
   c. Characters and character development
   d. Setting
   e. Plot development, cause and effect, problems and solutions, and logical conclusions

7. Understand the relationship of reading to writing and thinking

8. Tell or dramatize their versions of stories to show comprehension of what they have read

9. Create new endings for stories, drawing on logical elements of the original stories

10. Read familiar or memorized nursery rhymes, songs, poems, and plays

11. Distinguish between real and make-believe, fact and opinion, in written materials

12. Read their own writing

13. Expand their phonological and print awareness (e.g., identify upper- and lowercase letters, sight vocabulary, rhymes and rhyming words, segmentation, common blends, vowel patterns, common contractions, common digraphs, and concepts about letter–sound relationships)

14. Develop a sight vocabulary and read simple lists and stories

15. Read independently and construct meaning from both narrative text and expository text, using decoding strategies (e.g., picture cues, context clues, phonic analysis, and syntax) to predict what makes sense

16. Read fluently with expression and clarity

17. Develop general concepts of print:
   a. Books are read from front to back.
   b. Print is organized from left to right and from top to bottom; the order of print is relevant.
   c. Letters are used to write words; letters stand for sounds we say; letters can be used more than once to make words.
   d. Words are the things that we read.
   e. Spaces are used between words.
   f. Punctuation is used to inform the reader.

18. Identify the parts of a book—cover (title, author, and illustrator), dedication page, table of contents, chapters, headings, and index

19. Gain access to printed materials to seek information, ideas, enjoyment, and understanding of their

individuality, our common humanity, and the rich diversity of our society

20. Apply, to their lives and others' lives, knowledge, ideas, and issues drawn from texts

21. Become familiar with libraries as interesting places to find books and other materials for entertainment and information

22. Evaluate their developing literacy skills, identifying their strengths and needs

23. Use information gained from reading to compare, contrast, analyze, infer, and express ideas and to solve problems

TEACHING STRATEGIES

To optimize children's language and literacy acquisition, teachers may use the following eight strategies:

1. *Structure a communication-rich environment.*

a. *Model appropriate, rich language usage.* Although you cannot expect standard English usage from all children, you must have a good command of it yourself. In addition, your diction needs to be clear and understandable to the children, with interesting vocabulary that stretches the children's understanding of and interest in the language.

b. *Listen to and talk with each child daily.* The school day is busy from beginning to end, and neglecting children who do not expect or demand attention is far too easy. Make having a personal conversation with every child each day a habit.

c. *Take advantage of spontaneous events to promote children's language development through discussion.* Use these events to start conversations with children and to encourage children to talk with one another. Some of the richest teaching moments occur unplanned. If you are too "scripted" by your teaching plans, you may not notice how something a child brings to the class, a change in the weather, or a serendipitous event can be used more effectively to attain your immediate or long-range teaching goals.

d. *When a child states something, extend his or her phrase by repeating it and using a new term or adding an appropriate clause.* Often, you have the opportunity to extend a child's vocabulary by repeating all or part of what a child says and using an interesting synonym for a word or two or adding a related idea. Use open-ended questions and paraphrases as described in chapter 3 to accomplish this.

e. *Plan the learning environment and the curriculum to provide opportunities for children to communicate informally with one another.* Centers in the activity-oriented classroom provide a natural environment for peer interaction.

Take advantage of spontaneous opportunities to promote language development.

f. *Plan activities each day in which the primary goal is for children to use language to describe events, make predictions, or evaluate phenomena.* Not all your goals for children's language development will be attained through activity centers. Plan particular small- and large-group experiences that stretch children's abilities to express themselves in particular ways. Ensure that each child in the group has sufficient opportunities to speak and is developing the confidence and skill to do so.

2. *Create a print-rich environment.* Integrate language development activities and quality literature throughout all areas of the early childhood curriculum. Because all subjects require language for learning, plan content around the language forms of listening and viewing, speaking, reading, and writing. Make a variety of literature central in your classroom. The literature will have important meanings for the children when you help them explore its relationships to, or its contrasts with, their lives.

Consciously create an environment that highlights print in every area of the room. Some examples are charts, predictable charts (see Figure 12.7), book-making materials, labels, names, directions, recipes, menus, and children's writing. The print that children see around them becomes their primary resource for their reading and writing. In addition, make the environmental print serve real uses in your classroom. Place print materials at the children's eye level. Draw attention to print messages, pointing to letters or words and asking why the messages are important; refer to them at appropriate times. Model print concepts often, by cuing left to right, top to bottom, and page turning and by noting word and

FIGURE 12.7 Shared Reading and Writing on a Predictable Chart

My favorite thing to play with is my <u>tennis racket</u>.	(Mr. Landon)
My favorite thing to play with is my <u>steam shovel</u>.	(Jamel)
My favorite thing to play with is my <u>Barbie doll</u>.	(Abby)
My favorite thing to play with is my <u>bike</u>.	(Robert)
My favorite thing to play with is my <u>video game</u>.	(Demond)
My favorite toy is my <u>Harry Potter books</u>.	(Kelsey)
My favorite toy is my <u>Lego blocks</u>.	(Andrew)
My favorite thing to play with is my <u>little sister</u>.	(Lily)
My favorite toy is my <u>board games</u>.	(Gavin)

sentence formations (e.g., spaces between words, types of punctuation).

3. *Model and teach the importance of developing and using good listening skills as follows:*

a. *Model good listening behavior* by attending to the children and responding to their comments and questions. Stop; look at each child when he or she speaks. Ask relevant questions. Ask other children to respond to what a child has said.

b. *Give children appropriate cues* to help them listen better. Say, "Look up here" or "Watch me"; use voice inflections; change your volume appropriately for the small- or large-group setting. You cannot expect children to know how to listen well, although they often are more-attentive listeners than adults are. Clues to listening behavior will be useful for them and lessen your frustration over inattentive listening behavior.

c. *Introduce sound discrimination* by using common environmental sounds (e.g., telephone or doorbell). Gradually alert children to interesting sound–symbol relationships in written language. Alerting children to the sounds in their environment calls attention to common experiences that are easily overlooked and creates understanding about hearing and sounds. When parents helped these children to learn to speak, the children did not focus their attention on the individual sounds that made up the words they were learning. Sounds and the letters that represent them on paper are more readily understood when they are examined in the context of a song, poem, or story the children enjoy. Early, brief, and natural encounters with phonics, usually on a class chart or a white board, ensures that sound–symbol relationships will not be overwhelming or confusing.

d. *Maintain children's attention* by using props, gestures, proximity, and particular facial and vocal expressions, but also gradually help children maintain attention without extra elements. A book, a puppet, a picture, or your special action is a useful attention getter; often, it visualizes for the children a concept that is difficult for them to conceive. However, children must also learn to create their own mind pictures about the words they hear. Plan listening experiences that develop the children's imaginations from oral stimuli alone as well as with aids.

4. *Involve children every day in engaging reading experiences.*

a. *Read to the children* at least once every day, more when possible. Remember that children who may come from literacy-impoverished homes are in even greater need of read-aloud opportunities, including sitting on the teacher's lap during reading. Provide cues as to what to listen to before you read aloud. Pose one to three questions that can be addressed at the end of a story.

b. *Use a variety of literary forms* when you are reading to children (picture books, poetry, folk and fairy tales, and factual books). Plan your oral reading time carefully so that you "tune your children's ears" to the ideas presented in a variety of genres and to the vocabulary and sentence structures typical of different forms of writing.

c. *Draw attention* to story sequence and development, characters, cause and effect, main ideas, and details, but only when these discussions will not interfere with the children's enjoyment of the story. On appropriate occasions, take advantage of opportunities when you are reading to children to teach them these important concepts. Remember that preserving the continuity of what the children are listening to and the integrity of the overall meaning is also important.

d. *Involve children* in songs, chants, poems, finger plays, rhymes, choral readings, and dramatic play. Dramatic activity is a natural learning mode for children. Plan for the overt involvement of all the children as much as possible. Combine speaking or singing with reading the lyrics of these favorite songs or poems to lead children into intuitively learning about reading.

e. *Plan for silent reading (book time) and shared reading experiences for children.* Have them spend time each day looking through familiar books or picture books, putting their imaginations to work by rethinking what went on in the text. Allow children to work with a reading partner, each of them reading a paragraph or a page.

5. *Involve children every day in enjoyable writing experiences.*

a. *Write in front of them every day.* Daily, in large group, have children take turns dictating a message. The messages can be centered on the children's experiences and observations or even brief stories developed by the entire group. This approach allows the children to hear and see their words in print, written in "adult language." As they dictate, they can concentrate on what they want to say without struggling with writing these ideas and words. In this kind of activity, they can dictate longer, more-complex pieces than they can write on paper by themselves, and this activity models how messages are composed. Be sure to write what the children say; they need to know that you value what is said and how it is said. Ideas can come from the group about how something might be "fixed" until everyone is satisfied with the message.

b. *Provide daily opportunities for children to write* and share their writing with peers and their teacher because writing is learned only by doing it. Include ample writing activities and writing suggestions in daily play-based experiences. Provide access to a variety of materials for children to make their own print. Place writing materials in all centers of the room: order blanks for the pretend restaurant, sticks for making words in the sandbox, and so forth. Provide reference materials, such as a simplified dictionary, in some centers so that children can readily use them.

c. *Allow invented spelling,* introducing editing as appropriate on an individual basis. Each child's level of performance in writing will depend on the opportunities he or she has had to write at home and in previous grades at school, his or her understanding of the purposes of printed language, and the degree to which his or her efforts have been accepted by others. Avoid drawing attention to words and letters as the children write so that they can concentrate on the meanings they are trying to express. Avoid the common school practice of spelling words for children as they write because these "helps" turn children's attention away from the ideas they are trying to express. At other, more-appropriate times (such as Morning Message or Daily News time), point out similarities and differences in words, correct or unusual spellings, rhyming words, use of capital letters, and punctuation. Because their enthusiasm for writing grows as children hear responses to their efforts, display all children's writing on bulletin boards or in "published" books. Encourage children to share their pictures and writing by taking a turn in the Author's Chair.

d. *Provide writers' workshops or minilessons* for teaching the elements of the writing process that are developmentally appropriate for the children with whom you are working: topic selection, creation of drafts, and draft sharing. In earlier stages of emerging writing, children write best and write most about the topics they know and care about. Discuss places at which additional words and sentences could be added to their pieces. Show them ways to correct errors but allow them to make the corrections; expect older children to begin higher level revision strategies as they take increasing pride in what they have produced. Do not push the children into revising or editing too soon, or you may diminish their initial writing efforts. Asking the child to read a piece to you or the other children often helps him or her see changes that need to be made.

6. *Plan literacy games, songs, and other play-oriented activities to enhance children's phonological and print awareness.* Help children to develop the letter–sound associations and the phoneme–grapheme knowledge that they need to have by carefully embedding these activities in meaningful experiences. Call attention to letters individually and in words when you are reading charts of familiar poems, dictated writing, and so forth. Highlight the configuration of letters and familiar words by drawing around them and pointing out unique features of a particular letter or word. Also draw children's attention to various writing forms by providing examples (upper- and lowercase letters; manuscript, cursive, and italic forms; contractions; boldface, etc.) when they appear in contexts interesting to children.

Model strategies for determining how to read unfamiliar words.

7. *Accept children's risk taking in their listening, speaking, writing, and reading,* even when their efforts do not result in correct or useful production. Be careful about "taking over" too quickly to provide the correct answer. So that you do not destroy motivation or shortcut the thinking that children must do to internalize a concept, think about what the next small step is in the scaffolding process to help children become more independent and less reliant.

8. *Structure useful assessment strategies* to ensure that children are making progress in every area of the language domain. Observe, record children's developing strengths and needs, save work samples that indicate progress, and involve children in the evaluation process (see chapter 7 for specific suggestions).

ACTIVITY SUGGESTIONS

The following activities are structured to support children's growth in the language domain. Included are ideas for enhancing skills, processes, and concepts in each of the subareas of listening and viewing, speaking, writing, and reading. Clearly, more than one language objective is supported in any of the suggested activities, which is the hallmark of a well-designed activity. However, the *primary* purpose of each activity is to focus on the objective specifically cited. Doing so allows professionals to determine whether they are offering growth-producing experiences in each of the subareas and across the curriculum.

Because you may be working with children in any or all stages of emergent through fluent literacy and from 3 to 8 years of age, you will need to adapt these ideas to the developmental and experiential levels of the individual children with whom you are working. To aid this transition, we provide suggestions for simplifying or extending each activity. Also, each activity has been labeled for a specific group: younger and less experienced children, older and more experienced children, or children of all ages.

Listening and Viewing Activities

✎ Listen and Dismiss (For Younger or Less Experienced Children)

Listening and Viewing Objective 2 For children to enhance their listening skills.

Materials None

Procedure Once children have been together in a learning setting for several months, they begin to know one another's voices. This natural development can be used to help them focus their auditory senses to discover who is speaking to them without seeing the person. Model the listening game during large group by turning your chair around just before dismissing the children and having one child at a time say, "Good morning, Mr. (Ms.)_____. How are you?" As you recognize the child's voice, respond by saying, "Very well, thank you, (*Child's Name*)," and excuse the child from the large group. As children listen carefully, they pick up on the nuances of the other children's voices. They can then participate by closing their eyes during dismissal and trying to guess who is speaking to the teacher.

To simplify Significantly reduce the number of voices that must be discriminated by designating only four or five speakers from the large group before beginning the game; have the remainder of the children be the listeners. The game may also be played in a small group of only four or five children, which also reduces the discrimination difficulty.

To extend Choose individual children each day to play the role of teacher and be the dismisser.

✎ Going on a Sound Walk (For Younger or Less Experienced Children)

Listening and Viewing Objective 6 For children to improve their ability to focus on relevant oral content and ignore distractions.

Materials Chart paper, marker

Procedure Tell the children they will be going on a walk (either inside the building or outside) to "collect" all the various sounds they can hear. Once on the walk, have the children stop every 25 to 50 steps (a good counting exercise, also) and stand completely still, listening for 20 seconds to the different sounds they hear in that space. Before going on, ask the children what sounds they heard, encouraging them to listen carefully for unique sounds they may have never noticed before in that area.

To simplify Practice "collecting sounds" while sitting in large group in the classroom by having the children be as silent as possible for approximately 20 seconds and then discussing the different sounds.

To extend On returning to the room, record with the children on chart paper (or have children record in their journals) all the sounds they can remember hearing from the beginning to the end of the walk.

✎ Listen! Can You Hear It? (For Younger or Less Experienced Children)*

Listening and Viewing Objective 2 For children to enhance their listening skills.

Materials Pitcher of water, four same-sized crystal glasses

Procedure Have children watch you place a different amount of water in four crystal glasses of the same size. Tell them that you are going to show them how the glasses make different sounds but that they must listen very carefully to the music each glass makes. Show them how to wet a finger and then, holding the bottom of each glass, trace the finger around the rim of the glass. Remind them to listen carefully for the different sound each glass makes.

To simplify Start with only two glasses, each with a vastly different amount of water. Gradually add more glasses.

To extend Have the children line up the glasses from the highest tone to the lowest tone; have the children line up the glasses from the lowest tone to the highest tone.

✎ Packing My Suitcase (For Older or More Experienced Children)

Listening and Viewing Objective 8 For children to demonstrate auditory memory by repeating in correct detail and sequence the messages they hear.

Materials None

Procedure Seat the children in a circle. The teacher (or a child who has played the game previously) begins the process by saying, "I'm going on a trip, and in my suitcase I am taking a bathing suit." The person to his or her right then says the same thing, adding an article (e.g., "I'm going on a trip, and in my suitcase I am taking a bathing suit and a towel"). The speaker must remember all the articles in the correct sequence or is "out" of the game and moves inside the circle. The game continues until one person remains.

To simplify Be sure to eliminate the competitive aspect of the game with very young children. If they cannot remember the articles in sequence, have the group help them. Go on only as long as the children seem to be enjoying the challenge of remembering the number of items and then move on to another activity. The game can also be made simpler by playing it with a smaller group of children so that they have less to remember.

To extend Have the children think of other categories. For example, they can go on a "trip" to a specific place and collect things found in that place. They may elect to go to a zoo and collect zoo animals, to a farm, to a country outside the United States, and so on. They may play the part of a community worker and think of different items that person needs to do his or her work (e.g., a police officer will need a police car, handcuffs, a gun, a walkie-talkie, and a badge).

✎ Viewing a Story Through Different Lenses (For Older or More Experienced Children)

Listening and Viewing Objective 7 For children to develop their understanding of contemporary media (e.g., television, videos, CDs, DVDs, and computer technology) and the impact of media on learning and values.

Materials Copy of *Charlie and the Chocolate Factory,* by Roald Dahl (Puffin Books); DVD or video of *Willy Wonka and the Chocolate Factory* (available from Films Incorporated, 440 Park Ave. S., New York, NY 10016; 1-800-323-4222, ext. 234); VCR or DVD player and monitor

Procedure Using Dahl's book (or any other for which a video is available), read the story to the children (or have them read it independently), providing time for discussion after each section to talk about the way characters are portrayed and the plot is developed. Following completion of the written story, have children view the story on video. Develop a Venn diagram with the children, looking at ways the book and video are similar and different. For example, are the characters depicted differently? Is the story line the same or different? Which did they enjoy most and why?

To simplify Choose a highly familiar text for emerging readers, such as *Goldilocks and the Three Bears,* so that children have a good sense of the characters and plot. Eliminate use of the Venn diagram in the activity.

To extend Have the children role-play a familiar story and create a video of it.

Speaking Activity

✎ Imitating Clapping Patterns (For Younger or Less Experienced Children)

Speaking Objective 1 For children to experiment with language sounds.

Materials None

*Source: Herr and Libby (2000).

Procedure Ask children to listen carefully while you clap a pattern (clap-pause-clap-clap-pause) and ask them to try to repeat it. Move on to more-complex and longer patterns as the children gain experience. Eventually have the children clap one another's patterns.

To simplify Begin with simple patterns.

To extend Move on to having them clapping the syllables in their names and other words.

Writing Activities

✎ Book Making (For Younger or Less Experienced Children)

Writing Objective 2 For children to put their thoughts on paper, first through simple pictures and then progressing through the developmental stages of writing.

Materials Various kinds and colors of paper, markers, scissors, glue

Procedure Having very young children create their own books is one of the best activities to encourage them to write. A variety of books can be made, including "peek-a-boo" books, pop-up books, shape books (cover is in the outline of a particular animal or other theme), and accordian books (paper is folded accordian style, with each section illustrating separate parts of the story), and flip books (cut into three sections, with head of person or animal on top section, torso on middle section, legs and feet on bottom section). Provide examples of differently constructed books. Explain the tools and techniques needed to construct them. Provide help as needed. Encourage children to draw different pictures on each page. Have them dictate their thoughts about the picture, and encourage them to write as much as they can under each illustration. Remember that a picture book with no words is still a book in which ideas and a story can be expressed.

To simplify Provide very young children with a blank book that has been constructed, having them complete the book as appropriate, given their fine-motor and literacy capabilities. Focus on only one type of construction at a time.

To extend Challenge the children to devise their own themes and shapes relevant to the content of the particular story they have written.

✎ Putting Humpty Together Again . . . and Again . . . and Again (For Children of All Ages)

Writing Objective 3 For children to use their own temporary versions of writing, working gradually toward conventional spelling, handwriting, punctuation, and format.

Materials Paper, pencils or markers

Procedure As an assessment and evaluation procedure, periodically have children illustrate and write the rhyme "Humpty Dumpty." Standardize the assessment by having the children spend only 15 minutes on the task. Have them use a date stamp to date their work sample, put their name on it, and place it in their portfolio for future comparisons. When the work samples are dated and saved, they become an excellent vehicle through which the children can compare their earlier and later versions. Such comparison will reveal to you and them how they are growing in their ability to represent detail through their drawing and in qualitative movement toward conventional spelling, handwriting, punctuation, and format.

To simplify At first, very young children may be able to only illustrate the rhyme and later add their first name. Later, they may use temporary spelling to reproduce some of the words. Do not point out children's errors at this time. Simply encourage them to do their best.

To extend Once children can write all of the rhyme and spell many of the words correctly, have them begin to compare their samples with the original rhyme and make the corrections needed. Have them add an original story about why Humpty Dumpty could not be put back together and how it might be done.

✎ Morning Message (For Children of All Ages)

Writing Objective 1 For children to observe others' purposeful writing, thus extending their awareness that writing transforms thoughts, ideas, and feelings into print symbols to communicate meaning.

Materials White board or easel paper, markers

Procedure Using a white board or easel paper, write one to three sentences dictated by the children. Then ask the children to read the sentences back. As children become more familiar with the process, put some "question word" reminders in the upper left-hand corner of the paper (e.g., *how, what, who, why, when,* and *where*). Select a child to dictate a story about a personal experience while you write, purposely making some errors for the children to catch (e.g., ignoring some punctuation or misspelling some words). After each sentence is written, have the children go back to the beginning to read what has been written so far. When the story is finished, work with the children to correct any errors they see in the text or to make changes in the text to clarify or extend some points.

To simplify Start with only one sentence. As children's writing skills increase, make errors that should be apparent to most of the children. As you correct the errors on the advice of the children, children at a less sophisticated level are picking up skills by watching what the other children are catching and you are correcting.

To extend   Take dictation (about three or four sentences) from the group and then go back through each line of the text, asking if there are any errors that should be circled. As children call them out, circle them and then ask the children to write the message in their journals, individually making their own corrections where they believe corrections are needed.

✎ What's the Question? (For Children of All Ages)

Writing Objective 15   For children to use the writing process to create original stories, poems, and informational pieces.

Materials   Journals, markers, pencils, easel, easel paper

Procedure   After reading or telling a story, stimulate the children to imagine what something looks like that cannot be seen, such as a leprechaun. Have them take out their journals and draw a picture of the thing on the left-hand page of the journal. Afterward, have younger children dictate a question they have (e.g., "How big is the leprechaun?" "Where does he live?"); older children can write a question they would like to ask. Tell the children to leave their journals open to that page, and sometime after they leave the classroom and before they return the next morning, an answer appears on the right-hand page of the journal. Although children know that the teacher is providing the answer, they love the fun of imagining that the answer has come from the leprechaun. Some teachers add to the fun by making small footprints across the page to accompany the answer.

To simplify   Children at the prewriting stage may act as a group to dictate some of their questions, which you write on the left-hand side of a piece of easel paper. That evening, the questions are answered on the right-hand side. The next day, in large group, ask the children to help you read each question and answer.

To extend   Challenge the children to illustrate and write to other imaginary or mythical characters (e.g., unicorn, fairy, or man in the moon) or real objects that are difficult to see (e.g., germs or a mouse that hides). When answering the question they have written, add a question they must answer in turn.

Reading Activities

✎ Puppet Drama (For Younger and Less Experienced Children)

Reading Objective 8   For children to tell or dramatize their versions of stories to show comprehension of what they have read.

Materials   Children's storybook *The Little Red Hen* (or another familiar story), stick puppets of characters in the story, supplies to make puppets

Procedure   Read the story to the children several times during a number of days, having brief discussions afterward to learn whether the children have a good sense of the characters and plot. Select a story narrator and supply other children with stick puppets of the characters. Have the remainder of the children act as the audience. Have the players reenact the story, encouraging those in the audience to listen carefully and applaud at the end. Switch roles so that all children have a chance to be either an actor or a participant in the audience.

To simplify   In large group, supply each child with a stick puppet. Have the appropriate child stand when you come to that character and put his or her puppet in the air and say the character's line.

To extend   Have the children make the puppets from materials you provide. Choose other familiar stories and have them play with puppets provided to them or created by them.

✎ What's in a Name? (For Older and More Experienced Children)

Reading Objective 13   For children to expand their phonological and print awareness.

Materials   Magnetic or movable letters, paper, pencils or markers

Procedure   Have children work in dyads. Supply magnetic or movable letters that are in each of their names. Challenge them to use the letters to make as many words as they can. Have them record the words as they find them and total the number at the end of the time provided for the activity.

To simplify   Provide the 26 individual letters of the alphabet and encourage children to form any words they can from these letters.

To extend   Have older children work in groups of three or four and write as many words as they can during a certain time period. Use as a math exercise as well by having them assign 1 point to two- or three-letter words, 2 points to four- or five-letter words, and 10 points to words of six or more letters. Have them write the words they are able to make and total the number of points they have earned at the end of the time period. Second and third graders enjoy the competition of comparing their group results with those of other groups. Remember that *individual* competition is not appropriate; nor is group competition appropriate for children in Grade 1 or kindergarten.

✎ It's a Fact! (For Older and More Experienced Children)

Reading Objective 15 For children to learn to read independently and construct meaning from both narrative text and expository text.

Materials Expository texts containing facts and information about famous persons, 3 × 5 in. cards, pencils

Procedure Have children choose a famous person they would like to learn more about. Making available a number of expository texts at an appropriate reading level, have them search the books to find at least 10 facts of interest about the person. Have them record only 1 fact on each card. Have children report what they found out about the person to the rest of the class.

To simplify Have children work with a partner to find 3 or more facts about a particular person.

To extend Have children convert their facts into a set of questions and answers. These can be used by the children to set up a Trivial Pursuit or Jeopardy game to challenge one another about the facts. Some children may enjoy making up and illustrating a board game using the facts they gathered.

✎ Secret Message (For Older or More Experienced Children)

Reading Objective 13 For children to expand their phonological and print awareness.

Materials White board or easel paper, marker

Procedure Using a "Wheel of Fortune" approach, print out dashes where the letters for words in a "secret message" would be (e.g.,_ _ _ _ _ _ _ _ _ _ _ _ _ _ _ _ _ _ _!). Have children guess a letter, and, if it appears in the message, write it in. If the letter appears more than once in the message, print it in all places as it is guessed. As letters are guessed, write them on the right side of the board so that children can see which have been guessed. This exercise is valuable because it is so engaging for children. They learn letter–sound associations and sight vocabulary as they see words produced from the letters (in this case, the message was "This is a secret message!").

To simplify Limit the number and complexity of the words. Put in the vowels and have children fill in only the consonants, which are easier for them.

To extend Extend the complexity of the message, using words that have letters less often seen (e.g., *X* and *Z*). Do not put the guessed letters on the side of the board so that memory must be relied on more.

SUMMARY

A child's first word is a joyous experience for any family, signaling a lifetime of communication with others. Additional markers in language development are the child's first indications of interest in and emerging facility with symbolic language.

Although innate drives help children to develop linguistic abilities, the environment plays a critical role in the quality of children's developing capabilities to use language effectively, imaginatively, and confidently. Adults are important players in this unfolding process. Their role is to model listening and viewing, speaking, reading, and writing skills and to help the child gain access to a balanced variety of well-designed experiences to enhance understanding and independent use of the language.

To be as effective as possible, early childhood educators must have expertise related to the emergence of language and literacy skills. Because of the many ongoing controversies surrounding the teaching of reading and writing skills, they must also have a well-researched theoretical perspective about the best practices for guiding children's progress and the capability of articulating it to others. They need to have practical knowledge about structuring optimal learning environments that promote communication capabilities, an ability to draw the child's attention toward print in a variety of ways, and skill in providing the scaffolded experiences that children need to move to new levels of understanding and language usage.

If we want children to be competent readers and writers, they must be involved in quality writing and reading activities daily. Their phonological and print awareness can be fostered and extended through well-designed, meaningful activities that support their individual acquisition of skills and concepts. All this can occur most easily in a developmentally appropriate program in which educators appreciate the complexity of factors affecting language and literacy development, in which language can be naturally integrated across other developmental domains, and in which children's unique interests, strengths, and needs are considered.

✋ Applying What You Read in This Chapter

1. Discuss

a. Adding the information gained in this chapter to your experience with young children, reexamine the five questions that open this chapter.

b. If you were interviewing for a position in a school district as a first-grade teacher and a search committee member asked you to talk about your philosophy for teaching young children to read and write, how would you respond?

c. Name one of the strategies in this chapter that you feel confident about and another that seems more difficult to implement. Discuss why the second would be more difficult and what it would take to remove the barrier(s).

2. Observe

a. Observe a classroom of children who are 3 years old or younger, listening for examples of oral language. Notice whether any children appear to have significantly less-advanced or more-advanced skills relative to vocabulary, syntax, and ability to elaborate. Discuss your findings with the classroom professional.

b. Observe the classroom of an experienced early childhood teacher. What evidence do you see that supports a print-rich environment or the need for enhancing this aspect of the learning environment? What strategies do you see that match or disagree with the philosophical underpinnings about emerging literacy presented in this chapter?

3. Carry out an activity

a. Look at three basal texts for a specific grade level. Is a common vocabulary used among the three? What approaches do the authors support for making the reading experience developmentally appropriate? How viable are these suggestions on the basis of your understanding of differences in young children at this age? Can you suggest two or three additional ideas that would enhance the use of a basal text for children in this age group?

b. Identify one issue presented in this chapter that you continue to be unsure about. Refer to the latest issues of several professional journals such as *Phi Delta Kappan, Educational Leadership, Young Children,* and *Reading Teacher* to determine whether you can learn more about resolving the issue. Write a one- or two-page position paper following your investigation.

4. Create something for your portfolio

a. Develop a language-based lesson plan based on the format provided in chapter 3.

5. Add to your journal

a. Think about your earliest experiences with reading and writing. Which books were your favorites? What can you remember about the process of learning to read? How much do you think your earliest experiences are related to your leisure-time literature choices as an adult?

b. Identify one goal you have for either extending your expertise relative to understanding children's emerging literacy or planning for more effective application of teaching strategies. What steps do you plan to take to reach this goal?

The Physical Domain

You may wonder:

Is sending young children outdoors to play sufficient to support their physical development?

How do children develop the fine-motor skills necessary for writing?

What kinds of motor skills are appropriate for children to learn?

What information do young children need so that they can practice safety measures and make healthy choices?

In this chapter on the physical domain, we present information to help you answer the preceding questions.

PHYSICAL ACTIVITY

Mrs. Runningdeer scanned the room, where small groups of 3- to 5-year-olds were engaging in gross-motor activities. Smiling, she watched two girls swinging Styrofoam mallets at soft foam balls suspended by strings from the dropped ceiling.

Carrie, who was not quite 3 years old, held her mallet up and twirled it around and around. Sometimes the ball went swinging as her mallet made contact with it from the front or the back. Her arm and wrist did not appear to move. Each hit appeared to be entirely accidental. She was grinning joyously.

Tabby, at age 4 1/2 years, was also focused on her ball as she swung the mallet from her right shoulder with her forearm partially extended, moving her right foot with a half rotation of her whole body. When she connected, the force was great, sending the ball swinging out fast in the full arc of the string. Sometimes Tabby did not move back fast enough, and the soft ball hit her. She struck the ball about once every three or four swings.

Mrs. Runningdeer recognized that Carrie was just exploring the mallet and hanging ball and that Tabby was further along in learning to strike the ball but was by no means at a mature skill level. Mrs. Runningdeer moved forward to encourage the play and to encourage Tabby to step into the strike using the other foot.

Mrs. Runningdeer is very knowledgeable about the motor behavior of these preschool-aged children. Having arranged the equipment in the environment, she is providing encouragement and instruction as children play, with an understanding of each child's competence and which steps come next as the child increases in skill.

Importance of Physical Activity

Children benefit in many ways from regular physical activity, some of which are listed next. Physical activity does the following (V. Seefeldt & Vogel, 1986):

❏ Promotes changes in brain structure and function in infants and young children. Sensory stimulation through physical activity is essential for the optimal growth and development of the young nervous system.

❏ Assists in the development and refinement of perceptual abilities involving vision, balance, and tactile sensations.

❏ Enhances the function of the central nervous system through the promotion of a healthier neuronal network.

❏ Fortifies the mineralization of the skeleton and promotes the maintenance of lean body tissue, while simultaneously reducing the deposition of fat.

❏ Leads to proficiency in the neuromuscular skills that are the basis for successful participation in games, dance, sports, and leisure activities.

❏ Improves aerobic fitness, muscle endurance, muscle power, and muscle strength.

❑ Enhances self-concept and self-esteem as indicated by increased confidence, assertiveness, emotional stability, independence, and self-control.

❑ Effectively deters mental illness and alleviates mental stress (pp. 1–2).

Children obtain these benefits when they are able to participate in a variety of motor activities and are motivated to engage in regular, vigorous play (Leppo, Davis, & Crim, 2000). In addition, because physical play is an integral part of children's social life, competence as a participant enables children to interact with others, solve problems as they arise during play, and develop concepts of fairness.

With time, children also establish lifestyle patterns of safety, fitness, and healthy daily life practices that many individuals will maintain throughout their lifetime. As children begin to do more for themselves and learn how to keep themselves safe and healthy, they may have fewer contagious illnesses, may have sounder teeth, and may avoid preventable injury. Meanwhile, adults remain substantially responsible for maintaining a safe and sanitary environment, providing adequate health services, and teaching young children what they can do for themselves.

Principles of Motor Development

The principles of motor development, maturation, and learning apply to all aspects of physical activity: gross-motor, perceptual-motor, and fine-motor skills. Physical skills develop from head to toe and from the center of the body outward. Thus, children will be able to move their upper arms and hands before they will be able to engage in complex dance steps. In addition, youngsters scoop a ball with their arms and body before being able to catch it with their hands. We generally recognize that *locomotor movements* (going from one place to another) require the use of the large muscles in the trunk, legs, and arms, whereas *manipulative movements* require the use of the many small muscles of the hands. Fine-motor development of the feet is also possible for children who participate in dance and soccer, for which such control is needed.

Growth also influences children's play because taller children usually run faster and are generally stronger than shorter children. Rates of growth and maturation (qualitative changes) vary among individuals and are genetically determined. Children learn the specifics of each motor skill once their bodies are sufficiently mature. Instruction and practice of a motor skill before a child is sufficiently mature to benefit from it is ineffective and does not ensure the performance of the movement (Gabbard, Le Blanc, & Lowy, 1994). Because mat-

uration and the prerequisite learning required for performance differ for different skills, children may be advanced in one skill and just beginning the developmental sequence for other skills.

Fundamental Motor Skills

After the 1st year of life, children learn to walk on their own, exploring their environment, manipulating objects, climbing on furniture, and moving around their near environments with curiosity and interest. Their initial movements are short, and they fall often. Gradually, these skills improve qualitatively in a predictable sequence so that walking is more automatic and more mechanically efficient. Some gross-motor skills such as walking and striking are *fundamental motor skills,* which form the basis for games or other more-complex movements. The early childhood period is the time when children become mature enough to acquire these movement competencies. Children may acquire the fundamental motor skills on their own or with adult guidance. Unfortunately, not all children experience optimal conditions. Some children in Head Start (41%) demonstrate delays in fundamental motor skills, whereas others (16%) exhibit substantial deficiencies (Woodard & Yun, 2001). Evidence suggests that if children do not acquire proficiency by age 6 or 7 years, they may never acquire it during the elementary years (Gallahue, 1993). In Figure 13.1, we provide a summary of selected gross-motor skills that most youngsters can achieve (Gallahue, 1995; Ignico, 1994; V. G. Payne & Isaacs, 2002).

Most of the locomotor and manipulative skills listed in Figure 13.1 have inherent sequences that begin as exploratory movements and gradually evolve into more-mature forms of movement. The throwing sequence is presented in more detail in Figure 13.2 to illustrate the predictable stages that children go through while achieving competence in this skill. Additional skills are described in Table 13.1. Remember that children move through these sequences at different rates and that ultimate performance at the end of the early childhood period is determined by maturation, learning, and practice during this time. Note that many of these functions progress from the following positions: *bilateral*—usually forward facing, both hands at body midline; *unilateral*—one-sided, shift of body; *ipsilateral*—the foot, arm, and body move from the same side, some rotation; and *contralateral*—across the body, the movement is diagonal, involving both sides of the body and body rotation with stepping.

Summary of Fundamental Motor Skill Stage Characteristics The number of stages that a particular skill appears to involve varies; throwing and catching have five distinct stages, and galloping and

FIGURE 13.1 Select Gross-Motor Skills Usually Learned Between 3 and 7 Years of Age

Locomotor Skills

Walk	Run	Leap	Jump	Hop	Creep	Roll
Stop	Start	Dodge	Slide	Start	Skip	Gallop
Climb						

Manipulative Skills (Projecting and Receiving Objects)

Throw	Kick	Punt	Strike	Volley	Bounce	Roll
Dribble	Catch	Trap	Hug			

Nonlocomotor Skills

Bend	Stretch	Twist	Turn	Swing	Curl	Swivel
Whirl	Spin	Rock	Bend	Hang	Pull	Push
Lift	Sway					

skipping, only three. There does not appear to be carryover from one fundamental motor skill to another except for skipping, which is a combination of running and hopping. Clearly, a child who cannot hop cannot skip. However, children who can strike a ball at Stage 3 may be able to throw it only at Stage 2. The same child may function at Stage 1 of the long jump at age 7 years if the opportunity to learn the skill has not occurred. Once the final stage of each fundamental skill is reached, children continue to eliminate extraneous movement and increase in power and strength, and they may incorporate elements of style exhibited by skilled players. *Coordination* (the use of more than one set of muscles) of body parts and sensory information generally increases as the skills of typically developing children increase. Many more gross-motor skills exist besides those defined as fundamental; children may develop these as a part of ballet, horseback riding, or hunting with a spear, boomerang, or bow and arrow.

A written description of the characteristics of several fundamental motor skills is provided in Table 13.1. With conscientious reading, you can identify fine distinctions between stages. Children appear to need time to explore and practice movements in each stage before moving forward to the next. The length of time between Stage 1 and Stage 2 varies considerably, with an interval between 6 months for running and 36 months for kicking. The level of detail allows classroom teachers to determine which actions to encourage. Adults can plan for scaffolding that will permit the children to advance if they appear to need this level of support. Often, more-skilled children provide such support for less-skilled youngsters during informal play.

Children also begin developmental sequences at different times, and the amount of time that they need to perform at mature levels also varies considerably. Climbing begins in infancy, after crawling; babies rock forward and backward until they move their body over their arms in an anticipatory stage of climbing. Beginning attempts are followed by clambering onto something, hanging on and lifting a leg over, and rolling to the top. Then the initial attempt at real climbing begins with the child's holding on and pulling one leg up to another. The regular patterns of ipsilateral movement (action of limbs on the same side of body) followed by a transition into contralateral movement (action of opposing limbs) emerge with practice until the approximately 4-year-old is competent. Unfortunately, the ability to go up precedes the ability to come down because the child depends on being able to see his or her arms and feet in order to move effectively (Readdick & Park, 1998).

Throwing begins at age 1 year for both boys and girls, and 60% of all boys demonstrate a mature technique by age 5 1/2 years. Girls do not show this level of performance until much later. Catching does not begin until around age 2 years, and both boys and girls show a mature form by about age 7 years. Nevertheless, substantial individual differences can be seen in children at any age.

Perceptual-Motor Skills

Children always use all their sensory capacities as they engage with the environment, explore, move, or handle objects. When professionals speak of perceptual-motor development, they are usually referring to movement activities that will lead to academic or cognitive outcomes (V. G. Payne & Isaacs, 2002). However, the distinctions between general physical activity and perceptual-motor skills are unclear. Typically developing children use their sensory skills in every movement except when they are playing games such as Blind Man's

FIGURE 13.2 Developmental Sequence for Throwing

Stage 1
Vertical (upward–backward)
 windup
Little or no weight transfer
No spinal rotation
"Chop" throw

Stage 2
Windup in horizontal or oblique
 plane
Straight-arm throw (sling) in
 horizontal or oblique plane
Block rotation with weight shift to
 opposite foot
Follow-through across body

Stage 3
High (upward–backward) windup
Forward stride with ipsilateral foot
Hip flexion, arm movement in
 vertical plane
Little trunk rotation
Follow-through across body

Stage 4
High (upward–backward) windup
Forward stride with contralateral
 foot
Trunk–hip flexion, arm movement
 forward, elbow extension
Limited trunk rotation
Follow-through across body

Stage 5
Low (downward–backward)
 windup
Body (hip–shoulder) rotation
Forward stride with contralateral
 foot
Sequential derotation for force
 production
Arm–leg follow-through

Source: Haubenstricker (1991).

Bluff. In addition, movement is a part of most social and communication events as gestures, approaches, and mutual activity. Therefore, in the following discussion, we focus on a few skills that appear to be distinctive and particularly useful for children to learn fully.

The perceptual process improves with practice, generally improving rapidly during the early childhood period. All modes of receiving sensation from the environment are involved: sight, audition, scent, taste, and touch. Frequently, multiple modes of sensation come

TABLE 13.1 Summary of Fundamental Motor Skill Characteristics by Stage

Fundamental Motor Skill	Stage 1	Stage 2	Stage 3	Stage 4	Stage 5
Throw	Vertical windup "Chop" throw Feet stationary No spinal rotation	Horizontal windup "Sling throw" Block rotation Follow-through across body	High windup Ipsilateral step Little spinal rotation Follow-through across body	High windup Contralateral step Little spinal rotation Follow-through across body	Downward arc windup Contralateral step Segmented body rotation Arm–leg follow-through
Catch	Delayed arm action Arms straight in front until ball contact, then scooping action to chest Feet stationary	Arms encircle ball as it approaches Ball is "hugged" to chest Feet stationary or may take one step	"To chest" catch Arms "scoop" under ball to trap it to chest Single step may be used to approach ball	Catch with hands only Feet stationary or limited to one step	Catch with hands only Whole body moves through space
Kick	Little or no leg windup Stationary position Foot "pushes" ball Step backward after kick (usually)	Leg windup to the rear Stationary position Opposition of arms and legs	Moving approach Foot travels in a low arc Arm–leg opposition Forward or sideward step on follow-through	Rapid approach Backward trunk lean during windup Leap before kick Hop after kick	
Punt	No leg windup Ball toss erratic Body stationary Push ball and step back	Leg windup to the rear Ball toss still erratic Body stationary Forceful kick attempt	Preparatory step(s) Some arm–leg yoking Ball toss or drop	Rapid approach Controlled drop Leap before ball contact Hop after ball contact	
Strike	"Chop" strike Feet stationary	Horizontal push or swing Block rotation Feet stationary or stepping	Ipsilateral step Diagonal downward swing	Contralateral step Segmented body rotation Wrist rollover on follow-through	
Long jump	Arms act as "brakes" Large vertical component Legs not extended	Arms act as "wings" Vertical component still great Legs near full extension	Arms move forward, elbows in front of trunk at takeoff Hands to head height Takeoff angle still greater than 45 degrees Legs often fully extended	Complete arm and leg extension at takeoff Takeoff near 45-degree angle Thighs parallel to surface when feet contact for landing	
Run	Arms—high guard Flat-footed contact Short stride Wide stride, shoulder width	Arms—middle guard Vertical component still great Legs near full extension	Arms—low guard Arm opposition—elbows nearly extended Heel-toe contact	Heel–toe contact (toe–heel when sprinting) Arm–leg opposition High heel recovery Elbow flexion	
Hop	Nonsupport foot in front with thigh parallel to floor Body erect Hands shoulder height	Nonsupport knee flexed with knee in front and foot behind support leg Slight body lean forward Bilateral arm action	Nonsupport thigh vertical with foot behind support leg—knee flexed More body lean forward Bilateral arm action	Pendular action on nonsupport leg Forward body lean Arm opposition with leg swing	
Gallop	Resembles rhythmically uneven run Trail leg crosses in front of lead leg during airborne phase, remains in front at contact	Slow–moderate tempo, choppy rhythm Trail leg stiff Hips often oriented sideways Vertical component exaggerated	Smooth, rhythmical pattern, moderate tempo Feet remain close to ground Hips oriented forward		
Skip	Broken skip pattern or irregular rhythm Slow, deliberate movement Ineffective arm action	Rhythmical skip pattern Arms provide body lift Excessive vertical component	Arm action reduced, hands below shoulders Easy, rhythmical movement Support foot near surface on hop		

Source: Haubenstricker (1990).

from one source at the same instant, which requires *sensory integration*. For example, if a dog approaches a child, the child is likely to see (color, size, conformation, and demeanor), hear (footsteps, panting, or barking), and possibly smell (breath or fur) the dog. These sensations are transmitted to the brain through the nervous system. The brain uses the current information, organizes it, and integrates it into previously learned concepts such as *animals, brown things,* or *things that move with four feet*. After a decision is made about a course of action, the brain transmits signals through the nervous system to initiate the desired movement. Finally, the movement is performed. A very young child may decide to run to an adult from fear, approach the dog cautiously, or even approach joyfully, depending on the decision he or she makes. Last, relevant information is stored in the child's memory that will ultimately affect similar future experiences.

The perceptual process is rapid, continuous, and ongoing. The same set of events might constitute vastly dissimilar experiences for children. For example, if two children observe a large, inflated ball in the yard, one child might classify the ball as something to kick, whereas the other might perceive it as something to roll. Adults supervising the children will become aware of these differing understandings as youngsters disagree about how the play should proceed. Both children will enhance their concepts and skills as they learn to play successfully, using either or both responses. To the extent that perception of the environment is a steady component of living, all movement uses this capacity. Five aspects of perceptual-motor development are of particular importance: balance, spatial awareness, figure–ground perception, temporal awareness, and body and directional awareness.

Balance   *Static balance* is the ability to maintain a posture while holding still. Standing on one foot, leaning forward with one foot in front of the other, and teetering on the edge of a stair with the toes only on the tread are examples of static balance. *Dynamic balance* is the ability to remain in a desired posture while moving. Walking on a balance beam, hopping on one foot, running, and turning rapidly are all examples of dynamic balance. Balance is a component of most movements but is particularly important for complex movements in games or dance. Visual information is helpful in maintaining dynamic balance. Because children's center of gravity changes as they grow, youngsters require ongoing practice to adjust for changes in height and weight.

Spatial Awareness   Four-year-old Jeanne asked, "Why is my house little here and big when I get home?" as she looked out of the second-story window of the

school. She had not yet learned that objects appear smaller when they are farther away. Young children understand their surroundings in relation to themselves. With more maturity and experience, they can describe locations by using landmarks. In addition, an understanding of distance appears to increase with age. Inquiries such as "Are we there yet?" are typical of younger children at the beginning of a trip and occur later and less frequently with older youngsters, regardless of whether the children have made the journey before and regardless of the mode of travel: foot, bicycle, automobile, or airplane. Children also confuse distance with the time required to reach a destination. Thus, a six-block walk is longer than a 2-mile drive!

In practical terms, youngsters may bump into each other during play because they misjudge the distance between themselves and another. Beginning writers often run out of space on a piece of paper because they misjudge the amount of space they will need for all the letters. Most children in early childhood find getting a needed item easier than telling someone else where to find it in another room or a crowded cupboard. Experienced teachers learn that children are likely to be more appropriately separated for a dance experience if they stand with arms and legs outstretched and cannot touch another person than if the teacher simply asks the children to disperse so that they will have enough room to move. The space in the former strategy is defined by the child's body; in the latter, their strategy depends on a more abstract concept of their own and others' space.

Figure–Ground Perception   Determining what is in the foreground and in the background usually involves auditory or visual perception skills. The task in the visual modality is to find a specific object within a group. Three- to five-year-olds have difficulty selecting toys from crowded cupboards. They will choose to play with a toy on the table or a toy that someone else is using. They will also find locating a particular letter within a word challenging.

Equally difficult is hearing the voice of a particular instrument in the background of an orchestra. Similar challenges occur in perceiving a particular consonant within a word. Such skills develop with time, so that primary-age children can "find" animals in drawings in which the lines form other, more-obvious shapes. Early school-age children can also more readily discern directions spoken in an open classroom in which several muted conversations are occurring than preschool children can.

Temporal Awareness   Time relationships are not fully developed until late in the early childhood period or even into adolescence. However, the beginnings of the notions of speed and timing do begin to emerge. Rhythm is one aspect of organized time that most young children enjoy. Toddlers between the ages of 12 and 18 months will bob, bounce, or bend in time to music as an expression of their involvement. With guided practice, 2- to 5-year-olds may clap complex patterns and engage in increasingly challenging rhythmic activity. A steady beat is more felt than heard (Weikart, 1998). Moving to a steady beat helps the child develop inner control and coordinated competence and requires focused attention. When young children are engaged in dance experiences, they learn to explore time, space, and energy as they learn to express themselves and move their bodies (Koff, 2000).

Because young children's spatial awareness is not fully developed, and their senses of time and cause and effect are still immature (J. L. Frost & Sweeney, 1995), estimating the speed of an object is extremely difficult for 3- to 5-year-olds. You might observe that these youngsters close their arms after the ball has passed them. Many accidents occur on playgrounds because these children do not accurately judge the speed of objects and other people. Children do improve with practice, but an approximate estimation of an object's trajectory and speed emerges only during the primary years; some 8-year-olds even become adept at catching balls thrown at different speeds (V. G. Payne & Isaacs, 2002).

Children who learn to assess their speed as slower or faster than their previous performance experience pride and pleasure in their accomplishments. However, premature competition is generally discouraging to all but the one child who is recognized as the winner. During the preschool years, the feeling of moving rapidly through space is exciting on its own. As children move into primary grades, noncompetitive running games are most appropriate because children are developing their competence in efficient running (Sanders, 2002).

Body and Directional Awareness *Body awareness* is a part of the social-conventional knowledge about the names and functions of the various body parts. For most children, naming external body parts is primarily complete during the preschool years. Finger plays such as "Head, Shoulders, Knees, and Toes" or "Where Is Thumbkin?" can help familiarize children with the vocabulary. This vocabulary is most helpful to children when teachers give them suggestions such as "Billy, bend your knees when you land" while they are engaged in motor activity.

Directional awareness is a combination of the understanding of concepts such as *up and down* and *front and back* and the application of this information during a physical activity. Ideas such as *left and right* are related to a specific speaker and are much more difficult to understand than other concepts of direction or spatial relationships. For example, if two children are facing each

other at a table and an adult asks them to point up, the children would be pointing in the same direction, yet if the direction were to point to the left, they would point in opposite directions. Most children master this idea by the end of the early childhood years.

Children younger than 8 years may not have the directional awareness and spatial awareness necessary to perceive and reproduce print accurately. They may confuse *3*, *m*, *w*, and *E* and other combinations of handwritten letters because the main difference in this script is the direction of the lines. Reversals and inversions are common during the primary years, although with practice and support, children develop the necessary discrimination.

Practice in perceptual-motor learning continues throughout everyday life. Informed adults can support this informal learning through instruction and the provision of materials and equipment. Skilled coordination between perceptual information and muscle groups requires learning the movements until sequences are almost habitual. For example, movements of the feet to dance music, or movements of the hand during drawing or writing, require much practice and are linked to perceptual information.

Fine-Motor Skills

Using the hands to move objects precisely and accurately is the task most people refer to as *fine-motor skill*. As with gross-motor skills, maturity, instruction, and practice are necessary for optimal development. Coordination of sensory information with the motoric action is also necessary. Children's control of the head, trunk, shoulders, and arms is well established before their hands and fingers attain more than rudimentary skill.

Throughout the preschool period, children become fatigued easily, often feeling frustrated at their inability to accomplish tasks. Adult support and encouragement without pressure to perform to an external standard is helpful. An environment in which the opportunities to use fine-motor skills abound allows practice. Adults should provide information and demonstration informally as the need arises.

Six- to eight-year-olds can generally perform most manipulative tasks independently. They can make simple crafts, such as those involving straight sewing, cutting objects reasonably skillfully with scissors, and stringing fine beads into simple patterns. These children move to greater control, precision, and accuracy while refining earlier accomplishments. Girls tend to be more skillful at fine-motor tasks earlier than boys, who appear to excel earlier at tasks requiring strength or power (Berk, 2002b). Many boys find penmanship challenging but may draw objects of interest in greater detail.

TABLE 13.2 Sample Play Materials That Support Fine-Motor Control

Inexperienced and Younger Children	Three- to Five-Year-Olds	Six- to Eight-Year-Olds and More Experienced Children
Graduated, multicolored plastic doughnuts to put on a tapered post	Graduated, multicolored disks to put on a straight post	Graduated disks of one color to put on a straight post
Wooden puzzles with fewer than 10 pieces, if they have color and shape cues and clear segments such as the head of a horse	Puzzles with as many as 50 pieces, if they have many color and shape cues and a clear picture	Puzzles with more than 50 pieces and fewer built-in cues
Large beads to string on knotted plastic tubing (such as that used in fish tanks)	Medium to large beads to put on a string with a coated end	Small to tiny beads to string on a slender cord or thread (if jewelry beads are used, a blunt needle may be needed for stringing)
Various types of kitchen tongs to be used to move Ping-Pong balls, 1-in. balls, or small cubes from one container to another	Various types of kitchen tongs or tweezers to be used to move various materials of increasingly smaller size (such as beads or cotton balls) from one container to another	Tweezers or chopsticks to be used to move smaller items (such as rice grains) from one container into a smaller container (such as a 35-mm film canister)

Fine-motor skills can be fostered in settings in which the tools, children's experiences, and cultural expectations are supportive (Bredekamp & Copple, 1997). In Table 13.2, some sample play materials are suggested that typically support fine-motor skills while also supporting other aspects of cognitive development. Cultural expectations in the home also affect the quality of drawing and writing observed in preschool settings (Huntsinger, Schoeneman, & Ching, 1994).

Children who have the maturity to perform the tasks illustrated in Table 13.3 but not the experience using the tools or engaging in the activities will begin their skills as much younger children do. For example, 4-year-old Emily had never been given writing implements of any kind at home. When she entered the children's program, she first used a fist grasp on crayons and pencils, learning quickly and with practice to use a more mature grasp. At age 3 1/2 years, Vivian had always been fed by her parents to avoid a mess. Her use of a spoon and a cup in a child care program was immature for her age, but, in a climate of encouragement and support, she progressed rapidly. Healthy children do seem to catch up when their earlier experiences have not been conducive to the acquisition of skill. However, such situations require time, patience, support, and instruction. Adult expectations must be adjusted accordingly. Youngsters whose skills are first attempted between 2 and 3 years of age and are brought to greater control and accuracy by age 7 years are more likely to be more physically advanced than children who do not begin this process until age 4 or 5 years.

Handwriting as a Fine-Motor Skill. Children learn about the written language much as they learn oral language: They first observe it and then imitate it. Beginning attempts are so rudimentary that adults may fail to recognize that the child is beginning the process of handwriting. In environments in which children see adults write grocery lists, letters, holiday greetings, or notes to family members, toddlers will attempt to participate in the activity as soon as they obtain access to a writing implement.

Gwen, about 18 months old, played near her mother's chair as her mother graded papers. When her mother left the room for a few minutes, Gwen climbed on the chair, picked up a red pen, and marked every page of a stack of papers with a large mark. With mother's return, she smiled, pleased with herself for having completed this task so promptly!

The concept that meaningful messages may be written is discussed in chapter 12. However, handwriting involves a progression of fine-motor skills that entails maturation, learning, and practice.

Using Writing and Drawing Implements Children use tools to write. At first, fingers are useful for drawing and writing in finger paint and sand, and these techniques remain the easiest method of leaving a mark on something. However, even very young toddlers use a variety of tools to write or make graphic designs. Paintbrushes vary in diameter and length. Crayons vary in diameter and are available with and without paper wrapping. Pencils vary in hardness, diameter, and

TABLE 13.3 Expected Timing and Sequence of Fine-Motor Skills for Children in Supportive Environments

Age (yr)	General	Targeting	Cut and Paste	Self-Help	Graphic Tools
2–3	Fatigues easily Undresses Carries small objects easily Precisely picks up small objects Uses doorknob	Places one-piece knob puzzles accurately Puts shapes in appropriate holes Strings large beads on plastic tubing	Tears paper May put large globs of paste on top of the piece to be pasted instead of between the pieces of paper Snips with scissors Holds paper and scissors incorrectly Likely uses both hands with scissors	Eats with a spoon Drinks from a cup Undresses if fasteners are simple	Scribbles with pleasure Copies a cross or a circle May attempt simple capital letters such as *H*, *V*, and *T* May hold implement in fist
3–4	Opens doors, manages most latches Builds block towers Uses keyboard for simple programs Pounds, rolls, squeezes clay Turns pages of a book one at a time	Inserts large pegs into pegboards Strings large beads with a string Puts together simple puzzles with objects representing an object or a clear segment of an object (e.g., tail of a dog)	Uses large globs of paste Pours on lots of glue Uses index finger or paste brush to spread Cuts full length of scissors, may do two lengths Has little directional control May not use correct grasp of scissors	Pours liquid from a pitcher into a container with increasing accuracy and control Handles Velcro fasteners easily Puts on outdoor clothing but usually needs help zipping or buttoning Eats most foods independently	Tries three-point grasp of writing implement Is inconsistent and may grasp implement far from the point Uses circles, crosses, and horizontal and vertical lines in drawings May outline a scribbled shape of a rectangle
4–5	Builds complex structures with various construction materials May have problems with spatial judgments and directionality Practices to attain mastery of fine-motor tasks With practice may become very adept at computer programs or video games	Uses pattern cards skillfully in placing small pegs in pegboards Laces Sews May master multipiece puzzles if they have color and shape cues Threads large needle with help Threads small beads on a string	Holds scissors and paper correctly Cuts straight lines and turns corners Places appropriate amounts of glue or paste in correct spot and spreads with control	Dresses and undresses, buttons and unbuttons, zips haltingly Needs help starting coat zipper Uses a hanger if reachable Usually has complete toileting independence Eats with a fork Spills infrequently Washes and dries hands	Uses tripod grip on writing implement, although position may still be high Draws sun and tadpole people and scribbles Paints with deliberateness Writes letters anyplace on the paper May write name or initials or portions of their names on their drawings
5–6	Sculptures with dough, able to do a pinch or coil pot Shows increased precision and control	Inserts increasingly small objects with ease Manages a 12- to 15-piece puzzle without dependence on color	Usually can cut on a curve, cut out interior shapes, geometric shapes, or magazine pictures Uses scissors easily and accurately	Organizes and takes care of own materials Combs and brushes hair, washes face and hands without getting wet	Exhibits good control of pencil or marker Makes letters, both upper- and lowercase, crudely but recognizable

Age (yr)	General	Targeting	Cut and Paste	Self-Help	Graphic Tools
	Has few if any false starts Pounds nails with accuracy Uses keyboard with increasing skill		Uses glue and paste skillfully	Manages own clothing fasteners and ties shoelaces Spreads with a knife and can do simple cutting with a table knife	Makes inversions and reversals often Writes letters of name but not necessarily on a line or correctly spaced Draws cars, boats, houses, trees, and flowers with increasing detail Writes numerals
6–8	Has good basic skills Shows improvement in precision and accuracy Makes simple crafts, depending on interest	Does multipiece puzzles Uses shape and size to place pieces Places small objects more precisely	Shows good control and improvement in precision	Demonstrates mastery	Ninety-seven percent of children make acceptable letters Spacing and placement of letters on page acceptable Word, letter, and numeral reversals common, often self-corrected Drawings made with many media, increasing details

Source: Adapted from K. E. Allen and Marotz (2003); Bredekamp and Copple (1997); M. Cohen and Gross (1979); Ignico (1994); and O. McAfee and Leong (2002).

shape (round to many sided). Pens vary in texture and materials, in the point size, and in diameter. Markers vary in diameter and in point shape. All tools are available in many colors.

The least mature, least experienced child will more likely maintain interest in and explore the use of writing implements such as markers, nylon-tipped pens, or #2 pencils. These implements create clear, colorful marks with little effort by the child and respond to the slightest movement. Children enjoy causing something to happen, and early success is encouraging. With older, more experienced writers, pencils offer greater control. The general guideline suggested by experienced teachers is to move from larger to smaller diameter as the child matures and from implements that more easily make a mark to those that require more control. However, apparently, preschool-age children are as competent at managing a standard-sized pencil as they are at using a large pencil (Carlson & Cunningham, 1990).

Holding the Writing Implement The mature finger tripod associated with adult writing is usually present in children by age 7 years. In addition, writing posture improves with age, although visible tension increases with age as well. In the earliest phases of writing, the muscles of the head, neck, trunk, and shoulder are primarily engaged. Later, the muscles of the elbow, wrist, and fingers are brought into use as the child attains greater control. The progression from the earliest pattern to more-mature patterns is as follows (V. G. Payne & Isaacs, 2002):

❏ All four fingers and the thumb are wrapped around the implement, with the thumb up (away from the point).
❏ The palm is engaged with a full-hand grasp, with the thumb toward the point of the implement. The implement is often grasped well away from the point. The arm and shoulder control the movement, which is usually large.

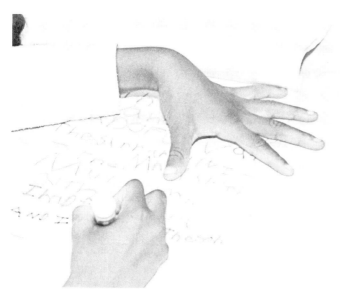

Early attempts at writing involve using large-muscle groups and result in the formation of large, skewed letters.

❏ The hand moves closer to the point of the implement. Control of the movement of the pencil shifts from shoulder to elbow to fingers as the grasp moves toward the tip.

❏ Tripod positioning of the fingers with noticeable wrist movement and minimal finger control is often combined with the fingers bent and the fingertips on the implement. (Children using this grip can tire easily, and their fingers may cramp.)

❏ The mature tripod, with the implement resting on the middle finger, allows rapid finger control of movements and is seen at about age 7 years for most children.

❏ Refinement of the dynamic tripod occurs between age 6 years and age 14 years, with the writing implement resting on the side of the middle finger and infrequent use of the fingertips to hold the implement.

The age at which children achieve a mature tripod grip varies widely; some youngsters achieve this milestone as early as age 3 years (48%) and 90% achieve it by age 6 years (V. G. Payne & Isaacs, 2002). The remainder may not achieve it until middle childhood. Parental expectations and opportunities for children to practice writing at home may account for such differences (Huntsinger et al., 1994).

Children need extensive practice with their hands before beginning to print letters, and they require opportunities to practice letter formation to develop the necessary motor skills. They learn to print from everyday experiences: observing adults print, observing letters and words in the environment, and "writing notes" of

one type or another during pretend play. One group of 3- and 4-year-olds were provided a writing table, unlined paper, and each of their names printed on a note card; the children were *invited* to "sign in" as they entered their preschool classroom. Their teacher observed carefully and made notes of their progress as they moved from controlled scribbles to scribbles and mock letters, to one or two letters of their names, to their first name with the letters placed randomly, to writing their first name. At the end of 7 months, none of the children wrote with only controlled scribbles, but their writing skills ranged across the various achievement levels (Green, 1998). The teacher's strategies were exploratory, with demonstration and paraphrased reflections used as each child progressed.

Handwriting is one example of a fine-motor skill that has been closely examined. Other skills such as keyboarding, piano playing, sewing, and paper folding have not been sufficiently researched to merit a similar discussion. In summary, these general principles might still be applied:

❏ The proximal–distal principle—in which the shoulder, arm, wrist, and then finger muscles are used in succession as children move on to greater control—is applicable in most instances.

❏ Maturation, learning, and practice are all significant factors in a child's ultimate success; maturation alone does not lead to skillful performance.

❏ Children acquire knowledge and skill gradually and are heavily influenced by the presence of models in the environment.

❏ Mature performance is the result of years of practice.

❏ Growth, or the increase of the size of the hands, may contribute to children's learning some skills, such as keyboarding and piano playing, because of the reach that is required to use the correct form.

❏ Children progress through the same developmental sequences, although considerable variation in rates can be seen.

Movement Concepts

Children use all the fundamental motor skills and perceptual-motor competencies together to produce movements of different qualities such as when variations of time, space, effort, or flow are explored. As children build their ideas and meanings, they must also learn the vocabulary of movement. Music may also support children's understanding of qualitative distinctions of movement. The teacher should select combinations of these movement ideas and incorporate them into an activity. An obstacle course in which children move through, around, under, and on top of objects at a slow pace until they reach a rug where they stop to rest is an example of a gross-motor array of movements. Similar combinations may be made by moving smaller items with the hands. For example, Mr. Towl asked a few kindergarten children to draw diagonal lines on tissue paper that they would later use to wrap around a shoe box to cover the inside and the outside of the box. Clearly, movement concepts apply to fine- and gross-motor skills and require the use of perceptual-motor skills as well.

Physical Activity of Children Who Have Special Needs

For many children who experience challenges in language and learning, physical play is an opportunity for more typical participation. Youngsters who have a disability may require more repetition to achieve success and often show delayed achievement in the fundamental motor skills (Doty, McEwen, Parker, & Laskin, 1999). However, for many children, vigorous play is one arena in which they may participate successfully with their peers (Figure 13.3).

Safety may require particular attention when children do not hear or see well. The arrangement of equipment, the structuring of activities, and the cooperation of other children usually suffice to enable most children to participate in large- and small-muscle activities.

Usually modifications in instruction are successful, such as gaining attention in the sensory modality that the child uses more typically to accommodate particular limitations. Clearly, children who do not see cannot develop visual discrimination tasks. However, touching a youngster with a hearing impairment and then demonstrating a skill, followed by pointing to the child is usually sufficient to give such a child instructions. The

FIGURE 13.3 Physical Activity of Children with Special Needs

Bettina

Bettina smiled as she ran into the playground. Her large hearing aid bumped on her chest as she moved, although she did not pay any attention to it. With some other children, she climbed the ladder and went down the slide, watching what the others did before trying it. Playing in the sand, she alternated between watching others and digging, filling a container, and tipping it over. Dusting off the sand that seemed to cling to her, she approached another pair of girls who were kicking a ball, watching first then joining the play. Ms. Goldbeck blew her whistle, which Bettina did not appear to hear, and walked toward her, moving in front of her, saying, "It is time to go inside."

---

physical domain is unique is that language may be optional in teaching.

Children with serious visual impairments are usually hesitant initially. In particular, balance seems to rely heavily on visual information. Continuous physical contact, oral encouragement, and spoken direction may provide sufficient security for the child to try new motor tasks.

Some children have impairments in the physical domain. A report from the physical or occupational therapist is useful for identifying the child's strengths and should be used as a guide by the general practitioner. If a child does not walk independently, walkers, wagons, or wheelchairs may enable the child to move and even engage in some games as wheelchair control improves. Public schools now provide consultants to classroom teachers to assist them in adapting programs and activities for children with special needs. Special interventions are necessary but not sufficient alone.

Heidi, a 7-year-old with leg braces, had sessions with the physical therapist once a week. She also went outdoors with the other children, one of whom was assigned to push open a heavy door. She could swing by herself and play catch with classmates, although her position was closer to a fence so that the balls that she did not catch did not roll too far. Her upper-body strength was excellent, which enabled her to hang from the horizontal ladder with ease. With encouragement and support during her primary years, she learned how to adapt many activities as she gained confidence and skill.

Most experienced teachers adapt their strategies to each child with special needs and build on what is easiest, safest, and most comfortable, with consideration for the child's particular disabling condition. Such teachers build on what each child can do, treating the children with respect and expecting them to try what is possible. Specialists design equipment and educational experiences involving problematic skills. For example, some very young children with hands that are impaired use computers as a means of communication by hitting keys with a stylus attached to the forehead. Increasingly, technology is enabling everyone to develop optimally.

Before children with disabilities reach the age of 5 years, adults should promote the development of basic skills before they incorporate technological resources. Tommy, who was motorically involved as a result of cerebral palsy, could not roll over, sit up, or support his head when he entered the classroom for 3-year-olds. He had attained control of two fingers, his eyes, and some facial muscles early in life, and he sat in a tilted support chair. When other children playing nearby had materials, they placed objects in his hand. He was initially frightened outdoors because of lack of experience, but eventually he enjoyed lying in the grass and rolling on the hill with support. His 3-year-old peers pulled him in a wagon from time to time and sometimes placed a ball on the ground for him to roll to another child. He could drop a die, and a child helper would move his piece on a board game, which he watched carefully. Using support equipment to hold him upright, he could finger paint and engage in a variety of sensory experiences. During his time with more typically developing peers in this preschool program, his strength improved and his hand control increased. He also learned to talk, although his speech continued to be difficult, slow, and infrequent. Therefore, even though some children have severe limitations, all children in the group may have a measure of success.

HEALTH, SAFETY, AND NUTRITION

Children require safe and healthy environments in which to learn and play, both indoors and outdoors. Likewise, well-balanced meals are essential to growth. Equipment and facilities should be hazard free. Children require medical monitoring to ensure health and well-being. Obesity in early childhood is being recognized as a serious public health concern (C. Garcia, Garcia, Floyd, & Lawson, 2002). These considerations are the responsibilities of parents, teachers, administrators, and the community. Unfortunately, people in the general community are not knowledgeable about the health risks for children. Forty-eight percent are unable to identify a single health issue (Blendon, Young, McCormick, Kropf, & Blair, 1998). Although policy makers, parents, and teachers have responsibilities for safeguarding children, children may take some responsibility for their own well-being. During the early years of development, they can learn to make safe and healthy choices and develop lifestyle attitudes that predispose them to maintaining healthy practices throughout their lifetime.

Fitness

Physical fitness is a value more admired than pursued for young children. A reasonable aspiration would be that children enjoy physical activity and see it as an ordinary, permanent part of their lives. Physical fitness and physical activity in childhood are protective health-related phenomena, and young children who are fit continue to maintain their fitness in adolescence (Janz, Dawson, & Mahoney, 2000). Endurance, speed, agility, coordination, reaction time, strength, flexibility, and balance are part of being fit (Leppo et al., 2000). Children increase in strength slowly between age 3 years and age 5 years, with few differences observed between boys and girls. Gains in speed are rapid, as might be expected

with the growth of their legs. Likewise, performance of tasks requiring agility, the long jump, and catching improves notably during the preschool years. Boys tend to excel at tasks that require power and speed, whereas girls usually excel at tasks that require balance, such as hopping. From 5 years of age onward, boys tend to excel in most of the fitness areas, although the variability within each age group of children is generally greater than the difference between boys and girls.

Adults can design successful activities that engage young children in physical fitness endeavors (C. Garcia et al., 2002). For example, one group of 4-year-olds enjoyed a carefully structured 9-minute walk–run to improve their cardiovascular fitness. Adults "ran" along with the children as they moved from one corner of the gym to the next, tapping helium-filled balloons as they passed the corners. All the children finished and appeared to enjoy themselves.

Children are generally active in preschool, but their level of activity decreases when they attend elementary school and engage in more sedentary activities in programs that plan for a balance of vigorous activity and quiet activity. Preschool-aged children tire easily, but they recover rapidly. Primary-aged children have better endurance, although they, too, benefit from opportunities to shift from vigorous activity to quieter pursuits. Often an option of a quiet activity in which they may come and go within a period of vigorous play provides them with sufficient rest (Werner, 1994). During outdoor play at most learning centers, which are usually designed to support fitness or skill development, a center for sand play (which requires minimal exertion) is suitable.

Youngsters do not necessarily have sufficient physical activity in their lives in preschool, in the primary grades, and at home (C. Garcia et al., 2002). A minimum of 30 minutes of moderate physical activity almost every day is recommended; however, 60 minutes of *accumulated* activity is an optimal standard for the early childhood period (Ignico, 1998). The accumulation includes moving up and down stairs, walking to and from school, engaging in vigorous play at home, and participating in any other active pursuit in which youngsters may engage in programs or at home. Even elementary schools that have physical education as a planned component for every grade frequently do not have it often enough to meet this physical fitness standard. Thus, educators in after-school programs and classroom teachers must plan to regularly contribute some time to fitness.

Children who are physically active maintain an appropriate weight more easily than do more-sedentary youngsters. Unfortunately, as mentioned, increasing numbers of children do not have much opportunity to play outside at home, nor are they accumulating the necessary exercise in early childhood programs (C. Garcia et al., 2002). Children in the United States are not as fit as their European counterparts (Zaichkowsky & Larson, 1995). Some children gain weight as they move from a more-active preschool level to the more-sedentary school age. Being overweight may interfere with the development of additional motor skills and with vigorous play. Any program designed to manage weight must also have an activity component for long-term success. However, just as an individual can be overweight and otherwise physically healthy and fit, an individual can be unfit at a normal weight. Therefore, professionals are responsible for encouraging all children to enhance their motor skills and to become or remain proficient in active physical pursuits.

Regular outdoor play is often a component of programs to promote physical activity and fitness. Free play is an effective part of the physical fitness program, but it alone is insufficient to ensure fitness. Demonstrations can provide appropriate modeling, and guided practice is necessary to ensure that all the children participate in the vigorous activity necessary for health. Some children as young as age 3 years have developed the patterns of sedentary behaviors, even outdoors. Many kinds of play occur outdoors, not only active play.

Safety During Physical Activity When playgrounds are provided with age-appropriate equipment and are properly supervised by knowledgeable adults, children are likely to be safe in their active play. However, the climate and daily weather may require specific considerations for safety during outdoor active play. For instance, 3- to 5-year-olds are vulnerable to heat-related illness (Taras, 1992). Heat appears to have a greater impact on their smaller bodies, and children in this age group do not perspire as effectively as adults do. In addition, some youngsters appear to lack the instinct to drink and replenish their fluids when they play hard. When children engage in vigorous physical activity during high outdoor temperatures, adults should ensure rest periods and adequate fluid intake. The use of hats, lightweight clothing, and light-colored clothing should also be encouraged to diminish the possibility of heat stress.

Extreme cold—with the potential of frostbite—should be avoided, even though the children may be engaging in vigorous activity. Otherwise, children should spend some time outdoors every day, even in winter. Cold weather does not cause colds and flu; rather, close contact with ill people carrying the contagion is the cause. Children are less likely to catch a cold outdoors than inside.

Other considerations for health and safety are addressed through the health curriculum. This curriculum is discussed next.

Comprehensive Health Curriculum

Even the youngest children participating in programs learn basic ideas about health, safety, and nutrition every day as a consequence of living and learning in an environment in which these issues are addressed and in which adults practice healthy behavior. In addition, educators teach specific knowledge that they know will help children to make safe and healthy choices. The *Michigan Model for Comprehensive Health Education* (George & Sellers, 1984) is an example of a written program that has content and materials to use with children in kindergarten through secondary school. An outline of the prekindergarten scope and sequence is shown in Table 13.4. This model includes some aspect of each of the basic content divisions for children during the early childhood years (Macrina, 1995). A health-promoting climate and a comprehensive health curriculum have significant positive outcomes for both the long-term health of children and their academic achievement. Other completely developed curricula for the preschool years are available, as are numerous other resources on specific topics.

Selected Health Topics

Do you recall if you washed your hands before and after the last meal you ate? Did you just splash your hands with water and wipe them with a towel, or did you do a thorough job? Do you routinely wash your hands before you enter into an interaction with children in the classroom and again as you leave? How often do you eat fast foods, which are high in salt and fat, instead of a well-balanced meal with fruits and vegetables? Do you select fruit instead of another dessert? Think about these questions as you read the following section.

Hand Washing The single most effective deterrent to contagious disease is the frequent and proper washing of hands (R. Newman, 1997). Adults may assume that children know the appropriate technique; however, this assumption is not always true. For this reason, the directions are listed next (Kendrick, Kaufmann, & Messenger, 1988):

Washing Your Hands

- ❑ Use soap and running water.
- ❑ Rub your hands vigorously.
- ❑ Wash all surfaces including wrists, backs of hands, between fingers, under fingernails.
- ❑ Rinse well from wrists to fingertips.
- ❑ Dry hands with paper towel.
- ❑ Turn off the water with the towel.
- ❑ Throw the paper towel in the basket. (p. 27)

TABLE 13.4 Scope and Sequence of the *Michigan Model for Comprehensive Health Education,* Prekindergarten Through Grade 2

Safety and First-Aid Education	Nutritional Education	Family Health	Consumer Health	Community Health
Prekindergarten				
Body rights and privacy and touch awareness Identifying and naming body parts Stranger awareness Strategies to use when lost How and when to seek help	Identification of foods and nonfoods Careful and varied food choices Food sources Body using food Introduction to nutrients	Family theme available as resource Family education activities or newsletters Family involvement guidelines How and when to seek help or report problems to parents	Health helpers and their roles Health product choices and functions	Environmental awareness Recycling Conservation
Kindergarten				
Fire safety rules for home and school Recognition of poisons Safety rules: school, playground, bus, pedestrian, bicycle, dangerous objects Traffic signs and signals Seat belts Appropriate and inappropriate touch Learning to say "no" to inappropriate touch; telling adults	Varieties in food Food characteristics Snacks	Individual uniqueness Identification of a family Family roles Family members as health helpers	Health helpers and their roles	Health helpers: roles and agencies Emergencies
First Grade				
Accident prevention and seat-belt safety Safety signs and signals Safety hazards and prevention: bus, pedestrian, bicycle, poisons, water, fire Emergencies Personal safety: secrets, actions that promote safety, avoiding dangerous situations Definitions of sexual abuse	Examples of food groups Snacks from each group Variety of foods needed for good health Food as source of energy and growth	Recognition that offspring resemble parents Examples of families Family roles, responsibilities, and abilities Differences in family eating habits Recognition of need for adult care Changes that affect families	Health helpers Effects of tobacco advertisement When to tell an adult	Personal medical procedures and instruments Immunizations Health checkups to prevent illness

Growth and Development	Substance Use and Abuse	Personal Health Practices	Emotional and Mental Health	Disease Prevention and Control
Body parts Senses Growth needs: own, plants, animals Introduction to body systems (heart, muscles, joints) Personal skills and choices	Definition of *drugs* Contrasts with medicines Care when accepting food from others Choice not to smoke or stay around smokers Identification of alcohol and cigarettes as drugs	Protective equipment (helmets) Care of teeth, skin, hair Grooming tools and their uses Care in handling of body wastes; nose blowing Exercise for muscles, heart, strength, flexibility Dental health theme as resource	Individual similarities and uniqueness Emotions and feelings Choices; problem solving How and when to seek adult assistance Self-help strategies	Introduction to use of medicines Health care professionals Care in handling body wastes Grooming and cleanliness routines and reasons Self-help strategies Appearance
Five senses Match body part with each sense Teeth	Definition of *drugs* Medicines as drugs Choice not to smoke Poisons How to say "no" to drugs	Eye protection Eye function Primary and permanent teeth Care of teeth Tooth decay and tooth brushing Individual health practices Sleep, rest, and exercise Seat belts	How to make friends Likenesses and differences How to name and identify feelings Ways to settle down Problem solving and decision making Adult help: when to seek it Identification of dangerous or destructive situations	Prevention of spread of germs Medicine: appropriate uses Recognition of systems How and when to seek adult help
Living and nonliving Living and growing Identification of growth needs New growth Personal skills and abilities Abilities of differently abled people External body parts Organs and their functions Body parts working together	Definition of *drugs* Identification of drugs Identification of alcohol and nicotine as drugs Harmful effects of tobacco and alcohol Poisons and medicines How to say "no" to drugs	Good health habits Exercises Protection of self and others when ill Health checkups and illness prevention Seat belts	How to name and identify feelings Ways to settle down Mixed feelings that accompany change How to show courtesy How to make friends Problem solving and decision making Adults to go to for help	Appearance and behavior associated with wellness and illness Factors changing health status and symptoms of illness Prevention of germ spread Head lice Immunization Communicable diseases

(continued on the next page)

TABLE 13.4   *(continued)*

Safety and First-Aid Education	Nutritional Education	Family Health	Consumer Health	Community Health
Second Grade				
Safety hazards and prevention: pedestrian, bicycle, sun, water, dental	Review of food groups	Similarities and differences of families	Aids for visual and hearing impairment	Definition of *environment*
Traffic signs	Food choices	Uniqueness of each person		Definition of *pollution*
Safety belt	Need to develop regular eating habits	Family members as health helpers		Noise and air pollution
Injury prevention	Combination foods	Changes that affect families		Effects of littering
Personal safety: dangerous situations, strangers, what to tell an adult	Healthy meals and snacks	Listening skills		Reduction of, reuse of, and recycling of materials

Food Selection   Opportunities to influence eating practices and food choices abound in full-day programs, Head Start, and elementary schools in which children eat together. Young children tend to eat foods with which they are familiar and reject foods that are new to them. When new foods are introduced slowly and along with other, more-familiar choices, children become interested and learn to enjoy a greater variety. For example, every culture has a variation on vegetable soup. Pea pods are an ingredient in Chinese vegetable soup but not in minestrone. A child familiar with one might be inclined to try the other, especially when it is served with a familiar sandwich. Adults who plan educational content should take every opportunity to teach nutrition in every context, including the school lunch.

In addition, children are often served differently in programs from the way they are served at home. When children are taught how to go through a cafeteria line or how to serve themselves family style, they are more likely to be successful in having a relaxed meal and are able to eat in a less stressful climate. In some busy families, some youngsters may not be familiar with sitting down to a meal with adults; therefore, they are unfamiliar with appropriate expectations at mealtime.

Finally, adults who accept children's contributions to classroom discussions will find learning the cultures of children in the classroom helpful. For breakfast, some youngsters may have soup, rice, and seaweed with milk and fruit. Others might have dry cereal and milk and an orange, and some children, cold pizza and juice. The conventional "American" breakfast is not the only adequate choice. Combinations of foods rich in nutrients are all good choices.

CURRENT EDUCATIONAL ISSUES

For each domain, educators must address some recurring issues in their practice. The physical domain is no exception. Following are discussions about the three most common issues raised about the physical domain.

1. *How can I teach gross-motor skills when I have neither a playground nor a gym. Won't teaching motor skills take time away from the "real" school subjects?* A child develops holistically. The body cannot be separated from the mind. In addition, physical fitness is a component of healthy functioning, mental well-being, and longevity. Therefore, when we compare the amount of time devoted to motor instruction—usually 15 to 20 minutes—with that of other activities, a quarter hour or so devoted to physical fitness appears to be reasonable. In addition, evidence is accumulating that moderate physical activity is associated with academic achievement because it improves the children's ability to focus their attention after participation (Pellegrini & Bjorklund, 2002).

Gyms and spacious playgrounds with developmentally appropriate equipment and a variety of other materials such as cones, riding toys, balls, and jump ropes are ideal but not required to incorporate physical activity into the program. Committed adults reduce the time that children wait for routine events and incorporate exercises into opening and closing routines as well as plan for activities during outdoor play. Even adverse conditions may be overcome if the early childhood educator is committed to the children's health and well-being.

Growth and Development	Substance Use and Abuse	Personal Health Practices	Emotional and Mental Health	Disease Prevention and Control
Five senses Function and compatibility of the senses Eye and ear development and function Eye and ear impairments and aids	Medicines and other substances that contain drugs Effects of nicotine, caffeine, alcohol, secondhand smoke How smoke enters the lungs Effects of alcohol on physical tasks or activities How to say "no" to drugs	Prevention of eye and ear injuries Healthy behaviors Self-responsibility and health status Exercise	Identification of feelings in self and others Ways to make friends Expressions of appreciation, annoyance, and anger How to handle strong emotions Problem solving and decision making Identification of personal skills and talents	Identification of eye problems When to use medicine Exercise and proper food for health

Ms. Rodd swept the broken glass off the square of asphalt behind the mobile classroom where her group was housed, picked up the trash, and planned interesting and vigorous activities that she supervised herself. She was always mindful of the risk of falls, but she carried out activities there all year long.

Mrs. Bronson placed orange cones in the church parking lot where the child care center rented space to keep cars away from a play area where she brought a mobile climber, mats to place under the climber, and assorted riding toys.

Ms. Stein set up a "bowling alley" in the hallway of an early childhood program that was used at various times of the day by different classrooms. In addition, she alternated physical activities and block play in a large-group area of her small classroom.

These teachers had to be creative problem solvers because their educational settings did not include playgrounds or gyms.

The combination of specifically planned activities and the moderate exercise children acquire as they engage in self-selected activity contributes substantially to the accumulation of the 60 minutes necessary for physical fitness. Regular physical activity can help prevent disease and improve the quality of life immediately and in the long term (Valentini, Rudisill, & Goodway, 1999) as well as contribute to the development of the brain, which may facilitate cognitive functions such as spatial perception, memory, selective attention, language, and decision making (Leppo et al., 2000).

2. *When should children begin to learn formal penmanship?* Children draw letters after they have learned to grip a writing implement and when they want to communicate across distance or time. Adults frequently prevent 1- and 2-year-olds from experimenting because of concern about painted walls and wallpaper, on which children are tempted to draw. By age 2 1/2 or 3 years, young children may be given crayons in restaurants, in early childhood programs, and at home when they are seated at a table. In the beginning, when children are scribbling and making large shapes, adults generally refer to the child's activities as "drawing." As children gain practice and observe adults write, their pretend writing becomes linear, with left-to-right progression, and a few letter shapes are randomly placed on the page. Children begin to distinguish between the "writing" and the drawing, although adults may not be able to make this discrimination.

If children have appropriate samples of manuscript print available, they will try copying some of the shapes on paper. This attempt usually occurs sometime between age 3 years and age 4 years. The letters most often available to children are their names. Because these letters are often scattered in random order, tilted on the side, or otherwise distorted, adults may or may not recognize some of these representations. They are very large and frequently misshapen. The lines appear to be jagged because these young children are using large sets of muscles instead of their fingers to shape the letters. Providing writing implements and paper and displaying as much manuscript printing as possible is sufficient to encourage children to explore drawing letters. Imposing premature adult standards for letter drawing is inappropriate until children have demonstrated a tripod grip and wrist and finger control during exploratory handwriting and drawing.

Informal instruction in short bursts when children ask, "How do I make a *k*?" is always appropriate as the adult draws the letter. Asking children if they want to write their name or if the adult should write it on a painting is also always appropriate as long as the adult accepts the child's approximation. The more exploration and practice the child has, the more probable that the skill will emerge.

Age alone is not the best criterion for skill emergence. Youngsters who enter kindergarten and have never held a writing implement need a lot of time using crayons, painting, and drawing with pencils before they have sufficient practice with finger and wrist muscles to produce credible approximations, whereas children with more experience may enter school drawing the letters of their name in a recognizable but imperfect form. If children's printing is decipherable, the focus of instruction should be on the message, not the mechanics. However, second- and third-grade children who tire easily and whose handwriting is indecipherable may need individualized strategies that focus on posture, trunk, and shoulder stability; pencil grip; and correct form to improve (Soderman, 1991).

Historically, beautiful cursive writing was the hallmark of the educated person. Penmanship was viewed as an art form. Such refined skills take much time and practice during many years to perfect. Educators are questioning the value of the time spent on penmanship as the range and depth of other content has increased with the years. Some children are taught to print, and cursive writing is omitted. Instead, children learn to print more accurately, smaller, and faster. Other children are given minimal instruction in penmanship, with print formation in kindergarten and first grade, followed by cursive instruction in second grade only. Except for the children who have not achieved basic letter formation, penmanship is not addressed again. Children are left to cultivate their own personalized form thereafter.

3. *Will I offend parents if I teach personal safety or talk to them about the child's obesity?* Early childhood educators may feel uncomfortable about addressing both these topics and may have assumed that such topics are within the family realm or are not appropriate subject matter for young children. However, a multilevel approach in which parents, teachers, and children cooperate is probably necessary to achieve the most desirable outcome. Preparing parents and involving them in discussions about personal safety, the nutritional needs of young children, and the importance of physical activity is always a sound practice. Parents can be effective at teaching their children and can integrate this information with what they already know in the context of the family. When families are treated with respect and early childhood professionals are culturally sensitive, families rarely become angry, especially if they believe that the professional is working with them toward a common goal. Professionals have access to accurate information and can ensure that the learning setting is consistently supportive of optimal health knowledge, attitudes, and practices. Family instruction on child sexual abuse is relatively rare (Finkelhor, 1984), and childhood obesity is likely ingrained in family culture, so both issues are challenging.

Childhood sexual abuse is a serious health problem and is widespread. Sexual abuse is more likely to begin during the preschool years than at any other time (Finkelhor & Baron, 1986). Professionals have had mixed success with teaching personal safety at the preschool level, although older children appear to understand the concepts and can describe a course of action that should be taken. Either teachers or parents may be effective in teaching the basic concepts of personal safety so that children can do the following (Wurtele, Gissispie, Currier, & Franklin, 1992):

❑ Know that they are the bosses of their bodies.
❑ Locate their private body parts.
❑ Distinguish between touching that is appropriate and touching that is not.
❑ Understand that touching an adult's private body parts is not appropriate.
❑ Say "no!" and then run away and tell someone what happened if a person tries to touch them inappropriately.
❑ Understand that they are not at fault nor are they bad if someone does touch them inappropriately.

Childhood obesity has also become an issue of national importance (C. Garcia et. al. 2002). Dieting is not recommended as a remedy for such obesity. Instead, a combination of physical exercise and sensible balanced food intake is most likely to be effective. Such a plan must occur consistently in all regular settings in which children live and work: homes, schools, after-school programs, and child care settings.

All adults can do the following (Eastman, 2002):

❑ Plan for daily physical activity
❑ Serve child-sized meals (one half to two thirds of the adult size in each food group)
❑ Serve low-calorie foods, such as fruits, for second helpings
❑ Serve low-fat snacks (fruit instead of a cookie)
❑ Minimize the amount of sugar-laden treats (foods and beverages) eaten
❑ Most important, encourage obese children to participate in sensible eating patterns

Young children can learn to do the following:

- ❑ Eat slowly and chew well
- ❑ Drink lots of water
- ❑ Try new fruits and vegetables in small quantities
- ❑ Stop eating when full
- ❑ Join in the fun of movement activities

GOALS AND OBJECTIVES

The ultimate goals of education in the physical domain are for children to develop confidence and competence in the control and movement of their bodies and to develop the attitudes, knowledge, skills, and practices that lead to maintaining, respecting, and protecting their bodies.

Intermediate Objectives

As children progress toward the ultimate goal, they will be able to demonstrate the following 23 competencies:

1. Gain confidence in using their bodies
2. Develop awareness of the location of their body parts
3. Develop spatial awareness (understanding of personal and general space and direction)
4. Develop temporal awareness (awareness of speed, timing, duration, and rhythm)
5. Improve total sensory awareness and integrate sensory information to solve movement problems
6. Distinguish the foreground from the background visually and auditorily
7. Engage in a variety of activities that require balance
8. Engage in a variety of activities that require coordinated movements with large- and small-muscle systems
9. Sustain vigorous motor activity with time to develop endurance
10. Engage in a variety of activities that require flexibility
11. Engage in a variety of motor activities that require agility
12. Use their whole bodies in appropriate activities to strengthen muscles and muscle groups
13. Develop fundamental motor skills such as jumping, hopping, throwing, kicking, striking, running, catching, and climbing
14. Coordinate wrist, hand, finger, finger–thumb, and eye–hand movements
15. Control the movement of their bodies in relation to objects
16. Use tools skillfully, including implements for eating, writing, dressing, and playing
17. Develop a positive attitude toward their bodies; appreciate their competence and that of others
18. Learn practices that keep their bodies and their environments clean and sanitary
19. Acquire attitudes, knowledge, and skills about physical activity that predispose them to maintaining physically fit lifestyles
20. Learn and practice sound nutritional habits and healthy, polite eating behaviors
21. Learn and practice appropriate safety procedures for school, playgrounds, home, and the neighborhood
22. Discriminate good and poor health, nutrition, and safety practices
23. Learn how to apply health, nutritional, and safety knowledge when making choices in daily life

TEACHING STRATEGIES

The two major components of the physical domain—skills and knowledge—utilize the strategies for teaching skills and those for teaching social-conventional knowledge. Both types of learning are addressed in chapters 3 and 4. Following are discussions of 24 specific strategies useful for this content.

Gross- and Fine-Motor Skills

1. Use learning centers to teach skills.   Young children have short attention spans, so movement from one activity to another allows them to participate in a variety of activities and maintain interest in as well as acquire and practice new skills. Depending on the facility, a motor skill may be the basis for a center in a classroom, with other centers representing other domains, or, if a gym is available, four to five motor skill centers may be set up at the same time. Usually classrooms are not large enough to contain more than one gross-motor center and one writing center. Often, several motor activities can be set up outdoors.

2. Provide opportunities for children to explore equipment and try out physical behaviors suggested by the equipment or materials.   Children should have time to explore equipment and materials before instruction begins. Such exploration promotes perceptual knowledge. In addition, adults have opportunities to observe what the children can do on their own. For example, in a preschool classroom, place pencils on a table with paper and watch how the children pick them up and hold them. Provide pencils of varying lengths and diameters. Place several large balls outside where they

Large, soft balls rolled along the floor help this preschool child learn to secure the ball by using only his hands.

are convenient for children to use, and watch what the children do. Younger children may need a lot of exploration time, but by the time youngsters reach age 6 or 7 years, only a few minutes may be necessary.

3. Observe children's performance of each skill of interest. To be effective and efficient, teachers must know children's current developmental level to know what to do next. Just how does the child throw, kick, or catch? What new information will help the child to move toward the next level? Patience is always required because skills are acquired slowly. Most children will use the next stage of a skill and then revert to more comfortable levels before they move forward more or less consistently. Establish specific objectives that move just ahead of the children and that are attainable challenges.

4. Demonstrate the skill to be mastered and incorporate do-it signals. The child may or may not be able to imitate your behavior. Let the child continue with the approximation of the motion. Repeat demonstrations as often as necessary to support the child's learning.

5. Provide suggestions and strategies to support the child's learning. Scaffolding for a large-motor task might be as simple as placing a silhouette of feet on the floor where the child is supposed to stand to be in position to strike a ball. Likewise, a piece of tape on a paintbrush indicating where to hold it may be helpful. Keep in mind that children must practice for long

periods before moving on to greater control or efficiency (Sanders, 2002).

6. Intersperse guided practice with modeling. We have described a several-year interval from beginning to success in acquisition of motor skills. Much practice is needed, as are intermittent demonstrations. Give oral cues that will help the child to attain greater control or efficiency (Sanders, 2002). Also provide many opportunities for the children to use their skills in free play with minimal adult guidance. Exploration of movement and creative use of the body often emerge as children experiment.

7. Emphasize qualitative movement over quantitative outcomes. Form is important. When you are teaching the formation of letters to 5- or 6-year-olds, the position of the paper and the student's posture become important to the eventual speed and quality of handwriting.

With throwing, the orientation of the body, the step on the foot opposite the throwing arm, the rotation of the body, and the follow-through are extremely important to eventual success. The distance thrown or the speed of the ball will improve with time.

In the early childhood years, basic skills and habits are established that last. As children grow and continue to learn, their skills become more refined; power and accuracy increase, and their motor activity becomes more complex.

8. Provide encouragement and feedback to children about their performance. As discussed in chapter 3, praise children by using specific descriptions when they are successful: "You took a step that time when you threw the ball!" Focus on the progress each child makes so that each experience is a success.

9. Use problem-solving strategies to explore movement concepts. After demonstrating high, medium, and low levels (see the Exploring Vertical Space activity at the end of this chapter), ask children to show how they could move across the floor on the low level. Then ask them to find another way to do so. Use reflections to support individual children and to encourage creative movements. Vary the problems so that children explore the space near their bodies without moving their feet. Generally, this strategy works well with whole-group instruction because of the amount of space required. Music and rhythm may be added but are not necessary as youngsters begin to understand the movements.

10. Encourage suggestions from the children. You will be able to assess children's movement vocabulary and concepts when you hear their suggestions. Ask children to assist in constructing an obstacle course that includes a variety of object–person relationships: under, through, behind, and on top of. Remind the children of safety considerations if necessary.

11. Establish guidelines for safety, level of participation, and respect for others.   Children must learn to be safe during physical play and must develop a concern for others' safety. Teach safety directly and provide practice so that each child knows what to do. Remember that the youngest children have difficulty stopping. In addition, because physical competence varies considerably across the group, each child should focus on his or her competencies and offer encouragement to others. Following are a few suggested guidelines (Sullivan, 1982):

❑ Hard or sharp objects must be left in lockers or on the sidelines. Dangerous items should not be worn or carried.

❑ Children should be aware of their personal space and avoid collisions or pushing if possible. They may not hurt one another deliberately.

❑ Words of self-praise and encouragement of or appreciation for others are appropriate. Children may not tease or ridicule one another.

❑ Children must come to the adult promptly when they hear a prearranged signal.

❑ Children should engage in the activities that are developmentally appropriate for them with some level of commitment. The "couch potato" pattern and the "I can't do it" pattern are unacceptable. (Adults must distinguish between real fatigue and a general pattern of no participation.)

❑ Children will "freeze" when called on to do so. Such freezing allows the adult to call attention to competencies and interesting or creative postures. Freezing is also a safety strategy.

Perceptual-Motor Skills

12. Provide opportunities to practice balance that are simple at first, then move on to more-challenging opportunities.   Walking on a taped line on the floor offers children an opportunity to practice balance beam skills without the risk of falling off a balance beam. Then move to the wide, low, balance beam and then to balance beams progressively higher from the floor. Be sure to place mats under the beams to absorb the force of falls. Under supervised conditions, children can incorporate a variety of movement skills, such as sliding, jumping, and hopping, on the balance beam at the end of the early childhood period. Always remain near the children so that you can support or catch them as they attempt new challenges.

13. Incorporate concepts of spatial and time awareness into other domains as opportunities arise.   Various strategies using small- and whole-group instruction are effective for helping children become more aware of space and time. However, only as these concepts are embedded in other ongoing activities do young children probably begin to understand the breadth of these concepts. All objects occupy space. Problems with space occur in the block area as a youngster shoves a long board along the floor, unintentionally interfering with another child's play. Sometimes adults and other children misinterpret a misunderstanding of the spatial concept as disregard for another child's rights. Make every effort to use time and space concepts accurately. A 5-minute warning should be given as close to 5 minutes before the children put away materials as is possible. Young children have sufficient difficulty estimating time that the intervals labeled as 5 minutes should not be between 2 and 15 minutes.

14. Select noncompetitive group games or modify familiar games to reduce or eliminate competitiveness.   Try to provide games in which all the children play all the time. For example, assist children to stand in a circle. Give the group one to three pillow balls (large, soft, cloth balls), and ask them to throw the ball to someone across the circle. Instead of having an "out" as in dodge ball, tell children to catch or pick up the ball and throw it to another person. The fun is in the throwing and catching. Children will have many opportunities to play competitively later.

15. Use directional language in context daily, including "left" and "right" for the older children of the early childhood period.   For preschool, modify dances such as "The Hokey Pokey" so that you sing "Put one hand in" instead of "your left hand." This approach allows the children to enjoy the dance and song and to participate in it fully. Put a piece of yarn on the left hand of kindergarten children and other primary children whenever they need it, and label it appropriately. Remember that some people have difficulty with the meaning of *left* and *right* into adulthood.

16. Use accurate language for naming body parts.   Most 2-year-olds know *head, knees, hands, arms,* and *legs* because caregivers use these terms when they are dressing children. Other body parts such as the chest, thigh, and forefinger are less frequently discussed and can easily be introduced. The genitals should be labeled with correct terminology: penis and testicles for males, labia and vulva for females. Sometimes children will surprise you with questions or comments. When an infant was being bathed by his mother during group time, one 3-year-old commented, "He's a boy 'cause he got balls." The teacher paraphrased the child's comment and responded by using accurate language: "You noticed that he had testicles. All boys do."

Joking and laughing about private body parts is normal in informal settings for 6- to 8-year-olds even though their understanding may be inaccurate or incomplete, just as 3- to 5-year-olds find comments related to elimination hilarious. Less appropriate behaviors generally diminish as children are provided with straightforward, factual information with accurate vocabulary.

17. *Provide safety information and guidance to prevent hazards as children explore their bodies' functions and capabilities.* Body awareness includes notions of what the body does. Body functions such as eating, drinking, eliminating, and sleeping are of interest, as are the internal body parts (Fleer & Careen, 1995). Include appropriate information within meaningful contexts or through direct instruction.

Delighted by their strength and increasing competence, young children explore the environment. As a result of less-than-accurate estimates of space, youngsters stick arms, legs, fingers, toes, and heads into amazingly small apertures and cannot get out again. For this reason, adults must always supervise children in this age group, pointing out hazards in matter-of-fact ways as children use equipment. As many parents and teachers know, children also experiment with stuffing objects into the orifices of their bodies. One teacher extracted five dried peas from a youngster's ear. The general rule is that food and water go into the mouth, but nothing is to be put into any other part of the body.

18. *With younger children, provide an uncluttered background for objects you want them to see.* High contrast in line, pattern, and color is easier to perceive than low contrast. Place play and work materials on uncrowded shelves so that children can find them. Point out relevant cues such as shape or color when the child is observing materials. Help children recognize how some plants and animals blend into the environment because of their shape and color. As children get older, they become better able to distinguish figure–ground relationships. For example, when teaching children about handwriting, use one letter or just a few letters on a whole page. Then the child can find and copy them. Usually the child's name is recognized first, but many youngsters focus on "their" letter—the initial of their first name. They are also aware of letters from the community, such as the *M* in the McDonald's sign. Using decorated or cute letters on the wall to stimulate interest in handwriting is not recommended because such decorations are too cluttered for the child to perceive the letter easily. Children often

find it easier to see letters on the same plane as that on which they are drawing them.

Similarly, children hear rhythm and melody from instrumental music more easily than from a combination of instrument and voice. The tune of the music line is less complex and easier to imitate. Children need guidance in learning what to attend to and what to ignore. More information on this topic can be found in chapter 9.

Health, Nutrition, and Safety

19. *Plan vigorous physical activity every day.* Incorporate stretching and moving opportunities as a part of group time and prolonged active play during outdoor time. Include motor skills instruction in daily schedules. Use balloons for tossing in the air, catching, and hitting upward with the hands or feet (E. Miller, 1999). Exercise tapes for children are widely available and can be used when weather inhibits outdoor activity.

20. *Demonstrate a concern for your fitness and health so that children can imitate what you do.* Teachers who have some difficulty with flexibility and stamina should tell the children about this and do as much as they can.

21. *Incorporate health and safety education when applicable.* Do not assume that children know such information. Statements such as "Use a tissue once; then throw it away" provide children with straightforward guides for functioning with greater safety and healthier practices. Place hand-washing pictograms near the sinks.

22. *Communicate regularly with families.* Give them the health and safety information you are teaching children. When families and teachers speak the same language about the same topics, children learn better and remember more. In addition, you will be reminding families of the basic concepts. For example, when you teach what to do in case of a fire, send home directions for family fire safety inspections and evacuations. When you attempt to expose children to a greater variety of vegetables in a tasting experience, send the list of selections home so that the children can tell parents which vegetables they liked. Collaborate with family members about strategies to help youngsters maintain an appropriate weight.

23. *Use mealtimes to teach nutrition and proper eating habits.* Children should learn to chew food slowly and to eat a variety of foods. Each child can taste a tiny portion (about 1 teaspoon) of the foods that are unfamiliar or disliked. Do not expect children

Mealtime should be a pleasant learning experience for children.

to clean their plates every day. Meal and snack time should be relaxing conversation time, not hurried. Teach socially polite behavior such as eating with the mouth closed and listening while chewing. Encourage children to drink plenty of fluids every day. When discussing what to eat for meals and snacks, focus on foods lower in fats and sugar and higher in other nutrients. For example, choose pretzels instead of potato chips. For the same volume of food, the child is better nourished with pretzels.

When children begin to participate in a school lunch program, rehearse the appropriate behavior with them at another time of day and then eat with them during the first few weeks and sporadically throughout the year. Many children do not know how to negotiate a cafeteria line or where to sit and are unfamiliar with the food. Children with free or subsidized lunches should always be indistinguishable from others. Help children to develop patterns of support and consideration by teaching them not to comment negatively on a child's food from home. Be alert to problems such as older children's taking lunch money away from younger children, and ensure supervision as necessary. Children should not be denied their food for behavioral transgressions; instead they should have a supervised eating area where they may learn more-appropriate behavior.

24. *When talking about food choices, use the phrase* a better choice *rather than* good foods *and* bad foods. The term *bad food* is best reserved for decayed, moldy, or otherwise unsafe food. Care should be taken not to undermine parents and cultural patterns. For example, a quarter cup of salted peanuts is not the best choice for a snack but is an excellent meat substitute in many main dishes such as curries or stir-fried mixtures.

ACTIVITY SUGGESTIONS

Most of the following activities are taught in small groups of children and become self-sustaining with intermittent supervision as children practice the skills. Some activities may be incorporated into whole-group sessions as a means for increasing physical activity in an otherwise sedentary experience. A few are for whole-group activities. Keep in mind that the typical patterns of motor skill acquisition range across the entire early childhood period and that children who do not have opportunities for instruction and practice are likely to perform as younger children do.

✎ Exploration With Balls (For Children of All Ages)

Objective 15 For children to control the movement of their bodies in relation to objects.

Materials 4–10 cardboard boxes of moderate size, several balls ranging in diameter from 2 to 10 in.

Procedure Outdoors, randomly place several moderately sized cardboard boxes on the ground. Put several balls ranging in diameter from 2 to 10 in. nearby. Observe as children play. Refrain from directing the play. The way in which children use the materials will vary with their age and experience.

✎ Fun on the Balance Beam (For Younger or Less Experienced Children)

Objective 7 For children to engage in a variety of activities that require balance.

Materials A steady 2×4 in. balance beam with fall-absorbent mats for indoor activity or a similar balance beam surrounded by fall-absorbent material outdoors; floor tape

Procedure Demonstrate a walk across the balance beam at a slow, comfortable speed. Invite children to walk across the beam. If they are successful, suggest that they find another way to cross the beam. Stand nearby to support children if necessary. If they cannot think of any ways that are challenging, try some from this list: forward; backward; sliding; step sideways, step together; forward, turn around, then go backward; forward, bend knees, collapse, stand, then move forward; forward, hop, forward. (Suggestions are in order of difficulty.)

Safety Allow only one person on the balance beam at a time. Children must be careful not to push or bump one another when they are on the beam.

To simplify Tape two lines (2–4 in. wide) on the floor and have the children walk between them with the suggested movements.

To extend Use a narrower balance beam or a higher one. Some extensions to easy levels are suggested in the preceding list of movements.

✎ Indoor Striking (For Younger or Less Experienced Children)

Objective 13 For children to develop fundamental motor skills such as jumping, hopping, throwing, kicking, striking, running, catching, and climbing.

Materials Four moderate-sized Nerf balls, heavy cord, large paper clips, Styrofoam mallets the size and shape of Ping-Pong paddles

Procedure Hang three or more Nerf balls from the ceiling with string so that the balls hang at approximately child waist height. Adjust the balls for the various heights of the children. The balls should be hung 3 or more feet apart and be well out of the pathway of other people. (They can be clipped up when not in use.) Give each of three children Styrofoam mallets and demonstrate how to hit the ball.

Safety A hard strike will send the ball the full radius of the string. Soft balls will not injure a child, but being hit by a mallet during the striker's follow-through may sting. Young children are not skilled at stopping in the midst of an action like this. For this reason, other players should remain outside the radius of the balls.

To simplify Ask the children to strike the balls with their hands. Encourage striking the moving ball as well as the stationary ball.

To extend After observing a child's exploratory hits, make suggestions about form so that the child moves from a straight approach with a chop to standing sideways to the ball to swing the mallet. If there appears to be any movement of the foot associated with the striking hand, encourage the child to move the foot and rotate the body. If the child is in the appropriate stage of striking, demonstrate the step, strike, and follow-through typical of more mature form. (See the description of stages for striking in Table 13.1.)

✎ Moving Standing Still (For Older or More Experienced Children)

Objective 3 For children to develop spatial awareness (understanding of personal and general space and direction).

Materials A list of instructions

Procedure Children need only their personal space—the amount of space they can take up within kicking or stretched-arm distance. Vary the movements, the body parts involved, and the tempo of the movements in the various directions. Ask children to stay standing on the same spot throughout the experience. Sample directions are as follows:

> Bend one part of your body while stretching another part.
>
> Stretch as many parts of your body as you can all at the same time.
>
> Keeping your feet still, twist around as far as you can.
>
> Discover how many directions in which you can push. Think of all the body parts that can be used to push.
>
> While standing, show all the body parts that can swing.
>
> Swing fast. Swing slow.
>
> Collapse to the floor slowly.
>
> Pull something heavy as you rise.

To simplify Demonstrate so that children can imitate, and gradually repeat directions so that they learn to follow the instructions without imitation. Use only a few directions.

To extend Increase the difficulty of the movements or the speed of transition from one movement to another or both.

✎ Mother/Father, May I? (For Older or More Experienced Children)

Objective 10 For children to engage in a variety of activities that require flexibility.

Materials None

Procedures This game is fun to play outside. Invite children to arrange themselves in a horizontal line so that they cannot touch anyone else as they move. The leader—Mother/Father—stands in front, facing the line of children. The starting line may be real, drawn in the dirt or grass, or imaginary. The leader presents the children with tasks that require flexibility as they move forward. The leader may say, "Israel, bend down and put your hands on the ground and walk them forward."

Israel must respond, "Mother/Father, may I?"

If the leader says, "You may," Israel may carry out the movement. If the leader says, "No, you may not," Israel should remain in place. If a child is caught moving without permission, he or she returns to the starting line. The object of the game is to reach Mother/Father first.

Some moves requiring flexibility are the following:

> Put your hands behind your neck and take two steps forward.

Squat and waddle four times.

Turn your body sideways and step sideways twice.

Swing your arms around and around and take three giant steps.

Sit down with your feet tucked under you and stretch your arms forward as far as possible, then move to where your arms reach.

To simplify Use only with a small group so that each child must not wait long for a turn. Younger children may need to practice the traditional steps before attempting the actions requiring flexibility. Doing so alters Objective 10 to Objective 13 (develop fundamental motor skills such as jumping, hopping, throwing, kicking, striking, running, catching, and climbing), although children do learn the rules of the game, which are as follows:

Baby step: Place toe to heel.

Giant step: Make the step as big as possible.

Banana split: Slide one foot forward as far as possible.

Umbrella step: Place your forefinger on top of your head and spin around once.

Frog leap: Do a two-footed jump.

Bunny step: Do a one-footed hop.

Fire engine: Run until Mother/Father says, "Stop."

To simplify further Use only forward and backward variations of *step* and *jump*.

To extend Older children may enjoy adding a game of tag at the end. The child tags the leader, who then chases the child back to the starting line. If the leader tags the child, that person becomes the next leader.

Encourage children to become the leader and invent twisty ways to move. Make suggestions to encourage flexibility.

✎ Mastering Cutting Techniques (For Children of All Ages)

Objective 16 For children to use tools skillfully, including implements for eating, writing, dressing, and playing.

Materials Magazines, pieces of scrap paper of various colors and textures, paste or glue, old sacks, classified ad pages, wallpaper scraps, scissors

Procedure Intersperse guided practice with demonstrations about how to use the scissors and encourage children to attempt more-challenging cutting tasks.

Draw lines on some of the scraps so that children cut increasingly difficult pieces:

Younger and Less Experienced Children	Older and More Experienced Children
No lines	Sharply curved lines
Straight lines	Corners
Long, wavy lines	Zigzag lines

Children may paste pieces on other reused products such as newspaper or paper bags.

To simplify Use unlined, small pieces of paper of moderate weight or tear the paper.

To extend Ask children who can cut all the lines listed in the preceding table to cut on the line simple shapes that they draw themselves or to cut out the inside space of two concentric circles or two concentric squares or pictures from magazines.

✎ Puzzles (For Children of All Ages)

Objective 14 For children to coordinate wrist, hand, finger, finger–thumb, and eye–hand movements.

Materials Puzzles, puzzle rack

Procedure Place a variety of puzzles in a puzzle rack or on the table where children can see them. Demonstrate how to take puzzles out by pouring puzzles of 50 to 100 pieces into a large tray or laying them out on a surface with the picture side up. Puzzles in frames should be removed one piece at a time and placed on a table. Do not flip them over because the pieces will slide and get lost on the floor or under furniture. Ask a child to look carefully at the picture, noting distinctive features. Guide the child as necessary to solve the problem. Point out curved and straight lines. Suggest tracing the edges of the shapes with a finger. Suggest looking for corner or edge pieces first because they usually have distinctive features.

To simplify Select easier puzzles: puzzles with one hole for each puzzle piece; 3- to 5-piece puzzles; 5- to 10-piece puzzles with the cuts in logical places such as a tail or a foot; 11- to 15-piece puzzles.

To extend Increase the number of pieces or the complexity of the picture. Three-dimensional puzzles are available and require a long time to complete but provide great challenge for older children.

✎ Pull a Friend (For Older or More Experienced Children)

Objective 12 For children to use their whole bodies in appropriate activities to strengthen muscles and muscle groups.

Materials Wagons, sleds, cardboard sheets with ropes making long bails, or tricycles that will carry passengers, blocks

Procedure Outdoors, suggest that one child pull or push another in the conveyance. Demonstrate and then suggest that another child take your place.

To simplify Provide blocks or other lighter objects for the children to transport.

To extend Increase the weight being transported, or suggest that the children try the cardboard-and-rope combination. Because of friction, this task is much more difficult, but it will work.

✎ Exploring Vertical Space (For Older or More Experienced Children)

Objective 4 For children to develop temporal awareness (awareness of speed, timing, duration, and rhythm).

Materials Tambourine, large balls

Procedure Ask the children to spread out so that they cannot touch anyone else. Tell them to put their hands on their shoulders and then raise their arms overhead and say, "This is your high space." Then ask them to touch their shoulders and then the area joining the leg to hip and say, "This is your middle space." Finally, ask them to touch the floor and then their hip joint and say, "This is your low space." Demonstrate, using your own body, while providing directions and defining the meanings of *high, middle,* and *low* spaces.

Making a slow walking beat on a tambourine, ask the children to start at their high space and move their bodies to their low space. Using words such as *smooth, jerky, bent,* or *twisted,* and denoting speeds such as *very slow* or *fast,* continue giving children movement directions. Alter the rhythm on the tambourine to match your directions. Intersperse "Freeze" or "Stop" directions when children make interesting forms with their bodies, then praise the performance.

To simplify Demonstrate most of the specific moves with the language cues if the children do not know the vocabulary.

To extend First, give the children large balls to hold as they move through vertical space. Next, provide simple music and then ask children to suggest ways to move. Last, include locomotor directions. Remember that the more directions the child must include, the more difficult the activity becomes; thus, leaping smoothly while holding a ball in high space is extremely challenging.

✎ Vegetable Tasting (For Younger or Less Experienced Children)

Objective 20 For children to learn and practice sound nutritional habits and healthy, polite eating behaviors.

Materials Variety of cooked and raw vegetables, serving spoon, tray, tasting spoons or toothpicks, small soufflé cups

Procedure Place a tray containing tasting spoons and a selection of vegetables where children can see it. Include small samples that you use to talk about and others that are used for tasting. Select combinations of common and less common vegetables so that children are familiar with some and not with others. Keep the portions tiny; one slender carrot coin or a kernel of corn is sufficient for children to explore the taste. To prevent children from dipping used spoons into a serving dish, use small soufflé cups. Put a little food in a cup and then allow the child to eat it. Name the vegetables and encourage children to comment. Within the context of this taste exploration, provide children with additional information such as "Raw, crisp vegetables help keep your teeth clean" or "Children should have several servings of vegetables every day to stay healthy." Maintain normal sanitary practices: clean hands, wash vegetables, and so forth.

To simplify Use fewer vegetables, and repeat the process several times. Deliberately include vegetables common to all cultural groups represented in the classroom.

To extend Increase the variety of vegetables to include those not commonly eaten by the children in the ethnic group being taught. Increase the information given so that children learn that some vegetables are really good or energy producing: potatoes of all kinds, corn, and peas. Tell the children that groups of vegetables such as leafy green and yellow vegetables have specific vitamins (particularly vitamin A) that people need, and some are mostly fiber and are also necessary for good health.

✎ Snowperson Walk or Run (For Older or More Experienced Children)

Objective 19 For children to acquire attitudes, knowledge, and skills about physical activity that predispose children to maintaining physically fit lifestyles.

Materials None

Procedure On brisk winter days, take the children outdoors and walk rapidly or run around the building. This activity is particularly effective after prolonged work at tables or quiet activities. Tell children that they are snowpersons in a hurry.

To simplify   Select a closer destination.

To extend   Gradually increase the length and speed of the walk. When returning inside, indicate how good you feel after you get out and really move.

SUMMARY

The focus of education in the physical domain is the development of motor skills, physical fitness, and health. The ultimate goal is to provide the knowledge and skills that children need to engage in developmentally appropriate activity safely and to maintain a healthy lifestyle. All physical skills are based on the maturation of the individual, instruction or the child's imitation of a model, and the opportunities to practice movements until efficiency and style are developed. Instruction without corresponding maturation of the body is ineffective, as is simply waiting until a skill emerges once appropriate maturation is attained. Skill increases in efficiency and refinement during the early childhood period.

Children acquire information and develop health and safety habits early in life. The teacher's role is to provide instruction when new information or new skills are needed and to provide an environment that supports healthy eating and safe playing. Direct instruction is sometimes needed, but concepts are also learned informally as children play, rest, and eat. Often, children who have disabilities in other domains can successfully engage in the physical domain once some adaptations are made.

Parents and teachers working together are better able than either working alone to be more successful at teaching children to have a healthy lifestyle. Children gradually learn to engage in play safely, eat sensibly, and use ordinary health habits such as hand washing and toothbrushing regularly as they begin to take some responsibility for their own health and safety.

✋ Applying What You Read in This Chapter

1. **Discuss**
   a. If children are allowed to play on a playground daily, will all of them develop the fundamental motor skills by the end of the early childhood period? Explain your answer.
   b. Ms. Cunningham wanted 2-year-old Phillip to be an athlete, so she showed him videos of tennis players and golfers, did infant massage, and engaged him in many bouts of training in jumping, kicking, striking, and throwing. What do you think was the outcome of all this effort and why?
   c. Describe how a dance experience for 5-year-olds that would enhance their nonlocomotor movement skills might be organized.

2. **Observe**
   a. Carefully watch two to five children engaging in gross-motor activity. Using the information in Table 13.1, try to determine each child's competence level for one of the fundamental motor skills. Record your findings as best you can. List the difficulties you had in doing this.
   b. Observe the fine-motor skills of two children at least 12 months apart in age. Compare your observations with the descriptions in Table 13.2. Explore why differences exist between the description and the individuals you observed.

3. **Carry out an activity**
   a. In pairs, try out the stages of each of the fundamental motor skills described in Table 13.1. One

adult student should read the description while the other tries to do it. If you can do it yourself, you will understand which muscles are involved for the children.
   b. Give a felt- or nylon-tip pen and paper to a preschool child, and suggest that he or she write you a letter. If the child informs you that he or she cannot write, tell the child that it is not necessary to do grown-up writing, only children's writing or pretend writing. Describe how the child gripped the writing implement. Compare this with the description in the text. Was there any apparent understanding of letters, left-to-right progression, or other aspects of written language?
   c. Select a fine-motor task such as sewing on a button, eating with chopsticks, or tying a fish lure, and write out step-by-step directions on how to perform the task. Teach this task to another adult who is a novice and evaluate your effectiveness. Reflect on the strategies you used. What scaffolding was necessary, if any?

4. **Create something for your portfolio**
   a. Write a lesson plan using the suggested strategies for any skill or movement concept. Prepare any visual aids that are necessary. Implement the plan if possible, and photograph a youngster carrying out the skill. Place these materials in your portfolio.
   b. Snap fast, multiple photographs of two children engaging in a fundamental motor skill to catch

the action. Write a short analysis of the stage that each child is in, and identify the next step necessary to advance the skill attempted.

5. Add to your journal

a. You are a teacher in a child care program. Your assistant is a picky eater and does not want to sit down with the children at lunch. When she does, she complains about the food selections and preparations, and she stirs the food around indifferently. What are the health implications for the children in the group? What is your responsibility in this situation, and what actions should you take, if any?

b. Examine the curriculum suggested for substance use and abuse. Think about the choices you have made. Considering the young children who will respect and emulate you, do you think you might reconsider some of your choices? Where does your personal freedom impinge on your professional responsibility? What will you say when they ask, "Do you . . . ?" or "Did you ever . . . ?"

CHAPTER
14

The Social Domain

You may wonder:

How do children develop social skills? Are such skills important enough to teach in school?

Why are children's friendships important?

When children enter into a conflict, what can I do to help them resolve their dispute peacefully?

What is the relationship between social skills and the social sciences?

What kinds of activities will teach social skills as well as the social sciences?

In this chapter on the social domain, we present information to help you answer the preceding questions.

From one corner of the preschool room comes the following interchange:

"I want that truck."

"But I had it first."

"I still want it."

"You can have it when I'm done."

"Be fast."

Ms. Roth's kindergartners are on their way to visit the local fire station. Their mission is to find out how the firefighters work and live and the ways in which they protect the community. The children have generated a list of questions they will try to answer through observations and discussion. One of their aims is to note diversity among the staff at the station. The children have brought paper, pencils, and markers so that they can record, in any way they can, what they discover.

The first-grade class at the Greenleaf Elementary School is embarking on a project to map the playground. Initially, they measure the space, choosing "footsteps"

as their unit of measure. After much discussion, the children decide to create three-dimensional models of the playground equipment by using boxes of various sizes and shapes. Small groups of children are taking responsibility for representing different areas of the schoolyard.

It is late October, and Mr. Hwang's second graders have been learning about the upcoming elections in their city, county, and state. The youngsters have demonstrated a great interest in voting, and lively discussions have arisen about issues of "fairness." When a guinea pig is offered as a class pet, the children ask if they can hold an election to choose a name for it.

Although these scenarios depict children of different ages in various school settings, they all represent a part of the social domain, which encompasses four essential aspects of children's development and education. First, *social skill development* deals with the ways in which children learn to interact with others. Second, *socialization* is the process by which children learn to understand and adapt to rules. Third, children's *social responsibility* is a measure of their respect for individual differences, their care for the environment, and their ability to function as good citizens (e.g., by resolving conflicts peacefully). Finally, *social studies*, or *social science*, is a curricular area with a focus on the whole of human behavior, now and in the past. Because

This chapter was written by Laura C. Stein, Early Childhood Consultant, Stein Associates, East Lansing, Michigan.

of its roots in the traditional social science disciplines such as anthropology, economics, human ecology, geography, psychology, and the like, social studies provides us with an organizing principle around which to plan programs for children. Thus, although each facet of the social domain is not the same as any of the others, they are inextricably linked.

Many possible approaches exist for addressing children's social development and teaching social studies in the early childhood curriculum (Brewer, 2001). One strategy is to treat social studies as a separate content area with a body of knowledge to be learned through formal experiences. Proponents of this approach believe that children could be learning more-specific knowledge than is traditionally taught to them. A second view is that the most important concepts of both social studies and social skills are best learned through the naturally occurring interactions within the classroom and that focusing on specific content is inappropriate. In this chapter we present a means for combining the best aspects of both these approaches so that children learn content related to social studies in ways that are relevant to them, while also developing the social competencies they need through productive interactions with others.

Teaching within the social domain provides children with opportunities to develop knowledge about and skills pertaining to themselves in relationship to people in their near environment and to extend this information to understanding human relationships in the larger world. The family provides the foundation for these learnings, while the classroom is often the place where children are confronted with ideas and people both similar to and different from themselves. During the early school years, children are discovering how to establish and maintain relationships with members of their group. As time passes, they explore their contribution to the well-being of the group. Throughout this period, they are continually working out how to value others and how to understand and cope with the differences they encounter. Thus, the classroom functions as a "human relations laboratory" in which children explore social knowledge, concepts, and skills through daily interactions, routines, activities, and on-the-spot instructions. It is the place in which they assimilate values and attitudes about other people from listening to and watching the adults around them. It is also the arena in which they practice citizenship in its most basic forms. Through their social encounters and activities, children build their understanding of history, sociology, economics, and culture. These are by no means the only issues they face, but they are so important that teachers must know how to address them.

To derive an understanding of the social domain, we must look at its individual pieces. Let us begin with a discussion of social skill development, including children's friendships and prosocial behavior, with an emphasis on the roles adults play.

SOCIAL SKILL DEVELOPMENT

Establishing relationships with others, learning to live within the bounds of societal expectations, and discovering your place in the group are all major tasks of children in early childhood and reflect aspects of children's social development. In fact, as children mature, more of their time and energy becomes devoted to this area of their development. This is especially true as they move beyond their family and neighborhood and come into greater contact with community institutions, such as early childhood centers and elementary schools. In these circumstances, children encounter new sets of expectations to which they must adapt.

How well children perceive, interpret, and respond to the variety of social situations they encounter is a measure of their social competence. A high level of social competence in our society means that a person exhibits responsible, independent, friendly, cooperative, purposeful, and self-controlled behavior. In contrast, youngsters with low levels of social competence act irresponsibly, timidly, hostilely, uncooperatively, or impulsively (Knapczyk & Rodes, 1996). Children who display socially competent behaviors are perceived more positively by society and are therefore treated in a more positive manner; these children thus experience more-satisfying interpersonal interactions and are happier than their less successful counterparts. Furthermore, research demonstrates that children's social competence influences their academic performance as well (Berndt & Keefe, 1995; Pellegrini & Glickman, 1990). Finally, children who are socially competent experience high self-esteem, viewing themselves as worthwhile, capable people, which has positive effects on their social performance.

Children are not born knowing how to make friends and influence people, nor do they come into this world understanding the rules their society has established. Time and many varied experiences are necessary for them to master the skills required for successful functioning in society (Kostelnik & Stein, 1990). Children spend much of their early lives trying out a panoply of strategies in order to make sense of their social world. Through experimentation, they begin to discover what works and what does not and under which circumstances. Once in school, their task becomes even more complex. Some of their actions may not lead to the same satisfactory outcomes as was true in former situations. For example, children may become bewildered when, after having been taught to work together with others on projects in preschool, their "team" efforts are suddenly viewed as "cheating" in higher grades. Or, youngsters accustomed to talking openly with adults about their playmates' transgressions may be labeled "tattletales" by their peers in school. Thus, children still have much to learn about the two major aspects of social development—socialization and social skills.

Children's social development can be looked at as the foundation on which other types of learning are built. Apart from nutrition and physical comfort, the need for human association is basic (Berk, 2000). This finding further implies that until individuals' essential needs, including positive association with others, have been met, they are unable to move beyond those realms into other areas of learning (i.e., academic, cognitive). Thus, instructional time spent on social development that has heretofore been regarded as "icing on the cake" must, instead, be treated as an essential ingredient of the cake.

Three critical issues of children's social development directly affect children's lives at school. The first of these primarily involves children's relationship with peers—that is, making and keeping friends and demonstrating prosocial behaviors, such as helping and cooperating. A second issue centers on children's interactions with adults, as they begin to determine how to fit their behavior to adult expectations and rules. Finally, learning to understand and appreciate differences in a diverse society and responding as a democratic citizen is a critical focus of youngsters' associations with both grown-ups and children as they develop. In this section, we address the first issue. The other two issues are addressed subsequently.

Children's Friendships

Five-year-olds Bo and Casey are playing with dinosaur models in the dinosaur habitat. They are deeply engrossed in their activity, moving the figures from place to place and actively communicating their ideas for the scenario with each other. Jimmy walks over, picks up a dinosaur, and tosses it into the middle of the play area.

"Hey," says Bo, "you can't put it there. That's the water hole."

"Yeah," adds Casey. "Besides you're not on our team!"

"I am so, if I wanna be," Jimmy asserts, angrily standing up with his hands on his hips.

"No, you can't," Bo responds.

"Teacher, they won't let me be on their team!" wails Jimmy.

Until fairly recently, most educators assumed that making friends and keeping friends were aspects of life that some children were better at than others but that nothing much could or should be done about it at school. These educators reasoned that the most appropriate place for children to deal with this issue was on the playground or before and after school, not during instructional time. At most, the playground supervisor was expected to deal with children who were having school problems. Youngsters having persistent difficulty were referred to the school counselor or administrator. We are now more aware of the negative impact that disharmony in social relations has on children's abilities to concentrate on school subjects and, as a consequence, their school achievement. Furthermore, we also know that teachers and classroom aides can accomplish much by helping children become more successful with their friendship strategies (Kostelnik, Whiren, Soderman, Stein, & Gregory, 2002). To effectively assist children in improving their friendship skills, adults must understand the role that friendship plays in children's lives.

Why Friends Are Important   As they mature, children become increasingly interested in establishing friendships (Hartup, 1996). In fact, researchers have documented that by age 7 years, most children find not having a friend almost unthinkable (Hendrick, 2000). Among other benefits, friends provide stimulation, assistance, companionship, social comparison, and affection. Furthermore, within a friendship children can experiment with a number of social roles, such as leader, follower, risk taker, and comforter. In essence, children develop a sense of belonging and security through the special relationship they have with a friend (Harter, 1999).

Life without friends can appear fairly bleak. Although truly friendless children are few, evidence exists that poor peer relationships in childhood lead to difficulties in later life (Newcomb & Bagwell, 1996). For instance, adolescent delinquency and emotional instability have been linked to friendlessness in the early years. Naturally, just as in the case of adults, children vary as to how many friends they want to have. Some are content with one "best" friend, whereas others seek a wide circle of friends. The quality of these relationships counts more than the quantity (Stocking, Arezzo, & Leavitt, 1980).

Children's Changing Ideas About Friendship
Children's ideas of what constitutes a friend change as they grow older. Significantly, children at various stages of development view friends very differently than adults do. Consequently, adults should look at this developmental process to assess and facilitate children's relationships with one another more constructively.

In the early stages of friendship, children are preoccupied with their own emotions. They concentrate on other youngsters on the basis of who is available, as well as on their physical attractiveness or other outward characteristics and their material possessions (Selman, Levitt, & Schultz, 1997). As part of their focus on the here and now, children between the ages of 3 and 7 years are better at initiating relationships than sustaining them, and they may also inadvertently rebuff others' advances because they are simply not good at picking up friendship cues. They sometimes have difficulty entering an ongoing play situation or accepting others who want to join, as illustrated in the example given previously (Kostelnik, Whiren, et al., 2002). Adults who observe these difficulties often view these children as being heartless and inconsiderate instead of recognizing that they are experiencing a cognitive dilemma—that of centering on one way to carry out the play episode.

Somewhat later in their understanding of friends, between the ages of 4 and 9 years, children begin to look for pleasing behaviors from others, such as giving one another turns, sharing toys, or deliberately choosing to sit together. Although children seem content with their choices, some of these relationships may not always appear equal in the eyes of an adult. Adults worry when children select friends that seem to be uncongenial companions—those that are bossy or overly compliant, for instance. Teachers and others have difficulty standing by when children persist in these types of friendships. Parents and educators are often tempted to separate these youngsters forcibly. However, they must remember that children are deriving benefits from these relationships that are not always apparent to adults. For example, they may use their companion as a model for their future behavior. Thus, the shy child may observe the bossy child achieve his or her aims through assertiveness and may ultimately try a few of these strategies. Similarly, the bossy child may admire the more modest approach of his or her peer. If, as the children assume different behaviors within the friendship, their relationship flexes to accommodate these new variables, youngsters may continue to remain close companions. If it does not, they will lose interest in each other and try out new relationships. Adults must allow children to decide for themselves when and if this change is to occur.

Children in this phase of friendship desire so much to have a friend that they often resort to bribery or threats. Furthermore, they still have difficulty having more than one close relationship at a time and are often heard to remark, "You can't be my friend—José is my friend." Adults are sometimes appalled at the tactics the children use toward one another. However, adults must recognize that children are merely trying out strategies to get what they want and will soon learn from their peers how well such strategies work; their aim is not to be deliberately mean or hurtful.

Because children at this stage actively seek friends that are like them, they are busy comparing themselves with others to determine likenesses and differences. They begin to choose same-sex and same-race playmates. This behavior becomes even more pronounced in the next phase, which describes children between the ages of 6 and 12 years. In this stage, children are finally beginning to understand that their behavior must please another person, not simply the reverse. They are deeply involved in what is fair and not fair (as viewed from their special viewpoint). In this stage children want to be most like their friends, and so conformity in dress, speech, and actions reaches a peak.

Furthermore, friendships at this stage tend to come in twos; girls especially form close-knit dyads, whereas boys travel in looser packs (Ladd, 1999). Both boys and girls are extremely possessive of their relationships, and conflicts and hard feelings often result. Adults express concern about the extremes of self-segregation by sex, race, and differing physical abilities that frequently occur at this stage. Although adults cannot mandate friendships, they can do much to help children recognize similarities between themselves and others despite certain obvious physical differences. Some common ground between children might include cognitive skills, degree of sociability, interests, and attitudes (Bukowski, Sippola, & Bolvin, 1995). These issues are especially relevant when adults are helping children develop nonprejudicial attitudes and behaviors. To promote these values, adults must think of ways to take advantage of children's growing abilities to observe and reason (Bergen, 1993; Deegan, 1993). (Strategies for helping children achieve a heightened awareness of similarity among people while recognizing and appreciating differences are presented in the Activity Suggestions section of this chapter.)

How children look at interpersonal relationships with peers across time is an important aspect of their growing capacity for friendships. Other crucial factors in their ability to make and keep friends are the skills they bring to the process. These skills can be divided into three distinct categories: establishing contact, maintaining positive relationships, and resolving conflicts (Kostelnik, Whiren, et al., 2002).

Friendship Skill: Establishing Contact To start a potential friendship, one child must first approach another. If the friendship has any chance of success, the second person must respond positively. How this contact is carried out influences each child's perception of the other. If both have a good impression, the interaction will continue; if they do not, it will terminate at this point. Children who are cordial—that is, who smile, speak pleasantly, offer greetings, and seek information—tend to elicit positive responses from others (Ladd & Coleman, 1993). These replies can be cast in the form of responding to others' greetings and questions, offering information, and inviting participation. Another successful strategy for breaking the ice is imitation. Very young children feel flattered when others mimic their actions by playing nearby or using the same materials, and they tend to welcome more direct involvement by the imitator. Older children are more leery of this tactic and may become irritated at someone who is "copying." Some finesse may be required on the part of the approaching youngster to recognize when he or she has breached the boundaries.

This kind of judgment may seem natural for all children to develop, yet many youngsters fail to recognize that even the seemingly simple strategy of acting friendly will gain friends. They may have the correct idea, but their timing may be off, or their actions may be misapplied. These children benefit greatly from friendship coaching (Kostelnik, Whiren, et al., 2002). This strategy involves pointing out the child's behavior and its effect on other youngsters by using specific, observable terms rather than generalizations. Then the adult should demonstrate the appropriate skill and explain the rationale for why it is effective. The next step is for the child to practice the skill and participate in an evaluation of how well it worked. Naturally, a great deal of time and practice is required for children to learn to make themselves more appealing to others.

Friendship Skill: Maintaining Positive Relationships The second level of friendship skills is to maintain positive relationships once they have been initiated. Children who speak directly to one another, are attentive to others in particular interactions, respond in an interested fashion, and offer suggestions, are pop-

ular with others (Rubin, Bukowski, & Parker, 1998). In addition, these youngsters demonstrate cooperation and helpfulness and are comfortable expressing emotions such as affection, empathy, and joy at their pals' accomplishments.

These children are able to sustain relationships because their behavior makes them fun and satisfying to be with. Children who lack these skills are far less successful in their abilities to sustain friendships with time. They annoy and antagonize their peers by showing off, being insensitive to people's reactions, becoming overly exuberant in their displays of affection, or taking over rather than being helpful or cooperative. Even though their intentions may be positive, their actions make viewing these youngsters as potential friends difficult.

Friendship Skill: Resolving Conflicts The most complex aspect of peer relationships is handling conflicts. Children's ability to deal with disputes in democratic ways such as recognizing and taking into account differences in another's viewpoint, compromising, bargaining, or suggesting nonviolent solutions to the problem is highly indicative of the future success of a relationship (Hartup, 1996). Children who forcibly demand that issues be decided their way or, conversely, who back down from establishing their legitimate rights lose their peers' respect and are often rejected by them.

Thus, children who use constructive means of resolving disputes while also satisfying their own needs are most successful in forming lasting relationships. The facets of this process are illustrated in Table 14.1 (Stocking et al., 1980).

Educators play an important role in helping children learn how to use these strategies. One way teachers can do this is by modeling the role of a conflict mediator in disputes between children. Doing so involves being a

TABLE 14.1 Negotiating Conflicts

Strategy	Example
Expressing your rights, needs, or feelings	"It's my turn to use the stapler."
Listening to and acknowledging others' rights, opinions, and feelings	"Oh, you haven't finished yet."
Suggesting nonviolent solutions to conflict	"How about giving it to me in 2 minutes?"
Explaining the reasons behind the solution suggested	"That way we'll both get to use it before lunch."
Standing up against unreasonable demands	"No, it's not fair if you use it the whole time. I want it, too."
Accepting reasonable disagreement	"OK, I hadn't thought of that."
Compromising on a solution	"I can use tape now, and you can use tape later when I'm using the stapler."

TABLE 14.2 Conflict Mediation

Step in the Process	Adult's Role
1. Initiating the mediation process	Assumes mediator role Stops aggressive behavior Neutralizes object or territory
2. Clarifying perspectives	Solicits statements from each party Paraphrases perspectives Establishes own neutrality
3. Summing up	Defines problem in mutual terms
4. Generating alternatives	Solicits ideas from combatants and bystanders Suggests possibilities, if necessary
5. Agreeing on a solution	Summarizes points of agreement Identifies resolution
6. Reinforcing the problem-solving process	Praises children for developing solution
7. Following through	Helps children carry out terms of agreement

nonjudgmental facilitator so that children learn to find peaceful solutions that are mutually satisfying.

The conflict mediation process consists of seven steps, summarized in Table 14.2. How to present this process so that children can practice the specific skills is discussed in the Activity Suggestions section of this chapter.

Children vary widely in their abilities to engage in this form of resolving conflicts. Success depends on their age, understanding of relationships, communication skills, and experiences. The technique has been used productively with children as young as age 3 years who could communicate their wants. As children mature, refine their abilities to express themselves, and become more familiar with how the process works, their capacity for staying with the process increases. They shift from the belief that disputes are caused by one person against another to a more balanced view of shared responsibility. The mediation model presented in Table 14.2 helps children move in this direction. They have opportunities to observe problem solving firsthand and experience the results of nonviolent solutions.

In addition, as the negotiation process becomes more familiar, the number of participating onlookers grows which increases the involvement of more children. Promising evidence also indicates that not only does aggression diminish, but positive prosocial behaviors increase in groups in which mediation is commonly used (Kostelnik & Stein, 1986). Furthermore, when adults take on the mediator role, the number and duration of children's conflicts decline with time and children take over the peaceful management of their disputes (Stein & Kostelnik, 1984).

Educators play an important role in helping children learn how to resolve disputes.

As stated previously, the give-and-take of children's relationships with their peers has a profound effect on their success at school. Also important is their understanding of how groups of people can live and work comfortably and productively together. Being kind toward one another by behaving helpfully and cooperatively makes group living a more positive experience for all.

Prosocial Behavior: Acting Positively Toward Others

Prosocial behavior represents the most positive attributes of society. Acts of kindness such as helping, sharing, sympathizing, rescuing, defending, cooperating, and comforting benefit all persons, the givers and the receivers. When children and adults cooperate with one another by working toward a common goal or help someone by alleviating his or her distress or facilitating work or play, they contribute to an environment in which friendly interactions and productive group efforts abound (Gazda, Asbury, Balzer, Childers, Phelps, & Walters, 1995). Furthermore, in such an atmosphere, routine or uninteresting tasks are easily handled because no single person is burdened with them. In essence, then, a classroom in which prosocial values and behaviors are transmitted and encouraged tends to produce participants with a positive self- and group image. Further, they are likely to view themselves and others as competent and congenial (Kostelnik, Whiren, et al., 2002). Finally, children who learn to be kind tend not to be selfish or aggressive. Thus, providing instruction in prosocial behaviors within the classroom creates the kind of setting in which all learning is enhanced.

Once, researchers believed that if people were taught to think prosocially, corresponding prosocial behaviors would follow automatically. Unfortunately, this correlation does not hold true. Good thoughts do not necessarily lead to good deeds. Although children can, on cue, proclaim, "We're supposed to share," all reason may go out the window in the midst of a race to get the red marker. Children must be helped to go beyond thinking and saying what is appropriate to doing what is right. To accomplish this, they must go through a series of steps. First, they need to recognize that help or cooperation is required; second, they must decide whether or not to do something. Finally, they must perform a prosocial action that is appropriate for the situation at hand.

Prosocial Skills: Recognition, Decision, Action
Sensitivity to someone's cues for help or cooperation is the initial skill children must acquire to learn to be prosocial. The messages sent by others can be non-spoken (panting, crying, or sighing) or the more obvious strategies of complaining or requesting assistance. Surprisingly, although these signals seem clear to most adults, some children appear to ignore them. Either these children misunderstand their meaning, or they do not think the signs are meant for them. Thus, adults cannot assume that just because children are in the presence of such cues they necessarily recognize them.

Once children realize a person is in need, they must decide whether to act. Several factors play a role in their decision. Youngsters are most likely to respond to people they know, like, or admire (Hartup, 1998). If they are in a positive mood, they will more likely act than if they are upset or in a neutral frame of mind. In addition, they feel more responsible toward a person who has extended kindness to them in the past or from whom they hope to reap future rewards (Denhan, 1995). In general, older children and adults will respond independent of personal gain because more-generalized notions of justice play a role in their thinking.

Finally, a child must perform an action. The suitability of the action that they choose is influenced by their ability to take another person's perspective into account and by their instrumental know-how (Berk, 2003).

At any stage of this process, children may experience difficulties. They may misinterpret cues or overlook them, they may miscalculate which behaviors would be appropriate, or they may act hastily or incompletely. As they mature and gain experience, their efforts will more likely meet with greater success.

Promotion of Prosocial Behavior As the primary conveyors of social values outside the family, educators play a key role in influencing children's prosocial behavior. Furthermore, educators have a profound effect on the degree to which children demonstrate prosocial behaviors in the classroom. Educators can increase children's kindness by creating an environment in which the educators model the behaviors they expect of children, look for instances of prosocial behaviors and reward them, and teach children directly to think and act prosocially (Gestwicki, 1998; Kostelnik, Whiren, et al., 2002).

In addition, children can be given many planned opportunities to participate in tasks and situations that allow them to rehearse prosocial skills. Children benefit greatly from these occasions and demonstrate a greater frequency of such positive behaviors in similar circumstances (Honig & Wittmer, 1996). This increase in positive behaviors occurs because children can better remember both the appropriate behavior and the cues that signal which conditions apply in a given circumstance when they have had a chance to practice. (Specific techniques that combine oral descriptions and explanations with practice are illustrated in the Activity Suggestions section of this chapter.)

The educator's role is significant in influencing children's prosocial actions. In the same vein, how educators teach children about expectations for behavior affects children's ability to understand and follow rules.

SOCIALIZATION: CHILDREN'S BEHAVIOR AND ADULT EXPECTATIONS

Many of children's interactions with teachers and other adults in school revolve around rules. Children are continually learning what the rules are and how to act in accordance with them. This process is not simple for children to master.

Educators often expect children to learn classroom and school rules within a few weeks and then be able to follow them consistently. Failure to do so has frequently been viewed as willfulness or resistance on the child's part, and such youngsters develop reputations that follow them throughout their school career. Although teachers believe that teaching rules is important, they often resent having to take class time to teach children about the rules more than a few times. Furthermore, because following rules is an expected behavior, infractions are often noticed more than compliance. Learning rules and being able to follow them takes time. Just as in other areas, children vary both in the rates at which they acquire the knowledge and skills and in the extent of adult intervention they require.

One major goal of early childhood educators is for children to be able to understand and then follow the rules even when adults are not present; in other words, for children to achieve self-discipline. How this can be achieved is such a vital aspect of children's social development that chapter 6 is devoted entirely to how children develop self-control and what the adult role is in the process.

SOCIAL RESPONSIBILITY

Many changes have occurred in the world during the past few decades, and more changes are to come. Families have become more mobile, youngsters with special needs are being integrated in ever-increasing numbers into classrooms, neighborhood boundaries are more permeable, and so children are exposed to a wider variety of people. In addition, the health of our planet has been brought into question. Furthermore, as a consequence of the impact of world events, we realize that we truly live in a global village (Swiniarski, Breitborde, & Murphy, 1999). At the same time, educators have become aware that social attitudes are formed when children are young. Given these facts, the question becomes how to prepare our young people to live in a pluralistic society in ways that uphold the democratic principles of fairness, equal opportunity, and justice. Thus, we have come to understand that we must teach children about their responsibility to the world beyond their doorstep. Doing so is the essence of encouraging children to become good citizens of their classroom, their neighborhood, and the larger society they will encounter as they mature. Through attention to social issues that are important to children's lives now, we are teaching them the attitudes and skills they will need to make reasoned decisions now and in the future. Through instruction in peaceful conflict negotiation, strategies for confronting bias, and the promotion of prosocial behaviors, we are giving them the tools.

Valuing Diversity

religion	ethnicity	gender role
race	age	family composition
language	abilities	lifestyle
interests	values	skin color

This list represents only a fraction of the variations children encounter among the people in the school setting. Some of these differences are immediately apparent to children, whereas others take longer for them to discover. Children's attitudes about issues of diversity have their roots in childhood. Even before they are 3 years old, children notice others' physical attributes and begin to compare these features with their own. As their experiences broaden and their cognitive and language abilities develop, young people also become aware of and comment on more-subtle distinctions (Alejandro-Wright, 1985; P. Katz, 1982).

Once, people thought that simply bringing children into contact with others who were different from them would lead to understanding and tolerance. Unfortunately, this hope has proven to be naive. In some cases, already-negative perceptions are strengthened rather than eliminated when diverse people are introduced into somewhat stable groups (S. Cohen, 1977). This negative effect occurs in part because adults neglect to take into account children's development and their own biases in teaching children positive responses to the differences.

The development of valid concepts of race, gender, and differing physical abilities appears to be age and stage specific, with older children displaying more-accurate understandings than those of younger children (Alejandro-Wright, 1985; P. Katz, 1982). As an example, until about age 8 years or older, children are not sure which physical attributes are constant and which will change with time. Furthermore, their rudimentary notions of causal relationships make determining what the process of change entails difficult for them. For instance, they may conclude that dark skin is dirty and, if washed, will turn white; that they may lose the function of their legs if they play with a child in a wheelchair; or that if a girl gets a short haircut she turns into a boy. Although exactly when children understand these issues is unclear, what is clear is that such understanding is gained during childhood.

Another developmental issue that comes into play is children's continuing efforts to sort out likenesses and differences. In their attempts to determine who is like them and who is not, their criteria may be based on obvious physical characteristics alone. At certain friendship stages, when children are seeking others who are like them, they may exclude children on the basis of these external attributes unless other similarities are brought to their attention.

In addition to developmental considerations, how children evaluate differences and how they consequently behave are highly influenced by the adults around them, their peers, and the societal values as expressed in the media and other outside sources. Children's opinions of both their worth and others' worth are affected by these forces, especially negative forces (W. E. Cross, 1985). Therefore, early childhood professionals must pay attention to the messages they convey about diversity in the settings they create, the teaching materials they use, and the manner in which they respond to children's behavior and words.

Creating Inclusive School Environments Inclusive school environments and teaching practices are those in which all forms of diversity are fairly and consistently represented. By virtue of the interpersonal interactions and planned activities that occur, the physical structure of the space, and the materials on walls and shelves, communities are created in which all people, adults and children alike, feel acknowledged, accepted, and valued (Sapon-Shevin, 1983).

One strategy for ensuring that diversity is valued is to make sure that classroom activities and materials represent different cultures, different ages, different lifestyles, people with differing abilities, and men and women in non-sex-stereotypical roles. Diverse people should be deliberately introduced and integrated into programs on an ongoing basis rather than on a special basis. Furthermore, all materials used in the educational setting must be examined so that stereotypical portrayals of groups are not unconsciously displayed or categories of people are not left out. In addition to the obvious (e.g., Native Americans shown with feathers in their hair or only at Thanksgiving), more subtle cues should be explored. For instance, classrooms and school hallways that feature only Christmas trees in December send the message to non-Christians that their holidays and traditional practices are not important. Furthermore, cultural awareness should focus on how people live today in the United States, not only on cultures and people in other nations. Thus, the focus of teaching should be on Asian Americans, African Americans, and Hispanic Americans rather than on people's countries of origin (Derman-Sparks & the ABC Task Force, 1989).

Adults have a responsibility to help children sort out valid conclusions from those based on incomplete or erroneous information. Educators can do this by providing accurate data for children to work with as well as deliberately setting up experiences that confound children's stereotypical assumptions. Answering children's questions honestly and carrying out frank and open discussions about the differences children observe is another way to help children gain important knowledge about others.

One additional strategy is to help children recognize the effects of their actions and words on others (Kostelnik, Whiren, et al., 2002). Pointing out instances of kindness and explaining how they made another child feel encourages further prosocial behaviors. In addition, children should be confronted directly when they show evidence of overtly biased behavior or opinions. Letting children know that insensitive remarks made someone feel hurt or angry is the first step in changing their behavior in a more socially responsible direction (Derman-Sparks & the ABC Task Force, 1989). The adult must be sure to indicate a positive alternative to the child and determine any appropriate acts of restitution.

Changing the Curriculum Several stages of curricular reform have been identified as teachers struggle with issues of inclusion in their programs (Banks, 1988). Although these approaches were originally designed to describe ethnic content, they can be generalized to encompass all areas of diversity. The first stage that teachers often go through is called the *contribution approach*. This approach focuses on heroes, holidays, and discrete cultural elements. For example, teachers introduce heroes into the program, treating their lives as exemplars with special abilities. They are not integrated into the curriculum, nor are the issues they confront as members of minority groups, such as discrimination, truly explored. Rather, their successes are promoted, and they are treated as exotic, exceptional human beings, not representative of their group.

Mr. Raymond used a popular first step to introduce concepts of racial diversity by presenting the life and work of Dr. Martin Luther King, Jr., during a week in which African-American history was celebrated. Pictures of Dr. King were prominently displayed in the classroom, his "I Have a Dream" speech was read to the second graders, and Dr. King was depicted as a singular human being. Once the week ended, the pictures were taken down, and no mention was made of voting rights or Dr. King for the remainder of the year. On reflection, Mr. Raymond concluded that the children had not learned much. He realized further that he had not given children information about what the absence of voting rights would mean to people within the fabric of a democracy and that, although introducing Dr. Martin Luther King, Jr., to the children represented a step for him as an educator, his method had made little impact on the children.

The *ethnic-added approach* is a second means teachers use to introduce content related to diversity into their programs. At this level, content, concepts, and themes are added without changing the curricular structure. That is, although important steps have been taken to integrate diversity, the curriculum is still based on a majority-centered view.

Ms. Somerset enjoyed a first-grade class that included children of several ethnic backgrounds. As the winter holidays approached, she made a special effort to encourage parents to demonstrate holiday celebrations representative of their cultures. Parents brought in special songs, stories, and foods, and demonstrated lighting candles as befit their specific holiday. Children and families enjoyed the celebrations. However, when the youngsters returned to school after winter break, all evidence of the diverse cultural artifacts that had been collected were gone, none of the songs were included in the classroom repertoire, none of the stories were added to the library, and the classroom had reverted to its "normal" state. Ms. Somerset was pleased to have involved so many families in the preholiday experience but decided that next time she would incorporate the activities on an ongoing basis.

The third stage is called the *transformational approach*. At this level, teachers have infused various perspectives, frames of reference, and content into their curricula. The result is that students will come away with a greater understanding of the complexities of our society and how society is a result of a synthesis and interaction among the diverse elements that compose it.

Mrs. Sterns often used literature to integrate diversity into the curriculum. For her kindergarten students this year, she focused on common themes, such as stories of origins—how the earth was formed, how the sun and moon got in the sky, how people and animals came onto the earth, and so on. She found tales from Native American, African, and European sources. She read these to the children. They discussed the similarities and differences among the various versions and wrote their own origin myths. In addition, children used art media to illustrate their ideas, created props to dramatize their stories, and struggled to understand why people might develop stories to make sense out of what might otherwise seem impossible to comprehend. In addition, Mrs. Sterns used parents as resources for both scientific and fanciful explanations. Acceptance of divergent thinking was a hallmark of the study, as no one person had the "correct" answers.

Banks' (1988) final stage is called the *decision-making and social action approach*. The most sophisticated of all, this approach includes all elements of the previous stage but requires children to make complex decisions related to their study and to take some action.

The year following his initial inclusion of Dr. Martin Luther King, Jr., in the second-grade curriculum, Mr. Raymond expanded his and the children's horizons. He helped children understand the context in which Dr. King and others worked by giving them background on the struggle for voting rights that had occurred in the communities in the South for many years before it became recognized nationwide. Then he tried an experiment to help children understand what not having the same right to vote as your neighbor would be like. Arbitrarily, he chose a physical characteristic, blue eyes, and declared that all children possessing this trait were ineligible to vote on a choice for a class treat on Friday. He separated the blue-eyed children from the rest, seating them at the back of the class, and proceeded with the election. After it was over, he monitored a heated discussion by the voters and the nonvoters about bias, discrimination, fairness, equality, and the like. As they discussed, they speculated on various options that might be available for remedying the situation. They found that no solution was simple. In this experiment, children were exposed to a taste of some of the issues that disenfranchised individuals face. This experience was the first of many hands-on strategies Mr. Raymond used to bring what might seem abstract and out of children's realm of experience into the focus of their lives.

Changing Adults' Thinking The paradigm set forth by Banks (1988) offers much information for the teacher. A blending of the approaches just described seems a reasonable way to tackle the difficult task of changing your thinking and practicing to be more inclusive. Professionals must examine their attitudes and practices for evidence of prejudice. This task is not easy because bias may rear its head in numerous subtle ways and emanate from sources that relate to early life experiences and learnings. Thus, by monitoring their behavior, as well as confronting children's stereotypical beliefs, reinforcing positive behaviors, and proactively teaching about the similarities and differences that make us all part of the human family, educators can help children make strides toward a bias-free society.

Becoming Environmentally Aware

Individuals on almost every side of every issue use a popular saying: "Think globally; act locally." In no area is this more apt than when we are teaching children about their responsibility for the indoor and outdoor environments in which they live and play.

Environmental ecology deals with the complex interrelationships among all living things and their surroundings (C. Seefeldt, 2001). Like most areas of study, awareness of the environment spans more than one domain. It involves principles from science and the broad goals of the social domain. In addition, affective development is

The beginnings of social responsibility develop as children contribute to their community.

involved because the problems of caring for the environment relate to how children's behavior affects others. Thus, although pollution in its most overt forms is a difficult concept for children to understand, youngsters can, and should, be made aware of the effects of their actions on their milieu. Attention to the environment has some far-reaching consequences in the lives of young children. Just as attitudes about differences are established at an early age, so, too, are attitudes toward the world. As we know, adults exert a powerful influence on children, and the behaviors that adults display are more significant in proclaiming their values than any words they profess. Thus, for children to become sensitive to the needs of the global community, adults must demonstrate their concern through their actions.

Specific planning within the classroom in terms of activities and routines is an effective way of conveying children's responsibility for their setting. Children can be taught to clean up their messes, either individually or with help from others. They can be shown how to generate less waste in school and at home and to find uses for scrap materials. A classroom recycling center is one way to prompt their excitement and to create a hands-on, concrete demonstration project for other classes to emulate. An activity as simple as planting, caring for, and harvesting plants can make an important contribution to the classroom as well. Activities such as these reveal important causal relationships to

children because the children can experience directly the results of changes in their actions.

In addition, children can be made aware of the conflicting needs of human beings for resources and society's concerns about the untimely depletion of these resources. The classroom can be a microcosm for learning how to resolve these dilemmas in democratic ways, through negotiation and compromise.

SOCIAL STUDIES

Social studies is defined as "the study of people in society, past and present, and their relations with each other and the world around them, both near and far" (National Council for the Social Studies, 1998). The goals for social studies focus on expanding children's horizons and teaching the elements of citizenship in a democratic society. The ultimate goal is to produce individuals who feel good about themselves and develop the necessary concepts and skills to make worthwhile contributions to society through thinking and decision making. Social studies curricula take their perspectives from a variety of disciplines, such as anthropology, economics, geography, history, human ecology, political science, psychology, and sociology. All these disciplines are similar in that they focus on the understanding of human behavior; however, the key concepts of each make unique contributions to children's knowledge (C. Seefeldt, 2001).

Anthropology is the study of human beings and their diverse cultures and lifestyles. Children begin to understand that people represent many cultures as they come in contact with others in their school and community. Even people who look the same may have different beliefs, different ways of celebrating holidays and festivals, and different family structures. Children also learn that people who seem unlike them may share similar ideas and values.

Economics informs us about how people produce and consume goods and services. Children can be made aware of the diverse kinds of work adults engage in by talking with and observing persons who fight fires, care for people, buy and sell goods, grow produce and livestock, work in factories and build useful products, and perform services for pay. Money exchange and the value of money is a topic that can be introduced to children at a young age. Consumer education, such as learning how to evaluate advertising, is critical for children to understand. One component of such education is for children to be able to distinguish their needs from their wants and to make informed decisions on the basis of the difference.

Geography illuminates the characteristics of the earth's environment and the relationship of this environment to the people who live in it. Where things are in children's near environment is important information for them to have as they move farther from their home. In addition, children develop a better appreciation for the natural world and its resources when they learn to be responsible for the waste they generate and the ways in which they dispose of this waste. Geography also relates to how people get from one place to another and the reasons they choose to move.

History deals with the past, the concept of change, and the forces that influence it. Important to the lives of young children is their personal history and that of their family. Every child has an ancestry, and becoming aware of their forebears helps children develop a sense of belonging and pride. History also deals with the passage of time and the sequence of events. In the early childhood setting, these elements are built into the structure of daily living. Bringing them to children's consciousness is the first step in their understanding temporal relationships (National Center for History in the Schools, 1994).

Human ecology is the study of the interplay between the individual and all systems with which that person comes in contact, both directly and indirectly. So, for example, the child is a member of both the home and the school setting and is indirectly affected by his or her parents' workplaces. Communication among individuals in these systems is also a part of the human ecological perspective and underscores the importance of regular contact between the child's family and educators at school. When children bring items or information from home to the classroom, and when messages are sent home about possible visitors or field trips, children are active participants in their social groups.

Political science relates to the management and governance of social units. This discipline very much relates to teaching children about living in a democracy. Children have opportunities to practice aspects of democratic living when they learn to understand the rules that govern the classroom and when they become involved in making some of these rules themselves. Within the social studies curriculum, children learn that everyone has rights and responsibilities and that sometimes they must negotiate and bargain for the things they need. Furthermore, they participate in group problem solving about issues that are important to them. All these experiences teach them how societies function for the benefit of all members.

Psychology reveals the internal workings of the mind—how people think, feel, and respond. Every time children approach an interaction, they are dealing with their emotions. They are busy learning to recognize what these emotions are, the variety of ways in which they are expressing them, and what the impact of such expression is on other people. As they develop and extend their prosocial skills, children are discovering more about others' emotions and needs. For instance, teaching children about the similar and different ways people respond to holidays gives youngsters experience in understanding their own feelings and others'.

Sociology helps us understand the social groups in which we live. Like adults, children belong to many social groups, such as their family, class, after-school activity group, and congregation. How people function within these different settings—as leaders or followers, initiators or passive observers, dependent or independent thinkers—provides a focus for discussion among children. Specific activities can be planned so that children will sharpen their awareness of the roles they and others play in their groups.

From the earliest inclusion of social studies in the early childhood curriculum, real experiences have been the appropriate vehicles for teaching social studies content and concepts (Bredekamp & Rosegrant, 1992). Children's active and direct participation in projects and activities is the necessary means of instruction because it is congruent with what we know about children's development (Bredekamp & Copple, 1997). The classroom is an ideal arena within which children learn the social skills, values, and rules required for living in society. Therefore, for young children, social studies is viewed as an extension of their social development. Understanding that children learn best that which is most important to them, educators can logically translate children's natural concerns about their relationships with others and the world around them into studies of the self, the family, the school, and the community (National Council for the Social Studies, 1998). Thus, the integrative nature of social studies promotes children's understanding of the society in which they live.

Goals for Social Studies

As with other curricular domains, the goals for social studies are grouped by knowledge goals, skill goals, and attitude goals (National Council for the Social Studies, 1998). *Knowledge goals* focus on concepts that reflect the content of social studies, such as the uniqueness of all people, the interdependence of people, the influence of environment on people's choices of habitats and work, and the function and operation of social groups. Other knowledge goals deal with the structure of the social science disciplines, such as what and how we learn about human history and how people make decisions. Additional knowledge goals reflect similarities and differences among individuals and groups and how people learn to live together. *Skill goals* focus on children's mastery of techniques related to gathering

TABLE 14.3   Implementing the Social Studies Curriculum in the Classroom

Social Science Discipline	Experiences for		
	3- to 5-Year-Olds	5- to 7-Year-Olds	6- to 8-Year-Olds
Anthropology	Children are provided with a wok, chopsticks, plastic models of sushi, and plastic plates with Asian designs as normal props in the Family Living Center.	Children are taught two versions of a similar singing game, each with a different ethnic origin.	Children interview family members about their cultural heritage. They record on tape or paper a story that represents their heritage and share it with the class.
Economics	Children participate in a theme entitled "The Work People Do."	Children set up a store in the classroom. Classmates are allotted a limited amount of money with which to buy goods. They are encouraged to bargain or to barter other goods and services to get what they want.	Children develop a plan for a class project to earn money for a special field trip.
Geography	After a walk in the neighborhood, children are encouraged to use blocks to reconstruct their experience.	After a walk through the neighborhood, children arrange photographs of features in the area in the order in which they observed them. Later, they make a return trip to check out their recollections.	After a walk in the neighborhood, children create a map representing the buildings and other landmarks near the school.
History	Children bring in pictures of themselves as babies and dictate stories.	Children bring in pictures of their parent(s) as youngsters. They write or dictate descriptions comparing their parents' past and present appearances.	Children create their individual family trees. They obtain the information by interviewing family members.
Human ecology	A local kindergarten teacher spends the day in the preschool classroom, whereas on another day, the preschool teacher teaches in the kindergarten room.	Children address envelopes to themselves, go to the post office to mail them, and trace the progress of their mail through the system by observing the sorting machines, seeing a mail deliverer in action, and so forth.	To conclude a study of the community, children create a diorama, depicting the interrelationships among all the community service agencies, such as the post office, fire department, police station, and the like.
Psychology	Each child wears a badge during the day that reads, "I'm special because I _____" (child decides what the special attribute or skill is).	Each child works on an "All About Me" book. They list in it favorite objects, favorite people, things they dislike, and other categories they choose.	On a table set aside for the purpose, children place favorite items brought from home. They display the items, along with guidelines that others must follow in examining them. Children describe the articles to one another and explain why the articles are special.

Social Science Discipline	Experiences for		
	3- to 5-Year-Olds	5- to 7-Year-Olds	6- to 8-Year-Olds
Political science	During interpersonal disputes, children participate in conflict negotiation, with the teacher as mediator.	Children establish classroom rules for the safe use of a microscope on loan from the museum.	Children hold a mock election for a town council seat. A campaign gives children the opportunity to influence their "constituency."
Sociology	Children take turns conducting a rhythm instrument band.	Children participate in a theme on friends and friendships, during which they identify and practice friendship-making skills.	Small groups of children work on solving a designated classroom problem (e.g., determining how to make sure children's possessions remain undisturbed). The groups present their solutions to the class, where these solutions are discussed and evaluated.

information, improving their interpersonal interactions within their group, and problem solving, both in terms of content and social relations. *Attitude goals* relevant to social studies emphasize respecting individuals both similar to and different from themselves, understanding and appreciating their own and others' culture and traditions, and caring for the world around them. These goals and their implementation across the early childhood age range clearly encompass the entire range of the social domain.

Social Studies in the Classroom

How might a social studies curriculum look in practice for children of different ages? Table 14.3 includes sample experiences appropriate for the youngest children (3- to 5-year-olds), somewhat older children (5- to 7-year-olds), and the oldest children (6- to 8-year-olds). Children's maturity and prior access to the materials and activities will affect which experiences are best suited to their needs. Therefore, the age range should be viewed as a guide.

Clearly, teachers have the responsibility of teaching social studies directly, as well as helping children learn to have positive interpersonal interactions. This learning must take place in the context of the child's daily experience in the classroom. This is best accomplished when teachers carefully plan activities that relate to children's lives and take advantage of the spontaneous occurrences that are a natural part of group dynamics to teach important lessons. Active participation by children in the exploration of these issues ensures that they will derive the meaningful knowledge,

skills, and attitudes that are the foundations of a social studies curriculum. As a result, these children will demonstrate good citizenship in their school, their communities, and, ultimately, their world.

RELATIONSHIP BETWEEN THE SOCIAL DOMAIN AND COGNITION

Many practitioners may have difficulty justifying spending classroom learning time on improving children's social skills and helping them become more aware of the social world around them. However, in fact, while children are engaged in these pursuits, they are exploring and sharpening their physical knowledge, intuitive knowledge, representational thinking, social-conventional knowledge, language, and critical thinking skills.

Let us use as an example an activity outlined toward the end of this chapter: The People's Choice. To summarize, children are offered an opportunity to negotiate a conflict or a difference of opinion in a democratic way by voting. In the activity, the adult poses a problem for the children to solve—naming a classroom pet, for instance. Children examine the animal in an effort to understand its physical characteristics (physical knowledge). They may discuss its characteristics and thus learn the appropriate descriptive vocabulary (language). Names are solicited from children, which requires them to link the physical object to an abstract idea (representational thinking) and to recognize that the names written on the chart represent the animal. Each child has the opportunity to vote for his or her favorite (critical thinking and decision making). Finally, children determine which name has the most number of advocates—first by viewing the groups of children and guessing; second by using one-to-one correspondence, as the groups line up next to each other (logical-mathematical knowledge); and finally by counting (social-conventional knowledge). Throughout the decision-making process, children must separate what they *want* from what they *think*. Doing so requires a high level of cognitive functioning.

This brief examination of the relationship between cognition and the social domain illustrates that the two are inextricably linked and that we cannot delve into social issues and skills without engaging children's minds.

CURRENT EDUCATIONAL ISSUES

Teachers working with young children confront several issues in relation to social development and social studies. These issues represent key topics regarding the social domain and the early childhood curriculum.

Understanding the Relationship Between Social Development and Social Studies

To live productively in the world, children must have satisfying relationships with the people in it. This means knowing about and following societal expectations, making and keeping friends, working out interpersonal conflicts, being kind to others and accepting kindness from them, and recognizing and valuing diversity among people. As children become aware of the impact of their ideas and behaviors on others, they gain an awareness of their own point of view and an understanding of the perspectives of people different from themselves. They can also appreciate their own culture and family history. In addition, children become increasingly aware of the complex interrelationships among all things, living and nonliving, in the world. Through numerous experiences, children can be made cognizant of the necessary interdependence of people in any society and the need for responsible behavior toward the environment. Teachers can help children develop the skills they need to live in a peaceful world and provide opportunities for them to practice democratic problem solving and decision making. Doing so empowers children to affect the world they live in. As children's concepts broaden, teachers may introduce children to issues that go beyond their immediate concerns, through a focus on greater world issues, such as peace and war, homelessness and poverty, and vanishing species. Thus, the social realm requires children to look both within and outside themselves as they build their repertoire of social studies concepts.

Teaching Peace: The Classroom and Beyond

The definition of social studies includes aspects of how we live in our social world (Sunal, 1993). For children in formal settings, this world includes the home, the classroom, and the school or community center in which they spend most of their waking hours. Teaching children to generate and carry out peaceful solutions to conflicts involves helping them develop interpersonal cognitive and behavioral problem solving. Many teachers have adopted the conflict resolution model illustrated in this chapter, or similar models, as they work with youngsters in their individual classrooms. The question has arisen whether these same strategies can be applied to larger groups of children—in whole-school settings.

In fact, many schools have used a systematic approach to teaching children to make more-productive decisions in handling conflicts. *Peer coaching* is one such method reported to have widespread success. Older elementary school children are trained as conflict mediators. They are identifiable by their peers and by younger children by means of armbands or T-shirts as they operate on playgrounds and lunchrooms to recognize conflicts as they occur and to assist children in reaching nonviolent solutions. Other strategies include using *peace tables,* where children come together to settle differences before an argument has reached the boiling point. *The conflict wall* is an effort by yet another district to assist children in learning conflict resolution skills. In this instance, a wall in the principal's office displays a *conflict escalator* chart and posters to remind children, for instance, what to do when they are angry (P. Phillips, 1997). Although this idea has been used with older children, it can be adapted for use with younger children.

In all cases, active student participation and involvement of the community as a whole and parents in particular have resulted in positive outcomes (Weissberg, Shriver, Bose, & DeFalco, 1997).

Embracing Diversity: Interpretations and Misinterpretations

Important goals for education are exemplified by children who demonstrate self-respect, display self-confidence, possess the skills necessary for mastery over ideas and materials, approach new ideas and problems creatively, develop their individual potential to its highest level, and are productive members of society. An essential value of a good early childhood curriculum is that children of all races, religions, home languages, family backgrounds, economic circumstances, and cultures be treated with understanding and consideration. These values of equality and respect reinforce the democratic foundations of the

U.S. Constitution in our pluralistic society. How these ideas are implemented in daily practice varies enormously from program to program. Some educators interpret these guidelines to mean that differences among children are to be acknowledged if they arise in the normal course of play or conversation; others prefer to be proactive and to seek out and introduce the variations in children's lives to them and to plan discussions and activities that emphasize the uniqueness of individuals and social groups. A different interpretation is to practice democratic principles in the classroom by involving children in making choices about what they learn. Others extend this idea to include classroom governance as a mutual agreement between adults and children. Wherever such interpretations fall within the spectrum, they are consistent with the values and goals of a democratic society.

During the past several years, criticisms of these ideas and practices have surfaced from a number of sources. Some educators interpret the notion of embracing diversity as eliminating the standards and values that it is wrong to teach youngsters that differences have no distinctions and that no one culture is superior to another. Others misinterpret acceptance of each child's family structure as active promotion of homosexual lifestyles. Still others misinterpret the practices of offering choices to children and of democratic governance in the classroom to mean that children are being taught to flout authority, which, they believe, will lead to acceptance of criminal behavior. Still others object to including diverse ethnic festivities in schools, claiming they dilute traditional Christmas and Thanksgiving practices. Such interpretations claim to uphold family values and the "American Way."

Misinterpretations of the goals and attributes of diversity education for young children may be addressed by examining the practical outcomes for individuals and society. Building self-esteem in youngsters through acceptance of who they are and whence they come enables them to overcome adversity because they have the confidence to try again. Offering numerous opportunities to attempt solutions to problems, evaluate these solutions, and seek other pathways if those routes are not fruitful develops perseverance and creative thinking. This quality leads to the ability to hold a job later in life and to be responsible to your family. In the same vein, practicing decision making as a child allows you to more easily make productive decisions when the stakes are higher. Exploring ideas creatively, taking risks, not assuming there is a "right" answer, and understanding that a "right" answer may not exist has led, for instance, to technological innovation. Practice in decision making, reaching compromises, and experiencing the consequences of decisions fosters increased involve-

ment in governance on every level. Thus, expanding the possibilities for children to participate actively in their school lives is to be welcomed rather than feared and avoided. Finally, exposure to a wide variety of people, ideas, and customs enriches the individual as well as society. Learning to recognize and appreciate differences among people by embracing diversity is a key to more harmonious living for all.

Determining How the Social Domain Fits Into the School Day

Teachers have numerous demands on their time and resources during school. They are expected to plan for instruction in all the domains and to fulfill many other responsibilities. Where, then, does teaching about the social domain fit?

One important factor to recognize is that social development is integral to every part of school life. It appears in both implicit forms and explicit forms. Fundamentally, teachers are conveying information and values related to social development in everything they do in the classroom. How they treat children both individually and in groups; how they interact with aides, volunteers, and parents; which disciplinary strategies they employ; and how they respond to diversity of all sorts within their school community directly affect children's social development. In addition, teachers influence children when they take advantage of spontaneous opportunities to make children aware of the effect of their behavior toward others and when teachers model, encourage, and promote helpful and cooperative behavior. Other ways in which implicit instruction is conveyed is when teachers set up routines and practices during which children are expected to care for their immediate environment and the school environment. In all these areas, teachers are addressing important aspects of children's social development.

In addition to the subtle attention to social development, teachers can deliberately plan for the inclusion of the social domain in their program. In New Haven, Connecticut, a districtwide project has achieved exciting success (Weissberg et al., 1997). In contrast, trying to teach a social skill or improve children's prosocial behaviors by using a predigested, 15-minute kit is not very effective. Kits alone are not useful teaching tools because we now know that even when children can tell us appropriate behaviors, they may not actually act in those ways without practice in real-life situations. A far better approach is to integrate social concepts throughout the day-to-day transactions of the classroom. Such concepts can also be highlighted within particular activities. Planning thematic units that revolve around social studies content, such as "Families" "People in Our Community," and "The Work People

Do," is another way teachers can underscore these significant understandings and help children comprehend the relationship between what they are experiencing and the processes in the world outside themselves.

GOALS AND OBJECTIVES

The ultimate goals of education in the social domain are for children to develop successful patterns of interaction with peers and adults, gain internal control, acquire and practice prosocial values, demonstrate positive attitudes toward diversity, and build social studies knowledge. For children to progress toward these goals, they must have opportunities to attain interpersonal skills, learn the expectations of school and society, learn about and practice prosocial behaviors, gain respect and appreciation for the wide variety of people in the world, and achieve understandings and skills that relate to social studies.

Intermediate Objectives

As children progress toward the ultimate goal, they will demonstrate the following 23 competencies:

1. Develop play skills (e.g., initiate play, join a group at play, make suggestions, take suggestions, recognize ways to deal with unpleasant social situations and the emotions associated with them, learn to play productively alone)
2. Develop peer friendship relationship skills (e.g., how to initiate, maintain, and terminate interactions and relationships constructively)
3. Become aware of other people's opinions, viewpoints, and attitudes
4. Learn to negotiate conflicts in democratic ways (e.g., compromising, voting, bargaining)
5. Develop empathy for others (recognize others' emotions, respect others' emotional responses)
6. Perceive adults as sources of gratification, approval, and modeling
7. Learn how to conform to reasonable limits set on behavior, play space, use of materials, or the types of activities in which they are involved
8. Identify the reasons for classroom rules
9. Distinguish acceptable from unacceptable classroom behavior
10. Use their knowledge of appropriate behavior in one circumstance to determine appropriate conduct in another
11. Begin to develop skills related to self-control (e.g., impulse control, resistance, delayed gratification, and positive social actions)
12. Learn approved behaviors related to social and ethnic customs (e.g., manners and other respectful behaviors)
13. Learn how to cooperate (work with others toward a common goal)
14. Learn how to be helpful (share information or materials, give physical assistance, offer emotional support)
15. Develop awareness of and concern for the rights and well-being of others
16. Develop positive attitudes about belonging to a group beyond the family
17. Become aware of similarities and differences among people
18. Develop positive attitudes toward people who are different from themselves
19. Develop an awareness of and a respect for the values, ethnic background, family traditions, culture, gender, differing abilities, and special needs of others
20. Become aware of how people live together in families, neighborhoods, and communities
21. Develop a sense of responsibility for the environment
22. Develop knowledge related to social studies content in the following areas (see Table 14.3):
    - Anthropology (e.g., culture)
    - Economics (e.g., money, consumerism, work)
    - Geography (e.g., home and school environs)
    - History (e.g., personal history, family history)
    - Human ecology (e.g., child–school–home connection)
    - Psychology (e.g., understanding personal emotions and those of others)
    - Political science (e.g., democratic principles and practices, conflict resolution)
    - Sociology (e.g., individuals and communities)
23. Develop skills related to social studies content, such as collecting data, mapping, and making decisions

TEACHING STRATEGIES

Following are 12 strategies that educators can use to teach children skills in the social domain.

1. *Help children make friends at school by using their names.* Children feel most comfortable interacting with people whose names they know. Thus, acquainting children with one another's names is a basic strategy for facilitating children's friendships. To accomplish this, use children's names frequently. Identify by name youngsters who are sitting near one another, working

together, and playing with one another. Unfamiliar or uncommon names will seem less strange with frequent repetition. Be sure you know how to pronounce every child's name correctly.

2. *Help children make friends at school by promoting social interactions.* To help children become more aware of others in their group, you can deliberately pair children to work on projects. Choose children who have something in common. Remember to point out these common attributes, attitudes, preferences, or shared experiences so that the youngsters will become more aware of them. Shy children, in particular, benefit from this technique, but it is effective with others as well. For the benefit of all children, remember to provide numerous opportunities during the school day for children to interact with one another informally. Another related idea is to plan activities that require more than one child's participation. Observe how children behave with one another and use this information in future planning.

3. *Provide activities that allow children to practice social skills.* Use the suggestions following this section to create activities that focus on specific social skills. For instance, use skits to teach children numerous ways to let others know that they want to play. Carry out discussions during which children generate alternatives and explore the effectiveness of different solutions. As a follow-up, create opportunities for children to practice the strategies in real-life situations. Then, provide them with on-the-spot information regarding their progress in applying their knowledge. This approach will help them determine which techniques are successful and encourage them to eliminate those that are not. Other examples include deliberately setting out materials in such a way that children must ask, bargain, or trade to get what they want.

4. *Help children become more helpful and cooperative.* A necessary first step in this process is to recognize and acknowledge the times when children behave in positive or prosocial ways. Pointing out such instances increases the chances that children will repeat the acts of kindness. Another strategy is to plan activities in which children have opportunities to practice helping or cooperating. For instance, activities in which children must work together cooperatively to reach a common goal are far more supportive of children's prosocial behavior than those that pit child against child or group against group.

5. *Help children understand and follow expectations for behavior.* Use the guidelines outlined in chapter 6 to establish appropriate rules. Promote the development of children's internalization of rules through the use of the positive guidance strategies outlined there.

Indira's horizons have expanded through her relationship with Mrs. Anna, a classroom volunteer.

6. *Help children develop positive attitudes toward diversity.* As is well known, familiarity with a wide range of people helps children be more accepting of differences. Therefore, one valuable strategy is to present children with opportunities to interact with adult members of their own and other cultural groups, individuals who display varying physical abilities, older people, and younger people. For example, invite grandparents into the classroom to talk with children about what life was like when they were growing up. Ask them to talk also about the activities that they engage in at present to dispel stereotypical attitudes about old people's being helpless. Ask parents in the group to come in to tell stories remembered from their childhood and, if possible, bring books in their language of origin. Send home a request to families for recipes from their culture. Finally, use neighborhood resources to acquaint children with people who are different from themselves. In sum, introduce and celebrate diversity by connecting it to children's common experience in the classroom.

7. *Provide children with classroom activities, materials, and discussions that address the wide range of diversity.* Ensure that diversity education and awareness is an ongoing part of your classroom by planning multicultural activities that are integrated into the daily routines of the program rather than reserving them only for holidays or special occasions. Check the

pictures, books, learning materials, and other classroom props for evidence of stereotypical portrayals of any group. In some cases, remove them; in others, use the biased depictions as springboards for discussions with the children. When appropriate, create new pictures that more justly represent the true diversity in the world. Finally, engage children in sending letters of criticism and concern to manufacturers who are producing and marketing toys and games that undermine a fair portrayal of an ethnic, a racial, a gender, or an ability issue.

8. *Help children deal with stereotypical ideas.* The first part of this process is to provide accurate information about the differences and similarities that children perceive. This means that you should respond openly and honestly to children's observations and to the questions they ask. Giving them chances to explore differences by providing direct experiences is an important component. For example, activities during which children compare and graph skin color or hair texture sharpens children's awareness while presenting variety in a positive light. Another aspect of this strategy is to build children's critical thinking skills so that they will become more attuned to evidence of prejudice—within themselves, in others, and as portrayed in the media. Increasing their prosocial attitudes will allow them to respond to these situations in positive ways. Furthermore, the more prosocial the child, the more likely that he or she can come to the aid of a friend. The final step is to assist children in defending themselves against bias directed toward them. School personnel are an important influence on how children view themselves and can therefore be effective in teaching children coping skills. Work with youngsters in designing spoken responses to name-calling. Allow them time in the classroom to practice with their peers in the safe haven of the classroom. Give them opportunities to talk about their experiences within school time.

9. *Help children learn to care for their near and far environments.* Give children practical experiences in cleaning up the classroom, the school hallways, the playground, and other areas in which they work. Use activities such as those suggested in this chapter to alert children to the uses of materials they would otherwise discard. When engaged in picking up litter, readying the classroom for the next day, and so on, use music to lighten the burden. Have children perform these tasks in groups so that they feel a sense of group participation and camaraderie and further develop their repertoire of shared experiences. Base themes around the issue of recycling. For example, prepare projects for children to ascertain the recycling efforts of their community, and invite local groups with interests in these matters to give presentations to the class.

Assist children in assessing what actions they, as young people, can reasonably take.

10. *Help children build social studies concepts by practicing democracy in the classroom.* Plan activities in which children have opportunities to identify, generate solutions for, and carry out solutions for problems inherent in group living. One way to do this is for children to create some of their own classroom rules and designate the appropriate consequences for infractions of these rules. When work is to be done in caring for the classroom, let children decide the means for handling them. In addition, promote children's abilities to evaluate the techniques they choose and to redesign the strategies as needed. Some school policies can also be decided by children and teachers working together. (An example of this in operation is described in chapter 6.) An additional way to practice democracy is for teachers to model strategies for helping children solve interpersonal conflict peacefully. Take on the role of mediator in the conflicts that arise in the classroom or on school grounds. Train peer coaches to assume this role. In either case, with experience and feedback, children develop skill in managing their disputes and the conflicts of others in nonaggressive ways.

11. *Help children build social studies concepts through theme choices.* When deciding on themes for teaching in the classroom, choose some that focus on social studies content. Such topics as the self, the family, the community, the interdependence of people, and caring for the environment are subjects in which children are naturally interested because these topics are directly related to youngsters' lives and activities. Other aspects of social studies can be addressed, for example, when you teach children that people learn about the past from evidence left by others and that they, too, can leave records for others to study.

12. *Help children build social studies concepts and skills across the curriculum.* Social studies is truly an integrative area of focus. For example, teach historical understanding and literature comprehension through the use of modern and old versions of the same story. Another idea is to compare the ways of living of two families during different periods in history, assessing both similarities and contrasts (e.g., *Little House on the Prairie* books can be read alongside a modern story by Judy Blume). Assist children in relating mapping skills both to geography and to mathematics when they represent an area of their school in a diorama after having determined the unit of measure they will use. Combine political understanding with increased self-esteem as you aid children in expressing their needs and wants during a conflict negotiation session. These suggestions are only a few examples of how social studies can pervade daily life in the classroom.

ACTIVITY SUGGESTIONS

Following is a set of activities designed to encourage children to practice the social strategies outlined in this chapter. Each subarea of social development has been addressed by at least one activity. Thus, plans are offered that touch on developing play and friendship skills, negotiating conflict, recognizing other viewpoints, establishing rules, cooperating, helping, recognizing similarities and differences between self and others, and solving problems of group living. These lesson plans are aimed initially at 5-year-old children, with suggestions for simplification and extension so that they can be used successfully with children 3 to 8 years of age. Easily obtained materials are listed for each plan, when appropriate.

✎ Using Skits to Teach Social Skills*
(For Children of All Ages)

Objective 1   For children to recognize and understand play skills.

Materials   Two dolls, puppets, or pictures of children; several small blocks or other objects

General information   An effective strategy for introducing to and reinforcing particular play skills of children is to use skits or short scenarios. Children enjoy watching these presentations and can learn a great deal about ways to interact with others. However, simply viewing them is not sufficient. Adults must point out the pertinent features of the interplay and pose questions that help children clarify their understanding. Older children benefit from opportunities to reenact the scenes and to generate their own. Following are some general guidelines for developing and presenting skits to children.

Procedure

1. Select one play skill on which you want to focus.
2. Decide on the medium of presentation. Use realistic props such as dolls, puppets, or photographs that look like children rather than animals or cartoon characters. Be sure the dolls or puppets represent both sexes (or are androgynous) and depict a variety of racial and ethnic groups and differing physical abilities.
3. Outline a script that is succinct but consists of five parts:
   a. Demonstration of a skill
   b. Demonstration of lack of the skill

_____

*Many of these ideas are based on skits developed for *Teaching Young Children Using Themes*, M. J. Kostelnik (Ed.), Glenview, IL: Good Year Books, 1991.

   c. Explanation by the adult
   d. Discussion by the children
   e. Opportunity for children to use the props
4. Write out the statements and questions you will use to facilitate discussion: which characters demonstrated the skill, which showed lack of skill, the reaction of each character, how viewers evaluated the behaviors and why, and what they think the characters could do to improve their situation. Be sure to include both effective strategies and ineffective strategies. Doing so is important for helping children distinguish appropriate from inappropriate behaviors in a variety of situations.
5. Before introducing the skit to children, rehearse it until you feel confident. Write the questions you want to ask on cue cards, if needed.
6. Present the skit. Seat children in a semicircle facing you so that everyone can see your face and hands and the space directly in front of you. Use a low bench or table to display the props.
7. Say, "Today we are going to talk about friends. Here are two dolls. We are going to pretend that these dolls are real children just like you. Their names are Sarvesh and Cathy. They are 5 years old and go to a school just like ours. Watch carefully and see what happens."
8. After you present the skit, ask the questions you prepared, adapting them to situations that arise. Paraphrase children's ideas. If children have difficulty thinking of ideas, prompt them by providing suggestions.
9. Once children suggest their ideas, replay the scene, using each suggestion, one at a time. Ask the children to predict how Sarvesh will react in each case. Play out the scene as they suggest. Provide further information as appropriate. "John, you said Cathy could help Sarvesh build. Let's try that." (Maneuver the dolls and provide appropriate dialogue.) "Tell me what you think Sarvesh will do now."
10. Help children evaluate how well their solution worked. For example, "Sarvesh still doesn't know that Cathy wants to be friends. Tell us another way that Sarvesh could ask Cathy to play." Continue trying out their ideas. As children find solutions, praise them for thinking of ways to help the friends determine what to do. Summarize for them the ways that were tried and which proved more successful. As unfriendly solutions are suggested and role-played, point out that the results may be confusion, hurt feelings, sadness, and anger.
11. Remember that children learn from repetition, so you should present each social skill numerous times

and in several ways across time. Each time you do a new skit or repeat an old one, change the roles that the characters play so that in children's minds particular behaviors will not be associated with a specific figure.

To simplify   Carry out the activity with a very small group of children. Keep the scenarios short and simple. As children suggest solutions, act them out and point out the results.

To extend   Encourage the children to reenact on their own the scenario you demonstrated. Introduce open-ended scenarios in which a problem is posed but no solution (effective or ineffective) is modeled. Invite the children to create a solution and then evaluate it. Make dolls available to the children so that they can role-play other scenarios of their invention.

✎ Conflict Mediation* (For Children of All Ages)

Objective 4   For children to learn to negotiate conflicts in democratic ways.

Materials   None

General information   This activity is to be carried out during a naturally occurring conflict between two children in the classroom or on the playground. The exact nature of the conflict will influence the specific words and phrases used by the adult. Be sure to follow the steps of the mediation process exactly.

Step 1: Initiating the Mediation Process   The adult in charge observes signs of a conflict taking place. He or she moves to the site and watches carefully. The adult takes action if children seem unable to resolve the dispute or if they behave aggressively toward one another. The teacher stops any aggressive behavior and separates the combatants, saying, for example, "Sookyong and Alonzo, you are both pulling the toy. It looks as if you both want it. You have different ideas about how to use it. I'll hold it while we're deciding what to do. I'll give it back when we've figured it out." The adult then removes the toy; if territory is at issue, he or she safeguards it from being taken over by other children by declaring it out of bounds. This procedure stops the children from continuing to hit or grab, helps them to listen, and assists them in approaching a highly emotional situation more calmly and objectively.

Step 2: Clarifying Each Child's Point of View   Ascertaining and paraphrasing each child's perspective vis-à-vis the conflict is the second part of the process.

*For a more detailed discussion of this strategy, see Kostelnik, Whiren, et al. (2002).

The adult asks each one, in turn, to tell his or her side of the story without interruption: "Alonzo, you think . . . ," "Sookyong, you wanted . . ." Then the adult paraphrases every statement as it is made. This step is critical. For the adult to be trusted not to make an arbitrary decision, he or she must establish neutrality. Thus, he or she must not make any evaluation or comment on the merits of either position. This step in the process may take considerable time; do not expect inexperienced children to complete it quickly because they may require repeated chances to fully express their viewpoints.

Step 3: Summing Up   The adult should state the problem in mutual terms: "You each want. . . . We have a problem. It is important that we figure out what to do so that each of you will be satisfied and no one will get hurt." The problem thus defined implies that both youngsters have responsibility for the problem and its solution.

Step 4: Generating Alternatives   The focus of the fourth step is for children to think of a number of possible solutions to the problem. At this point bystanders as well as the combatants can have their say. Every time a solution is offered, the mediator paraphrases it to the youngsters directly involved. Each is then asked for an opinion. Children often initially reject a solution they later find acceptable, so even repeat suggestions should be brought to the table. The mediator can make suggestions such as "Sometimes when people have this problem, they can decide to share or take turns" if children seem unable to devise their own ideas. However, to truly leave the solution up to the children, the adult must not indicate by words or tone of voice that any one plan meets with his or her approval or disapproval.

Step 5: Agreeing on a Solution   The ultimate aim of this step is for individuals to agree on a plan of action that is mutually satisfying. The mediator should help children explore the possibilities and find one idea or a combination of ideas that is acceptable. The final agreement should generally involve some compromise on the part of the children and may not represent anyone's ideal. The mediator then states the result: "You've agreed that you can take turns. First, Sookyong will have it for 2 minutes, then Alonzo. It sounds as if you solved the problem!"

Step 6: Reinforcing the Problem-Solving Process   The adult must praise children for their hard work in reaching a solution. The goal is to demonstrate that the ultimate solution is not as important as the process for reaching it. Thus, children's emotional investment in the problem and the compromises that were made should be acknowledged as well.

FIGURE 14.1 How One Teacher Adapted The People's Choice Activity for a Child with Down Syndrome

Ronna

Ronna, a child in Mrs. Scarpetta's kindergarten class, had Down syndrome. Down syndrome is a common genetic disorder, affecting 1 of every 800 to 1,000 newborns. As a result of her disorder, Ronna showed moderate mental disability and exhibited a range of medical problems, such as low muscle tone, some delayed speech, and vision problems. To help Ronna be successful in school, Mrs. Scarpetta adapted activities for her special needs. One example was The People's Choice activity. First, Mrs. Scarpetta paid particular attention to where Ronna was seated—ensuring that Ronna had an unobstructed view of the board or paper on which she (the teacher) wrote and making sure that Ronna was near it. Second, Mrs. Scarpetta limited Ronna's choices to two, instead of the four or five she allowed other children. Doing so lessened Ronna's potential confusion. In addition, Mrs. Scarpetta paired Ronna with Damian, a more skilled partner, someone with whom Ronna played, and a potential "coach" in the choosing process. Mrs. Scarpetta was prepared to take on this role if Damian could not or did not want to do so. Finally, because Ronna's speech was limited and Ronna was not yet comfortable speaking in front of other children, Mrs. Scarpetta allowed her to indicate a choice through gesture.

Step 7: Following-Through The mediator should help the children carry out the terms of the agreement. This step is especially important so that they will learn to trust that the mediation process is worth the time and effort they have put into it.

To simplify Shorten some of the procedural steps if you see signs of boredom or fatigue, such as extreme restlessness, turning away, or yawning. Keep the dialogue short and simple.

To extend Teach children the mediator role.

✎ The People's Choice* (Figure 14.1) (For Older or More Experienced Children)

Objective 4 For children to learn to negotiate conflicts in democratic ways.

Materials Chalkboard and chalk, or large piece of writing paper and marking pen; three to five $3 \times 12''$ pieces of oaktag or sentence strips

Procedure

1. Introduce the activity by explaining that the whole group will select a name for a class pet, their favorite story, or whatever. Tell them they are going to vote, which means that each person will have a chance to choose a favorite name or story, and at the end they will determine which choice most people liked best. This choice will be the most popular because the most people liked it best, and it will be the one that wins.

2. Begin the process of choosing the alternatives. Limit the number of possibilities to three to five, enough so that children can have a real option but not so many that the cluster of children for each group is too small. Explain the limit to the children. Solicit suggestions and write down the first ideas on the chalkboard or paper, reading each aloud. When the list is complete, read each entry; running your hand under the word as you say it so that children can "read" it.

3. Write each option on a piece of oaktag and place it in a corner of the group area, separate from one another. For younger children, place an adult with each tag.

4. Tell children they are going to vote. Explain that they will choose only one of the options and will then stand by the corresponding name. Say that they may not change their minds once they are in place, but assure them that they will have many opportunities to vote throughout the year. Ask each child in turn to pick a favorite from the list. You should read the list before each child chooses, to remind him or her of the options and to minimize the likelihood that children will simply repeat the last person's selection. Write the child's name on the chalkboard next to the appropriate station. Children may abstain from voting. In this case, direct the individual to remain seated and offer another chance when everyone is finished.

5. Once the group has divided into areas, instruct children to look at the groups and estimate which has the most people (which choice is the most popular). Make sure everyone who wants to has a chance to speak. Paraphrase and then summarize their ideas.

6. Tell children that there are several ways to find out which is most popular. Line up two groups and ask the children which line is longer.

7. Paraphrase children's responses. Compare another group's line with the longer line. Continue comparing

---

*Many of these ideas are based on skits developed for *Teaching Young Children Using Themes*, M. J. Kostelnik (Ed.), Glenview, IL: Good Year Books, 1991, and *Themes Teachers Use*, M. J. Kostelnik (Ed.), Glenview, IL: Good Year Books, 1996.

until the longest line is determined. Then ask children which line has the most people.

8. With the children assisting, count the members of each group and record the number on the board or chart. Ask children which number is largest.

9. Explain again that the group with the most members represents the most popular choice. Ask children to tell which entry won the voting. Announce the result and mark it on the chart or board.

A child may insist that the name he or she has chosen is the most popular (even if this is not the case). Differentiate what the child *wants* to be true from what he or she *thinks* is true. Carefully review the evidence (counting again if necessary) until the child can accept the answer. Be patient. His or her response is evidence of egocentric thinking, not stubbornness.

To simplify Younger children may tire of the process before the final decision. If you detect signs of restlessness, move to the final step quickly (you may have to condense a few steps) so that the children experience closure to the activity. Limit the children's choices to two or three.

To extend In the step in which children "vote with their feet," substitute using their names on the chalkboard to represent them. Ask youngsters to count these names and compare quantities. If this is your plan, print the names clearly enough for children to see them easily. If children are having difficulty, quickly move to the original procedure. At a later time, ask children to recap the decision-making procedure that occurred and discuss the results. After a period of days or weeks, revote and compare the results with the original outcome.

✎ Alike and Different (For Children of All Ages)

Objective 17 For children to become aware of similarities and differences among people.

Materials Standing mirror, paper and pencil for recording children's observations

Procedure

1. Invite children two at a time to look into a mirror at themselves and each other. Help them discover characteristics they have in common and things that are different. This opportunity is ideal for pairing children who may be different in physical ableness, sex, and appearance to help them discover similarities beyond the obvious.

2. Make two lists, one in which likenesses are indicated ("We are alike") and another on which differences ("We are different") are recorded. Urge the children to begin with physical appearance and to move on to other attributes, such as interests, ideas, preferences, skills, handedness, number of siblings, letters in their names, and so on.

3. Tell the partners that as they observe more things about themselves and each other, they can add to the list throughout the day. At this point, allow the children to continue the activity without interference.

4. At the end of the day, suggest that children review the list and count all the things they discovered. Let them find out if they discovered more similarities or differences.

5. Repeat this activity, mixing up pairs until all the children have had a chance to be paired with each other. If ample time exists, repeat the activity later in the year and compare the new lists with the original lists. Determine whether the categories increase as children learn more about each other with time.

To simplify Focus only on physical attributes, adding other dimensions as children mature.

To extend Without naming the children involved, read some lists to the class and have them guess the pairs in question.

✎ We Are a Family (For Older or More Experienced Children)

Objective 19 For children to develop an awareness of and a respect for the values, ethnic background, family traditions, culture, gender, differing abilities, and special needs of others.

Materials Photographs of children and adults in the classroom and members of their families, a board on which to display these, pen, paper

General guidelines Request photographs from each child's family well in advance (2 to 3 weeks may be necessary). Assure the families that their photos will be returned. Label the pictures with names and relationships of each person. When you have secured the pictures, mount them temporarily on a bulletin board or oaktag, taking care not to mar them. Label the pictures with names and relationships of each person. Numerous activities using these family pictures can then be planned.

Procedure

1. During a period of time, allow each person in the class an opportunity to talk about his or her family. Respond positively to children's comments about any similarities or differences they notice in family structures. Avoid using terms like *only* when describing a child's family, as in "Judith has only a grandma in her family." Talk with children about the range of possible family compositions.

2. Encourage children to write or dictate stories about their family, telling what they like to do together, how each person in the family works to help the family, how they celebrate special holidays or occasions, and so on. Tell children to read these stories to the other children. Elicit comments from children about these practices. Reinforce the idea that each family does things in ways that are meaningful to its members.

3. Instruct children to graph independently the various families in the group. These graphs can be compared with those of one another as children identify which families are composed of many people, which fewer; which families include pets, which do not; which family memebrs look like other members, which do not.

4. Put the pictures in a book called *The Families in Our Class*. Include stories and other descriptions that children have written or dictated. Make the book available for children to "read."

To simplify   Focus on what children can see depicted in the photographs, such as family composition.

To extend   Delve more deeply into family traditions by asking children to bring in and talk about important family artifacts. Elicit information from families about favorite stories, jokes, and so forth. Write this information out for children to see. Compare it with other versions.

✎ Match-Ups (For Older or More Experienced Children)

Objective 18   For children to develop positive attitudes toward people who are different from themselves.

Materials   One set of pictures portraying people of different ages, sexes, cultural groups, races, and physical abilities; one set of pictures of commonly used tools, household implements, or office equipment; two boxes, one for each set of pictures; cards or tagboard

Procedure

1. Mount the pictures on cards or tagboard so that they will stand up to repeated use.
2. Explain the procedure to children. Pair children or establish small groups. Say that they are to pick one picture from each container, decide whether that person could use the tools, and give a reason for their decision.
3. As they work, listen for indications of children's stereotypical thinking (e.g., that a person in a wheelchair could not work in an office or that a man could not, or should not, use a blender). Confront these erroneous notions directly at a later time by giving children accurate and relevant

information. Ask other children who may be standing by for their ideas. Facilitate discussions between children on these issues.

4. If children persist in their opinions, plan to introduce activities or visitors into your program that will confound their assumptions. For example, invite an individual in a wheelchair to demonstrate his or her abilities, or do a cooking activity with the boys as well as the girls.

To simplify   Select pictures that depict a limited range of tools. Focus on one personal attribute at a time in your pictures.

To extend   Write children's ideas on a sheet of paper. Discuss them with the group as a whole. Help children determine how they could find answers to the questions that arise.

✎ Recycle-Ickles (For Children of All Ages)

Objective 21   For children to develop a sense of responsibility for the environment.

Materials   Medium-sized plastic bags labeled with each child's name, safety pins to secure them to children's clothing

Procedure

1. Carry out a discussion with children about trash—what it is, how it is generated, what the effect is on the environment, and what people can do to recycle materials that are no longer wanted. Explain that each child will collect the trash he or she produces during a day and place it in the plastic bag. Tell children that at the end of the day they will examine their trash and make determinations about how to reuse it. Then allow children to proceed on their own.
2. Plan a time at the end of the day for children to examine the things they have collected in their bags. Ask each individual to state one way he or she can recycle the materials (include the collection bag as well). Tell children that they are now "Recycle-Ickles." Provide each child with a badge that says, "I am a Recycle-Ickle. I reuse my trash."
3. Set aside a recycling center in which to store the materials they have collected and encourage children to reuse it on the following day.

To simplify   Use a classroom collection bag rather than individual bags.

To extend   Carry out the activity during an extended period. Evaluate whether children are able to generate less trash as time goes on. Set this as a goal for the school year. Extend the activity to include a collection of schoolwide trash. Follow a similar procedure and acknowledge the efforts of each classroom as they cut down on the trash they generate with time.

SUMMARY

The social domain encompasses four essential aspects of children's development and education: social skills, socialization, social responsibility, and social studies. The most effective paradigm for integrating this body of knowledge and skills is through children's personal experiences at home, at school, and in the broader community in which they live.

Learning to get along with others, both children and adults, is a major task of children and is one on which they spend an increasing portion of their time and energy. Some children make friends easily, and some do not. Friendships are so vital to human beings that friendless children and those whose interpersonal relationships with peers are unsatisfactory lead unhappy lives. The development of friendship skills—such as establishing contact, maintaining positive relationships, and resolving conflicts—and how they view friendships with time are important aspects of children's ability to make and keep friends. Youngsters who behave prosocially (e.g., helping, cooperating, comforting, and sharing) develop feelings of competence, enjoy many successful personal encounters, and respond positively to offers of prosocial actions from others. Being sensitive to someone else's cues, deciding to help, and taking appropriate actions are the facets of successful prosocial behavior.

How well children understand and enact the rules and customs of society is a measure of their socialization. Chapter 6 is devoted entirely to this topic.

Societal factors in our modern world mandate that children become aware of and share responsibility for the world beyond themselves—become good citizens in their homes, schools, and communities. Doing so requires that children learn to recognize and embrace diversity in all its forms and that they learn about and care for their immediate environment.

Social studies is the study of people in society, past and present, and their relations with one another, both near and far. Thus, the social studies encompass anthropology, economics, geography, history, human ecology, political science, psychology, and sociology. Knowledge goals for social studies reflect the uniqueness of people, their interdependence, the similarities and differences among people and groups, and the ways in which people have learned with time to live together in democratic ways. In addition, skill goals focus on children's mastery of tools and techniques, whereas attitude goals emphasize respect for all people and efforts to make the world a healthier and safer place to live. Thus, social studies is the framework within which all the areas of social development are integrated.

Applying What You Read in This Chapter

1. Discuss
   a. On the basis of your reading and your experiences with children, discuss each of the questions that open this chapter.
   b. Discuss the educational issue "Embracing Diversity: Interpretations and Misinterpretations" raised in this chapter. Do you agree with the positions taken in the text? Explain your reasons. Include personal experiences you may have had.
   c. Using Table 14.3, create an additional activity in each category that is appropriate for the children with whom you work.

2. Observe
   a. Observe a group of children for signs of prosocial and antisocial behavior. Tally the incidents of each and summarize the results. Be sure to include the ages of the children in your report.
   b. Watch a group of children at play. Determine who is friends with whom. Give a detailed description of their relationship. Using the information about the characteristics of friendship in this chapter

and your observations, determine the children's level of friendship.
   c. Observe an early childhood classroom. Determine the degree to which children have decision-making opportunities by recording the number and types of choices that are offered or group problem-solving experiences in which children participate.

3. Carry out an activity
   a. Write a script using the guidelines in the activity section of this chapter. Choose a prosocial or a friendship skill on which to focus your teaching. Practice the skit at home or with friends. Present the skit to the group, using dolls or puppets to create the characters and the situation. Hold a follow-up discussion with the children and, if appropriate, replay the skit using information gleaned from them.
   b. Set up a recycling center in the classroom. Collect all scrap paper and paper products during a single day and plan for children to use the paper on the following day for an art project.

c. Carry out one or more of the activities you developed for the social studies chart. Evaluate the results.

d. Carry out one or more of the activities listed at the end of the chapter. Evaluate the results in terms of your preparation and the children's responses.

4. Create something for your portfolio

a. Videotape your presentation of a skit in which you focus on prosocial or friendship skills. Include the script with the tape. Limit the tape to no more than 10 or 15 minutes.

b. Write a summary of the skit, focusing on prosocial or friendship skills. Give a synopsis of the discussion that followed the skit and note any changes in children's behavior that you observed as a direct or an indirect result of the ideas presented in the script.

c. Keep a weekly or monthly record of children's friendships. Compare their relationships before and after you present specific information to them by means of skits, discussions, or literature.

d. Document ways in which you have integrated social studies and social development into your curriculum. Use photographs, examples of children's writing or drawing, and anecdotal records you have kept with time.

5. Add to your journal

a. What is the most significant concept that you have learned about the social domain on the basis of your reading and your experience with children?

b. Does the information presented in this chapter correspond to your personal and professional experiences in the field? Review consistencies and inconsistencies you perceive.

c. Think about ways in which you will integrate social skill acquisition, and instruction in prosocial behavior into your program.

d. On the basis of what you have read, would you like to see changes made in the social studies curriculum used in your program? What are they, and how might they be implemented?

Part 4

Integrating Curriculum

Integrating Curriculum Through Pretend and Construction Play

You may wonder:

Isn't play just natural for children?

How can I convince parents or colleagues that play is important?

How do we account for the differences in the way children approach pretend and construction play?

How do children use pretend and construction play to represent experiences or objects?

How do pretend and construction play contribute to all other domains of learning and development?

In this chapter on pretend and construction play, we present information to help you answer the preceding questions.

Four first graders were talking intently in the bushes near the corner of the playground. "Let's pretend we're lost and all alone and have to build our house," suggested Alice.

"Yeah, we'll have to build it here. This could be a place to sleep," contributed Diane.

"And nobody knows where we are. No grown-ups. And no boys can come in here. Right?" Joan queried. "Shari, you get started on the kitchen. We gotta have a kitchen. Tomorrow we can bring some food."

All play is a delight to the young children engaged in it. In fact, pretend and construction play are the hallmarks of the early childhood period. Piaget (1962) used simple pretend as one of the criteria for differentiating between the sensorimotor period (birth to age 2 years) and the more advanced preoperational period (age 3 to 8 years). Adults recognize such play immediately, frequently dismissing it as a trivial pursuit of young children. Some persons believe that block constructions and the little things children make to support their play are simply amusements. More recently, scholars have recognized that play has not only a formative function that enables children to adapt to the social

and physical environment, but also an expressive function that facilitates children's communication with others about their thinking and feelings related to their understanding of the world (J. L. Frost, Wortham, & Reifel, 2001). Early childhood educators have long perceived pretend play as a vehicle for integrating various developmental capacities. Growing increasingly complex during this period, children's pretend play allows for some skills to be practiced and new challenges to be mastered.

CHARACTERISTICS OF PLAY

Play is fun, carried out for the pleasure of doing it, free of externally imposed rules, spontaneous, and voluntary. It requires the player's active involvement and the suspension of reality. It is symbolic behavior that allows the player to treat objects as though they were something else. The spoon becomes the musician's baton; a block structure becomes a spaceship. Players assume roles as though they were performers or explorers and sometimes machines. Players establish rules consistent with the play theme and roles requiring one another to perform in patterns that fit the narrative. For example, any contribution to the establishment of a household, the protection of the group, or other survival topics would be appropriate to the scenario described at the beginning of this chapter. Extraneous events, comments, or behavior would be either rejected or ignored by the players or would cause the play to disintegrate. Reality is suspended, but the play is governed by internal rules; thus the play event has internal coherence. Children function in the enactive mode as they engage in simple make-believe, shift to the iconic mode when they need to construct an object to further their play, and use the symbolic mode in complex play scenarios. Thus, imaginative, abstract thinking, set within the play frame and composed of sequences of action events, is typical.

The Play Frame The *play frame* describes the scope of the pretend-play event. Inside the play frame are all the people and objects that the children are using to enact their imaginative episode. The people, objects, and pretend narrative are all relevant to one another and to the progress of the play event. If a photograph were taken of the pretend-play episode described at the beginning of the chapter, the photographer would automatically move back to include all the players and relevant objects, even though other persons might be in either the foreground or the background of the photograph. Players within the frame are those who have a communication link and are engaged in the play. All other persons and objects without a relationship to the pretend narrative in progress are not in the play frame.

The frames of play may be established by a variety of modes (Sutton-Smith, 1986). Establishing the frame of the play allows children to communicate the theme, roles, and specific story to be enacted. Children might establish the frame by announcing it—"This is the house"—or by announcing a play role—"I'm the policeman"—or simply by acting on objects such as putting the train track together and running the train on it. Sometimes a smile and a gesture are sufficient between familiar players revisiting a common action sequence.

Recognition of play frames is important to educators because, although pretend play has its own internal logic with a unique imaginative quality, the players' behavior must be understood from this frame of reference. However, usually, the "reality" described in the pretend play reflects the level of understanding shared by the children. For example, if children are pretending to be firefighters and they assign one of the players to set fires, they lack information about the causes of fires and the true functions of firefighters. Although everyone agrees that play within the play frame is not "for real," adults may gain insight into children's thinking by the content of the frames and the skill with which children play.

Elements of Pretend Play

Pretend play is composed of a set of skills or elements that may be used singly (by less skilled players) or in combination (by players with greater skill). All players

"...3,2,1, blast off!" Charlotte has transformed the computer station into mission control.

must be able to participate in *make-believe;* that is, they must be able to suspend reality, even momentarily, to engage in the simplest form of pretend play, which is pretending with an object. When children pretend with objects, they act as though a stuffed animal were a baby, as though bits of play dough were food, or as though toy cars were real vehicles. Often the characteristics of the object suggest the make-believe scenario to the child. For example, a classroom computer might inspire a child to play airport controller, mission control for a space launch, or a computer operator. Stuffed animals might suggest the pretend notion of a zoo, a farm, or a veterinarian in much the same way.

When the needed object is not at hand, children engage in *object substitution*. This is straightforward representational thinking in which the child represents one object with another closer at hand. Whereas one child might use a pencil and paper to take an order in a "restaurant," another might substitute a hand for the paper and a finger for the pencil. Object substitutions are signaled by either actions or narrative. Three-year-olds can readily substitute one object in their play, and older children can use more objects when they are playing alone. In addition, younger children are more likely to substitute objects that perceptually suggest the needed device. For example, a seashell or a can is more likely to be substituted for a cup than is a string or a stick.

Primary-age youngsters may not need an object for the substitution. Instead, they use *object invention* and represent the needed objects solely through pantomime. A 7-year-old may open the door of a cupboard (that does not exist), remove a bowl (that is not there), place it on a real table, and begin to stir with an imaginary spoon. Measuring cups and ingredients may be represented through either the narrative or actions alone. Three- to five-year-olds find playing with a variety of object inventions very difficult, although older children do so more easily. In addition, all children have difficulty, when they are playing in groups, with more than one imaginary person or object. They appear to need something as a placeholder so that they can engage in sharing imaginary objects. For example, three 6-year-olds who were playing out small-town life drew streets in the dirt with their fingers and used leaves for community buildings and small mounds for houses. One child had designated an empty area as the vacant lot early in the play, and later another started to construct a house on it. After much discussion, the children agreed to draw a ring around the vacant lot so that others would not forget what it was. The ring defined the vacant lot and became the placeholder for empty space. Frequently, when several players are involved, iconic representations of objects are used as placeholders to avoid the confusion these 6-year-olds experienced.

Children throughout the early childhood period take on *roles* of others. These roles may be based on television show or movie characters (Power Rangers); functional roles (someone who eats or someone who uses a computer); familial or relational roles (husband–father, wife–mother); or occupational roles (nurse, robber). Naturally, children must be familiar with the roles they assume. Pretending to be yourself in another setting occurs between ages 2 and 3 years. Family roles predominate during the preschool period, with presentations of primary caregivers portrayed with emotional meanings as youngsters begin to understand that other people think and feel (Fromberg, 2002). Nurturing roles may become elaborate with time as children incorporate more complexity into the action sequences they represent. Occupational roles emerge slowly in older preschool children as they become aware of the larger community. These roles are heavily influenced by children's experiences and their school curriculum. School-age children elaborate on earlier roles and include frightening fantasies and themes of victim and aggressor. Fictional roles—those developed for television, the movies, or literature—generate high-action, powerful roles particularly attractive to boys. Sometimes these portrayals lack the personal creativity that the children are otherwise capable of demonstrating.

Children's *transformations of time, place, and setting* enable them to pretend to be pioneers or space adventurers. The beach, stores, the circus, or the market might be a place "visited" in the classroom play space. Time and place are limited only by the information available to the players. For example, a 3-year-old who

remains at home while family business is transacted would not have sufficient information to pretend about banking or stores, whereas a second grader who had both a school social studies background and more community experience would be prepared to engage in these play themes with considerable elaboration.

Communications That Enable Play to Work   When children play make-believe together, they must engage in complex communications called *metacommunication,* which means a communication about a communication (Bateson, 1971). These communications tend to describe what is "play" and what is not. They may serve to construct the play frame ("Let's pretend to be hunters") or define roles ("We can be neighbors who don't like each other").

Metacommunication statements transform objects and settings. "This [puppet stage] is the post office window" or "I'm in a dark forest and lost" typically sets the stage for continuing the play and provides the beginning narrative and context for continuing communication.

Likewise, children use metacommunications to extend their play and elaborate on characters' feelings or actions. In each case, cues for the content of continuing communication are provided: "This is a very dark forest, and I hope there are no monsters here" or "Pretend that you are a really mean bad guy."

Metacommunications also end the framed sequence. Children may deny the role ("I'm not the bad guy anymore"), change the meaning of the props ("This window [puppet theater] is really a window out of a spaceship"), or redefine the setting ("Why don't we pretend we were rescued and put in the hospital?").

Metacommunications combine the basic elements of pretend play and the framing process so that all players in a cooperative play venture can participate knowledgeably. When children engage in make-believe by themselves, they frequently create a narrative for themselves so that role-play and transformation of objects, setting, and time are apparent to the observer. As children mature, such spoken communication gradually decreases. Metacommunication in this instance is not necessary but sometimes is used by younger children.

Types of Pretend Play

Pretend play is sometimes conceived of as unidimensional. The following listing of pretend-play types is not intended to be definitive. The quality and complexity of the play and the setting are important variables among the types of play, as is the number of players. Examples of each type of pretend play are listed in Table 15.1.

Make-Believe   Simple pretend is when a child takes on the characteristics of an object or a person and acts

TABLE 15.1   Activity Ideas to Support Pretend Play

Type of Pretend Play	Sample Activities
Make-believe	Imagining what the clouds might be
	Pretending to be animals, automobiles, or simple machines
	Imagining how a character in a story feels
Pretend with objects	Hunt for props to support child-initiated activity
	Imagine an object if no placeholder is at hand
	Pantomime nursery rhymes, songs, or short poems
Pretend with art materials	Create stories as part of the drawing experience
	Illustrate told or written stories
	Listen to "pictorial" music selections while painting
Pretend with construction materials	Build or make a prop for pretend play
	Use blocks to build a setting for a pretend episode
	Use leaves, sticks, and other natural materials to build boats or houses
Pretend with miniatures	Use models or replicas in enactments
	Make dollhouse play available
	Supply toy farm animals or miniature people with blocks
Dramatic, sociodramatic, and thematic play	Enact occupational roles related to class themes
	Enact house, neighbors, and school play
Story reenactment	Perform a simple ballad with a clear story line
	Select and act out a traditional folk tale or folk song
	Dramatize a more modern story such as "Ask Mr. Bear" or "Caps for Sale"
Write and play	Ask children to pretend they are the characters in a story that a classmate has written and act it out
	Once children have engaged in a sociodramatic play set for several days, ask them to write a story based on their play

out a sequence. For example, 3-year-olds might pretend to be balloons that are being blown up by another child. Five-year-olds might walk down the hallway connected to one another to form a train and say, "Chug-chug-chug" as they move. Eight-year-olds might pretend to be an airplane or a cloud moving over the mountains. Such episodes may be encouraged deliberately by the teacher or developed spontaneously by the children.

Pretend with Objects   Exploration of an object or any new material always precedes well-developed play sequences, regardless of the children's age, skills, or familiarity with the material. In exploration a child asks, "What is the nature of this object?" whereas in pretend the child wonders, "What can I do with this?" Unskilled players may vacillate between pretend play and exploration while learning how to pretend with an object. For example, Rico, age 4 years, picked up a stethoscope and correctly identified it as a "doctor thing." He swung it around, talked into it, hung it on his neck, and used it to

hit at Maria. Mark told him to put the earplugs in his ears and listen to his heart. Rico tried this. He listened to tables, a window, and a radiator before attempting to listen to another child. Then he engaged in a brief "doctor" episode while listening to a doll's chest. Alternating between listening to dolls, children, and other objects in the environment, Rico's play vacillated between pretending with an object and exploration. Older children may also pretend by themselves and focus on the object they are using. Children who have few playmates may be very skilled in developing a variety of pretend scenarios based on a single object. During several play episodes, Allison used an old-fashioned washbasin variably for a doll bath, a helmet, and a cooking pot. Even in the most traditional classrooms, teachers are familiar with children's tendency to use anything for play: bits of paper, pencils, articles of clothing, science equipment, and so forth.

Pretend with Art Materials   Some 3- to 5-year-olds are primarily concerned about the pattern, color, or form of their visual art experiences, whereas others typically have a story that the graphic portion represents. Children may orally express the pretend story component as the child produces the graphic: "And the scary spider dropped down . . . to the ground. And he moved around. He went up and the wind blew him. Almost hit the boy." Thus, they use the "movements of play, the lines of drawing, and the sounds of language to represent the people, objects, and events that comprise their world" (Dyson, 1990, p. 50). Children may even share a pretend-play sequence, talking and drawing at the same time. Five- and six-year-olds can draw, pretend, and converse while labeling real or imaginary events or objects as they stimulate one another (Coates, 2002).

Pretend with Construction Materials Probably the most complex of all play episodes are those in which children construct the necessary play props to support their pretend theme or action sequence. In this case, the play shifts back and forth from construction to pretend play. With younger children, this shifting is seen most frequently during block play, in which a child might build a house or a barn and then use cars and small dolls to enact a scene. Older children may continue the same play action sequence for several days, building additional components as they go. In one Indiana kindergarten, children reconstructed their small town during several weeks by using clay, small cardboard boxes, and other discarded materials. Throughout the elementary school period, children build snow forts, tree houses, stores, and homes in which to engage in increasingly elaborate pretend-play sequences.

Pretend with Miniature Buildings and People Dollhouses, barns and animals, vehicles with passengers, and other miniature pretend settings stimulate pretend play. Children imagine the story and manipulate the figures. Unlike basic dramatic play, children cannot use facial expression or body action to convey ideas and feelings. They become the narrator; although they might portray many parts, they are not actors with their own bodies. Children aged 5 to 8 years usually have the capacity to use their voices to portray a variety of emotions and characters. Younger children are likely to find some way to include larger movements, such as transporting farm animals in a truck.

Dramatic Play During dramatic play the child carries out a sequence of events or actions that are related to one another. Children pretend with objects, place, time, and setting as they enact a role. Younger children enact scenarios based on familiar, much-repeated routines—such as feeding or bathing a doll, or putting the doll to bed—although the order of such enactments may vary from time to time. An older child might play a more

distant role and pretend to be a bus driver or even a worker at mission control guiding spaceships (that are being constructed out of clay) in takeoff or landing sequences. The play may be solitary or in the company of other children but not necessarily interacting with them except through observation or shared space. Six- and seven-year-olds can pick up the play theme from day to day and continue, whereas 3- to 5-year-olds are more likely to start over. Such differences in skill and maturity influence the selection of the play topic and the duration and complexity of the play enactment.

Sociodramatic Play Sociodramatic play involves several children who are playing together for at least 10 minutes and sharing the same narrative sequence. The story is negotiated, and the roles are established by using metacommunications. Usually pretend with time, setting, and place are agreed on by the players as the play progresses and may be completely embedded in the script. "Gee, it's getting dark now" automatically calls for an evening sequence of actions by other players. A second child might respond, "Where will we sleep?" which draws the play into a housing or furnishing problem. All the players share the story line, with individual children both following others' leads and contributing new ideas. Children frequently prompt one another when factual errors are made in the play, such as one child's whispering loudly, "The store man collects the money for the stuff. Doesn't pay someone to take it."

Theme-Related Play A variation of dramatic and sociodramatic play, theme-related play is very goal directed and may center on a number of occupational themes: beauty shop, school, camping, hospital, restaurant, or fire station. When children are engaged in thematic instruction, some aspect of the theme is available for pretend play. Children may initiate it themselves (Fayden, 1997), or adults may instigate the play by providing the props, time, space, and information necessary for enactment. Sometimes even the action is suggested by supervising adults. However, once initiated, children should take it over or develop it themselves. Children who rarely participate in house play may readily engage in occupational or adventure roles that are more typical of theme-related play.

The detail and accuracy of portrayals increase with practice and maturity. In addition, children add problems that must be solved within the play. These problems are frequently reasonable for the setting, such as having a fire drill while playing school, running out of permanent solution in a beauty shop, or having a fire in a garage. Primary-age children may successfully incorporate themes from television, video stories, or literature within their play. Preschool children's most complex sociodramatic scenarios are based on settings with which they are the most familiar—such as home (babies, families, and neighbors)—although they sometimes also attempt fantasy characters.

Story Reenactment Variously called *creative dramatics, thematic play, fantasy play,* or *story reenactment,* this type of play involves children's developing the skills of taking on a role and re-creating a plot they have heard in a myth, legend, poem, or story. Through story reenactment children can assume a variety of roles they otherwise would have no way of experiencing—such as a princess or a space traveler. The scope of mood, setting, and plot structures in literature far exceeds what a small group of children can imagine without additional sources. Older children may read–play–read again as they engage in the story enactment. Discussions about character and other elements of literature are possible and comprehensible as children dramatize a written or traditional story.

Write and Play, or Writer's Theater In writer's theater, children dictate or write a story and then enact it. Unlike reader's theater, children create and write the story. Sometimes the story arises from a pretend-play episode, story dictation, or a story that a child has written. This form of pretend play builds on the skills of 6- and 7-year-olds to develop pretend-play story plots and characterization. The additional transformation to word stories connects this form of play to learning in the language domain. Children also face the dilemma of written dialogue and begin to use grammar rules they otherwise would never attempt.

Fundamentally, children's story writing and their pretend play are blended so that the strength of one can foster the other. For example, a simple story written by a 6-year-old was only two sentences: "My baby brother got in my room. He made a mess." Several first graders were asked to think about this basic plot and to pretend play it. The author was in the group and watched as various children played the roles of baby, older brother, and parents. More than one pretend sequence was tried, and several solutions to the problem were explored as children acted out their roles. The author had the choice of incorporating some details, problems, and solutions into the story or leaving it alone. The advantage of this play form is that the connection between the familiar play and the new tasks of writing are clear, meaningful, and obvious.

Pretend play is the symbolic representation of ideas through the enactive mode. Children portray their ideas about events by what they do and say and use props to support their scenarios. They also use the iconic mode when they symbolically represent their ideas through what they make. Objects that children construct represent processes, events, or other objects. By constructing a concrete representation, they gain greater understanding of their experiences. Construction play, although similar to pretend play in that it represents children's interpretation of the world around them, has distinctive characteristics. Both pretend play and construction play include symbolic modes of representation.

Construction Play

Four-year-old Kate spent several minutes studying a spiderweb in the fence of the play yard. When she returned to the classroom, she used Wikki Stix, which are flexible colored-wax strips that stick to many surfaces, to reconstruct the spiderweb in three-dimensional form. Then she drew the spiderweb on paper with crayons and announced, "I can make a spiderweb, too!" She was completely engrossed in her activity.

Aida was playing store with other kindergarten children. She seemed dissatisfied with simply pretending to offer money to the clerk and said, "I gotta get some real money to buy this stuff." Looking around the room, Aida walked to the paper supply shelf, selected a few sheets of green paper, carefully tore it into rectangles, wrote numerals on each piece, and returned to complete her purchases in the pretend store.

Mark, who had been participating in a unit on trees in his third-grade classroom, spent several days accumulating leaves from the trees in his neighborhood on his own. Each leaf was mounted on a sheet of paper and labeled with its name. He carefully drew several trees with some details of the surrounding environment and labeled them "Tree in front," "Mr. McDirmid's tree," and "On the corner." Then he arranged them into a book of leaves in his neighborhood.

All these children have demonstrated their ability to bring together a variety of skills and concepts to represent objects, events, or groups of objects that are meaningful to them in a concrete, physical way. For example, Kate demonstrated memory skills, imagination, perseverance, planning, and fine-motor skills. She used her knowledge of materials, whole–part relationships, and concepts of line, direction, and space in addition to her obvious understandings of the spiderweb. Her emotional satisfaction was expressed in her comment. Aida, who could not pretend play comfortably without a placeholder for the symbolic money she needed, used her knowledge about money and good problem-solving skills to make "money." Mark, who is much older, represented a group of trees, their location and environment, and their relationship to people and places familiar to him. He incorporated information that he had learned at school and used the skills of observing, recording, and communicating his experience.

Construction is the transformation of an experience or object into a concrete representation of this experience or object. Children use materials to make a product.

> Often these are symbolic products, such as drawings, paintings and three-dimensional creations that represent objects (e.g., house), ideas (e.g., friendship), or processes (e.g., war). Constructive and symbolic play can also be combined to create a poem, a dramatic production, a tape recording, or other visual or technological products. (Bergen, 1988a, p. 247)

When a child constructs an object in many different ways such as in a report, in a drawing, with cardboard, or as a clay or wood model, the child must take into account previous representations as new ones are created. Each rendition takes a perspective that when passed on to the next medium generates conflict, challenge, and change (Forman, 1996). Such multiple perspectives can be considered variations on the same system.

Most physical products are accompanied by children's commentaries. These comments complete the representation. For example, a child might name a particular block a "car," although it does not differ greatly from the block next to it. When children build machines, an adult may be able to identify them by the associated sound effects. Thus, auditory information may supplement the physical to represent the child's idea more adequately. Among the patterns of developmentally appropriate curriculum, perhaps construction play is the easiest for experienced traditional teachers to understand and emulate. To many educators, it appears to be related to both play and work, and the outcomes are observable and understandable (Chaillé & Silvern, 1996).

Types of Construction Projects

Three broadly defined types of construction projects are "1) those resulting from a child's natural encounter with the environment, 2) those reflecting mutual interests on the part of the teacher and children, and 3) those based on teacher concerns regarding specific cognitive and/or social concepts" (New, 1990, p. 7). In all three types, the products emerge from an intense interest, an acute investigation, or a hands-on exploration of an object or event that appeals to the children. Specific examples of each are presented in Table 15.2. Constructions are children's attempts to solidify their ideas or to communicate ideas to others through imagery.

Projects Stemming from Natural Encounters All young children are in the process of trying to understand their world. Often an ordinary object or some aspect of nature will capture a young child's interest. Drawings of people, houses, and animals are typical, as are modeling dough constructions of cakes, cookies, snakes, and bowls. Some constructions may be extremely simple, as when Sasha, age 3 years, watched raindrops flow down the pane and then painted the irregular vertical lines at the easel. At other times, children's constructions are more elaborate. For example, when three children noticed the movement and seemingly purposeful activity of ants on the playground, their teacher suggested that they make something to help them remember what they saw. Other children joined the discussion about the ants' behavior and were encouraged by their teacher to elaborate on their comments by making something with clay or illustrating their understanding of the ants by using paper

TABLE 15.2 Activities to Support Construction Play

Type of Construction Play	Sample Activities
Projects stemming from natural encounters	Use tissue paper, adhesives, egg cartons, scissors, and so forth to make worms, flowers, or bugs
	Build houses from hollow blocks
	Construct a village using unit blocks and miniatures
Projects stemming from mutual interests of teacher and children	Prepare a creation station as a learning center and allow children to make anything they want
	Allow children to report on another learning activity by making something related to it and explaining what they did and why
Projects stemming from teacher concerns	Transportation unit: Build paper airplanes, boats from assorted materials, or cars using wood, saws, and nails
	Energy unit: Build a circuit board with batteries, bells, lights, and so on; make a magnet using a nail and another magnet
	Holiday unit: Create a collage depicting the many ways people celebrate
	Nutrition unit: Make and paint papier-mâché "food" to be used in pretend play

and chalk. This group of children continued to observe the ants and document what they saw.

Projects Stemming from Mutual Interests of Teacher and Children Teachers often stimulate a construction experience based on common events in children's lives. For example, many young children are concerned about having a friend. Discussions of friendship enhanced with constructions of modeling dough or collages of magazine pictures representing children's ideas about friendship further mutual communication and understanding. Sometimes current events discussed at home or on television may stimulate both children and adults to read, discuss, and construct images related to the topic. For example, 4-year-old Emma filled a large paper with black, brown, yellow, and red tempera paint and then clawed strips out of it with her fingernails from top to bottom, commenting, "It's the New York fire" (Gross & Clemens, 2002). Teachers listen and respond to children's ideas and concerns. Teachers also provide accurate information, ignite the children's creative thinking and questions, and support further examination of ideas. Often children's constructions provide clues that suggest children have misinformation and misconceptions, to which the teacher then responds.

Projects Stemming from Teacher Concerns Regarding Specific Concepts Another type of construction focuses on ideas or concepts initially unfamiliar to children but perceived by adults as valuable for children to explore. Such construction activities are embedded in a theme or unit in which children learn about other aspects of the social and natural world by using various strategies described in previous chapters. For instance, children living in forested areas of the United States are exposed to ideas related to oceans and deserts. Children living in a homogeneous community may explore ideas about people of various ethnic and racial backgrounds. Children may generate construction activities that emerge from topics in science, social studies, mathematics, health, literature, or music. Children listen or read, discuss, and then construct a representation of their understanding. Both the children and the teacher have opportunities to share insights into others' thinking as the projects are examined and classmates communicate their interpretations (Gardini & Edwards, 1988). Constructions of this type are more typically products of the primary child, although some 4- and 5-year-olds may attempt them.

Comparison of Construction and Other Related Activities

Object exploration, practice in fine-motor skills, and craft projects are related to children's construction activities but are not the same. Each of these three activities involves knowledge or skills children use when constructing, but they do not require the level of representational thought and creativity associated with construction.

Construction Is Not Simply Object Play Object play is exploration and investigation. A child attempts to discover the properties of an object or to answer the questions "What is this object like?" and "How does it work?" The novelty of the object attracts the child's attention, and its complexity sustains interest. Repetitive actions, systematic examination, and attempts to use the object in a variety of ways are typical of object play. Thus, object play with materials usually occurs before construction becomes possible.

When children stop investigating the nature of objects and begin using them to build something, they shift into construction. The contrast between object play and construction can be seen in the behaviors of two 3-year-olds. Jerry John arranged several blocks in front of him and engaged in snapping them together in various combinations. He seemed most interested in determining whether any combination could be snapped and unsnapped readily and answering the question "How does this work?" In contrast, Alexi selected only the units that could be fastened in a linear pattern and commented, "See my snake."

Three- and four-year-old children may spend substantial time exploring a material, creating a combination that reminds them of a familiar object, and naming it, as Billy did in one of his rearrangements of the blocks: "Look here, I got this house." Sometimes youngsters are aware of this, as Dimitri was when he told an inquiring adult, "I'll know what this painting is when I've finished it." Regardless of age, all children move between object play and construction when they encounter new media or materials or those that they have not used in a long time. However, in general, as children mature, they spend less time exploring and more time using the materials to construct.

Construction Is Not Simply Fine-Motor Practice The imitation of hand skills such as holding a writing implement, cutting with scissors, sewing, weaving, and using various tools develop fine-motor skill. Something may be produced, but it is a by-product of the process and not intended to represent a child's idea or concept. Instead, it is the natural outcome of the process, such as fringe produced while snipping paper or a cutout of a pattern given to the child to practice cutting. Occasionally, preschoolers will name their by-products if they resemble a familiar object, such as labeling a spiral-cut paper "snake" when they pull the ends apart. Primary children may have the basic skills and refine them during the construction process as the need arises. Clearly, children must control the materials and tools used for construction and apply their knowledge to tasks skillfully.

Construction requires that the child have an image in mind that he or she then represents by using familiar processes. For example, Rebecca carefully cut along the lines of a pattern drawn for her. She focused her entire attention on the process of producing a smooth curve and turning corners neatly. In contrast, Marietta left a group of children looking at the visiting cat, walked to the center where materials were stored, and created a cat face by cutting into a paper plate to form eyes and ears and adding whiskers with a marker. Rebecca and Marietta both produced products, but only Marietta had a specific idea in mind when she engaged in the activity. The child's imagination is central to the reasoning process, and no activity is undertaken without some image of the result, whether his or her conception is accurate or not (J. Smith, 1990). As with object play, the skills with which to control the processes of construction are necessary but insufficient.

Construction Is Not Simply the Demonstration of Technique Children must also learn techniques. For example, a child who wants to adhere two pieces of paper must learn where to put the paste. Children also learn when to use which adhesive (e.g., white liquid glue, school paste, rubber cement, or a mixture of white glue and paste) that will adhere pieces of wood or cardboard. Skill in the use of tools and techniques generally precedes construction activities or is learned in the context of a construction project as the need arises. As children shift from one medium to another, the demands for technical knowledge and skills increase.

Construction Is Not Simply Following Directions for a Project In her kindergarten class, Diedra listened carefully as the teacher gave directions and demonstrated how to make a rabbit. Each piece had been reproduced on paper, and the rabbit would have movable legs. She cut, colored, and assembled the rabbit as directed, even though it did not quite look the same as her teacher's. Diedra used her language, memory, and motor skills to perform this task. In the kindergarten at another school, Fredrico had listened to the story of Peter Rabbit and studied several photographs of real rabbits. He constructed a rabbit from materials that he selected from the supply shelves. Fredrico also used language, memory, and motor skills to produce a rabbit. In addition, he made decisions about materials and used imagination and representational thinking to form his image of the rabbit. Both children created products, but only Fredrico was involved in the representational thought necessary for

construction. However, Diedra might have produced a rabbit more appealing to adults by copying her teacher's image rather than creating her own.

Knowledge of necessary processes or step-by-step operations necessary to achieve a specific end is useful to the construction process but not a substitute for it. Does the child-drawn image of the human figure with a very large mouth and exaggerated hands mean that the child is unable to perceive the difference in length between fingers, arms, and legs? Of course not. The specific proportions of the human body are not necessary to convey the idea, and children aged 3 to 8 years have no difficulty in readily perceiving such contrasting lengths. Yet adults sometimes behave as though children are functioning without sufficient information. The copyist theory of knowledge is that children learn by closely attending and that if the child were sufficiently skilled in perception, he or she could accurately duplicate the idea (Forman & Kuschner, 1983). If children only followed the directions with care, the product, and incidentally the idea, would be replicated.

Children during the early childhood period increasingly develop their abilities to perceive with accuracy and learn to use step-by-step procedures. Following directions, imitating, and copying enable children to acquire the techniques that provide them with the skills and procedures for carrying out their construction projects. For example, two 5-year-olds re-created their experiences with vehicles in the snow, using different media. One child drew a rectangle with circles on the side with a red crayon on blue paper and neatly glued cotton balls around it. The second child used two paintbrushes held side by side and made parallel wavy lines across white paper to illustrate car tracks in the snow. Both youngsters demonstrated their abilities to use materials and fashion a concrete representation of an idea. Both used appropriate techniques for the medium selected and worked with care and deliberation. Imitation of the technique might be important, but once the technique is mastered, children construct the product according to their own ideas and interpretation. Children increase in confidence as their sense of competence evolves as a result of successfully constructing.

A second-grade teacher who had provided models and detailed directions for products in the past commented about a marked change in children's behavior when she altered her approach. "I have been really surprised," she said. "The children used to be concerned that their pictures looked 'just like their friends' pictures'; now they are trying to be unique in what they do."

Arts and crafts are favorites of young children and their teachers. When children make holiday ornaments from printed fabric and canning lids, decorate orange juice cans with macaroni and paint, or weave potholders, they are participating in activities that have become traditional in some communities. These activities are legitimate exercises in fine-motor control and may be useful in promoting perceptual development or listening skills. They have a place in the curriculum but do not substitute for genuine opportunities for children to construct something on their own. They have independent value but do not require the transformation of an idea into a product.

Construction and Materials of Choice

Construction opportunities are facilitated when children have access to a large array of materials. For example, one 4-year-old wanted a "cape." He examined butcher paper that was stiff but could be wrapped around and taped. He tried some lightweight tissue paper. Then he discovered some yarn and a piece of fabric. The texture of the fabric made this his best choice for the purpose. Only the materials were necessary to provide for this problem solving.

Various Blocks Blocks abound in sizes, colors, and textures. Some fasten together and have pieces designed for wheels and axles. Others, such as unit blocks, are cut in regular, predictable intervals. Some sets have a color for each shape and provide a variety of angles in wedge-shaped pieces. Large, hollow blocks may be used to build structures that children may enter.

Commercial Sets Numerous commercial construction sets have sections that children can fasten together with nuts and bolts or pieces that fit together when laid in place. These sets often have extender sets that include more-complicated pieces and may even come with electric motors so that children can make more-complex machines that run. Products that have many pieces and can be assembled in different ways provide for more diversity than those with fewer pieces or that are limited to a predetermined outcome. Older children frequently want their constructions "to work."

Carpentry Supplies and Tools Woodworking benches with real hammers, nails, saws, drills, screws, screwdrivers, safety goggles, and other tools to enable a child to construct with real wood are an alternative in many programs for young children. Good-quality tools may be costly, but they have the potential for lasting a long time (Huber, 1999). Most toy tools do not work. In some programs, children are allowed to build with wood and later take the structures apart to reuse the wood for new projects. Soft woods are easier for children to use than hard woods. They are also less expensive and can be obtained as discards from local businesses.

Art Materials, Paper, and Common Discards A multitude of papers that differ in color, texture, and size are available for purchase and as discards from businesses or families, such as old wrapping paper, commercial sacks, forms, used computer printouts, and even trim cuttings from printers. The numbers and colors of available paint and writing implements are considerable as well. In addition, a variety of three-dimensional materials such as egg cartons, packing material, meat trays, and other throwaway objects with interesting patterns, colors, or textures can be obtained for children to use in their symbolic representations.

Open-Ended Materials Flexible materials such as sand, clay, and play dough can be used to represent a variety of ideas. Once children understand the properties of the materials, they can create a wide array of representations with the appropriate tools. The advantage of these materials is that they are three-dimensional, with an undetermined shape in the beginning. With sand, children can try out their ideas and erase them without fear of making mistakes. Children can have better control over such media at younger ages.

Natural Materials Children have long used stones, mud, sticks, leaves, and other plant materials to create little worlds in which pretend people carry out their lives. Snow is another excellent building material. These natural resources may be used outdoors or brought into the classroom as the occasion demands.

Materials Assembled with Specific Teacher Goals in Mind Older children can create board games from file folders, poster board, or shirt boxes with assorted stickers, markers, and pieces to move (Castle, 1991). The child is required not only to construct a product but also to establish the rules of the game. The problems they encounter, such as how to have moving pieces that can be distinguished from one another or how to make the game challenging and fun, engage their creative interest and require access to an array of materials.

Independence of Materials from the Ideas They Represent

At times, children use the same materials to represent a variety of ideas. Paint and play dough are particularly versatile. In one small group, children used play dough to make nests and eggs, dishes, cups with handles, a ring, a long snake, and a cake. The diversity of ideas that individual children expressed expanded the entire group's vision. Children see more and more possibilities as they practice with the materials and tools. In another group, children used paint to represent abstract ideas such as *friends*, *conflicts*, or *feelings* in more-concrete terms. Nevertheless, paint is also used to represent some of the first identifiable drawings of people, vehicles, and houses (Kellogg, 1969). Whether children depict their ideas in realistic or abstract constructions, they tend to become more versatile when they are thoroughly familiar with the material and are in control of the process. Yet, to some extent each material also limits the content of expression and the approach used (Forman, 1996). For example, representing the ocean would be easier using paints and paper or a paper collage than using blocks.

Children often depict the same idea by using a variety of materials. Children must use their problem-solving skills when they have a choice of materials for representing the same general idea. Different materials give different results, so the character, mood, or level of detail may vary from one depiction to another. Children must also solve a variety of problems relating to technique when materials are varied. Developing the theme of "houses," the same child made houses from sticks, straw, and string; sugar cubes; blocks; crayons and paper; paints; and small boxes. The gravest technical difficulties were experienced when the child tried to use the straw and finally tied it at the top and stuck a finger in to make an interior. Various adhesives were tried, and the sizes of the houses differed considerably. The block house had an interior and an exterior. When given crayons, the child drew only the face of the house. These activities, extended across several days, involved much peer cooperation and prosocial behavior. Children also compared their work on the same idea from one medium to the next.

As children increase in their ability to represent objects and events, they can also better select the appropriate material with which to achieve their desired end. With practice, they become more confident, more skillful, and often more creative.

Individual Differences in Children's Pretend and Construction Play

Maturity, family life experiences, style preferences, classroom context, practice, cultural background, and play quality all influence the content of pretend and construction play as well as the players' performance (Mellou, 1994).

Maturity Three-year-olds do not possess the vocabulary, life experience, or level of abstract thinking that older children demonstrate. Their play is usually solitary, beside another player who is playing similarly, or in short episodes of cooperative play. Frequently, they cannot express the metacommunication messages necessary for more elaborate pretend play. Younger children usually select content based on familiar roles, such as those of the family, rather than on fiction.

A few children will begin true construction with regular materials as early as age 3 years. If the structure is not named, the adult may have difficulty discerning whether the child is involved in object play or simple construction. As children mature, their structures become more complex (Gregory, Kim, & Whiren, 2003). Details of interest become elaborated and are often the subject of conversation among children. In addition, the child's intent is much clearer, being either announced in advance or obvious from the context of the ongoing play. Four- and five-year-olds regularly engage in pretend play during the construction process. Six- and seven-year-olds may discuss in detail what they plan to construct and even determine the relationship among the structures before they begin. At any point in time, children produce constructions that are more recognizable (drawing of a person) or abstract (whirling leaves in the wind). They may do so independently or as part of a larger, more complex play frame. The developmental stages of block play are presented in Table 15.3 because blocks are a familiar and typical construction

TABLE 15.3 Developmental Stages of Block Play

Stage	Description
1. Object exploration	*Carrying blocks*—Children move blocks around and discover properties of the material.
2. Learning techniques	*Piling and laying blocks on the floor*—Children arrange both horizontal and vertical sets of blocks. Sometimes completed arrangements suggest a use, such as a "road."
3. Construction	*Connecting blocks to create structures*—Children make enclosures, build bridges, and design decorative patterns and layouts.
4. Advanced construction	*Making elaborate constructions*—Children create complex buildings, often with many parts, using curved and straight lines, around or over obstacles. This stage is frequently associated with pretend play.

The "house" built by these 3-year-olds is a typical Stage 2 block construction.

These second graders have constructed an elaborate Stage 4 movie theater, complete with screen, seating, concession stand, and parking.

material. A more elaborate and complete description of block play can be found in *The Block Book* (Hirsch, 1996) and in *A Constructivist Approach to Block Play in Early Childhood* (Wellhousen & Kieff, 2001).

Family Life Experience   The general life experience of 3- to 8-year-olds varies considerably. Children from rural areas know more about farming than urban children do and can pretend appropriate roles much earlier than their city counterparts of similar maturity. Some

children have experienced police raids in their neighborhoods and have a working knowledge of street gangs by the time they are 5 years old, whereas other children of similar ages are completely ignorant of such occurrences. Ordinary factors such as family composition, presence of pets, modes of typical transportation, and occupations of adults in the home provide some children with information that others do not have. Children tend to play out the scenes and scenarios with which they are most familiar. In addition, the child's language and the caregiver's support of symbolic play positively influence children's collaborative play (Bornstein, Haynes, O'Reilly, & Painter, 1996).

Cultural Differences   Many classrooms are composed of children from various cultural backgrounds. The roles of mother and father differ from one family to another. This is true of the individual family culture as well as of nationality, such as Arabic, Japanese, or Spanish. Thematic content and the communicative strategies used to structure and maintain play are influenced by culture (Farver & Shinn, 1997). Players often need help in negotiating their play. Younger children do not usually realize that different people may come to the play with perspectives vastly dissimilar from theirs.

Practice or Skill Differences   Children who do not have access to a wide variety of materials will not be as skillful as those who do, regardless of age. For example, although many 3-year-olds can cut simple straight lines, 5-year-olds who have just acquired access to scissors may still be discovering how they work. High-quality construction play depends on the skillful use of

Stage 3 constructions such as this "skyscraper" are common in kindergarten.

the tools and materials used in the process. Construction with blocks requires skillful placement and organization; with graphic materials, construction requires control of implements.

Because pretend play begins very early, children often exhibit differences in learned skills. Smilansky (1968) was the first researcher to note that skill development in the elements of pretend play was limited or absent in lower socioeconomic groups in Israel. This finding was later verified in studies in the United States (Fein & Stork, 1981) and modified by Eiferman (1971) to indicate that the deficiency was that of developmental delay, not inability. These findings mean that some children may not possess even the rudimentary pretend skills at age 5 or 6 years that other children exhibit at age 3 years. However, children can and do learn the elements of pretend play with appropriate adult instruction in educational settings (Christie, 1986). Many children are skilled at pretend play by age 5 years, whereas others are just beginning to learn, which may be the result of parenting practice or of early child care practices.

Classroom Context The context of the classroom also accounts for individual differences among children in play performance. First, the materials, the equipment, and the organization of classroom space influence whether or not children play and the number of players engaged at one time (Wellhousen & Kieff, 2001). Even the subtle differences in play with hollow and unit blocks affect play content and social structure. Theme-related play is unlikely to occur without the necessary theme-related objects and sources of information (Fayden, 1997). The presence of peers with whom to play and the level of creativity and flexibility other players bring to the pretend-play situation often influence not only the existence of play, but also its quality (Monighan-Nourot, 1998). The presence of one or two "master players" capable of sustaining the play by adjusting play scripts, imaginative problem solving, compromising, negotiating, and suggesting play elaborations influences the other children's performance. An integrated classroom of 6- and 7-year-olds who have been in a mixed-age group for at least a year will play more skillfully together than an age-graded group that has just formed.

Play Style Some youngsters focus on form, line, color, design, and the general aesthetics of the construction. A 5-year-old with this style builds more-elaborate block structures, with turrets, corners, and arches, using lots of blocks and space. These *patterners* may show interest in maintaining structures for several days. In contrast, *dramatists* tend to focus on the narrative of the pretend play and might use only a few blocks as long as they represent the idea they have in mind. For a dramatist, the form is much less important than the function. As soon as the pretend sequence is complete, this child is finished with the materials and more readily returns them to the shelf. A youngster's characteristic style applies to all materials. Children can and should be encouraged to extend their constructions beyond the limits of their preferred styles. More than one third of all children use either style with equal ease (Shotwell, Wolf, & Gardner, 1979).

Differences in style also appear in pretend play: Some children are extremely focused on the materials being used, and others, on fantasy (Grollman, 1994). One child may be very careful about the arrangements of the house, the neatness of the dishes, or the clothes the doll has on. However, another may use words and gestures to create a fantasy in the same setting that is stimulated by but not limited to the objects therein. Both children might be imaginative and creative, but in different ways.

Quality of Play Finally, the quality of play differs. This difference centers on the ability to maintain a group play theme with time and the inclusion of problems to be solved by the players (Roskos, 1990). Children enact roles relevant to settings such as a bakery, hospital, beach, school, or library. When they include a problem such as a fire starting in the library basement or an emergency patient entering the hospital, the narrative and enactment of the pretend play has more-story-like qualities: (a) a beginning, (b) problem identification, (c) plot development, (d) problem resolution, and (e) an ending.

Increased complexity of play is possible for 4- and 5-year-olds in supportive environments if they are skilled in all the play elements. Maturity is necessary but not sufficient to enable children to engage in high-quality play. Skill, supportive environments, practice, and time are essential to achieve the most advanced levels of pretend play. Complex sociodramatic play is predictive of self-regulation during cleanup, whereas solitary dramatic play is not. The beneficial effect of complex sociodramatic play is particularly strong for high-impulse children (Elias & Berk, 2002).

The complexity of constructions and the degree to which they are deliberately built, as representations of children's concepts and ideas, are an indicator of quality in block play. In addition, when pretend play and construction play are integrated into the same scenario, higher quality play is achieved.

PRETEND AND CONSTRUCTION PLAY ACROSS THE CURRICULUM AND IN DEVELOPMENT

Although studies of construction and pretend play have been conducted independently of each other, both tend to show that they are systematically related to positive developmental and learning outcomes. Understanding the physical and social world is the result of high-quality play in which children demonstrate focused interest, attention, experimentation, and cooperation (Chaillé & Silvern, 1996). It requires considerable mental activity rather than the simple manipulation of materials. Play has the significant attribute of "uniting and integrating cognitive, language, socioemotional and motor aspects of learning and development" while "supporting children's positive beliefs in their own competency" (Kieff & Casbergue, 2000, pp. 8–9). The skills supported by pretend play and construction are presented next as they apply to all the curricular domains.

Cognitive Domain

Play may serve to consolidate children's constructs (Piaget, 1962) or stimulate the emergence of abstract thought (Vygotsky, 1967). Whether play mirrors children's cognitive processes or causes them is yet unclear. However, ample evidence exists that pretend play is a significant factor in children's intellectual functioning (Fromberg, 2002; J. L. Frost et al., 2001). Nevertheless, play with peers apparently creates the context in which children stretch beyond their usual levels of functioning (Monighan-Nourot, 1998). They try new roles and engage in experiences not otherwise available to them. Opportunities for problem identification and the generation of varieties of solutions to ordinary situations that are created during play abound. Children practice and consolidate their skills.

Children may also acquire new information, although such acquisition is not the primary function of pretend play. It is most likely to occur when children of differing backgrounds and experience confront one another in the play setting. Players tend to require their peers to play consistently within the theme and behave appropriately for their roles. To this end, they may inform, coach, or direct other players and teach one another, which is consistent with Vygotsky's (1979) ideas that one child can assist the processes of learning in another. Investigative play with blocks leads children to discover interrelationships among concepts such as balance, cause and effect, classification, counting, estimation, whole–part relationships, geometric solids, serration, predictions, and the understanding of simple machines such as ramps, fulcrums, and levers (Wellhousen & Kieff, 2001). It is not surprising then that in one study young children's block play reliably predicted mathematics achievement at the seventh-grade and high school levels (Wolfgang, Stannard, & Jones, 2001). Play also contributes to increasing concentration skills and the expansion of imagination, creativity, and curiosity as well as developing the capacity to be flexible (Oliver & Klugman, 2002).

Aesthetic Domain

Construction activities provide opportunities for children to apply creative-thinking skills. All creative efforts require two familiar elements of the active imagination: the generation of alternatives and a selection among these alternatives (J. Smith, 1990, p. 83). Children must choose among a variety of materials that may be suitable for their project. In addition, the materials may provide ideas for constructions. Given encouragement and time to think, children will propose many uses beyond the obvious for common materials such as paper (Tegano, Sawyers, & Moran, 1991). Even properly identifying the problem is a challenge for the very young, and the teachers' support and guidance of even older children may be necessary (Tegano et al., 1991).

Children also plan what they are doing (Casey & Lippman, 1991). They may do so briefly and casually at first, beginning with an idea or a goal. Once materials are assembled and implementation begins, children often start over or add and delete as they alter the direction of their work. Sometimes they comment on the criteria with which they judge their products. For instance, when Janet and Lanna, age 4 years, were building a house of blocks, Janet said, "We gotta get the bigger ones. These won't fit [across the roof]." Lanna replied, "Yeah, and get some little red and blue ones from the table to be flowers."

More-mature creative efforts are never haphazard. Older primary children may plan a "fort" or "clubhouse" for several days before beginning construction. If allowed to continue, such constructions may be transformed repeatedly as children think of new alternatives.

Children need information about texture, size, shape, weight, flexibility, and translucency of materials to carry out their projects. They also learn about part–whole relationships as they construct complex forms having many components (Reifel & Greenfield, 1983). Position in space and placement of objects in relation to one another are typical concepts developed during the construction process. Children may use their drawing constructions to facilitate memory of an important experience (Raines, 1990). Anne Janette's picture (see photo) is the painting of an 8-year-old child with disabilities that was produced shortly after she and her father built a snowman. The most complex construction that this child produced during the early years, this painting provided a source of many good memories as she grew. Construction is inevitably an outcome of children's need to understand their social and physical world in their own very active terms by making things (Franklin, 1994).

Similarly, children create music. They use rhythm, pitch, the voices of simple instruments, and their own voices to generate simple tunes within the context of

Anne Janette created this iconic construction to represent the snowman she had built the evening before.

play. They explore the concepts of duration and pattern and the use of repeated phrases in their chants. Often such chants are used to denote special effects during their pretend play or "magical" transformations such as when Sara chanted, "Grow, gro . . ow gro . . . . ow," to alter her pretend role from baby to someone who could iron clothes.

Affective Domain

Pretend play has long been recognized as a vehicle for children to express their innermost thoughts and feelings. Although most play episodes either are based on immediate past observations and experiences or occur in response to cues from the physical environment of the school, children can and do enact play sequences that express their concerns. Increasing evidence indicates that children's pretend play fosters their ability to simulate feelings and desires not currently held, which allows the child to understand that other people may hold different beliefs about the world and to perform correctly from that viewpoint (Jenkins, 2000). Sometimes the experiences they view on television may be so emotionally overwhelming that such tragedies are expressed only through their constructions (Gross & Clemens, 2002). Children achieve mastery of their feelings when they rework a scene to a happier conclusion, can express repressed feelings, and can try out solutions to normal daily crises. Play is also one of the most powerful and effective means of reducing children's ordinary stress (Jesse, Wilson, & Morgan, 2000). All children experience fears about being accepted (and may be temporarily rejected by their peers) or may have concerns about family members. For example, two 8-year-olds played out marriage, separation, divorce, courtship, and remarriage during a period of several weeks. One child came from a stable two-parent family, and her best friend had already lived through the divorce process, with her father remarrying and a mother contemplating a second marriage. Through multiple play sequences, the inevitable uncertainties that one child was experiencing were portrayed while the other learned about the social and emotional realities experienced by another. Pretend play is a normal process by which healthy children learn to cope with the problems of daily life.

Children gain self-confidence and demonstrate pride in their creations: "I did it!" "Look at mine!" "This, here, is my house!" Children have a sense of mastery as they work hard, solve problems, test their skills, and demonstrate patience and perseverance in the construction process. Construction play leads to a sense of confidence and competence as children have concrete evidence of their endeavors.

During play, children communicate their anxieties that cannot be simply explained to an adult that relate to and predict the status of their mental health (Warren, Emde, & Sroufe, 2000). Similarly, children develop their skills in expressing, controlling, and modeling emotional behavior through play as they come to better understand the contextual situations in which modulating emotional responsiveness is appropriate (Kwon & Yawkey, 2000). This skills set is generally termed *emotional intelligence*.

Language Domain

Research on the effect of pretend play on language development is extensive, and the results of most studies indicate positive relationships (Frost, 1991). In a detailed review of the literature, play was found to have the following specific effects (Levy, 1984, p. 167): Play stimulates innovation in language, introduces and clarifies new words and concepts, motivates language use and practice, and encourages verbal thinking. Apparently, the relationship between symbolic play and language increases with age because the play becomes more abstract and independent of real objects as a source of shared meaning. Good players are more verbal during play. In fact, examples of kindergartners' language at play were found to be better indicators of language ability than did formal assessments such as the Illinois Test of Psycholinguistic Abilities (Levy, 1984). Language fluency and the variety of language structures were even greater during block play than during housekeeping play (Isbell & Raines, 1991). Pretend play also enhances short- and long-term recall and the ability to comprehend stories (Kim, 1999).

When pretend or construction play is enhanced with appropriate materials, children incorporate literacy acts, such as looking at a cookbook while preparing a pretend meal or writing labels on their constructions (Goldhaber, Lipson, Sortino, & Daniels, 1997). When appropriate teacher guidance is added, the variety and frequency of such acts increases (Morrow, 1990). The free use of open-ended materials enables children to play with the forms of written language as a part of their constructions, supporting emergent literacy (S. Miller, Fernie, & Kantor, 1992). An even greater effect was observed as teachers played beside children in a literacy-enriched environment, informally modeling the use of books and helping children to produce signs (Pickett, 1998). In a mixed-age primary group (K–Grade 2) of children, youngsters incorporated reading environmental print, functional reading, reading for pleasure, academic reading (i.e., practicing letter recognition, etc.), reading aloud, engaging in other book-related activities with art or drama, and both recreational writing (self-expression) and academic writing (penmanship and spelling) during sociodramatic play with mixed-age classmates (Stone & Christie, 1996). Children also produce a variety of written language that is functional. They write to (a) serve instrumental purposes (making a list of things to get), (b) regulate the behavior of others (preparing a "Keep Out" sign), (c) meet interaction needs (writing a telephone number for a friend), (d) fill personal needs (putting their name on paper), and (e) relay information (making a "Telephone Broken" sign; Stroud, 1995). Children also engage in conversations about literacy within the play context, which might include using literacy conventions, naming literacy-related objects, or even coaching one another in some literacy task in order to achieve a play goal (Neuman & Roskos, 1990).

Primary-age children from low socioeconomic families are far more likely to benefit by attaining literacy competence from drama instruction than are students from average populations (Podlozny, 2000). This finding is particularly true for helping children learn the elements of a story (Creech & Bhavnagri, 2002). The linkages between aesthetics and pretence enhance children's ability to write stories.

Physical Domain

Motor development is perhaps the skill most obviously affected by pretend play and construction and therefore not typically the focus of research. Children manipulate fasteners when they dress up, develop the tripod grip and increase their control over writing instruments as they pretend to be writers, and coordinate eyes and hands with the rest of the body when moving objects as they engage in play. Perceptual-motor and fine-motor skills improve with time. Three-year-olds build with great concentration, but their blocks are haphazardly stacked, which leads to imbalance. Four-year-olds are more precise and straighten blocks that are not aligned. By five, these skills have become so refined and controlled that children can place blocks with precision and move more rapidly, making increasingly complex structures (Santrock, 2000). Older youngsters can achieve similar results with smaller blocks and less uniform materials. Construction with large blocks in particular strengthens muscles. Body awareness in relation to specific spaces as they stand, sit, crouch, or reach across other blocks contributes to understanding spatial relationships as they maneuver during construction activities (Wellhousen & Kieff, 2001).

Social Domain

Social competence, or the ability to function effectively in society appropriate to your age, comprises several aspects. Perspective taking, conceptions of friendship, interpersonal strategies, problem solving, moral judgment, and communication skills are all components of social behavior. Participation in sociodramatic play requires a high level of both social and cognitive abilities, including sharing and cooperation, appreciation of role reciprocity, and self-regulation of affect. Generally, increases in pretend-play skills are associated with corresponding increases in all three aspects of social cognition:

❑ Visual or perceptual perspective taking—How does another person see the world?

❑ Cognitive perspective taking—What are other people thinking? What are other people like?

❑ Affective perspective taking—What kind of emotional experiences is another person having? (Johnsen & Christie, 1984, p. 109)

The spontaneous play of pretend scripts provides the context and the practice for children to learn negotiation skills and achieve social acceptance. Children continually engage in social comparison as they encounter differing perceptions of a given situation. These checks are frequently in the form of tag questions ("You're not going to her house; right?") as a request for information. Correspondingly, they make requests for agreement ("Let's not play house today; OK?"), permission ("I need to make this street longer; right?" [moving into another's play space]), compliance ("You can put those babies to bed now; huh?"), verbal response ("You like to play cars; right?"), and attention ("This is a bridge; see?"; Chafel, 1986). As children initiate and respond to verbalizations that are essential to social play, they develop leadership skills (Trawick-Smith, 1988). In early childhood, children who rank high in leadership skills also rank high in following skills. They can contribute to the

TABLE 15.4 Analysis of an Experience of Primary-Age Children Creating a Postal Center

Domain	Intermediate Objectives	Immediate Objectives	Pretend Play	Construction
Aesthetic	Reflect on and discuss aesthetic experiences Appreciate art as a means of nonverbal communication	☐ Collect a variety of used postage stamps ☐ Discuss the images on the stamps ☐ Select stamps to use for pretend mail	Children contribute stamps for the post office. Customers select stamps for their letters.	Use postage stamp designs as a part of the display in the post office. Place as appropriate to the structure.
Affective	Gain experience and demonstrate independence in using age-appropriate materials and tools Assume responsibility for caring for classroom materials	☐ Use pretend money with the cash register and scales ☐ Put away materials at the end of the daily play session ☐ Use hollow blocks and long boards appropriately	Children will have scales to weigh the letters and packages, pretend money to purchase stamps, calculators to compute totals for multiple purchases, and writing materials for receipts.	Children build the postal center with blocks, boards, and furnishings.
Cognitive	Discover measurement relationships by using standard unit tools Add and subtract Identify numbers	☐ Base charges on actual weights and using current postal rates ☐ Use a rate chart ☐ Calculate charges either by hand or with a calculator	Most primary-age children can read the numerals for the postage stamps and charts. The challenge will be to figure cost per unit.	
Language	Demonstrate courteous listening behaviors Demonstrate comprehension of spoken language Use own version of writing Respond to written symbols in the environment	☐ Engage in polite exchanges between seller and buyer ☐ Ask appropriate questions in the pretend context ☐ Respond to written signs ☐ Write letters to classmates and others in the school; read own letters	Maintain the flow of pretend play through metacommunications. Use enactment to supplement visual symbols and create the narrative that supports the pretend story. Use reading and writing within the play frame.	Make signs, envelopes, or other props using written language or pictographs.
Physical	Coordinate wrist, hand, finger, finger–thumb, and eye–hand movements Maintain adequate levels of physical activity	☐ Use pencils, pens, tape, and other adhesives ☐ Wrap and unwrap packages	Children will be engaged almost continuously in fine-motor activity as they write letters, put stamps on them, organize the post office, and use the tools and props provided. Post office play is active, with postal deliveries and general movement in the setting.	Children will be moving furnishings and blocks, which requires coordination during the construction process.
Social	Learn how to cooperate Develop knowledge related to social studies	☐ Make plans for building the postal station together ☐ Build the station ☐ Collect information about postal services from the community ☐ Use accurate information in play	Many skills in play and social intercourse are required during complex thematic play in addition to those listed. Children must relate to one another in role-appropriate ways, settle disputes, negotiate roles, and use metacommunications to make the play move forward. Exchanges with one another must be mutual and balanced.	Cooperation is required for children to build the postal station with large blocks and furnishings. Work must be organized, jobs assigned, placements agreed to, and then implemented. Objects must also be collected and placed and signs made.

direction of play but do not dominate it. Kindergartners and primary-grade children use richer texts, more-contoured scripts, and more-elaborate plots than those used by preschool children. There is also more directing and stage-managing of the play at this age (Johnson, Christie, & Yawkey, 1999). Friendship grouping in play and construction is stronger and flows across activities.

The social skills practiced during pretend play are also used in construction play. Cooperation and teamwork are required in a variety of construction activities: building with blocks, painting murals, making a bus from a big box. Children negotiate ideas, share information, cooperate, share space and materials, and compare their performance with that of others (Chafel, 1986). For example, because large, hollow blocks are difficult to handle alone, they challenge 3- to 5-year-old children physically. Such blocks also afford opportunities for immediate holistic experiences requiring social organization and cooperation as youngsters build and later engage in pretend play.

INTEGRATION OF MULTIPLE DOMAINS

Construction and pretend play are integrative, requiring that children use all the information at their disposal, share it with others, and apply it in ways that reflect their understanding (Cooper & Dever, 2001; Phelps & Hanline, 1999). Children must synthesize ideas to enact or plans to build in this experience and utilize a variety of skills and abilities (Adams & Nesmith, 1996). The child is a meaning maker, the embodiment of knowledge rather than a passive recipient of it. One of the most salient characteristics of this type of play is that it facilitates the cross-fertilization of ideas and connections across traditional content areas (Chaillé & Silvern, 1996). Children must use logical-mathematical thinking about space relations, oral language skills, and techniques for negotiation and cooperation in order to build a fort and play in it. Like pretend play, construction play challenges children to use all that they know and can do to be successful.

Berry, Stan, Chico, and William labored with the large blocks. "We have to make this longer so everyone can get to Mars," noted William. His teacher had just shown this group of youngsters pictures of the space shuttle as a result of their interest expressed as the class studied the night sky.

"And wear space suits to build it," commented Stan who had interestedly watched a space walk recently on television. The boys collected some large boxes and used masking tape to make appropriate space suits.

Once the space-going vessel was built, Berry took the role of steering it. When Chico, who had removed his costume, stepped out of the structure, William cried, "Man lost!" as Stan commented, "You're going to just pop out there. You have to wait till we land!"

Chico entered the vessel and waited for the slow process of landing before heading off to another activity.

To illustrate the amalgamation of curriculum goals more completely through pretend play and construction, Table 15.4 has been compiled to analyze the relationship of specific goals to a particular scenario in a primary classroom—post office. The opportunity to learn does not guarantee that all children will learn the same things. Participants must actively engage in the activity and take advantage of the opportunities provided.

Many intermediate objectives within the domains may be addressed during pretend play or construction; objectives may be combined as described in Table 15.4. The children's maturity, their skills in pretend play and construction, their experience in playing with one another, and the topic of the pretend play are all relevant. For example, the goals addressed in the cognitive and language domains would not be as appropriate for 3- and 4-year-old children. In addition, the degree of the teacher's guidance and support would have to be adjusted for children of varying ages.

TEACHERS' QUESTIONS REGARDING PRETEND AND CONSTRUCTION PLAY

1. *Don't children get enough play at home?* For children who enter a program without pretend-play skills, the school is the only source of such information. If the parents of these children understood the significance of pretend play and knew how to support it, the children would have some of the skills at program entry. Children just turning 3 years old are just beginning to develop pretend play, which will peak sometime between ages 5 and 6 years; for older children, these skills are used in developing understanding of new information that they encounter in the primary grades. Families do not usually have the materials, information, and guidance techniques for developing a variety of play opportunities such as archaeologist, scientist, or space explorer. Families may supplement what early childhood programs do if they receive information and suggestions, although some children do not have access to a peer group in the immediate vicinity of their homes. Skill in play, information about the themes played, playmates who have similar information, time, materials, and supportive adults are all necessary to achieve optimal outcomes from pretend play. Similarly, effective constructive play requires similar conditions for optimal outcomes. As with other strategies that support learning, families generally are supportive and willing

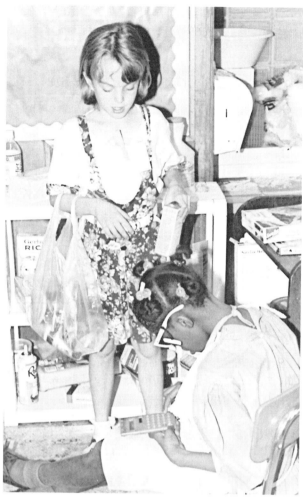

These second graders are combining mathematics, language, and social skills as they pretend "store."

within the limitations of time, skill, and their resources. If children who are very inexperienced or unskilled players enter a program, teachers may use some of the strategies listed in Table 15.5.

2. *What can I do without the proper equipment and materials?* Because pretend play for 3- to 5-year-olds is a priority, programs should allocate resources to this domain first. Quality unit and hollow blocks are expensive as an initial purchase, as are the furnishings to support pretend play. However, such equipment and furnishings last for 30 to 40 years and require minimal upkeep, which children can undertake themselves, so such items are a relatively low-cost investment in the long run. Unit and large blocks, as well as pretend furnishings, are flexible in supporting all the domains of learning and have the unique capacity for integrating children's experiences.

Many of the materials for pretend play and construction are found rather than purchased. For example,

teachers can gradually develop pretend-play kits as described in Figure 15.1 (on p. 422). The task of adding to and replacing materials in the pretend-play kits may be shared among teachers. Garage sales, flea markets, donations from parents, and discards from industry are sources of pretend-play props. File boxes are often useful for storage, and schools may install near-ceiling shelving to hold them. Industrial and household discards make excellent resources for construction projects. Figures and vehicles used in construction are inexpensive and may also be donated by families whose children have outgrown them.

3. *What do I do about superhero play and other play themes that make me uncomfortable? Sometimes it is violent.* Teachers are legitimately concerned about the level of violence in children's play. Several sources of violence might appear in pretend play, and each should be treated independently. First is violence that is simply the imitation of observed adult behavior at home and in the community. Second is violence portrayed as a result of events such as earthquakes, war, car accidents, and other catastrophes. Third is play that is related to children's inner needs to handle their feelings of aggression and helplessness. Fourth is the use of pretend-play toys and scripts from television; generally children select only the action sequences and violent scenes for reenactment. Last is *masked play*, in which the child engages in play for the purpose of behaving aggressively toward others without having to be responsible for the consequences of the aggressive act. Each source of violent play is briefly discussed next, individually.

Teachers of preschool children are likely to see youngsters enact events they have observed. Adults in some families have little privacy, so children are likely to incorporate behaviors such as parental arguments, physical fights, and sexual intercourse into play sequences. Young children simply do not understand what should remain private and what is appropriate for play in school. Teachers who observe inappropriate play have found simple redirection to be most useful. Focusing on other activities that adult men and women engage in is usually sufficient. An effort should be made to keep this redirection low key because children tend to imitate another's outstanding play sequences. By first grade, youngsters usually can distinguish between public and private family information and are less likely to enact the latter. Frequent, repetitive, or excessively detailed play sequences of violent or sexual behavior may be an indicator that the child is living in an unwholesome situation that requires additional attention.

Children who experience a natural disaster such as an earthquake or a flood or who witness serious accidents or violence on the street struggle with feelings of intense fear, anger, and helplessness. In the process of

TABLE 15.5 Common Child Behaviors Indicating Lack of Pretend-Play Skills and Selected Teacher Intervention Strategies

Behavior	Teacher Intervention Strategy
Avoiding the pretend-play area	Encourage participation directly.
	Assist the child in entering the area before others arrive.
Continuing a pattern of exploring materials without using them for play	Use open-ended questions: "What else do you think you can do with that?" "Show me how you might use that if you were a [role] policeman."
Manipulating play materials and discarding them	Engage the child in thinking about the materials: "Tell me about the _____." "How could that be used to _____?"
Misusing materials	Assess whether the material is appropriate for the child's age. If it has either too little or too much challenge, it may be misused.
	Ask children to tell you about an object. Some very young children may not "recognize" a common prop.
	Suggest appropriate object substitutions: "Pretend that the _____ is a _____."
Focusing on the reality aspects only; insisting that the stove will not cook something, for example	Explain that pretend-play props are not supposed to work. Demonstrate pretend play with the object.
Regarding other players with amazement; watching, staring, and appearing confused (common among 3- and 4-year-olds)	Move close to this child and provide comments about what the others are doing. "George and Alfie are pretending to be truckers. They are . . ."
	Engage in pretend play with this child.
	Select another child with slightly better pretend skills, and encourage them to play together.
Either coercing others or participating very passively; not engaging in mutual theme or shared goal	Often 3- and 4-year-olds will work out patterns of leadership on their own, but if this behavior occurs with older children or is persistent, play with the children and demonstrate mutual play.
	Discuss the play theme in a group, and explore possible ideas before children begin to play. Ensure that most of the children have the knowledge they need to play out the theme. In some instances intervene directly in the play and use the mediation strategies suggested in chapter 6.

enactment, the child can work out a variety of situations and solutions and perhaps master these emotions. Such play may require many repetitions before the child feels safe. Teachers may facilitate this process by providing accurate information and reassurance as children play out violent scenes. Listening to the real concerns of children as they depict this type of violence through either their constructions or their pretend play is key to helping them to understand and to cope with their fears (Gross & Clemens, 2002). The content of the play is the fear and violence itself, and other players often take on the roles of nurturer, rescuer, and comforter. Themes of family and friends, health care, and rescue workers of various sorts may be useful if such incidents occur in a community.

Five- to seven-year-olds are concerned with social position. Competent students and skillful players are accorded high status among peers. In some schools toughness or skill in fighting is another avenue to social position. Fighting has nothing to do with play and should be handled by adults as inappropriate behavior. However, children are also concerned about aggressor and victim roles in a more general sense, as in cops and robbers, good guys and bad guys. These roles are designed to be oppositional. Opposing-force pretend play may occur during children's recess or noninstructional time without real violence occurring. Frequently the bad guys are imaginary. If no injuries and no real violence will occur, dealing with the forces of good and evil as a play theme may allow children to work out their ideas of right and wrong in an acceptable framework (Boyd, 1997). Play around issues of justice, right and wrong, and fairness are important concepts for older children to explore.

FIGURE 15.1 Pretend-Play Kits with Associated Teaching Themes

Unit Theme: Living in Homes
Pretend-Play Theme: Real Estate
Props: Pictures of many kinds of homes, magazines, real estate brochures, desk, telephone, paper, pencil, chairs, "contract forms," "Real Estate" and "For Sale" signs

Moving Houses
Props: Wagons, small moving dollies, boxes with ropes, rags for wrapping goods, telephone, work order forms, pencils, child furniture, clothing, stuffed animals, dolls, "Moving Day" sign

Unit Theme: Clothing
Pretend-Play Theme: Washing Clothes
Props: Doll clothes, a tub or water table with soap, clothesline and pins, plastic aprons

Dress Up
Props: Scarves, hats, curtains, coats and capes, shoes, mirror, dresses, ties, shirts

Unit Theme: Vehicles
Pretend-Play Theme: Gas Station
Props: Gas pumps with hoses, windshield-washing equipment, tires, tire pump, wrenches, fan belts, screwdrivers, cash register

Vehicle Showroom
Props: Many vehicles arranged, car sales brochures, ads, calculators, pencils, forms, price stickers, balloons

Unit Theme: Insects
Pretend-Play Theme: Entomologist's Laboratory
Props: Insect pictures, specimens, tripod, magnifying glass, white coats, paper, pencil, insect books, dried insects, wasp nests, or other real things

Picnic Partners
Props: Dishes, pretend food, tablecloth, plastic or paper insects

Unit Theme: The Sky
Pretend-Play Theme: It's Raining, It's Pouring
Props: Sand-table village or miniature houses; rocks; seashells; twigs; miniature people for the houses; squirt cans; small drum for thunder; "Cirrus," "Stratus," "Cumulus," and "Nimbus" signs

Outdoor Slumber Party
Props: Sleeping bags or blankets, alarm clock, different phases of the moon to hang, stars, large pajamas (worn over clothes), stuffed animals

Unit Theme: Machines
Pretend-Play Theme: Repair Shop
Props: Wrenches, screwdrivers, pliers, old clocks, radios, toasters, pencil, paper, do-it-yourself books, "Repair Anything" sign

Bike Repair
Props: Wrenches, loose spokes, cogs and sprockets (donations from local bike shop, cleaned), rags, telephone, pencil, paper, bikes or tricycles

Unit Theme: Storytelling
Pretend-Play Theme: Storytelling Theater
Props: Chairs for seating, a "stage" marked off with blocks or tape, tickets, playbill, cash register, dolls for audience, dress-up clothes, hats, child-constructed costumes if desired, child-painted backdrops for older children

Bedtime Stories
Props: Dolls, doll beds, picture books, rocking chair, lullaby CDs.

Source: Adapted from material in *Teaching Young Children Using Themes* (Kostelnik, 1991).

The number of fantasy action heroes portrayed on television has increased with time. Considering that young children are exposed to as much television as schooling, the fact that children reenact media episodes is not surprising (Bergen, 1994). Working with parents to monitor television viewing may be the most practical solution to the least desirable programs (Boyatzis, 1997). Reenactment of film or video portrayals rarely entails more than the sequenced action scenes. With roles selected from commercial characters, children incorporate rough-and-tumble play into their pretend play. Enactment of fantasy heroes of this type is much more common in casual or illicit play than in teacher-initiated or teacher-guided classroom play.

Rough-and-tumble play, consisting of laughing, running, smiling, jumping, open-hand beating, wrestling, play fighting, chasing, and fleeing, looks aggressive to many adults. However, children engaging in this type of play do not get hurt or cry, nor are they confused about what is or is not play. Rough-and-tumble play apparently facilitates social cognition (Bjorklund & Brown, 1998). Frequently, rough-and-tumble play is a transitional activity leading to games with rules, especially for popular boys (Pellegrini & Perlmutter, 1988). Teachers apparently become distressed with excited, physically active play more than the children or other objective observers do, which may be related to teachers' appreciation of the more-gentle play forms typical of girls than the rough-and-tumble play regularly pursued by boys. Aggression, which includes fixation, frowning, hitting, pushing, taking, and grabbing, is more likely to occur in relation to possessions than in the fast-moving superhero play typically seen on playgrounds.

Violent play rarely emerges from the carefully planned play opportunities provided by teachers as a part of the curriculum (Boyd, 1997). Acting-out behavior, frequent violent outbursts, and excessive anger or hostility displayed by a child may be symptoms requiring special intervention and should be carefully assessed and the child referred to experts. In the meantime, even distressed children can learn to behave appropriately in the classroom setting. See chapter 6 for details.

4. *What do teachers do when children say, "You can't play!"* Even preschool-age children judge straightforward exclusion from activities on the basis of gender as wrong (Theimer, Killen, & Stangor, 2001). However, children who are engaged in making a project, who are building a complex structure together, or who are involved in an ongoing pretend scenario are likely to reject new players unless they contribute something unique to the activity. Sometimes the new players would be rejected anyway, or if accepted, the play would disintegrate. In such a case, their inclusion would be similar to adding a fifth player to a partnered card game. However, individual children cannot control the materials from one day to the next. When teachers want particular children to engage in either a construction or a pretend-play episode, these children should begin the activity period in that area as part of the daily plan. When children do not know how to play, planning for moderately skilled players to engage in play with unskilled players is generally effective. As with other scaffolding tasks, the level just above the current level of performance is the goal for the less skilled.

Children may exclude others on the basis of language, social group, race, ability, or sex. When such exclusion occurs, teachers should take the opportunity to help children understand biases better and to develop together several rules based on fairness. Typically, primary-age children prefer to play in single-sex groups,

which is both supportive of sex-role socialization and acceptable. However, one first-grade teacher helped her group to develop the rule that space and materials had to be shared fairly but that individuals could choose with whom to play. Children understood the "fairness" issue and were cooperative.

5. *What if the child has worked with blocks or wet sand and has nothing to carry home?* An instant photograph taken periodically to represent the child's construction is useful. Although doing so frequently is too expensive, the child might select one or two constructions to be preserved in this way. Occasionally, youngsters may take dough products home, especially when the dough needs to be replaced anyway. Children who produce music as a creative effort may consent to tape it if the teacher is unable to write the notation. Older children are often less concerned with carrying something home than they are with saving it from one day to the next. Block or box structures may be saved for a short time to maximize the opportunities for elaboration and expansion typical of these activities. Often the class as a group can establish its own ground rules and propose solutions.

6. *What will the parents think if children are playing in school rather than engaging in real learning?* Parents are very supportive of children's playing in child-centered programs for 3- and 4-year-olds but generally believe that the time spent in play should decrease as children get older (Rothlein & Brett, 1987). Parents do not indicate that play should be eliminated for 6- to 8-year-olds, merely that the amount of time dedicated to play should be less than that for 3- and 4-year-olds. Therefore, parents are likely to express their concerns and will have a particular interest in how much school time is devoted to play. The value of play to the development of a competent child has considerable support in research and can be presented understandably to parents (Nourot & Van Hoorn, 1991). For example, if birds are being studied, young children might pretend to be birds in the nest, and older children, scientists studying birds. In pretend play, children use the information that they have to solve problems. In addition, teachers can assess children's level of understanding about the topic on the basis of their play. If children are unable to incorporate information into pretend-play sequences, they do not understand it well. Other intellectual skill development is also needed. Guided-theme pretend play and construction play that use ideas from science, social studies, or other domain content are logically coherent components of curriculum. Teachers of primary-age children in rural areas provide more opportunities for play than their counterparts in suburban areas, who in turn provide more time than urban teachers do (J. Newman, 1996).

Furthermore, the practice of separating tasks down to skills and drilling them separately has not been a spectacular success (Peck, McCaig & Sapp, 1988). Teaching is more than telling and setting up drill experiences; it is also more than going through textbooks, as a group of Iowa teachers discovered when they set aside all their textbooks and shifted to unit instruction using developmentally appropriate goals (Barclay, Benelli, Campbell, & Kleine, 1995).

If children have had appropriate early experiences, 7-year-olds will be skilled players. They are in the strongest position to engage in creative problem solving and to explore a situation's possibilities in depth. They add detail and substance to their play, which may continue, even though interrupted, during several weeks. Play is a childhood competence that may be used to help them understand science, the humanities, and the world around them. Story reenactment is particularly useful for developing reading comprehension skills and for motivating children with more-limited reading skills. For most teachers, a combination of unit instruction including play and some of the more traditional practices is more typical.

PROMOTION OF PLAY SKILLS

As an infant grows into early childhood, play skills are learned from parents, siblings, and playmates. Some children enter programs with their abilities well devel-

oped, whereas other children are just beginning to gain preliminary proficiency. In this way, play skills are no different from skills in the six domains of the curriculum.

Providing an ample supply of materials, organizing them, and presenting them to children is usually sufficient to encourage exploratory, investigative, and testing play in 3- to 8-year-olds. The general ambience of the classroom is important for any kind of play (Chaillé & Silvern, 1996). To play productively, youngsters must be rested, free from hunger or other physical discomfort, safe, secure and comfortable. Thus, adults must let children know in many ways that child-initiated activity is acceptable. When adults show a lack of interest, fail to provide the materials necessary to support play, neglect skills assessment, or criticize processes in play, the climate is not conducive to experimentation or exploration, much less pretend play or construction.

Adults responsible for youngsters' development must attend to individual and group characteristics so that if children are not self-sufficient in this area, appropriate support and instruction are provided. The first step is to recognize what these skills are and then to examine how they can be taught. In Figure 15.2, specific behaviors are inventoried that are necessary for pretend play and construction. Strategies for actively supporting play are described in the following section.

FIGURE 15.2 Skills Children Need to Engage in Pretend Play and Construction

Children must be able to
 Mimic in their play the behaviors that they have seen or experienced.
 Engage in a wide range of experiences from which to draw their interpretations.
 Use their bodies to represent real or imaginary objects or events.
 Assign symbolic meaning to real or imaginary objects using language or gestures.
 Take on the role attributes of beings or objects and act out interpretations of these roles.
 Create play themes and engage in play themes created by others.
 Experiment with a variety of objects, roles (leader, follower, mediator), and characterizations (animal, mother, astronaut, etc.).
 React to and interact with other children in make-believe situations.
 Maintain pretend play for increasing lengths of time.
 Use narratives and metacommunications to structure the play.
 Dramatize familiar stories, songs, poems, and past events.
 Interpret events and reconstruct them in tangible ways.
 Use diverse approaches and materials to represent objects or events by
   representing a single object or event using different materials or techniques
   representing different objects and events using one material or technique
 Collaborate with classmates to construct a representative object.
 Integrate new information into play episodes.
 Integrate construction into pretend-play episodes.

Customary Strategies to Enhance Play

Educators can use the following 10 strategies to enhance play:

1. *Set the stage for children's play.* The teacher is responsible for establishing conditions that accept and encourage play. Suggestions for doing so are as follows:

a. Incorporate make-believe into transitional times such as cleanup, dressing, or moving from one room to another as a group.
b. Encourage pretend play in other aspects of the curriculum. Ask children to imagine what someone would feel like or how a setting would look, or to pretend that they are the character in the story.
c. Coordinate the theme of the dramatic play center to match other ongoing themes in your room. Provide theme-related props (see Figure 15.1) and materials for construction related to the theme. Add additional materials to the pretend-play setup to expand the play as needed.
d. Provide adequate space for play. Occasionally furniture may need to be moved, or room made for miniature play sets.
e. Provide enough time in any one segment for play to get under way.
f. Pay attention to what children say and do during play. Watch carefully and concentrate. Listen for children's appropriate application of concepts or misinformation.

2. *Create conditions of acceptance and safety by what you say and do.* In a psychologically safe environment, children can risk being wrong or having a project not work out as they had hoped. Creativity is the outcome of challenge and risk taking. The strategies described next include behavioral reflections and questions initially described in chapter 6. The concepts apply equally to pretend play and other forms of play, although for clarity, some specifics related to construction have been selected:

a. Allow children to engage in their activity without intervention or comment unless they contravene safety, property, or the social cooperation rules of the classroom. The play belongs to the children. Often acceptance, observation, and general support are sufficient.
b. Ask about a project or pretend event when children are seeking information or assistance; do not assume you know what the intent is (Cassidy, 1989). You might be wrong. "Tell me about your drawing" and "I don't quite understand what you are trying to do here" are general statements letting the child know that you are not able to interpret his or her construction. "Did you have something specific in mind?" is more direct and is responsive to the child's questions or comments when the teacher is unable to respond because the representation is not clear. These and other strategies will help you to provide the help sought without taking over the project.
c. Describe what you observe about the materials or technique being used or other specific characteristics of the project. Such statements should not be judgmental but might be comparative, such as "I see Harry has used all bright primary colors and George chose the pastels." Describing specifically what the child has done models the appropriate language and conveys respect for the unique characteristics of each child's work. Examples of respectful comments on children's block constructions are listed in Table 15.6. Similar statements could relate to other constructions or to pretend-play events. Such observations may assist children in opening conversations so that both adults and children may understand. Note that the statements are descriptions of the observation.
d. Provide opportunities for children to share their projects with others. Display drawings, paintings, and sculptures regularly. Ask the child who made the construction to talk about his or her ideas at group time. Encourage relevant peer questions and comments. Color, line, mass or volume, pattern, shape or form, space, and texture are appropriate topics for discussion

TABLE 15.6 Respectful Commentary on Children's Block Constructions

Observation	Statement
Which blocks were used	"You found out that two of these make a half circle."
Where the blocks were placed	"You used four blocks to make a big square."
How many blocks were used	"You used all the blocks to make the building."
Whether the blocks are all the same	"All the blocks in your tower are exactly the same size."
How the blocks are connected	"All your blocks are touching."
How the blocks are balanced	"Those long blocks are holding up the shorter ones."

Source: Adapted from Dodge (1991, p. 91).

(Moyer, 1990). Demonstrate how to give feedback or ask questions about the construction. "You selected interesting colors for the [purple] cow" and "The size of this drawing is very small; tell us why you chose to do it that way" are statements based on observations of the construction as well as openings for explanation if the child wants to provide it. Never use sarcasm; the child's feelings will be hurt, and no educational goal can be reached. Do not allow children to provide gratuitous negative comments without making them accountable. For example, if a child says, "That's ugly!" respond by saying, "You think that drawing is not attractive; tell us why you think that." If the child responds with detail, then discuss how the same characteristics that appeal to one person may not be attractive to another.

e. Support children who are feeling frustrated and angry when their work appears unsuccessful to them. Help them define the problem ("Tell me why you think this isn't going to work." "What's wrong?" "What do you think you can do about it?" "Is there anyone else in the class who might be able to assist you?"). Children should be able to achieve their goal by their own actions when they work together. Occasionally offer assistance, but allow the child to make the decisions.

f. Provide display opportunities to everyone. Keep the displays posted for a few days and then dismantle them. Avoid selecting the "best" construction for display. Sometimes the most appealing product does not indicate the most creative thinking.

g. Teach children to respect one another's work. Help them to understand that having respect is why they do not kick down someone's blocks, make noise while someone shares a song, or jeer when someone hangs up a drawing (Kostelnik, Whiren, et al., 2002).

h. Help other children focus on the play potential of the construction. If a child has made a particularly

effective supplement to pretend play, recognize his or her contributions. When children are working together on a construction, encourage them to discuss what they plan to do and how the construction will fit into their continuing play plans. Demonstrate respectfulness yourself. Make statements that recognize children's positive contributions to the ongoing play of their peers.

3. *Actively help children improve their level of performance in pretend play.* Table 15.7 lists procedures that increase in the level of intrusion and power exercised by the teacher. Usually, the teacher selects the least intrusive strategy that will accomplish the change. For example, either active observation or nondirective statements may facilitate the children's becoming more focused or the teacher's starting to develop the theme for skilled children. Inexperienced youngsters may need stronger measures such as modeling and physical intervention (Wolfgang & Sanders, 1986).

Modeling is always done inside the play frame. The teacher becomes a player and assumes a role. Physical intervention during the play usually requires that the teacher enter the space of the play frame, if only briefly, to provide or take away materials. Removing materials is usually more effective if the adult assumes a role ("I'm the plumber and I have come to get the sink [full of water] for repair. You will get it back in a day or two."). This would be done only if there were sufficient reason to intervene—say, if children began adding real water to pasta the teacher had provided for pretend cooking. The water would ruin the pasta and make a sticky mess.

Nondirective statements, questions, and directive statements can quickly offer suggestions or assistance from outside the play frame. Usually the teacher watches, makes the verbalization, and listens to the children's response but does not move into the play directly.

TABLE 15.7 Methods of Instruction from Least Intrusive to Most Intrusive

Methods of Instruction	Example
Active onlooking	The teacher intently observes what children are doing and saying as they play.
Nondirective statements	"It looks like you're going to the beach" or "You're a cloud floating in the air."
Questions	"What do heroes really do?" or "When you go to the store, does the customer pay the storekeeper, or the other way around?"
Directive statements	"Tell me about the family that lives in the dollhouse" or "Think about the middle Billy Goat Gruff and show me how he crossed the bridge."
Modeling	"I'm your new next-door neighbor [knocking at the pretend door]" or the teacher picks up a stethoscope and says, "Is your baby sick?"
Physical intervention	The teacher adds or removes props during the play.

These strategies are effective before and after a play sequence for assisting in the planning and evaluation process. Avoid rushing older children. They frequently take 30 minutes to plan a scenario and 10 minutes to enact it. This planning requires both skill and knowledge.

4. *Teach children the technical skills needed to use materials when they are engaged in construction activity.* Showing the child how to use materials appropriately does not impede creativity. On the contrary, lack of skill inhibits children's ability to do construction. For example, show children how much paste to use and where to place it; show them how to cut; demonstrate sewing; model the use of a wire cutter on potter's clay; and deliberately mix paints so that they can see the effect. Then let them use the skills to implement their own goals (E. Cole, 1990).

Nondirective statements, questions, suggestions, and demonstrations that help the child to do what he or she has in mind are always appropriate. Discrimination between a statement that specifies an outcome and a technique that enables a child to achieve his or her chosen outcome is necessary. As in pretend play, use the least intrusive strategy necessary to support the child's activity.

5. *Allow children to create their own sociodramatic play independently.* Prepare the environment, provide information and resources, then allow the children to

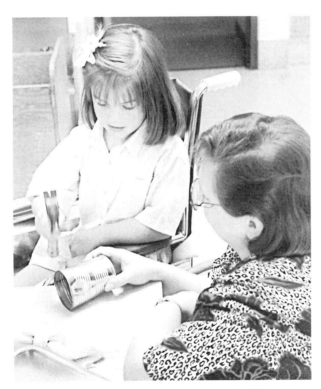

Learning how to use a variety of tools expands children's construction skills.

create their own scripts. If intervention is necessary, intervene and withdraw promptly. Most 5-year-olds have all the basic skills and can elaborate on them within an appropriate setting; therefore, the sociodramatic play center may run smoothly for 5- to 8-year-olds and require limited adult intervention. Encourage experimentation and creative problem solving whenever possible.

6. *Provide information relevant to the play theme.* Use picture books, field trips, videotapes, photographs, and other sources of information so that children know what is supposed to occur in the pretend situation. Themes and topics from social studies, science, and literature support older children's knowledge needs and can be most easily incorporated into related pretend-play themes. Identify information gaps and misunderstanding. If children pretend that firefighters set the fires before putting them out, they need additional information on fire safety and community helpers. Strategies for providing information for pretend play also work for construction.

7. *Provide a solid base of information and experience from which children develop their constructions.* Projects of investigation should be a regular part of the curriculum, not an add-on or an extra. Build on children's interest, and use the surrounding community as a source of information and assistance. Both field trips and visitors to the classroom enhance the information base established by the teacher. Projects and themes, which are described in the next chapter, are another good avenue to support construction.

8. *Support children in their problem solving,* and encourage them to expand the number and diversity of potential solutions (Casey & Lippman, 1991). (The corollary is that teachers should not arbitrarily announce "That won't work!" before a child has had a chance to think about his or her plan.) The following strategies are useful:

a. Attempt to grasp the child's intent. Direct observation sometimes works, but you may need to ask ("It seems that you are trying to . . ."). Honestly inquire if necessary ("I don't understand . . .").
b. Ask about alternatives children considered ("Tell me what you thought about doing. . . Anything else?").
c. Inquire about the possible sources of information ("Has anyone done anything like this before? Might he or she help?"). Encourage the use of reference materials ("Where might you get a picture of the . . . ?" or "Is there anything else you might use to help you figure this out?"). In one instance a 4-year-old was attempting to build a pair of walkie-talkies. She had already nailed long spikes into the ends of two blocks of wood and was worried that "they won't work just like that." She had never seen a walkie-talkie up

close but knew they had more than an antenna to make them receive and transmit. The teacher could have just handed her a walkie-talkie. Instead, she carefully engaged the child in a conversation until the child recognized the scope of the problem and could quickly identify a potential solution.

d. Encourage children to participate in the general planning and decision-making process. When a child enthusiastically asks, "Can we build a . . . ?" respond, "Yes, and what materials [space, time] will you need?" or "Yes, and how will you do this?" Avoid "Yes, but . . ." Children cannot do everything just when they might like to. Older children are particularly sensitive to the competing needs for time and space. Involve them in making opportunities for carrying out and building projects.

e. Actively involve children who are less likely to initiate construction projects. Often the more timid child is left out of group constructions or does not initiate construction activities independently. Good ideas may be lost to the group and the timid child's abilities not acknowledged or recognized, even by the individuals involved. Watch for opportunities to suggest that the timid child participate in the group endeavor. Interact with the less forceful students, and encourage them to share their ideas with you and one or two others. Avoid telling them what to do or giving them solutions to problems. Standing by them (literally) when they approach other children is more likely to give them confidence and practice and to help them with the task at hand.

f. Allow time for children to think about and develop their ideas. Few problems are solved spontaneously. Little creative work happens on the spur of the moment. Sometimes more time is required to think about and plan a project than that required to carry it out. Rather than urging a child who is sitting quietly or abstractedly to "Get started on . . .", offer a listening ear: "Would you like to share what you are thinking about? Maybe that will help."

9. *Encourage the flow among play, construction, and information acquisition.* Given the appropriate circumstances, experiences that are intended as basic information generate construction. Equally often, children's desire to construct something for their play motivates them to seek the information. Topical reference materials are essential to every classroom, even for the youngest children. Older children may look up information for themselves, and younger children can watch teachers who "don't know, but I'll find out."

10. *Evaluate the level of skill development.* Observe all the children and determine whether each child is able to pretend play. If a child can do so, check such qualita-

tive aspects as posing problems to be solved, generating ideas, initiating play, following play, negotiating, allowing new players to enter the play, and creating objects to be used in the play. Check to see whether children are using metacommunication skills to structure pretend play. Because play is often an area of strength, skills developed in this context may be transferred to other areas of developing competence. Recall that the highest level of play has a story structure with a plot and resolution of a problem. Higher levels of construction incorporate artifacts into pretend play or other areas of learning.

The preceding 10 general tactics proposed to support pretend play and construction include approaches to creating an appropriate climate, instruction on interventions for less skilled children, methods for combining play and information, procedures for fostering cooperation and respect among the players, patterns of effective adult–child conversation, and recommendations for assessment. These components are essential for achieving desirable skills, yet more remains to be done. Adults must plan for play to occur, provide many opportunities for a variety of construction activities, and foster specific sociodramatic and theme play that enables children to make sense of their world.

One advantage of planning for pretend play daily is that once the basic plan is made and the center is operating, it can continue as long as the unit of instruction continues. The teacher may add props or materials occasionally or encourage children to bring household discards from home to supplement school supplies. The teacher's task is to encourage, guide, and assess children's accomplishments.

Construction activities may be short term for younger children or may involve weeks of work with primary-age children. Various materials representing the same objects and events with different media enhance children's understanding. Often construction and pretend play are a part of the same episode or activity. When children make their own props to enact a story with a problem and a resolution, they are involved in a very complex, intellectually demanding activity.

SUMMARY

At the beginning of this chapter you were asked a number of questions that you should now be able to answer readily. Play has unique characteristics that distinguish this behavior from all others.

Children integrate their understanding of experience through pretend play and construction and learn other things on their own. The relationships between specific areas of development and play are illuminated in this chapter, as are the areas in which expectations for individual differences can be anticipated. When teachers understand this, they are better prepared to plan for play experiences.

General strategies to support play and ideas for planning appropriate learning centers and projects are also presented. When themes are incorporated into pretend play and construction, much learning is consolidated in children's minds. As you learn how to develop themes and projects in the next chapter, keep in mind the role that pretend play and construction might play for each theme.

Applying What You Read in This Chapter

1. Discuss

a. What makes an activity playful or not playful? How can you tell the difference?

b. Why does resistance to including play exist in many public school settings, and what role might you play as a member of the teaching team in one of these settings?

c. Describe what you might expect to see in (a) a classroom in which guided play is a part of the curriculum and (b) a setting in which the teacher simply lets children play if they want to and treats it as a time filler until dismissal.

2. Observe

a. Observe children at play with materials that can be used for construction and find (a) a child exploring or investigating only, (b) a child who appears invested in the design (patterner), and (c) a child who appears to be pretending with what he or she has made (dramatist). How is their play similar? What distinguishes these approaches? Do children change in their approach during the observation?

b. Observe a 3-year-old and a child who is 5 years of age or older who are engaged in pretend play. What skills does each child have for pretending with an object; pretending about time, place, or setting; substituting objects; pretending with another child for at least 10 minutes; maintaining an idea or a topic in the play with another; and introducing a problem and resolving it in the pretend-play sequence.

c. Review Table 15.4. Organize a similar table for analyzing either pretend play or construction. Observe a group of children at play for at least 30 minutes and identify the specific intermediate objectives in each of the six domains that their play suggests. You should infer the relevant objectives from what the children do and say. You may not recognize all the learning potentials in each domain on any one occasion.

3. Carry out an activity

a. Examine the play ideas presented in Tables 15.1 and 15.2. Select one activity from each and write a long-form lesson plan to implement it.

b. Participate in the block area of a program. Use the strategies to support block construction suggested in the section on promoting children's play skills.

4. Create something for your portfolio

a. Using the information in this chapter, prepare a checklist to use to assess pretend play and construction play skills.

b. Write a newsletter for parents, explaining why you will include pretend play in the classroom. Explain briefly how such play will contribute to the children's learning. The newsletter should be well written and no longer than two single-spaced pages.

c. Review chapter 3, and select four teaching strategies that support pretend play and construction.

5. Add to your journal

a. Describe in detail one memorable play experience from your childhood in a program setting. Include details about what made this experience so memorable. Then review the chapter and reflect on the content in terms of your personal experience.

b. After interacting with a group of children who have had some opportunity to engage in pretend play or construction, contemplate your performance in terms of the suggestions offered in this chapter. In what areas were you more or less successful? What questions do you still have regarding children's performance?

Integrating Curriculum by Using Themes and Projects

You may wonder:

What is *theme teaching?* What is a *project?*

What are the benefits of using themes and projects?

What kinds of themes or projects are most suitable for pre-schoolers? for school-age children?

What are the steps involved in creating a theme or project from start to finish?

What are the pitfalls to avoid when I use themes and projects?

In this chapter on themes and projects, we present information to help you answer the preceding questions.

The children have been gathering a variety of rocks for their collection. With their teacher's aid, they create a graph depicting differences in the color, size, and shape of the rocks.

The children use smooth, round rocks as tools to grind corn into a coarse powder. Later, they make fried mush from the cornmeal.

A lively discussion takes place when the teacher asks the children to predict what will happen to two large rocks when one is placed in the shade and the other in the sunshine. She records the group's predictions, and after the experiments are carried out, the children compare their ideas with the results.

The children create a classroom book in which they draw, dictate, or write descriptions of rocks found on a recent rock hunt.

Following a field trip to a rock shop, the children transform the pretend-play area into their own "rock shop." They pretend to buy and sell rocks and minerals to people at a mall.

As an outgrowth of their interest in rocks, children in the class wondered, "Where do different rocks come from?" and "Why are some rocks shiny and some rocks dull?" These questions led to individual and collective investigations by the children (also known as project work*) that lasted several days.*

These are typical activities you might see occurring in any early childhood classroom from preschool through the second grade. All involve hands-on experiences for children and provide them with information about rocks. They also give children opportunities to observe, compare, count, predict, remember, role-play, express ideas, and develop fine-motor skills.

In one classroom, these activities might be dispersed throughout the year; in another, they might be offered within the framework of a multiweek theme focusing on rocks. Children experiencing either approach will probably profit from the activities and increase their knowledge. However, youngsters involved in several rock-related activities concentrated within a month-long theme have the added advantage of being able to make connections among these activities that could be more difficult to make if the lessons were more spread out across time. The creation of such linkages is the essence of theme teaching (Kostelnik, 1996).

WHAT THEME TEACHING IS

Theme teaching involves creating an array of educationally sound activities planned around a central idea. These activities are integrated into all aspects of the curriculum and take place within a concentrated time frame, ranging from several days to several weeks. Such integration creates a common thread among activities that facilitates children's generalization of knowledge and skills from one experience to another (Eliason & Jenkins, 2003; Machado & Meyer, 2001). Early childhood educators who successfully implement themes incorporate the principles of developmentally appropriate practice described throughout this volume into their teaching. Such practices form the foundation for effective theme teaching.

HOW THEMES CONTRIBUTE TO CHILDREN'S CONCEPT DEVELOPMENT

Using themes to organize young children's educational experiences is not a new idea. It has been a popular teaching method since Dewey first proposed that curriculum be related to children's real-life experiences. Since then, educators have looked to themes as a way to help children gain an overall sense of direction and consolidation in their learning. Through participation in theme-related activities, children form connections among individual bits of information. These connections contribute to children's concept development and are the most important reason to use themes as part of your program.

Conceptual Development

Concepts are the fundamental ideas children form about objects and events in the world. They serve as the cognitive categories that allow children to group perceptually distinct information, events, or objects (Eliason & Jenkins, 2003). As such, concepts serve as the building blocks of knowing, thinking, and reasoning.

Children form concepts through firsthand experiences (Berk & Winsler, 1995). Each time they act on objects or interact with other people, they extract relevant bits of meaning from the encounter. They combine the new information with previously acquired knowledge and perceptions to clarify or modify current understandings and later to construct new ideas. By mentally cataloging a growing number of experiences and making finer discriminations and more-abstract connections among them, children build, adjust, and expand their concepts with time.

Link Between Concepts and Themes

The natural process of mentally connecting bits of information into more unified ideas is enhanced through children's involvement in thematic instruction. As children engage in activities permeated by a theme, they can more easily link what they have learned in one activity to what they have learned in another. In this way, theme teaching provides children with opportunities to integrate learning across the curriculum (Bergstrom & O'Brien, 2001). For instance, participating in theme-related aesthetic, language, and cognitive activities enables children to combine the individual elements of the curriculum into a cohesive whole. Similarly, when children carry out math, science, and social studies activities linked by a theme, they go beyond the bounds of traditional subject matter to form more holistic, comprehensive understandings. These understandings represent increasingly elaborate concepts. Because young children are continuously striving to make sense of their environment, the early childhood years are years of rapid concept development. Consequently, educators have become increasingly interested in helping young children make conceptual connections through an integrated curriculum that also provides concept organizers such as themes (Chard, 2001; Kovalik, 1997).

ADDITIONAL BENEFITS FOR CHILDREN

In addition to enhancing children's concept development, themes provide other advantages to young learners. First, they offer children a means for exploring a central pool of information through many different avenues. Regardless of whether children prefer small- or whole-group activities, more or less active modes of interaction, or auditory, kinesthetic, visual, interpersonal, or intrapersonal experiences, they can gain access to a topic in ways that suit their individual needs. If one activity is unappealing or does not match their learning style or fails to fit their capacities, children have other options for learning about the concept. They may pursue alternative activities instead, gaining similar insights. This is not the case when ideas are presented only once or in only one way.

Second, themes encourage children to immerse themselves in a topic. As youngsters become interested in an idea, they often want to know *all* about it. Exploring a theme-based concept satisfies this desire. It also enhances children's disposition to become mentally absorbed in pursuing ideas (Katz & Chard, 2000a).

Keeping the early childhood curriculum varied and interesting is a third value of theme teaching. Both children and teachers experience a sense of novelty with each new topic. As themes change, so do props, activities, and room decorations, which reinvigorates daily routines. Not only do new themes spawn original activities, but the same or similar activities (such as grouping objects or writing in journals) are given a fresh emphasis when they are used to support different topics.

Fourth, group cohesiveness is promoted when several children focus on a particular topic simultaneously. Children who have common experiences and knowledge develop a nucleus of mutual interests that provides a natural context for cooperative learning. As children discover classmates whose interests match theirs, their social circles widen. Their perceptions of one another also broaden because with each theme change, different children act as novices and experts; youngsters who are leaders for one topic may be followers for another. Thus, their patterns of interaction vary, which allows each youngster an opportunity to experience different social roles.

Finally, children's changing interests are accommodated year-round through theme teaching. As children become excited about new ideas, these ideas can be highlighted throughout the curriculum, which conveys to children the message that their ideas are valuable and worth exploring. Also, themes developed in response to the expressed interests of some children in the class may spark their peers' curiosity and enlarge children's notions of what is worth investigating.

TEACHERS' BENEFITS

By acting as a focus around which to plan, themes help practitioners organize their thinking, choose relevant activities and vocabulary to support theme-related goals, and locate resources prior to unit implementation (Brewer, 2001). All these factors increase teachers' confidence in planning an integrated array of educational activities for young children.

Another advantage is that theme teaching enables early childhood educators to address topics in sufficient breadth and depth to ensure that each child has had a chance to learn something new. Both these dimensions are enhanced by having multiple theme-related activities in a variety of curricular domains. Such cross-coverage allows teachers to structure the presentation of concepts more coherently and to devise sequential plans that gradually challenge children's thinking (Eliason & Jenkins, 2003).

In addition, teachers who approach theme planning appropriately research each topic, generating a pool of factual information. Doing so increases their knowledge base as well as the accuracy of the information they provide to children. Further, it allows practitioners to consider in advance how to handle sensitive issues associated with the theme and prompts them to think of original activities, a process that teachers find intellectually stimulating. The collegiality that sometimes arises when they collaborate with fellow staff members on developing thematic units is also pleasing. Brainstorming theme-related activities, solving problems in relation to the theme, sharing props, and swapping written plans are timesaving, invigorating activities that teachers find rewarding.

Themes also provide a unifying framework for measuring children's progress. An important teacher responsibility is to continually assess children's grasp of concepts addressed by the curriculum (Bredekamp & Copple, 1997). Teachers do this by observing children and interacting with children individually and in groups. Attempting to evaluate children's concept development

on a child-by-child basis, with no unifying framework within which to make judgments, is extremely difficult because it is so fragmented. Such assessments are more easily accomplished when practitioners have a single concept on which to focus. Seeing and hearing many children within the group demonstrate varying interpretations of the same concept provides a context for the teacher's judgments. For instance, an adult is better able to determine whether children's incomplete or erroneous ideas are universal or particular to an individual. He or she can also gauge which of several activities enhances or detracts from children's grasp of a particular idea. This is more difficult to accomplish within a totally unrelated set of activities. For all these reasons, practitioners report that theme teaching is extremely self-satisfying (Hurley & Blake, 1997).

PROGRAM EFFECTS

As you can ascertain, theme teaching enhances both children's and practitioners' educational experiences. Themes also yield programwide benefits. First, theme teaching can be implemented across diverse program structures, among children of all ages, with youngsters whose needs differ greatly, and by teachers whose philosophies and styles vary (Bergstrom & O'Brien, 2001; Gould, Thorpe, & Weeks, 2001). This universal applicability provides a common bond among programs and increases the potential for collaboration among professionals. Conversely, because educators create themes with a specific group of children in mind, instruction is individualized.

Second, family members who are informed of upcoming themes are better able to contribute their knowledge, expertise, and resources to children's educational experiences. They can more easily envision how to participate in children's education when they have a particular topic in mind than to do so in terms of the more generalized instruction that takes place from day to day. Consequently, family support for the program may go beyond the traditional donations of discarded meat trays and toilet paper rolls. For instance, knowing that the class is studying birds, a family may send in a bird's nest they found, a photograph of a bird taken at their feeder, or a magazine article about birds. An older sibling may help the children build bird feeders, or a grandparent may show the children how to care for a baby bird fallen from its nest. This kind of family involvement promotes constructive home–school relationships and helps parents and other family members feel more involved in the educational process.

The third and perhaps most important programwide impact of theme teaching is that it provides a tool by which content learning and process learning can be integrated within the curriculum. Often treated as mutually exclusive categories of knowledge, content and process can be combined by means of theme teaching without violating the integrity of either.

Focusing on Content

Content learning encompasses all the factual information relevant to the theme. Learning content requires such mental abilities as attending, listening, observing, remembering, and recounting (Hendrick, 2003). Thus, a group of first graders studying wild birds might engage in a variety of experiences to learn the following facts:

❑ Birds live in a variety of places: in the woods, meadows, plains, and deserts; near ponds, lakes, and oceans; and in cities.

❑ Each species of bird builds a nest characteristic of the species.

❑ Birds build nests to protect their eggs, which contain baby birds.

❑ Birds build nests of varying complexities.

❑ Different bird species build their nests in different places: on the ground, above the ground, in the open, or hidden.

As you already know, simple exposure to factual content such as this does not teach in and of itself. Only when children become physically involved in, talk about, and reflect on their experiences do they learn from them. Children might gain access to factual knowledge about wild birds through firsthand activities such as going outdoors to watch birds fly, observing a nesting bird, recording the numbers and kinds of birds they see, or examining several different abandoned bird nests. Teachers might also give children make-believe wings and straw to use to act like birds caring for their young, or teachers could work with children to construct a replica of a bird's nest. Throughout these activities, teachers and children would discuss which type of bird might build which type of nest, which would further extend children's content learning.

Focusing on Process

All the aesthetic, affective, cognitive, language, social, and physical operations and skills that form the basis for children's experiences within the early childhood curriculum constitute process learning. Because they encompass the "whole" child, such processes range from imagining, creating, and performing, to grouping, differentiating, inferring, and concluding, to pretending, representing, and constructing. Just as with content learning, children gain proficiency in process learning through hands-on activities. In fact, the same bird activities cited in the preceding section could pro-

vide the means for children to increase their competence and understanding in any domain.

Integrating Content and Process

Content and process come together in the activities teachers plan. These activities form the basis for instruction and offer children an applied means for experiencing the curriculum. Thus, two children acting out the roles of wild birds not only gain factual insight into bird life, but also have opportunities to practice social and cognitive processes such as offering ideas ("You be the baby bird. I'll be the mommy"), reaching compromises ("OK, I'm the mommy bird first, and then you"), and drawing conclusions ("If we have two mommy birds, we'll need two nests"). In fact, during the early childhood period, often the content included in each activity is simply the medium through which children explore other, more process-oriented operations and skills (Hendrick, 2003). Consequently, even when children are involved in theme-related activities, the thematic content is not always what captures their attention. They may be much more involved in the process learning represented within that experience. In this case, the children may eventually ignore the bird theme to concentrate on the dynamics of their social relationship. Even so, they are continuing to learn and benefit from the activity.

Furthermore, although teachers have a domain-specific goal for each activity they plan, children frequently proceed from the original aim to exploring aspects of the activity related to other domains. Moving from content to process or from one process to another is a natural, appropriate way for children to expand their knowledge and skills. Such adaptations do not mean teachers should simply provide generic activities with no real content-learning or process-learning goals in mind. Rather, practitioners must be purposeful in their planning so that they assist children in exploring facts and processes they might not otherwise experience and ensure a coherent, comprehensive set of activities from which children may choose. The integrative nature of such activities is well suited to the holistic manner in which children learn.

NEGATIVE ASPECTS OF THEME TEACHING

Considering all the benefits cited thus far, theme teaching might appear to automatically translate into developmentally appropriate practice. Unfortunately, this is not always true. Themes can be enacted poorly (Freeman & Sokoloff, 1996). For instance, some teachers violate the principles of developmentally appropriate practice by failing to accommodate children's needs for movement and physical activity, social interaction, and independence. These educators may try to get across the "facts" of the theme by reciting them to children or by creating a mountain of theme-related work sheets for children to complete. Teachers using such approaches ignore the importance of hands-on learning and self-discovery.

Some topics are too narrow or too contrived to make good themes. Examples are weekly plans centered on letters of the alphabet, such as *g*. As children paint with green tempera at the easel, eat grapes for a snack, and growl like lions, the teacher may confidently believe that youngsters are learning all about the letter *g*. In reality, the children may be focusing on the subject of their paintings rather than on the color, they may be thinking of grapes as fruit rather than a *g* word, and they may be more aware of the loudness or mock ferocity of their growling than the consonant sound they are making. Because *g* is not a concept and does not directly relate to children's real-life experiences, it is not a worthy theme.

Another problem occurs when teachers fail to adequately research the theme they are planning. Relying on their personal store of knowledge, they may omit critical aspects of the topic or present erroneous information to children as fact. For instance, assuming she knew enough about opossums to handle the interests of the 3-year-olds in her class, Ms. Miller told the children that opossums are mammals (they are marsupials) and that wild opossums have as many as 20 babies at a time (not so). Such misinformation undermines the conceptual value of theme planning.

Finally, some teachers assume they are theme teaching well when they simply relate several activities to a central prop, such as "pockets." Children may sing about having a smile in their pocket, hear a story about pockets, eat "pocket bread" for a snack, and decorate paper pockets. Unfortunately, children are not learning content that is particularly useful or interesting. The process learning involved is also perfunctory. Children are not being challenged to think, problem solve, expand their literacy skills, or develop their social and physical abilities. Although the activities may keep children busy and entertained, they fail to engage childrens' minds and bodies in the excitement of real learning. This type of theme planning is trivial—it addresses neither content learning nor process learning and does not fit the definition of the term *themes* that we espouse.

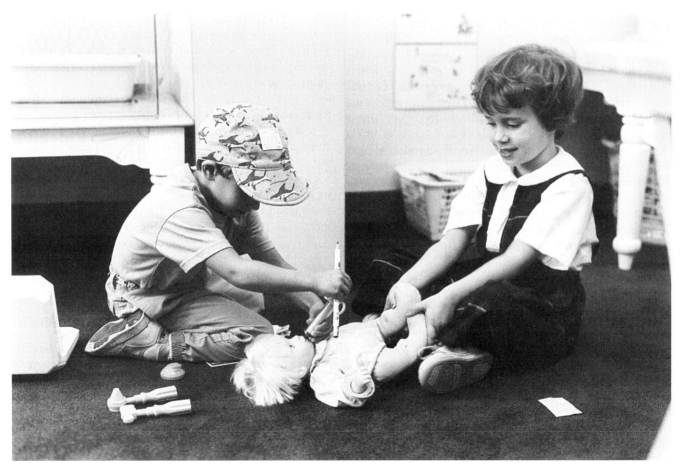

The children's interest in medicine led their teacher to introduce a theme on medicine.

PRINCIPLES OF EFFECTIVE THEME TEACHING

Effective theme teaching is much more complex and comprehensive than any of the misdirected approaches just described. It is characterized by the following principles (Jalongo & Stamp, 1997; Katz & Chard, 2000; Kostelnik, 1996). Themes are most likely to be effective when they

- Are directly related to children's real-life experiences, building on what children know and what is readily observable in their immediate environments
- Are age appropriate and culturally sensitive
- Represent a concept for children to investigate
- Are supported by a body of factual knowledge that has been adequately researched by the teacher(s)
- Involve firsthand, direct investigation
- Address all six curricular domains and promote their integration
- Address thematic content and processes more than once and in different kinds of activities (exploratory play, guided discovery, problem solving, discussions, demonstrations, direct instruction, small-group and whole-group activities)
- Integrate content learning with process learning
- Give children a chance to practice and apply basic skills appropriate for their age
- Expand into projects that are child initiated and child directed
- Encourage children to document and reflect on what they are learning
- Involve children's families in some way

HOW TO CREATE THEMATIC UNITS

Exploring Sources of Ideas

Cats, gardens, art and artists, storytelling, people in our neighborhood, insects, measuring—all these topics are potential themes or subjects of study. As an early childhood educator, you will have to decide which topics are best suited to the children in your group. Many ideas are available from which to choose. These ideas have many sources: the children, special events, unexpected happenings, program-mandated content, and teachers and parents.

The Children The best sources for thematic ideas are the children and what they are experiencing day to day. The things children frequently enact, discuss, or wonder about offer a relevant basis for selecting and implementing themes in early childhood programs. You

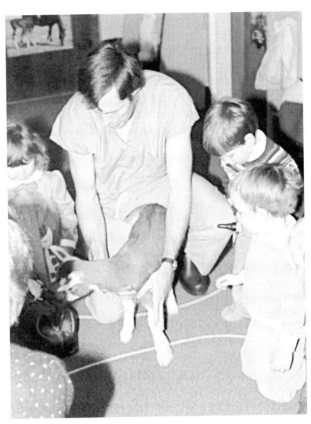

These visitors came because of the children's interest in animals and gave the children firsthand experience with the "real thing."

will discover children's interests by talking with children informally, observing them, and listening as they talk with one another. You may use more-formal means to assess children's interests, such as interviewing children or using the KWHLH brainstorming strategy described in chapter 4. Information from parents regarding upcoming events in children's lives or events at home provide additional clues about concepts that will be important to children in your class throughout the year.

For instance, you might introduce the theme "machines" because children are curious about the heavy equipment they observed at a nearby construction site. The birth of new siblings to one or more families in the class might prompt a unit on babies. Children's frequent discussions about who can play with whom could serve as the stimulus for a theme on friends. Ordinary events like these are important to young children, which is why they provide such a strong foundation for planning and implementing themes in the classroom. No matter what age group you are teaching, child-initiated topics are a valuable source for themes and should be the basis for many of the themes you teach about.

Special Events Occasionally, out-of-the-ordinary occurrences such as the program's annual farm trip, an assembly featuring guide dogs for the blind, or the celebration of Arbor Day also serve as a spark for theme development. Occasions like these, which teachers know about in advance, may be integrated into or serve as the cornerstone for related units of study such as "farm products," "working dogs," or "trees."

Unexpected Happenings Sometimes unanticipated events stimulate children's thinking in new directions. This was the case for second graders intrigued by the habits of a grackle whose nest was in the rain gutter above their classroom window. The teacher responded to their curiosity by introducing a unit on wild birds, using the grackle as a firsthand example. Along similar lines, a sudden hailstorm prompted so many questions from children that a theme on weather evolved naturally.

Program-Mandated Content In addition to child-inspired content, many school districts require particular subject matter to be addressed at given grade levels. This is also true for other early childhood programs in which certain topics such as dental care or fire safety are regularly mandated by the administrator or board of directors. Such required content can also serve as a basis for thematic teaching. Social studies, science, health, math, or language arts concepts can be used as the core around which a variety of theme-related activities are created and integrated throughout the day. This approach has the advantage of ensuring that important but sometimes neglected subjects like science, social studies, and health receive adequate attention. Moreover, teachers gain the satisfaction of covering prescribed material in ways that are meaningful to children.

Teachers and Parents Theme ideas may also have their source in concepts that teachers and parents find exciting or valuable. A teacher enthralled by clouds may share his or her enthusiasm through a unit on the daytime sky. The teacher's desire to teach children constructive ways of working together could be the motivation behind the theme "cooperation." Likewise, apprehension expressed by parents regarding child sexual abuse might stimulate the development of a unit on personal safety.

Considering Essential Theme Criteria

With so many sources of themes and so many ideas to choose from, the number of potential topics usually exceeds the amount of time available to teach them. Certain additional criteria will narrow your choices and

help you pick the most appropriate themes. When finalizing an idea for a theme, consider five factors:

1. Relevance
2. Hands-on activities
3. Diversity and balance across the curriculum
4. Availability of resources
5. Potential for project work

Relevance Of the five criteria, the most important is relevance. Themes are relevant when the concepts they represent are directly tied to children's real-life experiences and build on what children know. If relevance has been properly considered, themes are age appropriate, individually appropriate, and socioculturally appropriate. Relevant themes highlight concepts with which children have initial familiarity and provide new insights into their daily experiences. Themes such as "self," "home," "family," "foods," "plants," and "night and day" are pertinent to preschoolers and early elementary–aged children because such themes help the children understand their lives and the world around them. In contrast, some themes are inappropriate for this age group. "Life in ancient Rome" and "penguins" are too far removed from most children's day-to-day living to be relevant. Gravity and electricity are too abstract to constitute an entire theme, especially for children younger than 5 years old.

Naturally, themes are most meaningful when they match the needs and interests of particular groups of children. Locale as well as family and community resources or traditions will influence which aspects of the concept are most pertinent. For instance, the theme "plants" has relevance for most children no matter where they live. However, children growing up near a marsh would naturally focus on cattails, marsh grass, and milkweed as examples of plant life, whereas youngsters living in an arid region would find studying desert vegetation such as cacti, sagebrush, and yucca plants more relevant. Likewise, the relevance criterion makes backyard birds, rather than exotic varieties, with which most children have had no experience, more appropriate. Moreover, entire topics that are relevant to one group of young children may be irrelevant to others. For example, studying tidal pools could be a significant learning experience for children living in Kennebunk, Maine (which is near the ocean), but not so for those in Lincoln, Nebraska (which is landlocked). Having never seen a tidal pool, the Nebraska group would benefit from studying a more familiar water habitat, such as a pond or a river.

In each of the preceding examples, relevance is determined by the suitability of the subject. Timeliness is another factor to consider. Timely themes build on children's current interests. What are children talking about? What has piqued their interest? The answers to these questions should shape your choice of themes. Consequently, effective theme planners do not plan a year's worth of themes in advance. Instead, they create one theme at a time that reflects children's curiosity or concerns. Timeliness may also prompt teachers to substitute one theme for another to take advantage of current events or to respond to shifts in children's needs and interests. The reasoning behind early childhood professionals' decisions to change themes is illustrated in the following situation.

A group of first graders attending the International School in Hong Kong were deeply engrossed in a theme on folktales. During that time they learned that a dinosaur skeleton had been found in the Gobi Desert of China. While discussing these events, several children wondered whether the dragons they heard about in Chinese stories were based on real dinosaurs, a notion that elicited much interest among the group. Capitalizing on their excitement, the teacher substituted a dinosaur theme for the poetry unit she had originally planned to come next.

In the preceding example, delaying attention to dinosaurs or ignoring children's hypotheses would have resulted in missed learning opportunities. The timeliness of the dinosaur theme in relation to the children's expressed interest made it relevant to these youngsters.

Hands-On Activities Another criterion for selecting a theme is how well the content lends itself to the creation of related hands-on activities. Only themes whose content children can experience through the direct manipulation of objects are suitable for children 3 to 8 years old. This hands-on instruction *must* include firsthand experiences but may also involve some simulations. Both forms of hands-on instruction could be offered through exploratory activities, guided discovery, problem solving, discussions, cooperative learning, demonstrations, and direct-instruction activities. However, the emphasis must be on exploratory play and inquiry if children are to truly expand their concepts with time.

Firsthand experiences are those in which children become directly involved with the actual objects or phenomena under study. These experiences are real, not analogous or imaginary. Consequently, they give children opportunities to derive relevant bits of information from the original source of the concept. For instance, youngsters engaged in the theme "pets" would gain firsthand insights into the life and activities of pets by observing and caring for pets in the classroom. A visit to a pet shop to see the variety of pets available and

a trip to a veterinarian to see how pet health is maintained are other examples of real-life experiences. Simply looking at pictures or hearing about these things could not replicate the richness or stimulation provided by firsthand involvement. Firsthand activities are so essential to children's concept development that teachers should avoid themes for which few such lessons are possible. In other words, when teachers know that children have had no direct experience with the theme and that related firsthand activities cannot be provided in the program, they should consider the theme inappropriate for their group.

Simulations are another hands-on activity type. They approximate but do not exactly duplicate firsthand experiences. Providing make-believe ears and tails so that children can enact life as a pet and working with children to construct a replica of a veterinarian's office using toy animals are examples of simulations. In each case children act directly on objects or carry out activities that resemble the real thing. Although one step removed from the original concept, simulations give children access to data that, for safety or logistical reasons, they have no other means through which to discover the data.

Once you have determined that a theme suggests a wealth of potential hands-on activities, consider also the *variety* of hands-on experiences children will have. For example, themes that prompt many craft ideas but are not well suited to pretend play, games, or problem-solving activities are best rejected as too limited. A more appropriate topic would encompass a wider range of learning opportunities for children.

Diversity and Balance Across the Curriculum
Throughout the year, children should experience a broad array of themes. Thus, diversity and balance across the curriculum is another criterion for consideration. For example, some themes are primarily scientific (seasons, machines, leaves, insects, and fish); others reflect a social studies emphasis (families, friends, occupations, and the neighborhood); still others highlight language arts content (storytelling, poetry, and writers); some focus primarily on mathematical ideas (stores, measuring, numbers, and numerals); and some are more health oriented (foods, dental hygiene, and fitness). Furthermore, many topics can be adapted to fit one or more of these foci depending on what intrigues the children and what the teacher chooses to emphasize. For example, a unit on stores could stress the mathematical content of money and counting, the more-social aspects of employees' working together toward a common goal, or the health-related focus of safety in the store. Teachers can deal with these ideas separately, sequentially, or in combination.

When selecting themes, teachers should choose a cross section of topics in which all the previously mentioned content areas are eventually addressed. With time, children will then have opportunities to expand their concepts and skills across a wide range of subjects, with no one topic predominating. For instance, a teacher has both diversity and balance in mind when, in response to second graders' fascination with the space shuttle, he or she plans a natural science unit on the sky to be followed by a theme on space exploration in which social cooperation is the primary focus. In this case, children initiated the original idea for the themes, and the teacher influenced their direction.

Resources The availability of support materials is another factor to consider when you are determining what themes to select (Katz & Chard, 2000). Because children need objects to act on, teachers should choose themes for which several real items are obtainable. Relevant materials may be accumulated with time as well as solicited from families, community resources, libraries, museums, and so forth. Also, when early childhood colleagues pool or trade props, the number and variety of materials at their disposal greatly increase. Themes for which no real objects are available for children to use should be dropped from consideration. This is also true for themes that depend on one spectacular prop, such as a hang glider or a spinning wheel, which, if suddenly unavailable, would deny children their only access to direct firsthand investigation of the topic. Better themes are those for which a variety of real materials are easily accessible.

Project Potential The best thematic topics are those that have project potential. Projects are open-ended activities in which youngsters undertake, during a period of days or weeks, the in-depth study of some facet of the theme. Ideas for projects emerge as children gain experience with a concept and become curious about particular aspects of it (Chard, 1998a). As children's interests evolve, individual or small groups of children, in consultation with the teacher, plan and then carry out a relevant project. These projects are primarily child initiated and child directed. For example, children involved in a pet theme might wonder about pets owned by classmates and adults in the group. In response, the children could decide to conduct interviews and create a catalog of all the different pets represented in the class. They might use the information they glean to create graphs, stories, and displays related to their investigation. Later, the children could share what they have learned with family members in a celebration at the conclusion of the unit. Project work requires sustained effort and involves learning processes such as exploring, investigating, hypothesizing, reading, recording, discussing, representing, and evaluating. Consequently, projects give children many chances to plan, select manageable tasks for themselves, apply skills, represent what they have learned, and monitor their personal progress. More structured than spontaneous play and more self-determined than teacher-planned instruction, projects provide a bridge between the two. They offer children strategies for exploring topics in ways that are individualized and therefore more personally meaningful.

Because projects are such a valuable learning tool, we invited Sylvia Chard, a noted expert on the project approach, to offer a brief description of how projects can be implemented in early childhood classrooms.

The Project Approach

Sylvia C. Chard, Ph.D.

University of Alberta, Canada

A *project* is an in-depth study of a real-world topic. Teaching strategies associated with the project approach are designed to help children develop a fuller understanding of the world around them. Through collaborative projects, children carry out investigations and learn many ways to represent new information. As children study topics in depth, they apply language and math skills as they build new understanding in the areas of science and social studies.

Origins

In the 1960s and 1970s there was interest around the world in "infant schools," where young children were educated in Great Britain. These programs featured the "integrated day." Young children experienced no separation of curricular subjects and learned incidentally with the guidance of the teacher as they carried out in-depth studies of local buildings, businesses, services, and features of the natural environment. The book *Engaging Children's Minds: The Project Approach* (1989) was written to rekindle interest in what Katz and Chard believe to have been an important part of early education in mid-20th-century Britain.

Methods

The teacher selects a topic on the basis of the children's interests, curricular goals, and the availability of local resources. The teacher brainstorms his or her experience, knowledge, and ideas, representing them in a topic web. The potential scope of the project is assessed. A web of ideas is developed throughout the project and continues to be useful for planning and recording its progress.

Three Phases in the Life of a Project

Projects generally develop through an introductory phase, a research phase, and a review phase. This three-phase structure helps the teacher organize and guide the study in ways that match the children's interests and personal involvement.

Phase 1

The teacher discusses the topic with the children to find out about their previous experiences with the content. The children represent their experiences in a variety of ways and show how well they understand the concepts involved. The teacher helps the children ask questions about what they would like to investigate. A letter is sent to parents about the study, inviting them to talk with their children about the topic and to see if anyone can offer special expertise.

Phase 2

The teacher arranges opportunities for the children to do fieldwork and to speak to experts. Resources are provided to help children with their investigations: real objects, books, and other research materials. The teacher suggests ways for children to carry out a variety of investigations. Children are involved in representing what they learn and in participating in learning centers at their own developmental levels in terms of basic skills, drawing, music, construction, and dramatic play. Different representational possibilities can be suggested and provided for. Children share their work with classmates in class meetings at the beginning and end of project work sessions. The teacher helps children be aware of all the different work being done through class or group discussion and displays of work around the classroom. The topic web developed earlier provides a shorthand means of documenting the progress of the project.

Phase 3

Once the teacher decides that the work of the project is almost complete, he or she arranges for the children to share what they have learned. They feature the highlights of their project for another class, the principal, or the parents. In preparing such an event, the teacher helps the children purposefully review and evaluate the whole project. The teacher also offers the children imaginative ways of personalizing their new knowledge through art, stories, and drama. Finally, the teacher uses children's ideas and interests to make a meaningful transition between the project being concluded and the topic of study for the next theme or project.

Assessment

Assessment is carried out daily as the children plan their work and implement their plans. The teacher notes how well the children understand the information they are learning, how well they can apply the skills they have acquired, and how well they can account for what they have learned, explaining it to other children at class meetings and in the final sharing or celebration of learning. The teacher makes anecdotal notes about dispositional learning and how children approach their work, collaborate with peers, and develop their strengths and interests.

Distinctive Features

Projects involve in-depth investigation. Teachers encourage children to develop interests and work on their strengths. Projects are energized by questions the teacher has helped the children to formulate. Activities are chosen for their representational contribution to the evidence that the whole class group has collaboratively achieved a significant depth of understanding. The project approach offers teachers a powerful way to address many aspects of the early childhood curriculum.

Where Readers Can Find Out More

A comprehensive Web site about the project approach can be found at http://www.project-approach.com

In addition, the project approach is described in more detail in Chard (1998a, 1998b, 1999, 2001, 2002) and Katz and Chard (2000a, 2000b).

Although projects can be carried out independent of a theme, we suggest that they serve as an extension of theme planning. In this model, projects evolve after children have had exposure to a thematic concept in the ways described so far. As a result of participating in teacher-planned activities and group discussions, children begin to suggest related topics they would like to examine. These investigations become their projects. While children carry out projects, the teacher promotes their learning by using many of the teaching strategies found in chapter 3, such as reflections, scaffolding, questions, and silence. Teachers also help children document their work and prompt them to reflect on what they have discovered. Although not every theme will lead to a project, the best themes are those that would allow projects to develop in accord with children's interests.

Let us now turn our attention to the 21 steps necessary to develop a thematic unit from start to finish.

Creating an Information Base

The core of every theme is the factual information on which it is founded and that is embodied in a comprehensive list of terms, facts, and principles (TFPs) relevant to the theme. These TFPs are similar in form to the TFPs you learned about in chapter 3. Although the TFPs embody the theme, adults do not formally recite them to children. Instead, educators provide hands-on activities through which children derive factual information, learn relevant terminology, and engage in theme-related conversations with peers and adults. Through such experiences, youngsters gain meaningful insights that enlarge their concepts.

To be useful, TFPs must be accurate and thorough. Five steps are suggested for creating a suitable listing.

Step 1 Select a topic of study. Keep in mind relevance to children, hands-on activities, diversity and balance across the curriculum, the availability of theme-related resources, and project potential.

Step 2 Brainstorm logical subtopics for the theme. You may do this on your own or in conjunction with colleagues or the children. For instance, a unit on cats might include the subtopics depicted in Figure 16.1. Although developed with first graders in mind, these subtopics are relevant to children in preschool through second grade.

Step 3 Use reference books, trade books, program-adopted textbooks, children's books, or other people as resources. From these, generate a list of TFPs to support the various subtopics in the topic web you created. Begin by writing down every item that seems relevant to the theme. At this point, do not worry about differentiating terms, facts, or principles. (Some teachers reverse Steps 2 and 3, beginning with a general list of TFPs and then developing a topic web. Choose the sequence that makes the most sense to you.)

Step 4 On the basis of your understanding of the children's interests and abilities, decide whether a general overview or a more in-depth study of one of the subtopics is best suited to your class. If the former is true, choose a few TFPs from each of the subcategories; if the latter is your choice, focus primarily on one subset of TFPs.

Step 5 Pick 5 to 10 TFPs on which to focus directly. Use the others simply as background information or as a guide for responding to children's questions regarding the topic.

Developing Activity Ideas

The steps for developing appropriate theme-related activities are straightforward and not nearly as time consuming as those required to create TFPs.

Step 6 Brainstorm activities for each of the 5 to 10 TFPs you selected. Go through the TFPs one at a time, generating at least two or three activities per TFP. Do this with a colleague or in a small group to enhance the richness and variety of the activities generated. For instance, you might want children to learn that "People who own cats are responsible for providing them with food, shelter,

FIGURE 16.1   Initial Topic Web for "Cats" Theme

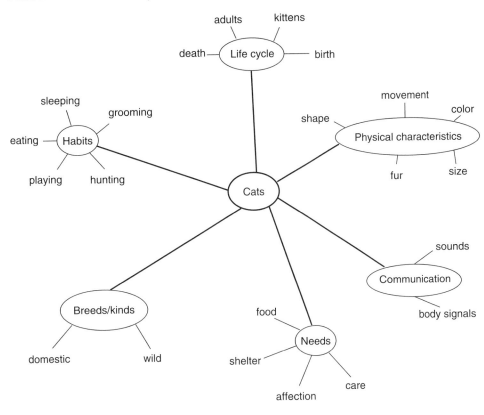

attention, and medical care." Sample activities to support this information could include (a) having children take care of a visiting cat for a day or a week, (b) having children take care of pretend cats in the housekeeping area, (c) reading books about cat care, (d) visiting a veterinarian's office to witness cat care, (e) inviting a cat owner to visit the class to talk about how he or she takes care of a cat, and (f) creating collages that represent the different things people do to care for their cats.

Step 7   Assign each activity to one of the six curricular domains described in this text. Make sure to have no less than one activity per domain per week. You might have a different number of theme-related activities in each domain. However, you should strive for some balance among them.

Depending on how you structure it, the same activity could be adapted to more than one domain. Thus, a collage designed to help children represent different ways cat owners care for their cats takes on a social focus if children are asked to cooperate as a group to create one large collage. In contrast, giving each child his or her own collage to work on, along with several cutting tools, emphasizes the fine-motor aspects of the activity, which makes it more physical. Alternatively, if the structure of the collage activity emphasizes children's following oral directions step by step, the focus shifts to listening skills (the language domain). With this example in

mind, you can use the same activity to teach more than one skill on the same day or on different days.

Step 8   Make certain that the activities represent varying types of instruction as listed in chapter 3 (i.e., exploratory play, guided discovery, and problem-solving opportunities). If you become aware that watching or listening dominates the activities, redesign them to include more hands-on involvement.

Making a Plan

Once the TFPs and activities are fully developed, assemble them into a thematic plan. Such a plan typically covers no less than 2 weeks' instruction and may be extended for several weeks after that, often in the pursuit of child-initiated projects. The following steps outline the planning process.

Step 9   Commit your ideas to paper, incorporating several theme-related activities into your lesson plans. Some teachers plan each day on a separate sheet of paper; others put an entire week's activities on a single sheet. Consider what time of the day certain activities will take place and whether each will be presented once or on several days. Design additional non-theme-related activities to fill in the rest of the instructional time and to give children some respite from the theme. Remember, having fewer well-developed theme-related activities is better than contriving to make activities fit.

Step 10 Check your plan to ensure that at least three theme-related activities are included every day and that by week's end all the domains have been included.

Step 11 Consider classroom management issues such as availability of materials, numbers of adults available to help, and special events. Adjust your plan as necessary. For instance, if you have scheduled easel painting and tie-dying for the same day and time but have only three smocks in your room, move one of these activities to another time in the day or to another day so that you will have enough smocks for children at both areas.

Step 12 Plan for a portion of group time to focus on the theme each day. Such whole-group activities allow children to become aware of certain concept-related information simultaneously, which provides a common foundation for exploration. Carried out at the beginning of class time, circle activities serve as an introduction to the day's experiences. Conducted at the end, they give children a chance to review and summarize their current understanding of the theme.

Step 13 Make a final check of your written plan, focusing on how well you have addressed the TFPs. Tally how often you have used each. Refer to your original brainstorming list if you need a reminder of which activities relate to which TFPs. Verify that each TFP receives attention at least three or four times during the week. Also make sure that individual TFPs have been addressed within different domains across the plan. If you notice that some domains are seldom theme related or that certain TFPs are always addressed within the same domain, revise your plan to achieve better integration. In addition, if some TFPs have been left out or are underrepresented, either add a few related activities or extend the theme another week, focusing on these TFPs as well as some additional TFPs, to give the children more time to explore the concept. In this way you will create 2-, 3-, and 4-week units.

Step 14 After your plan is complete, gather your materials and create any props you will need. To minimize preparation time, use some props for more than one activity.

Step 15 Create a thematic atmosphere in your classroom. Post theme-associated pictures at children's eye level. Choose compact disks, videotapes, audiotapes, books, finger plays, or songs related to the topic.

Implementing the Theme

Once you have a sound plan, implement the theme. Let the following steps guide your actions.

Step 16 Carry out your plan. Also, take advantage of spontaneous events to further children's understanding of the concept they are exploring.

Step 17 Assess children's understanding of and interest in the theme through observations, interviews, group discussions, work samples, and constructions. Make note (mentally and through written anecdotes) of times when children talk about the theme, when they exhibit theme-related behaviors and knowledge, and when family members mention incidents illustrating children's awareness of and reactions to the topic. During the free-choice or learning center portion of your day, keep track of the activities children choose and the amount of time they spend there. A participation chart can help maintain this type of record (described in chapter 7).

Step 18 Help children reflect on their understanding of thematic content and processes. Invite them to make drawings, graphs, murals, maps, constructions, journal entries, paintings, charts, and reports to represent what they have learned. Take photographs of the children's work. Keep work samples and include them in portfolios or display them for children to refer to. See Figure 16.2 for an example of how one preschool class documented their investigation of a transportation unit.

Step 19 Extend the thematic unit if children's interest remains high. As children demonstrate understanding of and curiosity about the subject, introduce additional TFPs in subsequent weeks or move into the project phase of investigation. An example of a project carried out by teacher Jennifer Heaton and her kindergarten class at Beech Hill Elementary School, Summerville, South Carolina, is presented in Figure 16.3. It grew out of a unit on transportation and took 2 months to complete.

FIGURE 16.2

FIGURE 16.3 The Truck Project

Introduction

The kindergarten children had been involved in a thematic unit on transportation. They collected ideas in a topic web, generated questions, and shared experiences. Their teacher was able to bring in a tire from a Mack truck. The size of the truck tire captured the children's attention and provided the starting point for the "truck" project.

Phase 1

The teacher scheduled a field experience at the trucking company where her mother worked in the payroll office. The children planned questions to ask at the trucking company field site, ranging from "How do you hook the truck and the trailer?" to "How do you pay for the trucks?" The children's interests were in the truck and the company. The teacher prepared personnel at the field site for the types of questions the children would have and the experiences they were hoping for.

Phase 2

The children had previously learned about questioning, sketching, and investigating. Before leaving school, the children chose specific areas of the truck and the company that they wanted to investigate. They toured the grounds of the company, including the fueling lane, the tire shop, the maintenance shop, the tank-washing area, and the office. The president of the company, a safety specialist, and the comptroller accompanied the class on the tour and answered the children's questions.

One truck was cleaned and parked in an area where the children could examine it thoroughly. The children recorded their observations in field sketches. Some sketched inside the truck, some the tires, and some the tank they saw being washed. A few children tallied how many trucks they saw in the yard. A small group of children went into the office area and investigated the dispatch process.

On returning to their classroom, the children discussed the idea of building their own truck. To begin, they made a basic frame for the truck from cardboard and drew lines for the doors and windows. After several discussions, they designed the hood so that it opened. The engine had to be accessible. They referred to pictures and finally decided where the teacher should cut so that the hood would open correctly. They painted the truck.

A few children worked on making the tires for the truck. They determined how to trace a circle on cardboard, then painted the circles. Once they made the tires, they wanted to attach them to the truck so that the tires would actually turn. With the teacher's help, they tried four ways and then decided on the one that they could do by themselves.

As their work continued, the children thought about how they could set up a trucking company in the learning centers in the classroom. The children used various materials to make the things they needed, including a toolbox, fan belts, fenders, windshield wipers, tools, forms, money, a fuel tank, and a fuel pump.

Three children worked on the fuel tank and pump. They wanted to make numbers that really turned. It took them several attempts, but they finally achieved what they had envisioned.

The children paid great attention to the details of the truck. They were careful to include the grill, an engine, a steering wheel that turned, a driver's seat that bounced, a bed behind the seats, a fifth wheel, mud flaps, tail lights, side mirrors, and a horn that worked (a bicycle horn!).

As the truck was being constructed and the trucking company developed, the children wrote a poem and made books about trucks. One large area of the classroom wall was devoted to a display of the children's work. The wall area displayed the children's field sketches as well as photographs of the areas the children had sketched. This area became the working area for construction of the model truck. The truck eventually became so large—6 feet long and 4 feet tall—that the teacher and the children moved it into the hall to complete work on it.

Phase 3

As a culminating event, the class made a presentation of their truck and gave a tour of their trucking company. The model truck was exhibited in front of the work on the wall display. The truck tire was displayed with the diagram showing its dimensions.

At first, the children wanted to invite everyone at school to see their work. Instead, they agreed with the teacher to give their presentation to four classes ranging from kindergarten to fourth grade, a special education class, and several administrators and office personnel. The teachers also made a video of the presentation for the children's parents to view at home. Each child had a part in sharing his or her knowledge of trucks. It was clear that they enjoyed their involvement and had learned a great deal about the important work done by truck drivers and trucking companies.

Source: Chard. (2001).

The children examine a truck on their field trip.

The number on the tank is 1145.

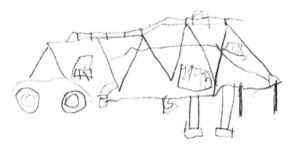

One kindergartner's field sketch will help the children remember what they saw at the truck company.

Shown is a truck tally made by the children.

The children point out many things on the truck they made.

Step 20 Establish two-way communication with families about the theme. Provide theme- and project-related information to them through newsletters. Invite family members to contribute materials or their talents to the classroom. Suggest ways for family members to support the theme or project at home. Create opportunities for family members to share the children's discoveries.

Step 21 Evaluate the theme by using the theme-teaching checklist presented in Figure 16.4. Write down the changes you made and how you might alter your plan if you decide to repeat it later.

Adapting "Apples in the School Yard": An Apple Theme

All the steps involved in theme planning are illustrated in the following example of an "apple" theme. As you read through this approach, consider how to adapt the theme for the children in your class.

Step 1 The 4- and 5-year-olds in Hannah Solomon's preschool class noticed that two apple trees in the play yard were heavy with fruit. Eager to pick the apples, the children watched each day as the fruit grew riper. Hannah decided that a theme about apples would interest the children and would promote their observation skills and problem-solving abilities. Because the children lived in a community known for its apple orchards, she also thought that such a theme would provide a good chance for the children to become more aware of resources in their environment.

Steps 2 and 3 She prepared for the apple theme by looking up information about apples and making a list of TFPs related to the concept. By not simply relying on her own knowledge, she discovered some facts about apples she had not known previously. As the list grew to around 25 items, she divided it into the following subsections: varieties of apples, physical characteristics, apples as food, apples' development from blossom to fruit, apples' journey from orchard to home, and apples as a cash crop.

Steps 4 and 5 Next, she narrowed the list to include 12 TFPs that would provide a general overview for the children to explore for at least 2 weeks. Following are 5 of the 12 she chose:

1. There are many kinds of apples.
2. Apples vary in size, shape, color, texture, smell, and taste.
3. People eat apples in many forms.
4. Apples grow on trees.
5. Apples are the fruit of the apple tree.

Step 6 Hannah brainstormed activities to go with each TFP. Would you add others to this list?

❑ *There are many kinds of apples.* ACTIVITIES: Select different varieties of apples at an orchard or a store, examine the apples firsthand, match the different apple types to their names, look at paintings that include apples, create apple paintings, and look through seed and fruit catalogs that show various kinds of apples.

❑ *Apples vary in size, shape, color, texture, smell, and taste.* ACTIVITIES: Examine different kinds of apples, make a chart graphing apple differences, generate a list of words that describe apple characteristics, create apple books with one page for each variety—list the characteristics, sort apples, taste apples (seriate the apples from sweetest to most sour; seriate the apples from juiciest to least juicy), and select favorite apples.

❑ *People eat apples in many forms.* ACTIVITIES: Examine different apple products (raw apple, applesauce, apple juice), make an apple product such as applesauce, create a lotto game using apple product pictures or labels, and create a grocery store in which children pretend to buy and sell apple products.

❑ *Apples grow on trees.* ACTIVITIES: Examine an apple tree, examine apple leaves, do a bark rubbing, trace or paint with apple leaves, read fiction and nonfiction books about how apples grow, create a make-believe orchard in which children pretend to pick apples, go on a field trip to pick apples, read a book about how apple trees appear during the different seasons, construct apple trees out of art materials, and make apple tree puzzles.

❑ *Apples are the fruit of the apple tree.* ACTIVITIES: Examine seeds inside apples, examine dried apple blossoms, read a story about how the blossom becomes fruit, and predict how many seeds will be in the different varieties of apples.

Steps 7 and 8 Hannah could see that she had a wide array of firsthand activities to support children's learning. Next, she assigned the activities to different domains, referring to the intermediate objectives for each. For TFP 1 she developed the following list:

❑ Select different varieties of apples at an orchard or a store—affective (focus on the choosing process).
❑ Examine the apples firsthand—record the children's observations—cognitive (focus on observation).
❑ Match the different apple types to their names—language (focus on language labels).
❑ Look at paintings that include different kinds of apples—aesthetic (focus on the color and design elements of the art).

FIGURE 16.4 Theme-Teaching Checklist

Purpose:	To help teachers assess the effectiveness of theme teaching in their classrooms
Directions:	Put a *1* by each item that accurately depicts the classroom. Total the items to achieve a final score.

Score	*Level of Effectiveness*
22–24	Excellent use of themes
19–21	Good use of themes; minor additions could make it better
16–18	Reasonable start; gradually address missing items to improve
15 and less	Poor use of themes; major revisions necessary

Theme-Related Activities

❑ 1. The theme planner can describe the relevance of the theme to the children.
❑ 2. Theme-related information is accurate.
❑ 3. Two or more theme-related *firsthand experiences* are available each week.
❑ 4. At least three theme-related activities are available every day.
❑ 5. Theme-related activities take place at different times throughout the day.
❑ 6. Every week at least one theme-related activity is included for each of the six domains.
❑ 7. Children have opportunities to apply, synthesize, and summarize what they have learned about the theme through-out the week.

Child Involvement

❑ 8. Children are talking about the theme (offering information, asking questions, conversing with peers and adults).
❑ 9. Children are pretending in relation to the theme.
❑ 10. Children are creating theme-related products of their own invention.
❑ 11. Children express a desire to learn more about some aspect of the theme.
❑ 12. Children link the theme to their past or current experiences through their actions and words.
❑ 13. Family members report that children have discussed or played out the theme at home.
❑ 14. Children continue to refer to the concept represented by the theme after the unit ends.

Classroom Environment

❑ 15. Terms, facts, and principles are posted or otherwise available for adult reference.
❑ 16. Children's theme-related creations (projects, writings, etc.) are displayed in the room.
❑ 17. Theme-related props are available to the children each day.
❑ 18. Theme-related pictures, songs, poems, books, and so on are used to create a thematic atmosphere.
❑ 19. One circle time each day is theme related.
❑ 20. Theme-related circle-time activities include active child participation.

Family Involvement

❑ 21. Family members receive information about the theme.
❑ 22. Family members are invited to contribute to the theme.
❑ 23. Family members receive feedback regarding children's interest and participation in the theme.
❑ 24. Families are included in theme- or project-related celebrations.

❑ Create paintings that include different kinds of apples—aesthetic (focus on color and design elements while painting).

❑ Look through seed and fruit catalogs that show various kinds of apples—cognition (focus on the social-conventional knowledge related to the different varieties).

Hannah repeated this process for each TFP. She looked over the complete list to make sure she had included many exploratory-play, guided-discovery, and problem-solving activities as well as some demonstrations,

discussions, and direct-instruction activities. Convinced that she had a good selection of activities, she began to commit her ideas to paper.

Steps 9 Through 13 Hannah created the weekly plan, presented in Figure 16.5. She made adjustments to ensure that she did not have too many "star" activities (those involving a lot of adult supervision) on any one day and that both theme-related and non-theme-related activities were provided daily. She also paid attention to the sequence of thematic activities throughout the week, so that certain activities could lead up to or build on others. For instance, in the art area on Tuesday, Hannah hung three still-life paintings of apples by different artists in different styles for the children to enjoy. During the next few days, she drew the children's attention to the paintings, especially their color and design. The following week, Hannah provided a bowl of apples of different varieties along with watercolors and poster paints for the children to make their own still-life arrangements and paintings. In this way, she used the Week 1 art activity to lead to another activity planned for Week 2.

Steps 14 and 15 Hannah gathered relevant materials and prepared the classroom. She asked families to contribute any materials they might have (such as favorite stories or songs) and invited a parent who was a fruit grower to visit the class.

Steps 16 Through 18 Hannah implemented the theme according to her written plan. However, on Tuesday a child brought in two pieces of fruit that resembled apples but were actually Korean pears. Intrigued by their similarity, some children spent much of the free-choice time comparing the fruits and graphing their similarities and differences. During the second week, they created pictures, paintings, and charts of their experiences.

Step 19 After 2 weeks, Hannah conducted a circle time in which she and the children talked about what they had learned, what they still wanted to learn, and how they might go about doing so. Several children were interested in finding out more about how apples from Oregon went to stores across the United States. Others were interested in finding out people's favorite apple recipes. Some children wanted to know if people had apples everywhere in the world. Hannah and the children carried out investigative projects to answer these questions. These projects took several weeks and included a field trip to a produce distribution center and visits to the class by family members with recipes to share. The group created a time line that went along one whole wall of the classroom and showed the various steps in the distribution process. The children also made a cookbook of classroom recipes with apples as an ingredient. Trying some of the recipes in class and documenting the process was also part of the project phase of this theme.

Step 20 While the children were involved in learning about apples, Hannah communicated with families through individual notes home and a classroom newsletter. Family members were invited to provide favorite apple recipes for the class and to join the field trips to the orchard and the distribution center. As the thematic unit neared its conclusion, children, teachers, and family members gathered to see and hear what the children had learned. They examined the time line, marveled over the children's written interpretations of family recipes, and sampled apple butter made by the class.

Step 21 Hannah formally evaluated the theme by using the theme-teaching checklist and anecdotal records in some activity areas each day. She also kept a journal to remind herself of points she wanted to remember and reflect on:

September 20: *The children enjoyed making apples to put on the trees in the pretend orchard. It was exciting to see them consult the catalogs to determine which variety to make. Having several different catalogs on hand was a good idea. Albert and Johan argued about whether two kinds of apples could grow on the same tree. We added this question to our chart on what we want to know more about. This point will be important to follow up on at the orchard.*

October 6: *We're putting a lot of time into Phase 1 of the project portion of this theme. The children had several opportunities at circle time and throughout the week to share their knowledge and stories as well as what they continue to wonder about. It became clear today that learning how apples get from our orchard to stores throughout the country is of keen interest to several children. We'll begin a topic web at circle time tomorrow to see how this plays out.*

Later, as the apple unit drew to a close, Hannah made a note to herself to periodically take the children out to observe the apple trees in the play yard throughout the late fall, winter, and spring. She believed that ongoing observation would promote their interest in the seasonal cycle of the apple trees and in how the trees provide shelter and food for various animals and insects.

The next theme undertaken in this class could be a spin-off from the apple theme, such as "trees," "insects," or "stores." In this way, one theme could lead to another, which would provide conceptual links among several topics and a sense of intellectual coherence for children and teachers. Alternatively, the class's interests may move in an entirely different direction. "Poetry," "pottery," and "physical fitness" may be topics that intrigue them next. What prompts the development of each new theme will be unique for each group.

Now that a sample thematic unit has been described from start to finish, let us consider the most common questions teachers have about theme and project planning, implementation, and evaluation.

FIGURE 16.5 Sample Weekly Plan: Apple Theme, Week 1, Introduction

Time/Routine	Area	Monday	Tuesday	Wednesday	Thursday	Friday
8:30–8:45 A.M. Greeting Time	Group-time rug	Children arrive	Greetings, job chart		Introduction to	Day's activities
8:45–10:00 Free choice	Art area	Making play dough; tools available include apple cookie cutters and apple shapes to trace	Easel painting on apple shapes Apple still-life pictures to enjoy		Sponge painting with apple shapes and red, yellow, and green paint (1,2,3)	Cooperative color mixing
	Blocks	Unit blocks with	vehicles		human figures	cardboard trees
	Library	Apple catalogs	Apple posters Flannel board: "The Apple and the Worm"	Field trip to the orchard	*How Do Apples Grow?* by B. Maestro *The Seasons of Arnold's Apple Tree,* by G. Gibbons	Big Book: *Down the Road,* by Alice Schertle
	Writer's nook	Class surveys	Apple adjectives		Apple books	
	Fine motor	Making apple tree puzzles with a friend Lacing apple shapes	Cutting activity		Peeling apples for snack	Cutting activity
	Math and science	Numeral bingo Pulleys and levers Apple sorting	Magnets Apple seed estimates		Ramps with rollers Seriating apples by taste, touch, smell, size, and look	Counting apple seeds Making applesauce
	Open snack	Apple juice, crackers, and peanut butter	Dried apples, toast, and low-fat cheese cubes	Snack at orchard	Tasting three kinds of apples	Charting apple favorites (juice, sauce, raw)
	Pretend play	Pretend orchard— trees, apples, bushel baskets, cash register, materials for sign making plus housekeeping	Add pie-making materials to house		Add props to orchard as suggested by children	

Time/Routine	Area	Monday	Tuesday	Wednesday	Thursday	Friday
9:55—Warning for cleanup		Pairs of children clean up			Children self-select cleanup area and decide what needs to be done	
10:00–10:10 cleanup						
10:10–10:30 Large group	Group-time rug	Flannel board: "The Apple and the Worm" Two little apples hanging on a tree	Preparation for orchard field trip Discussion		Thank-you note to orchard—group writing experience and reflection on trip	Book: *Down the Road*, by Alice Schertle
10:30 to 10:35 Transition outdoors						
10:40–11:20 Outdoor time	Playground 1	Apple tree investigations— materials for bark rubbings, magnifying glasses, small plastic bags for collecting apple tree items, chart paper for recording observations		Return from orchard during this time— transition to playground if weather is good	Apple tree investigations— materials for bark rubbings, magnifying glasses, small plastic bags for collecting apple tree items, chart paper for recording observations	
			Musical hoops			Wheeled carts
11:20–11:30 Transition indoors	Bathroom hand washing					
11:30 A.M.–12:00 P.M. Lunch	Classroom	Set a place for a friend			Set a place for a friend	
12:00–12:15 Transition home	Saying farewell to friends					

Items listed here are provided in addition to the standard materials always available to children indoors and outside.

Tally of theme-related activities: Aesthetic activities = 3, affective activities = 3, social activities = 6, cognitive activities = 6, language activities = 6, physical activities = 3, social activities = 4.

COMMON QUESTIONS ABOUT THEMES AND PROJECTS

Must Every Activity Relate to the Theme?

As noted, effective daily and weekly plans include both theme-related and non-theme-related activities. However, this question is so commonly asked that the answer bears repeating. Although having several theme-related activities each day is important, creating a mix of theme- and non-theme-oriented activities each week is preferable. In half-day programs, the minimum number of theme-related activities is three or four, one of which should occur during a group time. For full-day programs, an average of two or three activities in each half day works reasonably well. At least some portion of a group time should also be devoted to an aspect of the theme.

If the class is saturated by a given topic or the thematic unit goes on for too long, the subject loses its appeal for children and teachers alike. Moreover, the link between activities and the concept becomes contrived rather than obvious and real. Some non-theme-related activities interspersed throughout your teaching plan will provide a respite from the topic and enable you to address necessary skills unrelated to the theme. Reprising children's favorites, reviewing past experiences, and including subject-based activities whose content is mandated by the program curriculum are appropriate alternatives. Take time also to create activities that introduce children to new content that might be expanded on in the future. These activities will allow you to gauge children's interest in and knowledge of untried topics.

How Long Does a Typical Thematic Unit or Project Last?

The length of a thematic unit or a project depends on the children's needs and interests and how you have structured the topic. Some thematic units and projects may last only a week or two; most others will last much longer. For instance, spending several days on "pumpkins" might cover the topic well. In contrast, 3 or 4 weeks devoted to "seeds" may barely scratch the surface of possible information or children's curiosity about the topic. Moreover, one class could find 2 weeks devoted to the "kitchen" to be sufficient, whereas another group of children might be so intrigued by the kitchen and what goes on there that they will choose to carry out a variety of projects regarding this important place in their center or school. The less experience children have with a concept, the more time they need to explore it. For example, youngsters who have had many opportunities to go to their local library or bookmobile may find that 3 weeks is enough time to learn more about these book-lending opportunities. However, children who have few books at home and have never visited a library may enjoy and profit from an additional week or two focusing on these related ideas.

Exercise judgment in determining the most fitting approach for your class. Many teachers report that 2- to 3-week themes (with an optional follow-up week or two) work well. If you anticipate that children will become involved in projects as a result of the theme, even more time will be necessary.

Beware of teaching an entire year of themes that last only 1 week each. One-week thematic units are too brief to do more than survey a few bits of information. The short time frame denies children opportunities to become absorbed in a topic, conduct personal investigations into the concept it represents, and come away with new understanding. Different weekly themes also force teachers to shift gears too quickly to put together a cohesive, well-considered set of plans.

Is There a Difference Between Planning Themes for 3- and 4-Year-Olds and Planning Themes for 6- to 8-Year-Olds?

The process of planning and implementing themes is the same regardless of children's ages. Selecting a topic, creating the TFPs, generating activity ideas, planning the unit, and carrying it out are steps required for every theme. However, themes vary—in terms of the TFPs selected and the concepts chosen for study—according to the children's ages and their prior experience with the theme. To make age-appropriate and individually appropriate differentiations, divide the TFPs into two categories: simple and advanced.

Simple TFPs consist of terms or facts that can be observed or experienced by the children directly through their own activity (although they might not be able to put these terms or facts into words). Existing in the here and now rather than the future or past, simple TFPs do not require teacher explanations. Adult talk may reinforce children's self-discoveries, but it is never a substitute for direct experience. Principles, because they often involve abstractions, are not identified as simple. For example, the theme "clothing" could be supported by the following simple terms and facts:

Terms Specialized names for certain articles of clothing are *poncho, helmet, yarmulke, kimono, vest, kilt, turban, kaftan,* and so on.

Facts Certain articles of clothing go on certain parts of the body. Clothes have different fasteners: buckles, buttons, snaps, zippers, ties, and Velcro. Clothing comes in a variety of sizes, shapes, colors, patterns, and textures. People wear clothing for different reasons.

Children engaged in activities and routines in the classroom could incorporate all these terms and facts into their concept of clothing on the basis of actual experience.

Advanced TFPs are those that children often learn about through representational experiences such as pictures, models, or discussions. Advanced TFPs may refer to past or future events or events that occur outside the classroom and may require children to envision something mentally in order to comprehend them. That cows have four legs is a simple fact because it is readily observable both in real cows and in toy cows in the classroom. The fact that cows have multiple stomachs is advanced because it must be represented by a picture, diagram, or discussion and requires children to envision the internal workings of a cow without experiencing them directly. Advanced TFPs consist of more-elaborate or enigmatic vocabulary and more-complicated facts and principles. Because of the complexity or abstractness of these TFPs, children generally need more opportunities and time to grasp them than is usually required for simple TFPs. Advanced TFPs related to the theme "clothing" are given in the following examples:

Terms When two pieces of fabric are sewn together, the joining point is called a *seam. Natural* fibers are made from animals or plants. *Synthetic* fibers are made from chemicals.

Facts People make leather from the skins of various animals. People created synthetic fibers for many reasons: strength, durability, ease of care, and so on.

Principle When choosing clothing they like, people may be influenced by advertising or others' opinions.

This designation of simple and advanced TFPs will help you to identify which category of TFPs to emphasize when you are working with a particular group of children. Simple TFPs should be used with 3-, 4-, and 5-year-olds and older children who have little experience with the theme. Advanced TFPs are more appropriate for kindergartners who know the theme well and for children in the early primary grades as well as for youngsters beyond the early childhood period. This stratification allows you to choose a subset of TFPs that best corresponds to the needs of your class. Depending on the concept to be addressed, the subset may be composed of TFPs representing either or both levels of difficulty.

The criteria that differentiate simple TFPs from advanced TFPs may also be applied to concepts overall. Concepts that deal with the here and now and that youngsters can explore through numerous hands-on experiences are most suitable for young children. Examples are clothing, water, plants, textures, books, and people at school. Children can explore all these topics in the near environment of their classroom, play yard, or neighborhood. These topics do not rely on a one-time field trip or visitor as the children's only real experience with the concept. Neither must children try to remember or mentally envision something they have never experienced directly in order to think about the concept meaningfully. Concepts dependent on these latter forms of experience are more abstract and would be considered advanced. Samples are the circus (dependent on children's remembering or envisioning a circus experience), communicating (focuses on actions rather than tangible objects), and the eye (focuses on representations such as models and diagrams to illustrate how the eye functions). Advanced concepts are better used with children toward the latter phases of the early childhood period and beyond.

How Do I Use Themes and Projects with so Much Required Content to Cover?

Theme teaching and project work are not add-ons. They are not additional strands to be incorporated into the day's instruction, nor are they an extra layer to be added to an already-bursting curriculum. Themes and projects are strategies for breaking away from rigid compartmentalization of subject matter and the traditional use of designated time blocks.

Because time is limited in early childhood classrooms, efficient teachers do not confine subjects to certain slots in the day. Teachers who attempt to use time slots find they run out of time without having adequately addressed all areas of the curriculum. In particular, we have learned during the past decade that knowledge, processes, and skills related to science, social studies, health, and the arts suffer most in this regard (Bergstrom & O'Brien, 2001; Jalongo, 1990). Yet the concepts associated with these subjects are essential to children's understanding of their experiences and the world around them. In response to this dilemma, professionals in a variety of disciplines are advocating a more holistic, interdisciplinary approach to educating children at all grade levels and across all subjects (Freeman & Sokoloff, 1996; Kovalik, 1997). Consequently, one good idea is to create some thematic units each year focusing on concepts generally associated with underrepresented portions of the curriculum. Also, by using required content as a source for themes and the development of related projects, you can combine previously isolated subjects or skills (e.g., science and writing; social studies and math; health and reading; speaking, reading, and writing; or art and critical thinking). Doing so makes the day less fragmented, which allows children and teachers more time to explore topics in depth.

Is Repeating a Theme Ever Appropriate During the Year?

Repeating a theme is appropriate, but remember that concept learning does not stop simply because a particular unit ends. Children will continue to explore and apply related knowledge and skills within subsequent themes. Although they will do this spontaneously, teachers should plan some activities throughout the year that call for children to retrieve content and processes explored previously.

Some concepts are greatly enriched when they receive formal instructional attention for several days at different times of the year. As a good example, a leaf theme could be introduced in the fall and then repeated in the spring, building on what children learned earlier as well as contrasting leaves and leaf growth during two seasons. Likewise, some teachers begin the year with a unit on friends, the primary aim of which is to help children "discover" one another and create a sense of cohesiveness within the class. Later in the year, these teachers return to the concept "friends" as a means of reinforcing social harmony and addressing more-advanced TFPs that the children, now more thoroughly acquainted, are ready to explore.

What About Repeating Themes from One Program Level to the Next?

Sometimes teachers and family members worry about children's revisiting certain themes as they move from the 3-year-old room to the 4-year-old class or from kindergarten to first grade. Thinking children may get bored or will not learn anything new, they need to remember that children learn through repetition. Having opportunities to explore familiar concepts further is not only worthwhile, but also the best way for children to expand their understanding by building on what they already know. Each time children participate in a given theme, they glean new insights and skills from the experience. No single period of investigation is ever complete or offers children all they want or need to know about a topic. In addition, the projects that evolve out of a theme will vary from one year to the next as children build on what they know to investigate new aspects of the topic. Consequently, repeating some themes from one year to the next is an effective instructional strategy.

In contrast, simply rehashing the *exact* material year after year may not provide enough stimulation to hold children's interest or enhance their concept development. To avoid this problem, teachers within the same program can plan similar themes to draw children's attention to different facets. They can also use multiyear themes to help children move from focusing on simple TFPs to more-advanced TFPs. For instance, dinosaurs,

Educators find working together on theme ideas satisfying and stimulating.

a topic beloved by children throughout the later early childhood period, is a theme they often request. It may be covered 2 or 3 years in a row, which makes it an ideal vehicle for collaborative planning among teachers at different program levels. Such a plan could be formulated, keeping in mind that 6-year-olds are fascinated by the terms associated with dinosaurs, especially their names. Simple facts regarding dinosaurs' physical characteristics are also appealing to these children. Second graders, already familiar with dinosaur names, continue to be intrigued with the physical attributes of dinosaurs as well as where they lived and how they protected themselves. By third grade, children who have experienced the theme twice before tend to be no less enthusiastic about dinosaurs, but they may have moved on to exploring more-advanced facts (e.g., why dinosaurs became extinct) as well as considering principles (e.g., attributes of the jaw and teeth are what distinguish meat eaters from plant eaters). Creating a programwide plan that incorporates this developmental progression from simple to complex and from concrete to more abstract supports children's interest in the theme. It also gives each teacher a chance to offer children opportunities for new insights. The more often teachers within the same program talk to and collaborate with one another regarding theme planning, the more likely it is that they will complement rather than duplicate one another's efforts.

Is There One Best Way to Cover Particular Concepts?

Every theme can be approached from a variety of angles, each of which has potential benefits for children. For instance, a unit on storytelling could be carried out in either of the following ways.

Option 1

Week	Content
1–2	Fictional stories
3–4	True stories
5	Children as storytellers
6	Children select projects
7	Children's projects continue this week and the next 2 or 3 weeks as appropriate

Option 2

Week	Content
1	Story of the week (e.g., "The Three Bears") or author of the week (e.g., Ezra Jack Keats, Barbara Cooney)
2	New story or new author or previous author continued
3	Children select projects
4	Children's projects continue this week and in the future as dictated by the children's interests and productivity

Another approach is to choose a major concept such as "the pond" or "people living together" to guide your planning for several months or even all year. These overarching concepts provide a unifying mechanism that not only permits choice, but also creates a link from one theme to another. Thus, children and teachers together might choose "insects," "frogs and toads," "waterfowl," "aquatic plant life," and "water," all as part of the comprehensive concept of "the pond." In this fashion, one teacher planned an entire year around the idea of "life beneath, on, and above the Earth's surface." At the beginning of the year, she and the children chose "soil," "rocks," and "worms"—themes they associated with life beneath the surface of the Earth. By midyear, their investigations had moved above the ground. "Mapping," "water," "plants," "animal habitats," and "human habitats" were topics they explored. As the year came to a close, children and teacher turned their attention to life in the sky as they explored "clouds," "air transportation," "birds," and "sky legends."

Clearly, more than one way is effective for approaching thematic teaching. The children's interests, their prior knowledge, what they want to know more about, the availability of support materials, and resource people will influence your choices.

What About Having All My Themes and Projects Revolve Around Holidays?

One practice still common in many early childhood programs is to use holidays as a primary framework for developing curriculum (Myers & Myers, 2001–2002). Weeks at a time center around Halloween, Christmas, St. Patrick's Day, Washington's Birthday, Groundhog Day, and so forth. A number of potential problems are inherent in this approach.

First, such themes run the risk of being little more than a convenient backdrop for children's participation in numerous craft projects, with minimal attention paid to either content learning or process learning (Kostelnik, 1996). Youngsters usually come away from these units without having increased their skills or expanded their conceptualizations.

Second, when children spend an entire month focusing on Halloween or St. Patrick's Day, these times come to dominate children's lives. They take on a disproportionate importance in comparison to the more common and relevant phenomena that constitute children's real-life experiences.

A third risk is the inadvertent teaching of cultural or religious stereotypes. For instance, in many schools across the United States, November marks the time when children hear about pilgrims and Native Americans. All too often, Native Americans are depicted as wearing feathers in their hair, dancing, and war whooping, while their real contributions—helping the pilgrims—are overlooked. Moreover, Thanksgiving is presented as a time of universal celebration and feasting. Although true for many people, some Native Americans fast at this time and view the day as one of mourning in remembrance of the many tragedies suffered by native people following the arrival of the first White settlers (Little-Soldier, 1990; Ramsey, 1979). Equitable treatment of the subject demands a balanced point of view that would be too abstract for most young children. Yet, promoting the traditional stereotypes, assuming they will be altered or undone when children are older, is risky because such corrections may never happen.

Similarly, a theme that promotes children's creating Easter baskets and Easter rabbits, parading in Easter finery, and playing Easter bunny math games presupposes that every family celebrates this particular holiday or that such items and activities are nonreligious symbols of spring. Both notions are erroneous. These practices trivialize the day and violate the principle of respect for religious differences, which makes such practices inappropriate.

Finally, because so little time is available in formal group settings to cover every important topic, teachers should omit topics that focus on social-conventional knowledge to which children are heavily exposed outside the classroom (Neubert & Jones, 1998). Many holidays fall into this category and thus are not the worthiest topics for large chunks of instructional time. Having fewer holiday themes allows more opportunities to explore concepts for which program support adds richness, variety, and a dimension not so easily obtained elsewhere.

Eliminating holidays as the *sole* basis for theme planning does not mean ignoring them altogether. Instead, teachers may incorporate these special times into the context of a larger concept such as "celebrations" or "family traditions." Both these themes could support a wide array of TFPs, as illustrated in Figure 16.6. Such concepts tend to be inclusive rather than exclusive. They support children's growing awareness and appreciation of similarities and differences among people.

In addition, integrating Valentine's Day into the more global theme "friends," using Halloween to pique children's interest in "costumes and masks," and exploring and comparing home rituals associated with Christmas, Hanukkah, and Kwanza through a unit on "families" or "homes" are all ways for the class to acknowledge and enjoy holidays as they occur. Such themes simultaneously allow more-relevant connections to be made to children's lives.

Finally, holiday customs need not be confined only to holiday times. Instead, a variety of observances could be highlighted within such generic themes as "clothing," "seasons," "storytelling," or "healthy foods" and could be carried out at any time of the year, with rituals, games, props, and foods associated with various holidays incorporated as appropriate.

How Do I Know That Children Are Developing More Sophisticated, Complex Concepts?

Children reveal their conceptual understandings through play, conversations with peers and adults, questions, errors, methods of investigating objects and events, products, and representations. To find out what children know, observe and talk with them about the concept. Use the KWHLH brainstorming technique described in chapter 4 to give children a chance to describe what they have learned and what they still wonder about. Give children opportunities to talk and interact with their peers, and provide open-ended activities through which they can explore the concept in their own way. Encourage them to

FIGURE 16.6 Terms, Facts, and Principles (TFPs): "Family Traditions"

1. A family tradition is an activity families repeat in much the same way time after time.

2. Traditions are an important part of family life.

3. All families have traditions, such as special songs, celebrations, foods, activities, stories, recollections, routines, rules, beliefs, and values.

4. Family celebrations are often influenced by tradition:

   ❏ Particular foods may be prepared.
   ❏ A certain sequence of events may be followed.*
   ❏ Special clothing may be worn.
   ❏ Special songs may be sung.
   ❏ Special stories may be told.
   ❏ People may have special roles within the celebration.*
   ❏ Special activities may be carried out

5. Families vary in the traditions they observe.

6. A family's religious and/or cultural heritage influences the traditions they adopt.*

7. Traditions help family members feel close to one another.

8. Some family traditions have been carried out for many years, and some are relatively new.*

9. Some traditions are very elaborate; others are quite simple.

10. Sometimes outsiders are invited to participate in a family tradition, and sometimes only the family participates.

11. Every family has stories or anecdotes about how certain traditions developed or how certain family members were involved in family traditions.

12. Photographs, home videos, or cassette recordings are often used to record traditional family events.

Source: These TFPs were developed by Laura C. Stein, M.S., Early Childhood Consultant, Stein Associates, East Lansing, Michigan. Those marked with an asterisk are advanced.

represent what they have learned through drawings, charts, writings, dictation, and so forth. Create displays of these items so that children can refer to them as the unit progresses. Make these displays available to family members in an end-of-unit celebration or get-together. Make notes about what you see and hear, using the assessment techniques described in chapter 7.

SUMMARY

Coordinating activities around a central theme has long been a tradition in early childhood education. The benefits to youngsters, practitioners, and programs are many. Nonetheless, the greatest value of theme teaching lies in its use as a concept organizer. As young children engage in activities permeated by the same basic idea, they connect individual bits of knowledge and perceptions and form more comprehensive, accurate concepts. However, such positive outcomes result only when practitioners keep in mind principles of developmentally appropriate practice as well as those of effective theme teaching. The latter include relying on children's interests and capacities to influence theme selection and direction; focusing on the conceptual nature of thematic teaching; using an accurate, thorough body of factual information to support the theme; emphasizing firsthand learning as well as real objects in carrying out the theme; integrating thematic activities across domains, subject areas, and parts of the day; and using the theme as a foundation for child-initiated and child-directed projects.

Creating thematic units involves several steps. The first is to select a topic. Ideas for themes most often originate from the children. Themes may also reflect special events or unexpected happenings, school-mandated content, or teacher or family interests. The best themes are relevant to children and make significant use of hands-on experiences. They contribute to diversity and balance across the curriculum, include a variety of theme-oriented resources, and prompt children to engage in projects of their choosing.

Once an idea has been settled on, the second step is to create a topic web as well as an accurate information base to support the concept under study. To do this, practitioners research relevant terms, facts, and principles (TFPs). These serve as the basis for activity development. To increase their educational value further, activities related to the theme also represent a variety of domains and modes of learning.

Making a plan is the third phase of theme teaching. It involves distributing theme-related activities throughout your weekly lessons and across all parts of the day. Although having several theme-related activities in the plan is important, not every activity in a day or week must focus on the theme.

The last phase of theme teaching involves implementing, evaluating, and revisiting the theme as children become engaged in the topic. Themes usually evolve from teacher-initiated planning to child-initiated projects. Projects have three phases: (a) beginning the project, (b) developing the project, and (c) concluding the project. Within this chapter, a theme-teaching checklist is provided as a tool for assessing theme implementation in classrooms as well as children's theme-related learning. Educators' potential questions regarding theme teaching and project work are also posed and answered.

In sum, theme teaching and project work are valuable instructional tools when used properly. Practitioners who have never engaged in this kind of teaching may find it time consuming at first. Nevertheless, as familiarity with the process increases, so will the teacher's speed and efficiency in carrying it out. Helping to make sense of what could otherwise be fragmented educational events is an advantage both children and teachers will enjoy.

Applying What You Read in This Chapter

1. Discuss
  a. On the basis of your reading and your experiences with young children, discuss each of the questions that open this chapter.
  b. The children in your classroom are excited about the new apartment building under construction across the street from the early childhood program building. What thematic ideas does this suggest? On the basis of what you learned in this chapter, how would you plan a thematic unit?
  c. Your colleague is planning to develop a thematic unit about the circus. Is this a developmentally appropriate theme for 3-year-olds in your commu-

nity? Is it a developmentally appropriate theme for 7-year-olds in your community?
  d. Using the apple activities generated by Hannah Solomon for the children in her preschool class, create a 1-week overview of activities for a class of children you know. Add or subtract activities as necessary. How does your plan compare with Hannah's? What is the rationale behind your plan?

2. Observe
  a. Observe a group of children for no less than 30 minutes. On the basis of what they talk about and seem greatly interested in, what themes or projects might this suggest for this group?

b. Observe a group of children in a classroom that uses theme planning. What do you notice about the children's involvement in the theme? What implications do your observations have for your approach to theme planning?

c. Observe a group of children carrying out a project. What do you notice about their involvement with the project? What implications do your observations have for your approach to facilitating projects?

3. Carry out an activity

a. Read an article on theme planning or the project approach. Summarize the primary points the author makes. Describe the extent to which the article supports or disputes what you read in this chapter.

b. Interview two early childhood educators who work with children of different ages. Ask these teachers to describe some of the topics their students are most interested in learning more about. Ask them to talk about how they incorporate children's interests into their teaching.

c. Participate in a classroom in which thematic teaching or projects are offered to children. Describe how you supported children's involvement with these topics.

d. Using the guidelines in this chapter, choose a thematic topic for a specific group of children. Explain why you selected the topic, and discuss how it is age appropriate, individually appropriate, and socioculturally appropriate for these children.

e. Using the guidelines in this chapter, create a thematic unit for a specific group of children in which you identify a topic, TFPs, a week's activities, and methods for evaluating the plan's effectiveness.

4. Create something for your portfolio

a. Take pictures of and record children's reactions to a theme or project you supervised.

5. Add to your journal

a. What is the most significant concept that you have learned about themes and projects on the basis of your readings and your experience with children?

b. What is your initial reaction to the idea of theme planning or project implementation with young children?

c. List the most pressing concerns you have about planning and implementing appropriate themes or projects for children. Describe how you will address your concerns.

Appendix: Sample Lesson Plans

SAMPLE GUIDED-DISCOVERY PLAN

Domain: Cognitive   **Activity Name:** Sea Life Observations

Intermediate Objective: The children will examine natural objects by using their multisensory abilities.

Immediate Objectives

The child will

1. Examine an object by using multiple senses.
2. Talk about what he or she discovered.
3. Record his or her observations for future reference.
4. Describe how he or she examined the object.

Content

1. People learn about objects in nature by examining them closely.
2. Some ways to examine an object include looking at it, touching it, smelling it, and listening to it.
3. The more senses people use in their investigations of natural objects, the more they learn.
4. People improve their investigative skills through practice and by thinking about how they will remember what they observed.
5. People record their observations so that they can refer to them later.

Materials: One large, dead starfish; a Dungeness crab or another hard-shelled crab, preserved on ice; strands of wet seaweed on a tray; a horseshoe crab shell free of insects; paper towels that cover the objects prior to use and that the children can use to wipe their hands on as necessary; pads of paper for the children to use; pencils or markers

Procedures

Examine and Talk

1. Gather the children in a large circle. Begin the activity with a discussion about all the ways that the children have been examining objects during the week. Remind the children of some of the strategies they have used.
2. Divide the children into four small groups, each assigned to a different table.
3. Give each group a towel-covered tray that holds a natural object. Explain that everyone will have a chance to examine the natural object very closely. Make sure that the children know that the objects are safe to touch. Invite the children to examine the object *before* taking off the paper towels. Ask this question: "What did you find out?" Paraphrase the children's comments.
4. Ask the children, "How did you discover _____?" Paraphrase the children's comments.
5. Tell the children to remove the towels and continue their investigation. Ask open-ended questions to prompt the children's use of various senses. Paraphrase the children's discoveries. Add factual information if the children desire it.

Record

6. After several minutes, give each child a piece of paper and ask him or her to make a mark on the paper as a reminder of what he or she discovered. Such marks could take the form of pictures, words, or symbols. They need have no meaning to anyone other than the child.

Describe

7. Invite the children to return to the large-group area with their marked papers. Conduct a discussion of what the children discovered. Create on chart paper a master list of the children's discoveries. Post this list where the children can refer to it and add to it throughout the day. During this discussion, continually refer to the investigative methods the children used and how they used them.

8. Tell the children that all the trays will be in the science/math center so that they can explore items they did not have a chance to investigate.

Simplification: Divide the large group of children into small groups; give each group a specimen of a similar object (e.g., give all the groups a starfish).

Extension

1. Have the children examine a different object each day, keeping a journal of the properties of the object.
2. Ask the children what they would still like to know but have not yet discovered about the objects. Brainstorm with them about how they could find out.
3. Adapt the activity to involve natural objects the children find outdoors or those in which they spontaneously express interest.

Evaluation

1. What properties were the most common among the children's observations?
2. What different strategies did the children use to investigate the objects?
3. What different ways did the children use to record their observations?
4. How might you revise the activity in the future and why?

SAMPLE PROBLEM-SOLVING PLAN

Domain: Affective   **Activity Name:** Making Plans

Intermediate Objective: The children will make a plan and carry it out.

Immediate Objectives

The child will
1. Establish a goal.
2. Create a plan for meeting the goal.
3. Carry out the plan.
4. Evaluate the plan.

Content

1. A *plan* is a guide for decision making and action.
2. A *goal* is something a person wants and tries to reach.
3. A goal can be better accomplished when we have thought about a plan of action to reach the goal.

Materials: A wide array of art materials; scraps of wood or cloth; glue, paste, and other fasteners; scissors, markers; crayons; paint

Procedure

1. Invite the children to look at the materials available.
2. Tell the children they will have a chance to make something of their choosing.
3. Ask each child to think of something he or she would like to make from the materials. This can be an object, such as a car, or something abstract, such as a collage.
4. Ask the children what they would have to do first, second, and third to make their projects. Write down their ideas, making a sample plan.
5. Have the children implement their plan.
6. After the children have made something, review their plan with them and ask them if they kept to their plan or changed it.

Simplification: Work with the child to scaffold a two- or three-step plan.

Extension: Invite the children to make plans of four or more steps.

Evaluation: Complete the following evaluation sheet by putting a check mark beside the objectives that each child demonstrated. Note how many steps each child included in his or her plan.

Children's Names	Established a Goal	Created a Plan	Carried Out the Plan	Evaluated the Plan	Number of Steps in the Plan
Alonzo					
Cathy					
David					
Dwayne					
Hallie					
Jorge					
Mark					
Maureen					
Olivia					
Rita					
Talia					
Veronica					
Vincent					

SAMPLE DISCUSSION PLAN

Domain: Social   **Activity Name**: Rules for the Block Area

Intermediate Objective: The children will create rules for the classroom and identify reasons for their rules.

Immediate Objectives

The child will

1. Participate in a group discussion about classroom rules.
2. Identify reasons for classroom rules.
3. Suggest an idea for a rule.
4. Provide a reason for his or her rule.

Content

1. A *rule* is a guide for behavior.
2. People make rules to protect property, to protect people's rights, and to ensure safety.
3. People in groups agree to follow certain rules to help them get along with one another.
4. People discuss things to better understand them and to reach agreement about them.
5. In a discussion, sometimes people talk, and sometimes they listen.

Materials: Easel and easel pad; dark, thick-tipped marker

Procedure

1. Open the discussion by talking about some of the current problems in the block area (people running, blocks all over the floor). Introduce the idea of rules as guides for behavior.
2. Invite the children to suggest ideas for rules that might involve play in the block area.
   a. Paraphrase the children's ideas.
   b. Use questions to stimulate the children's thinking.
3. Guide verbal turn taking.
   a. Remind the children to listen carefully when another child is speaking.
4. Record the children's ideas on a large sheet of easel paper.
   a. Restate each idea after it has been written.
5. Draw the discussion to a close by summarizing the children's rules.
6. Post the children's rules in the block area.

Simplification: If the children cannot think of ideas, offer suggestions to get the discussion started.

Extension: After a week, ask the children to evaluate their rules and revise them as necessary.

Evaluation

1. Who contributed to the group discussion?
2. Which children met which objectives?
3. What surprised you about the discussion?

SAMPLE DEMONSTRATION PLAN

Domain: Cognitive   **Activity Name:** Body Patterns

Intermediate Objective: The children will reproduce patterns.

Immediate Objectives

The child will

1. Explore a variety of body movements.
2. Imitate simple body movement patterns consisting of two elements.
3. Imitate complex body movement patterns consisting of more than two elements.
4. Suggest, create, or demonstrate a pattern of their own to the rest of the group.

Content

1. A *pattern* refers to the ways in which colors, shapes, or lines are arranged or repeated in some order.
2. The way that the elements of a pattern are organized determines the pattern's design or how it sounds. A pattern can be a set of repeated actions.
3. The same elements may be organized in a variety of ways to create different patterns.

Materials: None

Procedures

Explore

1. Invite the children to participate in the activity. Gain their attention by asking them to explore different ways to move their bodies.
2. Encourage the children to imitate a single motion that you or another child makes.

Imitate Simple Patterns

3. Invite the children to watch you as you show them a body movement pattern. Create a simple pattern of movements and words involving two body parts and single motion. For instance, tap your body and say the word for the body part in a rhythmic fashion: "Head, head, shoulders, shoulders, head, head, shoulders, shoulders."
4. Using a do-it signal, have the children respond by imitating your actions.
5. Repeat Steps 3 and 4 using two different body parts and different number combinations. Keep the numbers the same for each body part, such as two taps and two claps.

Imitate Complex Patterns

6. Gradually increase the complexity of the patterns by increasing the number of body parts and motions (tapping your head, clapping your hands, and stomping your feet). Another way to increase complexity is to vary the number of motions (two taps, three claps, one stomp). Have the children imitate the pattern you create.

Simplification: Use simple patterns slowly. Use major body parts such as head, hands, and feet.

Extension

1. Increase the complexity of the pattern and the speed of your movements, using body parts such as wrist, neck, and ankles.
2. Demonstrate a repetitive movement. Ask the children to predict what comes next, and then do it.

Evaluation

1. Which children participated in this activity?
2. What objectives did each child achieve?
3. Was the procedure carried out as described? If so, what was the result? If not, what did you change and why?

SAMPLE DIRECT-INSTRUCTION PLAN

Domain: Cognitive   **Activity Name:** Earthworm Facts

Intermediate Objective: The children will acquire scientific knowledge related to life sciences, specifically animal life.

Content

1. Earthworms are cylindrically shaped, segmented animals.
2. Earthworms have a mouth (no teeth), a headed end, and a tailed end (the head is more pointed than the tail).
3. Earthworms have no ears, eyes, legs, or skeleton.
4. Earthworms live and burrow in the soil.
5. Earthworms move by waves of muscular contractions traveling along the body.

Materials: A shovel full of soil in a bucket or in the water table; worms; a large picture of an earthworm depicting its segments, specifically, head end and tail end; a children's reference book about earthworms that includes pictures and simple facts about earthworm movement and habits; a clean piece of white paper on which to place an earthworm to watch its movements more easily; paper on which to write and markers or pens; cheesecloth

Procedures

Preparation: To prepare for this activity, dig up some large earthworms or buy some at a bait store. Keep the soil moist and covered with cheesecloth prior to asking the children to participate.

Learning Phase	Immediate Objectives	Adult Does	Adult Says
Explore	Given a shovelful of soil containing some earthworms, the child will	Invite the children to participate.	Hi. Look at what's in this water table. It's not water! Today we have some soil dug out of our yard.
	1. Gently pick through the soil, searching for earthworms.	Remind children to be gentle.	Look carefully through it and tell me what animals you find.
Acquire	2. Talk about the earthworms as he or she observes them.	Ask children what they are noticing about the earthworms. Paraphrase the children's comments.	Tell me what you see.
			You noticed that some of these worms are red and some are black. You see skinny worms. The worm in your hand is very thick all the way around.
	Given an opportunity to observe and handle an earthworm while hearing an adult describe some of its features, the child will	Provide information to the children as they examine the earthworms. Talk about the shape, size, and movements of the earthworms.	Earthworms have a mouth at the head end of their bodies. Look for the mouth on your earthworm.
	3. Differentiate the head end from the tail end of the worm.	Ask the children to look for the earthworm's mouth.	Earthworms move head first. Look at that worm. Show me the head end.

Learning Phase	Immediate Objectives	Adult Does	Adult Says
		Refer to the picture of the earthworm to help children know at which end to look.	Look at this picture. See if your earthworm has segments on it like this.
		On a piece of paper, record the parts of the worm the children are able to identify.	So far, we have found heads and tails on these earthworms. Let's write that on our earthworm facts chart.
	4. Identify body parts earthworms do not possess.	Ask the children to tell you what body parts people or other animals have that they do not see on the earthworms they are examining.	Look to see if your earthworm has legs. Look at this picture; this earthworm has no ears. Look to see if that is true for your earthworm.
		Ask simple questions to help children focus on the body parts earthworms do not possess.	
		Provide correct information to children who have erroneous ideas.	You think your earthworm has eyes. Those dark colors on the tail are not eyes.
	5. Describe ways the earthworms move.	Show the children how the earthworms move by contracting their bodies. This may be done in the soil and on a clean piece of paper where the worm's undulating motion is easily seen. In addition, the worm will leave a faint imprint on the paper that will show the wavy way in which it propels itself.	Let's look closely at how these earthworms get from place to place.

Tell me what you see.

Notice how the earthworm pulls in and then stretches out to move. |
Practice	6. Observe and talk about earthworms outside on the playground throughout the week.	Guide the children's attention to earthworms outside.	Let's see if any earthworms are out here today.
		Review what the children discovered earlier in the week.	You remembered that earthworms come in different colors.
		Add new information to the chart the children had dictated.	You discovered that earthworms have tiny bristles on the underside of their bodies. Let's add that to our list of earthworm facts.

To Simplify: Focus primarily on color and shape and the variety among earthworms.
To Extend: Have the children compare earthworms with garter snakes, identifying similarities and differences.

Evaluation

1. What strategy was most successful in engaging the less assertive children in the activity? the more assertive children?
2. Which children achieved which objectives?
3. What did the children seem to know about earthworms in the exploration stage? What erroneous information did the children possess? About what were they most curious? What new facts did the children acquire during the week?

References

Abrams, H. (1985). *The Museum of Modern Art, New York*. New York: Harry Abrams.

Adams, P., & Nesmith, J. (1996). Blockbusters: Ideas for the block center. *Early Childhood Education Journal, 24*(2), 87–92.

The adventures of Sherlock Holmes [Motion picture]. (1939). United States: 20th Century Fox Studios.

Alejandro-Wright, M. N. (1985). The child's conception of racial classification. In M. B. Spencer, G. K. Brookins, & W. R. Allen (Eds.), *Beginnings: The social and affective development of black children* (pp. 185–200). Hillsdale, NJ: Erlbaum.

Allen, K. E., & Marotz, L. R. (2003). *Developmental profiles: Pre-birth through twelve*. Clifton Park, NY: Delmar Learning.

Allen, S. K., & Johnson, R. R. (1995, June). A study of hazards associated with playgrounds. *Journal of Environmental Health, 57*, 23–26.

Alvino, F. J. (2000, May). *Art improves the quality of life: A look at art in early childhood settings*. East Lansing, MI: National Center for Research on Teacher Learning. (ERIC Document Reproduction Service No. ED447936)

American Psychiatric Association. (2000). *Diagnostic and statistical manual of mental disorders* (4th ed., Text Revision). Washington, DC: Author.

American Public Health Association & American Academy of Pediatrics. (1992). Caring for our children: National Health and Safety Performance Standards: Guidelines for out-of-home care. Washington, D.C.: American Public Health Association.

Andress, B. (1998). *Music for young children*. Upper Saddle River, NJ: Delmar.

Archbald, D. A., & Newmann, F. M. (1988). *Beyond standardized testing*. Reston, VA: National Association of Secondary School Principals.

Association for Supervision and Curriculum Development. (1998). Teaching to the brain. *ASCD Update, 33*(8), 1–8.

Baker, R. J., & McMurray, A. M. (1998). Contact fathers' loss of school involvement. *Journal of Family Studies, 4*(2), 201–214.

Bandura, A. (1989). Social cognitive theory. In R. Vasta (Ed.), *Annals of child development* (Vol. 6, pp. 1–60). Greenwich, CT: JAI.

Bandura, A. (1991). Social cognitive theory of moral thought and action. In W. M. Kurtines & J. L. Gewirtz (Eds.), *Handbook of moral behavior and development* (Vol. 1, pp. 45–103). Hillsdale, NJ: Erlbaum.

Banks, J. A. (1988, Spring). Approaches to multicultural curriculum reform. *Multicultural Leader, 1*(2), 1–4.

Barab, S. A., & Landa, A. (1997, March). Designing effective interdisciplinary anchors. *Educational Leadership, 54*(6).

Barbour, N. H. (1990). Flexible grouping: It works! *Childhood Education, 67*(2), 66–67.

Barclay, K., Benelli, C., Campbell, P., & Kleine, L. (1995). Dream or nightmare? Planning for a year without textbooks. *Childhood Education, 71*(4), 205–211.

Baroody, A. J. (1987). *Children's mathematical thinking*. New York: Teachers College Press.

Baroody, A. J. (1993). Fostering the mathematical learning of young children. In B. Spodek (Ed.), *Handbook of research on the education of young children* (pp. 151–175). New York: Macmillan.

Bateson, G. (1971). The message "This is play." In R. Herren & B. Sutton-Smith (Eds.), *Child's play* (pp. 261–266). New York: Wiley.

Batshaw, M. L. (2002). *Children with disabilities* (5th ed.). Baltimore: Paul H. Brookes.

Batzle, J. (1992). *Portfolio assessment and evaluation: Developing and using portfolios in the classroom*. Cypress, CA: Creative Teaching Press.

Baumrind, D. (1967). Child care practices anteceding three patterns of preschool behavior. *Genetic Psychology Monographs, 75*, 43–88.

Baumrind, D. (1973). Current patterns of parental authority. *Developmental Psychology Monographs, 4,* 1.

Baumrind, D. (1978). A dialectical materialist's perspective on knowing social reality. In W. Damon (Ed.), *Moral development* (pp. 349–373). San Francisco, CA: Jossey-Bass.

Baumrind, D. (1983). Rejoinder to Lewis's reinterpretation of parental firm control effects: Are authoritative families really harmonious? *Psychological Bulletin, 94*, 132–142.

Baumrind, D. (1991). The influence of parenting style on adolescent competence and substance use. *Journal of Early Adolescence, 2*, 56–95.

Baumrind, D. (1995). *Child maltreatment and optimal caregiving in social contexts*. New York: Garland.

Begley, S. (1997, Spring/Summer). The brain. *Newsweek,* (Special ed.), 28–31.

Bergen, D. (1988a). *Play as a medium for learning and development*. Portsmouth, NH: Heinemann.

Bergen, D. (1988b). Using a schema for play and learning. In D. Bergen (Ed.), *Play as a medium for learning and development* (pp. 169–180). Portsmouth, NH: Heinemann.

Bergen, D. (1993). Teaching strategies: Facilitating friendship development in inclusion classrooms. *Childhood Education, 69*(4), 234–236.

Bergen, D. (1994). Should teachers permit or discourage violent play themes? *Childhood Education, 70*(5), 302–303.

Berger, E. H. (1999). *Parents as partners in education: Families and schools working together* (5th ed.). Upper Saddle River, NJ: Merrill/Prentice Hall.

Bergstrom, J. M., & O'Brien, L. A. (2001, April). Themes of discovery. *Educational Leadership, 58*(7), 29–33.

Berk, L. (2000). *Child development* (5th ed.). Needham Heights, MA: Allyn & Bacon.

Berk, L. (2002a). *Infants, children, and adolescents* (4th ed.). Needham Heights, MA: Allyn & Bacon.

Berk, L. (2002b). *Infants and children: Prenatal through middle childhood* (4th ed.). Boston: Allyn & Bacon.

Berk, L. (2003). *Child development* (6th ed.). Boston: Allyn & Bacon.

Berk, L. E., & Winsler, A. (1995). *Scaffolding children's learning: Vygotsky and early childhood education*. Washington, DC: National Association for the Education of Young Children.

Berndt, T. J., & Keefe, K. (1995). Friends' influence on adolescents' adjustment to school. *Child Development, 66*(5), 1312–1329.

Bernero, T. (2003). *Intermediate results of a school-wide discipline policy*. Report on the Community School, East Lansing, MI.

Berns, R. M. (2001). *Child, family, school, community: Socialization and support* (5th ed.). Fort Worth, TX: Harcourt College.

Bernstein, P. S. (1998, April). Why dads should be more involved in school. *Family Life,* 32.

Bickart, T. S., Dodge., T. D., & Jablon, J. R. (1997). *What every parent needs to know about 1st, 2nd, and 3rd grades*. Naperville, IL: Sourcebooks.

Biddle, B. J., & Berliner, D. C. (2002, February). Small class size and its effects. *Educational Leadership, 59*(5), 12–23.

Bjorklund, D. F., & Brown, R. D. (1998). Physical play and cognitive development: Integrating activity, cognition, and education. *Child Development, 69*(3), 604–606.

Blendon, R. J., Young, J. T., McCormick, M. C., Kropf, M., & Blair, J. (1998). Americans' views on children's health. *Journal of the American Medical Association, 280*(24), 2122–2127.

Bobbitt, N., & Paolucci, B. (1986). Strengths of the home and family as learning environments. In R. J. Griffore & R. P. Boger (Eds.), *Child rearing in the home and school* (pp. 47–60). New York: Plenum.

Bodrova, E., & Leong, D. (1996). *Tools of the mind: The Vygotskian approach to early childhood education*. Upper Saddle River, NJ: Merrill/Prentice Hall.

Bogart, J. (1994). *Gifts*. Richmond Hill, Ontario, Canada: Scholastic Canada.

Bollin, G. G. (1989, Summer). Ethnic differences in attitude towards discipline among day care providers: Implications for training. *Child & Youth Care Quarterly, 18*(2), 111–117.

Bornstein, M. H., Haynes, O. M., O'Reilly, A. W., & Painter, K. M. (1996). Solitary and collaborative pretense play in early childhood: Sources of individual variation in the development of representational competence. *Child Development, 67*(6), 2910–2929.

Bowman, B. (1994). The challenge of diversity. *Phi Delta Kappan, 76*(3), 218–225.

Bowman, B. T., Donovan, M. S., & Burns, M. S. (2001). *Eager to learn: Educating our preschoolers*. Washington, DC: National Academy Press.

Boyatzis, C. (1997). Of Power Rangers and v-chips. *Young Children, 52*(7), 74–79.

Boyd, B. J. (1997). Teacher response to superhero play: To ban or not to ban? *Young Children, 74*(1), 23–27.

Bracey, G. W. (2001). School involvement and the working poor: Summary of research by S. J. Heymann and A. Earle. *Phi Delta Kappan, 82*(10), 795.

Brainard, A., & Wrubel, D. H. (1993). *Literature-based science activities*. New York: Scholastic.

Brandt, R., & Epstein J. (1989, October). On parents and schools: A conversation with Joyce Epstein. *Educational Leadership, 47*(2), 24–27.

Bredekamp, S. (1987). *Developmentally appropriate practice in early childhood programs serving children from birth through age 8*. Washington, DC: National Association for the Education of Young Children.

Bredekamp, S. (1991). Guidelines for appropriate curriculum content and assessment in programs serving children ages three through eight. *Young Children, 46*(3), 21–38.

Bredekamp, S., & Copple, C. (1997). *Developmentally appropriate practice in early childhood programs*. Washington, DC: National Association for the Education of Young Children.

Bredekamp, S., & Rosegrant, T. (Eds.) (1992). *Reaching potentials: Appropriate curriculum and assessment for young children* (Vol. 1). Washington, DC: National Association for the Education of Young Children.

Bredekamp, S., & Rosegrant, T. (Eds.) (1995). *Reaching potentials: Transforming early childhood curriculum and assessment* (Vol. 2). Washington, DC: National Association for the Education of Young Children.

Brendtro, L. K., Brokenleg, M., & Van Bockern, S. (1997). *Reclaiming youth at risk: Our hope for the future* (Rev. ed.). Bloomington, IN: National Educational Service.

Brewer, J. A. (2001). *Introduction to early childhood education: Preschool through primary grades* (4th ed.). Boston: Allyn & Bacon.

Briggs, N. R., Jalongo, M. R., & Brown, L. (1997). Working with families of young children: Our history and our future goals. In J. P. Isenberg & M. R. Jalongo (Eds.), *Major trends and issues in early childhood education* (pp. 56–69). New York: Teachers College Press.

Bronfenbrenner, U. (1989). Ecological systems theory. In R. Vasta (Ed.), *Annals of child development* (Vol. 6, pp. 187–249). Greenwich, CT: JAI.

Bruer, J. T. (1999). *The myth of the first three years*. New York: Free Press.

Bugental, D. B., & Goodnow, J. J. (1998). Socialization processes. In N. Eisenberg (Ed.), *Handbook of child psychology* (Vol. 3, pp. 389–462). New York: Wiley.

Bukatko, D., & Daehler, M. (2001). *Child development: A thematic approach.* (4th ed.). Boston: Houghton Mifflin.

Bukowski, W. M., Sippola, L. K., & Bolvin, M. (1995, March). *Friendship protects "at risk" children from victimization by peers*. Paper presented at the meeting of the Society for Research in Child Development, Indianapolis, IN.

Bundy, B. F. (1991). Fostering communication between parents and schools. *Young Children, 46*(2), 12–17.

Burns, M. (2000). *About teaching mathematics: A K–8 resource* (2nd ed.). Sausalito, CA: Math Solutions Publications.

Burts, D. C., Hart, C. H., Charlesworth, R., & Kirk, L. (1990). A comparison of frequencies of stress behaviors observed in kindergarten children in classrooms with developmentally appropriate versus developmentally inappropriate instructional practices. *Early Childhood Research Quarterly, 5,* 407–423.

Burts, D. C., Hart, C. H., Charlesworth, R., & Kirk, L. (1992). Observed activities and stress behaviors of children in developmentally appropriate and inappropriate kindergarten classrooms. *Early Childhood Research Quarterly, 7*(2), 297–318.

Busink, R. (1997). Reading and phonological awareness: What have we learned and how can we use it? *Reading Research and Instruction 36*(3), 199–215.

Cardellichio, T., & Field, W. (1997, March). Seven strategies that encourage neural branching. *Educational Leadership, 54*(6), 33–36.

Carlisle, A. (2001). Using the multiple intelligence theory to assess early childhood curricula. *Young Children, 56*(6), 77–83.

Carlson, K., & Cunningham, J. L. (1990). Effect of pencil diameter on the graphomotor skill of preschoolers. *Early Childhood Research Quarterly, 5*(2), 279–293.

Carnegie Foundation for the Advancement of Teaching. (1988). *The conditions of teaching: A state by state analysis.* Princeton, NJ: Author.

Carta, J., Schwartz, L., Atwater, J., & McConnell, S. (1993). Developmentally appropriate practices and early childhood special education: A reaction to Johnson and McChesney Johnson. *Topics in Early Childhood Special Education, 13*(3), 243–254.

Casey, M., & Lippman, M. (1991, May). Learning to plan through play. *Young Children, 46*(4), 52–58.

Cassidy, D. (1989). Questioning the young child: Process and function. *Childhood Education, 65*(3), 146–149.

Castle, K. (1991). Children's invented games. *Childhood Education, 67*(2), 82–85.

Castle, K., & Rogers, K. (1994). Rule-creating in a constructivist community. *Childhood Education, 70*(2), 77–80.

Chafel, J. (1986). Call the police, okay? Social comparison by young children during play in preschool. In S. Burrows & R. Evans (Eds.), *Play, language and socialization* (pp. 115–130). New York: Gordon & Breach.

Chaillé, C., & Silvern, S. (1996). Understanding through play. *Childhood Education, 72*(5), 274–277.

Chang, H., Salazar, D., & DeLeong, C. (1994). *Drawing strength from diversity: Effective services for children, youth and families.* Sacramento: California Tomorrow.

Chard, S. C. (1998a). *The project approach: Making curriculum come alive.* New York: Scholastic.

Chard, S. C. (1998b). *The project approach: Managing successful projects.* New York: Scholastic.

Chard, S. C. (1999, Spring). From themes to projects. *Early Childhood Research and Practice, 1*(1). Retrieved June 10 from http://ecrp.uiuc.edu/v1n1/chard.html

Chard, S. C. (2001). *The project approach: Taking a closer look* [CD-ROM].

Chard, S. C. (2002). The challenges and the rewards: Teachers' accounts of their first experiences with the project approach. In D. Rothenberg (Ed.), *Issues in early childhood education: Curriculum, teacher education, and dissemination of information.* Proceedings of the Lilian Katz Symposium, Champaign, IL.

Charlesworth, R. (1998). Developmentally appropriate practice is for everyone. *Childhood Education, 74*(5), 274–282.

Charlesworth, R. (2000). Mathematics in the developmentally appropriate integrated curriculum. In C. H. Hart, D. C. Burts, & R. Charlesworth (Eds.), *Integrated curriculum and developmentally appropriate practice: Birth to age eight* (pp. 51–73). Albany: State University of New York Press.

Charlesworth, R., Hart, C. H., Burts, D. C., Thomasson, R. H., Mosely, J., & Fleege, P. O. (1993). Measuring the developmental appropriateness of kindergarten teachers' beliefs and practices. *Early Childhood Research Quarterly, 8,* 255–276.

Charlesworth, R., & Lind, K. K. (1995). *Math and science for young children* (2nd ed.). Albany, NY: Delmar.

Charney, R. S. (1998). *Teaching children to care: Management in the responsive classroom.* Greenfield, MA: Northeast Foundation for Children.

Chipman, M. (1997). Valuing cultural diversity in the early years: Social imperatives and pedagogical insights. In J. P. Isenberg & M. R. Jalongo (Eds.), *Major trends and issues in early childhood education: Challenges, controversies and insights* (pp. 43–55). New York: Teachers College Press.

Christie, J. (1986). Training of symbolic play. In P. Smith (Ed.), *Children's play: Research development and practical applications* (pp. 55–64). New York: Gordon & Breach.

Clarizio, H. (1980). *Toward positive classroom discipline.* New York: Wiley.

Clay, M. (1979). *Reading: The patterning of complex behaviour* (2nd ed.). Auckland, New Zealand: Heinemann.

Clay, M. M. (1995). *Reading recovery: A guidebook for teachers in training* (Rev. ed.). Portsmouth, NH: Heinemann.

Clayton, M. K. (1989). *Places to start: Implementing the developmental classroom.* Greenfield, MA: Northeast Foundation for Children.

Coates, E. (2002). I forgot the sky: Children's stories contained within their drawings. *International Journal of Early Years Education, 10*(1), 21–35.

Cochran, M., & Henderson, C. R., Jr. (1986). *Family matters: Evaluation of the parental empowerment program.* Ithaca, NY: The Comparative Ecology of Human Development Project.

Cohen, M., & Gross, P. (1979). *The developmental resource: Behavioral sequences for assessment and program planning* (Vol. 2). New York: Grune & Stratton.

Cohen, S. (1977). Fostering positive attitudes toward the handicapped: New curriculum. *Children Today, 6*(6), 7–12.

Cohen, S. (1994). Children and the environment: Aesthetic learning. *Childhood Education, 70*(5), 302–303.

Coladarci, T. (2002, June). Is it a house . . . or a pile of bricks? Important features of a local assessment system. *Phi Delta Kappan, 83*(10), 772–774.

Colbert, C. (1997). Visual arts in the developmentally appropriate integrated curriculum. In C. H. Hart, D. C. Burts, & R. Charlesworth (Eds.), *Integrated curriculum and developmentally appropriate practice: Birth to age eight* (pp. 201–223). Albany: State University of New York Press.

Cole, E. (1990). An experience in Froebel's garden. *Childhood Education, 67*(1), 18–21.

Cole, M., & Cole, S. R. (2000). *The development of children* (2nd ed.). New York: Scientific American Books.

Coleman, C. A. (2001). *Balancing literacy*. Huntington Beach, CA: Creative Teaching Press.

Conezio, K., & French, L. (2002). Capitalizing on children's fascination with the everyday world to foster language and literacy development. *Young Children, 57*(5), 12–18.

Consortium of National Arts Education Associations. (1994). *National standards for arts education: Dance, music, theatre, visual arts: What every young American should know and be able to do in the arts*. Reston, VA: Art Educators National Conference.

Cooper, J. L., & Dever, M. T. (2001). Sociodramatic play as a vehicle for curriculum integration in first grade. *Young Children, 56*(3), 58–63.

Cost, Quality, and Child Outcomes Study Team. (1995). *Cost, quality, and child outcomes in child care centers* (Public Rep.). Denver: Economics Department, University of Colorado at Denver.

Courtney, S. M., Ungerleider, L. G., Keil, K., & Haxby, J. V. (1997, April 10). Working memory. *Nature, 386*, 608–611.

Cowley, G. (1997, Spring/Summer). The language explosion. *Newsweek: Your Child* (Special ed.), 16–22.

Crary, E. (1996). *Help! The kids are at it again: Using kids' quarrels to teach "people" skills*. Seattle, WA: Parenting Press.

Creech, N., & Bhavnagri, N. (2002). Teaching elements of story through drama to 1st-graders. *Childhood Education, 78*(4), 219–223.

Crews, D. (1991). *Bigmama's*. New York: Trumpet.

Cross, T. (1995). The early childhood curriculum debate. In M. Fleer (Ed.), *DAP centrism: Challenging developmentally appropriate practice* (pp. 87–108). Watson, Australia: Australian Early Childhood Association.

Cross, W. E. (1985). Black identity: Rediscovering the distinctions between personal identity and reference group orientations. In M. B. Spencer, G. K. Brookins, & W. R. Allen (Eds.), *Beginnings: The social and affective development of black children* (pp. 155–172). Hillsdale, NJ: Erlbaum.

Crosser, S. (1992). Managing the early childhood classroom. *Young Children, 47*(2), 23–29.

Crosser, S. (1994). Making the most of water play. *Young Children, 49*(5), 28–32.

Cunningham, P. (2000). *Phonics they use: Words for reading and writing* (3rd ed.). New York: Longman.

Currie, J. R. (1988, Winter). Affect in the schools: A return to the most basic of basics. *Childhood Education, 65*(2), 83–87.

Curry, N. E., & Johnson, C. N. (1990). *Beyond self-esteem: Developing a genuine sense of human value*. Washington, DC: National Association for the Education of Young Children.

Curry, N. E., & Johnson, C. N. (1998). *Beyond self-esteem: Developing a genuine sense of human value*. Washington, DC: National Association for the Education of Young Children.

Curwin, R. L., & Mendler, A. N. (1999). *Discipline with dignity*. Reston, VA: Reston Publishing.

Dahl, K. L., Scharer, P. L., Lawson, L. L., & Grogan, P. R. (1999). Phonics instruction and student achievement in whole language first-grade classrooms. *Reading Research Quarterly, 34*(3), 312–341.

Damon, W. (1995). *Greater expectations: Overcoming the culture of indulgence in America's homes and schools*. New York: Free Press.

Davidson, J. (1996). *Emergent literacy and dramatic play in early education*. Albany, NY: Delmar.

Deegan, J. G. (1993). Children's friendships in culturally diverse classrooms. *Journal of Research in Childhood Education, 7*(2), 91–101.

DeHart, G. B., Sroufe, L. A., & Cooper, R. G. (2000). *Child development: Its nature and course* (4th ed.). New York: McGraw-Hill.

Deiner, P. L. (1993). *Resources for teaching children with diverse abilities*. New York: Harcourt Brace Jovanovich.

Delpit, L. D. (1991). Interview with W. H. Teale, editor of *Language Arts. Language Arts, 68*, 541–547.

Delpit, L. (1995). *Other people's children: Cultural conflict in the classroom*. New York: The New Press.

Dempsey, J., & Frost, J. (1993). Play environments in early childhood education. In B. Spodek (Ed.), *Handbook of research on the education of young children* (pp. 306–321). New York: Macmillan.

Denham, S. A. (1995, September). Scaffolding young children's prosocial responsiveness: Preschoolers' responses to adult sadness, anger and pain. *International Journal of Behavioral Development, 18*(3), 485–504.

Derman-Sparks, L., & the ABC Task Force. (1989). *The anti-bias curriculum: Tools for empowering young children*. Washington, DC: National Association for the Education of Young Children.

Derscheid, L. E. (1997, Spring/Summer). Mixed-age grouped preschoolers' moral behavior and understanding. *Journal of Research in Childhood Education, 11*, 147–151.

DeVogue, K. (1996, March). *Conflict resolution with children in grade school*. Presentation, Forest View Elementary School Teachers, Lansing, MI.

DeVries, R., & Kohlberg, L. (1990). *Constructivist early education: Overview and comparison with other programs*. Washington, DC: National Association for the Education of Young Children.

DeVries, R., Zan, B., Hildebrandt, C., Edmiaston, R., & Sales, C. (2002). *Developing constructivist early childhood curriculum*. New York: Teachers College Press.

Dickinson, D. K., & Tabors, P. O. (2001). *Beginning literacy with language: Young children learning at home and school*. Baltimore: Paul H. Brookes.

Dinkmeyer, D., Sr., McKay, G. D., Dinkmeyer, J. S., Dinkmeyer, D., Jr., & McKay, J. L. (1997). *Parenting young children: Systematic training for effective parenting (STEP) of children under six*. Circle Pines, MN: American Guidance Service.

Dodge, D. (1991). *Creative curriculum for early childhood*. Washington, DC: Teaching Strategies.

Dodge, D. T. (1995). *The creative curriculum for early childhood*. Washington, DC: Teaching Strategies.

Doherty-Derkowski, G. (1998). *Quality matters: Excellence in early childhood programs* (2nd ed.). Reading, MA: Addison-Wesley.

Doty, A. K., McEwen, I. R., Parker, D., & Laskin, J. (1999). Effects of testing context on ball skill performance in 5-year-old children with and without developmental delay. *Physical Therapy, 79*(9), 818–826.

Doyle, R. P. (1989, November). The resistance of conventional wisdom to research evidence: The case of retention in grade. *Phi Delta Kappan, 71*(3), 215–220.

Dreikurs, R., & Soltz, V. (1991). *Children: The challenge* (Reprint ed.). New York: Plume/Penguin Books. (Originally published in 1964, New York: Hawthorn Books)

Driscoll, A., & Nagel, N. G. (2002, January). *Early childhood education birth–8: The world of children, families and educators.* Boston: Allyn & Bacon.

Duckworth, E. (1987). *The having of wonderful ideas and other essays on teaching and learning.* New York: Teachers College Press.

Duffelmeyer, F. A. (2002, April). Alphabet activities on the Internet. *The Reading Teacher, 55*(7), 631–634.

Dunn, L., Beach, S. A., & Kontos, S. (1994). Quality of the literacy environment in day care and children's development. *Journal of Research in Childhood Education, 9,* 24–34.

Dunn, L., & Kontos, S. (1997). What have we learned about developmentally appropriate practice? *Young Children, 52*(5), 4–13.

Dyson, A. (1990, January). Symbol makers, symbol weavers: How children link play, pictures, and print. *Young Children, 45*(2), 50–57.

Eastman, W. (2002, May/June). Working with families around nutritional issues. *Child Care Information Exchange, 145,* 42–45.

Eaton, M. (1997). Positive discipline: Fostering self-esteem in young children. *Young Children, 52*(6), 43–46.

Educational Productions. (1988). *Super groups.* Portland, OR: Author.

Ehlert, L. (1989). Eating the alphabet: Fruits & vegetables from A to Z. San Diego: Harcourt Brace Jovanovich.

Eiferman, R. (1971). Social play in childhood. In R. Herron & B. Sutton-Smith (Eds.), *Child's play* (pp. 270–297). New York: Wiley.

Eldridge, D. (2001). Parent involvement: It's worth the effort. *Young Children, 56*(4), 65–69.

Elgas, P., Prendeville, J., Moomaw, S., & Kretschmer, R. (2002, January). Early childhood classroom setup. *Child Care Information Exchange, 143,* 17–20.

Elias, C. L., & Berk, L. E. (2002). Self-regulation in young children: Is there a role for sociodramatic play? *Early Childhood Research Quarterly, 17*(2), 216–238.

Eliason, C., & Jenkins, L. T. (2003). *A practical guide to early childhood curriculum* (7th ed.). Upper Saddle River, NJ: Merrill/Prentice Hall.

Elkind, D. (1989, October). Developmentally appropriate practice: Philosophical and practical implications. *Phi Delta Kappan, 7*(2), 113–117.

Emde, R. N., Biringen, Z., Clyman, R. B., & Oppenheim, D. (1991). The moral self of infancy: Affective core and procedural knowledge. *Development Review, 11,* 251–270.

Epstein, J. L. (1978). Growth Spurts During Brain Development: Implications for Educational Policy and Practice. In J. Child and A. Mersey (Eds.), *Education and the brain* (pp. 135–161). Chicago: University of Chicago Press.

Epstein, J. L. (1984, April). *Effects of parent involvement on student achievement in reading and math.* Paper presented at the annual meeting of the American Research Association, Washington, D.C.

Epstein, J. L. (1986). Parents' reactions to teacher practices of parent involvement. *Elementary School Journal, 86,* 277–293.

Epstein, J. L. (1998). *School and family partnerships: Preparing educators and improving schools.* Boulder, CO: Westview Press.

Essa, E. (2003) *Introduction to early childhood education* (4th ed.). Clifton Park, NY: Delmar Learning.

Evans, E. D. (1975). *Contemporary influences in early childhood education* (2nd ed). New York: Holt, Rinehart & Winston.

Faber, A., & Mazlish, E. (1995). *How to talk so kids can learn at home and school.* New York: Simon & Schuster.

Fagen, J. (2000). African American and Puerto Rican American parenting styles, paternal involvement, and Head Start children's social competence. *Merrill-Palmer Quarterly, 46*(4), 592–612.

Farver, J. A. M., & Shinn, Y. L. (1997). Social pretend play in Korean- and Anglo-American preschoolers. *Child Development, 68*(3), 544–556.

Fayden, T. (1997). Children's choice: Planting the seeds for creating a thematic sociodramatic center. *Young Children, 52*(3), 15–19.

Fein, G., & Stork, L. (1981). Sociodramatic play: Social class effects in integrated preschool classrooms. *Journal of Applied Developmental Psychology, 2,* 267–279.

Feuerstein, A. (2000). School characteristics and parent involvement: Influences on participation in children's schools. *Journal of Educational Research, 94*(1), 29–39.

Fields, M. V., & Spangler, K. L. (2000). *Let's begin reading right: A developmental approach to emergent literacy* (4th ed.). Upper Saddle River, NJ: Prentice Hall.

File, N. (2001). Family–professional partnerships: Practice that matches philosophy. *Young Children, 56*(4), 70–74.

Finkelhor, D. (1984). *Child sexual abuse: New theory and research.* New York: Free Press.

Finkelhor, D., & Baron, L. (1986). High-risk children. In D. Finkelhor & Associates (Eds.), *A sourcebook on child sexual abuse* (pp. 60–88). Beverly Hills, CA: Sage.

Flavell, J. H. (1977). *Cognitive development.* Upper Saddle River, NJ: Prentice Hall.

Fleer, M. (1995). *DAP centrism: Challenging developmentally appropriate practice.* Watson, Australia: Australian Early Childhood Association.

Fleer, M., & Careen, L. (1995). *What do I look like on the inside? Developing children's understanding about their bodies.* (Australian Early Childhood Association Resource Book Series, Vol. 2, No. 1). Watson, Australia: Australian Early Childhood Association.

Ford, S. (1993). The facilitator's role in children's play. *Young Children, 48*(6), 66–69.

Forman, G. (1996). A child constructs an understanding of a water wheel in five media. *Childhood Education, 72*(5), 269–273.

Forman, G., & Kuschner, D. S. (1983). *The child's construction of knowledge: Project for teaching young children.* Washington, DC: National Association for the Education of Young Children.

Fox, C. L. (1993). *Let's get together: Activities for developing friendship and self-esteem in the elementary grades.* Rolling Hills Estates, CA: Jalmar.

Franklin, M. (1994). Art, play, and symbolization in childhood and beyond: Reconsidering connections. *Teacher's College Record, 95*(4), 526–541.

Franz, C. E., McClelland, D. C., & Weinberger, R. L. (1991). Childhood antecedents of conventional social accomplishment in mid-life adults. A 36-year prospective study. *Journal of Personality and Social Psychology, 60,* 586–595.

Freeman, C. C., & Sokoloff, H. J. (1996, Fall). Children learning to make a better world: Exploring themes. *Childhood Education, 73*(1), 17–22.

Freiberg, H. J., & Driscoll, A. (2000). *Universal teaching strategies* (3rd ed.). Boston: Allyn & Bacon.

Friedrich, L. K., & Stein, A. H. (1973). Aggressive and prosocial television programs and the natural behaviors of preschool children. *Monographs of the Society for Research in Child Development, 38*(4), serial no. 151.

Fromberg, D. P. (2002). *Play and meaning in early childhood education.* Boston: Allyn & Bacon.

Frost, J. (1991). *Play and playscapes.* Albany, NY: Delmar.

Frost, J. L., & Sweeney, T. (1995). *Causes and prevention of playground injuries and litigation case studies* (pp. 60–88). Washington, DC: ERIC Clearinghouse. (ERIC Document Reproduction Service No. ED394648)

Frost, J. L., Wortham, S., & Reifel, S. (2001). *Play and child development.* Upper Saddle River, NJ: Prentice Hall.

Frost, L., Talbot, J., & Monroe, M. (1990). Playgrounds. In L. Ard & M. Pitts (Eds.), *Room to grow: How to create quality early childhood environments* (pp. 149–160). Austin: Texas Association for the Education of Young Children.

Gabbard, C., Le Blanc, E., & Lowy, S. (1994). *Physical education for children: Building the foundation* (2nd ed.). Upper Saddle River, NJ: Prentice Hall.

Gable, S., & Cole, K. (2000, October). Parents' child care arrangements and their ecological correlates. *Early Education and Development, 11*(5), 549–572.

Gallahue, D. (1993). Motor development and movement skill acquisition in early childhood education. In B. Spodek (Ed.), *Handbook of research on the education of young children* (pp. 24–41). New York: Macmillan.

Gallahue, D. (1995). Transforming physical education curriculum. In S. Bredekamp & T. Rosegrant (Eds.), *Reaching potentials: Transforming early childhood curriculum and assessment* (Vol. 2). Washington, DC: National Association for the Education of Young Children.

Garcia, C., Garcia, L., Floyd, J., & Lawson, J. (2002). Improving public health through early childhood movement programs. *Journal of Physical Education, Recreation and Dance, 73*(1), 27–31+.

Garcia, E. (1993). The education of linguistically and culturally diverse children. In B. Spodek (Ed.), *Handbook of research on the education of young children* (pp. 372–384). New York: Macmillan.

Gardini, L., & Edwards, C. P. (1988). Early childhood integration of the visual arts. *Gifted International, 5*(2), 14–18.

Gardner, H. (1985). *Frames of mind: The theory of multiple intelligences.* New York: Basic Books.

Gardner, H. (1991). *The unschooled mind: How children think and how schools should teach.* New York: Basic Books.

Gardner, H. (1993a). *Frames of mind* (Rev. ed.). New York: Basic Books.

Gardner, H. (1993b). *Multiple intelligences: The theory in practice.* New York: Basic Books.

Gardner, H. (1994). *The arts and human development.* New York: Basic Books.

Gardner, H. (1997). *Extraordinary minds: Portraits of exceptional individuals and an examination of our extraordinariness.* New York: Basic Books.

Gardner, H. (1998). Are there additional intelligences? The case for naturalist, spiritual, and existential intelligences. In J. Kane (Ed.), *Education, information, and transformation: Essays on learning and thinking* (pp. 111–131). Upper Saddle River, NJ: Prentice Hall.

Gardner, H. (2001, January 15). Constant testing isn't the way to measure education. *Lansing State Journal,* 5A.

Gardner, H., Kornhaber, M. L., & Wake, W. K. (1996). *Intelligence.* Fort Worth, TX: Harcourt Brace.

Gartrell, D. (2003). *A guidance approach for the encouraging classroom* (3rd ed.). Clifton Park, NY: Delmar.

Gazda, G. M., Asbury, F. R., Balzer, F. J., Childers, W. C., Phelps, R. E., & Walters, R. P. (1995). *Human relations development: A manual for educators* (5th ed.). Boston: Allyn & Bacon.

Genisio, M., & Drecktrah, M. (2000–2001). Emergent literacy in an early childhood classroom: Center learning to support the child with special needs. In K. M. Paciorek (Ed.), *Annual editions: Early childhood education* (22nd ed.). Guilford, CT: McGraw-Hill/Dushkin.

George, M. A., & Sellers, W. (Eds.) (1984). *Michigan model for comprehensive health education.* Mt. Pleasant: Central Michigan University Educational Materials Center.

Gestwicki, C. (1998). *Developmentally appropriate practice: Curriculum and development in early education.* Albany, NY: Delmar.

Ginsberg, H. P., & Baron, J. (1993). Cognition: Young children's construction of mathematics. In R. Jensen (Ed.), *Research ideas for the classroom: Early childhood mathematics* (pp. 3–21). Reston, VA: National Council of Teachers of Mathematics.

Glasser, W. (1985). *Control theory in the classroom.* New York: Perennial Library.

Glickman, C. (1991). Pretending not to know what we know. *Educational Leadership, 48*(8), 4–8.

Goldberg, S. (1997). *Parent involvement begins at birth.* Boston: Allyn & Bacon.

Goldhaber, J., Lipson, M., Sortino, S., & Daniels, P. (1996–1997). Books in the sand box? Markers in the blocks? Expanding the child's world of literacy. *Childhood Education, 73*(2), 88–91.

Goleman, D. (1995). *Emotional intelligence: Why it can matter more than IQ*. New York: Bantam Books.

Goleman, D. (1997). *Emotional intelligence: Why it can matter more than IQ* (Reprint ed.). New York: Bantam Books.

Gonzalez-Mena, J., & Widmeyer Eyer, E. D. (2001). *Infants, toddlers, and caregivers* (5th ed.). Mountain View, CA: Mayfield.

Gordon, A., & Browne, K. W. (1996). *Guiding young children in a diverse society*. Boston: Allyn & Bacon.

Gould, J. C., Thorpe, P., & Weeks, V. (2001, November). An early childhood accelerated program. *Educational Leadership, 59*(3), 47–50.

Grace, C., & Shores, E. F. (1991). *The portfolio and its use: Developmentally appropriate assessment of young children*. Little Rock, AR: Southern Association on Children under Six.

Graves, S., Gargiulo, R., & Sluder, L. (1996). *Young children: An introduction to early childhood education*. St. Paul, MN: West.

Green, C. R. (1998). This is my name. *Childhood Education, 74*(4), 226–231.

Greenberg, P. (1989). Parents as partners in young children's development and education: A new American fad? Why does it matter? *Young Children, 44*(4), 61–75.

Greenman, J. (1988). *Caring spaces, learning places: Children's environments that work*. Redman, WA: Exchange Press.

Greenman, J. (1995). Of culture and a sense of place. *Child Care Information Exchange, 101,* 36–38.

Gregory, K., Kim, A. S., & Whiren, A. (in press). The effect of verbal scaffolding on the complexity of preschool children's block structures. In D. Lytle (Ed.), *Play theory, children's playfulness, and educational theory and practice*. Westport, CT: Praeger.

Griffore, R. J., & Bubolz, M. (1986). Family and school as educators. In R. J. Giffore & R. P. Boger (Eds.), *Child rearing in the home and school* (pp. 61–104). New York: Plenum.

Grollman, S. (1994, September). Fantasy and exploration: Two approaches to playing. *Child Care Information Exchange,* 48–50.

Gross, T., & Clemens, S. G. (2002). Painting a tragedy: Young children process the events of September 11. *Young Children, 57*(3), 44–55.

Guild, P. (2001). *Diversity, learning style and culture*. Seattle, WA: New Horizons for Learning.

Gullo, D. F. (1994). *Developmentally appropriate teaching in early childhood*. Washington, DC: National Education Association of the United States.

Gunnar, M. R., Brodersen, L., Krueger, K., & Rigatuso, J. (1996). Dampening of behavioral and adrenocortical reactivity during early infancy: Normative changes and individual differences. *Child Development, 67*(3), 877–889.

Haberman, M. (1994, Spring). Gentle teaching in a violent society. *Educational Horizons, 72,* 131–135.

Hale, J. E. (1994). *Unbank the fire: Visions for the education of African American children*. Baltimore: Johns Hopkins University Press.

Hart, C. H., Burts, D. C., & Charlesworth, R. (1997). Integrated developmentally appropriate curriculum: From theory to research to practice. In C. H. Hart, D. C. Burts, & R. Charlesworth (Eds.), *Integrated curriculum and developmentally appropriate practice: Birth to age eight* (pp. 1–27). Albany: State University of New York Press.

Hart, C. H., Burts, D. C., Durland, M. A., Charlesworth, R., DeWolf, M., & Fleege, P. O. (1998). Stress behaviors and activity type participation of preschoolers in more or less developmentally appropriate classrooms: SES and sex differences. *Journal of Research in Childhood Education, 12*(2), 176–196.

Harter, S. (1999). *The construction of the self: A developmental perspective*. New York: Guilford Press.

Hartley, R. E., Frank, L. K., & Goldenson, R. M. (1952). *Understanding children's play*. New York: Columbia University Press.

Hartup, W. W. (1996). The company they keep: Friendships and their developmental significance. *Child Development, 67*(1), 1–13.

Hartup, W. W. (1998). Cooperation, close relationships, and cognitive development. In W. M. Bukowski, A. F. Newcomb, & W. W. Hartup (Eds.), *The company they keep: Friendships in childhood and adolescence* (pp. 213–237). Cambridge, UK: Cambridge University Press.

Hatch, T. (1997, March). Getting specific about multiple intelligences. *Educational Leadership, 54*(6), 26–29.

Hatch, T., & Gardner, H. (1988, November/December). New research on intelligence. *Learning, 17*(4), 36–39.

Haubenstricker, J. (1990). *Summary of fundamental motor skill characteristics: Motor performance study*. Unpublished document, Michigan State University, East Lansing, MI.

Haubenstricker, J. (1991, May). *Gross motor development in preschoolers*. Paper presented to Michigan Council of Cooperative Nurseries, East Lansing, MI.

Hayes, C. D., Palmer, J. L., & Zaslow, M. J. (Eds.) (1990). *Who cares for America's children? Child care policy for the 1990s*. Washington, DC: National Academy Press.

Haywood, K. M., & Getchell, N. (2001). *Life span motor development* (3rd ed.). Champaign, IL: Human Kinetics.

Hein, G. E., & Price, S. C. (1994). *Active assessment for active science*. Portsmouth, NH: Heinemann.

Hendrick, J. (2001). *The whole child: Developmental education for the early years* (7th ed.). Upper Saddle River, NJ: Merrill/Prentice Hall.

Hendrick, J. (2003). *Total learning: Developmental curriculum for the young child* (6th ed.). Upper Saddle River, NJ: Merrill/Prentice Hall.

Henninger, M. (2002). *Teaching young children: An introduction*. Upper Saddle River, NJ: Delmar.

Herr, J., & Libby, Y. (2000). Creative resources for the early childhood classroom. New York: Delmar.

Hetherington, E. M., & Clingempeel, W. G., in collaboration with E. Anderson, J. Deal, M. Hagan, A. Hollier, & M. Lindner (Eds.). (1992). Coping with marital transitions: A family systems perspective. *Monographs of the Society for Research in Child Development, 57*(2–3, Serial No. 227).

High/Scope Curriculum. (1998). *Supporting children in resolving conflicts*. Ypsilanti, MI: High/Scope Press.

Hildebrand, V. (1997). *Guiding young children: A center approach.* Palo Alto, CA: Mayfield.

Hildebrand, V., & Hearron, P. (1999). *Guiding children's social behavior.* Upper Saddle River, NJ: Prentice Hall.

Hirsch, E. S. (1996). *The block book* (3rd ed.). Washington, DC: National Association for the Education of Young Children.

Hirsh-Pasek, K., Hyson, M. C., & Rescorla, L. (1990). Academic environments in preschool: Do they pressure or challenge young children? *Early Education and Development, 1,* 401–423.

Hoffman, M. L. (1970). Moral development. In *Carmichael's manual of child psychology* (Vol. 2, pp. 262–360). New York: Wiley.

Hoffman, M. L. (1990). Empathy and justice motivation. *Motivation and Emotion, 14*(2), 151–172.

Hohmann, M., & Weikart, D. P. (1995). *Educating young children: Active learning practices for preschool and child care programs.* Ypsilanti, MI: High/Scope Press.

Hohmann, M., & Weikart, D. P. (1997). *Educating young children.* Ypsilanti, MI: High/Scope Press.

Holt, B. G. (1989). *Science with young children.* Washington, DC: National Association for the Education of Young Children.

Honig, A. S., & Wittmer, D. S. (1996). Helping children become more prosocial: Ideas for classrooms, families, schools, and communities. *Young Children, 51*(2), 62–70.

Hsue, Y., & Aldridge, J. (1995). Developmentally appropriate practice and traditional Taiwanese culture. *Journal of Instructional Psychology, 22,* 320–323.

Huber, L. K. (1999). Woodworking with young children: You can do it! *Young Children, 54*(6), 32–34.

Hudson, S., Thompson, D., & Mack, M. (1997). Are we safe yet? A twenty-five year look at playground safety. *Journal of Physical Education, Recreation and Dance, 68*(8), 32–34.

Huffman, L. R., & Speer, P. W. (2000). Academic performance among at-risk children: The role of developmentally appropriate practices. *Early Childhood Research Quarterly, 15*(2), 167–184.

Huntsinger, C. S., Schoeneman, J., & Ching, W. (1994, May). *A cross-cultural study of young children's performance on drawing and handwriting tasks.* Paper presented at the Midwestern Psychological Association, Chicago, IL.

Hurley, R. S., & Blake, S. (1997). Animals and occupations: Why theme-based curricula work. *Early Childhood News, 9*(1), 20–25.

Hymes, J. (Narrator). (1980). *Hairy scary* [Film]. Silver Spring: University of Maryland.

Hymes, J. L. (1998, May). A child development point of view: Excerpts from the writings of James L. Hymes, Jr. *Young Children, 53*(3), 49–51.

Hyson, M. C., Hirsh-Pasek, K., & Rescorla, L. (1990). The classroom practices inventory: An observation instrument based on NAEYC's guidelines for developmentally appropriate practices for 4- and 5-year-old children. *Early Childhood Research Quarterly, 5,* 475–494.

Ignico, A. (1994). Early childhood education: Providing the foundation. *Journal of Physical Education, 65*(6), 25–56.

Ignico, A. (1998, May). Children's sedentary lifestyle: A forerunner of unhealthy adulthood. *USA Today, 126*(2636), 58–59.

Inhelder, B., & Piaget, J. (1964). *The early growth and logic in the child.* London: Routledge & Kegan Paul.

International Reading Association (IRA) & National Association for the Education of Young Children (NAEYC). (1998). Overview of learning to read and write: Developmentally appropriate practices for young children. A joint position paper of the IRA and the NAEYC. Washington, DC: NAEYC.

Isbell, R., & Raines, S. (1991). Young children's oral language production in three types of play centers. *Journal of Research in Childhood Education, 5*(2), 140–146.

Jackman, H. (2001). *Early education curriculum: A child's connection to the world.* Albany, NY: Delmar Learning.

Jackson, P. W. (1997). Child-centered education for Pacific-rim cultures? *International Journal of Early Childhood Education, 2,* 5–18.

Jalongo, M. R. (1990). The child's right to the expressive arts: Nurturing the imagination as well as the intellect. *Childhood Education, 66*(4), 195–201.

Jalongo, M. R., & Stamp, L. N. (1997). *The arts in children's lives: Aesthetic education in early childhood.* Needham Heights, MA: Allyn & Bacon.

Jambunathan, S., Burts, D. C., & Pierce, S. H. (1999). Developmentally appropriate practices as predictors of self-competence among preschoolers. *Journal of Research in Childhood Education, 13*(2), 167–174.

Janz, K. F., Dawson, J. D., & Mahoney, L. T. (2000). Tracking physical fitness and physical activity from childhood to adolescence: The Muscatine study. *Medicine and Science in Sports and Exercise, 32*(7), 1250–1257.

Jenkins, J. M. (2000). Theory of mind and social behavior: Causal models tested in a longitudinal study. *Merrill-Palmer Quarterly, 46*(2), 203–220.

Jensen, E. (1998). *Teaching with the brain in mind.* Alexandria, VA: Association for Supervision and Curriculum Development.

Jesse, P. O., Wilson, H., & Morgan, D. (2000). Medical play for young children. *Childhood Education, 76*(4), 215–218.

Johnsen, E. P., & Christie, J. F. (1984). Play and social cognition. In B. Sutton-Smith & D. Kelly-Bryne (Eds.), *The masks of play* (pp. 109–118). New York: Leisure Press.

Johnson, J. E., Christie, J. F., & Yawkey, T. D. (1999). *Play and early childhood development* (2nd ed.). Boston: Allyn & Bacon.

Juel, C., Griffith, P. L., & Gough, P. B. (1986). Acquisition of literacy: A longitudinal study of children in first and second grade. *Journal of Educational Psychology, 78*(4), 243–255.

Kagan, J. (1997/1998). The realistic view of biology and behavior. In K. L. Freiberg (Ed.), *Human development annual editions* (pp. 54–56). Sluice Dock, Guilford, CT: Dushkin.

Kagan, S. (2000). The changing face of parenting education. In M. Jensen & M. A. Hannibal (Eds.), *Issues, advocacy and leadership in early education* (pp. 156–157). Boston: Allyn & Bacon.

Kalb, C., & Namuth, T. (1997, Spring/Summer). When a child's silence isn't golden. *Newsweek: Your Child* (Special ed.), 23.

Kamii, C. (1985, September). Leading primary education toward excellence: Beyond worksheets and drills. *Young Children, 40*(6), 3–9.

Kamii, C., & DeVries, R. (1977). Project for early education. In M. Day & R. Parker (Eds.), *Preschool in action* (2nd ed.) (pp. 393–420). Boston: Allyn & Bacon.

Katz, L. G. (1987). *What should young children be learning?* Urbana, IL: ERIC Clearinghouse on Elementary and Early Childhood Education.

Katz, L. G. (1995). The benefits of mixed-age grouping. *ERIC Digest*, No. ED382411. Retrieved from http://www.ericfacility.net/ericdigests/ed382411.html

Katz, L. (1996, March). *The essence of developmentally appropriate practice for children from birth to age 8.* Keynote address, Michigan Association for the Education of Young Children, Grand Rapids, MI.

Katz, L. G., & Chard, S. C. (1989). *Engaging children's minds: The project approach.* Norwood, NJ: Ablex.

Katz, L. G., & Chard, S. C. (2000). *Engaging children's minds: The project approach* (2nd ed.). Norwood, NJ: Ablex.

Katz, L. G., Evangelou, D., & Hartman, J. A. (1990). *The case for mixed-age grouping in early education.* Washington, DC: National Association for the Education of Young Children.

Katz, L. G., & McClellan, D. E. (1997). *Fostering children's social competence: The teacher's role.* Washington, DC: National Association for the Education of Young Children.

Katz, P. (1982). Development of children's racial awareness and intergroup attitudes. In L. G. Katz (Ed.), *Current topics in early childhood education* (Vol. 4, pp. 17–54). Norwood, NJ: Ablex.

Kauffman, J. M., & Burbach, H. J. (1997, December). On creating a climate of classroom civility. *Phi Delta Kappan, 79*(4), 320–325.

Kellogg, R. (1969). *Analyzing children's art.* Palo Alto, CA: National Press Books.

Kellogg, R. (1979). *Children's drawings/children's minds.* New York: Avon Books.

Kemple, K. M., & Johnson, C. A. (2002, Summer). From the inside out: Nurturing aesthetic response to nature in the primary grades. *Childhood Education, 78*(4), 210–218.

Kendall, F. E. (1995). *Diversity in the classroom: New approaches to the education of young children.* New York: Teachers College Press.

Kendrick, A., Kaufmann, R., & Messenger, K. (1988). *Healthy young children: A manual for programs.* Washington, DC: National Association for the Education of Young Children.

Kennedy, L. M., & Tipps, S. (1999). *Guiding children's learning of mathematics* (9th ed.). Belmont, CA: Wadsworth.

Kessler, S. (1991). Alternative perspectives on early childhood education. *Early Childhood Research Quarterly, 7*(2), 183–197.

Kibbey, M. (1988). *My grammy.* Minneapolis, MN: Carolrhoda.

Kieff, J. E., & Casbergue, R. M. (2000). *Playful learning and teaching: Integrating play into preschool and primary programs.* Needham Heights, MA: Allyn & Bacon.

Kilmer, S. J., & Hofman, H. (1995). Transforming science curriculum. In S. Bredekamp & T. Rosegrant (Eds.), *Reaching potentials: Transforming early childhood curriculum and assessment* (Vol. 2, pp. 43–63). Washington, DC: National Association for the Education of Young Children.

Kim, S. (1999). The effects of storytelling and pretend play on cognitive processes, short-term and long-term narrative recall. *Child Study Journal, 29*(3), 175–191.

Kindergarten Curriculum Guide and Resource Book. (1985). Victoria, British Columbia: Curriculum Development Branch, Ministry of Education.

King, M. L., & King, C. S. (1984). *The words of Martin Luther King, Jr.* New York: Newmarket Press, 92.

Klein, E. L., Murphy, K. L., & Witz, N. W. (1996). Changes in preservice teachers' beliefs about developmentally appropriate practice in early childhood education. *International Journal of Early Childhood Education, 1,* 143–156.

Klein, J. (1990). Young children and learning. In W. J. Stinson (Ed.), *Moving and learning for the young child* (pp. 23–30). Reston, VA: American Alliance for Health, Physical Education, Recreation and Dance.

Knapczyk, D. R., & Rodes, P. G. (1996). *Teaching social competence: A practical approach for improving social skills in students at-risk.* Pacific Grove, CA: Brooks/Cole.

Koff, S. R. (2000). Toward a definition of dance education. *Childhood Education, 77*(1), 27–31.

Kohlberg, L. (1964). Development of moral character and moral ideology. In M. L. Hoffman & L. W. Hoffman (Eds.), *Review of child development research* (Vol. 1, pp. 381–431). New York: Russell Sage Foundation.

Kohn, A. (1993). Choices for children: Why and how to let children decide. *Phi Delta Kappan, 75*(1), 8–20.

Kohn, A. (1996). *Beyond discipline: From compliance to community.* Alexandria, VA: Association for Supervision and Curriculum Development.

Kohn, A. (2000). *The case against standardized testing: Raising the scores, ruining the schools.* Portsmouth, NH: Heinemann.

Kolbe, U., & Smyth, J. (2000). *Drawing and painting with under-threes.* Watson ACT, Australia: Australian Early Childhood Association.

Kolodziej, S. (1999). Block building: Architecture in early childhood art education. In J. K. Guilfoil & A. R. Sandler (Eds.), *Built environment education in art education* (pp. 151–152). Reston, VA: National Art Education Association.

Kontos, S., & Wilcox-Herzog, A. (1997). Teacher's interactions with children: Why are they so important? *Young Children, 52*(2), 4–12.

Kontos, S., & Wilcox-Herzog, A. (2001). How do education and experience affect teachers of young children? *Young Children, 56*(4), 85–91.

Kostelnik, M. J. (1990, February). *Standards of quality for early childhood education: Implications for policy makers.* Keynote address, Michigan Department of Education Early Childhood Conference, Detroit, MI.

Kostelnik, M. J. (Ed.). (1991). *Teaching young children using themes.* Glenview, IL: Good Year Books.

Kostelnik, M. J. (1992). Myths associated with developmentally appropriate programs. *Young Children, 47*(4), 17–23.

Kostelnik, M. J. (1993, March). Recognizing the essentials of developmentally appropriate practice. *Child Care Information Exchange, 73–77.*

Kostelnik, M. J. (Ed.) (1996). *Themes teachers use.* Glenview, IL: Good Year Books.

Kostelnik, M. J. (1997, October). *Spaces to learn and grow: Indoor environments in early education.* Paper presented at the Samsung International Early Childhood Conference, Seoul, Korea.

Kostelnik, M. J. (1998). Misconstructing developmentally appropriate practice. *The Early Years, 18*(1), 19–26.

Kostelnik, M. J., Onaga, E., Rohde, B., & Whiren, A. (2002). *Children with special needs: Lessons for early childhood professionals.* New York: Teachers College Press.

Kostelnik, M. J., & Stein, L. C. (1986, November). *Effects of three conflict mediation strategies on children's aggressive and prosocial behavior in the classroom.* Paper presented at the annual meeting of the National Association for the Education of Young Children, Washington, DC.

Kostelnik, M. J., & Stein, L. C. (1990). Social development: An essential component of kindergarten education. In J. S. McKee (Ed.), *The developing kindergarten: Programs, children, and teachers* (pp. 145–179). Saginaw: Mid-Michigan Association for the Education of Young Children.

Kostelnik, M. J., Whiren, A. P., Soderman, A. K., Stein, L. C., & Gregory, K. (2002). *Guiding children's social development: Theory to practice* (4th ed.). Albany, NY: Delmar.

Koster, J. B. (1997). *Growing artists: Teaching art to young children.* Albany, NY: Delmar.

Kovalik, S. (1997, August). *Integrated learning: Integrated teaching.* Keynote address, Multi-Age Conference, Kalamazoo, MI.

Kovalik, S., & Olsen, K. (1997). *Integrated thematic instruction* (3rd ed.). Kent, WA: Susan Kovalik & Associates.

Krogh, S. L., & Slentz, K. L. (2001a). *The early childhood curriculum.* Mahwah, NJ: Erlbaum.

Krogh, S. L., & Slentz, K. L. (2001b). *Early childhood education: Yesterday, today and tomorrow.* Mahwah, NJ: Erlbaum.

Kwon, J. Y., & Yawkey, T. D. (2000). Principles of emotional development and children's pretend play. *International Journal of Early Childhood, 32*(1), 9–13.

Lach, J. (1997, Spring/Summer). Turning on the motor. *Newsweek: Your Child* (Special ed.), 26–27.

Ladd, G. W. (1999). Peer relationships and social competence during early and middle childhood. *Annual Review of Psychology, 50,* 333–359.

Ladd, G. W., & Coleman, C. C. (1993). Young children's peer relationships: Forms, features, and functions. In B. Spodek (Ed.), *Handbook of research on the education of young children* (pp. 54–76). New York: Macmillan.

Larsen, J. M., & Haupt, J. H. (1997). Integrating home and school. In C. H. Hart, D. C. Burts, & R. Charlesworth (Eds.), *Integrated curriculum and developmentally appropriate practice: Birth to age eight* (pp. 389–415). Albany: State University of New York Press.

Lawton, J. T. (1987). The Ausubelian preschool classroom. In J. L. Roopnarine & J. E. Johnson (Eds.), *Approaches to early childhood education* (pp. 85–108). Upper Saddle River, NJ: Merrill/Prentice Hall.

Lay-Dopyera, M., & Dopyera, J. (1993). *Becoming a teacher of young children.* New York: McGraw-Hill.

Lee, L. (1997). Working with non-English-speaking families. *Child Care Information Exchange, 116,* 57–58.

LeFrançois, G. R. (2001). *Of children: An introduction to child and adolescent development* (9th ed.). Belmont, CA: Wadsworth.

Leong, D. J., & Bodrova, E. (1995, Fall). Vygotsky's zone of proximal development. *Of Primary Interest, 2*(4), 1–4.

Leppo, M. L., Davis, D., & Crim, B. (2000). The basics of exercising the mind and body. *Childhood Education, 76*(3), 142–147.

Levy, A. K. (1984). The language of play: The role of play in language development. *Early Child Development and Care, 17,* 49–62.

Lewin, K., Lippitt, R., & White, R. (1939). Patterns of aggressive behaviors and experimentally created "social climates." *Journal of Social Psychology, 10,* 271–299.

Lind, K. K. (1997). Science in the developmentally appropriate integrated curriculum. In C. H. Hart, D. C. Burts, & R. Charlesworth (Eds.), *Integrated curriculum and developmentally appropriate practice: Birth to age eight* (pp. 75–101). Albany: State University of New York Press.

Little-Soldier, L. (1990, January). *Anthropology in education.* Keynote address, Michigan Association for the Education of Young Children, Grand Rapids, MI.

Little-Soldier, L. (1992). Working with Native American children. *Young Children, 47*(6), 15–21.

Loeffler, M. H. (2002, Winter). The essence of Montessori. *Montessori Life, 14*(1), 34–36.

Love, J. M., Ryer, P., & Faddis, B. (1992). *Caring environments: Program quality in California's publicly funded child development programs.* Portsmouth, NH: RMC Research Corp.

Lowenfeld, V., & Brittain, W. L. (1965). *Creative and mental growth* (4th ed.). New York: Macmillan.

Lubeck, S. (1994). The politics of developmentally appropriate practice: Exploring issues of culture, class and curriculum. In B. L. Mallory & R. S. New (Eds.), *Diversity and developmentally appropriate practices: Challenges for early childhood education* (pp. 17–43). New York: Teachers College Press.

Lubeck, S. (1998). Is developmentally appropriate practice for everyone? *Childhood Education, 74*(5), 283–292.

Maccoby, E. E. (1984). Socialization and developmental change. *Child Development, 55,* 317–328.

Machado, J. M. (2002). *Early childhood experiences in the language arts.* Albany, NY: Delmar Learning.

Machado, J. M., & Meyer, H. C. (2001). *Student teaching: Early childhood practicum guide.* Albany, NY: Delmar.

Macrina, D. (1995). Educating young children about health. In C. Hendricks (Ed.), *Young children on the grow: Health, activity and education in the preschool setting* (pp. 33–42). Washington, DC: ERIC Clearinghouse on Teacher Education.

Magid, K., & McKelvey, C. A. (1990). *High risk: Children without a conscience.* New York: Bantam Doubleday Dell.

Mangione, P. L., Lally, R. J., & Signer, S. (1993). *Essential connections: Ten keys to culturally sensitive child care.* Sacramento, CA: Far West Laboratory.

Mantzicopoulos, P. Y., Neuharth-Pritchett, S., & Morelock, J. B. (1994, April). *Academic competence, social skills, and behavior among disadvantaged children in developmentally appropriate and inappropriate classrooms.* Paper presented at the annual meeting of the American Educational Research Association, New Orleans, LA.

Marcon, R. A. (1992). Differential effects of three preschool models on inner-city 4-year-olds. *Early Childhood Research Quarterly, 7,* 517–530.

Marcon, R. A. (1995). Fourth-grade slump: The cause and the cure. Principal, 74(5), 17–20.

Marcon, R. A. (1999). Differential impact of preschool models on development and early learning of inner-city children: A three-cohort study. *Developmental Psychology, 35,* 358–375.

Marion, M. (1999). *Guidance of young children* (5th ed.). Upper Saddle River, NJ: Prentice Hall.

Maslow, A. H. (1954). *Motivation and personality.* New York: Harper & Row.

Mason, J. M., & Sinha, S. (1993). Emerging literacy in the early childhood years: Applying a Vygotskian model of learning and development. In B. Spodek (Ed.), *Handbook of research on the education of young children* (pp. 137–150). New York: Macmillan.

Maxwell, L. E. (2000). A safe and welcoming school: What students, teachers, and parents think. *Journal of Architectural and Planning Research, 17*(4), 271–282.

McAfee, D. (1985). Circle time: Getting past five little pumpkins. *Young Children, 40*(6), 24–29.

McAfee, O., & Leong, D. J. (2002). *Assessing and guiding young children's development and learning* (3rd ed.). Boston: Allyn & Bacon.

McBride, B. A., Rane, T. R., & Bae, J.-H. (2001). Intervening with teachers to encourage father/male involvement in early childhood programs. *Early Childhood Research Quarterly, 16*(1), 77–93.

McDevitt, S. C., & Carey, W. B. (1978, July). The measurement of temperaments in 3–7 year old children. *Journal of Child Psychology and Psychiatry, 19*(3), 245–253.

McGee, L. M., & Purcell-Gates, V. (1997). Conversations: "So what's going on in research on emergent literacy?" *Reading Research Quarterly, 32*(3), 310–318.

McGee, L. M., & Richgels, D. J. (2000). *Literacy's beginnings: Supporting young readers and writers* (3rd ed.). Boston: Allyn & Bacon.

McGuinness, D., Olson, A., & Chaplin, J. (1990). Sex differences in incidental recall for words and pictures. *Journal of Learning and Individual Differences, 2,* 263–286.

McIntyre, E., & Pressley, M. (1996). *Balanced instruction: Strategies and skills in whole language.* Norwood, MA: Christopher-Gordon.

Meisels, S. J. (2001). Readiness and relationships. *The Beacon, 23*(3), 8.

Meisels, S. J., & Provence, S. (1989). *Screening and assessment: Guidelines for identifying young disabled and developmentally vulnerable children and their families.* Washington, DC: National Center for Clinical Infant Programs.

Mellou, E. (1994). Factors which affect the frequency of dramatic play. *Early Child Development and Care, 101,* 59–70.

Michigan Family Independence Agency. (1996). *Child care licensing regulations.* Lansing: Author.

Michigan State University Child Development Laboratories. (1997). *LPS parent handbook.* East Lansing: Author.

Miller, D. F. (2004). *Positive child guidance* (4th ed.). Clifton Park, NY: Delmar Learning.

Miller, E. (1999). Balloons, blankets, and balls: Gross-motor activities to use indoors. *Young Children, 54*(5), 58–63.

Miller, S., Fernie, D., & Kantor, R. (1992). Distinctive literacies in different preschool play contexts. *Play and Culture, 5,* 107–119.

Milne, A. A. (1995). *Pooh's little instruction book.* New York: Dutton Books, 24.

Moll, L. (1996). *Vygotsky and education.* Cambridge, MA: Cambridge University Press.

Monighan-Nourot, P. M. (1998). Sociodramatic play: Pretending together. In D. Fromberg & D. Bergen (Eds.), *Play from birth to twelve and beyond: Contexts, perspectives, and meanings* (pp. 378–391). New York: Garland.

Moore, S. G. (1986). Socialization in the kindergarten classroom. In B. Spodek (Ed.), *Today's kindergarten* (pp. 110–136). New York: Teachers College Press.

Moriarty, R. F. (2002, September). Helping teachers develop as facilitators of three- to five-year-olds' science inquiry. *Young Children, 57*(5), 20–25.

Morrison, G. S. (2001). *Early childhood education today* (8th ed.). Upper Saddle River, NJ: Merrill/Prentice Hall.

Morrow, L. (1990). Preparing the classroom environment to promote literacy during play. *Children's Quarterly, 5,* 537–554.

Moyer, J. (1990). Whose creation is it, anyway? *Childhood Education, 66*(3), 130–131.

Mulcahey, C. (2002). Take-home art appreciation kits for kindergartners and their families. *Young Children, 57*(1), 80–88.

Music Educators National Conference. (1994). *Opportunity to learn standards for music instruction, preK–12.* Task force chair P. Lehman. Reston, VA: Author.

Musson, S. (1994). *School-age care: Theory and practice.* Reading, MA: Addison-Wesley.

Myers, M. E., & Myers, B. K. (2001–2002, Winter). Holidays in the school kindergarten: An avenue for emerging religious and spiritual literacy. *Childhood Education, 78*(2), 79–83.

Nash, J. M. (1997, February 3). Fertile minds. *Time Special Report,* 48–56.

National Association for the Education of Young Children. (1986). *Early childhood teacher education guidelines for four- and five-year programs.* Washington, DC: Author.

National Association for the Education of Young Children. (1996a). *Guidelines for appropriate curriculum content and assessment in programs serving children ages 3 through 8.* Position statement of the National Association for the Education of Young Children and the National Association of Early Childhood Specialists in State Departments of Education. Washington, DC: Author.

National Association for the Education of Young Children. (1996b). *Guidelines for preparation of early childhood professionals.* Washington, DC: Author.

National Association of Elementary School Principals. (1990). *Early childhood education and the elementary school principal: Standards for quality programs for young children.* Alexandria, VA: Author.

National Association of State Boards of Education. (1988). *Right from the start*. Alexandria, VA: Author.

National Center for History in the Schools. (1994). National standards: History for grades K–4. Los Angeles: Author.

National Council for the Social Studies. (1998). *Expectations of excellence*. Washington, DC: Author.

National Council of Teachers of Mathematics. (1989). *Curriculum and evaluation standards for school mathematics*. Washington, DC: Author.

National Council of Teachers of Mathematics. (2000). Standards for grades pre-K–2. In *Principles and standards for school mathematics* (pp. 73–78). Reston, VA: Author.

National Research Council. (2001). *Eager to learn: Educating our preschoolers*. Washington, DC: National Academy Press.

Neill, D. M., & Medina, N. J. (1989). Standardized testing: Harmful to educational health. *Phi Delta Kappan, 46*(8), 688–697.

Neubert, K., & Jones, E. (1998, September). Creating culturally relevant curriculum: A negotiation. *Young Children, 53*(5), 14–19.

Neuman, S., & Roskos, K. (1990). Peers as literacy informants: A description of young children's literacy conversations in play. *Early Childhood Research Quarterly, 6*, 233–248.

New, R. (1990, September). Excellent early education: A city in Italy has it. *Young Children, 7*, 4–8.

New, R. S. (1994). Culture, child development, and developmentally appropriate practices: Teachers as collaborative researchers. In B. L. Mallory & R. S. New (Eds.), *Diversity and developmentally appropriate practices: Challenges for early childhood education* (pp. 65–83). New York: Teachers College Press.

Newberger, J. J. (1997, May). New brain development research—A wonderful window of opportunity to build public support for early childhood education! *Young Children, 52*(4), 4–9.

Newcomb, A. F., & Bagwell, C. (1996). The developmental significance of children's friendships. In W. M. Bukowski, A. F. Newcomb, & W. W. Hartup (Eds.), *The company they keep: Friendships in childhood and adolescence* (pp. 289–321). Cambridge, UK: Cambridge University Press.

Newman, J. (1996). Teachers' attitudes and policies regarding play in elementary schools. *Psychology in the Schools, 33*(1), 61–69.

Newman, J. M., & Church, S. M. (1990). Myths of whole language. *The Reading Teacher, 44*(1), 20–26.

Newman, P. R., & Newman, B. M. (1997). *Childhood and adolescence*. Pacific Grove, CA: Brooks/Cole.

Newman, R. (1997). Learning healthful habits for a lifetime. *Childhood Education, 73*(4), 234–235.

Nicholls, J. G., Cobb, P., Wood, T., Yackel, E., & Patashnick, M. (1991). Dimensions of success in mathematics: Individual and classroom differences. *Journal of Research in Mathematics Education, 21*, 109–122.

Nickelsburg, J. (1976). *Nature activities for early childhood*. Menlo Park, CA: Addison-Wesley.

Nikoltsos, C. (2000, January). *The art of teaching art in early childhood education*. East Lansing, MI: National Center for Research on Teacher Learning. (ERIC Document Reproduction Service No. ED443575)

Nourot, P. M., & Van Hoorn, J. (1991). Symbolic play in preschool and primary settings. *Young Children, 46*(6), 40–50.

Oliver, S. J., & Klugman, E. (2002). Playing the day away. *Child Care Information Exchange, 145*, 66–70.

Ong, W., Allison, J., & Haladyna, T. M. (2000). Student achievement of third-graders in comparable single-age and multiage classrooms. *Journal of Research in Childhood Education, 14*(3), 205–215.

Paciorek, K., & Munro, J. H. (1995). *Notable selections in early childhood education*. Guilford, CT: Dushkin.

Paley, V. (1988). *Mollie is three*. Chicago: University of Chicago Press.

Paley, V. (1995). *Kwanzaa and me*. Cambridge, MA: Harvard University Press.

Palincsar, A. S., & Brown, A. L. (1989). Classroom dialogues to promote self-regulated comprehension. In J. Brophy (Ed.), *Advances in research on teaching* (Vol. 1, pp. 35–71). Greenwich, CT: JAI.

Patterson, G. R., & Stouthamer-Loeber, L. S. (1984). The correlation of family management practices and delinquency. *Child Development, 55*, 1299–1307.

Payne, K. (1991, Spring). Principles of parent involvement in preschool classrooms. *National Organization of Laboratory Schools Bulletin, 18*, 8–9.

Payne, V. G., & Isaacs, L. D. (2002). *Human motor development: A lifespan approach* (5th ed.). New York: McGraw-Hill.

Payne, V. G., & Rink, J. (1997). Physical education in the developmentally appropriate integrated curriculum. In C. H. Hart, D. C. Burts, & R. Charlesworth (Eds.), *Integrated curriculum and developmentally appropriate practice: Birth to age eight* (pp. 145–170). Albany: State University of New York Press.

Peck, J. T., McCaig, G., & Sapp, M. E. (1988). *Kindergarten policies: What is best for children?* Washington, DC: National Association for the Education of Young Children.

Pellegrini, A. D., & Bjorklund, D. F. (2002). Should recess be included in a school day? In Paciorek, K. (Ed.), *Taking sides: Clashing views on controversial issues in early childhood education* (pp. 174–175). Guilford, CT: McGraw-Hill.

Pellegrini, A. D., & Glickman, C. D. (1990). Measuring kindergartners' social competence. *Young Children, 45*(4), 40–44.

Pellegrini, A. D., & Perlmutter, J. C. (1988). Rough and tumble play. *Young Children, 43*(2), 14–17.

Pena, D. C. (2000). Parent involvement: Influencing factors and implications. *Journal of Educational Research, 94*(1), 42–54.

Perkins, D. N. (1995). *Outsmarting I.Q.: The emerging science of learnable intelligence*. New York: Free Press.

Peterson, R., & Felton-Collins, V. (1991). *The Piaget handbook for teachers and parents*. New York: Teachers College Press.

Petrakos, H., & Howe, N. (1996). The influence of the physical design of the dramatic play center on children's play. *Early Childhood Research Quarterly, 11*(1), 63–77.

Phelps, P., & Hanline, M. F. (1999). Let's play blocks! Creating effective learning experiences for young children. *Teaching Exceptional Children, 32*(5), 62–67.

Phillips, C. B. (1991). *Culture as process.* Unpublished paper.

Phillips, P. (1997, May). The conflict wall. *Educational Leadership, 54*(8), 43–44.

Piaget, J. (1962). *Play, dreams and imitation in childhood.* New York: Norton.

Pica, R. (2000). *Experiences in movement with music, activities, and theory* (2nd ed.). Albany, NY: Delmar.

Pickett, L. (1998). Literacy learning during block play. *Journal of Research in Childhood Education, 12*(2), 225–230.

Podlozny, A. (2000). Strengthening verbal skills through the use of classroom drama: A clear link. *Journal of Aesthetic Education, 34*(3–4), 239–275.

Powell, D. (1994). Parents, pluralism and the NAEYC Statement on Developmentally Appropriate Practice. In B. L. Mallory & R. S. New (Eds.), *Diversity and developmentally appropriate practices: Challenges for early childhood education* (pp. 166–182). New York: Teachers College Press.

Powell, R. (1989). *Families and early childhood programs* (Research Monographs of the National Association for the Education of Young Children, Vol. 3). Washington, DC: National Association for the Education of Young Children.

Pulkkinen, L. (1982). Self-control and continuity from childhood to adolescence. In P. B. Baltes & O. G. Brim, Jr. (Eds.), *Life-span development and behavior* (Vol. 4, pp. 63–105). Orlando, FL: Academic Press.

Raines, S. C. (1990). Representational competence: (Re)presenting experiences through words, actions, and images. *Childhood Education, 66*(3), 139–144.

Ramsey, P. G. (1979). Beyond "Ten Little Indians" and turkey: Alternate approaches to Thanksgiving. *Young Children, 34*(6), 28–52.

Ratcliff, N. (2001). Use the environment to prevent discipline problems and support learning. *Young Children, 56*(5), 84–88.

Read, K. H. (1966). *The nursery school: A human relations laboratory.* Philadelphia: Saunders.

Read, K., Gardner, P., & Mahler, B. (1993). *Early childhood programs: Human relationships and learning.* New York: Harcourt Brace Jovanovich.

Readdick, C., & Bartlett, P. (1994). Vertical learning environments. *Childhood Education, 71*(2), 86–91.

Readdick, C. A., & Park, J. (1998). Achieving great heights: The climbing child. *Young Children, 53*(6), 14–19.

Reifel, S., & Greenfield, P. (1983, Spring). Part–whole relations: Some structural features of children's representational block play. *Child Care Quarterly, 12*(1), 144–151.

Reisman, B. (1996). What do parents want? Can we create consumer demand for accredited child care programs? In S. Bredekamp & B. Willer (Eds.), *NAEYC accreditation: A decade of learning and the years ahead* (pp. 139–148). Washington, DC: National Association for the Education of Young Children.

Resnick, L. (1996). Schooling and the workplace: What relationship? In *Preparing youth for the 21st century* (21–27). Washington, DC: Aspen Institute.

Revicki, D. (1982). The relationship among socioeconomic status, home environment, parent involvement, child self-concept and child achievement. *Resources in Education, 1,* 459–463.

Reynolds, E. (2001). *Guiding young children: A problem-solving approach* (3rd ed.). New York: McGraw-Hill.

Richgels, D. J. (2001). Invented spelling, phonemic awareness, and reading and writing instruction. In S. B. Neuman & D. K. Dickinson (Eds.), *Handbook of early literacy research* (pp. 142–158). New York: Guilford Press.

Rivkin, M. (1995). *The great outdoors: Restoring children's right to play outside.* Washington, DC: National Association for the Education of Young Children.

Roehlkepartain, J. L. (1998). *150 Ways to show kids you care.* Minneapolis, MN: The Search Institute.

Rogers, F. Cited in Gestwicki, C. (1997). *The essentials of early education.* Albany, NY: Delmar, 135.

Rosenthal, D. M., & Sawyers, J. Y. (1996, Summer). Building successful home/school partnerships: Strategies for parent support and involvement. *Childhood Education, 72*(4), 194–200.

Roskos, K. (1990). A taxonomic view of pretend play activity among four and five year old children. *Early Childhood Research Quarterly, 5,* 495–512.

Rothlein, L., & Brett, A. (1987). Children's, teachers', and parents' perceptions of play. *Early Childhood Quarterly, 2,* 45–53.

Routman, R. (1996). *Literacy at the crossroads.* Portsmouth, NH: Heinemann.

Routman, R., & Butler, A. (1991). *Transitions.* Portsmouth, NH: Heinemann.

Rubin, K. H., Bukowski, W. M., & Parker, J. G. (1998). Peer interactions, relationships, and groups. In W. Damon (Series Ed.) & N. Eisenberg (Vol. Ed.), *Handbook of child psychology: Vol. 4. Socialization, personality, and social development* (pp. 619–700). New York: Wiley.

Rushton, S. (2001). Applying brain research to create developmentally appropriate learning environments. *Young Children, 56*(5), 76–82.

Rylant, C. (1985). *The relatives came.* New York: Bradbury.

Sanders, S. (2002). *Active for life: Developmentally appropriate movement programs for young children.* Washington, DC: National Association for the Education of Young Children.

Santrock, J. W. (2000). *Children* (6th ed.). Boston: McGraw-Hill.

Sapon-Shevin, M. (1983). Teaching young children about differences: Resources for teaching. *Young Children, 38*(2), 24–32.

Saracho, O. N. (1993). Preparing teachers for early childhood programs in the United States. In B. Spodek (Ed.), *Handbook of research on the education of young children* (pp. 412–426). New York: Macmillan.

Sattler, J. (2001). *Assessment of children: Cognitive applications* (4th ed.). La Mesa, CA: Sattler.

Scherer, M. (1997, April). Perspectives/Negotiating childhood. *Educational Leadership, 54*(7), 5.

Schirrmacher, R. (1986). Talking with young children about their art. *Young Children, 41*(5), 3–7.

Schmoker, M. (1996). *Results: The key to continuous school improvement.* Alexandria, VA: Association for Supervision and Curriculum Development.

Sciarra, D. J., & Dorsey, A. G. (1998). *Developing and administering a child care center.* Albany, NY: Delmar 355.

Seefeldt, C. (Ed.). (1987). *The early childhood curriculum: A review of current research.* New York: Teachers College Press, 144–197.

Seefeldt, C. (1995). Art—serious work. *Young Children, 50*(3), 39–45.

Seefeldt, C. (2001). *Social studies for the preschool/primary child* (6th ed.). Columbus, OH: Merrill/Prentice Hall.

Seefeldt, V., & Vogel, P. G. (1986). *The value of physical activity.* Reston, VA: American Alliance for Health, Physical Education, Recreation & Dance.

Seligman, M. E. (1995). *The optimistic child.* New York: Houghton Mifflin.

Selman, R. L., Levitt, M. Z., & Schultz, L. H. (1997). The friendship framework: Tools for the assessment of psychosocial development. In R. Selman, C. L. Watts, & L. H. Schultz (Eds.), *Fostering friendships* (pp. 32–52). New York: Aldine DeGruyer.

Sendak, M. (1963). *Where the wild things are.* New York: Harper & Row.

Seven styles of learning: Clip-and-save chart. (1990, September). *Instructor Magazine,* 52.

Shaffer, D. R. (2000). *Social and personality development* (4th ed.). Belmont, CA: Wadsworth.

Shaffer, D. R. (2002). *Developmental psychology: Childhood and adolescence* (6th ed.). Belmont, CA: Wadsworth.

Shapiro, L. (1997). *How to raise a child with a high EQ.* New York: Harper Collins.

Sharp, C. (1987). *Now you're talking: Techniques that extend conversations.* Portland, OR: Educational Productions.

Sherman, C. W., & Mueller, D. P. (1996, June). *Developmentally appropriate practice and student achievement in innercity elementary schools.* Paper presented at Head Start's Third National Research Conference, Washington, DC.

Shoemaker, C. J. (1995). *Administration and management of programs for young children.* Upper Saddle River, NJ: Merrill/Prentice Hall.

Shore, R. (1997). *Rethinking the brain: New insights into early development.* New York: Families at Work Institute.

Shotwell, J., Wolf, D., & Gardner, H. Y. (1979). Exploring early symbolization: Styles of achievement. In B. Sutton-Smith (Ed.), *Play and learning* (pp. 127–156). New York: Gardner Press.

Slentz, K. L., & Krogh, S. L. (2001a). *Early childhood development and its variations.* Mahwah, NJ: Erlbaum.

Slentz, K. L., & Krogh, S. L. (2001b). *Teaching young children: Contexts for learning.* Mahwah, NJ: Erlbaum.

Smart, M. S., & Smart, R. C. (1982). *Children: Development and relationships* (Rev. ed.). New York: Macmillan.

Smilansky, S. (1968). *The effects of socio-dramatic play on disadvantaged preschool children.* New York: Wiley.

Smith, J. (1990). *To think.* New York: Teachers College Press.

Smith, S. S. (2001). *Early childhood mathematics* (2nd ed.). Needham Heights, MA: Allyn & Bacon.

Smith, T. M., Young, B. A., Bae, Y., Choy, S. P., & Alsalam, N. (1997). *The condition of education, 1997.* Washington, DC: National Center for Education Statistics, U.S. Department of Education.

Snow, C. E., Tabors, P. O., & Dickinson, D. K. (2001). Language development in the preschool years. In D. K. Dickinson & P. O. Tabors (Eds.), *Beginning literacy with language: Young children learning at home and school* (pp. 1–25). Baltimore: Paul H. Brookes.

Snow, V. R., Burns, M. S., & Griffin, P. (Eds.). (1998). *Preventing reading difficulties in young children.* Washington, DC: National Academy Press.

Soderman, A. (1991, May). *Facts about brain growth.* Unpublished paper delivered to the East Lansing public schools.

Soderman, A. K. (1995). Brownell Community School and Gundry Elementary School: Reading accuracy assessment: A baseline study of grades 1–3. East Lansing: Michigan State University.

Soderman, A. (1997, August). *Multi-age classrooms: Accommodating gender differences among children.* Paper presented at the Michigan Multi-Age Conference, Kalamazoo, MI.

Soderman, A. K. (2001, Fall). Statewide testing: Problem or solution for failing schools? *Michigan Family Review, 6*(1), 55–66.

Soderman, A. K., Gregory, K., & O'Neill, L. (1999a). *Creating phonological and print awareness: Developmentally appropriate practices.* Needham Heights, MA: Allyn & Bacon.

Soderman, A. K., Gregory, K. S., & O'Neill, L. T. (1999b). *Scaffolding emergent literacy: A child-centered approach for preschool through grade 5.* Boston: Allyn & Bacon.

Spangler, C. B. (1997). The sharing circle: A child-centered curriculum. *Young Children, 52*(5), 74–78.

Spear-Swerling, L., & Sternberg, R. J. (1994). The road not taken: An integrative theoretical model of reading disability. *Journal of Learning Disabilities, 27,* 91–103.

Spodek, B. (1973). *Early childhood education.* Upper Saddle River, NJ: Prentice Hall.

Spodek, B. (1985). *Teaching in the early years* (3rd ed.). Upper Saddle River, NJ: Prentice Hall.

Spodek, B., & Brown, P. C. (1993). Curriculum alternatives in early childhood education: A historical perspective. In B. Spodek (Ed.), *Handbook of research on the education of young children* (pp. 91–104). New York: Macmillan.

Spodek, B., Saracho, O. N., & Davis, M. D. (1991). *Foundations of early childhood education.* Upper Saddle River, NJ: Prentice Hall.

Stanovich, K., West, R. F., & Cunningham, A. E. (1991). Beyond phonological processes: Print exposure and orthographic processing. In S. A. Brady & D. P. Shankweiler (Eds.), *Phonological processes in literacy: A tribute to Isabelle Y. Liberman* (pp. 219–235). Hillsdale, NJ: Erlbaum.

State of America's Children: Yearbook 1997. Washington, D.C. Children's Defense Fund, 1997.

Stein, L. C., & Kostelnik, M. J. (1984, Spring). A practical problem solving model for conflict resolution in the classroom. *Child Care Quarterly, 13*(1), 5–20.

Steinberg, L., & Belsky, J. (1991). *Infancy, childhood, and adolescence: Development in context.* New York: McGraw-Hill.

Steiner, J., & Whelan, M. S. (1995, December 29). *For the love of children: For people who care for children.* St. Paul, MN: Redleaf Press.

Stephens, K. (1996, May). You can make circle time developmentally appropriate. *Child Care Information Exchange,* 40–43.

Stewig, J. W., & Jett-Simpson, M. (1995). *Language arts in the early childhood classroom.* Belmont, CA: Wadsworth.

Stiggins, R. J. (2002, June). Assessment crisis: The absence of assessment for learning. *Phi Delta Kappan, 83*(10), 758–765.

Stipek, D., Feiler, R., Daniels, D., & Milburn, S. (1995). Effects of different instructional approaches on young children's achievement and motivation. *Child Development, 66,* 209–223.

Stocking, S. H., Arezzo, D., & Leavitt, S. (1980). *Helping kids make friends.* Allen, TX: Argus Communications.

Stone, S. J. (1997). *ACEI speaks: Understanding portfolio assessment. A guide for parents.* Wheaton, MD: Association for Childhood Education International.

Stone, S. J., & Christie, J. F. (1996). Collaborative literacy learning during sociodramatic play in a multiage (K–2) primary classroom. *Journal of Research in Childhood Education, 10*(2), 123–133.

Stritzel, K. (1995). Block play is for all children. *Child Care Information Exchange,* 42–47.

Stronge, J. H. (2002). *Qualities of effective teachers.* Alexandria, VA: Association for Supervision and Curriculum Development.

Stroud, J. (1995). Block play: Building a foundation for literacy. *Early Childhood Education Journal, 23*(1), 9–13.

Sullivan, M. (1982). *Feeling strong, feeling free: Movement exploration for young children.* Washington, DC: National Association for the Education of Young Children.

Sunal, C. S. (1993). Social studies in early childhood education. In B. Spodek (Ed.), *Handbook of research on the education of young children* (9th ed.). Upper Saddle River, NJ: Merrill/Prentice Hall.

Sutton-Smith, B. (1986). *Toys as culture.* New York: Gardner Press.

Swiniarski, L., Breitborde, M.-L., & Murphy, J.-A. (1999). *Educating the global village: Including the young child in the world.* Columbus, OH: Merrill/Prentice Hall.

Sylwester, R. (1995). *A celebration of neurons: An educator's guide to the human brain.* Alexandria, VA: Association for Supervision and Curriculum Development.

Tabors, P. O., & Snow, C. E. (2001). Young bilingual children and early literacy development. In S. B. Neuman & D. K. Dickinson (Eds.), *Handbook of early literacy research* (pp. 159–178). New York: Guilford Press.

Taras, H. (1992). Physical activity of young children in relation to physical and mental health. In C. Hendricks (Ed.), *Young children on the grow: Health, activity and education in the preschool setting* (pp. 33–42). Washington, DC: ERIC Clearinghouse on Teacher Education.

Tarr, P. (2001). Aesthetic codes in early childhood classrooms: What art educators can learn from Reggio Emilia. *Art Education, 54*(3), 33–39.

Taylor, B. J. (2003a). *A child goes forth: A curriculum guide for preschool children.* Upper Saddle River, NJ: Prentice Hall.

Taylor, B. J. (2003b). *Science everywhere: Opportunities for very young children.* New York: Harcourt Brace Jovanovich.

Taylor, J. A., & Baker, R. A., Jr. (2002, January). Discipline and the special education student. *Educational Leadership, 59*(4), 28–30.

Taylor, S. I., & Morris, U. G. (1996). Outdoor play in early childhood education settings: Is it safe and healthy for children? *Early Childhood Education Journal, 33*(3), 153–158.

Tegano, D. (1996). Designing classroom spaces: Making the most of time. *Early Childhood Education Journal, 23*(3), 135–144.

Tegano, D., Sawyers, J., & Moran, J. (1991, Winter). Problem finding and solving in play: The teacher's role. *Childhood Education, 68* (2), 92–97.

Theimer, C. E., Killen, M., & Stangor, C. (2001). Young children's evaluations of exclusion in gender-stereotypic peer contexts. *Developmental Psychology, 37*(1), 18–27.

Thelen, P., & Soderman, A. K. (2002). *Running a successful kindergarten round-up: A guide for elementary principals and teachers.* Lansing, MI: Lansing School District Safe Schools/Healthy Students Initiative.

Thomas, A., & Chess, S. (1977). *Temperament and development.* New York: Brunner/Mazel.

Thomas, A., & Chess, S. (1980). *The dynamics of psychological development.* New York: Brunner/Mazel.

Thomas, A., & Chess, S. (1984). *Origins and evolution of behavior disorders.* New York: Brunner/Mazel.

Thomas, A., Chess, S., Birch, H. G., Hartzig, M. E., & Korn, S. (1963). *Behavioral individuality in early childhood.* New York: New York University Press.

Thompson, C. M. (1995a). Transforming curriculum in the visual arts. In S. Bredekamp & T. Rosegrant (Eds.), *Reaching potentials: Transforming early childhood curriculum and assessment* (Vol. 2, pp. 81–98). Washington, DC: National Association for the Education of Young Children.

Thompson, R. A. (1998). Early sociopersonality development. In N. Eisenberg (Ed.), *Handbook of child psychology* (Vol. 3, pp. 25–104). New York: Wiley.

Tierney, R. (1991). *Portfolio assessment in the reading–writing classroom.* Norwood, MA: Christopher-Gordon.

Tisak, M. S., & Block, J. H. (1990). Preschool children's evolving conceptions of badness: A longitudinal study. *Early Education and Development, 4,* 300–307.

Torgeson, L. (1996, May). Starting with stories: Building a sense of community. *Child Care Information Exchange,* 55–57.

Trawick-Smith, J. (1988, July). Play leadership and following behavior of young children. *Young Children, 43*(5), 51–59.

Trepanier-Street, M. (1991). The developing kindergartner: Thinking and problem solving. In J. McKee (Ed.), *Developing kindergartens: Programs, children and teachers* (pp. 181–199). East Lansing: Michigan Association for the Education of Young Children.

Turbiville, V. P., Umbarger, G. T., & Guthrie, A. C. (2000, July). Fathers' involvement in programs for young children. *Young Children, 55*(4), 74–79.

Turiel, E. (1998). The development of morality. In N. Eisenberg (Ed.), *Handbook of child psychology* (Vol. 3. pp. 863–932). New York: Wiley.

Turner, J. S. (1992). Montessori's writings versus Montessori practices. In M. H. Loeffler (Ed.), *Montessori in contemporary American culture* (pp. 17–47). Portsmouth, NH: Heinemann.

Unger, D. G., Jones, W., & Park, E. (2001, Winter). Promoting involvement between low-income single caregivers and urban early intervention programs. *Topics in Early Childhood Special Education, 21*(4), 197–212.

U.S. Census Bureau. (2001, October 3). *Population by age, sex, race, and Hispanic or Latino origin for the United States: 2000* (Publication No. PHC-T-9). *In United States Census 2000.* Washington, DC: Author. Retrieved from http://landview.census.gov/population/www/cen2000/phc-t9.html

U.S. Department of Education. (1986). *What works: Research about teaching and learning.* Washington, DC: U.S. Government Printing Office.

Valentini, N. C., Rudisill, M. E., & Goodway, J. D. (1999). Incorporating a mastery climate into physical education: It's developmentally appropriate! *Journal of Physical Education, Recreation and Dance 70*(7), 28–32.

Vance, B. (1973). *Teaching the prekindergarten child: Instructional design and curriculum.* Pacific Grove, CA: Brooks/Cole.

Vandell, D. L., & Corasanti, M. A. (1990). Variations in early childcare: Do they predict subsequent social, emotional and cognitive differences? *Early Childhood Research Quarterly, 5,* 555–572.

Vasta, R., Haith, M. M., & Miller, S. A. (1998). *Child psychology: The modern science* (3rd ed.). New York: Wiley.

Viadero, D. (1996, September 18). Brain trust. *Education Week on the Web.* http://www.edweek.org

Viadero, D. (1997). Fathers play unique role in schooling, study finds. *Education Week, 17*(13), 3–5.

Vygotsky, L. (1929). The problem of the cultural development of the child. *Journal of Genetic Psychology, 36,* 415–434.

Vygotsky, L. S. (1962). *Thought and language* (E. Hanfmann & G. Vakar, Eds. & Trans.). Cambridge, MA: MIT Press. (original work published 1934)

Vygotsky, L. (1967). Play and its role in the mental development of the child. *Social Psychology, 12,* 62–76.

Vygotsky, L. (1978). *Mind in society: The development of higher psychological processes.* Cambridge, MA: Harvard University Press.

Vygotsky, L. (1979). The genesis of higher mental functioning. In J. V. Wertsch (Ed.), *The concept of activity in Soviet psychology.* Armonk, NY: Sharpe.

Wagner, T. (1996, October). Bringing school reform back down to earth. *Phi Delta Kappan, 78*(2), 145–149.

Waite-Stupiansky, S. (1997). *Building understanding together: A constructionist approach to early childhood education.* Albany, NY: Delmar.

Ward, S. (1986). *Charlie and grandma.* New York: Scholastic.

Warren, S. L., Emde, R. N., & Sroufe, L. A. (2000). Internal representations: Predicting anxiety from children's play narratives. *Journal of the American Academy of Child and Adolescent Psychiatry, 39*(1), 100–107.

Washington, V., & Andrews, J. D. (Eds.). (1998). *Children of 2010.* Washington, DC: National Association for the Education of Young Children.

Watson, R. (2001). Literacy and oral language: Implications for early literacy acquisition. In S. B. Neuman & D. K. Dickinson (Eds.), *Handbook of early literacy research* (pp. 43–53). New York: Guilford Press.

Weikart, P. S. (1998, May/June). Facing the challenge of motor development. *Child Care Information Exchange, 121,* 60–62.

Weinstein, C. S., & Mignano, A., Jr. (2003). *Elementary classroom management: Lessons from research and practice* (3rd ed.). New York: McGraw-Hill.

Weissberg, R. P., Shriver, T. P., Bose, S., & DeFalco, K. (1997). Creating a districtwide social development project. *Educational Leadership, 84*(8), 37–40.

Weissbourd, R. (1996). *The vulnerable child: What really hurts America's children and what we can do about it.* Reading, MA: Addison-Wesley.

Wellhousen, K., & Kieff, J. (2001). *A constructivist approach to block play in early childhood.* Albany, NY: Delmar.

Werner, P. (1994). Whole physical education. *Journal of Physical Education, Recreation and Dance, 65*(6), 40–44.

Whiren, A. P. (1995, August). *Play and children's learning.* Paper presented for the Korean Association for the Education of Young Children, Seoul, Korea.

Whitebook, M., Sakai, L., & Howes, C. (1997). *NAEYC accreditation as a strategy for improving child care quality.* Washington, DC: National Center for the Early Childhood Work Force.

Whitehurst, G. J., & Lonigan, C. J. (2001). Emergent literacy: Development from prereaders to readers. In S. B. Neuman & D. K. Dickinson (Eds.), *Handbook of early literacy research* (pp. 11–29). New York: Guilford Press.

Wieder, S., & Greenspan, S. I. (1993). The emotional basis of learning. In B. Spodek (Ed.), *Handbook of research on the education of young children* (pp. 77–104). New York: Macmillan.

Wilcox, E. (1994). Unlock the joy of music. *Teaching Music, 2,* 34–35.

Williams, C., & Bybee, J. (1994). What do young children feel guilty about? Developmental and gender differences. *Developmental Psychology, 30*(5), 617–623.

Wilson, R. (1995). Environmental education: Environmentally appropriate practices. *Early Childhood Education Journal, 23*(2), 107–110.

Wiltz, N. W., & Klein, E. L. (2001). "What do you do in child care?" Children's perceptions of high and low quality classrooms. *Early Childhood Research Quarterly, 16*(2), 209–236.

Winfrey, O. (1996). *About us: The dignity of children.* Fred Berner Films and the Children's Dignity Project: CDP Films.

Wittmer, D. S., & Honig, A. S. (1994, July). Encouraging positive social development in young children. *Young Children, 4,* 4–12.

Wolery, M., Strain, P., & Bailey, D. (1992). Reaching potentials of children with special needs. In S. Bredekamp & T. Rosegrant (Eds.), *Reaching potentials: Appropriate curriculum and assessment for young children* (Vol. 1, pp. 92–111). Washington, DC: National Association for the Education of Young Children.

Wolfgang, C. H. (1996). *The three faces of discipline for the elementary school teacher.* Boston: Allyn & Bacon.

Wolfgang, C. H., & Sanders, L. (1986). Teacher's role: A construct for supporting the play of young children. In S. Burroughs & R. Evans (Eds.), *Play, language and socialization* (pp. 49–62). New York: Gordon & Breach.

Wolfgang, C. H., Stannard, L. L., & Jones, I. (2001). Block play performance among preschoolers as a predictor of later school achievement in mathematics. *Journal of Research in Childhood Education, 15*(2), 173–180.

Woodard, R. J., & Yun, J. (2001). The performance of fundamental gross motor skills by children enrolled in Head Start. *Early Child Development and Care, 169,* 57–67.

Wright, S. (1997). Learning how to learn: The arts as core in an emergent curriculum. *Childhood Education, 73*(6), 361–365.

Wurtele, S. K., Gissispie, G., Currier, L., & Franklin, C. (1992). A comparison of teachers vs. parents as instructors of a personal safety program for preschoolers. *Child Abuse & Neglect, 16,* 127–137.

Yopp, H. K., & Yopp, R. H. (2000, October). Supporting phonemic awareness development in the classroom. *The Reading Teacher, 54*(2), 130–143.

York, S. (1991). *Roots and wings: Affirming culture in early childhood settings.* St. Paul, MN: Toys 'n Things Press.

Zahorik, J. A. (1997, March). Encouraging—and challenging—students' understandings. *Educational Leadership, 54*(6), 30–32.

Zaichkowsky, L., & Larson, G. (1995). Physical, motor, and fitness development in children and adolescents. *Journal of Education, 177*(2), 55–79.

Zavitkovsky, D. (1986). *Listen to the children.* Washington, DC: National Association for the Education of Young Children.

Zentella, A. C. (1981). Ta bien you could answer me en cualquier idioma: Puerto Rican code-switching in bilingual classrooms. In R. Duran (Ed.), *Latino language and communicative behavior* (pp. 109–132). Norwood, NJ: Ablex.

Name Index

Subject Index

Physical activity (*continued*)

    fine-motor skills and, 348–352

    fundamental motor skills and, 343–344

    goals and objectives of, 361

    health, safety, nutrition and, 354–358

    importance, benefits of, 342–343

    motor development principles and, 343

    movement concepts and, 352–353

    perceptual-motor and, 344–348

    special needs children and, 353–354

    teaching strategies of, 361–365

Physical domain, 10, 41, 69, 70, 155, 270–271

    Children's Comprehensive Curriculum and, 236–237

    construction play and, 417

    direct instruction use in, 369

    education focus in, 369

    exploratory to goal-directed activity within, 59

    pretend play and, 417

    ultimate goal of education in, 369

Physical experience, social interaction, reflection principle

    constructing knowledge internally and, 49

    implications of, 50–51

    memorizing and, 50

    zone of proximal development and, 50

Physical knowledge

    aesthetic experiences and, 245, 246

    affective development and, 270–271

    cognitive development and, 295, 305

Physical learning activity

    Exploration With Balls as, 365

    Exploring Vertical Space as, 368

    Fun on the Balance Beam as, 365–366

    Indoor Striking as, 366

    Mastering Cutting Techniques as, 367

    Mother/Father, May I? as, 366–367

    Moving Standing Still as, 366

    Pull a Friend as, 367–368

    Puzzles as, 367

    Snowperson Walk or Run as, 368–369

    Vegetable Tasting as, 368

Piaget, Jean, 312

    assimilation, disequilibrium, cognitive theories of, 292

    cognitive maturation theories of, 292–294, 297

    concrete operational perspectives, Vygotsky v., 294

    mental operations, four stages and, 292–293

    preoperational children and theories of, 293

    preoperational children, centration and, 293

    preoperational children, reversibility and, 293

Pictorial Story Problems, 310

Pitch Play, 262–263

Place-Value Pocket Game, 311

Plan component(s), 69. *See also* Planning

    activity name as, 70–71

    behavior's role in, 71

    content as, 71–72

    developmental direction and, 71

    domain as, 70

    evaluation as, 73

    extensions as, 72–73

    immediate objectives as, 71

    intermediate objective as, 71

    materials as, 72

    procedures as, 72

    simplifications as, 72

Plan-do-review process, High/Scope learning approach and, 27–28

Planned lessons, instruction mode, self-discipline, 166

Planning. *See also* Plan component(s)

    advantages to lesson, 66–67

    assessing development through, 67

    basics of, 69

    characteristics, components of effective, 67, 69–73, 88–89

    common teaching strategies and, 72, 73–82

    congruence of goals, objectives and, 89

    ecological nature of, 67

    flexibility and, 67

    implementation of, 88–89

    negative results, lack of, 67

    teachers and, 67–69, 89

    typical activity plan as example of, 89

    whole group activities, avoiding pitfalls in, 105–110, 116

    whole group activity, 93–95

Planning pitfalls, whole group

    engagement, ineffective pacings as, 109–110, 116

    excessive routinized activities as, 109, 116

    inadequate preparations as, 105–108, 116

    inappropriate activity lengths as, 110, 116

    materials, inappropriate selections as, 109, 116

    small groups, ill-suited instruction and, 108, 116

Plants or Animals, 310

Play. *See also* Construction Play; Individuality, construction and pretend play; Pretend play

    characteristics of, 402–403

    construction, 407–429

    curricular and developmental, 414–419

    directed, 54

    free, 53–54

    guided, 54

    individual differences, construction and pretend, 412–414

    pretend, 402–407, 412–429

    solitary and collaborative, 54

    work disguised as, 54

Play enhancement strategy. *See also* Pretend play

    creating proper conditions as, 425–426

    improving children's level of performance as, 426–427

    independent sociodramatic plays as, 427

    play, construction and information flow as, 428

    providing solid base for construction as, 427

    relevant information provision as, 427

    setting the stage as, 425

    skill development evaluation as, 428

    supporting problem solving as, 427–428

    teaching technical skills as, 427

Play frame, 403

Political science, social study of, 383, 388

Portfolios, authentic assessment. *See also* Authentic assessment

    individual, 200–201

    institutional, 201

    showcase, 201

    teacher, 201

Practice

    direct instruction and, 87

    exploratory to goal directed development through, 59

    self-motivation/initiation of children through, 59

Preoperational stage, 299

    centration and, 293

    Piaget's stages of cognitive maturation and, 292–293

    reversibility and, 293

Preparation and strategies, group times

    active involvement, factor in, 97

    adult roles and responsibilities during, 98

    focus, importance in, 96–97

    location consideration, factor of, 96

    materials, factor of, 97

    pace and variety, factor of, 97

    teaching methods and, 97–98

    teaching strategies applicable to, 97

Pretend play. *See also* Individuality, construction and pretend play; Play; Play enhancement strategy

    aesthetic domain and, 415–416

    affective domain and, 416

    cognitive domain and, 415

    communication enabling, 404

    elements of, 403–404

    individuality in, 412–414